PENGUIN BOOKS

THE LIFE OF GRAHAM GREENE
VOLUME II: 1939–1955

Norman Sherry is a Fellow of the Royal Society of Literature and Mitchell Distinguished Professor of Literature at Trinity University in San Antonio, Texas. In addition to the first volume of this biography, he is the author of *Conrad's Eastern World*, *Conrad's Western World*, *Charlotte and Emily Brontë*, and *Jane Austen*.

Acclaim for *The Life of Graham Greene Volume II: 1939–1955*

"Norman Sherry brings to the pursuit of Graham Greene an obsessional, relentless passion for detail and the sifting of ambiguous evidence worthy of the curious object of this unremitting investigations. In this book we meet the biographer as bloodhound, relishing the thrill of the chase . . . what Mr. Sherry gives us in this second volume of his massive study of a grotesquely complicated life is a compulsively readable, astutely humane account." —*The New York Times Book Review*

"Professor Sherry is in many ways the ideal biographer. . . . [He] is not in the least bit shocked by Greene's eccentric taste for prostitutes and brothels and opium dens, and studiously avoids any moral judgement."
—Auberon Waugh, *The Spectator*

"Sherry's major biography takes us deep into the 'heart of the matter,' where love, pity, sin and redemption struggle so powerfully on the human plane, often with God as a distant antagonist. It is an adventure to read, an adventure not to be missed." —*Houston Chronicle*

"It confirms the promise of his widely-acclaimed first volume. It is constantly entertaining, filled with fascinating and well-researched detail, generous and sympathetic." —John Wells, *The Daily Mail*

"Engrossing and always readable, it is a masterly example of the biographer's craft." —*Newsday*

"Volume two of Norman Sherry's authorized *Life* . . . shows how biography has become today's equivalent of the Victorian triple-decker novel . . . intimate in its discussions of its hero's most raw emotions. . . . Sherry's book is unputdownable." —*The Financial Times*

"Like a detective, Sherry has tracked Greene's journeys around the globe and has searched his life for the sources of his fiction."
—*The Philadelphia Inquirer*

"Norman Sherry brings many skills to the biographer's art. He's a wonderful synthesizer, a canny stylist and a sharp reader. Above all, Sherry perceives Greene fully and clearly, showing him many angles and capturing the different facets of his personality." —*Chicago Tribune*

"The second volume of Norman Sherry's life of Graham Greene . . . confirms the promise of his widely acclaimed first volume. It is constantly entertaining, filled with fascinating and well-researched detail, generous and sympathetic."
—*Evening Standard*

"Compelling reading . . . Sherry has done his work well and honorably."
—Allan Massie, *The Daily Telegraph*

THE LIFE OF
GRAHAM GREENE

Volume II: 1939–1955

Norman Sherry

PENGUIN BOOKS

PENGUIN BOOKS
Published by the Penguin Group
Penguin Group (USA) Inc., 375 Hudson Street, New York, New York 10014, U.S.A.
Penguin Books Ltd, 80 Strand, London WC2R 0RL, England
Penguin Books Australia Ltd, 250 Camberwell Road,
Camberwell, Victoria 3124, Australia
Penguin Books Canada Ltd, 10 Alcorn Avenue, Toronto, Ontario, Canada M4V 3B2
Penguin Books India (P) Ltd, 11 Community Centre,
Panchsheel Park, New Delhi – 110 017, India
Penguin Group (NZ), cnr Airborne and Rosedale Roads,
Albany, Auckland 1310, New Zealand
Penguin Books (South Africa) (Pty) Ltd, 24 Sturdee Avenue,
Rosebank, Johannesburg 2196, South Africa

Penguin Books Ltd, Registered Offices:
80 Strand, London WC2R 0RL, England

First published in Great Britain by Jonathan Cape Ltd. 1994
First published in the United States of America by Viking Penguin,
a division of Penguin Books USA Inc., 1995
Published in Penguin Books 1996, 2004

1 3 5 7 9 10 8 6 4 2

Copyright © Norman Sherry, 1994
All rights reserved

LIBRARY OF CONGRESS CATALOGING IN PUBLICATION DATA
(Revised for Vol. 2.)
Sherry, Norman.
The life of Graham Greene.
Vol. 2. includes index.
ISBN 0 14 20.0421 9 (v. 2)
Contents: v. 1. 1904–1939—v. 2. 1939–1995.
1. Greene, Graham, 1904–1991—Biography.   I. Title.
PR6013.R44Z845   1990
823'.912—dc20   90-7026

Printed in the United States of America
Set in PostScript Adobe Sabon

for

Max Senyi, a great bookman

Harry Smith, a true gentleman

Ian Watt, a superb scholar

If anybody ever tries to write a biography of me, how complicated they are going to find it and how misled they are going to be.

— GRAHAM GREENE

Contents

Illustrations

LINE ILLUSTRATIONS   *page*

Seeking Greene

As this work bears down quickly on the twentieth year, I am aware of the expense of spirit, and of the difficulties of transforming raw research into a life, but the compensation for this biographical endeavour lies in those serendipitous discoveries which, for one crazy moment, bring fate to heel.

Whilst recognising that Greene still has that splinter of ice in the heart, remaining elusive, aloof, and inaccessible, I am seeking in the period following (1939–55) to move from his public reputation to an understanding of his inner vulnerabilities. Numerous and extensive interviews, as well as a study of his letters, diaries, journals and major novels, force a central question to the surface: why was life so impossible for Greene? Why was suicide a constant thought? Herein lies the paradox: that this author, thought by many to be the greatest novelist of his generation, and also the most successful (his books have sold more than twenty million copies and have been translated into over forty languages), should yet suffer from a despair that seemed beyond success, beyond money. At the height of his fame as a writer, and at the height of his grand passion for Lady Walston, he was suicidal. Sometimes he set the date for death, saving up his sleeping pills because he wanted a termination point for his unhappiness. Although he did not succeed in committing suicide, the fact remains that Greene had a formidable desire for self-annihilation.

Clearly, the territory of his mind was radically different from that revealed in Volume One. He suffered from a deep-seated personal disturbance, a fall in spirit of an unalterable intensity, a kind of plague spot.

During this period Greene produced his known masterpieces – *The Power and the Glory*, *The Heart of the Matter*, *The End of the Affair* – novels which have a strong religious dimension and are conspicuous in providing us with a sense of human isolation, passion and death. It is a world where his scapegoat heroes have a capacity for damnation; where the flames of Hell seem to touch them; where others seem destined for Purgatory, and where some seem to be, in spite of their sins, candidates for sainthood. For the biographer, these novels are a rich mine, and if he can dig deep, striking that which is soft and that which is granite in Greene's nature, he will be probing secrets that reveal the painful nature of Greene's existence.

Greene was a professional spy, working during the Second World War for MI6. By nature he was the perfect spy; he was an intensely secretive man. His whole life remained a mystery even to those closest to him: his brothers, Herbert, Raymond and Hugh, didn't understand him; his mother and sister Molly were often mystified by him and even his favourite sister Elisabeth, loved and trusted by Greene, admitted to me that her favourite brother was not easily understood. His family were earthbound before his leaping mind.

Who understood Greene? His wife? Shrewd as her comments were, he did not release his spirit to her. His mistress Dorothy Glover? Definitely not. His greatest love Catherine Walston? If anyone knew him, surely she did. His love for her was a fever: to her he confessed – but only selectively.

Greene remained a mystery because the masks he wore, except with intimates, were very real and necessary to him. In the 1950s when he went to various sleazy night clubs and strip joints, he would present a business card which had printed on it the name of one of his characters. Two of the cards he used bore the names Major Scobie (*The Heart of the Matter*) and Mr Tench (*The Power and the Glory*).

In life he was not willing to allow full entrance even to those familiar with his secret life. A man who would write two versions in his diary was not a man who would give up easily the secrets of his existence. When Greene was a leading contender for the Book Society award for *Stamboul Train*, he went to London while the committee was in session. Two separate pages covered the events of the same day giving two different versions. Greene intended to destroy the first, true version (and in part did) and replace it with the more conventional version. I believe his Vietnam diaries were also doctored, so I fancy it was not an unusual habit.

In one version, after learning that he had won the award, he finishes his day by writing a poem and then goes quietly to bed. The first version begins in the same way: 'Caught 7.15 to London' – but adds that he telegraphed 'A' to expect him at 6.15 in the evening (this was Annette, one of two prostitutes he often visited when on business in London). We know no more since the rest of the original version has been torn out of the diary – only carelessness allowed this fragment to survive – but it seems likely that his evening was not spent as quietly as his rewritten version suggests.

His love-life included many lovers. Its essentially painful nature was revealed at the end of a weekend I spent with Greene at his sister's. Early on Sunday morning, Elisabeth left us at the railway station in Tunbridge Wells and we waited quite alone on the platform. Greene suddenly told me in his clipped, slightly hoarse voice that he'd heard his wife intended to write a book about their marriage (they had been separated for many years). However, once Greene had said that, his face took on a look of total dismay, and he opened his mouth and sang high-pitched from an old music-hall song: 'Shovel the dust on the old man's coffin and take up your pen and write.' He sang with such melancholy that I stood the entranced spectator of another's mortal sadness.

Between the completion of the first volume of his life (1989) and the writing of the second Greene died, joining what he once called 'the dignified and disciplined ranks of the dead'. My hope is, at the end of the second volume, that readers will be able to say: this was a living man, described as many knew him, as I knew him. Greene is a literary creature of our historical period, revealing it and yet, in an extraordinary way, as typical of it as Churchill. I want to be able to say: here is the public man but here also is the tormented private man unadulterated. I have not, to repeat what Boswell said of Johnson, cut off his claws, nor made this tiger a cat.

San Antonio, Texas   N.S.
1994

Before the War, 1904–1939

Born in Berkhamsted on 2 October 1904, the fourth of six children, Henry Graham Greene entered the cloistered world of upper-middle-class Edwardian society. His father, Charles Greene, headmaster of Berkhamsted School, was a man of sharp intelligence and naïve innocence. His mother, Marion, though somewhat remote in character, offered her children security and confidence. Although sheltered, the knowledge of death came early to Greene. He remembered how his sister's dead pug was carried home beside him in the baby carriage and recollected witnessing a suicide.

Greene was an odd child, given to nightmares and strange imaginings, painfully sensitive, and very shy. These qualities were an affliction when he moved from his family's home at School House to become a boarder at Berkhamsted. His shyness and physical awkwardness prevented him from excelling at games, and the total absence of solitude made life beyond the green baize door, that separation between home and school, unbearable for him.

His subsequent breakdown was brought about by a boy only three months older than himself – Lionel Carter, who looked even younger and more inoffensive. Beneath that look of innocence lay Carter's recognition of the conflict between Greene's need to be loyal to his father and his desire to befriend the boys of his school. Carter was like some dark magician able to shut down Greene's contacts, halt friendships, put barriers around him, so that on entering the classroom Greene experienced mockery from the chorus of Carter's friends.

Greene was different from the pack. He had a funny voice, with a bit of a lisp; he was the headmaster's son who could be suspected of being a spy and driven out. Isolated, disliked, distrusted, and fearing humiliation, Greene saw death as a release from an impossible situation and the only way of escape was self-injury. He first tried to saw open his knee and, when that failed, swallowed different potions in order to poison himself, including hyposulphite, hay-fever drops, a whole tin of hair pomade, and even a bottle of eye-drops. He picked the deadly nightshade plant and survived after eating it. When nothing else worked, he took fourteen aspirins and swam in the school pool. He recalled his legs feeling like lead – but he did not drown. He did not know then, but he had found his theme for his greatest novels and stories: 'In the lost boyhood of Judas / Christ was betrayed.'

Charles Greene sent his disturbed son to a London psychoanalyst, Kenneth Richmond, and the six months Greene spent under Richmond had a profound effect on him. Richmond and his wife, Zoe, were Jungian psychologists, spiritualists, and involved in the London literary community. They presented Greene with his first experience of a family environment where every issue was open to conversation and debate. Under Richmond's influence Greene explored the darker side of human nature and acquired his first literary contacts.

On his return to Berkhamsted, Greene was surer of himself and became rigorously keen in his observations, a characteristic which helped to distinguish him as a novelist. In 1922 he went up to Oxford, to Balliol College, where he revelled in the escape from the conventionality of his middle-class home. He was a founder of the Mantichorean Society, the exploits of which included a number of episodes in disguise, and one in particular when he and his friend Claud Cockburn disguised themselves as organ-grinders and went unrecognised even in Berkhamsted. These escapades reflected Greene's obsessive need to flee from the creeping boredom of everyday life.

Fascination with disguise and espionage led Greene on the first of many adventures in the world's trouble spots. The Ruhr Republic lured him under the sponsorship of German Intelligence. Greene covered his travel expenses by promising articles based on the journeys and with a youthful recklessness ventured into perilous situations almost without care.

At university, both before and after his twentieth birthday, Greene flirted with death. He played Russian roulette six times in five months: 'The revolver would be whipped behind my back, the chamber twisted, the muzzle quickly and surreptitiously inserted in my ear . . . the trigger pulled.'

The cool objectivity used to describe so terrible an action against his own person is astonishing. It is as if a third person were doing this to him, as if the revolver had a will of its own, exacting that penalty from this particular ear. Behind the deed lay a strong sense of despair and a desire for annihilation. Greene's attempt to shoot his head off was a necessary testing of himself – the uninspired weakling on the playing fields of Berkhamsted becomes the inspired adventurer off them, an example of his need to live on the dangerous edge of life, what he called 'life reinforced by the propinquity of death'.

More significantly, perhaps, during his last two terms at Oxford his first volume of verse, *Babbling April*, was published and he began his first novel, *Anthony Sant* (never published). In 1925 he fell in love with nineteen-year-old Vivien Dayrell-Browning, who was employed by his publisher, Basil Blackwell.

Vivien was handsome, independent minded and a devout Catholic convert. Greene deluged her with almost 2,000 letters in thirty months, sometimes as many as three a day. Initially she treated him with reserve, but her feelings for him gradually warmed.

But most important, on graduating, was his need to find work. Uncertain whether to choose a domestic or a foreign job, Greene sought employment with the British American Tobacco Company hoping to leave for China, but the tedium of work, the crassness of his co-workers, and his fear of losing Vivien made his resignation inevitable. He next turned to journalism, but, lacking experience, was unable to land himself a job with any London daily. Instead, he accepted a position as a trainee, sub-editing on the *Nottingham Journal* without salary.

Nottingham provided Greene with a rich reservoir of experience of working-class life from which he created memorable, sometimes mysterious, and often seedy characters. Here he also received instruction from Father Trollope which led to his conversion to the Catholic Church, though the motivation was chiefly his love for Vivien. The domestic atmosphere of the sub-editor's room at the *Journal* provided a peaceful interlude, but Greene soon began seeking work in London.

In March 1926, with less than five months' experience on the *Nottingham Journal*, Greene was offered a post as a sub-editor with *The Times*. By supplementing his income with reviews, marriage was beginning to be within his financial reach. However, Vivien's commitment to him was still in question. To overcome her fear of sex, Greene, in an extraordinary gesture, offered a celibate marriage.

It was while Greene was sub-editor at *The Times* that the country experienced the General Strike, and London ground to a halt with mass pickets and riots. Young Greene was exhilarated by working as a packer, manual labourer, and member of the newspaper's 'shock troops' during the nine-day strike, but the excitement ended too quickly and monotony loomed. The possibility of unending years of sub-editing at *The Times* gave impetus to his literary efforts. He finished his second novel, *The Episode*, but encountered repeated rejections and the novel remained unpublished. Having forsaken any hope of his first two novels being published, he started a third, *The Man Within*.

Greene and Vivien were married on 15 October 1927. They honeymooned in France and returned to live in London at a house affectionately known as 'the basket', a reflection of Vivien's passion for cats.

At the age of twenty-four, still working at *The Times*, and only ten days after *The Man Within* was submitted, Greene was telephoned by Charles Evans of Heinemann with the news that his novel had been accepted. It was an immediate success, with two reprints sold before publication. Within six months the novel went into six impressions and was translated into five languages. On publication day in June 1929 a literary star had been discovered.

Overconfident as a result of the success of *The Man Within*, Greene persuaded Heinemann to take him on salary in order to write full time. He resigned his position at *The Times*, but his next two novels, *The Name of Action* and *Rumour at Nightfall*, were failures. *The Name of Action* hardly sold 2,000 copies and *Rumour at Nightfall* barely 1,200. Financial pressures forced Greene and Vivien to move from London to a primitive cottage in Chipping Campden. Greene became increasingly depressed by the growing debt to his publisher, but for Vivien this isolation and financial struggle was an idyllic period.

The 1930s were difficult times and the Greenes were not unaffected by the Depression. Although temporarily elated that his next novel *Stamboul Train* was selected as a Book Society choice, Greene was forced to share the expense of reprinting twenty pages of the soon-to-be-released book on threat of a libel action from J. B. Priestley (then at the height of his fame), who concluded that the character Mr Savoy was based on him.

In spite of the last-minute difficulties *Stamboul Train* was the Christmas rage and a breakthrough success for Greene. Excellent reviews poured in and by late January sales had passed the 16,000 mark. Greene, still facing financial hardship, applied for a position at Bangkok University (unsuccessfully) while continuing to review for the *Spectator*.

The central metaphor of his next novel, *It's a Battlefield*, was of life as 'a battlefield in which individuals, ignorant of the extent of the whole war, fought their own separate battles . . . ' The romantic relationships of *It's a Battlefield* with their premise that love complicated a simple act of lust suggested that Greene, though still in love with Vivien, frequented prostitutes.

After moving from Chipping Campden to Oxford and finishing *It's a Battlefield*, Greene spent three weeks in Sweden trying to concoct a biography of the Swedish Match King, Ivar Kreuger, which never materialised. Instead, Greene began *England Made Me*, set in Sweden, which condemned the antiquated precepts of 'honour' so central to the public school system in which he had suffered. A major character, Anthony Farrant, was modelled on his eldest brother Herbert, the black sheep of the family.

Shortly after his first child Lucy was born in December 1933, Greene impulsively decided to explore Liberia. Over a glass of champagne his 23-year-old cousin, Barbara Greene, agreed to accompany him to a country still largely unexplored by Westerners. The attraction for Greene was that the most reliable map available was an American military one with sections blank except for the word 'Cannibals'.

At Freetown, Sierra Leone, he found that everything ugly and seedy was European and everything beautiful was native. At the start of his journey Greene was a novice African traveller, but by the time he reached Monrovia he was seasoned, as a result of overcoming endless difficulties. He led his small expedition with vigilance, walking hour after hour through perilous terrain, sometimes getting lost. In spite of the heat and the difficult conditions, he dutifully recorded his observations, which had the qualities of nightmare – the old man he'd seen beaten with a club outside a poky little prison at Tapee-Ta, the naked widows at Tailahun covered with yellow clay, the great wooden-toothed devil swaying his raffia skirts between the huts.

Greene pushed himself to the limit, physically and mentally, nearly exceeding even his formidable determination. He contracted a strange disease and became profoundly exhausted from constant travel. The travellers had very little medicine and they had to rely on Epsom salts. One night Barbara was certain that Greene would die, but curiously his fever broke and the next morning, discovering a renewed interest in living, he was anxious to travel. After weeks of pressing through dense jungle they emerged at Grand Bassa and by April were back in England. Greene found a compelling new desire to succeed as a writer, and his book *Journey Without Maps*, probably one of the best travel books of our time, was published in 1936.

Greene moved from Oxford to London in order to be at the hub of the publishing world. Having experienced the unknown and survived by his own wit and determination, he had a surge of creative energy. He began the thriller *Brighton Rock*, edited the short-lived magazine *Night and Day*, and reviewed films for the *Spectator*. It was his review of the Shirley Temple film *Wee Willie Winkie* which hastened the financial downfall of *Night and Day*. In its libel action Twentieth Century Fox claimed that Greene 'had accused

[it] of "procuring" Miss Temple "for immoral purposes" ', a bizarre comment.

With *Brighton Rock* published and the libel suit threatening, Greene departed for Mexico under the patronage of Longman's to write about religious persecution there. His hatred of Mexico started at a ceremonial cockfight in San Luís Potosí, with the beggars of Mexico City, and the unnerving *abrazo* (embrace) grown men used when meeting each other. With little knowledge of the language and less of the terrain, Greene journeyed by mule from Salto to Palenque recording his extreme suffering.

In Villahermosa, decrees were passed insisting that priests should marry. God was denounced from his own pulpit, people were forced to destroy altars, religious ornaments were smashed, even torn from people's necks. Priests in Tabasco were hunted down and eventually shot, except one who wandered for ten years under cover in the forest and swamps and became the itinerant 'whisky' priest. Greene knew that 'The greatest saints have been men with more than normal capacity for evil, and the most vicious men have sometimes narrowly evaded sanctity.'

PART I

War

I

Rumours at Nightfall

Just fear of an imminent danger, though there be no blow
given . . .

— FRANCIS BACON

AFTER Greene's devastating trip on a mule through the state of
Chiapas, he returned to Mexico City (in early May 1938) in
very poor health. He'd had dysentery on the interminable journey
back. He had to go into a stony field to relieve himself and be sick.
He had kept himself going with thoughts of a luxurious hotel, 'all
brandy cocktails and bourbon'. Instead, in the Hotel Canada, he read
the newspaper clippings about the Shirley Temple libel case ('it looks
as if I shall be arrested when I land [in England] if the L[ord] C[hief]
J[ustice]'s bite is as bad as his bark'),[1] worked on the proofs of the
American edition of *Brighton Rock*, and while applying heated
beeswax to his behind to extract ticks embedded there during his
journey, listened to a hysterical woman screaming and sobbing in the
room below.

He returned to England in May 1938 with vital material, which
enabled him to produce his brilliant travel book *The Lawless Roads*
and his greatest novel *The Power and the Glory*, but it was material
which reflected his dislike: 'I hate this country and this people.'
Hatred was certainly very much part of the tone of *The Lawless
Roads*, yet it became modified by the time he was writing *The Power
and the Glory*, and his response to England was perhaps an indicator
of why this happened. He sailed for Europe on the *Orinoco*, longing
to see his wife and children again, and arrived in England on 25 May,
only to suffer another culture shock.

He began to wonder why he had disliked Mexico so much, as he
compared the Catholic religious observances in England with those
in Mexico: 'Mass in Chelsea seemed curiously fictitious; no peon
knelt with his arms out in the attitude of the cross, no woman

3

dragged herself up the aisle on her knees. It would have seemed shocking, like the Agony itself. We do not mortify ourselves. Perhaps we are in need of violence.'[2]

London was a culture shock for him on his return:

> One jolted through the hideous iron tunnel at Vauxhall Bridge, under the Nine Elms depot and the sky-sign for Meux's beer. There is always a smell of gas at the traffic junction where the road is up and the trams wait; a Watney poster, a crime of violence . . . In the grit of the London afternoon, among the trams, in the long waste of the Clapham Road, a Baptist chapel, stone and weed.[3]

And war seemed to be brewing, but perhaps, not yet.

Upon returning, he gave himself too much to do: 'I see no further for the next twelve months than the grindstone.' He knew war was inevitable ('How could a world like this end in anything but war?') yet curiously hatched a plan of escape as if it were not so: 'In about two years or so, I want to go & stay up the Amazon with an odd delightful German whom I met on the way home, but he has to serve a short sentence in Hamburg first.'[4]

Greene's 'odd delightful German' was a rare creature. They had met on the *Orinoco*, and Greene discovered that Kruger had been wrongfully gaoled in Mexico and had endured appalling conditions – an open cell crowded with thieves and murderers, the floor crawling with worms, covered with urine and excrement, and no food or water for eight days. What struck Greene about him was his gentleness, his amazing gratitude for life and the extraordinary sense of goodness surrounding him. This sense of essential goodness Greene passed on to his whisky priest in *The Power and the Glory*, Kruger being one source for the famous fictional figure.*

On the *Orinoco*, Kruger and Greene made vows to meet in two years' time in Iquitos. It was not to be. With the war intervening, it was not possible to visit the Amazon nor did he ever hear what happened to Kruger after he returned to the Fatherland to finish his sentence.

*

In London, the telephones were cut off, the anti-aircraft guns set up on Clapham Common, and trenches were being dug. Air-raid

---

* Kruger's passion was for a life on the Amazon, especially a simple life among the Indians – 'a man could have ten wives if he wanted wives', he told Greene. Greene answered that he had a wife. Kruger replied, 'Never mind. You will never want to go home, never. You can get another wife there.'

wardens had been appointed and air-raid posts set up in anticipation of war and the inevitable onslaught of German bombers. Greene believed that under the conditions of war novels, short stories, reviews and articles would not , be saleable products, and the subsequent loss of earnings would make it difficult to support his family. Thus he forced himself to take on extra writing commitments. His urge to make money stemmed from a fear that his family might experience the poverty he and Vivien had known in the early 1930s, with the added fear that with his family increased by two he would not be able to provide for them.

At home his two lively small children made it difficult to concentrate on writing and he sought ways of getting his family from under his feet. His mother took them off his hands for a holiday: 'It's very good of you to have all my family & domestic.' He pleaded with her to look after Vivien: 'See that she takes regularly her particularly foul medicine, that she goes to bed early and that she has a car to take her on Sunday to Mass.' At the beginning of August he asked his mother to approach his sister Molly to take his daughter for ten days – 'She can really dress herself now' – for he was planning to go to a country pub for a week or two in the hope of getting a lot of work done – 'there are so many interruptions in town'. He wanted to visit his mother: 'I wish I could come down, but there isn't a chance. As well as going to the office [of the *Spectator*] every day as literary editor,* I've signed up again for at least four weeks with Denham [film studios] at 125 pounds a week . . . ' But a more serious concern was soon to vie with the urge to work.

By 14 September 1938 war seemed inevitable and Greene wrote in his diary: 'A curious air of unreality – a rather silent [Clapham] Common – too many strangers talking together in pairs. The papers: CRISIS LATEST, FRENCH WAR CHIEFS HERE, HITLER CALLS HIS GENERALS, THE NEXT FEW HOURS WILL DECIDE PEACE OR WAR.' It was the day after his son's second birthday and there was thunder in the air and later slow rain fell. In the context of impending war Graham, the least domesticated of men, found some peace in domesticity: 'The nursery – everything – looking prettier than I remembered it.' Yet in spite of the distractions of the time, he did complete a review of *The History of the Film*, but in his diary questioned, 'Who on earth will bother about that?' Indeed, he wondered whether his review would appear once war started and whether he would be paid: 'Nothing to do but go out and look at

* Greene did not officially become literary editor of the *Spectator* until October 1940, so it must be that the editor, Derek Verschoyle, was temporarily away from the office.

the latest posters. This heavy day, one feels, *can't* end in peace.'[5]

September was filled with fear and uncertainty. But it was clear that there were to be many more such months, when Hitler occupied the Sudetenland, an area of Czechoslovakia containing three million Germans, which he called his 'last territorial demand in Europe'. The Czech response was to impose martial law on the Sudetenland and to send troops there. On 14 September, the Prime Minister Neville Chamberlain flew to Berchtesgaden to meet Hitler as tension grew in France and Britain. But instead of confronting Hitler, Chamberlain conceded areas of Czechoslovakia. On 22 September, Chamberlain returned to Germany and met the German leader again at Godesberg. Two days later Greene wrote in his diary: 'Chamberlain's second meeting with Hitler apparently ended in failure . . . Back again where we were on September 14 with war almost certain . . . Rain pouring down: a dreadful unreality over everything.'[6] In London parks there was what amounted to panic trench-digging, and thirty-eight million gas masks were issued.

On 29 September plans were published to evacuate two million people, mostly children, from London. Greene recalled a 'small, rather timid-looking man, the headmaster of an L.C.C. school, while an aeroplane droned low overhead', explaining evacuation plans: 'Railways to be taken over, children to be sent to unknown destinations – the parents informed later by telegrams. The Mother Superior, an old lady with a bone-white face and a twitching upper lip, sat taking notes . . . Most of the London boroughs fitting gas masks . . . ' Greene recorded in his diary: 'Had to pack a bag for Lucy to take to school in case of evacuation. Blanket, one change of underclothes, food for one day. Marked H 105, the mark of the school.'[7] That night was grim and wet. Greene's younger sister Elisabeth came to dinner and they played poker dice for pennies. In Berlin Hitler made a belligerent speech. The next day, 27 September, Greene told his mother how he had 'to drag the old cook almost by main force to be fitted for a gas mask. Vivien and the children are being done this morning. We had an hour's wait in a queue. Nasty smelly things!'

Two days before Munich, his diary reflects a suspicion: 'The Macaulay telephone exchange not working [his number was Macaulay 2529] (Deliberate?)', and the Government's (and his own) preparations for war: 'Anti-aircraft guns set up on Common and trenches apparently being dug. Have planned to evacuate family by car with Eleanor [his brother Raymond's wife] tomorrow afternoon.'[8]

In spite of the fact that the schools had their future evacuation of children well planned, Greene intended to move his own family out of London himself: 'Don't worry too much about arrangements,' he wrote to his mother, 'Vivien, Lucy and Francis are going down with Eleanor tomorrow afternoon, in case Parliament declares a state of emergency right away.' In the same letter, he commented coolly on how he saw his future if war was declared:

I see things rather as follows:
    Immediate conscript is certain. Therefore
    a. one may find oneself in the army with or without a commission. This means small earning power and only a small allowance. In that case one must make one's savings go as far and as long as possible. Under those circumstances I should feel very grateful if my family were boarded out either with Eleanor or you on some sharing basis: we'd contribute of course to rates, labour, etc. as well as board. And this house [14 North Side] would be shut up or let.
    b. one would find oneself in some ministry – of information or propaganda at a reasonable salary. In that case I should take as cheap a lodging as possible in town or get someone to share expenses of this house, and find a cottage, perhaps at Campden, for the children.[9]

But there was no need for immediate evacuation, the day being saved (or lost, depending on your point of view) by Chamberlain's visit to Munich. Britain and France sold out the Czechs and Chamberlain returned to London a hero, waving a piece of paper, a copy of the agreement in which Hitler renounced all belligerent intentions against Britain.

There was a great sense of relief in Britain – many felt that Chamberlain had saved civilisation. In London streets people burst into tears and the Mall and Whitehall swarmed with joyful crowds celebrating because there was to be peace and there would never be another world war.

Greene was not taken in. To his mother he wrote:

I can't say I felt any jubilation about the way things went. We've lost every friend we had in Central Europe, Hitler has got all the supplies necessary for war and when we fight on the next issue I doubt if we shall win. And presumably he'll be confident enough then not to let us creep out of it. The Czechs very naturally are already preferring German friendship to ours. Altogether I feel rather gloomy.[10]

But there *was* to be peace – for one more year.

The difficult months of 1938 over, Greene, on what was to be the last peacetime Christmas for some years, wrote to his mother, thanking her for her presents to the children, asking her to convey his thanks to his sister and aunt for their presents, and adding: 'I ought to write, but the proofs of the Mexican book [*The Lawless Roads*] were unloaded on Christmas Day and I'm hard at the grimmest job of all.' Having children of his own, he realised how his father and mother must have felt with *their* children at Christmas: 'the delicious sense of peace which must come over you when Christmas is safely over, without colds . . . or tears . . . We had a very nice Christmas dinner with Pat [Vivien's brother] and sat drinking brandy to a late hour.'[11]

Three months' respite from the fear of impending war followed. In February, Greene was still involved with the proofs of *The Lawless Roads*, this time the American edition, and anxious to make changes where he felt there was a danger of libel, especially in the case of 'the dentist at La Frontera' called Tench in *The Power and the Glory* and Dr Winter in *The Lawless Roads*, but actually called (ominous name) Carter! In an unpublished notebook Greene wrote, 'I always seem to come across dentists, in life and in my work. They always crop up. The first person I met in Mexico was one. He took me to a brothel and showed me his own girl's teeth. Like most things, one doesn't invent one's dentist – they happen.'[12]

At this point in time, Greene was not sanguine about his career. In a letter now missing, Ben Huebsch of Viking had asked Greene to forgive him. We don't know for what peccadillo, but Greene's answer gives a sense of the novelist's feelings of failure. 'Forgive you? It's you who I hope forgive an as yet unprofitable author.'[13]

By March 1939 Hitler had swallowed up the rest of Czechoslovakia and was now demanding the return of the colonies Germany had lost in the First World War. At last the message percolated through to Britain that Hitler's desire for domination was insatiable. The Government responded by offering guarantees of support to Poland. In the next month, Greene returned the American proofs of *The Lawless Roads*, the book's title being changed to *Another Mexico*, because his American publisher felt that the British title was too critical of their neighbour, Mexico.

Greene was never a man who could live in uncertainty: 'I begin to wish that the war would come . . . only the selfish thought that it would stop the autumn production of *Brighton Rock* gets in the way!'[14] The play, based on the novel, was not to be produced until February 1943. The notoriety that the novel brought Greene expressed itself in a curious way. On 7 April 1939 he wrote to his brother Hugh: 'A new shade for knickers and nightdresses has been named *Brighton Rock* by Peter Jones. Is this fame?'

*

As war again seemed inevitable, Greene (always seeking ideas and future topics) posted off to Huebsch the suggestion that he might write a blow-by-blow account of life in bombed London:

> It has occurred to me that in the event of this silly war coming off, you might be interested in a book called something like THE FIRST HUNDRED DAYS which would be a personal account of conditions in a bombed London – what is happening in newspaper offices, suburban homes, accounts of raids, rumours, gossip, all the things that newspapers leave out because they don't consider them important. It will be a very queer city indeed, down to Victorian size in population. An empty Piccadilly, what a dream! I think a fascinating and bizarre piece of reportage could be done.[15]

Greene wasn't trying to pin Huebsch down as to terms. He simply wanted to know if something of the kind would interest him and then he added, 'these words like "interest" sound horribly cold-blooded, but one's got to treat the whole thing with some indifference if it breaks'.[16]

Huebsch replied at once: 'That's a fine idea of yours to write the history of the first hundred days while the history is actually in the making – or in the devastating – and we will be ready to go with you if, when the time comes (and I hope it won't), the plan should still be feasible.' But, practical to the last button, Huebsch added:

> Considering, however, that every big news gathering organisation would be trying to do the thing that you propose, such understanding as we may have should include arrangements for the immediate printing of your dispatches in a suitable daily or weekly; thus, if civilisation collapses before the hundred days are over we will have collected some money for you and ourselves (even though the money will be worthless after the collapse).[17]

But until money did become worthless, Greene – as all writers without a fixed income must be – was ever watchful as to who owed him money. His literary agents, Pearn, Pollinger & Higham, were never allowed to be slack: 'Dear David,' he wrote to Higham on 16

May, 'this is to remind you that 50 pounds was due to us from Penguin Books on 11 May.' He added, 'Any news from Frere or Albatross?' To which Higham promptly replied: 'we are after the Albatross and the Penguins – both are accursed birds to deal with I am afraid'. With Greene, a contract was a contract to be kept to under all circumstances. He had written to Higham on 1 February: 'Albatross contracted to publish *Brighton Rock* [as a paperback] not later than Feb. 1 & 30 pounds & three copies are now due to us.' He must have expressed his money worries to his wife (evacuated just before war was declared) for she wrote understandingly: 'Darling I know about money & how one must follow it into the darkest & squalidest cavern where it may lurk.' Vivien's letter ends with her usual animal imagery: 'Precious, noblest Timmy, most gallant Mongoose of them all, nobler in stratagem than Mingo's, more faithful & braver than Rikki-Tikki, I salute your quivering nosetip & sensitive ears scarred in many battles for your nestful.'[18]

So there was Greene, in 14 North Side, Clapham Common, living his life and incidentally leaving us a description of that pre-war summer in the 1951 novel *The End of the Affair*.

the daily newspaper, the daily meal, the traffic grinding towards Battersea, the gulls coming up from the Thames looking for bread, and the early summer of 1939 glinting on the park where children sailed their boats – one of those bright, condemned pre-war summers . . . drinking bad South African sherry because of the war in Spain . . . in those years the sense of happiness had been a long while dying under the coming storm . . . The eighteenth century church stood like a toy in an island of grass – the toy could be left outside in the dark, in the dry unbreakable weather.[19]

In the middle of 1939 Greene wrote to Huebsch about his brother Hugh: 'My younger brother who was *Telegraph* correspondent in Berlin has just been expelled after ten years in Germany. He thinks the optimism here is rather blind and we shall get trouble in the autumn.'[20] Hugh Greene understood the Nazi menace. He had visited Dachau concentration camp prior to the incarceration of Jews, when it was mostly filled with communists opposed to National Socialism. To his mother Hugh wrote, 'The guards were quite the most brutal and criminal looking collection of men I've ever seen, quite different from the prisoners . . . The eyes of the prisoners were horrible. I shan't forget that . . .'[21]

In July Huebsch decided to visit London, to discuss directly the book *One Hundred Days*. Greene had yet another idea for a book to discuss with Huebsch, *Refugee Ship*, already sold to Heinemann: 'I want to get on one of these Greek tubs that fill up with refugees at Constanzia [in Romania] and try to smuggle their [Jewish] load into Palestine . . . if only I can get seven feet by three of deck space.'[22] These appalling voyages were in old wooden Greek boats, each carrying 300 or 400 Jews. He saw the original work under three headings: 'The port, the voyage, the landing – or the arrest.' Greene was never to write it, for once war was declared, public interest in Jewish pain disappeared. An in-house memo from his agent Laurence Pollinger records that 'PANAMA FLAG [Greene's final title] didn't go through owing to the war and I expect it will now be washed out or held over till after the war.'[23]

A month before war was declared, Greene went on a six-hour flight on practice bombing manœuvres in a Wellington – his first such experience – from which came an article for the *Spectator*. He described the Wellington as 'the noisiest bomber these pilots have handled', passing Blackwater, Gravesend 'with the oil tanks like white counters'. The target was in Berkshire and they flew at a maximum height of only about 200 feet at 200 mph, too low for gunfire; 'nor could any fighter squadron in the upper air observe us as we bumped just above the hills and woods the same colour as ourselves'. Greene observed that while travelling thousands of feet up, objects below moved slowly across the window-pane, but at fifty feet above the ground 'the world really does flash by – county giving place to county, one style of scenery to another, almost as quickly as you would turn the pages of an atlas'. In Hampshire they were so close to the turf that 'it was like combing a head, up the forehead and over'.

For Greene it was a good day. Even if it had been a real wartime flight, it would still have been a good day. The six-hour flight, sweeping them along to buttered toast and eggs with tea and the radio playing in the mess, led him to conclude that 'action has a moral simplicity which thought lacks'.[24] This seemed a light-hearted adventure, but Greene took it very seriously. Before departure, he left Vivien a sealed envelope at the bottom of which was written: 'To be opened only in the event of death.' She kept this letter unopened until 1947 when Greene and she separated. The letter is dated 'Thursday aft.' and affirms his love for her: 'Darling, dearest heart for ever, this is just a hasty line to say how much I love you. Don't let anything ever make you doubt that. And forgive anything I've ever done to hurt you if this flight ends badly.'

Mostly, Greene kept his head down and worked. In a letter to his mother in the middle of June, whilst admitting that he had an ineradicable antipathy to the physical act of writing, he remarked that in the last twelve months he'd got through a quarter of a million words – 'the travel book, a thriller for the autumn, two-thirds of a novel for the spring, short stories, a B.B.C. play [on Jowett] and weekly reviews'.

And he had plans for travel. His brother Hugh had just been posted to Warsaw and some time earlier had interviewed Dr Goebbels. Greene, no doubt with his brother's assistance, for they were good comrades all their lives, considered a working visit to Poland, but it was too much for him: 'I was going to dash off to Danzig this weekend and see Hugh and Goebbels (with articles for the *Spectator* and *Tablet*), but the thought of 80 hours in a third-class carriage in the end put me off.' And in London it was all go:

> we have a long parade of cocktail parties. Last Thursday Aunt Polly came to lunch: I met her and V. at the Aeolian Hall for the Hawthornden prize-giving . . . Afterwards we filled up time at an exhibition of early English water-colours and tea at Stewarts. Then V. went home, and I took Aunt P. to the Café Royal and we both drank gin till it was time to take her to the train. I enjoyed my two days walking with Hugh in spite of hay fever Yesterday there was an A.R.P. demonstration on the Common, and a barrage balloon went up. Both [children] were excited, but Francis said, 'Saw ballooloo afore long time.' This must be a memory of last September.[25]

With the war fast approaching, Greene had a presentiment that he would die before completing his greatest novel *The Power and the Glory*. He feared this would deprive his family of financial security and so wrote Vivien a second letter to be opened only in the event of his death. She kept this letter also unopened until her marriage was breaking up. She thought it would express his great love for her, a love often promised and still longed for. 'It was not what I hoped for. All it did was to tell me how his novel was to be completed. I was so very disappointed.'[26] From a literary point of view, it is fascinating to see that Greene had worked out in detail how he would end his novel long before he completed it, but perhaps he worked the conclusion of the novel out in detail so that some money could be paid for unfinished work. Indeed, he insisted upon this, suggesting Vivien could write a synopsis, which he then promptly supplied himself:

Darling will you see that David [Higham] makes Heinemann pay up for the unfinished book – it's novel length as it is & you know roughly how it was to end & could write a synopsis: The dying American exists, but of course he's a trap. A long scene was to follow between the priest & the lieutenant in which their different ideas of what's good for the people really come into the open. They are stranded all one night by rain. The priest teaches the lieutenant card tricks & they both grow to appreciate something of the other's position. The priest is brought back to Villahermosa, he is given permission to confess – to Padre José (a good scene!) & dies believing in his own wickedness – the lieutenant gives the *coup de grace*. Then we have a final section of the onlookers – Captain Fellows & his sick wife in a hotel waiting for a boat (we gather without any direct statement that it's the child after all who had died); the Spanish mother reading to her children the absurd account of Juan's martyrdom – so different from the priest's in its stilted piety, & last Mr Tench who heard the shots in the prison yard as he was fitting in a new tooth for the jefe 'With the death of that little man it seemed to him for a moment that all the blood had drained out of the world.' [This last statement does not appear in the novel.]

Greene's fear about their poverty led him to end his 'final letter' with a note on his financial position:

> I'm sorry – so sorry – to leave you in a hole, my heart. Insurance about 2,800 pounds, house value about 2,300 pounds. Overdraft about 1,500 pounds. Securities between us of about 2,000 pounds. Leaves 5,000 odd. I hope *Brighton Rock* [the play] will help there.
> Goodbye, my darling, for a while.
> Your lover.

It was his continued fear that he'd leave his family short that determined Greene to write yet another 'entertainment'* (*The Confidential Agent*), working on it in the mornings, while he 'ground' on slowly with *The Power and the Glory* in the afternoons. To create a proper atmosphere for work, free from telephone calls and the cries of children, he took a studio in Mecklenburgh Square – 'a lovely

---

* In his preface to *Three Plays*, Greene writes, 'The strain of writing a novel, which keeps the author confined for a period of years with his depressive self, is extreme and I have always sought release in "Entertainments" for melodrama as much as farce is an expression of a manic mood' (p. xiii). An entertainment is generally a melodramatic thriller where there is an almost exclusive concentration on outward action and less on character development.

eighteenth century square in those days, but most of it, including my
studio . . . blown to pieces two years later'.[27]

Soon after renting it, he met Walter Allen, the critic and novelist,
unexpectedly: 'I was at a loss because I sensed that Greene was. What
was he doing in that part of the world at that time of day? We
walked across Guilford Street to a pub on the corner of Millman
Street, where in the saloon bar you could hear Welsh spoken. He
told me he had taken a room in Bloomsbury to write in. He planned
to keep office hours. It was a secret; only his wife knew of it and the
address and telephone number.'[28] His wife knew and approved:

> I don't think he wanted to see the children much – that was why
> he found a workshop elsewhere – they were quite good and very
> small. No, I think that he just needed to – and I can understand
> that. You want enough [freedom] to make you feel you are
> working and starting something fresh. You don't want to hear
> doors opening and shutting, and you don't want to step out of
> your room for a minute and feel you are back in a domestic
> setting. You want to be quite separate.[29]

Vivien could not have anticipated the dangers that would arise from
such an arrangement.

The pressure of writing two separate books told on him and to
keep up the pace he used benzedrine. For six weeks he started each
day with a tablet, renewing the dose at midday:

> Each day I sat down to work [on *The Confidential Agent*] with no
> idea of what turn the plot might take and each morning I wrote,
> with the automatism of a planchette, two thousand words instead
> of my usual stint of five hundred words. In the afternoons *The
> Power and the Glory* proceeded towards its end at the same leaden
> pace unaffected by the sprightly young thing who was so quickly
> overtaking it.[30]

By early May (an incredible six weeks) Greene had completed *The
Confidential Agent*.* Charles Evans and A. S. Frere of Heinemann
liked it and he then offered it to Viking: 'You've heard from Mary

---

* He was not home two weeks before he told Huebsch that he'd begun a novel while
in Mexico – 'scene England & West Africa, but have laid it aside for the moment & have
started a thriller instead [*The Confidential Agent*] with the idea of writing it simultaneously
with the Mexican book, so that when I get stuck on one I can turn to the other.' Greene
laid aside the manuscript – 'scene England & West Africa' – so effectively that to his dying
day he could no longer remember it, and the fragment has disappeared.

[Pritchett, his agent in America] about a thriller . . . Evans and Frere like this and think it very saleable over here,' but he admitted, with his usual honesty, that it was a lightweight affair: 'I'm giving it to [Heinemann] outside my contract for 300 pounds instead of 500. I feel it's only fair not to ask for the full advance from you.'[31]

Charles Evans particularly liked the book: 'Charlie had seized "THE CONFIDENTIAL AGENT" off his desk and read and liked it very much,'[32] wrote Greene's agent, who therefore hoped to receive the full contracted sum. However, Greene's last novel, *Brighton Rock*, had only earned £256 in the nine months since publication, and the publishers decided to exercise caution and pay a smaller advance.

It did not receive immediate praise and even his friend, Derek Verschoyle, in reviewing it admitted that 'Mr. Greene, with his eyes fatally fixed on Hollywood, has slapped his hero down against a merely formal background and handed out action neat.'[33] Greene disowned it himself in a gentle way: 'perhaps it is not really one of mine. It was as though I were ghosting for another man. D, the chivalrous agent and professor of Romance literature, is not really one of my characters, nor is Forbes, born Furtstein.'[34] The book moved rapidly because he was not struggling with his own technical problems. 'I was to all intents ghosting a novel by an old writer who was to die a little before the studio in which I had worked was blown out of existence.'[35] The 'old writer' Greene had in mind – he died on 26 June 1939 at Deauville – was Ford Madox Ford, whom Greene admired immensely.

In spite of his demur, *The Confidential Agent* is characteristically Greene. Verschoyle criticised Greene's emphasis on violence ('[it] has become an obsession') and on those 'parts of the human nature that are mirrored in the police courts'. Also, it is a world where there is 'no nobility, no beauty (except of female appearance), no integrity unless allied to incompetence, in which trust is absent and suspicion ubiquitous, confidence and generosity unknown and greed and fear universal'.[36] The review appeared soon after war had been declared, and it was war which taught us about perfidious man and his partiality for violence, a lesson Greene already knew.

Greene's serious doubts about the significance of the novel rose again in the 1950s when he was considering which novels to include in the Uniform Edition of his work. He wrote to John Hayward (whom he had known since 1931 and whose judgment he trusted) asking him if he would take a look at *The Confidential Agent* ('written in a great hurry . . . because I thought war was coming and wanted money in the bank'), to see whether he should include it in the Uniform Edition. Greene's own feeling was against inclusion (it is significant that in the manuscript Greene used not his own name but the pseudonym Henry Gough) and he promised to take Hayward's judgment as final.[37]

But if it was money that was of such importance, and if, as Verschoyle suggested, Greene had his eyes 'fatally fixed on Hollywood', then Greene played his cards right because Warner Brothers bought the book before publication. The film caught the spirit of the book and Charles Boyer was splendid as the world-weary Spanish loyalist. Greene especially admired Boyer's ability to wear 'worry like a habit on his forehead'. In an undated letter to her husband, Vivien recalled opening *Vogue* and seeing *The Confidential Agent* listed under 'Books to Beat the Blackout' and being thrilled.

*

Greene, forcing the pace, suffered for it: 'At five o'clock I would return home with a shaking hand, a depression which fell with the regularity of tropical rain, ready to find offence in anything and to give offence for no cause.'[38] He broke himself of the benzedrine habit by taking smaller and smaller doses. In looking back, he felt that 'those benzedrine weeks were more responsible than the separation of war and my own infidelities for breaking our marriage'.[39] However, although his marriage was still far from over, there were difficulties in the offing since Greene was highly sexed and his wife less so. But neither benzedrine nor his infidelities led to the break up of his marriage during the war – that process was infinitely slow.

On 23 August 1939 communist Russia signed a non-aggression pact with Nazi Germany, disillusioning many who thought Russia the natural enemy of Germany. Immediately the Molotov–Ribbentrop treaty was signed, Greene, thinking war would now come quickly, evacuated his family. He moved his wife and two children to his mother's home in Crowborough, Sussex. Vivien recalled the event:

> We went from Clapham Common in a taxi to Crowborough. I had a kitten and a canary in a cage and my children and a German refugee called Lore. Lucy was sick in the taxi. We had the dear little cat and the children's bird and clothes and blankets. Toys, clocks, furniture, books or valuables were left. That's how we went to Crowborough. Graham's mother's house was very cold and there wasn't much room really. The cat was never allowed in the living quarters of the house. The canary we had to give away at Crowborough.[40]

The final act leading to war was Germany's invasion of Poland on 1 September 1939. Hearing the news, the well-known literary editor John Lehmann remembered that he had the feeling he was slipping down into a pit, clutching at grass, which did not stop his accelerating descent into darkness. Thousands of children were evacuated from London. Reluctantly, and only after a revolt by his cabinet, Chamberlain issued an ultimatum that unless German forces withdrew from Poland, a state of war would exist. There was no response from Germany and on Sunday 3 September, war was declared: 'Everything that I have believed in during my public life has crashed in ruins,' Chamberlain said movingly. He at last recognised that the country would be fighting 'evil things . . . brute force, bad faith, injustice, oppression and persecution'.

Greene continued to live at 14 North Side, Clapham Common, troubled by the sudden departure of his family, but seeing no alternative. Separation because of war was, he felt, much worse for Vivien. 'I've always had a feeling for a physical anarchy,' he wrote to Vivien, 'to match the philosophical anarchy!' And because they were short of money, Greene told his wife that he was being frugal: 'I'm living very economically, 6d breakfast, 8d lunch, & 1/6d supper at the outside!'[41] Perhaps he was hinting to Vivien that she too should be frugal: she had a passion for antiques and for jewellery.

Only a few days before the declaration of war, Greene described a changed city: 'London very odd. Dim lighting, pillar boxes turned into white zebras in some parts. The [Clapham] Common a mass of tents and nobody about on North Side. All the old shabby pound notes which would have been destroyed are being stored in the country in case the printing works (used by the *Spectator*) are destroyed.'[42]

Once war was declared, it was believed that devastating raids would be made immediately on London: 'My imagination', said Churchill, 'drew pictures of ruin and carnage and vast explosions,' but it was a year before the Luftwaffe attempted the destruction of London. Londoners began to make preparations the day war was declared. Pubs had cardboard stuck over their windows, providing a total blackout so that German bombers flying at night received no assistance. Greene himself had an odd-job man put plywood under the skylight of 14 North Side to prevent broken glass falling into the house.

That first day there were two false alarms when the sirens sounded and policemen riding bicycles blew whistles. They had placards around their necks advising everyone to take cover. Somewhat jokingly, Greene wrote to his wife: 'An historical document, a first war impression. I heard it on the radio, and Ronald [Matthews] rang up before it finished. So I said, "You've heard the war's begun," and he hadn't.' Something of Greene's self-discipline comes out when we realise that in spite of the declaration of war he had to review H. E. Bates's *The Flying Goat*: 'Awful to sit down this morning to a review of Bates.' But, like a true professional, he wrote it.

Greene was struck by the fact that there was no panic of any kind and no scurrying about. He himself went out to the Prince of Wales theatre to see Douglas Byng ('very funny') and Nelly Wallace. He found the night very lovely and impressive 'with all the sky signs gone and little blue phosphorescent milk bars and a hurdy-gurdy invisibly playing – rather like a Paris back-street':

A newspaperman calling, "Ave a paper tonight,' plaintively. Another one very conversational, 'Reminds me of the trenches. Never knew which way you was going.' . . . After the all-clear went last night it was curiously like Christmas morning: the voices of air raid wardens going home like people returning from Midnight Mass.[43]

2

Enter Dorothy

Against the beautiful and the clever and the successful,
one can wage a pitiless war, but not against the un-
attractive.

— GRAHAM GREENE

THE letter which Greene had left Vivien, on the occasion of his
flight in the Wellington, his plea for forgiveness for anything
he'd ever done to hurt her, she took as a reference to his wartime
affair with Dorothy Glover.

> Dorothy began in 1938 or 1939, when I found it impossible to
> work at home because of the children. I saw an advertisement for
> a studio to be rented in Mecklenburgh Square. I went there where
> Dorothy was living with her mother. It was just a work room . . .
> it wasn't a studio in the French sense with a bed . . . It was simply
> a room to work in. That is how we met. And she reduced the
> price because she thought I looked rather poor and I was a poor
> struggling author.[1]

It is possible to date the beginning of that affair more accurately.
In a letter written to Vivien on the day war was declared, Greene
recounts the first air-raid warning and his immediate visual
experiences — seeing a woman, in an unhurried manner, pass down
the street; watching the huge barrage balloons rising in the sky;
noting the odd scene of pigeons making a mass dive for shelter and
his feeling that this was the end of civilisation.* Behind this
experience lay another secret, one which he confided to Malcolm
Muggeridge: 'Greene told me that he was working in his rented
work room when the war was declared and he looked out of the

---

* In the same letter he provided his wife with an account of his activities: 'I'm very
snug: work in the morning, then go out and see people; and have my three halves, and
wander round.'

window. There were all the barrage balloons rising into the sky and a sort of exaltation seized him. Looking behind him, he saw Miss Glover looking out of the window too and there was the beginning of this rather weird affair.'[2] Here was the truth hidden from Vivien. Greene rented the work room in early May when he began writing *The Confidential Agent*, which he finished in six weeks. Thus he rented it at the end of March or the beginning of April 1939, well before the first air-raid and the declaration of war. There is also one conflicting piece of information which perhaps confirms that the beginning of the affair was earlier than the first air-raid on London.

Hugh Greene suggested in April 1939 that Graham and he should meet in Paris. Greene turned his brother down even though he longed to escape from London and felt 'a passionate nostalgia for Paris': 'In confidence life at the moment is devilishly involved, psychologically. War offers the only possible solution.'[3] If Greene had lived in the same house as Dorothy since the end of March or the beginning of April, this cryptic note might well refer to an affair already begun and of such seriousness that war offered the only possible solution – war and the immediate evacuation of his family, not only to his mother's home in Crowborough, but out of the country altogether.

Quite soon after his family's evacuation to Crowborough, Greene tried to send them abroad. This was not to give himself a free hand with his affair, though this may have been a factor, but because he was deeply concerned for their survival. An undated letter shows him trying to persuade Vivien to leave the country:

Rupert's [Hart-Davis] just been on the phone to say he's sending Comfort [his wife] & children to U.S. So if it does happen you'll find half our world on the other side . . . I absolutely agree with you about Winnipeg. That's only our last straw. Toronto is far preferable. Laurence [Pollinger] says it's a lovely city, full of parks & lakeside, & he has a great friend there who'll help you. You're only a few hours too from New York & [I] might be able to transfer there.[4]

The wealthy were sending their families abroad in great numbers to escape the expected German air onslaught on London. Angus Calder reports that 5,000 people left for America in the first forty-eight hours after war was declared.[5] Something of the anxieties of the time is reflected in a letter written to Vivien by an unknown friend; it also shows how advanced Greene's plans were to move his family out of the country:

It's all absolute Hell and I'm miserable & exhausted with the effort of a decision. However, we feel it's best anyway to get our permits to go. We shall both go to New York & then on if we do. What is your Canadian address? A friend of ours is going at the end of this month and perhaps she will be on your ship.[6]

Greene also considered Jamaica. There was a suggestion that H. V. Morton's family would go to Jamaica and Greene's family would follow suit.[7] Greene returned to the topic of overseas evacuation on a number of occasions.

Cable last night from Mary [Pritchett]: 'Trying another angle getting Vivien and children here. Business connection impossible.' That refers to my guarded message about you acting as my representative. Temporary dependence seems required, and two affidavits from host and bank. I think you ought to send a long explanatory cable too to your Canadian relatives, getting their address by phone or wire . . . Shall try and get U.S. immigration form today at lunch time. Such a rush. Don't be scared or unhappy, dear heart. Here's Mary's address in case of need.[8]

The more pressure Greene put on his wife to leave, the more she was inclined to resist, for she began to wonder (as she told me) whether she would ever be brought back.

Vivien was right to sense danger and to feel instinctively that it came from Graham's affair with Dorothy. Its seriousness is reflected in a scene in *The End of the Affair*. Sarah, wife of a leading Civil Servant in the Department of Home Security (the irony does not escape the hero Bendrix) falls in love with Bendrix and he with her. It happens when Sarah and Bendrix are dining at Rules.* At the moment of helping themselves to onions, they fall in love: 'It wasn't of course, simply the onions – it was that sudden sense of an individual woman, of a frankness that was so often later to make me happy and miserable. I put my hand under the cloth and laid it on her knee, and her hand came down and held mine in place.'[9]

The sense of love coming at the time both are eating onions is sufficiently bizarre to be based on a real model. After the war, when his long-standing affair with Dorothy was beginning to wane, he fell in love with a married woman, Catherine, later Lady, Walston, love revealing itself when they were eating onion sandwiches. But what

---

* Rules, a popular restaurant in Maiden Lane, was a favourite with Hugh and Graham Greene. Until recently a huge caricature of them both, done by the cartoonist Low, hung above what was known as the 'Greene table'.

follows the eating of the onions in *The End of the Affair*, when they leave Rules restaurant, is based on his experience with Dorothy not Catherine. Greene was moving between two lovers in his life and using the experience for fictional purposes.

In the fictional affair 'there was no pursuit and no seduction' and they leave half the good steak on their plates and a third of the bottle of claret and come into Maiden Lane with the same intention. By the doorway and the grill, they kiss:

> I said, 'I'm in love.'
> 'Me too.'
> 'We can't go home.'
> 'No.'
> We caught a taxi by Charing Cross Station and I told the driver to take us to . . . Leinster Terrace, the row of hotels that used to stand along the side of Paddington Station with luxury names, Ritz, Carlton, and the like. The doors of these hotels were always open and you could get a room any time of day for an hour or two. A week ago I revisited the terrace. [The hero is writing at the time of the blitz.] Half of it was gone – the half where the hotels used to stand had been blasted to bits, and the place where we made love that night was a patch of air. It had been the Bristol; there was a potted fern in the hall and we were shown the best room by a manageress with blue hair: a real Edwardian room with a great gilt double bed and red velvet curtains and a full-length mirror . . . I remember the trivial details very well: how the manageress asked me whether we wanted to stay the night: how the room cost fifteen shillings for a short stay: how the electric meter only took shillings and we hadn't one between us, but I remember nothing else – how Sarah looked the first time or what we did, except that we were both nervous and made love badly. It didn't matter. We had started – that was the point.[10]

This incident in a hotel near Paddington station is based on fact. It was not the first time that Greene and Dorothy had made love, but Vivien Greene recalled her husband's experience:

> He took Dorothy to a lodging house in the road that's opposite Paddington Station, and when they got there found it was kept by somebody who had been on the set, not acting but in some other capacity, of the film or play of *Brighton Rock*. I don't know why he went to a lodging house with her. But I know that he did go to this house and the door was opened by this woman. He told me

all this, and said how taken aback, and what a sort of strain of superstition he felt. It was so extraordinary that out of the thousands and thousands of houses that he could go to, that this person should turn up there. Dorothy was one of the great loves of his life, he told me.[11]

Greene thought that Dorothy was slightly younger than his wife, but her birth certificate shows that she was born on 17 May 1901, so was older than Graham by three years and Vivien by four. She was already thirty-eight when she met Greene. David Low, the bookseller who knew Greene and Dorothy during the blitz, recalled that she was 'happy, small, rather stoutish, not smart but very friendly – she radiated friendliness. She gave you a sense of feeling at home in her company – she had a nice laugh.' David Higham's account tallies with Low's:

I used to know Dorothy. She was a strange little person – very small. Greene was kind to her – she was always hard up: she was an accident-prone girl. She was always breaking her leg or her wrist or something. She was short and a bit stout (though not fat), stocky more than anything. I could see no sexual attraction at all. She was nice. I liked her, but that's a different thing.[12]

Greene's brother Hugh, admitting she was very small, less than five foot (Hugh was six foot six), remembered her as thin and boyish with short bobbed hair.[13]

Many people were mystified by Greene's interest in Dorothy, in particular Malcolm Muggeridge: 'I was thinking of old Glover who rather strangely enough was very intimate with him and whom he was extraordinarily good to. She was a person who, on the grounds of attractiveness, was absolutely a non-starter. I mean, she was alright but she was a very ordinary kind of person and not the sort of person you'd think in worldly terms he'd be attracted to, and yet he was devoted to her.'[14] But Muggeridge also stressed Greene's enigmatic nature:

He's a curious man in the sense that there is no one who has any ultimate intimacy with him, not any man, perhaps some woman. [Later Muggeridge doubted even this.] The characteristic of Greene is that he has shunned intimacy, even with his brother Hugh, his closest friend. He would know more about him in the sense that they were brothers and shared the same background but he'd be the same enigma to him also.*[15]

A partial account of Dorothy, though no less accurate, was provided by Vivien Greene. Dorothy was in her fifties when Vivien met her for the first and only time; the 'thin, little girl' Hugh Greene admired (and Greene's brother did admire her enormously) had long since disappeared, though Graham Greene's love had not. Greene had been separated from his wife half a dozen years at the time of this meeting. Vivien came to London and visited him unexpectedly – something she normally did not do:

> We went upstairs and came in. I don't think we went much further than the hall, and we were just chatting. He was a bit uneasy and presently a small stoutish woman in blue glasses, like a character in a Victorian novel, came up the stairs. She was quite small and roly-poly, and she came up and was taken aback and said, 'Oh! Graham, I came to ask if I could borrow your telephone – I wanted to telephone my furrier.' At once I thought, 'Fancy climbing three flights of stairs to borrow a telephone and then to telephone your furrier at about 6.45.' He introduced us, and I made a get-away. He was taking her out to dinner obviously, and this ridiculous story about a furrier.[16]

Very little is known about Dorothy's background, though by the time Greene met her she was a book illustrator and, probably, along with her mother, a landlady as well. Vivien remembered Greene telling her that Dorothy had danced in the chorus of *Chu Chin Chow* and that she had married an American soldier in the First World War (she would have been very young to have done that), but that the marriage broke up.[17]

A theatre review of the revival of *Chu Chin Chow* appearing in the *Spectator* on 1 August 1941, and signed D. M. Glover, stated: 'During the last war I watched every performance of *Chu Chin Chow* from the stage – as a small urchin in any scene; where there was an odd corner to fill . . . Last week I watched the revival of *Chu Chin Chow* at the Palace Theatre from the stalls.' The First World War version of *Chu Chin Chow* was popular between the years 1916 and 1919, so Dorothy was not a small urchin but a teenager; perhaps she was hiding her real age from her lover.

* Greene's sister Elisabeth was in my company during the interview and did not disagree with Muggeridge's judgment.

Vivien recalled Dorothy with a dispassionate air: 'She was quite a lot older and looked it. She was square and small, but Graham said something about the most terrific sort of sexual thrill he had was seeing her sitting in a red dressing gown in front of a dressing table. He did tell me such things. I think there was a certain element of seeing what my reaction would be. I think very largely too as a novelist.'[18]

*

But if Vivien suspected an affair, her letters early in the war reveal only her love, often expressed in small domestic ways. At one point Greene had asked about a present she'd sent him which he believed hadn't arrived: 'Oh you poor, poor darling – the tiny present was only Jaeger socks. Didn't you notice you sent 1 sock & 2 came back?'

Greene's letters also contain no hint that he was no longer living at 14 North Side. On one occasion, she telephoned him in the morning without catching him. Graham explained, rather dubiously, why this was so: '9 is a bad time to ring up: I'm either shaving in the bathroom & can't hear, or out getting my breakfast. And at night there's always the chance that I'm in bed or out . . .'[19]

His affair with Dorothy was thriving, but his love for Vivien still flourished and sometimes there is a faint whiff of guilt in the phrasing of a letter:

> Your letter today made me miss you so much . . . I've been to a bad film and it's pouring with rain and I was cut off from you on the phone because of a trunk call . . . Now there's lightning and a drum, drum, drum on the skylight. Lightning in November. The whole world's crazy . . . It's like when I go to Mexico or Liberia or some place: I only know how deeply I love you when you are not at hand to speak to.[20]

The New Year came in with bitter cold – 'it is so cold', Vivien wrote three days into 1940, 'that one isn't much enticed out, even for a jaunt'. But her concern was for her husband's welfare: 'Darling . . . keep warm, don't economise on warm food. You must eat well & have Nescafe or "Camp" & Bovril in the house when you want a hot drink . . . awfully important to have one the moment you feel chilled or seedy.'

When Vivien worried about their future together – 'There's no one to nuzzle up to. Will we ever have our teas together, I wonder? It will take years after the war for things to come right again, won't it?' – he replied gently, 'Darling, don't feel so sad. It won't take any time to get back to normal and our teas. Things are strange and unshipped, I know: one doesn't feel properly oneself. But cats can see in the dark, and we'll come creeping along to find each other.'[21] Vivien immediately responded: 'Your letter was so perfect & made me so consoled & happy. I put it in the gold envelope with the telegram & shall carry it about & keep it under my pillow.'[22] Believing that true love had returned, she expressed herself in her 'special' language, not realising that both cat imagery and cat-like activities (which early in his marriage pleased him as evidence of her love), now felt 'sticky' – much too sentimental and too physically close. She did not know that what she wrote had the opposite effect to the one she intended: 'Darling, it is always & will always continue to be touching & wonderful that "Sourpuss the Jamesian" likes being loved and purred over. Well, I do purr over you and stroke you . . . & wish to burnish your fur with much caressing & soft words of trust and affection.'* [23]

What Vivien was working up to was to return to 14 North Side, for the blitz had not yet materialised and people were returning to London in droves:

> I would like to come & look after you, especially if it wouldn't destroy the romantic . . . feeling. You wouldn't see much of me. I would banish you to work & only notice you *really* at tea time. You could have a meal on a tray in your study when you liked, if you didn't want to stop the 'run' – absolutely no bother. And it wouldn't cost *very* much more, as you'd have the 15/- for me here, & we'd live very simply. I'd not open any A/Cs for us two but trot out with a basket & buy just what was wanted & pay so when I went back to Crowb[orough]., there'd be no complications.[24]

Greene handled the threatened return of his wife by suggesting that Vivien visit him once a fortnight. Her desire to return is palpable: 'I must come & see how you are & do a cake,' but one senses her fear also: 'I have a key & shan't trouble you. I would arrive about 11 I suppose after buying materials. If you can remember to tell me measurements of window & door-window in kitchen as I will order blackout blinds.' Her anxiety grew as the time

---

* Greene hated being purred over or stroked or having his 'fur burnished' or being called 'Sourpuss the Jamesian', though Greene's love of James was central and he often mimicked James's style in letters.

for her short visit came near – the first since she'd been forcefully evacuated. Clearly she saw it as a period when love would be renewed since the children would be staying at Crowborough: 'I do love you. You *will* telephone if you want me? I will come home in about 10 days for my first fortnight.' The visit was only a week away and whilst admitting that owing to the cold weather, her brain was functioning very slowly – it was one of the coldest Januarys on record – she went on to say pathetically: 'I do feel Stupe & that is vaguely dispiriting. As we haven't been to Tenerife or Fez together you don't know & can't imagine how amusing I might or could be or what an affectionate Love! These are true words.'[25]

On the occasion of their twelfth wedding anniversary, Greene still asserted his love 'as I have always said & shall always say – how dearly I love you & how glad I am we got married', and he urged his wife not to be depressed: 'There are good times coming I feel sure. We'll all be snug again together with your objects [Victorian *objets d'art*] & my books.'[26]

Greene, I should imagine, had little hope that good times were coming for he was never sanguine about his future. Always sensitive to another's pain, he was simply trying to comfort Vivien. However, at this time he was involved in an ordinary, rather shabby deception, but one practised casually enough in many lives.

*

Vivien, though often under strain, was not always unhappy and she cleverly presents us with the tedious character of living as an evacuee in wartime Britain with in-laws: Greene's mother is M, Father is Da, and N is his Aunt Nora:

M: Oh, Nora, remind me I must ring up Miss Hazlett about the sandwiches for Weds W.I.

Da: (Ponderously) One thing the War *has* done is to draw the Empire together . . .

N: Are you having rock cakes as well for the soldiers?

Da: I wonder what Stalin is thinking *now* about the Petsavo peninsula . . . ! (Very Slowly)[27]

Greene's father was a diabetic and Marion Greene attended to his every need, religiously giving him injections of insulin. She also read aloud to him countless detective stories, which were his passion.

Vivien recalled a further scene: 'Aunt N is resting with a [hot water] bottle, Mumma is faithfully reading aloud to Da, I hope for her sake Trollope & not Scott. Did I tell you that she read [Dorothy Sayers's] BUSMAN'S HONEYMOON aloud!! Helga [Hugh's wife, also living at Crowborough] and I insisted she must have skipped for the sake of Da's delicacy: he said quite interested – "I didn't notice you skipping. Did you skip?" Mumma smiled rather mysterious & said It was too long ago to remember.'[28]

But 'Da's delicacy' was his wife's also. Little wonder that Greene broke away from the limiting conventions of the household. On one occasion Marion Greene, reading *Old Moore's Almanack* for 1939 and noticing that it failed to suggest that war would break out that year, expostulated, 'He doesn't seem to know *anything* . . . ' Vivien wanted to read the almanack, but was not allowed to because Greene's mother felt that the advertisements were indecent. She intended to tear it up and later did so.[29]

Marion Greene treated Vivien as if she were not yet old enough to make adult decisions: 'It is so awful,' she explained to her husband, 'being a schoolgirl after having been a proud 'ook [Vivien's nickname for being a wife].'

Greene's early letters to his separated family often listed incidentally what he saw:

Steel helmets on sale in fashionable hatters in Jermyn St. This explains men with steel helmets waiting for buses; prostitute ensconced for custom in a sandbag dog trot outside Swan and Edgar's in the black-out. Yesterday afternoon I saw a lovely sight in a blue sky. Eleven planes making an enormous diving arc with their exhausts, pursued apparently by our fighters in another huge circle. They were like skaters on blue ice & their tracks stayed in the sky for about ten minutes afterwards.[30]

Vivien's letters were about domestic happenings, and her love for her husband and children, but she could express her isolation delicately: 'Bizet wrote Carmen, Wagner wrote Lohengrin. Nobody writes me: Gee, I'm lonesome!'[31]

*

In London, Greene was looking for new and exciting ways to be employed: 'I've written to Frere who is now some big gun in Whitehall to do with man-power,' he wrote to Vivien, 'suggesting that a group of younger writers should be formed, parallel to that of the war artists in the last war, to record various aspects of all the fronts.' And he added, 'Seems to me something might be pulled in that way.'[32]

He was as busy as ever writing reviews of fiction and films for the *Spectator*; he was working on *The Power and the Glory*, while his agent Nancy Pearn was trying to place his work in the popular press – unsuccessfully as it turned out. Greene sent Pearn a short synopsis of stories for the *Daily Herald*, but it wasn't acceptable. The synopsis was offered to the *Strand* magazine and again turned down: 'After all, five hundred words is mighty little in which to outline five stories,' wrote the editor, 'for everything depends on the plot and treatment of each story.' But the editor's chief objection was that the outline was depressing, such insistence being made on the sordidness and squalor surrounding the whole concern. 'I should love to have a Graham Greene story set in a London scene, and if needs be I wouldn't mind it reasonably tough, but I don't want the atmosphere to be just gloom.'[33]

The month war was declared, Greene's thriller *The Confidential Agent* (a perfect title to attract a nation entering upon the uncertainties of conflict) appeared, and in October was published in America.

He was still working on *The Power and the Glory* when 'during the Winter of 1939' he received a summons to meet the draft board for emergency reserve officers. The days of anxiety which had driven him to write so fast and which had led to an addiction to benzedrine were over and he passed A1 in health. The board consisted of a major-general and two colonels.[34] They first asked him how he 'visualized' himself. On Greene not giving them the answer they wanted, they rephrased the question, 'but how do you *see* yourself?'

All three watched with anxiety. I was aware of their bated breath, and I felt some sympathy for what they had endured day by day from all my fellow reservists . . . I believe they dreaded the thought that once again they were to suffer that word 'Intelligence'. They leaned a little forward in their chairs and I had the impression that they were holding out to me, in the desperation of their boredom, a deck of cards with one card marked. I decided to help them. I took the marked card and said, 'I suppose . . . the Infantry.'

One of the colonels gave a sigh of relief and the general said with unmistakable pleasure, 'I don't think we need ask Mr Greene any more questions, do you?'

I had so evidently pleased them that I thought I could safely make a small request. I only needed a few more months to complete *The Power and the Glory*. Could my call-up be postponed for a few months?

The general positively beamed. Of course I should have those precious months – 'Shall we say until June [1940]?'[35]

Greene's vagueness about the date of this meeting ('Winter of 1939') was perhaps deliberate. We know the meeting took place in September because a letter to Vivien, though undated, refers both to his board ('I was a little surprised at the Medical Board giving me Grade one. I thought weight, chest expansion and eyes would prevent that') and to his involvement in a *Spectator* competition, an account of which appeared in the magazine on 29 September 1939.

Suggesting a more exact date for the meeting is significant, for if he went in front of the board in late September, he must have already completed *The Power and the Glory*. Indeed, a letter to his wife dated 19 September indicates this: 'It feels awfully peaceful – to have a book [*The Power and the Glory*] finished on the day another one [*The Confidential Agent*] comes out.' Thus Greene persuaded the draft board for reserve officers to give him a further six months to finish *The Power and the Glory* when it was already completed. No doubt he felt it necessary to seek a further reprieve from the draft in order to find extra cash for his family before being called up. In his letter of 19 September to Vivien, Greene added: 'I really do have time to look around. On the chance of a boom I think I shall get a volume of essays ready & see if Mary can sell a volume of short stories in U.S. I feel I can take 3 months before I start another novel or thriller . . . Say 2 months holiday.'

His call up delayed, Greene promptly offered his agent a suggestion for a future volume of essays. He called this *The Heroic Age* and it was to include chapters on Rider Haggard, Stanley Weyman, G. A. Henty, and crime and detective novels (touching on Raffles and Guy Boothby), but alas no wartime publisher wanted it. He then tried out the notion of an anthology: 'It would attempt to give the general view of life as seen by a Catholic mind . . . The reader might find on one page a passage of Crashaw and on another such a murderer's statement as I printed on p. 14 of *Lawless Roads*,* a passage from St. Augustine's City of God might jostle a coroner's report on a suicide.'[36] Greene intended a general picture of the world 'full of horror, grotesqueness, courage, meanness, spirituality, the

---

* 'I went upstairs. My husband was lying on his back. I pulled back the bedclothes, and holding the knife in both hands I made sure to get him in the right place . . . It seemed as if someone hit my hands down with a mallet. The knife went in as if his body was rotten. He sat up in the bed and hollered out, "Hi, hi, hi."'

shadow of the City of God would as it were fall across the whole'.
This also was turned down.

Then Tom Burns, a director of Longman's, suggested that Greene
write the biography of Father Joseph Damien, the Belgian leper
missionary who had himself died from the disease. Greene had long
been interested in this martyr to Christian compassion and dedication, but discovered, under conditions of war, there wasn't enough
material available.

In spite of writing and trying his hand at different forms, he was
ever in need of finding himself a more adventurous life, and he
responded with excitement, in a letter to Vivien, to Bishop David
Matthew's 'wild idea' that he could get Greene 'sent to Central or
South America to look for German submarine bases!' When this fell
through, he expressed the wish to be sent either to the army training
centre (Aldershot) or the front ('the Siegfried Line').[37]

Greene kept busy: he filled the *Spectator* with his incidental pieces
(twenty-one book reviews and thirty-eight film reviews during 1939
alone); he won first prize for a competition in the *Spectator*, using
the pseudonym Hilary Trench (last used when he was writing in the
Oxford Outlook as an undergraduate in 1925). The prize was for the
best letter to the Divisional Petroleum Controller claiming a
supplementary petrol ration in the style of a famous writer. Greene
chose Henry James:

Dear Sir,

The papers 'inform' – if one can use in connexion with our
dear delightful old backward English Press a word which conveys
the vulgar and voluble idea of news – that in less than a week's
time (our days now so hurry on under the pressure of universal
calamity) a law is to be enforced which will prevent even so
modest, so innocent, I was going to say so 'green' a creature as
myself, from purchasing more than a modicum of what my
compatriots call in their gross vivid style, so like their own streets
all concrete foundation, glittering surface and brutal echo, gas.

My wants are humble: far be it from me in a time of ferocious
inquisition and rigid self-examination to lay claim to further
benefit on grounds that are not the most urgent, the most
impelling: I simply beg you as one bred in the bureaucratic
corridors, acquainted as my poor friends are not with the *mœurs*,
conditions and relations responsible for the inconceivably
portentous questions handed to me yesterday, to tell me *tout
doucement* whether I, aged, infirm, out of the vast crowded political
canvas as I am, may yet retain – practically and not as a mere fond

memento of the kindest, the most amiable of ladies – a small gay gorgeous object that goes, so I am told, in the huge hideous undiscriminating world by the abrupt name of a 'lighter'.

Believe me, very truly yours,
Henry James

Greene wrote to his wife afterwards: 'Note in the *Spectator* that your clever Tom has won a guineas-worth of books.'

3

The Ministry and the Glory

The law is silent during war.
— CICERO

THE first six months of the war passed with only limited military action. In December there was the battle of the River Plate, in which the *Admiral Graf Spee*, a German pocket battleship engaged by British ships, sustained heavy damage and took refuge in Montevideo. Ordered to leave the safe harbour, the *Graf Spee* was scuttled, and the captain committed suicide. There were casualties at sea when the destroyer *Exmouth* was torpedoed, but the home front was comparatively safe and quiet, though in January 1940 rationing of butter, sugar and bacon was introduced. Even the IRA (who were promised by the Nazis that, if they helped Germany, the government of Ireland would be handed over to them), exploding two bombs in London in February, killed no one.[1] And because there were no air-raids, family and business life, which had left London with the outbreak of war, began to return. 'Life here', Greene admitted, 'is really rather restful; so pleasant to be free from all the crises of 38–9.' What was the 'restful' Greene like in 1940?

In the early months of the year there was pressure on Chamberlain to retire so that a more vigorous Prime Minister could be appointed. Walter Allen recalled the 'Chamberlain Must Go campaign' when Labour Party members, trade unionists and academics marched in procession through the streets of London and other cities bawling out their slogans. And he also remembered Greene suggesting two practical (and comic) ways of getting rid of Chamberlain:

In one, you had visiting cards printed bearing the names of members of the Cabinet and then you got hold of a selection of dirty books from Paris which you parcelled and sent to Mrs

Neville Chamberlain, Lady Simon, Lady Inskip and the wives of other Cabinet ministers, each parcel containing the visiting card of the ostensible sender, as it might be by Leslie Hore-Belisha or Sir Samuel Hoare. A cross-traffic of such parcels, Graham asserted, would cause the government to cave in in a matter of days.[2]

Greene's second idea was more droll. It was a daring scheme involving a Chamberlain impersonator from the Unity Theatre, half a dozen out-of-work actors made up as Chamberlain and a devilishly tricky timetable. Greene suggested that they find out the date of the next Tory meeting Chamberlain was to attend in Birmingham Town Hall. An hour before the meeting, a wire as from Chamberlain would be sent to the organisers:

'Delayed stop Shall arrive Birmingham thirty minutes late stop Do not hold back start of meeting.' By the time the first ersatz Chamberlain was on the train, the others would follow at half-hourly intervals. Thirty minutes or so after sending the first telegram, a second is despatched: 'Urgent stop Have reason to believe Chamberlain due to arrive Town Hall now not genuine stop Arrest.' Chamberlain would arrive with three or four other Chamberlains angrily denouncing one another as imposters, and in the confusion would be promptly arrested and clapped in handcuffs.[3]

Barbara Wall, then a young married writer in London, with two babies and two novels to her credit, recalls that she was 'infatuated' with Graham Greene, 'as a writer, critic, a person, everything'. She met him at a time of his increasing fame. A friend arranged for them to meet in a Bloomsbury pub at noon:

I arrived first, sat watching the door, my heart going pit-a-pat. At a certain point, in came a tall lean man in a belted mack and a brown trilby with the brim turned down all round. He was in profile to me so I only saw the side of his face between turned-up collar and turned-down brim, but it had a tenseness and a bright-eyed look that made me know *at once* that it was he.

What struck her then 'was his own surprised and wondering look that anybody should want to pay him homage. He was like an astonished child, he being the startled pleased person rather than oneself.'

They went to a restaurant together and she discovered how bad his French was and they talked about Claudel and his famous phrase 'sin also serves':

> Graham didn't know this phrase and was very pleased when I told him of it – meaning as it does, that God can re-cycle sin in a mysterious way to make it work for good – the very essence of *The Power and the Glory*. I recall my amazement at his surprised and almost shy look at things, so totally at variance with the stereotype of the master's attitude vis-a-vis the disciple.[4]

*

Two months before he was due to be called up into the army, Greene warned Huebsch in confidence that he'd been offered the job of looking after the authors' section of the Ministry of Information. Accepting the post, he resigned from the emergency reserve and his chances of becoming an infantry officer abruptly ended. Greene was to stay with the Ministry of Information for only six months, but he must have felt some guilt because only eight months earlier he had criticised London intellectuals in general and one poet in particular: 'The faint susurrus of the intellectuals dashing for ministry posts. [Stephen] Spender feathered his young nest in the Ministry of Information.'[5]

The Ministry of Information was a quaint, amorphous organisation which was disliked by press and public alike. It was set up in Bloomsbury in the University College buildings in Gower Street. The place, according to Muggeridge, was 'teeming with people with briefcases, dispatch riders roaring up to the entrance on motorcycles and commissionaires in blue'.[6] Muggeridge watched the Ministry grow: 'departments mushrooming, and old ones expanding'. He remembered the Ministry's 'thronging corridors, fraudulent output, and voices prophesying peace'.[7]

What Greene recalled appears in a piece ironically entitled 'Men at Work'. It was in a 'heartless building with complicated lifts and long passages like those of a liner and lavatories where the water never ran hot and the nailbrushes were chained like Bibles'.[8] The huge staff of the Ministry accumulated like a kind of fungoid life, 'old divisions sprouted daily, new sections broke away and became divisions and spawned, in turn'. Soon the 500 rooms of the great block became inadequate, as corners of passages were turned into rooms and corridors disappeared overnight.[9] Ultimately, the Ministry employed a thousand members of staff. Greene's own room was little, dark and built of plywood in a passage.

It was Greene's view that the work done at the Ministry was all a game played in a corner under the gigantic shadow of war: 'Propaganda was a means of passing the time: work was not done for its usefulness but for its own sake – simply as an occupation.'[10] Neither Muggeridge nor Greene felt their work had very much use. Muggeridge remembered that he had written feature articles to raise enthusiasm for the Allied cause, though the only tangible evidence of this was a single cutting in a Ceylon newspaper under the title 'Eternal Vigilance'.

Also there was a general air of inefficiency at the Ministry well remembered by Greene. He recalled minutes about a pamphlet to be written on the French war effort still circulating indecisively right up to the time Germany broke the line and occupied Paris. Greene admitted to me that he did very little during his months there. But Muggeridge's view of Greene's performance was different: 'He took a highly professional view of what was expected of us, coolly exploring the possibility of throwing stigmata and other miraculous occurrences in the battle of the mind in Latin America to sway it in our favour.'[11]

Certain letters have survived which show him at work. He wrote to his agent Nancy Pearn that the popular Howard Spring should 'do a pamphlet on German Press and Radio Methods for a series with the general theme of "Life under the Nazis"'. To persuade him, Greene listed others who had made their contribution, politicians and writers: Herbert Morrison, E. M. Delafield, Vernon Bartlett and H. V. Morton.* He asked Spring for 7,000 words and offered a fee of only twenty-five guineas. The pamphlets were to be produced with illustrations in gravure and were intended to reach a popular market; the price was to be threepence.[12] Patriotism touched Mr Spring and he offered to write his pamphlet without a fee. Greene replied with exactly the right tone for a Civil Servant, 'The Minister, I feel sure, will much appreciate your generosity.'[13]

Greene sought others to do propaganda work. He wanted Storm Jameson to write a book about *Woman at War* and wrote to Nancy Pearn about Dorothy Sayers:

We are very anxious to secure a pamphlet from her pen . . . I should like her to take the humorous rather than the minatory line, and that is why I suggest that the pamphlet should take the

---

* Greene recalled to me the illustrated series of pamphlets, published by Collins. H. V. Morton provided an imaginary picture of what England would be like under the Gestapo: 'I rewrote the whole thing because I was afraid that H. V. Morton's style was a bit too popular to be good. It apparently so impressed Churchill that H. V. Morton was invited to go with Churchill on the meeting in the Atlantic with Roosevelt.'

form of a little detective work by Lord Peter Wimsey's wife-mother. The object I think should be to make people laugh at the absurdity of rumours rather than warn them of their dangers.[14]

While asking others to contribute to the war effort, Greene also wrote a propaganda piece. In one sense it was a straightforward morale booster entitled 'The Lieutenant Died Last', a story which tells how a poacher brought about the successive deaths of a small German contingent, an advance guard for a Nazi invasion. It's a minor story but it reveals Greene's commendable moral courage in wartime: the showing of sympathy for the enemy. After the poacher has shot the German lieutenant, he finds in the officer's pocket a photograph of a naked baby on a hearth rug, and his stomach turns over. The poacher can never forget that he killed the baby's father.

It was published in *Collier's*, an outlet for material produced by the Ministry of Information. The poacher, an unlikely hero, had one wall of his cottage repaired with petrol tins and slept on a bed of rags with his windows obscured by sacking. He was based on Charles Sykes, a one-time educated man who after a breakdown became a tramp and used to parade in rags through the village of Campden when Greene lived there in the early 1930s. His cottage contained a broken chair, straw where he used to sleep, and a sink.[15]

On 28 May 1940 Evelyn Waugh, arriving in London and hearing the news of the Belgian surrender, went to the Ministry of Information. Greene's desire to escape from the Ministry to more active duty is clear in a scheme he propounded to Waugh for official writers to the forces. Greene himself hoped to become attached to the Marines.[16] He wanted to be engaged in a real war, a war which was becoming increasingly grim. If he could have established writers at the Front, he could have remained a writer but spent his time physically in the front line – an ideal solution for him. It was not to be.

Barbara Wall also visited the Ministry in the company of Michael Richey (an outstanding navigator).

Wednesday, 5 June 1940: Mike on leave, came round to see us. Mike and I went to the Ministry of Information to visit Graham Greene and Tom Burns. We hadn't got passes but Mike said we were parachutists so we were let in. Had a nice chat with G. G. and a horrified one with Tom. Bernard [Wall] and I dined with the Graham Greenes at the Fifty [small restaurant in Charing Cross Road] and went to the Lamb and Flag [pub off Garrick St] and played darts and shove penny. Talked of little but the war.[17]

France had just fallen and British troops were being evacuated from Dunkirk in barges and small vessels, what J. B. Priestley called during his famous broadcast on the night of 5 June 'these fussy little steamers'. He spoke of the loss of the *Gracie Fields* of the Isle of Wight ferry service: 'This steamer, like all her brave and battered sisters, is immortal . . . holiday steamers made an excursion to hell and came back glorious.' Those steamers through the last days of May rescued troops in their thousands, culminating in the evacuation of 68,000 on the 31st. On 4 June the rearguard left Dunkirk. That night Churchill spoke to the Commons: 'Wars are not won by evacuation. Dunkirk is a colossal disaster,' but then came his splendid peroration: 'We shall not flag or fail . . . we shall fight on the beaches . . . we shall fight in the fields and in the streets, we shall fight in the hills; we shall never surrender.' Indeed, England stood alone and for Churchill this was Britain's finest hour. Barbara Wall's modest comment – 'talked of little but the war' – must have been true for the whole of Britain that night.

Muggeridge and Greene were not the only critics of the Ministry of Information. When Duff Cooper was appointed Minister of Information, the *Spectator* in an unsigned article admitted that he had a 'bewildering task in reorganising a top-heavy institution whose functions at the start had been determined less by the work that was crying out to be done than by finding occupations for its motley crew'. The author of this article in the *Spectator* on 9 August 1940 knew the Ministry from the inside, knew of its sluggishness, its failure to act promptly and knew also of its overpopulated staff. The writer granted that it had important work to do, 'to release it from the incubus of the subtle lies which the Nazis have planted and fostered and from the fears it has conjured up in millions of minds. And now that France has been overrun by the Germans France has been deluged with lies by Nazi agents . . . millions of French people . . . are longing to hear the truth.'

Greene had recently left the Ministry of Information and it was he who wrote the unsigned *Spectator* article. His leaving was rather abrupt. 'It was not a question of choice,' he wrote to his mother in October, 'my post at the M. of I. was abolished by Pick.' 'There was a man called Frank Pick,' Greene told me in 1983, 'who belonged to London Transport, was appointed Director General and he purged, quite rightly, the Ministry of a lot of unnecessary people, and I was one of those sacked. I was very relieved to be out of it because the job seemed such rubbish.'

*

On 4 March 1940 *The Power and the Glory* was published. This novel about a hunted, driven, desperate priest is probably Greene's greatest. Eight days later he sent a copy to Vivien and instead of autographing it in the usual way, wrote the following on plain notepaper and stuck it into the edition:

> My darling heart, just a line in pencil to say it's good to see you even for a few minutes. In a confused and confusing world I am certain of one thing: I can't live without you & I can't be happy for very long without seeing you. Whatever happens that's true. I shall like being old with you!
>> God bless you my darling one
>> Your Tyg

On the opposite page, near the dedication FOR GERVASE, Greene had written in ink, 'but far more for you dear love – March 4 1940'. The Reverend Gervase Matthew, brother of Bishop David Matthew (both close friends of Greene), had read the book in proof and, on his advice, Greene cut out a Wordsworth quotation, leaving another by Dryden: 'the sagacious power / Of hounds and death drew nearer every hour'.[18]

Also in Vivien's copy was the preface to the French edition of *The Power and the Glory* (*La puissance et la gloire*) with a short note from Greene: 'This may interest you – Preface by Mauriac.' Underlined by Greene, in the preface, was this passage – '*C'est dire que ce livre s'adresse providentiellement à la génération que l'absurdité d'un monde fou prend à la gorge. Aux jeunes contemporains de Camus et de Sartre, proies désespérées d'une liberté dérisoire, Graham Greene révélera, peut-être, que cette absurdité n'est au vrai que celle d'un amour sans mesure.*'[19]

In spite of his affair with Dorothy, Greene continued to rely on his wife's judgment. Although Vivien thought the title of the book fitted it admirably and was easy to remember, she had qualms about it. She had the uneasy feeling that it had been used before (actually by Phyllis Bentley a few months earlier). Vivien was also working on the galleys: 'I did your proofs very snugly in the study during News & Mr Chamberlain.'[20] By the 29th she could promise, 'Proofs will be sent tomorrow – without fail.'

His greatest novel, however, had to wait ten years for success. The print run of the first edition, according to Greene, was 3,500 copies, only a thousand copies more than his first novel eleven years before.[21] He suggests the book's modest failure was because it 'crept out' a month before Hitler invaded the Low Countries, but the newspaper headlines at this time were about Finland, which Russia had invaded in late November. There was great sympathy for that small, vulnerable country. Britain and France sent an expeditionary force of 100,000 men; in America Herbert Hoover raised $1,600,000, and the *Spectator* offered a small prize for a poem of not more than twenty-four lines, entitled 'Finland'. The first prize went to Hilary Trench, Greene's old alias. Though it was not one of his best efforts it does show an interesting and unexpected anti-Soviet slant:

> We were liberators: so the bands played,
> Ice on the mouthpiece and the fingers . . .
> They were our friends, so they gave us bullets:
> They were liberators, so they freed us,
> Here in the blizzard from the shared room,
> The awful repetitions of the how-many years plan,
> The edited texts of Lenin and the million sale of Marx.
> Here died fear, clutching a child's toy from Petsamo . . .
> And the bodies stiff like logs
> Are freed at last from the loudspeaker,
> In the land where White is only snow,
> And Red is only blood.[22]

Greene really had little chance, bringing out his greatest book in the middle of this vast war, of its becoming a bestseller. The day before publication the headlines were 'FINNS SET FIRE TO VIBORG. RED FORCES IN OUTSKIRTS: CITY'S EARLY FALL EXPECTED.'

And the news in April (a few weeks later) was the seizure of Oslo by the Germans, where they set up a National government under Vidkun Quisling, the occupation of Denmark and Sweden's acceptance of a Nazi ultimatum. Unless books either allowed the general reader to escape from war (the popularity of Jane Austen in wartime was an unexpected phenomenon) or provided information about war or spies, the chances of their becoming bestsellers were remote. The *Observer*'s book advertisements show which titles, published at the same time as *The Power and the Glory*, Greene's brilliant novel had to compete with: books with titles such as *I Was Stalin's Agent* or *Hitler Versus Germany* ('Sensational Facts' brought to light for the first time) or *The Gestapo in England* (Hitler's spy ring) were heavily advertised by publishers. There was a thirst for secret intrigues and the calamities of war; there was no interest in faraway Mexico or the tribulations of a betrayed whisky priest.

While recognising that any publisher would have difficulties in selling *The Power and the Glory* in wartime, Greene knew that the novel had to be pushed *now*, and felt Heinemann were not doing enough: 'The intense irritation that at intervals tempts one to leave Heinemann's', he wrote to his agent, 'is overcoming one again. Apparently when Frere rang me up at the beginning of last week the book was selling better than any other Heinemann except the Maugham, but they never seize the moment to plug home. They still carry the same ad. as they did the first week, except that it's reduced in size.' And while Greene admitted that he hated to pester the publisher 'because it seems self-important', he nevertheless felt 'this time they've got the chance which may not recur to get away with me'.[23] Greene felt that his publishers only marginally recognised the book's merits; by their advertising, they were giving a signal that *The Power and the Glory* was just another steady goodish Heinemann novel.

Because of his sufferings in Mexico (the whisky priest's sufferings often parallel Greene's) he would probably never be entirely satisfied with the efforts his publisher made to sell *The Power and the Glory*. These sufferings were especially severe when he was travelling by mule across mountain ranges in Chiapas. It was a spell-binding landscape, but the journey took Greene to the end of his endurance: climbing to 7,000 feet in the immense, serrated, almost uninhabited wastes with only the crack and pad of the mule's feet on stone and turf for company; the terrible heat, the brutal sun, his feelings of sunstroke; the merciless and unending bump of the mule's back; the sense that he'd become a bundle of bones without a brain, unable to go on but having no choice. These experiences entered into the making of *The Power and the Glory*. He longed for the novel to have its just reward, but feared it would drop into obscurity.

Five days later Pollinger replied: 'I had an up and downer with Frere yesterday morning. The sales to date are about 5,000 – the sales for the last two weeks being 245 and 704. For the first three days of this week 371, so that the graph is running the right way.'[24] This was no mean achievement, but if Heinemann had already sold 5,000 (the book had been on the bookstalls for five weeks), it had already sold above the print of 3,500 claimed by Greene. The print run was in fact 12,600.

Greene's complaints worried his publishers. They promised his agent an increase in advertising so that he'd again appear in the *Observer*, and they would also run a big one in the *Sunday Times*. 'I think I must have stirred Frere up pretty considerably,' asserted his agent, 'for he came through on the phone about 5 o'clock yesterday saying that he and Charlie [Evans] were really putting their backs into selling the book.'

The advertising shows that his publishers were now making strenuous efforts to sell the book. When they came to advertise it in the *Sunday Times* they quoted from Sir Hugh Walpole: 'Graham Greene's new novel proves that he is the finest English novelist of his generation. Simply magnificent,' and followed up with two further quotations: 'Beyond question his best novel. Nothing in his previous work has quite prepared us for the accomplishment in *The Power and the Glory*' (*The Times*): 'It filled my life for the last month more than any book since *The Brothers Karamazov*' (*Catholic Herald*). But the war news was deteriorating daily and sales had to be made at once, not two months ahead, for by then the interest in the book would have all but disappeared.

In the end the book did not sell well during the war, though immediately after it Heinemann printed a further 18,650 copies for their pocket edition and another 23,450 copies for the uniform edition in 1949. Its best sales were in France, thanks to the introduction by François Mauriac.

Its popularity in France led two Catholic French bishops to denounce it to Rome on two different occasions. No doubt these criticisms were kept alive in Rome because some fourteen years after the book's publication, it was condemned by Giuseppe, Cardinal Pizzardo, of the Holy Office, on the grounds that it was 'paradoxical' and 'dealt with extraordinary circumstances'.

In 1953 Greene was summoned by Cardinal Griffin to Westminster Cathedral, where Griffin read him a letter from the Holy Office in which Pizzardo required changes to be made to the text. Greene politely refused on the casuistical ground that the copyright was in the hands of his publisher.[25] Cardinal Griffin added that he would have preferred it if they had condemned *The End of the Affair*, and continued, 'You and I receive no harm from erotic passages, but the young . . . '[26] Greene responded by admitting that one of his earliest erotic experiences had been awakened by Dickens's *David Copperfield*. This brought the uneasy interview to an abrupt end and Griffin's parting shot was a copy of a pastoral letter which he had written, and which was being read in the churches of his diocese, 'condemning' not only *The Power and the Glory* but also, by implication, *The Heart of the Matter* and *The End of the Affair*, the trinity of novels upon which Greene's reputation rests:

It is sadly true that a number of Catholic writers appear to have fallen into this error [i.e. sin against the sixth commandment in thought and word]. Indeed, novels which purport to be the vehicle for Catholic doctrine frequently contain passages which by their unrestrained portrayal of immoral conduct prove a source of temptation to many of their readers . . . the presentation of the Catholic way of life within the framework of fiction may be an admirable object but it can never be justified as a means to that end the inclusion of indecent and harmful material.[27]

Greene, though he spoke lightly of the event in both *A Sort of Life* and *Ways of Escape*, was in fact troubled by being called in by the highest 'headmaster' of them all and in his anguish confessed the episode to his friend Evelyn Waugh. Waugh supported Greene strongly and even offered, almost in a literal sense, to take up the cudgels on his behalf, this in spite of his deeply conservative nature and profound dedication to the Catholic Church. 'Dear Graham,' he wrote on 2 May 1954, 'Since you showed me the Grand Inquisitor's letter my indignation has waxed. It was as fatuous as unjust – a vile misreading of a noble book. Do you want any demonstration by the admirers of *The Power and the Glory*? I shall be delighted to take any part in it.' While it was Waugh's view that Greene wouldn't want a demonstration, nevertheless if Greene felt that any protest was needed, Waugh urged, 'please count on me'. His further advice was typically sardonic:

> It seems to me, as a layman, that it is the business of the Inquisitors to make every move. You have not asked for an *imprimatur*. It is their business to propose detailed alterations & to make themselves ridiculous in doing so. They have taken 14 years to write their first letter. You should take 14 years to answer it.

Later, when Greene had an interview with Pope Paul VI, the Pope told Greene that among the novels of his he had read was *The Power and the Glory*. Greene responded that it had been condemned by the Holy Office:

> 'Who condemned it?'
> 'Cardinal Pizzardo.'
> He repeated the name with a wry smile and added, 'Mr Greene, some parts of your books are certain to offend some Catholics, but you should pay no attention to that.'[28]

*

After Dunkirk, after the fall of France and the Low Countries,

Britain braced itself for German invasion. Because of this threat, Greene moved his wife and children away from Crowborough, which was too near the south coast, to Oxford: 'I thought there was a chance that Oxford would remain an open city and not be bombed, that there would be an invasion and I had to protect my family,' said Greene. 'We left July 1, 1940, to Oxford, having been at Crowborough since August 1939,' said Vivien to me. She did not have a happy time with her mother-in-law, as sentences in a letter from Marion Greene to Vivien indicate: 'What will you do? We miss you all very much. I feel I was often cross and upset about things which don't matter but it is old age. We miss you all.'[29] In later life Vivien remembered her wartime experiences: 'A long war, twelve years of rationing, moving house,' but mostly 'being an evacuee in another person's house'.[30]

Vivien agreed to move to Oxford because she believed her husband intended otherwise to send her and the children to Jamaica. She wrote to Stella Weaver, an old friend whose husband was President of Trinity. The Weavers wanted 'some decent people in the lodgings'. So Vivien and her children went to Trinity to stay. Vivien recalled: 'I helped run the house. There were no domestics and it is a huge house, and we were always having guests. We grew tomatoes and kept ducks.'[*31] In a letter to her husband dated 27 September 1941, Vivien writes: 'Last week we ate poor Jeremiah the duck and Ballard (the parlourmaid) *recognised* him on the dish although she hadn't known he had been liquidated. It was rather awful but one gets callous by the third duck.'

In February the *Spectator*'s literary editor, Derek Verschoyle, was called up and Greene was offered the post: 'I'm so proud & happy with you as Lit. Ed.' wrote Vivien, '& it is exactly your sort of job & I like the feeling of security.' What follows indicates something of her understandably cautious middle-class nature: 'I simply long for you to stay put in something: the changing about fills me with dread & depression.' Her desires and hopes were not Greene's, but in her excitement perhaps, she revealed them too directly:

I think it would be so harmful to have the reputation of instability – (Yes, but he never stays in anything). It is what everyone begins by thinking of anyone of great talents & if they have any basis for thinking it, it is fatal. I do wish you could be an Editor, not of a daily paper but something like the 'Sp'. It has some *prestige*, too.[32]

* However, Francis Greene remembers there being a number of domestics; and 'the only livestock my mother had anything to do with were pet white mice'.[33]

She had other impossible hopes: 'You might seriously think of putting in for a "real" Ministry that would last after the war & be a Civil Servant. I think it is necessary to make up our minds not to live precariously – i.e., not on possible film deals & so on.'[34]

Vivien sometimes cautioned Greene, speaking to him as if he were an impetuous boy (which in some senses he always remained): 'I do wonder what the show-down with the Ed. was. I hope it was a *serious* issue, & after all, policy & choosing contributions to a large extent, is his business.' Greene was not the kind of man to allow a general editor to determine which contributors he as literary editor should use. But Vivien kept on – 'it doesn't seem the time to make changes: you may be called up soon enough'.[35]

4
The Blitz

Blood alone moves the wheels of history.
— BENITO MUSSOLINI

THE blitz on London began on 7 September 1940. An air-raid warden recalled that first raid: 'the miniature silver planes circling round and round the target area in such perfect formation that they looked like children's toy models of flying boats . . . at a fair'.[1] The miniature silver planes like children's toy models were in fact 1,300 bombers escorted by 600 fighters, which arrived over London at five at night and did not leave until four in the morning. The raid was successful – the bombers did terrible damage. The London Docks and Woolwich Arsenal were set alight, but then bombs were released on the East End, Poplar, Stepney and West Ham. A. P. Herbert, on patrol by the river Thames, recalled that night: 'after Lambeth it was nearly the light of day . . . The Pool, below London Bridge, was a lake of light.' At Limehouse corner, he was witness to 'a stupendous spectacle. Half a mile or more of the Surrey shore was burning . . . smoke and sparks of all the fires swept in a high wall across the river.' Going through that wall of smoke 'was like a lake in Hell. Burning barges were drifting everywhere . . . We could hear the hiss and roar of the conflagration, a formidable noise.'[2]

The fires they set ablaze were larger than any ever experienced before. The chief fire officer, seeing the sea of fire ascending up to the heavens, sent a message demanding 'all the bloody pumps you've got; the whole bloody world's on fire'. On the docks they were breathing the fiery smoke of cargoes – pepper, burning rubber and burning wheat. Barrels of rum were exploding and drums of paint. Over all was the sickly smell of burning sugar. Two-thirds of all telephones were put out of order and messengers had to carry messages.[3] The traitor William Joyce, known facetiously by the British as Lord Haw-Haw, broadcast from Germany on the occasion of the beginning of the blitz, telling Londoners that 'Jews today are shaking in their shoes, but tonight there will be no more Jews.' His prognostication was inaccurate, though on that first night the raiders killed 430 civilians and seriously injured a further 1,600: thousands were made homeless.

The massive raid was treated humorously by newspapers, aware that the whole truth could have a disruptive effect on morale. The headlines in the *Observer* ran 'Big Air Battle Over London: 65 Raiders Shot Down' but then treated it as a lucky extra to the afternoon's sport:

> Despite the boom of AA guns and the drumming of machine-gun fire London remained calm, and thousands at football matches and greyhound races treated the desperate fight being waged in the air as a spectacle: 'That was a near shave' was the comment of one man among several hundreds at the greyhound track where 3 bombs fell, one outside the ground, one behind the stand and one right on the track. Four thousand people at a football match had a grandstand view of one air battle. They forgot the risk of falling shrapnel and cheered when one plane fell in flames.[4]

The newspapers wrote very circumspectly, but the Germans had succeeded in devastating working-class homes in Stepney. British newspapers stressed the wonderful spirit of the British at war, but some little touches of the real situation leaked out. Of course, the British working class *were* genuinely defiant, the defiance of bombed-out people, and improvised signs revealed their spirit: 'Bombed but not Beat', 'Hitler may get us up, but he'll never get us down.' A woman told how she had been married only two days when their house went up in smoke: 'Now all I've got left is my wedding ring and my cat, and even my cat's turned grey.'[5]

There was a temporary collapse of authority due to the flight of bombed-out people living close to the docks. The *Picture Post* was almost alone in its willingness to give some indication of how badly the East End was hit: 'The search for household possessions, the pulling out broken fragments of household treasures. Some leave the East End loading their belongings and leave for the woods – anywhere to get an undisturbed night's rest and some trek aimlessly away.' One woman remembered, 'It was one steady stream. We got to the hopfields and there's this wonderful sense of peace.'[6] Sometimes, the true state of affairs reached print in minor newspapers like *A Kentish Independent*. The newspaper, speaking of those whose houses had collapsed around them, referred to the state of mind of those bombed: 'The shock of their experience seemed to have numbed their minds and reduced them to despair.'

But Londoners survived seventy-six consecutive devastating raids (apart from one clouded evening). Everything, and everybody, was in the 'front line': 'The present ordeal', the *Observer* declared, 'welds London and her people in a unity of feeling like no experience in their history.'[7] When the blitz was only thirteen days old, the *Spectator* admitted that 'London is deeply scarred. Bombs, explosive and incendiary, cannot be rained on the city day and night without leaving their tragic mark. Blackened or crumbling walls greet the eye in London streets where great business houses or humble dwellings lately stood.'

The devastation was caught in a film entitled *London Can Take It*. In it was heard the rich voice of Quentin Reynolds:

Now it is eight o'clock Jerry's a little bit late tonight. The guns are ready . . . Here they come. The heavy broken drone of German engines closer and louder. The guns begin to cough. Now the searchlights are poking long white inquisitive fingers into the blackness of the night. This is the music they play every night in London – the symphony of war.[8]

It was through such films, and the American radio programme *London After Dark*, that great numbers of Americans hearing the recorded sounds of war were deeply moved. Ed Murrow of CBS, suddenly in love with the sheer courage of the British under fire, stood suicidally on rooftops during raids, joined his neighbours in fire-watching duty, and left the studio for the front line of London burning: 'This . . . is London. This is Trafalgar Square. The noise you hear at this moment . . . ' This was the world Greene knew intimately: an empty London with sudden bursts of noise, incessant bombing, an umbrella shop burning at the corner of Oxford Street.

On seeing his first bombed house, 'one in Woburn Square neatly sliced in half', Greene recalled his sense of shock:

With its sideways exposure it looked like a Swiss chalet: there were a pair of skiing sticks hanging in the attic, and in another room a grand piano cocked one leg over the abyss . . . In the bathroom the geyser looked odd and twisted seen from the wrong side, and the kitchen impossibly crowded with furniture until one realized one had been given a kind of mouse-eye view from behind the stove and the dresser . . .⁹

In *The Ministry of Fear*, Greene drew on his experience of what a direct hit was like:

and then the bomb went off.

They hadn't heard the plane this time; destruction had come drifting quietly down on green silk cords: the walls suddenly caved in. They were not even aware of noise.

Blast is an odd thing; it is just as likely to have the effect of an embarrassing dream as of man's serious vengeance on man, landing you naked in the street or exposing you in your bed or on your lavatory seat to the neighbours' gaze. Rowe's head was singing; he felt as though he had been walking in his sleep; he was lying in a strange position, in a strange place. He got up and saw an enormous quantity of saucepans all over the floor: something like the twisted engine of an old car turned out to be a refrigerator. . . .¹⁰

Greene's hero Rowe looks up and sees Charles's Wain (the group of seven bright stars in the Great Bear), below him a water-colour intact at his feet, and he feels as if he were in a strange country, without maps to help him, trying to find his position by the stars.

Three flares came sailing slowly, beautifully, down, clusters of spangles off a Christmas tree: his shadow shot out in front of him and he felt exposed, like a gaolbreaker caught in a searchlight beam . . . They were machine-gunning the flares: two broke with a sound like cracking plates and the third came to earth in Russell Square; the darkness returned coldly and comfortingly.

But in the light of the flares Rowe had seen several things; he had discovered where he was – in the basement kitchen: the chair above his head was in his own room on the first floor, the front wall had gone and all the roof, and the cripple lay beside the chair, one arm swinging loosely down at him. A warden called from the street, 'Is anyone hurt in there?' and Rowe said aloud in a sudden return of his rage, 'It's beyond a joke: it's beyond a joke.'

'You're telling me,' the warden called down to him from the shattered street as yet another raider came up from the south-east muttering to them both like a witch in a child's dream, 'Where are you? Where are you? Where are you?'¹¹

Greene remembered another incident of seeing 'a man laughing outside his house where his wife and children were buried'.

Night after night, people invaded the tube stations seeking shelter from the raids above. The nightly exodus was recounted by Tom Hopkinson, one-time editor of *Picture Post*:

> The platform lights are dim, and what they reveal looks like the result of some terrible catastrophe – a battlefield, or a city stricken by the plague. A path barely a yard wide allows passengers to leave the train, but all the rest of the platform is a mass of bodies. Sleepers of both sexes and all ages lie or sprawl around on coverlets or rugs. Most appear to be awake, not talking but gazing mutely up at the curved ceiling. The men are mainly in shirt-sleeves, having folded their coats for pillows, but most of the women are fully-dressed. Two or three in a group are pouring tea out of a Thermos flask . . . The children are mostly asleep, with arms flung out . . . in the dismal light even their fresh faces appear grey and hollow.

The heat was terrific and the smell appalling, the smell coming partly from the sheer crowd of bodies in so confined a space, but mainly from the lavatory buckets, one for men and one for women, hidden from view by two hessian screens.

Like the Morlocks, the people of London lived out their nights underground. Greene's hero, Rowe, on the run finds himself an air-raid shelter: 'somebody had tied a red silk scarf over the bare globe to shield it. All along the walls the bodies lay two deep, while outside the raid rumbled and receded. An old man snored across the aisle and at the end of the shelter two lovers lay on a mattress with their hands and knees touching.'[12]

In an undated letter to his mother, Greene speaks of the massive raids and nights spent in a shelter: 'I can't get back to Clapham [14 North Side], and spend the night with friends [Dorothy, who was a shelter warden] in a public shelter off Gower St.' In that shelter there were always the same two dozen inhabitants. 'Occasionally one gets shaken as when the landmine went off in Tottenham Court Road – the night they got University College and St. Pancras and Oetzmann's. I've never seen such fires. Montagu Square has lost a tooth, and most of those lovely Marble Arch squares.'[13] It is this public shelter that Greene (using the pseudonym Henry Trench) describes in an article, 'The Strays'.[14]

After a month of aerial war, the group had coalesced like a platoon. Indeed, it was this solidarity rather than the 'bunks and free earplugs' that made life underground bearable: 'A routine grows naturally like a plant; in the first week tea was always made after a particularly close explosion; later the close explosions didn't matter so much, so we had tea and biscuits at 9 (everyone paid a penny and took it in turns to supply tea and sugar); lights were shaded at 10, and snorers ceased to rouse angry feelings – toleration developed.'[15]

Sometimes chance-comers were made welcome: an old philosopher with a white beard spent the night, 'he had a little birdlime on his hat . . . and handed round picture postcards of himself with sparrows nibbling the food from his lips'; a drunk, scandalised at the sight of husbands and wives sharing mattresses: 'If I hadn't seen it with me own eyes, I wouldn't have believed. Disgusting, it's disgusting.' Between the thuds of the barrage a young man explained to a girl the secret of contentment and a Czech told fortunes in a teacup. '"A bomb will fall," he said, and everyone laughed.'

But this small, tightly knit group themselves became strays: 'There was no warning whistle when the bombs exploded; they tore the air like calico. The fourth bomb wiped away the house next door. There wasn't time to be afraid; only the silence afterwards was a little shocking, and the smell of hot metal', before they found refuge in another shelter.

It was in this shelter that there had been complaints about the 'goings on'. An official came down and asked Chief Warden Jacobs to accompany him on a tour of the shelters. 'Just look at that pair,' said the official in disgust at a couple entirely engrossed in embracing. 'But,' responded the Chief Warden, 'that is Mr. Greene, one of our best wardens, and his nice wife.' Mr Greene's 'nice wife' was Dorothy.[16]

One of Greene's great enjoyments after a raid was coming above ground when the all clear went at 5.45 and seeing the latest damage and the early morning sky:[17] 'Along the . . . roads men and women [were] emerging from underground; neat elderly men carrying attaché-cases and rolled umbrellas appeared from public shelters.'[18] London had changed. It had become a 'strange torn landscape where . . . shops were reduced to a stone ground-plan like those of Pompeii . . . '[19] In Gower Street they were sweeping up glass and the buildings smoked into the new day.[20] There were 'the tank-traps by the roadside, fields bristling with stakes, blacked-out place names – and the first bombed houses, the shelter signs, the diversions, the paper labels, each bearing the new address of a bank or a shop, dangling from a rope which bars off a devastated street, the first black-out – the dramatic change from the day-world to the night-world, peace or war separated by a short twilight.'[21] Walking through the streets meant avoiding piles of rubble. Greene would see craters in the street, obscure tangles of wires and cables normally hidden from view. 'Wet hoses would still be spread around like giant spaghetti,'[22] buses overturned, gas mains broken, burst sandbags littering the streets, houses now only heaps of brick and stone.

The air war was made more terrible by its domestic familiarity: 'It happens in the kitchen, on landings, beside washing baskets; it comes to us without us stirring a yard from our own doorsteps to meet it.'[23] It was a London known since August, people emerging from a bombed block 'covered with that peculiar cement-like dust that seems to be the accompaniment of all bomb debris', people sleeping in the crypt of St Martin's, the Thames inky black as it ran by the burning buildings; the patience of the poor and the maddening inertia of the Civil Service; the sense of freedom from anxiety among those who had lost their homes; the growth of a routine so that very soon the nightly raid was just an uncomfortable part of life like Monday morning.[24]

Greene and Muggeridge found something curiously compelling about the nightly blitz. It was the great fires in the City and Fleet Street, a great illumination, a mighty holocaust, the end of everything, that led Muggeridge to feel a joy and exaltation at the 'sight and sound and taste and smell of all this destruction'.[25]

Greene appeared to relish destruction and death: indeed, he seemed to believe that the world deserved it. He *was* at home in the London blitz (as the article entitled 'At Home' stresses), and to him it was not odd to wake up on a cement floor among strangers in an air-raid shelter. The collapse of a whole way of life was, for Greene, inevitable: 'Violence comes to us more easily because it was so long expected – not only by the political sense but by the moral sense. The world we live in could not have ended any other way.'[26]

So Greene felt at home in the nightly air-raid shelter: 'some beast in [us] has prepared each man for this life':

That . . . is why one feels at home in London . . . or any of the bombed cities – because life there is what it ought to be. If a cracked cup is put in boiling water it breaks, and an old dog-toothed civilization is breaking now. The nightly routine of sirens, barrage, the probing raider, the unmistakable engine, the bomb-bursts moving nearer and then moving away, hold one like a love-charm. We are not quite happy when we take a few days off. There is something just a little unsavoury about a safe area – as if a corpse were to keep alive in some of its members, the fingers fumbling or the tongue seeking to taste. So we go hurrying back to our shelter, to the nightly uneasiness and then the 'All Clear' sounding happily like New Year's bells and the first dawn look at the world to see what has gone: green glass strewn on the pavement . . . and sometimes flames . . . lapping at the early sky.[27]

As for the victims, 'if they have suffered pain it will be nearly over by this time. Life has become just and poetic, and if we believe this is the right end to the muddled thought, the sentimentality and selfishness of generations, we can also believe that justice doesn't end there. The innocent will be given their peace, and the unhappy will know more happiness than they have ever dreamt about, and poor muddled people will be given an answer they have to accept.'[28] In his journal Muggeridge described Greene at the time of the blitz: 'a sinner manqué. In the Blitz we used to spend a good many evenings together, and I remember the longing he had for a bomb to fall on him. . . .'[29]

There is a tremendous feeling that these *were* Greene's best years. The world for him was 'all much of a piece engaged everywhere in the same subterranean struggle . . . there is no peace anywhere where there is life; but there are quiet and active sectors of the line'. He was now living in the active sector, was excited at such an existence and happily engaged in a life seen as a continuous battlefield.

In a letter written to Anthony Powell in December 1940, he seemed on a high, in manic phase, as he summed up his 'chequered and rather disreputable life'. His stint with the Ministry of Information is described as 'an absurd hilarious time I shouldn't have had the vitality to break'. Here is the happy Londoner during the blitz:

Luckily Pick axed me at the end of September, and I am now literary editing this rag [the *Spectator*] . . . which isn't quite as I pictured war. However London is extraordinarily pleasant these days with all the new open spaces, and the rather Mexican effect of ruined churches . . . All my family are parked in Trinity: and I sleep on a sofa in Gower Mews. As I'm under a skylight I go into a basement when the barrage is heavy. A direct hit next door and escaping gas and a midnight flight has been the most exciting evening yet. I find it impossible to write anything except reviews and middles, but there's nothing to spend money on and I find one can live admirably on about 500 . . . which I suppose is a fortune to a soldier.[30]

And in the shelter, dreaming of his life before the war and of his dead mother, Rowe reflects Greene's own sense of the difference between the peace he and his mother knew in Berkhamsted and the blitz in London:

'This isn't real life any more,' he said. 'Tea on the lawn, evensong, croquet, the old ladies calling, the gentle unmalicious gossip, the gardener trundling the wheelbarrow full of leaves and grass. People write about it as if it still went on . . . but it's not there any more.' His mother smiled at him in a scared way but let him talk . . . 'I'm hiding underground, and up above the Germans are methodically smashing London to bits all round me. You remember St Clement's – the bells of St Clement's. They've smashed that – St James's, Piccadilly, the Burlington Arcade, Garland's Hotel, where we stayed for the pantomime, Maple's and John Lewis. It sounds like a thriller, doesn't it, but the thrillers are like life – more like life than you are, this lawn, your sandwiches, that pine. You used to laugh at the books Miss Savage read – about spies, and murders, and violence . . . but dear, that's real life: it's what we've all made of the world' . . . he put his mouth to the steel frame of his bunk and kissed the white cold cheek. 'My dear, my dear, my dear. I'm glad you are dead. Only do you know about it? do you know?' He was filled with horror at the thought of what a child becomes, and what the dead must feel watching the change from innocence to guilt and powerless to stop it.

'Why, it's a madhouse,' his mother cried. 'Oh, it's much quieter there,' he said . . . [31]

5

The Destructors

And the crack in the tea-cup opens
A lane to the land of the dead.
— W. H. AUDEN

GREENE's journal for 16 April 1941 records the madhouse
remembered by Londoners as 'The Wednesday'. In a single
night 2,000 civilians died and 100,000 homes were destroyed, as
central London experienced its worst raid.

In spite of the terrible loss of life and property, the *Sunday Times*'s
headlines would not disturb its readers: 'FIRE FIGHTERS PARRIED BIG
RAIDS: HOUSES OF PARLIAMENT DAMAGED AGAIN'. The report
which followed – of the bodies of men, women and children (one, a
dead child in a wrecked perambulator) uncovered from underneath
the wreckage of four apartment houses in a working-class district –
would have stiffened the resolve of Londoners. So often newspaper
articles sought to find heroes and this time it was the Auxiliary Fire
Service. That Wednesday 20,000 firemen prevented the blaze
becoming a conflagration. The AFS men, who bore the full brunt of
the fire-fighting and bombing, the newspaper reported, 'had their
tails up!'

When the air-raid siren went on 16 April, Greene and Dorothy
were having a drink in the Horseshoe.[1] Leaving the pub, they went
to Frascati's and then to Victor's, hoping to have dinner before the
raid got under way, but both were closed. They ended up in
Czardas, sitting apprehensively next to plate-glass windows. An hour
into the raid, bursting bombs in Piccadilly shook the restaurant in
Dean Street, and they left, walking back to the home they shared in
Gower Mews. Dorothy was on duty fire-watching and Greene went
with her to her post on the roof of a garage. Before they reached the
garage, they saw flares from enemy planes drifting down 'like great
yellow peonies'.

Greene watched the flares flattened up against the wall of Maple's store. At first very little happened in the area he patrolled as air-raid warden. This was bounded in the south by New Oxford Street and in the north by Euston Road, Gordon Square on the east and Gower Street on the west. His station was No. 1 post under the School of Tropical Medicine in Gower Street. He had anticipated signing off by two-thirty in the morning, but the succession of flares made that seem impossible. A big raid was clearly in progress. Flares came down again right above them as he stood at the corner of Alfred Place and Tottenham Court Road. Further flares came down across Charlotte Street and suddenly there was a huge detonation. He and other wardens had only time to get down on their haunches before the shop window showered glass upon their helmets. Running down Alfred Place, they shouted at a dangerous uncovered light at the corner of Ridgmount Gardens. Then confusion descended. They found Gower Street ravaged on both sides.* A parachute bomb had fallen on the Victoria Club in Malet Street where 350 Canadian soldiers were sleeping. Ordered to the club, Greene and Dorothy found soldiers coming out in grey, blood-smeared pyjamas, some barefoot, though the road was littered with glass.

Greene and another warden took a stretcher and went in to find a man trapped on the stairs. The building on one side had disappeared and in front of them was a twenty-foot drop into the foundations. But the trapped man was a goner: only his head and shoulders were visible and a clot of blood by the head. When they decided to take the corpse out of the building, trained stretcher-bearers arrived and Greene lighted their way down the stairs. They all feared the building would collapse since it was held together solely, it seemed to Greene, by wishful thinking.

Earlier, hearing from women wearing dressing-gowns and bleeding from cuts on the face that someone was hurt on the top floor above RADA (the Royal Academy of Dramatic Art), two other wardens, a policeman and Greene, ran up four littered flights. They found a girl, very heavy, on the floor, bleeding and with stained pyjamas. There was room for only one man to lift her at a time. Greene took her down two flights, but the burden had to change

---

* Greene recalled this many years later when he gave Jones, that fraudulent but wonderful character in *The Comedians*, the following dramatic monologue entitled 'A Warden's Patrol' (the popular quality of it reflecting Jones's character): 'The flares came down over Euston, St. Pancras, / And dear old Tottenham Road / And the warden walking his lonely beat / Saw his shadow like a cloud . . . Maple's is hit, Gower Street's a ghost, / Piccadilly's alight . . .'

hands three times. The girl was in pain but apologised for being heavy.

Outside there were flames everywhere. Another stick of three bombs whistled down and Greene lay on the pavement, a sailor falling on top of him. Broken glass cut his hand and he bled a great deal so he had to go back to No. 1 post to have it dressed. As it was being dressed, another stick of three came down. Again Greene and his companions dropped, this time to the floor of the post. The windows blew in and Greene felt that this was the end and ceased to believe in the possibility of surviving the night. He began an Act of Contrition. When interviewed he admitted he was afraid of being wounded, but not of being killed: 'In the blitz, one was very frightened to begin with but then one gave up the idea that one was going to survive and one wasn't frightened any more.'[2] With Greene it was a great deal more complex than this.

As no further bombs fell, he went out again into the night with his companions. This time they found Dallas, the big factory in Ridgmount Gardens, ablaze. Behind every window and on every floor a wall of flame was blowing up. The bombing had only gone on for an hour. Greene felt the appalling thing about these nightly raids was that they never seemed to end.

In spite of the severity of the raid, in all that terrible night, Greene met only one person who lost his nerve. He was 'a large fat foreigner'. He had one foot crushed and was crying to be taken to the hospital. The wardens crossed hands to carry him, but he was so heavy that they had to rest in spite of his cries. It was now three o'clock in the morning, but because of the continuous flares it seemed like broad daylight. At one point the Chief Warden told the 'fat foreigner' that there were others more injured than him and he would have to be left. However, his mixture of moaning and crying was such that, with the help of a soldier, they got him to the Ministry of Information, which was being used that night as a temporary dressing station.

After three minutes' rest, Greene was sent to the fire station to warn them of the all-encompassing fire at Dallas's, though they were unable to come for three hours. Going down the iron steps into the well round the building, he heard another bomb coming down. He crouched down once more and heard it fall away. He was then involved in rescuing an old man in a basement in Gower Street, the back wall of whose house had been blown out. The old man was just out of hospital with a tube in his bladder and had been told he would never walk again. He did so that night and was happy. Greene finally had time to call at the shelter in Gower Mews, where Dorothy

Glover, along with her fire-watching duties, was shelter warden. She was delighted to see him, having heard rumours that he had been wounded and was covered in blood.

The raid died away about five in the morning. One survivor remembered that 'the Strand looked amazed and broken in the morning light. Buildings we had known for twenty years were no more than cracked walls . . . Little tongues of flame still licked the edge of great advertisements . . . Even the trees were wounded.'[3] Later it was discovered that a parachute bomb had landed at the end of Bloomsbury Street and a high explosive bomb had hit the Jewish Girls' Club in Alfred Place: the club, changed into a black hole belching fumes, was choked with smashed brickwork and mutilated corpses. More than thirty had been killed and rescuers were taking out the bodies for a long time. For days there was the sweet stench of corruption from the bodies in the rubble.

Two days later Greene wrote to his mother about the Wednesday raid:

It really was the worst thing yet. On my beat which only consisted of about three quarters of a mile of streets, we had one huge fire, one smaller fire, one H[igh] E[xplosive] and, worst of all, a land mine. The casualties were very heavy, as the landmine which got the Canadian soldiers' home by the M. of I. blasted houses right through Gower St. The fires are not quite out yet. I got off with a cut hand from having to flop down flat on the pavement outside the landmine place. One thought the night was never going to end. Hardly three minutes would pass between two and four without a salvo being dropped. I feel very stiff and bruised . . . One's first corpse in the Canadian place was not nearly as bad as one expected. It seemed just a bit of the rubble. What remains as nastiest were the crowds of people who were cut by glass, in rather squalid bloodstained pyjamas, grey with debris, waiting about for help. I was very lucky when the mine went off as I was standing with two other wardens in Tottenham Court Rd. We got down on our haunches, no time for more, and a shopwindow showered on top of us without cutting any of us. One felt rather pursued. I was having my hand bound up at my post under the School of Tropical Medicine in Gower St. when a stick [of bombs] came down again, and we were all over the floor again with the windows blown in . . . I shall be glad to get away for three nights. The whole place still smells horribly of burning.[4]

The sights of that night supplied the images for what one day,

Greene felt assured, would happen to him. His mother was greatly relieved to get his letter, and a message from her younger daughter (she was sleeping outside London that night), for she feared neither might have survived. 'It seemed to me,' his mother wrote, 'it must have been everywhere . . . I thought it was worse [than the worst raid]. Paper has just come and we see how awful it was. St. Paul's at last. Will it ever end.'[5] But even at Crowborough they had a bad raid:

> Never heard such planes, the noise went on steadily. Guns shook the house so much that at 10 we went down to the shelter. Then a bomb dropped . . . We stayed down till 1 when there was a lull and luckily Da went to sleep but Aunt Nono and I not till after 3. A big crash was one of our planes which came down at Redbridge Farm. Love from your loving mother.[6]

The incidents were manifold. Greene recalled after a raid police dogs searching the ruins for the living and the dead and recalled also a body in Tottenham Court Road which three fire engines drove over. He remembered a body was laid bleeding on a door in the road to escape glass. Warden Charlie Wix took a fur coat from a broken shop window and put it over the man. When Wix returned some time later, he discovered the body had been removed to the pavement and a thief was going through the man's pockets. In *The Confidential Agent*, Greene's knowledge of death is gathered particularly from his wartime experiences:

> She lay there stiff, clean and unnatural. People talked as if death were like sleep: it was like nothing but itself. He was reminded of a bird discovered at the bottom of a cage on its back, with the claws rigid as grape stalks; nothing could look more dead. He had seen people dead after an air raid, but they fell in curious humped positions – a lot of embryos in the womb.[7]

Inevitably, after the raids Dorothy and Greene needed emotional release. David Low recalled that one of the biggest bombs fell and hit the corner of Bloomsbury Street, and a great furniture shop took a direct hit:

> Coming from my shop in Cecil Court, I saw Graham and Dorothy walking up Bloomsbury Street. As a result of the bomb, there were papers flying everywhere, office correspondence and papers about this and that. Graham and Dorothy were picking up

the papers whatever they were and reading them to each other in the street and roaring with laughter.[8]

*

Greene was very happy with Dorothy as a comrade in arms, another soldier under fire. Vivien, writing on the sixteenth anniversary of their first meeting in Oxford, expressed her deep loneliness and her strong desire to join her husband: 'Dear heart, I do miss you especially much when I think of our anniversaries & the breakup of all the warm basket [home] . . . snails without snailshells especially miss their stable companions. I so miss our conversations, walking, or in our chairs in our own house.' They had been parted a year and a half and she felt 'quite dwindled away from being a wife and am only an inefficient nursery governess'.[9]

She signed herself 'Pusska', a cat name for 'wife'. Three days earlier, she had asked Graham if she could come to London to be with him during the blitz, but he must have successfully dissuaded her:

Darling Love, So disappointed, as I feel I ought to have heard one raid & barrage, but certainly I would not like to be without you [he would need to be out during raids as a warden]. In a hotel cellar we could be quite cosy, but I should be dreadfully worried knowing you were in it: I am now, but it would be worse *hearing* it, silly as it sounds.[10]

In an undated letter she had spoken of raids in the area of Oxford: 'A stick of bombs was dropped, no damage – on Weds, just before 11. about three miles off, a stunning event for country mice.' Vivien might have faced the blitz with courage but she was never tested. Her rival Dorothy was spunky and courageous during the blitz, and Greene loved her for it – a truly independent creature, able to stand up to the worst raids, and never panicking under the conditions of war. Dorothy was with Greene from the beginning: 'From the first raid, she was courageous, oh yes, and showed no fear of any kind.'[11]

Vivien, in contrast, though a woman of remarkable fortitude, showed by her manner a need for dependence. She desired to be a Victorian wife, accepting whatever the strong male determined, though perhaps part of her reacted in this way because she thought it was a means of retaining her husband's love. It was not.

She continued pressing to come to London, though in her own modest way: 'I *may* possibly have Fri. in London independently for snuffling round & prob. ring you up to hear your voice & any news but don't stay around purposely.'[12] She also offered to visit him on their anniversary, but because of the unusually severe and persistent raids, the meeting did not come off. One senses that she was making a last-ditch attempt to join her husband whatever the danger in London – after all, if Dorothy could face the hazards of war, Vivien must have wanted to, though she had a prior responsibility to care for her young children. Her brother Pat turned up – he was going to Staff College – and suddenly on 4 April 1941 she sprang her surprise in a daringly direct letter:

Do you ever *really* miss me or am I the termly tea out with relations: faint thoughts of keeping house for Pat if he went to Staff College . . . I think I would be quite useful there! If you give a baffled Woof & come lolloping up bristling I'd have to reconsider it, but make up that big brilliant mind of yours because you'll turn round & see what you THOUGHT was Pussy purring on the mat was *really* just the white enamel refrigerator turning on & off – if you know the difference.[13]

Sometimes Greene visited his family in Oxford: 'He'd come down for a day, and a day was enough, once a month. I don't think he ever felt, "Oh, if only I could be with the children," or anything like that. He didn't really care for them until they were grown up. I never got the impression that he took any notice of them, you know.'[14] His children thought otherwise. Francis Greene recalled that, on these visits, Greene spent a great deal of time with them. He would take them on long walks through the back streets of Oxford, playing a game which they called 'Left, right or straight on'.[15]

Vivien told me that she believed that she had married a tiger (in later years she became a member of the Protection of Tigers League): 'I must have realised, quite unconsciously, his undomesticated nature, realised that he was the wildest of creatures and the least domesticated.'[16] But Greene's visits were also made under difficult circumstances, not of his making. Stella Weaver never had him to stay in Trinity and he used to stop at the King's Arms: 'I'll try to get ⌐ooms for you for 18–20th (i.e. nights of 18th & 19th). Come anyway as I may not have time to write again.'[17]

Two weeks later, his four-year-old son had a fever and Vivien was up hourly through the night tending her child: 'At 4 he was quite normal-looking & said, "Hullo, my blessing," when I came in, the angel.' While he was preparing to visit his son, Vivien wrote to Greene insisting that he 'MUST bring some sugar & if possible a few rashers!'[18] because of the difficulty of food rationing.

There was another reason, apart from the blitz, for Greene's irregular visits. Dorothy didn't like him to go often: 'I don't know why he was interested in Dorothy, attracted to an older woman,' Vivien said.

He talked about her, yes. I think he enjoyed this. He told me that when I darned his socks, and he took them back, she would cut out the darn – probably because my darns were so bad, but he said she did it in a rage. Nevertheless, I never felt anything against her. For a long time I felt on a precipice. He once said to me that I was suspicious and I answered that, 'I'm not suspicious, I'm apprehensive.' That seemed to come like a flash before I could bite it back and he said nothing, but I think he felt the truth of that.[19]

But Vivien felt then that if she didn't take any notice of the affair, it would blow over and after the war everything would be different.

You see, you can't think of it now, but then one thought – other people's houses, everyone disturbed, children changing school. After the war things would settle down and it would all be part of the past and so forth. But of course things got worse, much more alarming and frightening – but no, I never said a word . . . not one word. I suppose, in a physical sense the marriage ended just before war was declared.[20]

*

Greene once described his house at 14 North Side, Clapham Common as 'the most beautifully decorated house I've ever been in' and Herbert Read's wife described it to me as 'a most enchanting house – like a Mozart opera – with the double step': but it did not survive the blitz unharmed. Greene wrote to his mother the day after his house received a direct hit:

Alas! our house went at 1.30 a.m. on Friday. I arrived to collect some objects at 8.30 to find a scene of devastation. There has been no fire & no flood & the structure is still standing, so something may be salvaged when the demolition people have made it safe to enter. Either a landmine at the back or else a whole load of bombs. The secret workshop in the garden next door destroyed, part of the L.C.C. flats & damage all along the row, but the back of our house got the worse blast. Impossible to get beyond the hill for wreckage. I only hope some of my books & some of V's things will be saved. But there was still an unexploded bomb nearby to go off, & the whole place is likely to tumble at much more shock. Rather heartbreaking that so lovely a house that has survived so much should go like that. And I feel one-armed without my books. No hope of salvage starting before Monday. However there were no casualties.[21]

Malcolm Muggeridge records in his diary how, finding his house seriously damaged and roped off, Greene had gone down to Oxford to break the news: 'When he told Vivien, he said, she rebuked him for mentioning what had happened in front of the children, which seemed to him unreasonable.'[22]

Years later when asked about this, Vivien answered that the reverse was true. She was rebuked by Greene for crying in front of the children on learning of the loss of her home. 'Graham told me', said Vivien, 'how he'd gone to North Side and seen all the fire engines and police and it was all being sort of guarded, because he had been living in Bloomsbury with Dorothy and had simply come to fetch books and things like that and found it had been bombed. His life was saved because of his infidelity.'[23] By the same token Greene, by evacuating his family, had saved their lives.

When salvaging what remained of his possessions, Greene's primary concern was the missing first editions of his work, which many years later turned up at Sotheby's:

The extraordinary thing, it was a Queen Anne house and it had a staircase supposed to have been influenced by Vauban. This great curved staircase kept up by pressure on the wall and this pressure is what held the staircase up and it remained. The floors had gone in from the backrooms and where most of my books were. In the sitting room there was a big hole there. There was only a narrow little piece of floor around and I had to abandon those books. Just that big hole and the room had lost everything except one foot of skirting going all the way round.[24]

His study, however, was safe and Greene made a chute and pushed down the books he kept there.[25] He was unable to rescue most of his first editions, which were signed and inscribed, and he assumed that later somebody with ladders had managed to get hold of them. But in the end Sotheby's let him buy them back at the price they had paid for them.

Vivien came up from Oxford with a van and took away the most valued objects; she placed Greene's books in Trinity library and some furniture with friends. She recalled her visit: 'I walked in tears on the edge of the front room looking down at the deep frightening cavity two floors below and all the rafters and rubble and dirt. Some furniture was dragged out of the house by thieves – my grandmother's little davenport was one.'[26] Her own books were among the broken glass at North Side; her diaries, letters, and photographs were destroyed by the bomb (as was a native harp which Greene had carried throughout his journey in Liberia).

The loss of the house took place at the height of the blitz, a time that was doubly exhausting for Greene because, as well as working at the *Spectator*, he was on nightly air-raid-warden duty. There is no evidence that he found the loss of the house as heartbreaking as he suggested in his letter to his mother. Muggeridge recorded a different reaction in his diary: 'Graham . . . when he heard that his house at Clapham Common had been destroyed in the blitz . . . experienced a sense of relief because there was a mortgage on it and it had represented a heavy financial liability.'[27] Greene expressed relief to me:

I used to go back during my lunch time, sometimes with Dorothy, to see if the house was there in Clapham Common, until it wasn't . . . I think it was rather slightly absurd. I mean I simply felt relieved that I didn't have to be backwards and forwards, backwards and forwards all day, and lose my lunch every day, whenever there had been a raid and there were raids most days, to see that the thing was there. So then it wasn't . . . [28]

That his reaction was relief seems clear from his comments about the loss immediately after it happened. On 4 October 1940, in reviewing the memoirs of Mrs Compton Mackenzie about life in Capri in the last year of the First World War, Greene was severely critical: 'The collapse of a whole way of life can be read into Mrs. Compton Mackenzie's book of gossip.' He also asserted: 'It makes one more reconciled to the cement floor [of the basement and air-raid shelter]: this had to happen?' In responding to Mrs Compton Mackenzie's distress at his review, he referred to the loss of his house, but in a curious way: 'A few days after your letter arrived, my house (alas, a Christopher Wren one) was destroyed . . . but that too I expect had to happen. I admit the cement floor is hardly likely to make things better . . . except that I can't help feeling discomfort does have its value.'[29]

Greene's attitude towards the loss of his house also comes out in a number of letters. To Anthony Powell he wrote starkly: 'My house has been blasted into wreckage by a landmine':[30] to his American literary agent, Mary Pritchett, he spoke of his crowded life:

> I've been very remiss in writing to you, but . . . life is quite crowded. I'm literary editing this paper [*Spectator*], acting as dramatic critic, reviewing a good deal, completely failing to write any books, doing some B.B.C. scripts, and at least three nights a week act as an air raid warden from 10 [p.m.] till 2 in the morning, or until the 'Raiders Passed [siren]' goes.

But he wrote only incidentally about the loss of his home: 'I'm glad to say I saved practically all my books from the house, though poor Vivien lost most of her Victorian furniture and objects. It's sad because it was a pretty house, but oddly enough it leaves one very carefree.'[31] Perhaps he felt justifiably bombed, after all so many had suffered this fate. After asking Mary Pritchett to write to his wife ('She has the thin end of things') he concluded his letter, in spite of his being daily witness to terrible nightly destruction, with two extraordinary, even bizarre sentences: 'I have a most interesting and agreeable time in London. It all seems most right and proper.'

Malcolm Muggeridge's continued analysis in his diary about Greene's loss of his Queen Anne house is shrewd:

> I said I didn't think it was unreasonable [that Vivien rebuked him], because, obviously, Vivien felt that the destruction of their house was an outward and visible manifestation of the destruction of their marriage, and that Graham's satisfaction at the destruction of the house was not really because it released him from a financial burden, but because he saw in it the promise of being relieved of a moral one.[32]

For Vivien the loss was very real. She had lost so much with that beautiful house: it was to be the last house that she lived in with her husband on a permanent basis. She had always been fascinated by antiques and particularly by Victorian antiques but now, because of this trauma, she became obsessed by dolls' houses: 'The loss of that house certainly had something to do with my growing interest in dolls' houses.' Neither the war nor a 'missing' husband could take away her small homes for small dolls. These at least were hers. Like Ibsen's Mrs Solness, the Master Builder's wife who lost her children yet continued to keep up empty nurseries, Vivien lost her last happy marital home, but persistently bought dolls' houses. She is considered a leading authority on seventeenth-, eighteenth- and nineteenth-century dolls' houses and her private museum contains one of the finest collections in England.

*

We have seen the sense of freedom that Greene felt in the loss of his beautiful Queen Anne house. If his short story 'The Destructors' is anything to go by, his relief had aspects of psychic violence about it. Written in 1954, it reflects Greene's partiality for the anarchy and violence released by the war. Diana Cooper once concluded that Graham Greene was a good man possessed of a devil. This demon for destruction was linked to the imaginative deracination of his own house, 14 North Side. 'I remember telling him', Vivien recalled, 'that in his story "The Destructors" he was writing about *our* house, 14 North Side. It angered him extremely. Perhaps he didn't realise that or perhaps he was angry because I had found it out.'[33]

'The Destructors', when it was televised by Thames Television in 1978, brought a hostile response. Vivien placed a newspaper cutting about the film in her journal for that year. The headline was PROTESTS OVER 'WICKED' PLAY: 'Many viewers telephoned Thames Television last night complaining about scenes of violence in a play called "The Destructors". The play, a dramatisation of Graham Greene's story, was described as wicked, corrupt and frightening by about 200 callers.' Above this cutting, Vivien wrote in her own hand:

> *The Destructors:* The house was 14 North Side: when we lived there, Graham fell in love with Dorothy Glover . . . When the short story was published it distressed me considerably & I cried, & next time I saw Graham said how upsetting it was. He was very brusque & rough: 'I don't know what you mean.'

In a note below the cutting, Vivien added the audience 'objected to the vandalism. I minded because the writer seemed to hate the house (our home) which was destroyed in 1941 by incendiary.'[34]

*

In the story, a gang of working-class youths with an upper-middle-class leader called 'T' tear down an old man's home. The house is a Christopher Wren, Queen Anne house and, like Greene's own, was badly damaged in the blitz. The owner, an old man the gang calls Old Misery, one day gives the boys chocolate. That is his undoing; from that moment, his only possession, the wrecked house, is doomed – evil is to be returned for good. A photograph of Greene's bombed house fits the description of the house Greene gives in his story, the side walls similarly supported by wooden struts:

'We'd do it from inside. I've found a way in.' ['T'] said with a sort of intensity, 'We'd be like worms, don't you see, in an apple. When we came out again there'd be nothing there, no staircase, no panels, nothing but just walls, and then we'd make the walls fall down – somehow.'[35]

By lunchtime, 'Chaos had advanced. The kitchen was a shambles of broken glass and china. The dining-room was stripped of parquet, the skirting was up, the door had been taken off its hinges and the destroyers had moved up a floor.' 'T' discovers hidden bundles of pound notes and then decides that they are not to be thieves. The gang will not share out the money, but will, in ritual celebration, burn it: 'taking it in turns they held a note upwards and lit the top corner, so that the flame burnt slowly towards their fingers. The grey ash floated above them and fell on their heads like age.' Blackie, to explain to himself why 'T' has taken these terrible actions against Old Misery, suggests that he must hate him, but the strange boy 'T' answers, 'There'd be no fun if I hated him . . . All this hate and love,' he said, 'it's soft, it's hooey. There's only things, Blackie. . . .'[36]

Such nihilism in a child was not new in Greene and unquestionably was derived from his experience of what he saw as unadulterated evil in his schoolboy enemy Carter. Carter was able to exercise authority over others to make them do his bidding, to restrict human sympathy in his fellow schoolboys. 'T' in this story does just this, by abiding by no rules and feeling no love.

Yet in the characterisation of 'T' there is something of young Greene himself. In his youth, Greene played with working-class boys, taking with him cricket bat and wickets which they couldn't afford in order to win them over, so the theme of the story could be said to reflect an experience in his own life. Of course, no comparable vicious actions were committed by Greene. What we are speaking of here is his living in an imaginative world, one which is anarchistic, violent and destructive.

Even so, the name 'T' is a strange one. When Greene felt particularly desperate or felt the need to express unpleasant aspects of his character (either in poems or in letters to Vivien), he revealed the Mr Hyde side of his personality under the pseudonym 'Hilary Trench'. This gloomy and morbid double personality never left him, though when he was courting Vivien he was often at pains to assert the death of Trench. Trench was nasty and brutish, and his mood was one of bitter raillery: 'And . . . you need never be afraid of meeting H. T. I've got to convince you that he's dead.'[37] But this secret personality sometimes took over, however much he regretted the sudden assumption of his alter ego. Muggeridge put it somewhat differently:

> February 24, 1948: Greene, we agreed, is a Jekyll and Hyde character, who has not succeeded in fusing the two sides of himself into any kind of harmony. There is a conflict within him, and therefore he is liable to pursue conflict without. I remember him saying to me once that he had to have a row with someone or other because rows were almost a physical necessity to him. This pursuit of disharmony is wrong . . . [38]

This Trench or 'T' was a disturbing inheritance. To Vivien he wrote: 'Miserableness is like a small germ I've had inside me as long as I can remember. And sometimes it starts wriggling [inside me].'[39] These insidious little worms periodically crept into his brain, gnawing away at the foundations of his belief so that he was left with 'only things'. On such occasions, Greene felt a total sense of emptiness and hated the initiator of life — God.

6

Trivial Comedies, Shallow Tragedies

My life's amusements have been just the same
Before and after standing armies came.
— ALEXANDER POPE

GREENE was almost single-handedly running the arts section of the *Spectator* in 1941, for as well as writing book and film reviews, he was going to whatever live theatre was on offer, especially revues, both before and during the evening blitz. Greene had always been a lover of revues, he had gone to them since childhood and enjoyed them without any sense of smugness; he understood them on their own simple terms.

He was also aware of the difficulties of reviewing live entertainment: 'One must write quickly before one forgets, jot notes upon one's programme as the songs and the jokes pass on their rapid way, in at one ear and out of the other.' Of the *New Ambassadors Revue* at the Ambassadors, Greene admitted remembering only a few sketches and one especially: a savage little song about English exiles escaping the war in New York ('We're holding the torch for England, each night in the Rainbow Room').[1] In reviewing S. N. Behrman's comedy *No Time for Comedy*, he made the point that at this time in the crisis of London, 'Trivial comedies are better than shallow tragedies. Millions of people already have learnt how to die: they don't need any more lessons. To be gay is also a duty.'[2]

His differences with his colleagues were made clear when, almost alone, he praised *Wednesday After the War* at the New Theatre, which was rather chillingly received by the West End audience: 'After a great deal of heart-searching I recommend *Wednesday After the War* as the best musical entertainment in town.' He admitted that the musical needed the faint smell of bottled beer from the bar and gala nights with coloured balloons floating down from the ceiling:

the fish-like faces, the applause like damp hand-clasps. Somebody behind me – who probably liked his demure and *Punch*-like Farjeon – said, 'It's pretty grim, isn't it?' Grim? with Mr. Jerry Verno singing a song which would have set all Islington whistling:

> I'm a Home Guard man on duty,
> And I'm no blinkin' beauty,
> With me tin-hat, with me gas-mask,
> with me gun.

Grim? with Miss Robina Gilchrist singing charmingly the title song that contains all the nostalgia of our time, 'Wednesday after the war', with all the cuties waving flags and chanting, 'Please Mr. Churchill'? This is exactly what a war-time revue should be.[3]

Even revues bombed out of London the previous year were now returning like homing birds. Greene commended especially *Up and Doing* at the Savile Theatre: Mr Cyril Ritchard 'in a blonde wig and a slinky gown with an unreliable Zip, hungry and horrible and prehensile as a torch-singer, or clumsy with ostrich feathers as a fan-dancer', or Ritchard in red tabs, singing with jerky ferocity of the 'Whitehall Warriors':

> Whenever the sirens start to blow,
> I'm the one of the first to go
> Below.[4]

Greene's attitude had mellowed. The crushingly dismissive film reviewer of 1937 (when he was editing *Night and Day*) had all but disappeared, to be replaced by a kinder critic, imaginatively and emotionally sympathetic. He was one of the few critics to praise the many story lines of Kim Peacock's domestic play, *Under One Roof*, involving the unhappy love-life of one of the daughters. She is in love with a celibate clergyman, but finds herself pregnant by a married man: 'Mr. Peacock's play contains a whole *Molotov* bread-basket of incendiary situations . . . like an expert fire-fighter, [he] extinguishes every bomb in turn before it has time to start a fire.' Moreover, 'his lines are witty and savage . . . [but] he refuses to take even his savagery seriously and ties everything up in the last scene with a Dickensian sentiment that has the effect of a shoulder-shrug.'[5]

In the same column, he praised *Black Vanities*: 'Miss Frances Day

. . . that graceless face under the battered crownless straw, those dirty ducks sagging below slack braces are the perfect foil for beauty – the thin Venetian glass figure, the undine smile, the long brittle fingers tossing a flower to an officer in a box, something for the troops to dream about as she sings *Silver Wings*:

> He with his wings on his tunic
> Me with my heart on my sleeve.'[6]

But Greene went to more than theatre comedies and revues. With Muggeridge in tow, he went at the height of the blitz to the famous Windmill Theatre (reputed never to close) where nudes were then bound by law to keep absolutely still. The spectacle appealed to Greene for its tattiness: '[Greene] explained how the *cognoscenti* knew just where to sit to get the best view, and how, as the front rows cleared, spectators at the back pressed forward to take their places; wave upon wave, like an attacking army.'[7] In his review, Greene expressed himself more prosaically: 'The mixture-as-before goes smoothly down the throats of the lonely men in macintoshes. . . . one man in a macintosh gets up and goes out and another takes his place . . . there is almost a religious air of muffled footsteps and private prayers . . . the rites are rather sombre.'[8]

Greene extolled the Windmill nudes, especially Dela Lipinska with her bawdy eyes; young, lovely, mischievous and irresistible (a rarity at the Windmill), she woos the man in the macintosh in the front row.[9] He was less friendly towards the revue at the Prince of Wales:

> From two till ten every day of the week the small hooves of the Dancing Vanities beat the boards, and the Glamour Lovelies as tall as grenadiers walk lazily with a slight sneer in at one wing and out at the other. Nothing ever disturbs the arrogant poise of these monumental lovelies . . . their eyes remain as empty as statues.[10]

His friend Muggeridge reported that before such expeditions during the blitz, Greene 'made a special act of penitence and other appropriate liturgical preparations in case death came upon him unawares'.[11]

*

Greene loved the Windmill, and was good-humoured and full of admiration for revues plugging a simple propaganda line. But, as if his kindliness had its limits, he suddenly, and without warning, began to assail one of the original talents of the world of theatre – Noël Coward. There was no obvious reason for seeing Coward as his *bête noire*. Perhaps for Greene the ever-popular Coward was a suspect talent, though periodically Greene felt an almost insane urge to lash out, working off some of his bile in a review.

The first assault took place while Greene was reviewing, and fulsomely praising, J. M. Barrie's *Dear Brutus* in the *Spectator* on 24 January 1941. He applauded the fact that 'Mr. John Gielgud's production of *Dear Brutus* is the kind of theatrical "event" which we had almost forgotten: an all-star cast, a play which occupies in the affections of many older people the position of a minor classic . . . ' Greene would have liked to compare the present revival to the original, also produced during wartime (but the *Spectator* for some reason had failed to review *Dear Brutus* during its first production in 1917), to see whether the original critics 'really swallowed the great sentimental scene between the artist-wastrel and his dream-daughter without protest'.

Greene suspected that

we have since those days – superficially at any rate – toughened; our literature has become less fanciful and self-pity is less prominent; but after the lapse of disappointing years *when no sustained talent more important than Mr. Noël Coward's has appeared in the theatre* [emphasis added], it is possible to recognise how superbly Barrie knew his job. Mr. Coward's works already bear the lines of time more deeply.[12]

In April, reviewing *Women Aren't Angels* by Vernon Sylvaine at the Strand, while telling us that 'Mr Sylvaine's new play is almost perfect of its kind,' he adds, 'and surely its kind is superior to the smart Coward comedies like too expensive cigarette cases'.[13]

Only a month passed before Greene had another go at Coward. Coward had been asked by the Ministry of Information to visit America with the specific task of countering anti-British propaganda put out by the Nazis, which was 'spreading all over America'. It was Coward's job to 'travel about the country to gauge the feelings of Americans in different States towards England and the British war-effort generally'. He was then invited to visit Australia and Greene quoted from Coward's diary:

Friday, arrival such and such a place – Civic reception – Lord Mayor very nice – wart on forehead – visited aeroplane factory, seemed fiercely efficient – Red Cross Garden Party Government

House – Governor and wife charming – garden lovely – shook hands with several hundred people – matinée theatre, audience fine, sang all right but a bit woolly – drove to X camp – dinner Officers' Mess – troop concert – Diggers terrific – too many officers' wives in front seats – long drive home – bed – exhausted.

Greene suggested that the Australian trip not only taxed Mr Coward's physical powers, but taxed far more his integrity:

Patriotism is not enough: he had to talk about England at war, and he had not seen England at war. If he had experienced the daily autumn blitz it is doubtful whether he would have said so easily: 'During the last two months, in America, I have often felt how infinitely preferable it would be to be kept awake by bombs and sirens than by the clamour of my own thoughts.' It would have been well to have waited to make the comparison until he had experienced both . . . Lack of tact was never more evident than when he rebuked – from Australia – 'the pink parlours of Bloomsbury' already gaping from the German bombs and declared (exhausted, it may well be, by shaking hands): 'We must watch the future and see to it that our new young writers and poets are a little more robust . . .'[14]

Noël Coward dealt with these attacks by sending Greene a private screed entitled 'The Ballad of Graham Greene' some time in June 1941:

> Oh there's many a heart beats faster lads
> And swords from their sheathes flash keen
> When round the embers – the glowing embers
> Men crouch at Hallowe'en
> And suddenly somebody remembers
> The name of Graham Greene.
> (A literary disaster lads
> The fall of Graham Greene.)
>
> Oh there's many a Catholic Priest my boys
> And many a Rural Dean
> Who, ages later – long ages later
> When all has been, has been,
> Will secretly read an old 'Spectator'
> And pray for Graham Greene.

(Let's hope its sales have decreased my boys
Because of Graham Greene.)

Oh one asks oneself and one's God my lads
Was ever a mind so mean,
That could have vented – so shrilly vented
Such quantities of spleen
Upon a colleague? Unprecedented:
Poor Mr Graham Greene.
(One's pride forbids one to nod my lads
To Mr Graham Greene.)

Oh there's many a bitter smile my boys
And many a sneer obscene
When any critic – a first-rate critic,
Becomes a 'Might have been'
Through being as harsh and Jesuitic
As Mr Graham Greene.
(Restrain that cynical smile my boys,
To jeer is never worthwhile my boys.
Remember the rising bile my boys
Of Mr Graham Greene.)

At the bottom right-hand corner, Coward had typed the following explanation: 'Perhaps it is unnecessary to state that the above was written following two very unpleasant attacks on me and my work by Mr Graham Greene in "The Spectator"'.

But Coward followed this with a letter in verse:

Dear Mr Graham Greene, I yearn
So much to know why you should burn
With such fierce indignation at
The very fact that I exist.
I've been unable to resist
Sitting up later than I need
To read in 'The Spectator' what
Appears to be no more, no less
Than shocking manners. I confess
Bewilderment. I've seldom seen
Another brother-writer press
Such disadvantage with such mean
Intent to hurt. You must have been
For years, in secret, nourishing

A rich, rip-snorting, flourishing
Black hatred for my very guts!
Surely all these envenomed cuts
At my integrity and taste
Must be a waste of your own time?
What is my crime, beyond success?
(But you have been successful too
It can't be that) I know a few
Politer critics than yourself
Who simply hate my lighter plays
But do they state their sharp dispraise
With such surprising, rising bile?
Oh dear me no, they merely smile.
A patronising smile perhaps
But then these journalistic chaps
Unlike ourselves, dear Mr Greene,
(Authors I mean) are apt to sneer
At what they fear to be apart
From that which they conceive as art.
You have descried (also with keen,
Sadistic joy) my little book
About Australia, one look
At which should prove, all faults aside,
That I had tried, dear Mr Greene,
To do a job. You then implied
That I had run away, afraid,
A renegade. I can't surmise
Why you should view your fellow men
With such unfriendly, jaundiced eyes.
But then, we're strangers. I can find
No clue, no key to your dark mind.
I've read your books as they appear
And I've enjoyed them. (Nearly all.)
I've racked my brains in a sincere
But vain endeavour to recall
If, anytime or anywhere,
In Bloomsbury or Belgrave Square,
In Paris or Pekin or Bude,
I have, unwittingly, been rude,
Or inadvertently upset you.
(Did I once meet you and forget you?)
Have I ever been your debtor?
Did you once write me a letter

That I never got – or what?)
If I knew, I shouldn't worry.
All this anguish, all this flurry,
This humiliating scene
That I'm making, Mr Greene,
Is a plea for explanation
For a just justification
By what strange Gods you feel yourself empowered
To vent this wild expenditure of spleen
Upon yours most sincerely
Noël Coward.

Neither Noël Coward's ballad nor his verse letter brought Greene's attacks to an end. Coward's next play, *Blithe Spirit*, opened at the Piccadilly a month after his ballad and verse letter were sent to Greene. It also received the chop from Greene. While admitting that Coward's first act was magnificent, he thought his handling of death unsavoury:

> One cannot draw a picture of a normally happy marriage and try to chill the blood at the idea of the harmless, aggravating wife driving to her death in a car with which her ghostly predecessor has tampered, and then a moment after the catastrophe dissolve an audience into laughter as the new ghost sets about her rival, pulling hair and hacking shins. The sudden transitions are not only maladroit; they show a tastelessness with which Mr Cecil Parker, Miss Fay Compton and Miss Kay Hammond were powerless to cope.[15]

Greene finds other examples: 'When the curtain rises for nearly the last time, Condomine is wearing a black band on either arm – perhaps Mr Coward's most meaningless exhibition of bad taste – a bad taste which springs from an ability to produce the appearances of ordinary human relationships – of man and wife – and an inability to feel them.'[16]

Part of what Greene was objecting to here was Coward's homosexuality, which inevitably prevented him, in Greene's view, from really 'knowing' about the relationship between man and woman. But another aspect was that Coward, in Greene's view, ran away from the blitz and the experience of death (so much the experience of every Londoner), but boasted of his patriotism abroad: 'We're holding the torch for England, each night in the Rainbow Room.'

No need to follow the plot to its silly and wordy end: apart from the first act it has been a weary exhibition of bad taste, a bad taste all the more evident now when sudden death is common and dissolves more marriages than the divorce courts. It would be charitable to suppose that Mr. Coward conceived his play in the crude peaceful sunlight of Australia, between the patriotic broadcasts, and that when he has been longer in this country he will feel less blithe about this spirit world of his where dead women behave like characters in *Private Lives*, and a saint is 'rather fun'.[17]

The novelist Rosamond Lehmann, who was a friend of Greene's, found his review intolerable. Her response must have pleased the disturbed heart of Coward: '[Greene] says . . . that one cannot draw a picture of a happy (second) marriage, cause the ghost of wife number one to bring about the death of wife number two, "and a moment after the catastrophe dissolve the audience into laughter as the new ghost sets about her rival . . . " to which the only reply is, "Can't one!": for Mr. Coward can and does.' To her mind, moral indignation was altogether the wrong approach to this piece; and Coward succeeded in pulling off his fantasy without offence 'by maintaining the subject of death at a consistent level of outrageous improbability, and not for one instant allowing genuine emotion to rear its head'. She made a wonderful point: 'Never having to feel, we never have to shudder. If the cracks aren't always of the highest class, they succeed each other with such dash on the part of both author and actors that they get across triumphantly; and Mr. Coward's technical skill and brilliance are greatly to be admired.'[18] She also dealt with the question of 'taste': 'There is obviously no standard criticism by which to judge tastelessness . . . I merely wish to say that if *Blithe Spirit* is in bad taste, then I am led to conclude, not for the first time, that I like bad taste.'[19]

Rosamond Lehmann was not alone in liking *Blithe Spirit* and Coward had the last laugh. The play ran for almost 2,000 performances, the longest straight run at that time of any play in London's history. It was still running when Graham Greene was sent abroad, and while on board a small cargo vessel wrote a book about drama. In it, Greene admitted that Noël Coward had all his contemporaries beaten for craftsmanship, was indeed the best craftsman since Barrie, and was able to disguise his sentimentality (unlike Barrie). Nevertheless, he left us with a sense of Coward's essential literary impermanence: 'Only as the years pass and the contemporary idiom changes does his sentimentality begin to show, emerging as the dye washes off, like the colour of a stolen horse.'[20]

A dozen years later, when Greene rented Coward's house in Jamaica as a holiday home, they met for the first time. Coward commented in his diary: 'He is very agreeable and his beastliness to me in the past I have forgiven but not forgotten.'[21]

*

Greene could be equally relentless when he was dealing with publishers, magazines and even the BBC. In June he had written a programme for the BBC entitled 'London in Spring'. The contract department felt able to question Greene's offering. They wrote the following autocratic Civil Service letter to Greene's agent:

> LONDON IN SPRING as sent by Mr. Greene was not found to be suitable for broadcasting, and neither was it adaptable for our purpose. It is suggested, however, that Mr. Greene should be asked to re-write the programme, and I shall be very glad to know if you will ask him if he is prepared to do this. In that case, we would agree to pay half the original fee now, the other half to be payable on completion of the re-written programme. Perhaps you would let me know what Mr. Greene feels about this suggestion.[22]

Miss Cooper, of Pearn, Pollinger and Higham, asked Greene what he would like her to say to the BBC. Greene made certain that she caught the exact tone and tenor of his meaning by writing the letter for her:

> Mr. Greene was commissioned to write a certain programme and his first sketch of it was approved by Mr. Potter. The BBC were in such a hurry over this programme that he was only allowed a few days to complete it. Its imperfections were the result of what was obviously a quite unnecessary rush. He is far too busy to work on the script again, and would certainly in any case not consent to do so without extra fee. Under the circumstances he would do no more work for this department even if offered another fee. Unless the money for work commissioned and carried out is paid very shortly, Mr Greene will have to put the matter in the hands of the Authors Society and will cancel the fortnightly Spanish talks he is doing for another section of the BBC. There is no question at all about this programme. It was commissioned and carried out. In literary matters of this kind a risk always attaches to a commission but no publisher after commissioning a book which then proved unsuitable would refuse to pay the sum contracted for.[23]

The fact that Greene was still in love with Dorothy Glover did not prevent him from visiting London prostitutes, who, around Piccadilly, wore special heels on their shoes so that they tapped like tap dancers. They shone torches on their silken legs, or showed their presence by little quick flashes of light. Greene used this experience in his novel *The End of the Affair*, when describing Bendrix's adventure with a prostitute:

It was dark and quiet by this time in the streets, though up in the moonless sky moved the blobs and beams of the searchlights. You couldn't see faces where the women stood in doorways and at the entrances of the unused shelters. They had to signal with their torches like glow-worms. All the way up Sackville Street the little lights went on and off . . . A woman flashed on her light and said, 'Like to come home with me, dear?' I shook my head and walked on. Further up the street a girl was talking to a man: as she lit up her face for him, I got a glimpse of something young, dark and happy and not yet spoiled: an animal that didn't recognise her captivity. I passed and then came back up the road towards them; as I approached the man left her and I spoke. 'Like a drink?' I said.
'Coming home with me afterwards?'
'Yes.'[24]

Prostitutes were especially numerous in wartime London, as soldiers, sailors and airmen, separated from home and family, found sex in a doorway, or, for more money, a night in the prostitute's room. There was also much open-air activity. Hyde and Green Parks were often invaded by an army of prostitutes turning that green and pleasant land into a battlefield of sex.

But Greene's days of soliciting prostitutes in the middle of the blitz were numbered. Soon he was to be engaged by British Intelligence, MI6, and, after suitable training, sent out to West Africa. No one was better suited for such a posting, for how would it be possible to find an agent who had already travelled throughout Sierra Leone and Liberia as Greene had done?

He was returning to Africa, but first he had to be sent to a school for spies.

PART 2

Africa

Travel ✓

SIERRA LEONE.
IDENTIFICATION CARD FOR EUROPEAN BRITISH SUBJECTS.

District......FRE.......   No. 395

1. Christian Names (in full)......Graham
2. Surname (in block capitals)....GREENE
3. Address......Police H.Q. Freetown
4. Address outside SIERRA LEONE 99 Gt Russell St. London. W.C.1.
5. Occupation...C.I.D. Special Branch
6. Nationality...English
7. Sex...Male
8. Date of Birth...Oct. 2. 1904

I declare the above particulars to be correct.

......Graham Greene......
                                                    Signature.

(Office Stamp)

Date...Apr. 24. 1942.   ....
                                    Signature of Issuing Authority.

Greene's identity card for Sierra Leone

7

School for Spies

In the final analysis a spy has no protection but the faith
of his friends.
— B. PAGE, D. LEITCH AND P. KNIGHTLEY

IN April 1941 Greene knew that the gravity of the war demanded
more of him than being the literary editor of a distinguished
journal, and that he could not remain a civilian under troubled
London skies much longer. He hinted as much to his mother: 'Now
they are conscripting for police and firemen, I may find myself not a
private in the Guards after all.'[1] But conscription into the police or
Auxiliary Fire Service would not have been greatly different from the
dangers faced daily as an air-raid warden. In any case, unbeknown to
his mother, Greene had been considering the possibility of joining
MI6 as an intelligence officer. A letter in December 1940 to Anthony
Powell revealed that he had conceived an ambition 'to do Free
French propaganda in French Guinea and the Ivory Coast from a
base in Liberia', but he had not been contacted.

Yet moves were afoot. His younger sister, Elisabeth, already in
Intelligence, had pressed her brother's case. She was secretary to
Cuthbert Bowlby, then regional head of the Secret Intelligence
Service (SIS/MI6) in the Middle Eastern theatre. Malcolm
Muggeridge reported Elisabeth Greene's influence in his
autobiography: 'We [Greene and Muggeridge] hoped that she would
recommend us both to her boss as suitable overseas representatives,
and be able to pull the requisite strings to get us accepted.'[2]

MI6 was slow to accept Greene, which was surprising since his
uncle, Sir Graham Greene, was one of the founders of Naval
Intelligence in the First World War, and was still, at a great age,
involved in Intelligence in the Second. What probably delayed the
process was that Greene's eldest brother, Herbert, the black sheep of
the family, had acted as an agent for Japanese Intelligence prior to the

war and had provided them with information of a minor kind about naval matters (information, it must be added, mostly taken from published journals). Herbert, for a time, successfully duped the Japanese, and incidentally provided himself with needed pocket money – £50 monthly. In December 1937 there appeared in the British communist newspaper an article headlined, 'I WAS IN THE PAY OF JAPAN: A SECRET AGENT TELLS HIS STORY TO THE *DAILY WORKER*.'[3] What Herbert had hoped to do by making these very minor revelations, was provide publicity for his book *Secret Agent in Spain* which had recently appeared.

But Greene was not being ignored. Initially, he didn't realise the meaning of the many parties given by a man he called the 'mysterious Mr. Smith' to which he had been invited. In spite of the blitz and rationing, there was never a lack of liquor at Smith's parties and everybody seemed to know each other.[4] Greene was being vetted. The 'mysterious Mr. Smith' was known as 'Smith of China' because his business wealth had originated from China. He was renowned for his parties, which often began one night and were still going the next. They were used to bring suitable civilians into the SIS: 'Your name was mentioned,' Rodney Dennys told me, 'and you'd be invited to a Smith party to allow certain SIS men to look you over privately.'*[5]

On 20 August 1941 Greene told his mother he was going out to West Africa for the Colonial Service, a comment insufficient to alert her as to the nature of his job. He gave notice to the *Spectator* and mentioned to his mother that he'd not be leaving for West Africa for two or three months but would work in London first.

Greene was sensitive to his mother's fears about the war, and aware that both he and Elisabeth would soon be leaving the country. He tried to assuage her anxieties by making an unlikely prognostication about when the war would end: 'I'm afraid your family is being rather scattered, but I feel myself that the war will be over by next autumn and that we'll all be back again by Christmas 1942.' He added that Elisabeth would be much safer in Cairo than in her London apartment in Vauxhall Bridge Road. He also tried to give his mother the sense that her children were in close contact: 'I lunched with E. yday: she's looking very well I thought, and I'm seeing Hugh tonight and Raymond on Thursday. Much love in all this haste.'[6]

---

* Rodney Dennys, later married to Greene's sister, Elisabeth, became a successful head of station, section 5 in Cairo, then went to Turkey, where he was the senior SIS officer at the time of Guy Burgess and Donald Maclean's flight to the USSR.

To his mother he admitted feeling the rather agonising conflict between his responsibilities to his family and the appeal of an interesting, well-paid job, but argued that if he had waited to be called up he might have gone abroad under far less happy circumstances.[7] It may be that leaving his family was disturbing Greene, but he did not make enough effort (according to Vivien) to see them since the war began. Probably more troublesome to him was that he was leaving Dorothy Glover. However, the fact that the 'shadow of a private's pay – or even a lieutenant's – was raised' attracted Greene and meant he'd be able to leave his family without financial worries.

Vivien was unhappy about his decision to go abroad, though she expressed her opposition in feline fashion and her threats were not intended to bear much weight. She may even have felt that his departure from England might be a godsend if it led to the end of his affair with Dorothy:

I do love my precious Stripey. I love his ruff & the rings round his tum & his sensitive whiskers & luminous pale eyes, & consider myself lost without him. Would *object* therefore (but with a hopeless sense that my objections would be merely swept aside) to Stripey going to a foreign clime: only punishment in my power would be NOT TO WRITE TO HIM. There.[8]

Vivien's babyish opposition melted and soon she was fussing over her husband, advising him to fix up with someone about the injections well beforehand, telling him she was unable to find his raincoat, but hoped his suit would do.

By October he was writing to his parents from Oriel College, Oxford, explaining to them that he was back in OTC (as he had been for a while in school), wearing battledress in the morning, and doing stick drill with the officers. An agent recalled watching him and commented how he was everyone's comic notion of how *not* to drill (Greene was unable to slope arms). His letters to his parents reveal nothing of his training as an intelligence officer. He wrote only of unimportant matters: 'Motor byking is a real trial – today, my second go. I got on a little better, fell off less – 1st worse . . . I shall be a "cripple" this week, inconvenient as I go up to town tomorrow to report.'[9] The head of the course had to abandon the idea that Greene would ever be able to learn to ride a motorcycle after he had damaged two.[10] Training was strict. He had three periods in the morning, three in the afternoon, took an enormous number of notes and did homework.

*

But what might his training have been to demand that he take voluminous notes? In the British Intelligence Corps Library a memorandum entitled 'Notes on the Working of Agents'[11] has survived, which reveals information the 'teachers' at Oriel would have imparted to nascent secret intelligence officers. It presents a strange world where 'trust' is on the side of the used agent and not on the side of the intelligence officer; where your informants are expected to provide you with valuable espionage information, but in spite of this, it is your duty to discover something in their past which will give you a hold over them for as long as you need them.

The first step is rather obvious: engage prospective agents in conversation with the object of finding out what type of person they are; i.e., talkative, indifferent or an enthusiast on a particular subject. Proceeding gently to the second step, make small offers of cigarettes or beer and ask very casually for a little information. The questions should be harmless, but of such a nature that the answer will indicate whether they are likely to become an agent or not. An important point to remember is that when the agent is considered reliable, and the information accurate, you must tell the agent the truth in return as far as is consistent with safety.

The paper gives three possible reasons why people give away information: (1) the desire for money; (2) dislike of the person or persons about whom the information is given; (3) desire to try and win a position which would obtain them protection from their own people or police.

The following are examples given of the various types of agents:

(a) Pacifist informers on militarists or republicans on monarchists, Communists on the police or vice-versa. (b) Agents in the pay of the political police who are 'put on to' [a British agent] to find out what [his service] is trying to find out, or in what he is interested. This type may be told to sacrifice some true information in order to gain confidence of [a British agent]. (c) Indiscriminate agents, who are continually asking if there is anything they can do, if there is any information they can provide. This type can be either dangerous or merely annoying. (d) Men of the same type as (b) whose aim is to make friends with [a British agent], offering to give information in order to find out his system of work and facts about the routine of his office. (e) Lastly, there is the casual informer.

The rules for running agents are as sound today as they were then. First, keep the agent's identity secret to avoid exposure to unnecessary risks. Never give an agent too much money at a time; the spending of it will only draw attention to the agent and to you. Never tell the agent more than he needs to know; there is always a risk that an undesirable person may obtain the information. If possible, the intelligence officer should hide his real identity and address in case it becomes necessary to cut off all communications with the informant. The intelligence officer needs to gain some influence over the agent by finding out something private about him that would disturb him if it got into the hands of the police or his party. It may prove useful later if he tries, or threatens, to go over to the other side.

The memorandum cautions the British agent about situations the agent must try to avoid:

Precautions.

(a) An agent sometimes urges [a GHQ agent] to meet him in some hotel, café, or restaurant, and becomes embarrassing in his demands. Probable reason: There is someone there from the other side, who wants to identify the [GHQ agent] as a [GHQ agent], and your agent is trying to give you away. (b) Whenever possible, do not interview someone, particularly in a discreet enquiry, with a set plan in your head. Certainly try to turn the question round to the subjects in which you are interested, but do not force it. He may be cleverer than you. (c) Try to find out something beforehand about the person to be approached, his interests, etc. (d) Avoid arousing suspicions by doing silly things: e.g. smoking obviously English cigarettes, etc . . . Once you have made a statement keep to it. Contradictions make you nervous and the agent suspicious. The general principle is to obtain as much information as possible, without giving any away.

From the difficulty I had in deciphering Greene's shorthand from this period, it appears that he certainly took to heart the following advice: '*Making notes.* Make as few as possible. Write on a newspaper or with a short piece of pencil on a piece of paper in the pocket. Never carry documents likely to connect you with the Army.' Agents are also cautioned never to trust porters, waiters, or hotel proprietors. When making enquiries in hotels, they must try to make friends with the victim by sitting at the same table with him. They must also intercept the victim's letters.

The memorandum is filled with other useful pointers:

(a)   Do not masquerade as someone about whom you know nothing, i.e. do not say you are a Dutchman unless you speak perfect Dutch; the other man may be one too.

(b)   Never use a telephone when speaking to agents. Danger of being overheard or intercepted.

(c)   It is easier to get information out of a woman, but more dangerous. Make use of jealousy if possible. Information about one woman through another.

It is difficult to know specifically what Greene was taught, but by studying what is known of the training of the Office of Strategic Services' (OSS) agents (the forerunner of the CIA), we can establish a general routine, for the Americans modelled their training methods on those used by the older, more experienced intelligence service, the SIS.

No doubt Greene and other trainees at Oriel took notes on how to find and evaluate potential agents to carry out espionage against their own country   local government officials, military personnel, representatives of intelligence agencies opposed to their own. Sometimes, businessmen, students, reporters, even missionaries were used. There would probably be lectures regarding how money might be used to bring about the downfall of another country; how to recognise an anti-Nazi dissident or someone opposed to the Hitler regime; how to use blackmail and exert influence over foreign officials in neutral countries. British agents would be told to look for those officials living beyond their means or with a weakness for alcohol, drugs, or women (or men). Greene would have received training in security precautions, the avoidance and detection of surveillance, the use of specialised equipment, such as miniature cameras, and he would learn new terminology – 'dead letter drop', 'cutouts', etc.

However, the primary lesson for OSS, CIA, MI5 and MI6 agents was how to live effectively within another identity. A standard training school exercise between novice agents is to fool your colleague – maintaining a false identity and cover is a requisite. Each agent must develop a passion for secrecy, deception and manipulation. These must become second nature.

*

Greene's family were at Oxford, but he saw little of them, though he did have dinner with his wife on his thirty-seventh birthday: 'V. & I had dinner in the evening with the Taylors. Otherwise we have rather snatched moments before dinner,' he wrote to his mother.[12]

He was still in frequent contact with his literary agent, especially about royalties: 'As you can imagine I'm keen on gathering in any shekels before my departure.' He wanted to know whether Heinemann owed him money on the Guild paperback of *Stamboul Train* and whether they would allow him to transfer *England Made Me* to Penguin, since they had already sold about 120,000 copies of *It's a Battlefield*.[13]

Greene's training was rigorous, but he didn't complete the course, going down with a serious virus: 'Just getting over an attack of flu in the discomfort & squalor of a military depot,' he wrote from the North Oxford Nursing Home in Banbury Road.[14] That did not prevent his agent, Miss Pearn, seeking him various commissions: the new *Strand* editor, an admirer of Greene's, wanted him to inject more humour and satire into the magazine, and enquired whether Greene could provide them with a piece before he left England. Miss Cooper, working for the same agency, wanted to know if he would write a story for *Modern Reading*: 'as a great admirer of your work, this editor would very much like to have something more of yours to publish . . . the editor is definitely prepared to commission a short story of approximately 3,000 words in length, if you feel able to do this.'[15]

Writing from his hospital bed, Greene advised Miss Cooper to 'tell Miss Pearn that she must be living in a happy dream world. *I am probably leaving for West Africa in about 3 weeks* – during which time I have to buy clothes & make all my family arrangements. I shall have *no time* to write a word before I go.'[16]

Greene returned to town on 4 November still pretty wobbly on his feet and stayed with Dorothy at Gower Mews: 'Back in town but not worth very much. My departure has been postponed a little,' he wrote to Pollinger. Before he left for Africa, he met the film producer Alberto Cavalcanti, and their meeting led to friendship. Cavalcanti wanted to make a film of one of Greene's stories, expressing an interest in the story 'The Lieutenant Died Last'. Greene was excited, for here was a means of leaving his family in good financial fettle:

I saw Cavalcanti yesterday who has two feature films to make for Ealing Studios [he wrote to Laurence Pollinger]. I told him about 'The Lieutenant Died Last', the story I had in *Collier's* and *Britannia & Eve*, & he seemed very keen on the idea. B&E have had their files destroyed [in the blitz], haven't they? The only way of tracing it is to let Cavalcanti have the date it appeared in *Collier's* . . . Could you cable Mary [Pritchett] asking her whether she could send us a copy of *Collier's*?[17]

Finally, Ealing Studios came through, though by that time Greene was already in convoy to West Africa: 'Thank you very much indeed', wrote Vivien the day after Christmas to Pollinger, 'for the good news and the cheque from Ealing Studios.' The film appeared with the title *Went the Day Well* in 1942. Greene was still in Africa and never saw it. Cavalcanti's film caused controversy when it was released, no doubt because it showed England being invaded at a time when invasion by Hitler was an ever-present possibility.

Greene went down to the country for a last two weeks to be with his family, though he intended to spend the final few days before departure with Dorothy at Gower Mews. Before leaving, he decided to make a will, asking Pollinger and his brother Raymond to be executors, and leaving all to Vivien. Dorothy was not a beneficiary, though he did throughout their relationship do her various favours. When working for the Ministry of Information, he introduced his lover into the Ministry as his secretary. When Pick sacked him, he persuaded them to put Dorothy in charge of a section: 'Her job was to get people to do cartoons, caricatures and things. She went on to the end of the war there.'[18]

One of the last trips Greene took before leaving England was to the army camp in Aldershot. He went with his friend Basil Dean, the head of ENSA troop entertainments, on a lightning tour in the company of the then powerful socialist Minister of Labour in the Churchill government, Ernest Bevin. Greene warmed to Bevin, and recorded in his journal how Bevin innocently pushed into dressing rooms, talking excitedly, 'I'm Mr. Bevin' – to the ENSA leading ladies: 'Very likeable, very unselfconscious.' In the urinal he said: 'This reminds me of the old Socialist who said: "Now I've really got my hands on the means of production."'

After dinner, they had champagne at The Anchor at Liphook, and drove back after midnight. What Greene especially remembered was how beautiful it was 'to see the London guns playing from the outside'.[19]

He would soon be unable to see 'London guns playing from the outside'. Across the seas in Africa he would no longer be part of the army of air-raid wardens protecting a London still sporadically under attack. He was leaving his wife, he was leaving his mistress, but his training at the school for spies was over and the apprentice was ready for further training in Africa.

8

Return to Africa

Under the cope of storms, with waves disputing
On the free crossway of the sea.
                              — ALEXANDER PUSHKIN

GREENE arrived in Liverpool on 8 December 1941, the day the
Japanese landed in Thailand and north-east Malaya, and the
United States declared war on Japan. He spent the night at that vast
Liverpool hotel, the Adelphi. He had last stayed there in January
1935 at the start of his remarkable journey to Sierra Leone and
Liberia with his cousin Barbara, which resulted in his brilliant travel
book, *Journey Without Maps*. Then he had thought the Adelphi was
designed without aesthetic taste but with the right ideas about
comfort and a genuine idea of magnificence: 'Beneath the huge cliff-
like fall of its walls, the idea of an English inn existed; one didn't
mind asking for muffins or a pint of bitter, while the boats hooted in
the Mersey and the luggage littered the hall.'[1]

In the journal he kept during his second voyage to West Africa, he
wrote briefly (often using a telegraphic style), but the feeling
engendered, even in wartime conditions, was still the same:
'Breakfast in the Adelphi – the great comfort and security';[2] then the
taxi drive 'through battered streets to the dock. Empty Sabbath-like
wastes with nobody about to ask the way. The difficulty of finding
something as large as a ship. At last the ship. The bright clean little
staterooms.'[3]

There were only twelve passengers on the unnamed Elder
Dempster cargo ship: 'The passengers: two fleet air arm officers: two
RNVR; a Naval officer who had only twice been at sea in his life –
as far as Hamburg; also an odd foreigner in the strangest plus fours
and very little English – a great square face and square plus fours, and
two oil men who keep together.'[4] One in particular, because of the
red-carpet treatment he received, was carefully noted by Greene. He

91

reappeared as a character in *The Comedians* a quarter of a century later: 'W., a rather mysterious elderly American travelling under the wing of the F.O.: farewell party in London as [Averell] Harriman's guest. Fetched by car by the port admiral – and yet the great authority on Byzantine art. Speaks Arabic, knows Turkey very well and possibly bound there, a vegetarian.' In a letter to his mother from Lagos, Greene again referred to the mysterious elderly American in a more direct manner: 'Nice old Professor Wittemore of Harvard, who was my shipmate, and a friend of the Matthews brothers, had looked [Elisabeth] up in Cairo. He recognised her immediately she came to his hotel by her likeness to me! This is very nice for me, but less so for E.'5

At about 2.30 p.m. they left port to anchor in the Mersey. The submarine menace was an ever-present concern and boat drill a serious rehearsal for what might well happen: 'I am No. 1 boat with the Fleet Air Arm officer, two or three blacks, etc.' and 'all day two rafts are suspended on a slope each side of the ship ready to be cut loose . . . On the poop the anti-aircraft men in khaki and any old sweater keep watch round the Bofors gun . . . Every passenger is morally compelled to volunteer for submarine and machine gun watches.'6 He ends his first day: 'Tonight one will sleep safely quiet in the Mersey.'7

The journey was not a pleasure cruise. This was war and passengers had to man three four-hour watches during the day, two men on machine-guns above the deck for aircraft, and two below the bridge for submarines. The sailor who showed the passengers how to fire the guns had been on the ship's previous convoy and told Greene that on that convoy two ships had been torpedoed the first night out of the Mersey. The warning to boat stations was seven short blasts of the siren and one long.

That first day was bitterly cold: 'The sea getting up: soldiers in Balaclavas by the Bofors.' Greene noticed the 'black steward making water in the bilge'. In his journal he wrote that 'even a bird can look like a periscope'. At dinner the chief told them that in weather like this it was easy for a submarine to follow a ship unobserved during the day above water and submerge at night for the attack. The hour with the machine-gun was less cold: 'One climbs a short vertical steel ladder into a kind of conning-tower containing a gun with steel shield.' He was less uncomfortable there: 'The steel shields like the wings of black angels', and perched up above the deck, 'one hears the wind in the wires like choral singing from inside a church'.8

The passengers listened every night to the news on the steward's radio and that first day heard the desperate report of a great victory by the Japanese, the sinking of the British carriers the *Prince of Wales* and the *Repulse* with terrible loss of life. Coming so soon after Pearl Harbor, and with the Germans only five miles from the Kremlin, the news left each listener with an overwhelming sense of the forces now aligned against the Allies. In an unpublished part of his journal, Greene recorded: 'At 6 listened to the wireless in the Chief Steward's cabin. Germany's declaration of war on America, following on the loss of our warships made me feel suddenly sick.'[9]

At tea, Greene felt a different kind of sickness: 'Awful prospect – duty while seasick,' and in the biting cold of the bows, he recited 'Hail Marys' to try to distract himself. About midnight, the sirens woke him. He counted seven blasts but no long blast. It was the approach to Belfast:

> Little white lighthouses on stilts: a buoy that seems to have a table tied to it: a sunken ship right up in the dock. Cranes like skeleton foliage in a steely winter. The flicker of green flame in the bellies of building ships. Hundreds of dock-yard workers stop altogether to see one small ship come in.[10]

At Belfast they waited for other ships to join the convoy; perhaps they gained a modest sense of safety. Greene noted with some astonishment the general anxiety to get ashore in so dull a place. Nevertheless, he went ashore too, thinking it wise to go to Confession before facing the submarine-filled Atlantic. It was difficult finding a Catholic church in Protestant Belfast, but he came across one, a hideous structure:

> At the Presbytery a tousled housekeeper tried to send me away when I asked for a confession. 'This is no time for confession,' trying to shut the door in my face. The dreadful parlour hung with pious pictures and then the quiet nice young priest who called me 'son' and whose understanding was of the simplest.[11]

Later Greene and two others plus the purser (whom Greene had known on the *David Livingstone* when he first sailed to Sierra Leone) went ashore again after dinner to the Globe, an oyster house where they had a dozen and a half of Galway oysters and a pint and a half of draught Guinness.

They left Belfast on 13 December, but lay all day in the lough. Gathering there were a dozen cargo ships, smaller than their 5,000 tonner, plus a destroyer, a cruiser and a little corvette, which steamed round the ships in the late afternoon taking charge. They discovered that the fourth engineer had skipped ship. He was ten pounds in the company's debt and couldn't get a drink until the debt was paid off. Greene wrote in his journal: 'How oddly dramatic ships are. My last voyage [when he returned from his trip to Mexico, which led to *The Power and the Glory*] – in a German ship from Vera Cruz – the cook committed suicide rather than return home.'[12]

The little ship now travelled in the direction of Greenock. It was cruelly cold: 'Leave the lough and join a line of about seven ships. Submarine watch 9 to 10.15: with the machine-gun 10.15 to 11.30, and then after a rather scanty lunch relieved someone at the gun from 1 to 1.30. The last watch high wind and icy sleet. Couldn't get warm afterwards. Lay down.'[13] The next two days, 15 and 16 December, were rough for Greene. The ship was making no more than four knots against a head wind going south-west. Greene was sick both days. Coming off duty from the well of the ship, he slammed the door of the cabin and caught his thumb: 'The whole nail will go. Bled a good deal and felt like hell. Luckily my left but difficult enough [to write].'[14]

As usual, writing was Greene's most important activity, a discipline never to be relaxed, even on board. Although involved in the daily protection of the ship, and often seasick, he used the time between the day watches to write a short book called *British Dramatists*. He had signed the contract in April 1941 (his payment was only £50 for the world rights), undertaking to write no more than 12,000 words. The quality of the book, which is now out of print, is greatly in excess of the sum of money offered. His journal reveals the effort he made to write. 11 December: 'So far in spite of nausea and watches I have kept up an average of 500 words a day on *British Dramatists*.' 15 and 16 December: 'Rough both days . . . No writing either day.' 22 December: 'disposed of Congreve in *British Dramatists*'. He wrote of the great Restoration dramatist: 'Shadwell had more life, and Wycherley more stagecraft – Congreve like the smooth schoolboy stole the prize.'[15] Greene completed the manuscript before he landed at Freetown: 'I finished off the *British Dramatists*', he wrote to his mother, 'on the ship without reference books & typed it laboriously on a machine with a French keyboard when I got to Lagos.'[16]

Greene's journal reflects his fascination with character. On 19 December he recorded the second steward's conversation:

The second steward – the cracked one – was a prisoner for two years in the last war – according to him in Siberia . . . He explains his paunch by it. 'I hate them,' he says, blocking the way in his

94

white jacket. 'I'd kill a German child that high. I'd kill a German woman who was pregnant with one. If I'm alive, you'll hear of me after the war in Lord Beaverbrook's paper . . . And if I die, I've left a letter for my two daughters – they'll carry on. There'll be two rebels in England if they try to let them off this time.'

'Don't talk of dying.'

'I'll never die. I live by prayer, I pray at sunrise and sunset like a Mohammedan.' (He is a Catholic.)[17]

In his published account of the journey, Greene called one troublesome fellow 'Glasgow' for obvious reasons. He was the drunk traditionally found on board every West Coast boat. He had a 'hooked bird's nose and his sudden tipsy release of mental activity was like a minor prophet'. Early in the voyage 'Glasgow' had everyone penned in the small smoking room:

Well, gentlemen . . . we're going to be together for five or six weeks, and there's going to be a wonderful interchange of mind . . . We've come into this ship all thinking different things, but when we go out of that door we'll all think the same . . . I'm not interested in what *you* think: I'm interested in what I think . . . It will be the most wonderful experience of my life, the deepest experience. I'll impose on you all what I think. I won't disguise it from you, gentlemen, I'm a drinker. I buried my wife last August and since then poor Joe's had nothing to do but get drunk.[18]

'Glasgow' is often quoted directly in Greene's journal: '"I'm drunk and proud of it. I hate criticism. Why shouldn't I be drunk? It feels good to be drunk and it sharpens the intellect." The Fleet Air Arm warrant officers watch him disapprovingly.' Apparently, 'Glasgow' was joining a friend at Basra as second in command of all naval transport through the Persian Gulf.[19]

On 21 December the weather was rough and though they had left the Mersey eleven days before, Greene doubted they had reached the latitude of Land's End. On 22 December some of the convoy turned off over the 'south-western horizon'. Soberly, Greene added, 'We missed their presence.' The day before, with the heavy mist and visibility of only 100 yards, the ships' sirens were blowing different tones. When the mist rose at 8.15 the next morning, each ship was still in its exact place, chugging slowly on. To frighten off possible submarines, the destroyer dropped depth charges and later raced towards the head of the convoy. It was at this point that Greene discovered from the chief steward that, in addition to the cargo of aeroplanes, they carried TNT. The 'CS' was nervous: 'this is his first trip after being torpedoed and his cabin looks exactly like the previous one'. He felt 'jittery at night. Hasn't gone to bed but lies on his couch. The cargo of depth charges and TNT under his cabin.'

The chief steward had every reason to be afraid. Between June 1940 and March 1941 German submarines sank two million tons of shipping, sinkings which if continued would have prevented England from feeding her population. U-boats off West Africa attacked not only at periscope depth by day but by night on the surface, making use of their greater surface speed. They were hunting convoys down in 'wolf-packs'. Beyond the range of air cover, the available escorts could not protect convoys from terrible losses from such mass attacks.[20]

Despite the concern about submarines, there were constant parties. On 18 December it was stormy again, but that did not stop the revelry: 'Party began in chief steward's cabin when I went to get thumb dressed at 10 and continued till I went to duty on guns at 12.30. The second engineer played the piano, the purser tried to sing, and the second steward served what he called 3d. cocktails – rum and milk – giving a dramatic recitation in a tin hat.'[21] That day, the American professor related an anecdote about Gertrude Stein. Asked at a lecture why it was that she answered questions so clearly and wrote so obscurely, Stein replied: 'If Keats was asked a question, would you expect him to reply with the "Ode to a Grecian Urn"?'

By 23 December the ship had moved at last out of the cold into warm sun and blue sea. As an additional diversion, Greene began to play chess with a Polish passenger, Kitzkuran. 'It is not to be avoided. If I lie down in the afternoon, he pokes his shaven Mongolian head through the cabin door and says, "Check?" During the game he sings all the time to himself: "Good. Very good. It is very good," and tries to take back his pieces.'[22] Kitzkuran turned out to be a confirmed polygamist. He explained the advantages of three wives: 'One wife, she rule. Three, I am king.'[23]

As Christmas approached, there were more parties: '24 December: Warmer and sunnier. Passing between the Azores in sight of land. A party again with the steward, the purser and "Glasgow" before lunch. The steward showing how to test a French letter.'[24] Greene started Christmas Eve with a half-bottle of champagne, then had Beaune for dinner followed by port and brandy. He went down to the steward's to help with Christmas decorations and another party developed, which lasted until 2.30 a.m.:

French letters blown up the size of balloons and hung over the

captain's chair. The black steward Daniel's gentle song, his shyness
. . . stands on his hands and put his feet round his neck. Sinclair
bossy & too free with his patronage, Fraser noisy, 'Glasgow'
himself. The Fleet Air Arm's songs – 'Danny Boy', 'When Irish
Eyes are Smiling' . . . and the like. The cracked second steward
became boring with over-repeated turns: we had heard so often
already the poem in praise of the Merchant Service said to be by
his eleven-year-old daughter – the recitation in a tin helmet . . .
Cookie, in his dirty white apron, thin consumptive fanatical face
with long razor nose and three days' beard. His magnificent ballad
about the E.D. ship which went down, & Captain Kerry . . .

Major Cripps's circular letter to all officers & men: 'Remember
what you have been told about V.D. & do your duty in the
lifeboats.'[25]

Christmas Day was uneventful; Greene decided to start at eleven in
the morning with a bottle of champagne to cure his hangover. At
lunch the passengers heard the Empire broadcast followed by the
King's speech on the radio. They enjoyed a generous Christmas
menu and made toasts to the King, Churchill and Roosevelt, as well
as the Polish leader Sikorski, included because of Kitzkuran. The
drinking and partying went on till midnight when they sang 'Auld
Lang Syne'.

It was not until 30 January 1942 that Vivien heard from her
husband about his Christmas activities (such was the delay in
transporting mail during the war): 'It was simply intoxicating to hear
from you – your lovely long Letter I, which was forwarded to
Sidmouth [Vivien had taken the children to Sidmouth for a holiday
so that they could convalesce after chicken pox] & I loved reading
about your Christmas. The champagne (which you can't spell)
sounds helpful but I know that the mere presence of the man
[Professor Wittemore, the mysterious American scholar] who knew
Henry & William James would irradiate any voyage.'[26]

On 28 December, his daughter's birthday, Greene drank
champagne in her honour before lunch, split two bottles of claret at
night, and attended a party in the chief steward's cabin afterwards. A
week before their scheduled arrival in Freetown, Greene wrote in his
journal: 'I feel as if I'm just coming out from under an anaesthetic, &
am scared of how lonely I shall feel when I leave the ship.' On the
30th more parties took place in the steward's cabin before lunch and
before dinner:

The usual West Coast tales are starting up like plants in the heat.

How one remembers them from eight years back. The doctor who cuts a tumour off a black girl's breast and tosses it to her waiting relatives: 'Here's a dash [gift].' The colonel & his girl in Lagos – of about 40! 'Soon as she saw me, she turns up her skirt behind.'[27]

At 10 p.m. that night the sighting of glimmering light on the horizon – caused either by a lighted ship or an island – generated excitement. It was the first time lights had been seen out of doors since leaving Belfast. The following day they saw their first real sign of land and a Sunderland flying boat above them took a look round for submarines. It gave everyone confidence as if they had up till now 'been lost on the empty sea'. Finally, the convoy divided. Some ships with railway engines on deck made for the Cape, and they were left to carry on alone. They felt the isolation and loneliness.

On 3 January 1942, shortly before noon, the ship entered the port of Freetown. The beauty of the scene as viewed from the ship was recalled in *The Heart of the Matter*:

From here the port was always beautiful; the thin layer of houses sparkled in the sun like quartz or lay in the shadow of the great green swollen hills . . . The destroyers and the corvettes sat around like dogs: signal flags rippled and a helio flashed. The fishing boats rested on the broad bay under their brown butterfly sails.[28]

Greene was deeply moved to return to Freetown after seven years: 'It felt odd & poetic & encouraging coming back after so many years. Like seeing a place you've dreamed of. Even the sweet hot smell from the land – is it the starved greenery and the red soil, the smoke from the huts in Kru town, or the fires in the bush clearing the ground for planting? – was oddly familiar.'[29] The printed version of his journal adds this final sentence: 'It will always be to me the smell of Africa, and Africa will always be the Africa of the Victorian atlas, the blank unexplored continent the shape of the human heart.'[30]

Greene's first visit to Africa had been made primarily as an antidote to boredom, an escape from Western civilisation. This time he came as an intelligence officer, a member of MI6 involved in counter-espionage against the German enemy:

landing in Freetown from a slow convoy four weeks out of Liverpool. I felt a strong sense of unreality: how had this happened? . . . The red Anglican cathedral looked down on my landing . . . Nothing in the exhausted shabby unchanged town of bougainvillaea and balconies, tin roofs and funeral parlours, had changed, but I never imagined on my first visit [in 1935] that one day I would arrive like this to work, to be one of those tired men drinking pink gin at the City bar as the sun set on the laterite.[31]

Greene was back. For a second time, he was to lose his heart to West Africa.

9

The Soupsweet Land

I speak of Africa and golden joys.
— SHAKESPEARE

EVERY passenger after a voyage longs to get ashore and stay ashore. Greene touched dry land but did not stay there. He was waiting to be contacted by someone (for the nature of his job and the reason for his presence had to be kept secret) – but by whom? His journal shows that he was not claimed for six days and continued to sleep on board ship.

Still, on arriving in port, he scrambled ashore like the rest of the passengers as his confusing journal entry reveals: 'The restlessness, the contrary rumours, the buttonholing of passengers in a port who want to get ashore. Finally after lunch gatecrashed with the launch which brought back the captain. The surly E[lder] D[empster] agent, the Field Security business: "This action is serious. Some people who thought it wasn't are in Freetown Gaol now." '[1]

The town in the bright sunlight, crowded with sailors and soldiers, looked a little less seedy than he remembered, though the kites still circled in the sky on the watch for carrion: 'The Sunday clothes. The Port. The officers' club – no alcohol between 2 & 4: in the port invasion ships, hospital ship, etc.'[2]

Journal entries following his arrival suggest that Greene was on the lookout for material for novels. His stay aboard gave him time to collect material for a book he never wrote, but he was watching and listening: 'The food of the men while we have been having soup, fish, two meats, sweet & perhaps a repeat: they had crackling off the roast pork we had for lunch & two small potatoes & a small bit of pudding.'[3]

One source, 'the shadow in the companionway with the pleasant, but rough accent', tells how half a dozen blacks got on board the previous night when he had left his watch for just a moment. The blacks could steal things through an open porthole by using long sticks with rubber at the end, or fish hooks. The same seaman was on the *Arandora Star* when she was sunk. Apparently, a prisoner kept putting his head out of the porthole while the boats were being lowered. The crew shouted to him to keep it in, but he took no notice and a falling raft took his head clean off. This started a panic among the other prisoners and seven were shot. The seaman was on a raft for seven hours before being picked up. ' "This West Coast route is the worst," he said.'[4]

Greene did not find all the crew as pleasant as the 'shadow by the companionway':

The third engineer, tall & slim with curly fair hair & conceited eyes, leans over rails & exposes everywhere with complacency his bottom in [position of] bugger absolute. A curious kink in his brain makes him talk as if he fought on the Somme, though his signing-on papers give him as 30 & he looks no more . . . Always the faint supercilious smile, the pathetic pose & the unreliability.[5]

Greene also went ashore the day following his arrival, a Sunday, but on the Monday waited all day for the RAF launch, which never arrived. In contrast Kitzkuran went ashore that day:

He was seen sitting in the park with two little black boys . . . The boys were offering him singing and dancing.
  'Gentleman & Ladies?'
  'Schoolgirls.'
  'How old?'
  'Oh fourteen to twenty-four.'
  'And drinks?'
  'Whisky & gin & port.'
  'Expensive?'
  'All drink expensive now.'
  'Is there anything else you can do?'
  'There are ladies.'
  'Expensive?'
  'Cheaper than London.'
  'Ten shillings.'
  'Oh no. You no get girl for 10/- in London.'
  'Fifteen shillings?'
  'Yes all right.'
He went off with them.[6]

On Tuesday Greene was able to go ashore to buy tropical trousers: a cockroach ran out of every pair he touched. He was alive to any gossip which might be useful both as intelligence officer and novelist: 'The passenger agent at E.D.'s showing off his friendship with a man called Coleman, son of Coleman's mustard: asking another agent about him he replied: "Oh, he's rather a big man here. We don't know quite what. A parcel to him came undone & it contained a lot of Tommy guns." '[7]

On the Wednesday (7 January) he was again left on board and played chess with Kitzkuran: 'All religions say a man must have woman two times a week.'[8]

*

Greene was eventually offered accommodation, until arrangements could be made to fly him to Lagos for a further three months' training: 'Difficulty of accommodation solved by my intro. to Dr. John Martyn, Food Controller, who invited me to stay with him from Friday.'[9]

Even though he was indebted to Dr Martyn, Greene was watchful, and witheringly cool in his examination of the Food Controller's character: 'A pompous little man very inclined to show off: monocle dubiously unnecessary. Known in certain quarters as Filthy Freddie. Gave him lunch at the City [hotel] & it only cost 6/-. Everywhere he goes they charge him cheap prices. He can't stop them.'[10]

That Friday, Dr Martyn's launch fetched him at about noon: 'The cook arranged a musical farewell as I got on the launch: the gong, tinpans, etc.' In an article years later Greene added further detail: 'A kitchen orchestra of forks and frying pans played me off the Elder Dempster cargo ship into a motor launch where my temporary host . . . awaited me, expecting something less flippant.'[11] Greene left his tin boxes with the customs, and had lunch with Dr Martyn at the City Hotel, and afterwards sat in the park for a while watching a fountain. Then Dr Martyn drove him to the hill station, where a family called Mackenzie were staying. Greene's observing eye is ever apparent: 'Mrs M. a tall pretty blonde girl who looked as if the climate was just beginning to pull down – inclined to a grumbling tone. M. a young man with a rather new moustache which he fingers a lot – intelligent. M. drove me round the station – the European hospital, the reservoir in a cup of the enormous nipple like hills. Very lovely up here with the excessive vegetation, the little sea birds the size of a wren with a long beak.' Back at the club Greene watched Martyn, Mackenzie and a Royal Naval volunteer play snooker, and he noted: 'Mrs M. a little tight & ever so much nicer when we left.'[12]

It seems as if Greene was casually offered temporary accommodation by Dr Martyn following an accidental introduction. An entry in his journal suggests otherwise: 'Dr. M[artyn] while we were out driving suggested I should take on the job at present done by one of his people an intelligence officer from the French Guinea & Liberian border, liaison with Wagon [MI5 agent under Martyn].'[13] In 1940, in a letter to Anthony Powell, Greene had expressed a private ambition to do propaganda work in French Guinea and the Ivory Coast from a base in Liberia,[14] and, a little over a year later, the same proposal was secretly but officially made to him.

In spite of his innocuous reference to Dr Martyn in his journal, Greene *was* waiting for someone to approach him, and Martyn must have been his contact, a contact which had to be kept secret because enemy agents were alert in Freetown: new arrivals were watched.

In an article, 'The Soupsweet Land', written ten years later, Greene described quite a different meeting with his contact. Here Dr Martyn (unnamed) is simply his host and quite unaware that he has an MI6 man in his midst:

> The sense of unreality grew stronger every hour. A passage by air had been arranged to Lagos where I was to work for three months before returning, and I thought it best to warn my host that he would be seeing me again. 'What exactly are you going to do here?' he asked, and I was studiously vague, for no one had yet told me what my 'cover' . . . was to be.[15]

His contact approaches him secretly. A major with a large moustache drops in for drinks and suddenly asks Greene to 'Come for a walk' in the middle of the day when the heat is greatest. Greene is struck by the oddity of the request at that hour. They set off walking down the road in the haze caused by the dry dusty wind from the desert. Suddenly the major swerves sideways into the garden of an empty house, whose owner has gone on leave. Sitting on a large stone together, the major provides Greene with his cover:

> 'Signal came in last Friday. You're an inspector of the DOT. Got it?'
> 'What's DOT?'
> 'Department of Overseas Trade,' he said sharply.
> Ignorance in this new intelligence world was like incompetence.[16]

Greene was now able to answer 'Filthy Freddie's' query: ' "As a matter of fact," I said to my host, "I can tell *you*, though it's not been officially announced yet, that I am to be an Inspector of DOT." '[17]

This must be a fictional account since his journal proves Martyn was MI5 and knew Greene as MI6. He could not have been happy with Greene's arrival since, for the first time, an interloper from the hated MI6 was to be active in *his* territory – there would be terrific wariness on both sides. Kim Philby mentioned to me the MI5 agent in Freetown, though not by name: 'What seemed to impress Graham most about Freetown was rain on the tin roofs and his MI5 opposite number, a tropical boozer of sub-homicidal tendencies which surfaced when he suffered visits of inspection from HQ in London.'[18]

*

In a backwater out of the danger and excitement of the war, with the intrigue of intelligence minimal, Greene's journal reveals a contempt for the colonial lifestyle of West Africa. Although he enjoyed his first afternoon (fishing with two colleagues of Martyn), the evening appalled him by its triviality. He went to a pantomime, *Royal Robes*, given by a medical unit with the help of two nursing sisters: 'Felt terribly depressed at the thought of life here – snobbery, sex & games I have no skill at.'[19]

The thoughts of his hero in *The Heart of the Matter* trying to cope with conditions in the terrible heat of the tropics are surely Greene's: 'Scobie walked rapidly back into the lounge. He went full tilt into an arm-chair and came to a halt. His vision moved jerkily back into focus, but sweat dripped into his right eye . . . He told himself: Be careful. This isn't a climate for emotion. It's a climate for meanness, malice, snobbery . . . '[20]

On Sunday, 11 January 1942, Dr Martyn took a party in his launch up-river first to Tasso Island, a swamp reclamation, and then to the famous Bunce Island, an old Portuguese slavers' fort. In his journal, Greene noted the disintegrating epitaphs found in the 'steamy graveyard':

10 guns lying on the grass stamped with George III's arms . . . the little steamy graveyard – the ship's cup . . . '18 years devoted service set up by the proprietor . . . se . . rus . . from Surrey, chief agent, renowned for his humanity' then the record breaks off 'A Danish sea captain married to the virtuous lady . . . ' who bore him 'two good-natured daughters'.

Ten years later Greene wrote: 'The phrase "The White Man's Grave" has become a music hall cliché to those who have never seen the little crumbling cemeteries of the West Coast like that on Bunce Island in Sierra Leone river.'

The party consisted of Martyn, Greene, the wife of the Commander-in-Chief, South Atlantic and her two charming daughters (aged about seventeen and nineteen), and an old convoy commodore: 'A sumptuous lunch before we got to Tasso & a lavatory rigged up on board for the ladies – the Commodore's failure to realise why they had gone on board alone. Note: the debased devil dancer at Tasso with just a sack on his head & exposing his body.[21] Afterwards the club . . . The club library has 3 of my books – *It's a Battlefield*, *A Gun for Sale*, & *The Power and the Glory*.'[22]

The Heart of the Matter also reveals an almost physical revulsion for the white colonials: 'His eye caught a snapshot of a bathing party at Medley Beach . . . the Colonial Secretary's wife, the Director of Education holding up what looked like a dead fish, the Colonial Treasurer's wife. The expanse of white flesh made them look like a gathering of albinos, and all the mouths gaped with laughter.'[23]

During his short stay, Greene felt an increasing dislike for 'Filthy Freddie': 'The dim Dr. Mac for dinner again, & a young Trinidadian officer from East Africa whose anecdotes of the Abyssinian campaign only temporarily deflected Dr. Martyn from sex – baring a girl bathing, etc.' Greene had an instinctive objection to lewd insinuations. When twenty-one and staying in Nottingham, he left his digs because of 'an awful man whose mind is the lowest cesspool of dirt I've ever come across . . . the hearty talks filth'. Sexual vulgarity dismayed him, though later entries in his journal, when he was partying in Lagos, show that he became a little more tolerant: 'The story of the toffee apple'; 'Stick your wooden leg up your arse'; 'Dinner . . . with S. Rather boastful, but many interesting professional stories. Petting the [waitress?] brings all to an end'; 'T's farewell party. Additional jokes. The frozen midget with the rigid digit. The massive vassal with the passive tassel. Obscene jokes have an unnecessary social elan, and the only way I can remember them is to note them down. Otherwise one has to remain dumb for they run out of my head at once.'[24]

Before Greene left for Lagos, he hoped to take a plane to spy out the land covering his area of operations, but on 12 January the plane failed to turn up. The next day Mackenzie drove Greene to Airways House, but again his name did not appear on the Pan-American passenger list. Greene, needing to make an initial survey of his territory, forced his way on to a Hudson and flew as far as Takoradi.

Over Monrovia, he photographed the river and the Firestone aerodrome: 'The Ivory Coast thick bush. The Gold Coast – the long stretch of sand & bush lawn-like rectangles out of the bush.' From Takoradi, he hoped to find transport to Lagos. Right up to the last moment because of hold ups, he felt he'd have to return to Dr Martyn's, but a lucky chance gave him the last seat on a plane.

His note before leaving refers to Dr Martyn: 'By British Airways to Lagos. Arrived about 2.30. Very congenial coy after Filthy Freddie.'[25]

*

Greene spent his days in Lagos coding and decoding in an office and his nights with a colleague in a disused (but not displeasing) police bungalow on a 'mosquito-haunted creek'.[26]

Three days after arrival, he received TAB jabs ('arm v. painful') and took the afternoon off, spending it in the bungalow. It all seems halcyon: 'A little boat with blue sail goes gently by outside window.'[27] 'This is really a very nice & luxurious place very different to Freetown,' he wrote to his mother. 'There are lavatories that flush & you can drink water from the tap – two luxuries I shall miss. I share a bungalow right over the lagoon: the water laps ten yards away at the bottom of the garden & we can see the ships coming into the port.'[28]

For those few months of further training in Lagos, Greene lived in comfort (but notice the identity of the man sharing his bungalow is kept secret): 'I & the other man have one boy [servant] each – & share a "small boy".' Both agent trainees lived well, and suffered the tedium of an orderly existence, as he wrote to his mother:

> We get our meals at the club for 5/- a day . . . We are woken with orange at 6.30 in the morning (also tea & sweet biscuits . . . even bourbons). Cold bath . . . walk to the club (two & a half miles) for breakfast . . . by car onto the office till 12.30 (orange juice at 11), then back to the club for lunch . . . to the bungalow for a siesta till 2.30 – back to office – tea at 4 . . . knock off any time according to work, between 5 & 7: back to another tea of our own in the bungalow – more fruit . . . warm bath: drink: back to club at 8 for dinner . . . then either to an open-air cinema or back to a quiet evening under the mosquito net with another grapefruit to end up the day.[29]

But he committed to his journal less quiet evenings:

After dinner with S. prowled around with L.P. & C. The Sugar Babies: little forced embraces. Black tarts have much the same manners of serving drinks & chatting with customers as white ones. The Royal Hotel roof garden – up one in the social scale. The lavatory palm frond open to the stars & George Formby's voice coming through on a microphone. The attempted seduction of the shy & excited L.P.[30]

While Greene was enjoying life in Lagos, at home Vivien received a disturbing note from an inspector of taxes which frightened her:

I understand [Tax Inspector Doyle wrote on 8 January] that your Husband received two thousand pounds for copyright from Alex Korda Film Productions during the year ended 5 April 1941 and also £1,331.8.6. literary royalties from Messrs Pearn, Pollinger, & Higham. As the total receipts shown in your husband's return for 1941–42 amounted to £1,193 only, it seems likely that the above-mentioned items were for some reason not included. I shall be obliged if you will ask your husband to let me have an explanation and also his agreement to the assessment of these items in due course.

She sent a copy of the letter to Greene, and another copy to his agent, Laurence Pollinger: 'I got a menacing sort of letter from the Income Tax . . . It seems evident there is a flaw somewhere: the Korda, if it ever came off, was surely before the war?'[31] The actual sum Greene received was £1,331.8s.6d and this *included* the Korda cheque. Three months later they were after Vivien again, but her fright had been replaced by anger: 'Income Tax: the bastards are completely muddled & trying to make me pay three times over what I've already paid.'[32]

Greene's journal entries contain mostly inconsequential matters, revealing a fascination with what others might find repelling. Having his Friday evening bath, he watches a beetle in the running bath: 'Haphazard struggles until it came near the whirlpool of the tap: then strong brave breast strokes which made it oddly human. Took it out & threw it away.'[33] He takes an interest in a lizard devouring its prey: 'The moth flutters round the globe, comes to rest & the lizard pounces. It seems to hold it by the head while the wings flutter less & less'; and is strangely amused watching two flies 'make love' on the staircase near his bedroom.

To keep a journal when one was a spy was a serious dereliction of duty, and necessarily the extracts were terse. When he was discussing 'secret' matters, the entry was so cryptic that it could only be understood by its author. Sometimes classified material and ordinary details lie cheek by jowl: 'Jan.16 (Friday) Went in to town & shopped. Stories of alluvial gold digging. Story of bath filling from the stopped lavatory. Jan.17 (Sat.) Appalling suggestions from London.'

Life was not completely uneventful – on 13 February Greene had an unexpected fall: 'All went well till the evening when I went to a very bad film . . . Ginger Rogers in *Having a Wonderful Time*: coming out I fell into a six foot open drain into African shit.'[34] He enlarged on this in a letter to his mother:

> I was just writing last night to somebody [again Greene carefully avoided naming names] saying that Friday the 13th had passed without mishap when I went out to a cinema. Coming out in the dark and hurrying to my taxi I suddenly trod on air and fell down a six foot open drain on top of unspeakable African muck; a nasty shock at the time and I thought I'd put my hip out. But after the drive, a stiff whisky and a cold bath I was all right, except for various scrapes – which in this climate takes ages to heal. My right thumb was rather torn . . . and I was a bit apprehensive of poisoning, but I swabbed it well with Dettol and all seems to be well.[35]

Vivien commiserated with the 'poor bedraggled miserable Tom'. She was also practical: 'I am very glad you had the Dettol: you should have poured a lot into a bath and soaked in it, not only dabbed the open scratches and bruises.'[36]

Ever meticulous, Greene observed the humans around him: 'The black boy with red [next word indecipherable] on his features. You could see fleetingly the stupid fear of his white father. How a child like that would horribly tie one to Africa out of pity and love';[37] and the lust to kill: 'Walking by the lagoon saw Syrian again with his gun & his children. Yday he killed a beautiful kingfisher & gives the body to his small children to play with: today there was a little heap of doves by the children's side.'[38]

The next day, walking with his colleague L.P. to the club for breakfast, he noted his conversation: 'L.P.'s conversation all bird observation & sex. "By Jove, look at that plumage. You know I shall have to do something about this soon. Look at those breasts."' Greene often became irritated by males whose company he had to keep – later he regretted his secret reactions for he kept his feelings to himself: 'Got very irritated by poor L.P. Deafness is so like stupidity that one forgets to differentiate.'[39]

In Africa Greene was disturbed by the same type he had been when a schoolboy: 'Dinner at Denton's – fat rugger bugger type with soft sentimental eyes, information officer whose ambitions are centred on the M[inistry] of I[nformation].'[40] It seems as if Greene was getting heartily sick of parties, but he briefly listed conversations in his journal: 'Mass at 8.30. Chop with Wormwold [This closely approximates the name of his hero in his spy spoof, *Our Man in Havana*, British agent Wormold]. The fat engineer & his family history of repression.'

Greene's journal suggests that whatever his training entailed, there was really little office work: 'No telegrams ever seem to arrive & be acknowledged.'[41] In his spare time he was writing:

25 Jan. (Sun.) Didn't go to office, but typed all day at B[ritish] D[ramatists].
27 Jan (Tues). Came home in evening & worked.

His journal entry concerning his involvement in a minor car accident reveals the professional writer: 'Slight motor crash coming back after siesta. Interminable 15 seconds waiting for the crash beside L.P. who was driving. Stupidly one made no attempt to duck but bent slightly sideways watching, as if one couldn't bear to miss seeing it happen.' This watchfulness appears everywhere: 'I woke up, switched on my torch & saw little white ants swarming on to the edges of my pillow. Simply moved into centre of pillow & went to sleep again. This is acclimatization.'[42]

*

The trivialisation of life by the trainee agents is perhaps best shown by the nightly activity Greene and L.P. engaged in: 'Every evening ends with a cockroach stalk. By making a sport of it one loses one's repulsion towards them. Last night one felt deserted as none appeared – as though one were a sinking ship.'[43] There is a further journal entry for 28 January: 'Came back alone & triumphantly killed four giant cockroaches in my bathroom. 3 were found together, but not one escaped. Becoming very deft with a gym shoe.'

The strength of the interest here is curious, even disturbing. These cockroach stalks were done in order to cheer up himself and L.P.: 'we used to hunt cockroaches by the light of electric torches, marking in pencil on the walls one point for a certain death, half a point if the roach had been washed down the lavatory bowl.'[44] As if to recall their repugnance, Greene cautioned himself to remember:

'The cockroach spreadeagled over the saucer of peanuts'.[45]

When Greene came to write *The Heart of the Matter* he used the cockroach stalk, which he'd been an original party to, and the rules of play, to reflect the limited nature of his characters Wilson and Harris. Harris is the cable censor, slightly pathetic and sanctimonious, but mealy-mouthed. He is a scandalmonger, attacking Scobie and at the same time getting in a clever dig at Scobie's wife: 'Perhaps if I had a wife like that, I'd sleep with niggers too.'[46] In contrast, the character Wilson pretends to a simplicity which takes Harris in. His false identity is that of the new accountant, but he is in fact a member of MI5 seeking out corruption among the police.

At the time Greene was literary editor of the *Spectator*, Wilson Harris was its editor. Greene simply separated the two parts of his editor's name to provide two characters with names. Greene had many passages of arms with the original Wilson Harris, though any sensitive person would have fallen out with the man. H. E. Bates recalls that Harris 'had about as much humanity as a clothes prop, was cold, ascetic, distant' to his employees and made Bates feel 'very small, very, very inferior, very, very unhappy'.[47]

It is Harris who approaches Wilson about turning cockroach killing into a sport, and the details in the novel reflect the game as it was played in Lagos, though the humour and anger are an imaginative addition:

> [Wilson] fixed his eyes on some symbols pencilled on the wall inside: the letter H, and under it a row of figures lined against dates as in a cash-book. Then the letters D.D., and under them more figures. 'It's my score in cockroaches, old man. Yesterday was an average day – four. My record's nine. It makes you welcome the little brutes.'
> 'What does D.D. stand for?'
> 'Down the drain, old man. That's when I knock them into the wash-basin and they go down the waste-pipe.'[48]

They decide to make a match of it for five minutes each night before bed: 'It needs skill, you know. They positively hear you coming, and they move like greased lightning. I do a stalk every evening with a torch':

> 'No use doing it like that, old man. Watch *me*!' Harris stalked his prey. The cockroach was halfway up the wall, and Harris, as he moved on tiptoe across the creaking floor, began to weave the light of his torch backwards and forwards over the cockroach.

Then suddenly he struck and left a smear of blood. 'One up,' he said. 'You have to mesmerize them.'

To and fro across the room they padded, weaving their lights, smashing down their shoes, occasionally losing their heads and pursuing wildly into corners: the lust of the hunt touched Wilson's imagination.[49]

To begin with, they are civilised in their responses, calling out 'Good-shot' or 'Hard Luck', but once they start to chase the same cockroach, their tempers become frayed – an example of the sudden effect the tropics can have:

A cockroach sat upon the brown cake of soap in the washbasin. Wilson spied it and took a long shot with the shoe from six feet away. The shoe landed smartly on the soap and the cockroach span into the basin: Harris turned on the tap and washed it down. 'Good shot, old man,' he said placatingly. 'One D.D.'

'D.D. be damned,' Wilson said. 'It was dead when you turned on the tap.'

'You couldn't be sure of that. It might have been just unconscious – concussion. It's D.D. according to the rules.'

'Your rules again.'

'My rules are the Queensberry Rules in this town.'

'They won't be for long,' Wilson threatened. He slammed the door hard behind him and the walls of his own room vibrated round him from the shock. His heart beat with rage and the hot night: the sweat drained from his armpits. But as he stood there beside his own bed, seeing the replica of Harris's room around him, the washbasin, the table, the grey mosquito-net, even the cockroach fastened on the wall, anger trickled out of him and loneliness took its place. It was like quarrelling with one's own image in the glass. I was crazy, he thought. What made me fly out like that?[50]

Harris's interest in Wilson springs from his discovery that Wilson and he were old boys from the same public school.

Harris shows Scobie a letter to the secretary of the school describing (vaguely) what he is doing in the tropics and talking about Wilson, the other old Downhamian boy: 'As I'm a cable censor you will understand that I can't tell you much about my work . . . We are in the middle of the rains now – and how it does rain. There's a lot of fever about, but I've only had one dose and E. Wilson has so far escaped altogether . . . We've got an old Downhamian team of two and go out hunting together but only cockroaches (Ha! Ha!)'[51]

Of course Greene *is* making fun of Harris. Later, Harris, looking through a copy of the school magazine, and skimming through an account of five matches, comes upon a fantasy entitled 'The Tick of the Clock'. This is the first story Greene wrote at the age of sixteen and it appeared in the school magazine, *The Berkhamstedian*. The description Harris conjures up of the school, as he lies on his bed in a tiny room in the tropics, is Greene's description of his own school, his own unhappiness, and is used by him on different occasions, especially the cracked bell, the boots beating on the stone stairs, though the phrase 'the loyalty we feel to unhappiness' is out of place when applied to Harris: 'The walls of Downham – the red brick laced with yellow, the extraordinary crockets, the mid-Victorian gargoyles – rose around him: boots beat on stone stairs and a cracked dinner-bell rang to rouse him to another miserable day. He felt the loyalty we feel to unhappiness – the sense that that is where we really belong.'[52]

It is difficult to imagine that the relationship between Harris and Wilson had its origin in life, for it smacks of being cobbled together, merely a plot device. However, Greene did meet (in Bathurst, Gambia, not Freetown) an old Berkhamstedian while he was stationed in Freetown:

> I forgot to tell you [he wrote to his mother] that I met an old boy from Uppers at Bathurst left about 1922: Harwood. He's intelligence officer with the R.A.F. there. He made one feel terribly old because he seemed so very young, though at school at the same time. He had a touch of fever before I left but everybody was having that. Nearly a 100 people down.[53]

Something of Wilson's dangerously youthful air is derived from Harwood. It was Harwood who invited Greene to Bathurst for Christmas 1942. Using his new skills, Greene replied by means of his code-books: 'As the chief eunuch said I cannot, repeat cannot, come.'[54]

On Sunday, 8 March, Greene made his last entry in his journal before leaving Lagos: 'A new sort of comfort – to lie in bed and realise that life is really running short. It seems such a short while since my first book was published: the same number of years & I shall be fifty.'[55]

His three months of training over, he was ready for action in Freetown.

10

Our Man in Freetown

There is all Africa and her prodigies in us.
— SIR THOMAS BROWNE

GREENE left Lagos in the middle of March and flew to Accra.
What he saw of it he didn't like 'except the superbly beautiful
old Danish fort in which the governor lives — like a stage set of
Elsinore in dazzling white with the surf beating below on two sides'.[1]
He stayed in an American transit camp for the night: 'a wind
blowing up the red dust all the time, bad food and . . . drunk tough
Americans belonging to the air line'.[2] Then on Sunday he went on
to Freetown, but first landed in Liberia and had lunch at a new
aerodrome that American personnel had made: 'the overcooked
steak literally a foot long'.[3] He flew in a freight plane for the first
time: 'The passengers sit upright facing each other the whole length
on little metal seats like lavatory seats. The heat until you get well up
is appalling and then the metal turns cold.'[4]

Greene arrived in Freetown, Sierra Leone, a parched land of
stifling heat. He had no accommodation arranged, but a kind
governor put him up for a couple of nights, which gave him enough
time to employ a 'couple of boys and a cook', and then he moved
into a 'dingy little Creole villa about two miles out of town'.[5] This
villa was to play an important part in his life, for it was both home
and his base for SIS operations. It stood on the flats below the
European quarter (there was no room on the hill) and had been
condemned by the medical officer of health. Unsought, the house
brought him into contact with a seedy Greeneland.

'It's terribly difficult to get anywhere to live alone in these days, so
one can't look a gift horse in the mouth,' he wrote to his mother.
'There is no water although there are taps.' Freetown receives 147
inches of rain a year, but the distribution is so bad that Greene's area

was without water until the rains began six weeks after his arrival. Drinking water was fetched in empty bottles from Freetown and then boiled; bath water was carried in kerosene tins from a native water hole: 'One tries not to think of germs and what the blacks do there and have done and pours in sanitas . . . '6

He told his sister in Cairo that he had no water at all, but that he had a 'plague of houseflies' because of the army camp just across the road. Worse still, the few acres of scrub were used as a public lavatory by Africans living in slum houses close by. 'It sometimes puts one off one's food to know where the flies have landed last. It's lucky I have a masochistic trend and a feeling for squalor.'7 Practically everything was unobtainable: for example, there was no ink or soda water, which was troublesome in a country where you had to boil and filter every drop of water (if, as Greene said, 'you could get a drop'). Even in town, the taps stopped running at about two in the morning. All the Europeans kept two inches of their morning bath to serve them again at night: 'This isn't so good when you've sweated all day,' he remarked.8

Greene succeeded in getting a public lavatory for the Africans. He wrote to the Colonial Secretary demanding one, but the official responded by telling him that his request should go through the proper channels by way of the Commissioner of Police. In reply, Greene quoted what Churchill said of 'proper channels' during wartime and the toilet was built. He also sent a final tongue-in-cheek letter to the Colonial Secretary, saying that 'in the annals of Freetown his name like Keats's would be writ in water'.*9

Those early days in Freetown, before the rains came, tested his vaunted love of Africa, and thanking his literary agent for a cable enquiring as to his well-being, he admitted that the enquiry had cheered him a lot 'in this God-forsaken hole, Freetown'. Two letters to his sister stressed his objections: 'Nothing that I ever wrote about this place is really bad enough.'10 After four months, he was still unhappy: 'Life here is pretty grim. The delights of Freetown are beginning to pall. I have a horrible fear that I'm being cured relentlessly of my *nostalgie de la boue*.'†11 His hatred of birds of any kind (a hatred stemming from a childhood fear) is reflected in his fascination with vultures. In the heat and humidity of the day, taking

---

* On Keats's tombstone are the words: 'Here lies one whose name was writ in water.'
† This phrase comes from Emile Augier's play *Le Mariage d'Olympe*:

| Marquis: | Put a duck on a lake in the midst of some swans and you'll see he'll miss his pond and eventually return to it. |
| Montrichard: | *La nostalgie de la boue!* |

a siesta (as is natural in the tropics), he would be disturbed by their heavy movement: 'when one took off or landed it was as though a thief were trying to break through the iron roof'. Sometimes he witnessed as many as six perched up on his roof 'like old broken umbrellas'.[12]

Once the rainy season arrives in Freetown, rain often falls daily, especially during July and August. The rains begin with a series of violent squalls, marked by thunder and lightning, and the ground on which Greene's house stood became a swamp. After rain, the night is filled with an intolerable plague of houseflies:

at night there are far too many objects flying and crawling . . . Wherever one wants to put one's hand suddenly, to turn on a switch or what not, there always seems to be a gigantic spider. Whenever one kills something which has flopped on the floor the ants come out and get to work, stripping the corpse and then heaving and pushing the skeleton towards the door.[13]

Writing to his mother, he recalled counting 'a slow procession of four hearse-like corpses: you couldn't see the ants underneath'.[14]

In 1959, seventeen years later, when visiting the leper colony at Yonda, Greene returned to his hut to find the floor covered with big flying ants and remembered how in Freetown they fell in showers over his food just before rain.

Still, the house suited Greene's notion of himself, someone who didn't quite fit in, who objected to his own class, bound by conventional values, instinctively. Greene had a longing to be an 'undesirable,' indeed thought of himself as such. Like Scobie, he regarded himself 'as a man in the ranks, the member of an awkward squad'.[15]

Greene used his 'creole house', which he described as just across the road from a transit camp in the process of erection with two steam shovels going all day, as the home of Scobie and his wife Louise in *The Heart of the Matter*. He kept descriptively close to it:

[Scobie] found himself relegated to a square two-storeyed house built originally for a Syrian trader on the flats below [the main European quarter] – a piece of reclaimed swamp which would return to swamp as soon as the rains set in. From the windows he looked directly out to sea over a line of Creole houses; on the other side of the road lorries backed and churned in a military transport camp and vultures strolled like domestic turkeys in the regimental refuse.[16]

Greene's life was a solitary one. Every afternoon he walked, before dusk fell, along an abandoned railway track up the slope towards the European bungalows. On one occasion, arriving back for a bath later than usual, he found a rat on the bath's edge defecating. Lying alone in bed under a mosquito net, at night he would watch the rats swing on his bedroom curtains. On nights of the full moon, the starving pye dogs kept him awake with their howling and he would rise, pull his boots over his pyjamas and throw stones at them in the lane behind his house. His boy told him he was known by the local poor as 'the bad man'. Before he left Freetown, he sent some bottles of wine to a wedding in the poor quarter hoping to leave a better memory behind.[17]

*

Greene started his life as secret agent 59200, by using a book code announcing his safe arrival: 'I had chosen a novel of T. F. Powys from which I could detach sufficiently lubricious phrases for my own amusement, and a large safe came in the next convoy with a leaflet of instructions and my codes.'[18]

When Greene returned to Freetown, he was unable to adopt the persona of an inspector of the Department of Trade (DOT) because the department refused to provide him with cover as a 'phoney inspector'. The British Council were then asked to provide a cover, but that came unstuck too. He was offered a naval or an air-force rank, but it was discovered that he'd need the higher rank of either commander or group captain before he could have a private office and a safe for his code-books. Thus it was that he turned up in Freetown, with what he describes as 'a vague attachment to the police force', a little difficult to explain to those who anticipated the arrival of an Inspector of Overseas Trade. In his archives I found his identification card, no. 395, used for travel by 'European British Subjects'. His address is given as Police HQ, Freetown, and his occupation CID Special Branch, and only as a member of the CID would Greene be known during his sojourn in Freetown. The card is dated 24 April 1942. Curiously it is printed on the reverse of an invitation card to the Governor's 'At Home' dated 8 March.

Greene spoke of the sense of unreality of living in Freetown; perhaps it was more a sense of not belonging because of his ambiguous position. He was not to be found on the Colonial Office list (where everyone's salary and position were set down);[19] he did not belong to the DOT; he was a curious member of the CID who spent very little time in the police headquarters.

But at least he was settling into his house, which was beginning to look habitable. He turned the minute dining room into an office, leaving the downstairs with one large living room. Upstairs were two bedrooms.[20] From letters to his mother we know how he entertained: 'It's pleasant having a house of one's own – one can relax. None of my china, cutlery, etc. & my car have yet turned up, so I live on a few things borrowed from my cook & in a taxi. If anyone comes to dinner, they have to bring their own plates, etc. so that I live a fairly retired life.'[21] Borrowing from his black cook! He would have been expelled from the club if fellow members had even suspected. To his sister, he expressed his anger more openly: 'My car and all my china, etc. have been sitting in Lagos for ten weeks waiting shipment. An energetic little man, my boss!'[22]

In another letter, he wrote of having been 'frantically social with dull people in every night for dinner or drinks, but this week thank God looks like being a little quieter'.[23] And then, we have recorded a simple bucolic African scene forever transfixed in memory:

I see my cook approaching in the distance proudly escorting two carriers: the Lord knows what he's been buying: one has a pail on his head and the other a large box. Things are a bit short here as we haven't had any ships in for a good while. Milk (tinned of course) has been unobtainable, and butter too. (I see now it's logs for the stove and not a box.)[24]

*

Greene started his day at six in the morning with breakfast, drove his little Morris into Freetown (his boy also drove him) to the market at seven, shopped for groceries at the Patterson Zachonias Company (known as PZ) or Oliphant's and then collected his telegrams at the police station, to which he was fictitiously attached.

The telegrams arrived in a code unintelligible to the police and were handed over to him by the Police Commissioner, Brodie. He would then return home, decode and reply to the telegrams, write reports, and rearrange the reports of his agents in an acceptable form. His work was normally over by lunchtime – unless an urgent telegram arrived or a ship in convoy brought a bag to be opened and dealt with.[25] But he could be (as his journal and letters tell us) 'ferociously' busy: 'I have no assistant or secretary, and God knows how I shall get through the work.' His work from London came in spasms: 'A day or two will be quite slack and then one will be hard at it round the clock from 8.30 to bedtime.'[26]

Part of Brodie's gentle character was used by Greene as a model for his hero Scobie. To begin with, there is a pseudo rhyme between the names Brodie and Scobie, suggesting that Greene had his friend in mind when creating the character. However, in Greene's time there was a railway station in Sierra Leone called 'Scobie'. Of course, there is much of Greene in Scobie, as there is in all of his scapegoat heroes. Brodie's friendship with Greene was, as he has said, 'the human thing I valued most during fifteen lonely months'.[27]

Greene's journal deliberately contains little about his activities as an agent. Like other agents, he would have acquired background knowledge of local conditions; he would have learned about fake documents for himself and his sub-agents, and would have mastered methods of recruiting and organising agents in the field. It is probable that he was also trained in sending secret encrypted radio transmissions, codes, and ciphers. Several methods of covert communications taught the use of secret inks, and should the raw material not be available, the use of an ink codenamed BS (bird shit). Greene made the ironic observation that 'vultures were the most common bird . . . but I doubt whether their droppings had been contemplated'.[28]

In *The Human Factor*, Davis asks Castle (who is also in part based on Greene) if he knows about secret ink:

'I did once – even to the use of bird shit. I had a course in it before they sent me on a mission at the end of the war. They gave me a handsome little wooden box, full of bottles like one of those chemistry cabinets for children. And an electric kettle – with a supply of plastic knitting needles.' 'What on earth for?' 'For opening letters.' 'And did you ever? Open one, I mean?' 'No, though I did once try. I was taught not to open an envelope at the flap, but at the side, and then when I closed it again I was supposed to use the same gum. The trouble was I hadn't got the right gum, so I had to burn the letter after reading it. It wasn't important anyway. Just a love letter.'[29]

Asked by Davis if in the old days he had been issued with a Luger or an explosive fountain-pen, Castle replied (as Greene, if asked, would have had to answer), 'I wasn't allowed to carry a gun, and my only car was a second-hand Morris Minor.'[30] But he would have had the standard issue of a potassium cyanide capsule in case he was captured by the Vichy enemy in French Guinea.

At this time Greene used a gold ring, which he wore on his left hand, as his private seal, dipping it in wax to seal his secret correspondence. The ring was a gift from his father on his twenty-first birthday and had a heraldic design on its surface.

Greene's main concern in Sierra Leone was the condition of the
battleship *Richelieu*, which was being repaired in Dakar and was seen
as a potential threat to British shipping:

> I think MI6 at that period was a little hazy in their geography
> because I was well over a thousand miles away from Dakar, and it
> was very difficult to know how one was going to get one's
> information of Dakar from a distance of over a thousand miles.
>   Then one was trying to get information out of the Vichy
> colony next door, in French Guinea. I needed to know about the
> state of air fields and so on, in case the Germans took over there
> and one was sort of organising, one had information about the
> smuggling of commercial diamonds on the Portuguese boats
> coming in for search in Freetown harbour on the way home, and
> agents were sometimes travelling on the boats there.[31]

Kim Philby, writing to me from Moscow, spoke of Greene's
knowledge and preparation for his work in Africa, for Greene was
under Philby before going out to Africa:

> At that time I was responsible for counter-espionage in the Iberian
> peninsula and parts of NW Africa. Graham's destination,
> Freetown, fell within my area, and it was my business to tell him
> what we knew of the German Intelligence services and of their
> connections with the corresponding services of the Vichy French.
> The latter, and a few Germans in the Spanish and Portuguese
> possessions in West Africa, were to be the main objects of his
> attention.[32]

Greene mentioned other MI6 schemes he tried unsuccessfully to
initiate: 'the rescue by bogus Communist agents of a left-wing
agitator who was under house-arrest.'[33] He was a communist gaoled
in Freetown, and Greene intended to have him planted in Vichy-
held Conakry. In Greene's journal, we find an entry that looks
strikingly like initial notes for a novel, but in fact these are notes,
with some deliberate distortion, of an actual SIS operation:

> The letter to the African agitator in his internment who has
> married again. In England he seems to have had relations with an
> ardent humanitarian Englishwoman who financed him. The letter
> is from an African in Gower Street – Gray's Inn district. First
> about letting him have collars left at the laundry. Reference to the
> agitator's new romance. 'Oh, she will be jealous when she hears

the news. You are a real heart-breaker.' The photo of the heart-breaker on the files. The respectable humanitarian names chiming in the right places – Victor Gollancz, Ethel Mannin . . . [34]

A month before Greene died in April 1991, he provided me with further details:

An African intellectual, a friend of Victor Gollancz, had been put in prison under the iniquitous 18B regulation which also imprisoned my cousin Ben. My idea was that he should be rescued from his prison by two purported Communists and in return for getting him out he would have to agree to send some harmless economic information from French Guinea. When we had sufficient of this, we would blackmail him and threaten to show it to the French if he did not provide more interesting material. The Commissioner of Police was ready to work with me on this, but London wasn't. Their objection was that a question would be asked in Parliament. [35]

Greene also intended to open a brothel in Bissau for visitors from Senegal. In his last days, he spoke further about this proposal:

My other rather wild plan was to open a brothel on a Portuguese territory Bissau just down the coast from Dakar where the *Richelieu* was stationed. The French were apt to take holidays on the Portuguese island. I had found an admirable Madame, French by origin but very patriotic, who was ready, given the money, to open the brothel. I felt that valuable information could be obtained from many of her visitors.

Of course, it wasn't a 'wild plan' but a very clever one. What better way to ferret out espionage information than by using local prostitutes? But it was not to be: 'The reply [from his headquarters in London] to that was that all brothels were very strictly under French Intelligence control which seemed to me dubious in the case of a Portuguese brothel.' [36]

When I asked Kim Philby about Greene's activities in Freetown, he replied: 'the only communication from him I remember was an operational plan to make use of a Madame who ran a peripatetic brothel much patronised, he reported, by Vichy officials and garrisons. For kicks, I put the plan to my superiors, and we discussed it seriously before rejecting it as unlikely to be what is now called cost-effective. When later I told Graham the story, he was loudly gratified.' The reason for rejection given by Greene differs from

Philby's, but the one doesn't exclude the other. However, perhaps Philby was being descriptively careless. In the seventeen years I knew Greene, I never witnessed him being 'loudly gratified' about anything. Perhaps Greene was too law-abiding here. At least two former SIS field agents I spoke to indicated that they would have ignored the fact that prior approval had not been given and gone ahead with the plan, hoping that the action would be a success.

It was certainly a pity that London did not allow Greene to establish a brothel in Bissau. If he had done so, what would he have uncovered?

Although Vichy France had a price on the head of any supporter of the Free French and their leader de Gaulle, ninety French citizens out of every hundred in Dakar wished success to the Free French. Governor-General Boisson was not trusted and his deputy was known to be pro-German. The British on the whole were not liked because they had tried unsuccessfully to take Dakar by storm in September 1940. Vichy power there lasted until November 1942 (at which time Greene was trying to leave Freetown for home), but that did not mean that de Gaulle and his Free French were welcomed by everyone. The following excerpt from a secret American report, written before French West Africa joined the Allied cause, gives some indication of this: 'We vomit de Gaulle – he has surrounded himself with dirty people from central Europe and with Jews.'[37] And when the British (an RAF contingent) and the Americans arrived, it was reported that practically every night in rue Raffnel (the red-light district of Dakar) there were fights between French and English sailors and between French soldiers and sailors and blacks. Though this report was from an American agent, its ring is authentic: ' "The American is blunt and to the point," said French civilians: "a poor diplomat, but you can trust him. You can never tell what an Englishman thinks. He says something with his mouth, but one is sure that he means something else." '[38]

As for the intelligence on the condition of the battleship *Richelieu* being repaired in Dakar which MI6 had requested Greene to obtain, Greene's brothel scheme would have probably uncovered the information which I found in the National Archives in Washington. The report of an American visiting the *Richelieu* in November 1942 revealed that the damage to the ship had been slight – a bent propeller shaft and a bent engine-room floor – and that even in that condition it was capable of twenty-six knots without difficulty, and was therefore a great threat to British shipping if it left port on active service.

Greene also tried to arrange a rendezvous with missionaries at

Bolahun whom he had originally had contact with when he was travelling through Sierra Leone and Liberia before the war in 1935. The Holy Cross Mission was run by American Episcopalian monks. To visit the mission Greene would have had to cross the border into Liberia, and that country had not forgiven his destructive attack on it in his travel book *Journey Without Maps*. Instead, Greene arranged for the monks to visit him at Kailahun just across the Sierra Leone border. It was at this time that a crisis developed between Greene and Alexis Forter, his boss in Lagos, 2,000 miles away.

It was the old argument: Forter, the professional at the last stage of his career, found himself having to deal with Greene, the amateur brought into the service as a result of the war. To make matters worse, Forter and Greene had disliked each other on sight. Forter was a sick man totally unacquainted with Africa. At that time, Greene didn't know how sick Forter was, or even that Forter would keep the Freetown bag sent by Greene unopened on his desk for days through fear of its contents. To clip Greene's wings, Forter tried to discipline him by cutting off his funds (funds Greene badly needed to pay his agents in the field). The crisis came when Forter interfered with Greene's operations. The date of Greene's rendezvous with the monks had already been fixed, and he intended to provide them with a radio transmitter so that information valuable to the SIS could be passed on to him.

Just prior to his journey to the border, Forter sent Greene a telegram forbidding him to leave Freetown because of the imminent arrival of a Portuguese liner. Portuguese ships from Angola had to be searched for industrial diamonds and illicit correspondence. The attempt by the Allies to reduce significantly Germany's stock of industrial diamonds was a matter of vital importance. They came almost entirely from South and Central Africa by illegal channels. It was the job of MI5 and the Special Operations Executive (SOE), and to a lesser degree MI6, to block these clandestine supply lines.

By 1943, Germany had only enough diamonds for eight months. Without them, precision tooling would not be possible and smuggling was the only source of replenishment. There were enemy smuggling channels throughout the Gold Coast, Mozambique, Angola, Cairo, the Belgian Congo, South Africa and Sierra Leone. Once a whole year's supply reached Germany from the Congo by way of Red Cross parcels organised by a Belgian Chief of Police. Germany desperately needed the diamonds, not least to meet the agreed date for their first operational rockets. It was known that Portuguese liners coming in and out of port, often from Angola, were used to smuggle them. Yet, in spite of careful searches, from the rice in the holds to the cosmetics in the cabins, few stones were ever turned up. Greene was involved in such searches, although he saw it as a police job belonging to his friend Brodie and MI5, and did not enjoy being involved in them.

After an inner debate, Greene decided *against* keeping the rendezvous with the missionaries. Instead, he wrote London an account of the unfortunate event which had kept him from his trip up-country and then offered his resignation, which was refused. This was both fortunate and unfortunate. London freed him from the control of Lagos, but his failure to keep the promised rendezvous made him an enemy.

In arranging for the missionaries to cross into British colonial territory, Greene suggested to them the excuse that they were collecting food brought specially from Fortnum & Mason, and held at Kailahun. He now had to telegraph the District Commissioner of the area, Richard Cox, to say that he was not coming. Cox, who had been party to the arrangement, was furious, taking Greene's failure to keep his appointment as an example of MI6's casualness, discourtesy, even sloppiness, in time of war. Greene anticipated the District Commissioner's response: 'I had to have his letters opened by the censor. I warned London that this would happen in my report and it did. He wrote such furious private letters that he had to be reprimanded by the Governor.' Cryptically, Greene mumbled in interview: 'He was an enemy from the beginning. I must have offended him in some way at Balliol.'[39]

Greene learnt that nothing pleased head office more than an addition to their agent's card in their Intelligence files. His report on a Vichy airfield in French Guinea was based on information from one of his agents, who was illiterate and could not count over ten (the number of his fingers and thumbs). Nor did the agent know any of the points of the compass except the east (he was a Mohammedan). A building on the airfield which he said housed an army tank was, Greene believed from other evidence, a store for old boots. He emphasised the agent's disqualifications, so that he was surprised when he earned a rating for his report of 'most valuable': 'Somebody in an office in London had been enabled to add a line or two to an otherwise blank card – that seemed the only explanation.'[40]

Greene felt a similar irritation when receiving coded instructions from London. His attitude towards his superiors is revealed in Wilson's receipt of materials in *The Heart of the Matter*, and the humour implicit in this passage reappeared in full flood in 1958 in *Our Man in Havana*:

[Wilson] took out the code books, 32946 78523 97042. Row after row of groups swam before his eyes. The telegram was headed Important, or he would have postponed the decoding till the evening. He knew how little important it really was – the usual ship had left Lobito carrying the usual suspects – diamonds, diamonds, diamonds. When he had decoded the telegram he would hand it to the long-suffering Commissioner, who had already probably received the same information or contradictory information from S.O.E. or one of the other secret organizations which took root on the coast like mangroves. *Leave alone but do not repeat not pinpoint P. Ferreira passenger 1st class repeat P. Ferreira passenger 1st class.* Ferreira was presumably an agent his organization had recruited on board. It was quite possible that the Commissioner would receive simultaneously a message from Colonel Wright that P. Ferreira was suspected of carrying diamonds and should be rigorously searched. 72391 87052 63847 92034. How did one simultaneously leave alone, not repeat not pinpoint, and rigorously search Mr Ferreira?[41]

One of the things Greene disliked about his job was that he seemed to be taking over what was traditionally the province of MI5. In a letter to me fourteen days before his death, he recalled an incident, minor to an interrogating policeman, but which continued to disturb him: 'All Portuguese boats had to be searched for commercial diamonds and information. In the papers on one boat I learnt that my friend and [French] literary agent Denise Clairouin had been arrested by the Germans as a member of the Resistance. One interrogation that I had to make of a prisoner disgusted me so much that I never made another.'[42]

The interrogation was of a young Scandinavian seaman from Buenos Aires who was suspected of being a German agent. Greene could not record the interrogation in his journal, but he elaborates on the event which sickened him in *Ways of Escape*:

I knew from a report about the girl he had loved in Buenos Aires – a prostitute probably, but he was really in love in his romantic way. If he came clean he could go back to her, I told him, if he wouldn't speak he would be interned for the duration of the war. 'And how long do you think she'll stay faithful to you?' It was a police job, an MI5 job again. I was angry that I had been landed with it. It was a form of dirty work for which I had not been engaged. I gave up the interrogation prematurely, without result, hating myself. He may even have been innocent. To hell, I thought then, with MI5.[43]

A note in his journal is probably related to this search: 'The suitcase of the suspect – the squalor and intimacy of a man's suitcase.'[44] Yet it was necessary work to identify German spies who were passing on intelligence about British shipping to German submarines.

Even five years after the incident, Greene's sense of disgust at the way he'd had to interrogate and search the man's cabin still strongly affected him. In *The Heart of the Matter*, he changed the character from a young Scandinavian seaman to a fat Portuguese ship's captain. On this occasion, one of the field security men has private information from the steward (who is under notice of dismissal), that the captain has letters concealed in his bathroom. Scobie searches the captain's cabin: 'A man's bedroom was his private life. Prying in drawers you came on humiliations; little petty vices were tucked out of sight like a soiled handkerchief.'[45]

Scobie comes to the end of his search of the cabin ('closing the box of French letters and putting them carefully back in the top drawer of the locker with the handkerchiefs') and comes to the bathroom. The captain assures him that there is not much cover there to conceal anything: 'The bathroom was bare and extraordinarily dirty. The bath was rimmed with dry grey soap, and the tiles slopped under' Scobie's feet. He begins to think the information might be false. Scobie opens the medicine-cabinet, unscrews the toothpaste, opens the razor box, dips his finger into the shaving-cream, he examines the taps (each funnel with his finger), the floor, the porthole, and the big screws. Each time Scobie turns he catches the captain's face in the mirror, 'calm, patient, complacent'. 'It said "cold, cold" to him all the while, as in a children's game.' Finally, Scobie comes to the lavatory, he lifts the wooden seat, he checks between the porcelain and the wood and he puts his hand on the lavatory chain. He notices in the mirror for the first time a tension in the captain, the brown eyes no longer on his face, they are fixed on something else. He pulls it and checks the 'gurgling and pounding in the pipes, the water flushed down'. He turns away and there is a relaxation of tension in the captain's face, even smugness: 'You see, major.' 'And at that moment Scobie did see . . . He lifted the cap of the cistern. Fixed in the cap with adhesive tape and clear of the water lay a letter.'[46]

It is Scobie's duty to take the letter and report it to the authorities, especially as it is a letter to a Frau Groener in Friedrichstrasse,

Leipzig. The captain insists it is a letter to his daughter, and of course, in wartime, as the captain says, he could be ruined because he had written a letter to his daughter: 'Open it and read. You will see.' Scobie, a stickler for duty, tells him he must leave that to the censors, but Scobie is touched though he does not tell the captain this:

> The man had lowered his bulk on to the edge of the bath as though it were a heavy sack his shoulders could no longer bear. He kept on wiping his eyes with the back of his hand like a child – an unattractive child, the fat boy of the school. Against the beautiful and the clever and the successful, one can wage a pitiless war, but not against the unattractive: then the millstone weighs on the breast.[47]

The captain discovers Scobie is also a Catholic, and he begins to plead for the first time, talking about his daughter and the way his mistress ill-treats him: ' "she will take away my trousers so that I cannot go out alone; every day it will be drink and quarrels until we go to bed. You will understand. I cannot write to my daughter from Lisbon. She loves me so much and she waits." He shifted his fat thigh and said, "The pureness of that love," and wept.'[48] Scobie takes a last look at the captain before leaving the cabin and sees him beating his head against the cistern, the tears running down his face. As Scobie joins the field security man in the saloon, he feels as if a millstone is weighing him down: 'How I hate this war, he thought, in the very words the captain had used.'[49]

'The letter to the daughter in Leipzig, and a small bundle of correspondence found in the kitchens, was the sole result of eight hours' search by fifteen men.'[50] In not reporting the letter, Scobie's 'own heart-beats told him he was guilty – that he had joined the ranks of the corrupt police officers', telling them that it was the usual thing: 'A dismissed steward with a grudge.'[51]

In the case of the Scandinavian seaman, Greene, like Scobie, burnt the letter, but not without qualms of guilt. His training in Oriel College and in Lagos was ignored for sentiment:

> Scobie felt no doubt at all of the sincerity of this letter. This was not written to conceal a photograph of the Cape Town defences or a microphotograph report on troop movements at Durban. It should, he knew, be tested for secret ink, examined under a microscope, and the inner lining of the envelope exposed. Nothing should be left to chance with a clandestine letter. But he had committed himself to a belief. He tore the letter up, and his

own report with it, and carried the scraps out to the incinerator in the yard – a petrol-tin standing upon two bricks with its sides punctured to make a draught.[52]

Greene was dismayed by the pressure brought to bear on the innocent: 'The story was sufficiently irrational to be true. Even in wartime, one must still exercise the faculty of belief if it is not to atrophy.'[53] It seems likely that this incident in the novel reflects Greene's own sense of guilt in allowing a possible German agent to slip through his hands. To the extent that Scobie is Greene, he does not handle the situation effectively. As an MI6 officer he should have employed the right mixture of flattery and threats, warmth and ruthlessness. Once Scobie found the offending letter his decision to take it to the censors should have been adhered to. Indeed, fifteen men had wasted their time searching the ship and Greene/Scobie had, through his sense of humanity, ruined the outcome of the operation. No wonder Greene felt he had to return home and that he could no longer be an officer in the field.

Greene's journal shows that enemy agents *were* found aboard ship. Again Greene suitably disguised his material in his journal so that it could easily be mistaken as notes for a future novel, since he was breaking strict rules in keeping a journal: 'The German agent's letters. Tell so-and-so he's too optimistic when he says no big ships can call here. The touch of pacifism: "What would Livingstone have said?" '[54] The only material which authentically refers to an SIS operation and the successful detection of incriminating material during a search of a Portuguese ship in port appears in the first sentence: 'The German agent's letters'. In the autumn of 1942, three Portuguese subjects who had accepted Abwehr [German Intelligence organisation] missions in southern Africa were arrested when their ship docked in Freetown.[55]

*

Greene badly needed secretarial assistance: 'I long for a secretary', he wrote to his mother on 4 May, 'to take off the donkey work of typing, etc.'; on 22 July he again wrote of the need for an assistant: 'I've been rushed off my feet as a result of being up in the Protectorate for a week. Stuff accumulates so, and although I've been promised an assistant, he or she hasn't materialised yet.'[56]

But on 12 August, when he knew that his assistant was aboard a ship bound for Freetown, he reported to his mother his anxiety (an anxiety typical of Greene): 'I'm expecting an assistant any day now, but in some ways I'm unenthusiastic. The office is very tiny and if we don't like each other it will be rather nerve-racking. However it will enable me to get about more.' To 'get about more' was essential as he was setting up agents across the border in French Guinea. Little is said about the young woman when she did arrive, but in a letter to his mother on 14 October, he wrote of returning from Bathurst (now Banjul) in Gambia to rather heavy arrears of work, 'I have an assistant now.' He also commented in the same letter about the amount of Intelligence work to be done: 'Even on Sunday there's work, and I always give my assistant Sunday off.' Her job was to do the coding and decoding and to send off reports.

Who was his secretary? When asked, Greene could no longer remember her name. However, surprisingly, a clue appears in an undated letter (probably written in June 1942) to Greene from his brother Hugh:

A girl called Doris Temple will be leaving soon for a government job in Freetown. She's a very nice piece & a good drinking companion. I think she might be quite a comfort to you . . . Don't be put off by the rather wide-eyed manner she puts on . . . I am telling her to apply for you at the Bank.

Greene's reply was unusually abstemious. He began by admitting that while in the ordinary course of things he should have been most grateful for Hugh's 'tasteful and reliable pimping', he had become 'terribly one-idea'd', and was 'getting grey, more and more bad tempered, and rather a bully'. Greene, normally at a high level of sexual excitement, disposed of his brother's suggestion in the following way:

I'll look out for the girl, but I don't feel inclined really for a playmate. Life's complicated enough as it is . . . A drinking companion would be a boon, if there was anywhere to drink and anything to drink. But there's only one hotel, and nothing to get but bad bottled export beer of uncertain kinds, Scotch if you are lucky, gin which is a depressant, and South African wines that make you feel like hell next morning . . . I should certainly warn the poor thing off these parts. They really are not a catch, unless she likes being swarmed around by subalterns.[57]

What Hugh could not know was that his brother's reply was disingenuous.

When I was in Freetown in 1980 trying to track down, among

other things, policemen who had worked under Police Commissioner Brodie at the time Greene was in Freetown, my contacts found Peter Turnbull, who, like Greene's fictional Deputy Commissioner Scobie, was known for his rigorous honesty. It is likely that Greene had Turnbull in mind when he told me that, before Brodie had a nervous breakdown, there was only one man he felt he could trust among his officers. The rains had begun and Brodie was under tremendous pressure from work, while dealing with the strain of controlling corrupt officers (most of them recruited from the British police serving in Palestine), and exposed to the badgering of MI5 bureaucrats at home.

Turnbull, in retirement in Sussex, had this to say about Greene and his secretary: 'Greene did not circulate amongst the resident European community. His secretary who was known as Shirley Temple – her name may have been Temple – was a pretty girl and very popular among the men.' Clearly, the subalterns did 'swarm around her'. Turnbull then added: 'She was looked upon as the eyes and ears of Graham Greene, in so far as local gossip was concerned.'[58]

The woman that Hugh Greene thought of as an 'ideal drinking companion', and who was expressly rejected by Greene as a possible 'playmate', was already known to him as his future assistant. Greene must have known about Doris Temple – the dates suggest that – because it had already been determined that she was to be his assistant in Freetown. London would have given Greene this information prior to her arrival. Perhaps with permission from London, or maybe out of a simple desire to know something about her new boss before she departed for Freetown, Miss Temple approached Greene's younger brother, Hugh. In his naïveté Hugh had thought he was just looking after his brother's interests, putting him on to 'a very nice piece'.

No doubt Doris was Greene's 'eyes and ears', picking up gossip at cocktail parties for him. In Freetown, government officials, officials from neutral countries, would be susceptible to her charms, and she would report to Greene. Greene told me that she helped in body searches of women on the various ships that had to be searched for industrial diamonds. However, up-country journeys were made by Greene alone.

Although she was attractive and good at providing him with information from a number of sources, alas, she was not efficient. In a letter written in his last days, Greene stressed that he 'was sufficiently overworked for them to send me a secretary, a young woman who unfortunately was very bad at coding which only added to our work. Too many telegrams were sent back asking for a repeat.'[59]

Rodney Dennys often wondered why Greene was sent out to a comparatively unimportant station like Freetown: 'My God, we could have used him in Cairo. He could have done wonders there.'[60] Philby also viewed Freetown's importance with some scepticism, and in covering Greene's career from trainee to officer in the field suggested that Greene's views chimed with his:

After very few sessions, I came to like and respect him as someone quite out of the ordinary run of SIS trainees. As I try to remember Graham's reactions to such 'training', the word 'bewilderment' occurs to me most readily. The mechanics of the work presented no problem to a man of his intelligence. But he showed, in flashes, profound doubts about the relevance of whatever he might do in Freetown to the war against Hitler. I confess I shared his doubts, although at the time I tried to dispel them with the suggestion that any of the ports of West Africa (Dakar, Bissau, Conakry) might harbour enemy agents doing us no good in the Battle of the Atlantic, and that Freetown should be a good observation post. He listened with invariable courtesy, but I am quite sure he remained unconvinced. I am also fairly sure that he sensed my own skepticism, though again he was too polite to say so. Or perhaps he realised that I was just saying my piece, and extended to me a slice of charity.[61]

Philby also felt that in the field Greene met with little success: 'The results of his work there were meagre, and he was kind enough not to overload the bag, too many overseas stations did so, creating a lot of useless work. As regards the enemy, Graham drew a blank, almost certainly because there *was* a blank.'[62]

But Greene did not think his posting was insignificant. Since the Mediterranean was completely closed, all convoys military or otherwise had to go to Egypt and North Africa via the Atlantic and the West Coast. Freetown was important because it was the main port of call. Also, after de Gaulle had attacked Dakar unsuccessfully the Allies were militarily at war with Vichy France, and Sierra Leone was more than half bordered by French Guinea, now in Vichy hands:

We had to be prepared at any time for a military assault. I had to have agents near the border on the look out for any possible movements by the French. This was why I was travelling a number of times in the interior to find agents and to check with them.[63]

These trips up-country were a godsend to Greene: 'I got up to the Protectorate for a week, and that saved my sanity, though I had to put in a 70 hour week afterwards to make up for it.'[64]

In *Ways of Escape*, Greene wrote of one trip up-country. A little narrow-gauge line ran up to Pendembu, near the Liberian and French Guinea borders. Greene had made the journey seven years earlier when he was just turned thirty, on the long walk through Liberia which he described in *Journey Without Maps*. Nothing had changed. He took his boy with him, took also his own supply of tinned food, his own chair, his own bed, and even his own oil lamp to hang on a hook in the train compartment when darkness fell. The train stopped at Bo for the night, where there was a rest house, and then it travelled laboriously uphill to Pendembu. At Pendembu was a rest house also, but it was not well maintained, and Greene preferred to take his evening meal on the railway line with his camp table set up on the track.[65]

Greene provides us in *The Heart of the Matter* with an intimate account of a journey into the interior, which is similar to many he made up-country. Scobie's journey is precipitated by the suicide of a young district officer. He is driven up-country by his 'boy' Ali, whose character mirrored that of Greene's own 'boy' – the boy in fiction and the boy in fact had the same name – who also drove him up-country:

When Louise [Scobie's wife] and Wilson crossed the river and came into Burnside [it was actually called Brookfield] it was quite dark. The headlamps of a police van lit an open door, the figures moved to and fro carrying packages. 'What's up now?' Louise exclaimed, and began to run down the road. Wilson panted after her. Ali came from the house carrying on his head a tin bath, a folding chair, and a bundle tied up in an old towel. 'What on earth's happened, Ali?'

'Massa go on trek,' he said, and grinned happily in the headlamps.[66]

The journey is precisely recalled, though Greene travelled up-country in his Morris car not in a police van: 'The police van took its place in the long line of army lorries waiting for the ferry. Their headlamps were like a little village in the night. The trees came down on either side smelling of heat and rain.' Scobie, no doubt like

Greene on such occasions, falls asleep, as they wait in the long line of traffic. When he opens his eyes, Ali is standing close by waiting for him to awaken: ' "Massa like bed," he stated gently, firmly, pointing to the camp-bed he had made up at the edge of the path with the mosquito-net tied from the branches overhead. "Two three hours," Ali said. "Plenty lorries." Scobie obeyed and lay down.'[67] An hour later Ali wakes him up with a cup of tea and plate of biscuits. They still have an hour to wait:

> Then at last it was the turn of the police van. They moved down the red laterite slope on to the raft, and then edged foot by foot across the dark styx-like stream towards the woods on the other side. The two ferrymen pulling on the rope wore nothing but girdles, as though they had left their clothes behind on the bank where life ended, and a third man beat time to them, making do for instrument in this between-world with an empty sardine-tin.[68]

Greene recalled with authenticity and love those journeys:

> Ali squatting in the body of the van put an arm around his shoulder holding a mug of hot tea — somehow he had boiled another kettle in the lurching chassis . . . He could see in the driver's mirror Ali nodding and beaming. It seemed to him that this was all he needed of love or friendship. He could be happy with no more in the world than this — the grinding van, the hot tea against his lips, the heavy damp weight of the forest, even the aching head, the loneliness.[69]

Greene was always happy away from civilisation: too much comfort appalled him. The absence of domestic pleasures pleased him, and 'Massa go on trek' meant a return to an isolation which he loved.

The same feeling of happiness and contentment came to him when he returned to his 'creole villa' after an up-country trip:

> It was past midnight when he drove into town. The houses were white as bones in the moonlight; the quiet streets stretched out on either side like the arms of a skeleton, and the faint sweet smell of flowers lay on the air . . . He was tired and he didn't want to break the silence . . . The small boy waved his torch from the door: the frogs croaked from the bushes, and the pye dogs wailed at the moon. He was home.[70]

A Mad Cook, a Suicide and a Nest of Toads

Sympathy is like rain on brown grass.
— SARAH COLERIDGE

IN his Freetown home, Greene had his share of domestic crises. Once he was aroused by the cries of his cook, who was chasing his first, unsatisfactory steward, a Mende, with a hatchet because the boy had borrowed the empty sardine tin in which the cook was accustomed to fry Greene's morning egg. Later, both boy and cook were gaoled. The boy was sent to prison for perjury ('an offence beyond his comprehension'),[1] despite the fact that Greene had him defended by the best black lawyer in Freetown. His cook also finished up in gaol when he went completely off his head.

One night, after a week's long trek up-country, Greene returned to find his house deserted, and his cook (who was a very good cook) in prison under medical observation. It all began when a woman complained to the police that she had paid him money to make a ju-ju (magic) for her and the ju-ju hadn't worked. The police superintendent refused to charge him, but Tamba, the cook, suddenly sat down on the floor of the police station and started ranting and wouldn't move. When charged with obstruction, he began to orate from the dock, so they gaoled him.[2] When Greene visited him, he couldn't bear to see him in a grim cell. He contacted the Vichy District Commissioner across the border in French Guinea (not easy in wartime, especially since he had agents operating across the border), and had the cook returned to his native village: 'where he would end his days well looked after, at liberty except for an iron ring round his ankle to show that he had been afflicted by God'.[3]

To his mother he wrote: 'I expect you heard of my domestic troubles: the cook who went insane and the steward who went to prison . . . I've settled down now . . . with a better boy and a tolerable cook – not the artist the other one was. The only thorn in the flesh is a completely useless small boy whom I picked up in the Protectorate and shall drop back there again when I go up the week after next.'[4] In *The Human Factor* Greene explained (though putting his comments in the mouth of Hargreaves, head of MI5) how he chose his servants: 'In Africa he had lived with intuition, he was accustomed to choose his boys by intuition – not by the tattered notebooks they carried with illegible references.'[5]

The loyalty of Greene's boy is reflected in the attention and faithfulness of Scobie's boy. The SOE man in Freetown tried to bribe Greene's boy to leave his employment. This might seem unusual, but each secret service (both British after all) meddled regularly in the affairs of the other. No doubt the SOE representative wished to know what Greene was up to. The SIS sometimes suffered casualties through the activities of the SOE.

In his spare time, Greene was reading Byron with great enjoyment: 'I'm in the middle of *Don Juan* (about the fourth time); I do think it's one of the greatest things from every point of view, poetry, politics and sense, as well as wit, in the English language. I'd far rather *Paradise Lost* disappeared than *Don Juan*.'[6] In late June he wrote to his mother about minor problems of health: 'One always has a few little festering bits – in my case at the moment a boil on the arm and a shaving cut that won't heal'; and colour changes to his hair at thirty-seven: 'I am going greyer with startling rapidity!' He told her he'd been reading 'Motley and the Old Testament, both with huge pleasure'. But he rationed his favourite author, Anthony Trollope, to one a month, so that he'd have some Trollope left to read throughout his tour in Sierra Leone: 'in a few days I shall have another rationed Trollope – *The American Senator*'.[7]

Reading Trollope in Africa is introduced into *The Human Factor* (written thirty-seven years later), and the references recall Greene's own experiences: 'During his service in West Africa, he had grown to appreciate the novels of Trollope . . . At moments of irritation, he had found *The Warden* and *Barchester Towers* reassuring books; they reinforced the patience which Africa required. Mr. Slope would remind him of an importunate and self-righteous District Commissioner [Richard Cox]; and Mrs. Proudie of the Governor's wife.' And reading Trollope many years later in England with a whisky at his elbow, darkness falling early in November:

he could even imagine himself in Africa, at some resthouse in the bush, on one of the long treks which he always enjoyed, far from headquarters. The cook would now be plucking a chicken behind the resthouse and the pye dogs would be gathering in the hope of scraps . . . The lights in the distance where the motorway ran might well have been the lights of the village where the girls would be picking the lice out of each other's hair.[8]

There are many random notes in his journal which look like preliminaries for a future novel, though never used:

My boy's brother's dying. Of gonorrhoea. My boy too has had the g. 'Cured now.' 'Injections?' 'No.' He makes an expressive gesture with his hands. 'Doctor throw it out.' His stilted walk with buttocks projecting and the smell of drink. 'You drink if you see your brother – own father, own mother – lying on bed, not seeing you. You drink to keep water out of eyes.' He cannot yet tell his brother's wife. If people know he's dying they'll all come in and steal his things. All night he's going to have a party at his brother's, drinking so that water doesn't come out of his eyes, and quietly checking on his brother's belongings and getting his small brother to write them down.[9]

At 4.30 daily, Greene would have tea, 'then take a solitary walk along an abandoned railway track once used by European officials, halfway up the slopes below Hill Station'.[10] From that point, he had a wide view of Freetown's huge bay and he could see the old liner *Edinburgh Castle* as it lay rotting on a reef (it was said) of empty gin bottles. This was the hour Greene loved best, when the sun began to set and the laterite paths turned the colour of a rose.

Greene took his evening walk alone, but we can see how he transferred his sights and experiences to *The Heart of the Matter*. When Scobie is asked why he likes the place he answers simply, 'It's pretty in the evening.' Later in the novel, when taking his wife Louise to the club on the hill, Scobie is again very much aware of the night:

In the evening the port became beautiful for perhaps five minutes. The laterite roads that were so ugly and clay-heavy by day became a delicate flower-like pink. It was the hour of content. Men who had left the port for ever would sometimes remember on a grey wet London evening the bloom and glow that faded as soon as it was seen: they would wonder why they had hated the coast and for a space of a drink they would long to return.[11]

And Greene was right. In 1948, soon after the publication of *The Heart of the Matter*, a Mr Northcott of London – he had served in Sierra

Leone at the same time as Greene – recalled 'that fleeting few minutes during the brief twilight, when everything seemed to be suffused with a pink glow: It was an amazing sight, and I often wondered what caused it.'

In *The Heart of the Matter*, Father Rank, a congenial gossip, takes the same walk along the railway track and, as he passes the abandoned station, unknowingly interrupts Wilson and Louise Scobie as they kiss:

> she pulled away and he heard the sad – to and fro – of Father Rank's laugh coming up along the path. 'Good evening, good evening,' Father Rank called . . . 'A storm's coming up,' . . . and his 'ho, ho, ho' diminished mournfully along the railway track, bringing no comfort to anyone.
>
> 'He didn't see who we were,' Wilson said.
>
> 'Of course he did. What does it matter?'
>
> 'He's the biggest gossip in the town.'
>
> 'Only about things that matter,' she said.[12]

Earlier in the novel, Wilson is made aware of Father Rank's gossiping nature, though the gossip is mild enough:

> 'You were saying something about a rumour?' Wilson asked.
>
> 'My head is a hive of rumours,' Father Rank said, making a humorous hopeless gesture. 'If a man tells me anything I assume he wants me to pass it on. It's a useful function, you know, at a time like this, when everything is an official secret, to remind people that their tongues were made to talk with and that the truth is meant to be spoken about.'[13]

The Heart of the Matter is infused with Greene's experiences and chance encounters. The nature of Father Rank reflects the nature of Father Mackie, a priest Greene admired and whose church he visited while in Freetown. Greene once recalled to me that Mackie was suspected of being a spy because he was overheard mentioning at dinner with the Colonial Secretary that the *Queen Mary* was in port. A man from the police (a type similar to Wilson in the novel) came to see Greene and asked him to warn Father Mackie not to speak so indiscreetly in front of the black boy. Greene pointed out the absurdity of this since everybody could see that the *Queen Mary* was in port – it came in regularly.[14]

Greene returned to Freetown in 1967 and called again at the Catholic church:

The Brookfield church was unchanged, where my friend Father Mackie used to preach in Creole: the same bad statue of St. Anthony over the altar, the same Virgin in the butterfly blue robe. At Midnight Mass I could have believed myself back in 1942 if in that year I had not missed the Mass. A fellow Catholic, the representative of the rival secret service, SOE, had come to dine with me tête-à-tête and we were soon too drunk on Portuguese wine to stagger to the church.[15]

*

The insufferable MI5 officer Wilson is based in part on Harwood, the old schoolboy contemporary of Greene's at Berkhamsted School. But the portrait is partly autobiographical, as Greene's journal shows, transferring the cockroach hunt with his colleague to Harris and Wilson in the novel. There is one further event which the fictional Wilson indulges in which is derived from Greene's own experience.

In the novel Wilson's 'melancholy lust' rises when his eye catches a young girl naked to the waist passing by 'gleaming through the rain'. Later he sees her again, the water trickling down between her shoulder blades and he decides to visit a brothel to slake his sexual thirst. His colleague Harris asks him what he will find to do in town at that hour. He answers brusquely: 'Business', and then admits silently to himself that 'it was business of a kind, the kind of joyless business one did alone, without friends'.[16]

What follows is a straightforward account of Greene's own experience later incorporated into the novel. It also refers to the first and only car Greene ever owned. Driving along, Wilson stops every few hundred yards to wipe the windscreen with his handkerchief because the wiper blades don't work. In Kru town the hut doors are open and families are sitting around the kerosene lamps. There is a dead pye dog lying in the gutter with the rain running over its white swollen belly. Because it is wartime, as in blitzed London, the headlamps of his car are blacked out to the size 'of a visiting-card'. In ten minutes Wilson reaches the great cotton tree (a well-known landmark in Freetown, then and now) near the police station, Greene's own ostensible office, and leaves his car outside the main entrance. Anyone seeing it would assume he was working inside. With his car door open he considers whether to return to Harris or go to the brothel close to the police station: 'He thought sadly, as lust won the day, what a lot of trouble it was.'

He had forgotten to bring his umbrella and he was wet through before he had walked a dozen yards down the hill. It was the

passion of curiosity more than of lust that impelled him now . . .
The brothel was a tin-roofed bungalow half-way down the hill on
the right-hand side. In the dry season the girls sat outside in the
gutter like sparrows . . . Now it turned a shuttered silent front to the
muddy street, except where a door, propped open with a rock out
of the roadway, opened on a passage . . . [17]

Wilson looks quickly this way and that and then steps inside the
brothel.

George Neal, serving in the British army in Freetown at the time
that Greene was an intelligence officer there, remembers meeting him
twice in the Cotton Wood bar (though Greene did not offer him his
name and Neal only recognised him when Greene's fame made
recognition possible). On one occasion, Greene (not willing to ask his
colleagues about the whereabouts of various brothels) asked Neal, who
gave him the address of the brothel, which Greene visited. Neal
offered me evidence of the location: 'The description [in *The Heart of
the Matter*] of the approach and location of the brothel is word
perfect.'[18]

What Neal remembers is that Greene was not attracted to black
women, but was clearly in need, and we know from various
comments that he was unhappy with the white women in Freetown:
'The consistent sexiness of the middle-aged begins to get one down.
The excitement over women who even in their prime were nothing
much.'[19] He was also depressed by the social life in Freetown and, as
he stressed in a letter to his brother, still in love with Dorothy Glover:
'I have become terribly one-idea'd.' So for sexual release he was left
with the black girls, but he feared even the nicest of them. What
worried him about them was disease. Sitting in a park on his first
arrival he noticed the young girls coming out of school: 'the lovely
small native girls', but added, 'who have got to grow up to syphilis
(98%)'.

Nicholas Elliott, a senior intelligence agent on his way to Lagos
whose ship called first at Freetown in June 1942, recalled Greene
lamenting that there were no French letters in Freetown. Elliott did a
collection for him among the passengers and handed him eleven
condoms. Greene now had the means of avoiding disease but, like
Wilson, it was a reluctant adventure.

The inside of the brothel does not measure up to the lovely small
native girl who passed Wilson in the rain. He is faced first with a
passage which years before had been whitewashed but where rats had
torn holes in the plaster and the walls 'were tattooed like a sailor's arm,
with initials, dates . . . even a pair of hearts interlocked'.[20] He notes

that on either side of the passage are little cells nine feet by four with curtains instead of doorways and beds made out of old packing cases spread with a native cloth.

Thinking the place deserted, Wilson intends turning at the end of the passage and leaving, but then discovers that the last cell is occupied: 'in the light of an oil lamp burning on the floor he saw a girl in a dirty shift spread out on the packing-cases like a fish on a counter . . . She lay there on duty, waiting for a customer. She grinned at Wilson, not bothering to sit up and said, "Want jig jig, darling. Ten bob." '[21]

The unsavoury nature of the girl in a dirty shift, her bare pink soles dangling over the packing-case bed, make him deny he wanted a 'jig jig' and he turns to leave, but finds his escape blocked by a big Mammy. He offers to come back after a drink but the Mammy, blocking the way out, sends the prostitute off for drink. The Mammy puts up the price to a pound and continues to block his way – she rules 'in the dark regions'. It is here that Wilson realises that 'a man's colour had no value: he couldn't bluster as a white man could elsewhere: by entering this narrow plaster passage, he had shed every racial, social and individual trait . . . '[22] Weakly Wilson asks, 'Let me by,' but she doesn't move, only occasionally repeating 'Pretty girl jig jig by and by.' He holds out a pound and she pockets it but goes on blocking his way. He tries to push by but she thrusts him backward 'with a casual pink palm, saying "By-an-by. Jig jig" ':

Down the passage the girl came carrying a vinegar bottle filled with palm wine, and with a sigh of reluctance Wilson surrendered. The heat between the walls of rain, the musty smell of his companion, the dim and wayward light of the kerosene lamp reminded him of a vault newly opened for another body to be let down upon its floor. A grievance stirred in him, a hatred of those who had brought him here.[23]

Greene certainly would have vehemently disagreed with Cyril Connolly when Connolly wrote: 'No one was ever made wretched in a brothel.' Curiously, Greene continued to visit brothels in every foreign country he went to. His attraction (and hatred and fear) to such places is similar to Father Damien's reluctant passion to live among the lepers – which Greene himself did in the late 1950s.

*

Another central incident in the novel, Scobie's trip up-country to investigate the suicide of Pemberton, a young district officer, is the result of hearsay and gossip remembered by Greene and cleverly worked into the story. For the purposes of plot, the Catholic priest needed to be morally bound by the rules: ' "Suicide," Father Clay said. "It's too terrible. It puts a man outside mercy." '[24] In Greene's journal we can see Father Clay's origin in Father B, whom Greene met in the interior: 'Poor little red-head north country boy neglected by his fellows. "I walk up and down here." ' Father B is transferred without change to *The Heart of the Matter*: 'Father Clay was up and waiting for him in the dismal little European house which had been built . . . in laterite bricks to look like a Victorian presbytery. A hurricane-lamp shone on the priest's short red hair and his young freckled Liverpool face. He couldn't sit still for more than a few minutes at a time, and then he would be up, pacing his tiny room . . . '[25]

This source is discovered by comparing journal and novel. More difficult to uncover is the source of Pemberton and his suicide, since Greene neither spoke nor wrote about it. Greene deliberately avoided making Pemberton a Catholic so that when Scobie the Catholic commits suicide, he does so in the full knowledge of his own personal guilt.[26] Pemberton lives an isolated life in a small village which has only one other white man, the red-headed priest. He hangs himself in his house by means of a picture cord which is still twisted over a brass picture hanger when Scobie inspects his room.[27]

In the novel the town is called Bamba. No such town exists, but Pejuhun could be described as Greene describes Bamba, as controlling 'one of the main routes across the border'. During Greene's stay in Sierra Leone two European suicides took place in Pejuhun. The district officer in charge during one of Greene's visits was C. J. Mabey, whom Greene visited in Pejuhun in his capacity as a military intelligence officer.[28]

One of the suicides – that of a retired medical doctor – doesn't fit the novel, but the second does. He was *not* a district officer like Pemberton, but worked for the PZ company. In the novel, Pemberton is in debt and has signed bushels of IOUs. Scobie can see how badly his office has been kept – 'filing cabinet was unlocked: the trays on the desk were filled by papers dusty with inattention'.[29]

My informant, who lived in Youmi, close to Pejuhun, described a situation quite similar to Pemberton's: the young man gambled, got deeply into debt, misappropriated company funds and decided he could not face the consequences. However, the model for Pemberton did not hang himself in his bedroom. He was found hanging from a tree in the bush, and his dog led the searchers to the scene. The unfortunate young man is buried near Youmi. When I stayed in Pejuhun, in the company of Father Peter Queally, the local paramount chief showed us the tree from which the PZ man hanged himself.

A Canadian living in Freetown told me in 1980 that he had heard from a number of authentic sources that Greene visited the home of the original suicide soon after the event. If this is the case, Greene's life mirrored Scobie's more closely than we could ever have suspected.

*

On returning to Freetown in June from a visit to the Protectorate, Greene heard the news that he'd been awarded a literary prize. Laurence Pollinger wrote proudly to Vivien on 9 June: 'The Hawthornden prizes for 1940 and 1941 have just been awarded and Graham's *The Power and the Glory* gets it for 1940. Isn't this exciting? Shall you be cabling him?' Vivien responded to Pollinger: 'How absolutely thrilling! I spent 16/- in cabling & am taking the children to a circus (which has fortunately arrived here).'[30] In the same cable Vivien also told Greene about the wonderful news that Paramount was to make a film of his book *A Gun for Sale*. Pollinger himself wrote to Greene about 'this good news'. Everyone was excited − but not Greene. His response to Pollinger was lukewarm:

> I was glad to hear that I'd won the Hawthornden; a hundred pounds is always useful. Otherwise the sole value, I feel, is advertisement among the middlebrows. One can't take an honour shared with Charles Morgan and Christopher Hassall very seriously!* I don't know whether in these days of paper shortage it's very possible to seize the chance of advertisement, but I feel Heinemann ought to do a little about it − after all it's building up for the next book and helps to fill the rather long gap.

He ended his letter with the following sentence: 'Write to me one day. One likes to have news of our dingy civilisation in this even dingier hole.'[31]

To his mother, he took a different tack at first: 'It's funny how things always seem to go well when I'm away; I've just heard about winning the Hawthornden prize and the film of *A Gun for Sale*. Vivien

---

* In June 1933, Greene went to a literary party given by Mrs Belloc Lowndes: 'Charles and Dwye Evans turned up and Charles Morgan. Dwye said: "I haven't read the paper. Who got the Hawthornden yesterday?" No one of us knew. Presently Morgan said dryly: "As a matter of fact I did." ' The previous year (10 July 1932) having read a new novel of Ford Madox Ford, Greene had noted in his diary: 'Finished Ford's novel. What a book . . . One is inclined to exclaim "genius", but the critics will not; they all go hunting the safe, literary stylists like Charles Morgan, who have no originality to speak of but a pretty style, dead as last year's leaves. But Ford's is as full of life as a flea.'

tells me it's an extremely good film.'[32] But the prize gave this curious man a sense of shame:

> One can't have the presentation and the speeches and so on of the Hawthornden, though the prizewinner always looks a little silly. And it's odd that one feels pleased . . . There's no real distinction in the prize: a few good books have won it, and a great many very bad ones – like Charles Morgan's. I suppose at the bottom of every human mind is the rather degraded love of success – any kind of success. One feels ashamed of one's own pleasure.[33]

In war-torn England, Vivien, her own home destroyed by bombing and her husband in foreign parts, was still very much in love: 'I pressed my red and blue taffeta evening dress yesterday and put it on to celebrate your letter coming.'[34] She had two children to attend to. Francis, then six, in the bath one night, asked a question his mother couldn't answer – they had been to see *Peter Pan*: 'What was Captain Hook's name before he lost his arm?' and another day asked: 'When Our Lord died, did his halo go out?'[35]

Vivien's longing for a proper married life was overwhelming:

> Darling, darling love, we do love you. Won't it be nice when we don't have to look forward to weekends again but all live together . . . Perhaps that alarms you. You will have been on your own for so long that family life is a bit claustrophobic? I believe I can see the whites of your eyes and your ears laid back, but think of the nice home made bread and the cubs thirsting for information . . . [36]

She came back to the same subject twice the following month: 'We live from day to day contentedly, but I do feel so impermanent and do so long after all these wasted years to have my own things round me.'[37] 'I do pine for my companion and next to that I pine for a little cat-basket of my own, nicely lined with compartments for kittens and an annexe for Toms when they turn up from foreign parts.'[38] In a letter to Greene on 14 April, Vivien told him of an argument she'd had with her friend Stella Weaver, who had criticised Greene, but in whose house she was living and whose powerful personality sometimes overwhelmed her. She had not allowed the criticism to stand: 'I prefer to be with my husband – he walks and I walk with him. We like doing things together.' And she added, 'After a slight underlining of this theme, I left it . . . it will be so nice when you are home and will plan and decide everything.' Vivien liked a dominating husband, something Greene did not like to be. In the following month of May, life was stirring in nature and in her: 'There is no one ever possible to be one millionth as precious and beloved,' she wrote.[39] 'Dear precious love for ever, you are so dear to me . . . keep well for starting our new and much longed for cat-and-dog basket again.'[40]

And Greene kept Vivien's love alive, giving her hope their love would continue, for though few letters have survived, what he wrote when sending his wife a Christmas present was: 'For My Dearest Love, Christmas 1941, the 14th [of marriage] & the only sad one.' He also deliberately misquoted lines from Edmund Blunden, ' "Oneness & Togetherness / A Conquest over Space no less", a misquotation you'll recognise.' Vivien did recognise it and recalled the occasion Greene had first used the phrase. It was in 1937. After ten years of marriage, Greene had bought Vivien a Roman missal dated 1815 and inscribed it with Blunden's lines correctly quoted: 'A Conquest over time no less.'

Vivien brings the war years back in her letters, in particular, the severity of food rationing. Taking a holiday during July at Wadebridge in north Cornwall, she told her husband how prostrate she would be on arriving, dizzy with the new ration books and their host of special regulations:

I have both sets of rations books, that is

1. The main ration book for each person   3

    Pink ration book (for things on 'points')   3

    Yellow ration book for jam, soap etc.   3

2. The new main ration book for each incorporating the Pink and Yellow   3

    The 'Personal Ration Cards' for wool, sweets and others   3

3. Clothing cards for three   3

    Identity cards for three   3

                        —

           21 separate documents

plus three railway tickets. Poor poor minnow.[41]

She betrayed her pleasure in small things, such as buying a gramophone: 'I am quite excited because I am going to fetch the gramophone from the store by taxi which is the only way to get it, and take it to be put in order and I am going to join the Record Society when I get back and make a small collection of records for myself too. Won't that be nice?'[42] On 1 August, Vivien's birthday – she was thirty-seven – she keenly felt her isolation:

> I will stop now precious love, with so much love, & telling you again how I miss you & pine for you & get tired of being alone & having no one to go about with. It is years & years now since *we* went to a film or an exhibition or a party *together* as a matter of course because we belonged to each other . . . You mustn't mind the birthday wail of a lone cat . . . Bless you thousands of times my own love – say you pine a bit & miss me especially 'of an evening'.[43]

She day-dreamed of things that held *no* spell for Greene: 'O to be in Charleston in an ice cream parlour with a magnolia tree in one's garden and sunshine coming in through striped sun blinds, the children pale brown and in pretty cottons, a white pekinese in a basket, one's hair just set by a good hairdresser, a nice dinner party to look forward to.'[44]

In the last surviving letter Vivien sent to Freetown, she had gone to London and was waiting for a train to take her back to Oxford and her children:

> Station cavernous but better lighted than I expected. Sat in waiting room till midnight. Very quiet. Woman cleaner swept the floor and went away. Presently I went out. There was a square formation of sailors sitting on the platform surrounded by gunny sacks, talking quietly. A policeman in a steel helmet told me they were waiting for the 2.30. In front of the gates of platform eleven were about a thousand soldiers, behind them a small queue of civilians: quite soon it moved and by 12.30 we were in the train, the troops on the platform having disappeared. Under the only light, at the barrier, a Military Policeman stood.[45]

Though no letters to or from Dorothy while Greene was in Sierra Leone have survived, there are two references to letters made in his journal when he was in Lagos: 'Very depressed & lonely. Depressed letter from D. made it worse.' 'Another letter from D. Perhaps the next after she knows I've arrived will be happier.' We can be certain, however, that her passion for Greene moved her to write. Six months later, in the same letter in which Hugh Greene refers to the possibility of Greene meeting Doris Temple, he also speaks of Dorothy: 'I see Dorothy for a drink every now and again. We've been working out an illustrated book, "Sights of London", to be published in Paris after the war. Among the characters: a milkman off Vine Street: a woman watching a flock of sheep in York Way behind King's Cross: an old man in Flask Walk, etc. Further details unfortunately impossible at this stage.'[46] Greene spoke of Dorothy to Hugh as if she were no more than a drinking companion. She was, in fact, much more to both of them. Here is Greene's reply to Hugh's news of Dorothy: 'Doll wrote me about the bawdy book she's planning with you as evasively as you. I long to hear more. I wish you'd told me how she was looking, whether she seemed well, could down her pint of Irish as readily, etc. Give her my love.' You notice that in writing about Dorothy, he calls her 'Doll' (both brothers did), after Doll Tearsheet in Shakespeare's *Henry IV*, and, like Doll, Dorothy was fond of her ale. Dorothy and Hugh were very close, as he always insisted during my interviews with him. Greene would probably not have objected to his favourite brother's congress with Dorothy, it was after all during the heady days of war.

But Greene was deeply in love with Dorothy, though, as usual, unwilling to share his intimate feelings even with the brother he was closest to. We can get some idea of his marital problems from a private letter he wrote to his sister in Cairo. Elisabeth Greene was in love with Rodney Dennys, but at this time their engagement was broken off – though they were later to marry happily and successfully. Greene wrote from Freetown: 'Things can be hell I know. The peculiar form it's taken with me the last four years has been in loving two people as equally as makes no difference, the awful struggle to have your cake and eat it, the inability to throw over one for the sake of the other . . . This of course is confidential.'[47]

In under three months his tour of duty in West Africa would finish, and Greene would be returning to England with nothing solved: his passion for two women, one his wife, the other his mistress, remained intense. He had always thought that war would bring death as a solution to his problems of divided love in one form or another – 'in the blitz, in a submarined ship, in Africa with a dose of blackwater',[48] but against his wishes, he remained alive.

*

In spite of numerous activities of a secret kind, Greene, calm on the surface and seemingly unhurried, was writing what was to be his most brilliant thriller, set in the London blitz. No doubt working furiously, he writes calmly enough to his mother in April: 'I try and do a minute portion of my own work every day – on a slack day more than a minute portion, so that I shall have something finished when I leave here.'[49]

The first reference to his entertainment comes in a letter Vivien wrote to Laurence Pollinger just before Greene left Lagos on 9 March 1942. Vivien asked if it was true 'that Paramount is going to make *A Gun for Sale* with Veronica Lake?' and then passed on a message from Greene: 'Tell Laurence I've started on an Entertainment & hope to let him have it by the autumn.' But protective of her husband, Vivien added, 'It is frightfully hot & the rainfall is 147 inches & mosquitoes & cockroaches (two & a half inches long) make life horrible in the evenings and it is a great effort to write letters even.'[50]

By 22 May Greene was 'two thirds through an entertainment which should be ready by August'.[51] Incredibly, in June he had almost finished it, though it was without a final title: 'Title as usual a problem: the only one I can think of *The Worst Passion of All* (referring to pity) seems a bit too serious.'[52]

As he was coming to the end of the book, Greene feared that the continued successful U-boat action against Allied shipping would result in the loss of his manuscript: 'I'm terrified of trusting a MS. to the ocean. Can one insure against war risk at Lloyd's? One would have to insure for 700 pounds. Perhaps you'd find out for me. Otherwise I'd better hang on to it till I come home myself.'*[53]

Greene's letter took three weeks to arrive and Pollinger replied that it was his understanding that parcels posted either by steamer or airmail could not be insured against war risk and that Greene should post by airmail. Also, he assured Greene that it was likely that the 37.5 per cent paper ration would be cut at the end of the month and that in 1943 fewer and fewer books would be published: 'Therefore, it's in your best interests to get the entertainment into Charles' [Evans] hands just as soon as possible, otherwise he will not have the paper for it.'[54]

'You don't quite get my difficulty about the entertainment,' Greene responded. 'I can't get it typed here, and seems a crazy thing to send the only MS., unless I can insure. One can insure against war risk – every bookseller does it, and I did it with my baggage. Will you find out from Lloyd's what they'd charge to insure a m.s. coming by air mail? I shall want to insure for 700 pounds if the book is going on

---

* Because of the terrible shortage of books, he asked his agent that, if he ran into his publishing friends, 'Michael Joseph, Charlie Evans, Hamish Hamilton . . . no, not Jonathan Cape, you might hint that any book would be welcomed with joy.' He then added, jokingly: 'I always encourage *other* people to cast their bread on the waters.'

contract.'[55] And five days later, he was telling Pollinger that the entertainment, God willing, would be ready for dispatch in August if the insurance could be fixed: 'About 65,000 words; only titles in my mind so far *The Worst Passion of All* . . . and *The Man Who Forgot* which is a bit banal.'[56]

By 4 August Greene excitedly told Pollinger that he had a good title for the entertainment: *The Ministry of Fear*. 'It will run probably to a shade under 70,000. I've finished 60,000 and have a clear run ahead.' The tone of Greene's letter is happy; he surely realised that he was writing the best of all his entertainments: 'There's a good cinematic idea in it.' In a letter of 12 August, he returned to this, asking Pollinger to 'drop a word into Paramount's ear, now that they've had a bit of success with *This Gun for Hire* [the American title of *A Gun for Sale*] that *The Ministry of Fear* has got a good filmable and new central situation, and it is not trash like *The Confidential Agent* was.'[57] The excitement of almost finishing *The Ministry of Fear* led him to think of starting and perhaps finishing another novel, incredible in the circumstances of war: 'I hope to get a novel done or nearly done by the time I get leave or the sack next year.' This was not to be.

Greene completed *The Ministry of Fear* and sent it off, but in parts, so that if one part went missing at least two parts might be saved. Moreover, he did not send the manuscript but a typescript. Somehow this slow and inexpert typist had been able to transcribe a complete manuscript, even though he was at times excessively busy with intelligence work.

By 20 September Greene was able to write to his literary agent: 'Here is about the first third of the book. I send it in bits, partly for security and partly because Heinemann may want to start setting.' He was going up-country for another week, yet was able to calculate that it would take another four weeks to complete the typing. His anxiety about his typescript is shown in his next letter: 'A third of the Ministry went off to you, a fortnight ago. Cable me if it doesn't come.'[58] There was no need to worry. Pollinger was able to send a cable twenty-six days later: 'FIRST THIRD FEAR RECEIVED.'[59] On 27 October, the second instalment arrived, and the last on 12 November, by which time Greene sent an extra copy by surface mail:

Will you have it bound up and let the film people see it . . . unless you think it better to wait and let them have page proofs? Will you acknowledge it by cable as surface copy to me 'Police Freetown'? I hope to see you fairly early next year. I haven't sent you a blurb, and if the quinine ridden brain doesn't function in time, I would much rather not have a blurb at all. [Here is a further example of

Greene's independence; if he is unable to write the blurb, it is not to be written.][60]

By 10 December Pollinger could report to Vivien that two copies of Graham's new book, *The Ministry of Fear*, had reached him: 'One is being read by Charles Evans [head of Heinemann] and the other I am showing to the film magnates here.' Only five days later, Pollinger sent Greene a cable: 'EVANS DELIGHTED WITH MINISTRY FEAR.'

As far as the film people were concerned, as early as 3 September Pollinger was reporting to Greene: 'Paramount have been told about THE MINISTRY OF FEAR and seem to be calling every other day asking if the typescript has reached me.' Two days after Evans's delight over Greene's new novel, Paramount made an offer: 'I first talked to Frank Farley of Paramount . . . Film Rights: The sale of THE MINISTRY OF FEAR to Paramount at 3,250 pounds is through and I now await their agreement.'[61]

On learning the good news (what an accomplishment: film rights to the novel accepted by Paramount *before* publication), Greene sent Pollinger a cable on 17 December: 'ACCEPT. I SUGGEST PAYING FIFTEEN INSTEAD OF TEN COMMISSION DIVIDED YOU AND MARY.' Pollinger cabled Mary Pritchett, who replied: 'PLEASE TRY ARRANGE PARAMOUNT PAY MY COMMISSION HERE CONGRATULATIONS GRATITUDE GREETINGS',[62] and Pollinger added: 'To say that I personally appreciate your thought and action in regard to this matter of commission is to put it mildly. Let me say simply and sincerely: "Thank you".'[63]

Greene was becoming the renowned author most of us have known all our lives. Pollinger ended his letter by saying, 'We are as busy as a dozen hives of bees, and business is good. Never before have I worked so hard, but I am enjoying it!'[64]

Greene must have felt that his professional life as a writer had come to some point of success in spite of the war. Two great religious novels had appeared, *Brighton Rock* and *The Power and the Glory* (and this last had won him the Hawthornden); the tropics and his activities as SIS Freetown had not prevented the completion of *The Ministry of Fear*. This entertainment is by any standards a remarkable novel, the best novel about the blitz written during the Second World War. Moreover, it brought him financial success even before its publication. With Paramount's offer of £3,250, he must have felt that he'd jumped ahead of the game, that he was on his way to making his family secure, possibly even that his purpose in life was achieved. On Christmas Eve, he wrote to Vivien that he'd had 'an apocalyptic dream':

I was going into a house which I knew was on the point of falling down: I remember saying aloud, 'People with experience of London cellars say they felt no fear if they knew their work was done. Now I have had many indications that my work is done.' Then the house began to collapse. I knew that outside there was an earth-quake & it was no use going out but all the same I made for the door and first got out before the house collapsed. I didn't feel in the least afraid. Outside there was wild stony chaos: mountains seemed to be collapsing & great rocks falling and one knew for certain this was the end of everything. One had just time to say 'God forgive my sins' and then the rocks and the wind came down on one and as it were blew one into vacancy, and on into wakefulness . . . The most interesting point of the dream was the conviction that one had done all one could do alive and that the indications were all set for death.[65]

*

It was not his own death but his father's that should have exercised his mind. Charles Greene retired from the headmastership of Berkhamsted School in June 1927 because of diabetes. Over fifteen years of retirement, his condition had worsened. A letter from a school friend of Elisabeth Greene recalled meeting her mother and father at Crowborough in their retirement: 'Your mother was a bit remote, very serene, and probably looked older than she was because of her white hair done in a bun. I remember she had a good sense of humour. Your Father always reminded me of a Teddy Bear with twinkly eyes, though I think we only saw him at meals and for the paper games, and I was probably incapable of carrying on a coherent conversation with him.'[66]

When a young boy at Berkhamsted, Greene didn't like his father, but he felt an increasing warmth towards him during his retirement. There was a sense of nobility, of simplicity and unworldliness about Charles Greene that was felt by almost everyone who knew him. Greene portrayed him in retirement in his abandoned novel *Across the Border*:

But Mr. Hands wasn't listening . . . his old tired grey face had peculiar nobility. For nearly seventy years he had been believing in human nature, against every evidence . . . He was a Liberal, he thought men could govern themselves if they were left alone to it, that wealth did not corrupt and that statesmen loved their country. All that had marked his face until it was a kind of image of what he believed the world to be.[67]

The love that Greene's parents bore each other lasted throughout their long lives. Greene's play, *The Potting Shed*, first produced at the Globe Theatre on 5 February 1958, presents the image of his mother: 'Mrs. Califer was his mother to the life, though the dialogue quoted didn't actually occur in real life,' asserted Vivien Greene. Greene suggested that the sources for Mr and Mrs Califer were the Webbs (Sidney and Beatrice), but Vivien felt he was only telling half the truth: 'Mrs. Califer cared for her husband and put him before her own children, as did Marion Greene.'[68] The fact that Greene wrote regularly to his mother throughout her life suggests that there was genuine love between mother and son, and that Vivien's judgment might be questionable.

Greene recalled his father's last diabetic years: 'always beside [my mother's] place at table there stood a weighing machine to measure his diet, and it was she who daily gave him his injections of insulin'.[69] Vivien, who lived with them during the early part of the war, recalled that Marion Greene petted her husband and looked after him even before his diabetes: 'She was very unmaternal to her own children. [Elisabeth, her youngest child, denies this] Charles was the child really.'[70] She read to him, but always censored her reading so that the world could remain both romantic and unsullied. In a late novel, *The Human Factor*, the relationship of Castle's mother and father is based on Greene's own parents: 'People did confess sometimes to his mother, who was much loved in the village, and he had heard her filter these confessions to his father, with any grossness, malice or cruelty removed. "I think you ought to know what Mrs. Baines told me yesterday." '[71] Both Greene and his wife Vivien remembered examples of Marion, when she was reading a thriller aloud to Graham's father, and especially when she was reading her son's latest novel, providing Charles with selected bowdlerised passages so as not to disturb him. But a letter Vivien wrote to Greene eight months before the death of Charles shows that the last years were hard for Marion Greene: 'poor Mumma unable even to go to Lewes Women's Institute meeting as she cannot leave him for half a day. She sounded tired and as if the coughing and illness had got her down a bit.'[72]

Charles Greene died on 7 November 1942, when Greene was still in Freetown:

I think that my parents' was a very loving marriage . . . their love withstood the pressure of six children and great anxieties . . . I was in Sierra Leone, running ineffectually a one-man office of the Secret Service, when my father died. The news came in two telegrams delivered in the wrong order – the first told me of his death – the second an hour later of his serious illness. Suddenly, between the secret reports to be coded and decoded, I unexpectedly felt misery and remorse, remembering how as a young man I had deliberately set out to shock his ideas which had been unflinchingly liberal in politics and gently conservative in morals.[73]

Charles Greene had never disputed by so much as a word Greene's decision to become a Catholic. Greene had a Mass said for him by Father Mackie, the Irish priest in Freetown. He thought that if his father could have known he would have regarded the gesture 'with his accustomed liberality and kindly amusement'. In payment for the Mass, Father Mackie asked Greene to provide a sack of rice for the poor African parishioners. Rice was scarce and severely rationed, but Greene was able to buy a sack clandestinely through his friendship with the Commissioner of Police. At least, Greene felt, his method of payment would have pleased his father.[74]

Because letters by sea during the war took a long time to arrive, Greene was only able to write back to his mother three weeks after his father's death. Perhaps it was his own guilt – being away from home, volunteering for service abroad when he need not have done – that brought him home soon after:

> I have only heard today about Da's death . . . I feel it was rather a selfish act taking on a job abroad at this time, and I ought to have been home . . . I can't write about how sorry and sad I feel: he was a very good person in a way we don't seem able to produce in our generation. I wish he could have seen the end of this wretched war and better times, but I'm glad all happened so quietly and suddenly . . . I'm glad too that I belong to a faith that believes we can still do something for him and he can still do something for us. It will be such a long time after that you'll get this letter, and that will hurt . . . I can't write more now, but I think I shall be seeing you before very long.[75]

Greene then added a postscript: 'This may seem Popish superstition to you, or it may please you, that prayers are being said every day for Da in a West African church & that rice is being distributed here in his name among people who live on rice & find it very hard to get.'

When Greene came to write *The Heart of the Matter*, long after his experiences in Sierra Leone, he made use of the cruel accident of being informed of his father's death first and of his illness an hour later in successive telegrams delivered in the wrong order. The telegrams in the novel are about the death of Scobie's daughter: ' "I had a child,"

Scobie said, "who died. I was out here. My wife sent me two cables from Bexhill, one at five in the evening and one at six, but they mixed up the order. You see she meant to break the thing gently . . . The cable said, *Catherine died this afternoon no pain God bless you.* The second cable came at lunch-time. It said, *Catherine seriously ill. Doctor has hope . . .* " [76]

Marion Greene's letter to her daughter Elisabeth about her husband's death is stoic and moving:

He had bad night, breathing bad. I read to him from 6–7 a.m. and then he thought he might get to sleep. I fell off but I don't think he did. I rang up Dr. E. who said he would come as soon as he could but had an operation . . . Da had some breakfast. He was very thirsty and had tea later. About 11. he insisted on going to the lavatory. I begged him not to lock the door. He did not come out and I went in and found him on the floor. Mrs. T., Noreen and I got him onto the floor of my room and covered him up but could not lift him onto the bed . . . He never recovered consciousness but I thought it was a diabetic coma . . . but Dr. E. and Raymond think as he fell like that it was thrombosis of the brain. When Dr. E. came he was dead. That was about 1. He died without a struggle, was lying just as I left him to come downstairs, I was not in the room, but he looked just asleep. I am so glad he did not know he was leaving me and so thankful he was taken before I was. We had such a perfect life together. There can never have been a more unselfish, good man. [77]

Charles Greene was cremated at Charing in Kent, a village they both thought beautiful:

A lovely afternoon. The trees are lovely this year. They took him down to their little chapel on Thursday afternoon. I put a bunch of roses and white heather in his hands. He looked so young, except of course for white hair . . . How pleased Da would have been with the news [The second Battle of Alamein marked the turning of the tide for Britain in its war against Germany]. I always took notes for him from the Wireless till that last morning. [78]

A passage in *The Potting Shed* is a little too sharp, but could well describe Marion Greene's marriage to Charles: 'For nearly fifty years I've looked after his laundry. I've seen to his household. I've paid attention to his – allergies. He wasn't a leader. I can see that now. He was someone I protected. And now I'm unemployed.' [79]

*

Greene swore in *Ways of Escape* that for the first six months in Freetown he was a happy man, for he was in a land he loved: though the evidence of his letters suggests his happiness and his love were intermittent. Yet in retrospect, he felt able to quote Kipling: ' "We've only one virginity to lose. And where we have lost it there our hearts will be." . . . At thirty-one in Liberia I had lost my heart to West Africa.'[80]

Greene's liking for West Africa is best expressed in Hargreaves's conversation in *The Human Factor*:

It's what the politicians call a realistic policy, and realism never got anyone very far in the kind of Africa I used to know. My Africa was a sentimental Africa. I really loved Africa . . . The Chinese don't, nor do the Russians, nor the Americans . . . How easy it was in the old days when we dealt with chiefs and witch doctors and bush schools and devils and rain queens. My Africa was still a little like the Africa of Rider Haggard.[81]

And the Africans liked the eccentric British. One provincial commissioner Greene knew, 'Old Sayers', came once a year to Freetown in a caravan with his black children and his mistress: 'The only reason that they were not married was that the mistress was a Catholic, probably converted by Irish missionaries. She wouldn't marry him because he was divorced. Everyone accepted this.'[82]

Perhaps his love for the people and land came out best when he recalled his return to Brookfield church in 1967, and watched, while inside the church, a young African girl:

the girl in front of me wore one of the surrealist Manchester cotton dresses which are rarely seen since Japanese trade moved in. The word 'soupsweet' was printed over her shoulder, but I had to wait until she stood up before I could confirm another phrase: 'Fenella lak good poke'. Father Mackie would have been amused, I thought, and what better description could there be of this poor lazy lovely coloured country than 'soupsweet'?[83]

The year ended and Greene prepared to leave Freetown. His activities as an SIS agent were coming to an end. Looking back on his life after the first few months in Freetown, he told his mother how on Good Friday four years before he went to a secret illegal Mass in Chiapas. Then unexpectedly and nostalgically, he commented on the quality of his existence on earth so far: 'I've had an odd life when I come to think of it. Useless and sometimes miserable, but bizarre and on the whole not boring.'[84]

Greene continued to expect that he would be home early in the New Year. How fed up he was becoming with the colonials is clear, on 19 January 1943, from his response to the news that London was being bombed again:

> I felt sick in the stomach when I heard the Germans had started on London again. I feel I'd be of much more use back wardening. One feels out of it in this colony of escapists with their huge drinking parties and their complete unconsciousness of what war is like. I had hoped at one time that we might have been bombed, but that hope has faded. Still I hope I shan't be here many more weeks.[85]

It might seem that Greene himself made the decision to leave West Africa, but the truth was a little different. As early as October he related to his sister that his working relationship with his boss had deteriorated: 'I had about two months ago a violent quarrel with my local boss and resigned. I was supported on the point at issue and offered a new position for which I was totally unfitted by lack of languages.' Greene was forced to reject this position and was concerned about his relations with London: 'I'm not quite sure or not whether I'm now going home under a cloud. I think not as I am not being replaced. This is a quite useless spot.' His uncertainty of his reception is shown by his give-away humour: 'Anyway you'll probably hear of me yet cleaning latrines on Salisbury Plain [a British army infantry training area].'[86]

Kim Philby (Greene's boss in London) described the situation succinctly: 'After the North African landings, SIS interest in West Africa waned, and we left MI5 in possession of the field. Graham was withdrawn from Freetown and posted to my Iberian sub-section, still in a large, ugly house on the outskirts of St. Albans.'[87]

Whatever else Africa had been for Greene, it was financially useful. His family suffered no diminution of income, so in this sense the war was a godsend. He was able to leave his whole salary behind and live on MI6 expenses. Moreover, he didn't have to pay income tax on his salary from the Secret Service. He was paid something like £1,000 a year, a reasonable sum in those days.[88]

In late January 1943 Pollinger wrote to Vivien: 'it is good to know that Graham hopes to be back here next month'.[89] In the first week of February, Vivien told Pollinger that she had had a cable from Greene advising that she 'STOP WRITING': 'It would still be worth cabling anything important, but not to send parcels or letters now.' She added that Greene might 'have to wait some time for transport still',[90] and this turned out to be true. The first letter of welcome is dated 3 March and is from Laurence Pollinger: 'Nancy has just told me the news. Welcome Home!' Greene had arrived on the first day of March.

He had closed his small office in Freetown and burnt his files and code-books with the help of celluloid sheets.[91] All the personal possessions he valued were put into one crate and sent home by sea. Mario Soldati, the Italian film producer and novelist, who went to Freetown with Greene in 1967, recalled Greene telling him what happened just prior to his departure:

Greene has a gift for discovering beauty, a truly existent and not imaginary beauty, in what everyone conventionally believes ugly, distorted and disagreeable. He is fond of rats, toads, and snakes. The other day [Greene] was telling me what had happened to him on leaving Freetown and giving up his job as an intelligence officer. He had been ordered to destroy a quantity of papers of no apparent further use. In the garden of his Brookfield cottage [*sic*], he lit a fire in a large tin drum into which he disposed of the documents. A few minutes later, when the flames began to blaze he was terrified to see the drum begin to shake violently as if it had taken on a life of its own. At first he did not realise and took no action. And soon the horrible, incomprehensible shaking stopped. A family of toads had built a nest at the bottom of the drum which was full of holes.[92]

He returned to England by plane, deeply troubled by the loss of the family of toads in the tin drum. On the journey back he could not sleep. In mid-war, with flights anything but safe, Greene was half-asleep and telling himself that he deserved to die; this would be his punishment for having so cruelly, though not wilfully, killed the poor toads.[93]

PART 3

The Long War Ending

Greene and Douglas Jerrold at
the publishers Eyre & Spottiswoode

12

Carving *Brighton Rock*

A cold coming we had of it.
— T. S. ELIOT

O N 15 June 1942, while Greene was still in Freetown, his agent wrote to him about the dramatisation of *Brighton Rock*, which had been on option for two years. As a result of the blitz, and the consequent erratic opening and shutting of London theatres, the play was still not in production. London theatres learned to live with the war: there was no heating and whilst the audience in winter could sit in their overcoats, mufflers and gloves, the actors were often bitterly cold. *Brighton Rock* also wasn't staged because theatre managers thought the public must be cheered up in wartime, and it was too serious to attract audiences.

The situation with the stage version of *Brighton Rock* was still chaotic. Greene suggested a number of manœuvres to Laurence Pollinger which would put pressure on the producers, and concluded: 'I am *not* prepared to extend the option free of charge any longer without a definite date for production.'[1]

Greene's letter produced several reactions. Margery Vosper, the drama agent, set out the difficulties of producing this kind of play in the early days of the war: 'The tremendous ups and downs in the theatre these last three years has [*sic*] made Linnit [Bill Linnit, a theatre manager] feel that it would be a waste to produce the play. Entertainment has swung with a metallic clang to the frivolous non-stop variety vein, and air raids make the theatre's troubles ever more acute.'[2] She felt the mood was changing and, though she took all London's theatre magnates 'with a large dollop of salt', she was convinced that Linnit's enthusiasm for the play was undimmed after this delay.

There were two problems, according to Linnit: the need for a good producer (Vosper suggested Emlyn Williams) who could give 'the proper balance to the atmosphere and undercurrents of a subtle play of this kind' and the casting. The casting of 'Pinkie' caused the greatest difficulty: 'I have been anti Johnny Mills [Sir John Mills] from the start, and have been begging Bill [Linnit] to consider trying a comparatively unknown actor in this part and relying on the two women for the names particularly essential for the play's success.' But they were up against a further snag: 'There is no big woman's name who is right for "Ida".' Nevertheless, Linnit promised that if Vosper could think of the right distinguished cast he would put the play into rehearsal tomorrow.[3]

A month later – letters took that long to reach Greene in Africa – Greene responded. He disagreed about Emlyn Williams: 'I only know him as an actor and don't care for him at that,' and he agreed about Mills. Although a great distance from the London theatre scene, Greene knew what he wanted. The two main parts should be cast with two young unknowns, 'almost children from Repertory or the R.A.D.A.' and that way, they could build up a ' "discovery . . . star overnight" kind of publicity'. The girl must be very young, 'and above all not glamorous'. The character of Ida should be played by a music-hall star ('a large pawky woman') with a good name, so that people would be curious to see her in a straight part. He believed that a music-hall star would be best since the part couldn't be harmed by overacting and 'it would give a touch of "amusement" to balance grimness'.[4]

As for casting for the young killer Pinkie, Greene felt they should choose: 'a youth who can look neurotic and seventeen and sinister, and the part's a give-away. It's simply a thing for typecasting and a good producer. Hollywood would produce a dozen types out of a hat or the nearest industrial school!'[5]

Greene kept for the postscript of the letter what was of singular importance to him: 'I still haven't seen or passed any finished version of the play. I can't help feeling that if Linnit is ready to put it on when he finds a cast, this preliminary should be got out of the way. I made suggestions over the first draft with which Harvey [who adapted the novel] agreed, but I never saw the result.'[6]

The fact that he had not read a finished version continued to trouble Greene and he sent a cable to Pollinger on 1 December 1942: 'I HAVE NEITHER SEEN NOR APPROVED SCRIPT ROCK. ARE ALTERATIONS IN FIRST VERSION INCLUDING EXTRA SCENE INCORPORATED IN MY ABSENCE. VIVIEN MUST APPROVE. ASK HER FORWARD SCRIPT QUICK WAY' (that is, by diplomatic bag).

Greene's next cable from Sierra Leone brought up the fact that

Brighton Rock was not in print: 'WILL HEINEMANN HAVE ROCK IN PRINT READY FOR PLAY OR WILL THEY RELEASE TO PENGUIN OR EYRE [& Spottiswoode]'. Greene left little to chance, assuming that publishers and agents have to be kept alert. But there were legitimate reasons for delays, and Pollinger felt the need to stress wartime conditions: 'I am not sure you appreciate how terribly short staffed everyone is these days: out of our own original staff of sixteen we now have only two, and that same state of affairs exists everywhere.'[7]

Vivien, whose task it was to vet the play script, asked Pollinger to send a duplicate to Greene in Sierra Leone: 'He hasn't seen it at all so far as I know – anyway not since 1940. I could then O.K. a final version with much more certainty. There would not be time to send a *final* version to him. Get this duplicate sent to me, marked MSS. ONLY and I will forward it by the quick route at once.'[8] One reason for speed was that Greene was expected home early in the New Year. However, Pollinger discovered there was only one script on which revisions were being made, and that it would take several weeks to do a duplicate – there were no copying machines then. He was firmly against having further copies made because it would interfere with or delay Linnit's plans for production. Moreover, there was a mad scramble going on to get in the long line of plays to London theatres, and nothing must be done to lose *Brighton Rock* its place.

> The old Playhouse, and The Winter Garden theatres have been re-opened, and I am told there are a number of plays waiting for London homes [wrote Pollinger to Greene]: that some of them have been waiting for several months, and are likely to have to wait for several months longer before West End theatres are available for them. Therefore, all things carefully considered, I do feel pretty strongly that if Linnit's plans are in any way held up we shall have to wait many months more before we shall see BRIGHTON ROCK produced and running vigorously within a stone's throw of Piccadilly.[9]

A copy of the script was at last sent to Greene by diplomatic bag and he cabled Vivien on 1 January 1943: 'SCRIPT APPROVED WITH YOUR OMISSIONS LAST SCENE NEEDS ATTENTION AND CAREFUL CASTING AVOID PIETY DO NOT APPROVE LINNITS PROPOSED ENDING SCRIPT ON WAY BACK WITH AMENDMENTS LAST SCENE LOVE GREENE.' On the same day, he wrote to Pollinger (with a carbon copy to Vivien) explaining in more detail what he meant:

I have read the script again and approve it in its present form. I think Vivien's suggested omissions improve it. I am not quite happy about the last scene: I'm so afraid of piety breaking in: and I have cut it a little, but I must insist on the ending being kept. Linnit had some crazy idea of getting Rose to consent 'to be looked after' by Ida – which means that he's lost the point of the whole thing as Ida is the real villain of the piece and Harvey has brought that out well. As I have written to Vivien, I'm convinced he is commercially wrong. The last part of the book did more than anything else to get it under people's skin, and so it will in the play. It's a magnificent curtain.[10]

Feeling financially sound after having sold the film rights to *The Ministry of Fear*, Greene felt he could insist on the play being well done or not done at all: 'I'd much rather the whole thing was indefinitely postponed than that a bad play should be produced.' He understood the necessity for alterations in dialogue which rehearsals demanded; but the theme, characters, plot and outline and, above all, the ending had to remain unchanged, and Vivien, on his behalf, had to be the final judge.

After almost three years rehearsals started on 25 January. The producer, in choosing who should play Pinkie and Rose, had not picked unknowns, but they were young 'knowns'. Rose was played by Dulcie Gray (then twenty-two) and Pinkie by Richard Attenborough. Attenborough was a particularly good choice. He was nineteen, and could look 'neurotic and seventeen and sinister'. The producer also felt he had found the perfect 'Ida' – Hermione Baddeley. On 11 February Pollinger sent a cable to Greene: BRIGHTON ROCK OPENING BLACKPOOL FEBRUARY FIFTEEN HERES WISHING IT EVERY SUCCESS.

Alas, Vivien, the final judge, had not been able to leave the children to see any rehearsals before it opened in Blackpool, and she feared the consequences: 'I suppose I can't see a rehearsal now till just before it opens in London?' she wrote to Pollinger. 'G. will be *furious*!!'[11] But Pollinger thought the play had gone well in Blackpool and that Greene would be pleased: 'They have kept the spirit of the thing excellently. It needs quite a bit of tidying up which they are doing. They were working under great difficulties in Blackpool. Two scenes require brilliant sunshine and stage lighting is controlled under the Fuel and Lighting Order.'[12]

Greene, returning from Africa on 1 March, attended the first night at the New Theatre in Oxford. He went with his family and it should have been a wonderful home-coming for his wife and children, but it was not. He was horrified by changes made to the play. Greene believed that Linnit, by adding certain lines, had destroyed the whole point: 'Now new lines have been inserted in Ida's mouth in Act 3, Scene 2, when she tells Pinkie that he belongs to a small crooked perverted world which can't beat her – *she* belongs to the real world.' But, 'the idea is that Pinkie & Rose belong to the real world in which good & evil exist, but that the interfering Ida belongs to a kind of artificial surface world in which there is no such thing as good & evil but only right & wrong.' Thus, the 'poor audience wonders what in hell the play's about'.

He believed that Hermione Baddeley was badly miscast: 'Her performance is on the overacted level of a revue sketch & her grotesqueness is all wrong for the part.' She was intolerable, but it was too late to do anything about that: 'she shouts all the time & has no variety in her voice. She shouldn't be dressed to get a laugh: she is meant to be a natural amateur bawd not an oddity whom nobody could possibly sleep with.' Also, certain passages added to her part enabled her to 'pull out an emotional stop . . . with grotesque inefficiency'. There comes a 'preliminary break in Miss Baddeley's voice which sounds rather like a gargle & can obviously be heard at the back of the gallery. The passages generally refer to her desire to be a mother to Rose.'[13]

What was tremendously painful to Greene was that the removal of the last scene and the priest's speech about 'the appalling strangeness of the mercy of God' made the play pointless:

Has this been removed in order to shorten the play – a case of Hamlet being shorter without the Prince of Denmark? We must have an explanation about this – I made an explicit condition of approving the script that the ending should be unchanged – & I am quite prepared to seek an injunction if I am not satisfied with Linnit's explanation. The last minutes of the last scene now are purely grotesque with Hermione rushing in with her fallen arches to the rescue.[14]

Greene's anger knew no bounds. He had criticised Noël Coward because Coward, in his view, was without any serious concern, had no sustaining values in his work except that he was clever and witty; he was fundamentally nihilistic. The play Greene had written had gone and something equally nihilistic had replaced it.

He insisted that his name be removed from all programmes and posters, and that no reference to him or his book be made in any publicity put out by the firm, if changes were not made. His threat to invoke the law gives some measure of his anger and is an indication of his rage when he felt his work was being 'carved up' by the ignorant. It makes clear what Vivien understood when she wrote: 'G. will be *furious*!!'

Greene was not even pleased with the production of the play: 'The production is extraordinarily careless. Time & again, Bird [the producer] ruins a good scene – the carving of the bookmaker. This is most effective, but is spoilt at the end because the bookmaker is allowed to drop the handkerchief from his face & we can see it isn't bleeding. The whole tension is lost in his exit.'[15]

Did anything please him? 'The gangsters are good & Harcourt Williams [as Prewitt] *very* good. It's a pity they should be spoilt by Hermione. Of course, the woman for Ida was Laura Cowie – who has been looking for a play.' Anything else? – yes. 'Pinkie is a most promising young actor. But he shouldn't be made so *violent*. He should be much more repressed – nerves coming out in the twisting of the string (a good touch this).'[16]

This led to another cable from poor Pollinger: 'EVERY LAST MINUTE EFFORT BEING MADE TO CARRY OUT YOUR WISHES . . . LINNIT AGGRIEVED BECAUSE YOU FAILED TALK WITH HIM AT OXFORD.'[17] Greene had not talked to Linnit because he could not face him in his anger. He did not go backstage after the performance but left the theatre, unable to praise hypocritically that which he intended to censure. In any case, Greene would always rather write out his anger than speak it. There was always in him this mixture of extreme sensitivity, polite reserve and excitability.

The reviews were not good. Greene wrote to Pollinger thanking him for his efforts, but maintained a defeatist attitude: 'So far the *News Chronicle* seems to possess the only dramatic critic of sense able to penetrate the awful eye-wash.' But the play did not sink; it prospered once it appeared at the Garrick Theatre. Greene, ever vigilant about his financial affairs, wrote to his agent on 5 May: '*Brighton Rock* has now been on for 10 weeks (7 in London) & the Vosper has not yet produced figures. Would you hurry her up & say that these must be produced regularly.'

*

Greene's ultimatum was written from the Clifton Place Hotel, Sidmouth, where he and his wife had gone for a fortnight's holiday. But he was not left alone. Paul Soskin wanted to see him about doing a film script of Howard Spring's *Fame Is the Spur*, as did Michael Balcon and Cavalcanti. Whilst Greene turned down the offer to do *Fame Is the Spur* ('I shall be at work about ten hours a day on a six day week [for the Secret Intelligence Service] for as far ahead as I can see'[18]), he was interested in meeting Soskin and Balcon in a general way.

Greene was so busy upon his return that he neglected friends and associates. In an undated letter to Charles Evans of Heinemann (probably written in April), he apologised guiltily for not getting in touch earlier: 'The truth is that after a couple of weeks' holiday with my family, I was pushed into really hard work [for SIS]'; he suggested dinner at the Reform Club and ended with a reference to Evans's cable: 'I never thanked you for your . . . cable which cheered me a lot in that God forsaken hole, Freetown.'

A letter from Vivien to Pollinger shows just how overwhelmed with work Greene was: 'We had only 10 days at Sidmouth & then G. was recalled. He is lent to the F.O. & is often out of London. He hopes to come to Oxford for the day next month.' Vivien suggested that Pollinger should let enquirers know that Greene had no time for private pursuits, worked on a Sunday and couldn't see anybody. Finally she explained how she would deal in future with her husband's correspondence: 'I am putting all letters for G. into a small suitcase & when it is full I'll send it to the Reform Club, where it can be picked up! Anyway, I *am* forwarding letters in one big envelope once a week. (No more secretarial work for me! – I'd rather clean windows or scrub steps!)'[19]

Vivien was irate, as was Pollinger. He wrote to Greene, telling him that Cavalcanti was desperately anxious to contact him and threatened to come to Sidmouth himself![20] And a further letter, addressed to the Reform Club, ends, 'Cavalcanti is cross with me because you are too busy to see and talk with him.'[21] But why Vivien's anger?

It developed in part because neither of them could escape from the demands made on Greene even on their first holiday together for many years. Undoubtedly Vivien had planned the holiday without the children carefully as a return to the 'love nest', but it failed. Greene was back in London working for MI6, and, most disturbing for Vivien, had returned to his old address, 19 Gower Mews, Dorothy's home. This is clear because the undated letter to Charles Evans has Dorothy's address on it. If in the past Vivien had hoped she could remain the loved one, in spite of his mistress in London, a feeling reinforced by Greene's warm letters from West Africa, she now knew that the affair had not died or even subsided. She sent his mail to the Reform Club because she couldn't countenance sending it to his lover's home. She knew she had failed.

13

Agents Three: Greene, Muggeridge and Philby

They can decipher a close-stool to signify a Privy Council,
a flock of geese a senate, a lame dog an invader . . .

– JONATHAN SWIFT

B Y the time the monsoon rain was falling upon Freetown and the land around Greene's home had become a quagmire, the spirits of the British were low. Tobruk had fallen to the Germans on 21 June 1942, and over 30,000 troops had been captured: 'Defeat is one thing, disgrace is another,' wrote Churchill. The British had lost 50,000 men in a fortnight and Field-Marshal Rommel had advanced almost 400 miles towards Cairo.

The turning point of the war was to be here, in North Africa. General Montgomery, newly appointed, raised the morale of the defeated British, though September and most of October were anxious months. Then battle was joined at El Alamein on 23 October 1942. A thousand guns bombarded the enemy lines at dawn. This time, Montgomery outnumbered Rommel's forces in men, tanks and armament. The British proved irresistible.

Yet, ironically, it wasn't only the British superiority in men and weapons or Montgomery's leadership that led to the defeat of the German forces; the secret activities of British Intelligence substantially helped to win the day. Since February 1940 some of the best minds in the country had been assembled at Bletchley Park in Buckinghamshire to break the cipher system of the German Enigma machine. Within weeks of doing this, the cryptoanalysts were decrypting, translating, and interpreting 1,000 intercepts of high-grade signals every twenty-four hours. A senior analyst remembered: 'What a moment it was! It was pure black magic.'[1] By March 1943, when Greene returned from Africa to work at SIS headquarters, there was confidence that the Allies would win the war.

Greene was posted to the headquarters at St Albans, where he was busy beyond expectations. Of his experiences here he wrote: 'I'm only allowed to come up for air at 8 every evening.'[2] The SIS complex was made up of three country houses on Lord Verulam's estate – the first, Prae Wood, was both the home and office of Felix Cowgill, head of Section V. The middle building, Glenalmond, housed the rest of the officers of Section V, and the third building was the General Registry, which served the whole of the SIS.

There was little formal training in counter-intelligence, rather one sat down at a desk and got on with it, and was asked if there were any questions or problems. Malcolm Muggeridge recalled:

My instructions at St. Albans were to familiarise myself with the working of Section V and generally . . . put myself in the picture. This involved going from room to room and from desk to desk, and listening to particular officers explaining what they were at; whether directing and supervising the operations of agents in the field or devising and planting deception material . . . [3]

Essentially, MI6 gathered enemy information and disseminated false information; the ultimate goal was to penetrate the enemies' secret operations, to become a part of them, to know their intentions. If you can persuade your opponents to believe the disinformation provided so completely that it enters their files and comes to be accepted, then the enemy can be misled and their reactions controlled.

Greene saw the work of MI5, which was more straightforward than that of MI6, as a form of spying on his colleagues. His dislike came out sharply in a letter to his friend David Low, the bookseller, who had accidentally suggested Greene was with MI5: 'You insult me when you suggest that I was ever MI5. I've never spied on my own countrymen!'[4]

Kim Philby wrote to me of Greene's work in Section V: 'We were six officers working in what had been a spacious drawing-room, so our paper work was interrupted by much shop-talk – little of it memorable.'[5] In those early days of 1943 Watts looked after Spain, Charles de Salis Portugal and Portuguese possessions, and Trevor Wilson Gibraltar, Tangier and Morocco. Trevor Wilson and Greene were both Catholics and friends. In the early 1950s it was to be Wilson, then British consul in Hanoi, who would open up Vietnam to Greene. Philby and Tim Milne (nephew of A. A. Milne) sat opposite each other at a large desk close to the window, which looked out on to a pond.[6] Milne handled special material related to Enigma. As de Salis's understudy, Greene worked at the Portuguese desk and when de Salis was drafted to Lisbon in August 1943, he took over.

Recruited for the duration of the war, these men were amateurs. Unlike the leading members of the SIS, experienced professionals who acted and dressed like diplomats, the men under Philby were more free-wheeling. Muggeridge explained their outlook:

> The prevailing fashion among the war-time MI6 intake . . . was to aim at being as unlike the conventional idea of a diplomat as possible; slouching about in sweaters and grey flannel trousers, drinking in bars and cafés and low dives rather than at diplomatic cocktail parties and receptions, boasting of their underworld acquaintances and liaisons. Philby, in this sense, may be taken as the prototype of them all and was, indeed, in the eyes of many of them, a model to be copied.[7]

At lunchtime the whole group retired to the local pub, The King Harry. They sat in the garden if it was fine, eating sandwiches and drinking draught beer and talking. It was the best moment of the day: 'I remember with pleasure those long Sunday lunches at St Albans [Greene wrote] when the whole sub-section relaxed under his leadership for a few hours of heavy drinking . . . '[8] Greene's estimate of Philby's character must have been formed in these favourable circumstances. As leader of the group and as a British intelligence officer, Philby was brilliant and won the respect and affection of all his colleagues.[9] He seemed to be against the Government, yet maintained relations with his tedious superiors, and was very much the new 'casual man'.

Philby praised Greene for working 'quietly, coolly and competently'. Moreover, according to Philby, Greene wrote 'terse, sometimes devastating, marginalia' on incoming correspondence: 'By some freak of memory, one of his marginal comments remains in my mind verbatim. "Poor old 24000, our Man in Lisbon [probably Cecil Gledhill, head of station in Lisbon] charging around like a bull in a china shop, opening up vast vistas of the obvious." '[10]

The purpose of Section V was to counter enemy intelligence activities.[11] Information would come in part from agents in the field – in Greene's case, chiefly from Lisbon and the SIS field officers in neutral Portugal – but much of it came from Enigma decodes.

Muggeridge, then SIS man in Lourenço Marques in Mozambique, provided evidence of the relationship between the officer in the field and Enigma. He was given the task of stopping the enemy's flow of information about convoys sailing to North Africa, where they were

1 Greene with the Finnish edition of *Brighton Rock*

2 London in the blitz

3–4 (left) 14 North Side, before it was hit by a landmine and shored up afterwards

5 (below) Greene in London, 1945

6 Catherine Walston's christening:
standing, John Rothenstein,
Vivien Greene;
seated, Catherine Walston,
the Reverend Vincent Turner

7 Dorothy Glover (right), with
Harry Walston behind her

8 Greene at the City hotel in Freetown, Sierra Leone

9 Freetown

10–12 Agents three: Graham Greene, Kim Philby
and Malcolm Muggeridge

13 Film director Carol Reed (*The Fallen Idol* and *The Third Man*)
discussing a script with Greene

14–15 (*above left*) The giant Ferris wheel in Vienna; (*above right*) a kiosk entrance to the sewers in Vienna – both used in filming *The Third Man*

16 Joseph Cotton and Orson Welles in *The Third Man*

17 Greene with François Mauriac

18 Correcting *The Heart of the Matter* at Thriplow

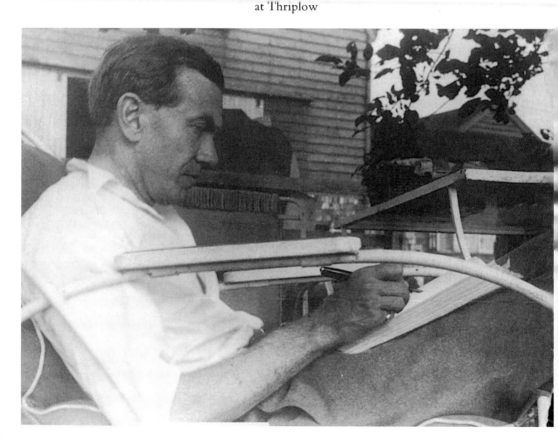

being torpedoed by German submarines. Both the German Consul-General, Wertz, and the Italian Consul-General, Campini, were, through their agents, providing German submarines with accurate information as to the whereabouts of British shipping. On arrival in Lourenço Marques, where he stayed at the same hotel as Wertz and Campini, Muggeridge first deciphered a long telegram from London:

> It came from Philby, as I knew from the style, and provided a résumé of the espionage scene in Lourenço Marques in the light of Wertz's and Campini's latest telegrams. All their traffic was being intercepted and cracked at Bletchley; so I had the advantage of knowing just what they were up to . . . It also meant, of course, that my activities showed in the Wertz–Campini traffic, so that any . . . pretence practised on my account without reference to London was bound to become known there at once . . . The Philby directive suggested that it might be a good idea to concentrate on infiltrating the Campini *apparat* rather than the Wertz one, since the personality of Campini, to judge from his boastful, high-flown style, seemed the more vulnerable of the two.[12]

Though Muggeridge judged the source of his directives to be Philby, his conclusion was based solely on his recognition of Philby's style. It must have been Greene controlling Muggeridge, among other agents, since he was in charge of the Portuguese desk, although his telegrams would need to be passed by Philby. Whilst suggesting that Greene was not entirely successful as an officer in the field in Freetown – 'He would need to have the qualities of gangsterism and he was too nice to be a gangster really, though he's good at describing them'[13] – Muggeridge none the less allowed that Greene was very able at headquarters:

> I mean he was tremendously good at dealing with agents and working out cover plans and things like that and justifiably was very highly thought of. He understood what he was about as his novel *Our Man in Havana* shows. It's the most brilliant book on intelligence that's ever been written because it gets inside the whole fantasy of the thing. He gives you the whole feeling of it, the ludicrousness of it and yet the way people get caught up in it. You have to take it seriously and yet it's all based on a fantasy.[14]

Even recruitment into the service had this sense of absurd fantasy. Greene had been brought into the 'firm' by attending special parties given by a Mr Smith. Another intelligence officer at St Albans recalled his recruitment into the SIS when he was an army officer with one pip. The 'firm' was looking for someone who could speak Spanish, and the interviewer, a Mr Carter, asked if he could pass himself off as a businessman in Madrid. He wasn't told what it was about, only that it was a War Office appointment. He had no idea of the set up, but was simply told that he'd just signed the Official Secrets Act and was to go downstairs at 5.30 and catch a bus.

'Someone shouted, "Anyone for Yoicks," and a lot of secretary types got up and finally we got to St. Albans, drawing up to a house called Yoicks.' Next morning a car took him to the Glenalmond office, and the recruit discovered that his Mr Carter was Kim Philby.[15] Another prospective agent also had little explained to him about his future work in SIS: 'I can't tell you what sort of a job it would be. All I can say is that if you join us, you mustn't be afraid of forgery, and you mustn't be afraid of murder.'[16]

Often MI6's devious work demanded that an agent give the enemy vital information prior to offering misinformation, thus, in a sense, acting out the part of a traitor. For example, Muggeridge's task in Lourenço Marques was to persuade the Abwehr (German Secret Service) that a highly regarded informer, successfully supplying the Germans with important information about British shipping, was in fact passing on suspect material. His immediate aim was to plant acceptable deception material. To do that he had to find out the German informer (his codename would already be known by the British through Enigma), find his sub-agents and suborn them by offering them information which in the first instance would be real and believable. Only later would false information be provided, making the German agent suspect to his masters.

Muggeridge did not have the best reputation as an agent in the field.[17] Greene, who was his direct contact man in London, and other ex-SIS officers, thought he was unreliable: 'In Lourenço Marques', Greene said, 'he tried to run a double agent in the German embassy. He was giving much too much information of greater value to his double agent than he was receiving in return. He was not a success which made him very anti the SIS and he *knows* that he was a bit of a flop.'[18]

Muggeridge returned to England and joined Greene and Philby in London in 1944. The SIS officer who succeeded him in Lourenço Marques inherited Muggeridge's car and found in it a loaded pistol and a top secret document.[19]

*

During the summer of 1943 Section V moved to London, to 7 Ryder Street, later to be the offices of *The Economist*. The front entrance carried the sign 'Charity House'. It was a building of some mystery. To gain entry, a pass was necessary which stated that the holder was a member of the Greenwood Country Club. Ryder Street runs into St James's Street close to White's. Sir Stuart Menzies ('C' – the head of the SIS) was a member of this exclusive club, as were other senior wartime intelligence officers.

'C' had his offices on the fourth floor of 54 Broadway. Set in one wall was a concealed door that led to a passage connecting his office to his official residence at 21 Queen Anne's Gate and he came through a door into his drawing room at Queen Anne's Gate. Thus 'C' could come and go between headquarters and his apartment without being seen.[20]

A number of visitors to this inner sanctum have given their impressions of it. Muggeridge described his first meeting with 'C': 'I made my way . . . [to] where I found two sedate, middle-aged secretaries who gave an immediate impression of being exceptionally well-bred.'[21] Muggeridge didn't give their names, but they have been identified as Kathleen Pettigrew (the model for Miss Moneypenny, secretary to 'M' in Ian Fleming's James Bond novels) and her assistant, Evelyn Jones. Jones was physically attractive, but Miss Pettigrew, according to Robert Cecil, was a 'formidable gray-haired lady with a square jaw of the battleship type'.[22] Every visitor had to wait until the red light outside 'C''s door changed to green before entering. The door was of double thickness, one of the layers being padded with quilted leather to make it sound-proof.

'C' was 'a regular officer in the Life Guards, sandy-haired, with a soft handshake and an air of indolence, belied by a glint of cunning in his brown eyes'.[23] He was formidable and to be summoned by him was disturbing. Yet by nature he was gentle, even generous. Kim Philby, who had little genuine admiration for his superiors and colleagues, spoke of an 'enduring affection' for his old chief. Professor Hugh Trevor-Roper had good reason to remember 'C''s generosity because he was court-martialled *in camera*:

> I was secretly denounced as being probably in touch with the Germans, and more openly – and more justly – accused of consorting with the more immediate enemy, MI5. I was once summoned to be dismissed. How well I recall that 'trial' . . . with Colonel Vivian [deputy chief of the SIS] as prosecutor and 'C' as judge! . . . [Vivian] maintained with increasing urgency, and in lamentable tones, that whatever the merits of the case, it was quite

impossible, after this, for me to remain in the organization. However, thanks to 'C', I did remain.[24]

Greene used his experience of 'C' and his offices in his novel *Our Man in Havana*, as the epilogue reveals. Wormold has admitted to the SIS that he has been fabricating all his supposed secret activities, and that his agents, for whom he was being paid, were imaginary. He is brought home to be court-martialled, *in camera*, just as Trevor-Roper was, though Greene makes some minor changes. He takes us not to 'C''s offices on the fourth floor, but to a long basement corridor, where of course the red light has to change to green outside the chief's door before Wormold has permission to enter. Greene has modified the appearance of 'C': no sandy hair, but a black monocle and a baby-blue glass eye, yet the mildness of response is quintessentially Menzies's.

Wormold doubts whether he can be charged under the Official Secrets Act: 'He had invented secrets, he hadn't given them away.' No one shouts at him and there is only the chief in the room. Far from being threatened he is offered a job: 'We thought the best thing for you under the circumstances would be to stay at home – on our training staff. Lecturing. How to run a station abroad. That kind of thing.'[25] And further, incredibly, Wormold is offered an OBE, a decoration also awarded to Kim Philby, for his service. Sir James Easton said that if Philby had been detected as a Soviet spy at an early date, he would not have been shot or sent to prison: "'C' would have posted him out of Broadway as a tutor' (like the offer to Wormold) and 'then arranged that he be placed on permanent sabbatical'.[26]

*

From Ryder Street Greene carried on his work of counter-intelligence against the Abwehr in the Iberian peninsula: 'By the end of the War, those Abwehr who were not working for us, we knew were working with completely imaginary agents and receiving pay to give to their agents, agents who did *not* exist. The Abwehr were wiped out in a sense.'[27] Greene admitted in *Ways of Escape* that his Secret Service comedy, *Our Man in Havana*, is based on what he learned from his work in 1943–4.[28]

The particular agent who inspired Greene's Wormold was an agent named Paul Fidrmuc, alias *Ostro*. Fidrmuc, a Czech businessman in his twenties, looked like a blond German. In 1940 he became a German citizen, worked for the Abwehr for a number of years in Denmark and Rome, and then settled in Portugal. His reports to the Abwehr originated in Lisbon and were then passed on to Berlin. British intelligence officers who knew him in the field in Lisbon called him 'the canoe man' because he was always 'hanging about the sea around Lisbon. We thought he was looking out for U-boats.'[29] By the autumn of 1943 Paul Fidrmuc was fully operative.

Fidrmuc first came to SIS notice when his secret reports to the Abwehr, found in the decrypts from Bletchley Park, reached St Albans.[30] Even before Greene arrived in St Albans in March 1943, the British had, through the Radio Security Service (RSS), intercepted thirty-seven *Ostro* reports. Ostensibly they came from a wide scatter of countries – Egypt, South Africa, India, the United States and Britain. *Ostro*'s reports on Britain were recognised by British Intelligence as fraudulent, but they were well written, carefully structured to give the impression that the reports came from various agents in the field. Certainly the Abwehr believed that *Ostro* had four or five agents in England and regarded him as one of their best sources of information. His imaginary agents were supposed to be communicating with him in Lisbon by secret writing. British Intelligence considered discrediting him on several occasions, though that would have been difficult since he had such a high reputation with the Abwehr. And all the time, Fidrmuc was studying English press reports, cooking up his information and seemingly handling his completely phoney agents.

Another agent, cover name *Garbo*, was as remarkable as *Ostro* and also contributed to the creation of Greene's Mr Wormold. In 1942 Bletchley realised that the Abwehr Enigma traffic between Madrid and Berlin contained reports, supposedly from a German agent in the United Kingdom, which were too ludicrous to be true – about drunken orgies in Liverpool, Glasgow dock-workers prepared to sell anyone out for a litre of wine. The British were right to believe that the agent was not even living in England. It turned out that *Garbo* was a brilliant amateur called Juan Pujol García, who was living in Lisbon. García, a 29-year-old Spaniard of good family, deeply devoted to the cause of British victory, approached our man in Lisbon. He also approached the Abwehr, was recruited by them, provided with secret ink, questionnaires and an accommodation address in Madrid – this last as a place to send his reports from England! In his room in Lisbon, he operated with a map and a *Blue Guide* to the United Kingdom, a Portuguese study of the British fleet and an Anglo-French vocabulary of military terms.

When the SIS arranged for *Garbo* to travel to the United Kingdom, he told the Abwehr that he was visiting London on behalf of the Spanish security services. Once in London, he continued his reports and his sub-agents grew in number to almost thirty, for many of whom *Garbo* asked payment. These non-existent agents were a mixed lot – a garrulous officer in the Royal Air Force, an official at the Ministry of Information of extreme left-wing views, a Venezuelan businessman living in Glasgow, a communist Greek sailor operating in eastern Scotland, a Gibraltese waiter working in service canteens, an Anglophobe sergeant with the US army service of supply and even Welsh nationalists in the Swansea area.

Sometimes the information *Garbo* sent to his controller in Madrid was absolutely accurate and would have been of inestimable value to the Germans, if it had been received *on time*. For example, he correctly reported the hot tip – supposedly from his Ministry of Information agent – that the Allies were about to invade French North Africa. Alas, the letters were somehow delayed in the post and did not reach Lisbon until 7 November, after the convoys had been spotted by German reconnaissance, and a few hours before the landing took place. The Abwehr trusted their remarkable agent: 'Your last reports are all magnificent but we are sorry they arrived late.'[31]

*

The business of spying, actual or fabricated, is not limited to the acts of individual agents – it extends to the highest levels of government. In order to prepare for the Portuguese desk, Greene's first job was to produce what was called a Purple Primer, a handbook containing a list of all persons in Portugal known to have been employed by Axis intelligence services, with a description of the roles they had played. This entailed going through the card index, which had been built up over the years, sorting out the true information from the false and compressing it into a usable form. It was a monumental task, for there were on file almost 2,000 confirmed enemy agents (by VE Day, the figure had reached 3,000) and 200 Germans living in Portugal with known Intelligence connections. Greene also had to deal with forty-six commercial firms in Iberia identified as commercial covers for enemy espionage.[32]

There was another reason for compiling the Purple Primer: it would have been immensely useful in the event of an Allied invasion of the peninsula. Working on the Purple Primer was an excellent preparation for dealing with the complications of Portuguese agents whom you could hardly trust, because, although they were working for the Allies, they were also in the pay either of the German or Portuguese Intelligence.

Greene's main purpose at the Portuguese desk was to collect intelligence concerning the peninsula, a labyrinth of spies and intrigue, and make some sense of it – an exercise for which his special abilities and experience had prepared him. To give some idea of the complexities he faced: Lisbon was used by UK and American agents as a departure point; German Intelligence used Lisbon as a base for collecting information about Allied Atlantic convoys which was passed on to German submarines; the Portuguese authorities, particularly the dreaded German-trained security police, PIDE (Polícia Internacional e de Defesa do Estado) headed by pro-Nazi Captain Lourenço, turned a blind eye to German clandestine radio stations which reported on the movement of Allied shipping. So long as the Axis forces seemed to be winning the war, every assistance was provided.[33]

German Intelligence activities were also condoned in 'neutral' Spain, not only because its government was fascist, but because the Spanish police force had been reorganised in 1940 by the head of the SS, Heinrich Himmler. The head of the Spanish police was on the German Intelligence payroll as were many of his subordinates. Admiral Canaris, head of the Abwehr, was a personal friend of General Franco and had set up observation posts at Algeciras and Tangier, on either side of the Straits of Gibraltar. Given the dominance of Himmler and the Abwehr, the Germans, in effect, had control over the intelligence and counter-intelligence of Spain.[34]

By the time Greene took over the Portuguese desk, the war was already turning in the Allied favour. It was possible to provide irrefutable evidence that Portugal was assisting the Axis powers and taking a pro-German stance, although Portugal's leader, Dr Salazar, was not initially receptive to the evidence that the British offered.

There had already been secret talks (to be found in the OSS files) between Salazar's Government and the British Foreign Office regarding the protection which could be given to Portugal in the event of an Axis invasion. They concluded that guerrilla warfare would follow an Axis invasion, including the active application of a scorched-earth policy and the turning over of the Azores and Portuguese colonies to the Allies for safe keeping and defence.[35] Whilst the police in Portugal were pro-fascist and unfriendly to the British, the Portuguese Legion, numbering some 150,000, were actively pro-British and sought arms from the SIS. Salazar himself was wary of the British.

To win Salazar over, the SIS built up a tremendous dossier proving that his police were not following a neutral policy. They named stevedores in sabotage operations, Portuguese police officers who were under German influence; they offered correspondence between the Abwehr and Portuguese agents proving how active the

Abwehr was; they listed the known German networks and radio stations in Portugal, thus establishing that German activities against British convoys stemmed from Lisbon. They presented Salazar with such impressive proofs of Portuguese collaboration during the spring of 1943 that he finally exercised his authority and made the Germans close down their radio stations and informer networks. This effectively brought Salazar on to the Allies' side. He became increasingly sympathetic to the Allies as it became apparent that they were winning the war.[36]

Once the tide turned in the Allies' favour, the SIS in Ryder Street had the brainwave of trying to 'turn' the German Security Service in Portugal, and Greene was involved in the operation as the head of the Portuguese desk. It was a daring procedure and great care had to be taken in selecting the type of German in the Security Service who could be approached to work for the Allies. Sir Dick White, then of MI5, told Philby that he had an agent, 'Klop' Ustinov,* who was originally Russian and had worked at the German embassy in London in 1934 as press attaché. He was an ardent anti-Nazi and *knew* who were and were not Nazis in the Abwehr.

Ustinov was sent to Lisbon in the spring of 1944. He had a comic-sounding cover name – *Middleton-Pendleton*. When he arrived, he was given a flat to share with an SIS officer and, with the names of the German embassy staff in Lisbon at hand, picked out various consular officials known to him as anti-Nazis who might respond to his overtures. He simply sent them 'Greetings from Klop' and arranged a meeting of the kind that seems to an outsider somewhat juvenile: 'Meet me by the 3rd oak tree at the top of the mountain.' Klop would return an hour later and say: 'Yes. He's willing to work with us.' It wasn't only high-ranking officers, but clerks and secretaries who were 'turned'. Klop would invite a secretary to lunch and advise the SIS officer to leave the flat and not come back until 1.30, by which time the girl would be sobbing and willing to offer the SIS inside information.[37]

As the Germans continued to lose the war, military and consular men who had also hated Nazis were increasingly willing to spy for the Allies. Some offered to work for the SIS without any persuasion. One was a German with the cover name *Artist*. *Artist*, a highly placed Abwehr official, had approached one of Greene's men in Lisbon and

---

* Ustinov, a brilliant agent, was tiny and round. A great impersonator (much like his son, actor Peter Ustinov), one of his party pieces was to imitate Queen Victoria with a white handkerchief over his head. He looked, I was told, like a bed bug imitating Queen Victoria. At the end of the war, he interrogated Paul Fidrmuc, whose activities inspired Greene's *Our Man in Havana*.

had arranged to meet him in the Monserrate Gardens at Cintra. He arrived dressed in a pin-stripe suit and an Anthony Eden hat, yet was every inch the Prussian. His greeting startled the SIS officer: 'I recruited three people to spy for me against Britain. I knew them to be pro-British and knew that they would double-cross me. I am pleased you are running my agents. Now run me.'

Artist proved valuable to the SIS in many ways, not least in protecting those Abwehr men who had defected, telling the authorities that they were not double agents. He was a courageous man who provided information about the organisation and operations of the Abwehr, and about political and economic conditions in Germany and occupied Europe. He protected some of Britain's best agents, some of whom escaped. *Artist* was not so fortunate. British Intelligence knew that he was not safe, but did not act promptly enough. He was kidnapped by the Sicherheitsdienst (SD) under Himmler, and taken back to Germany in the false bottom of a trunk. Almost fifty years after the event, there was still anguish in the voice of the SIS man who related his fate in Germany: '*Artist* perished at Oranienburg concentration camp, hanged by Hitler not because his cover was blown, but because the SD were closing in on all people not of their sort. SIS could have warned him. We let him down.'[38]

*

Greene gave a terse and somewhat random account of his activities at London headquarters:

It was an office job really . . . Giving directions to our man in Lisbon. For example, the thing which I have always wondered was whether Kim Philby smiled up his sleeve when I arranged to have Admiral Canaris, head of the Abwehr, harassed. I had him harassed, when he went to Portugal, by giving the police information about the meetings he was holding and so on. My telegrams had to be passed by Kim and he didn't prevent it and everyone knows *now* that Admiral Canaris was on our side. He was anti-Hitler. But there was talk on the German side of a separate peace which the Russians were very much afraid of. I wonder whether Kim knew this and was letting me harass him because the Russians feared a separate peace.[39]

Moscow was afraid that, if Germany were released from her war with Britain, she would be able to concentrate on defeating the Soviet Union, thus bringing an end to communism. Philby explains his attitude at the time in *My Silent War*: 'It often appeared that the British wanted a simple return to the status quo before Hitler, to a Europe comfortably dominated by Britain and France through the medium of reactionary governments just strong enough to keep their own people in order and uphold the *cordon sanitaire* against the Soviet Union.'[40] Philby had been instructed to frustrate moves toward a separate peace with Germany, at any cost, and did so.

These machinations are made clear in the intriguing defection of Otto John, the German who warned the British that plans were afoot to assassinate Hitler. Philby put paid to negotiations with John which, if they had succeeded, would have saved lives by bringing the war to a swifter conclusion.

Otto John came to Lisbon from Madrid and met with Tony Graham-Maingott, an agent under Cecil Gledhill at the Lisbon station. At first, the meeting was indirect:

I flew to Lisbon and Juan fetched me from my hotel. We first took a zigzag walk through the centre of Lisbon and then a taxi into the suburbs where my British interviewer was waiting for us in a car belonging to one of his Portuguese agents. Tony Graham-Meingott [sic] was a middle-aged, tubby, decorous-looking gentleman, radiating *bonhomie*. We drove out of the city into rolling country, left the car by the roadside and walked along country lanes between stubble-fields and vineyards with our eyes skinned for the approach of any unwanted observer. As we talked I gained the impression that he was not speaking freely and had been briefed for our meeting by London [Philby] . . . Without giving names I outlined to him the conspiracy to overthrow Hitler, its motives and aims together with its united political backing.[41]

The leader of the conspiracy wanted to know whether or not the British Government would be prepared to negotiate with the new Reich Government led by him. Maingott's answer was: 'The German opposition must soon *prove itself* [emphasis added] by doing something if it wishes to get a hearing in London.'[42].

John gives no date, but the meeting probably took place in November 1943 – when Greene was handling the Portuguese desk and thus involved in organising the meeting, though Philby would be supervising. What 'prove itself' must mean was that the assassination of Hitler was overdue. If it happened, London would reconsider its position. It would help to bring about the end of the war and even if it failed, it could still bring about extraordinary disaster for the Axis cause.

On 20 July 1944 Colonel von Stauffenberg made his unsuccessful attempt to assassinate Hitler which led to the death of thousands of Germans, including some of their great military leaders. Philby kept Otto John away from London for as long as possible so that the remaining opposition to Hitler was not precisely known, and the British Government was not enticed into making a separate peace with Germany. The communists wanted to install a puppet communist Government in Germany after the war and Philby, by scuttling Otto John's overtures to the Allies, was instrumental in seeing that that in part came about.[43]

Yet how much admired Philby was comes out in correspondence between *The Times* and the Foreign Office in 1944. The foreign news editor wrote to Sir Frank Roberts at the Foreign Office, requesting that Philby be allowed to become a war correspondent. Roberts's answer of 1 March indicates the favourable opinion the SIS had of Philby: 'We should be bound to recommend most strongly against his removal from his present job . . . his present work is so important, and he performs it with such exceptional ability, that his departure would be a real loss to us.'[44]

While Greene was at St Albans, Philby was actively burrowing for information for his Moscow masters. From 1940 to 1944 his KGB controller was Anatoli Gorsky, whose cover name was *Henry*. His meetings with Gorsky often took place quite casually on a park bench in Kensington Gardens, not far from the Soviet embassy.[45]

Philby admitted that after moving to Ryder Street, the intimacy at St Albans shared by Section V ended:

Instead of living at close quarters in a small country town, we were scattered all over the city. We even rose to the dignity of separate offices, which further diminished the feast of reason and the flow of soul. I cannot remember Graham ever visiting my quarters; I certainly never visited his. Our contacts were limited to the lunch hour, and to the after-hours drink at a pub before dispersing to our homes.[46]

Thirty-five years later, Greene's experiences are mirrored in the first sentence of his novel *The Human Factor*: 'Castle, ever since he had joined the firm as a young recruit more than thirty years ago, had taken his lunch in a public house behind St James's Street, not far from the office.' Greene identified the pub where he used to drink with Kim Philby as the King's Arms behind St James's Street.

Philby recalled Greene's somewhat adolescent urge to shock people. Some of the incidents were, said Philby, 'really funny': 'We were eating fish and chips in an overcrowded pub near Ryder Street and Graham roared, quite unnecessarily loudly: "This fish tastes of ammonia." There was a startled silence followed by the clatter of cutlery on china; then a swelling susurration – "You know, it *does* taste of ammonia," "Thought it smelt kinda funny meself," etc. – with Graham on his bar-stool, grinning in triumph.'[47]

Apart from meeting in 'their pub', Philby and Greene seldom spent time alone together. Philby regretted that he didn't get to 'know' Greene and that as a Soviet penetration agent, he could not allow Greene to get to know him:

There were usually colleagues to put a distance between us. But I felt in him a more personal factor: a deeply held sense of privacy on matters which seriously engaged him . . . not once did he refer to Catholicism in any context whatsoever. I had no wish to enter the forbidden zone. Any attempt . . . to probe his defences . . . would have exposed me to his probing of mine, which, for obvious, if melancholy reasons, was inadmissible.[48]

The curtain of privacy was raised at least once, when Philby unexpectedly met Dorothy Glover:

One afternoon his secretary, in great agitation, summoned me to his office: Graham was in great pain, rolling about on the floor. He told me not to worry, it was an internal haemorrhage which he had had before; could I just send him home? I got a taxi and went with him, to some address in Bloomsbury [this would be 19 Gower Mews]. On the way there, he asked me a favour. 'If when we get to my place you notice anything irregular, please keep it to yourself.' Of course! Well, what happened? When I rang his doorbell, a lady came out, scooped him up and took him inside. I wondered at such sensitivity from the tough man of the pub-talk. Incidentally, this is the first time that I have mentioned the incident to anyone.[49]

Apart from the fact that he was living with Dorothy, what could Greene have considered so irregular? In any case, it would hardly have troubled Philby, who was living at the time with Aileen Furse, when she was seven months pregnant with their fourth child and still unmarried.

Regardless of any friendship between Philby and Greene, everyone in Section V knew who was boss. Miss Kennard Davis, a secretary in the typing pool, remembered how cold-hearted Philby could be in his handling of staff. She recalled coming into Greene's office one day: 'He was gripping the chair and his eyes were glinting with anger. I asked him what was the matter and he said: "I've just had a caning from the headmaster." '50

*

By the end of 1944, by means of brilliant office manœuvring, Philby had got rid of Felix Cowgill, head of Section V, and had succeeded in taking over a new anti-communist section at a time when the Cold War was beginning to build up.* The irony of the situation was not lost on him. In his memoirs he wrote: '[Soviet] Headquarters had informed him [his control in London] that I must do everything, but *everything*, to ensure that I became head of Section IX.'

Cowgill had admired Philby enormously; everyone did. In his memoirs, Philby describes Cowgill as 'proud and impulsive, a man too big for his talents'.51 Robert Cecil later commented: 'Philby at one stroke had got rid of a staunch anti-communist [Major Cowgill] and ensured that the whole post-war effort to counter communist espionage would become known in the Kremlin. The history of espionage records few, if any, comparable masterstrokes.'52

Just prior to the Allied invasion of Europe on 6 June 1944, Graham Greene resigned from MI6. His departure came as a big surprise. He was not happy as an agent: 'it was a routine thing of collecting names and filing and making notes on cards and it was very dull. It was like working in an office.'53 Still, the question needs asking as to why Greene chose to resign at this dramatic moment in the war.

He gave his answer in two separate interviews:

I moved out of MI6 because Philby wanted to promote me and I didn't wish to be promoted, and I also wished to get abroad if I could. I quite unjustly thought it was a personal ambition on his part. He was moving up and I thought he was thinking of moving up his friends to guard his flanks as it were, for personal reasons. One knows now that they were not personal reasons.

And the man who should have been put in charge of the Iberian peninsula was a younger man than me, and had much more experience of dealing with the work. I refused the promotion and resigned.54

* Cowgill, nevertheless, remained on good terms with Philby's second wife, Aileen Furse, whom he deserted in England in the 1950s, to be with another man's wife in Beirut.

I transferred to PID [Political Intelligence Department] of the Foreign Office because they'd said that they would send me to France, as soon as the invasion took place, which they didn't do. They didn't keep their promise.[55]

Greene resigned in a gentlemanly fashion. He took Tim Milne and Philby to lunch at the Café Royal, ordered them a good meal and in the middle of it offered his resignation.[56] For Philby, Greene's resignation remained a deep mystery which still troubled him thirty-four years after the event. The situation revealed another aspect of Greene's character, though Philby was unsure just what it was:

In 1944, I received a promotion and, in the subsequent reshuffle of posts, the Iberian sub-section of Section V required a new head. The obvious man for the job on all counts was Graham. But when I raised the subject with him, he promptly resigned from the service altogether. He explained that he had not minded chivvying Portuguese on orders from above, but had no intention of taking personal responsibility for doing so. I did not find the explanation wholly convincing. Graham doing to order something he disapproved of? It sounded unlikely.[57]

It doesn't seem a likely explanation, but neither does Greene's.

Unquestionably, there was an obdurate side to Greene's nature. Job routine could easily become too much for him, and when it did, he got out. Philby offered a kinder explanation:

I prefer to think that the human factor in his job had been on his mind for some time. Pretty well all the Portuguese [agents] who played around with the Germans were of humble status and wretchedly poor; probably courting trouble for a new pair of shoes, and who could blame them? I could not think evil of them, and I am sure that Graham, with his greater charity and understanding, could not either. I also think that the wider futility of his occupation bore hard on Graham. The war was virtually won, nothing that he could do would hasten the end, and I had given him a pretext for cutting loose from a dreary and distasteful routine.[58]

Philby never understood why Greene refused a perfectly good promotion. If Greene's field officers in Lisbon were involved with Otto John in the early stages of plans to assassinate Hitler, it seems incredible that he should have suddenly resigned *before* the second front, before Stauffenberg's unsuccessful and tragic assassination attempt, and had himself transferred to the Political Intelligence Department (although Greene did have this itch to be near the front line and PID had promised that they would send him to France).

Comparing his old job with his new, however, it looks like a very curious decision. When Greene moved from MI6 to PID, he moved to an editorial job. At PID, he edited an anthology to be dropped over occupied France. Now Greene was an odd and brilliant man, but even odd, brilliant men accept promotion. In Ryder Street excitement must have been high – invasion pending and the possible assassination of Hitler – yet Greene got out. It is hard to believe that Greene would resign on the eve of D–Day, the emotional and strategic climax of a long war, without having a very important reason.

Perhaps Greene, always intuitive, resigned because he suspected that Philby was a Russian penetration agent. Greene once told me that if he had known that Philby was a Soviet counterspy, he 'might have allowed Philby 24 hours to flee as a friend, then reported him'. If Greene did suspect Philby, it would be just the kind of thing that would catapult him out of the service rather than share his suspicions with the authorities. And he would have had to contend with his own credo, established during his painful school years of divided loyalties. As a schoolboy, Greene had betrayed to his father the identity of his tormentor – Carter. He was not going to do that again.[59]

14

From Spy to Publisher

Times have changed since a certain author was executed
for murdering his publisher.

— J. M. BARRIE

As with mystics and soothsayers, Greene at times had dreams
which foreshadowed future events. He later described a dream
so vivid that, almost forty years on, the image remained in his mind:

> I woke up in bed and across the window went a small plane, with
> fire coming out of its tail, which then did a nose dive. Although I
> was working for MI6 and one heard stories that there was a secret
> weapon which was going to be unleashed by Hitler, I had, in my
> position, no knowledge of what kind of thing it was and so I was
> immensely surprised when the first night of the V1s came and one
> saw exactly the image that I'd seen in the dream.[1]

Almost a week after D-Day, on 12 June, the first V1 pilotless plane
crossed the English coast and fell on London. During the following
months 8,000 were launched against the city, 2,400 of which fell on
Kent.

The V1s had red tails and looked as if they were enemy fighters in
flames. The British cabinet christened them flying bombs, the man in
the street 'doodle bugs' for they seemed to doodle. When they ran
out of fuel they fell to earth and, being filled with high explosive,
burst with a roar and a blinding flash. The V1 was an unguided
missile, and it was, as Evelyn Waugh brilliantly described: 'as
impersonal as a plague, as though the city were infested with
enormous, venomous insects'.[2]

They came night and day; there was no warning, no time to seek
a safe shelter; abandoning dignity, all one could do was to throw
oneself on to the floor, under tables, into doorways. As many as

20,000 houses a day were damaged, and casualties were severe — 10,000 during the first week's bombing.

Greene's mother wrote of the missiles coming down near her home in Crowborough:

> Everybody in the village in a great state of excitement. People have been watching rockets all night. At any rate we lay in bed and rested our limbs if not our heads. The nights are awful. I don't mind the beasts [V1s] in the day time as you see our planes chasing them to open ground before firing [on them]. Then one hears a crash or not as the case may be. But at night we are surrounded by guns firing at them and I suppose planes. I just lie and shake. One's head feels awful. We go to bed very early to get some sleep. Last night we had slept till 2 before it started.[3]

June and July 1944 were months of heavy clouds, driving rain, leaden skies, and pilotless bombs. Greene was still living with Dorothy Glover, but no longer at 19 Gower Mews. They had moved to Gordon Square, an area regularly and heavily bombed. Surprisingly they rented the flat most vulnerable to attack: 'We got it very cheap during the flying bomb business,' Greene told me. 'It was a tiny rent and on the top floor. A bomb hits more easily if you're on the top floor and you are more likely to be killed than if you are on the ground floor,' hence the cheapness of the flat. The flat cost Greene 'something like three pounds a week, furnished'.[4]

In The End of the Affair, Greene describes the V1s first coming over and Bendrix (based on Greene) and Sarah (based on Catherine Walston) making love, but in this instance Greene used his experiences of making love to Dorothy under the threat of death from the V1 pilotless planes:

> the blitz had petered out with the great final raids of 1941. When the sirens went and the first robots came over, we assumed that a few planes had broken through our night defence . . . and at that moment, lying in the dark on my bed, we saw our first robot. It passed low across the Common and we took it for a plane on fire and its odd deep bumble for the sound of an engine out of control. A second came and then a third. We changed our minds about our defences. 'They are shooting them like pigeons,' I said, 'they must be crazy to go on.' But go on they did, hour after hour, even after the dawn had begun to break, until even we realised that this was something new.
>
> We had only just lain down on the bed when the raid started.

It made no difference. Death never mattered at those times – in the early days I even used to pray for it: the shattering annihilation that would prevent forever the getting up, the putting on of clothes, the watching her torch trail across to the opposite side of the Common . . . [5]

Greene wondered whether eternity might not after all exist as the endless prolongation of the moment of death, and that is the time he would have chosen, 'the moment of absolute trust and absolute pleasure, the moment when it was impossible to quarrel because it was impossible to think . . . the V1s didn't affect us until the act of love was over. I had spent everything I had, and was lying back with my head on her stomach and her taste . . . in my mouth when one of the robots crashed down on the common.'[6] That suspended moment of risk – 'the sudden waiting silence when the engine cut out' – was felt by all who experienced V1 bombing.

Since Greene was living in the midst of danger with Dorothy, one would expect that he'd be concerned about her future, but anxiety about Vivien and his family was uppermost. As Greene felt that the war made all expectations of life uncertain, he sent Laurence Pollinger some suggestions in the event of his death:

One would like to feel that a few pounds for one's impoverished family could still be wrung out of one's books, and I'd therefore be most grateful if you would help Vivien under those circumstances to produce:

a)   a book of short stories enlarging the Cresset volume.

b)   if Douglas [Jerrold] would consider such, a volume of essays of which I think there is ample material in store in a box of cuttings . . .

c)   Keeping *The Power and the Glory* in print and perhaps arranging Penguins or other rights for *The Man Within, Stamboul Train, A Gun for Sale.*

To go on to more cheerful matters . . . I suggest that I should write a preface to *The Lawless Roads* linking it up to *The Power and the Glory.* Presumably Douglas [Jerrold] would pay some kind of an advance in addition to the purchase price, but – except of course again in the event of death – I don't want him pressed hard about this.[7]

In July, Greene was still working for the Political Intelligence Department and his address was Editorial Unit, 43 Grosvenor Street, London. He ran a section with the novelist Antonia White,* producing a kind of *Reader's Digest* called 'Choix', to be dropped over France: 'It was supposed to have been a sort of secret, hidden propaganda of a cultural kind. I mean not obvious political propaganda but making the French aware of what had been going on in literature whilst their country had been occupied by the Germans. I was criticised severely by the chief of the department. The poem was called "Liberté". It was thought flippant to open with a French poem and take up the whole first page with a poem. It was not propaganda, you see, but I stuck to my guns.' Greene could not remember how many copies were produced, but he believed that none had survived: 'The aeroplane crews', he remarked mildly, 'probably threw them away rather than waste time dropping them.'[8]

On 14 July 1944 Greene wrote in high glee to his mother: 'My half-time release from Government service came through: starting on Monday as a publisher.'

*

Greene had known of the possibility of joining Eyre & Spottiswoode early in the war, for on 2 July 1940 he wrote to his mother: 'You'll be amused to hear that I've become a company director of a publisher – Eyre & Spottiswoode, who are also the King's Printers, so are soundly based. This will give me anyway £100 a year director's fees, if I'm called up. So long as I'm in London I shall be getting £100 free of tax entertainment allowance, whether in the Army or not.'

But it was what might happen after the war that pleased him most: 'After the war I shall go in to the office properly & learn publishing, & Douglas Jerrold, the managing director, indicates that he will be retiring reasonably soon, & that there is no other director who knows anything about books. So there may yet be a family-business open to Francis!' Greene's son was four years old at this time.[9]

During the war, Greene continued to receive his £100 tax-free

---

* Greene has his hero Mr Brown in *The Comedians* say: 'I served in the Political Intelligence Department of the Foreign Office, supervising the style of our propaganda to Vichy territory, and even had a lady-novelist as my secretary.'[10]

allowance, and it remained an enticement to him to go into the firm after the war. The understanding was that he would help to build up Eyre & Spottiswoode's fiction list (the firm's weak link) when 'the time was ripe'. According to David Higham, Douglas Jerrold thought he would be getting Greene's future novels. And Greene toyed with the idea of signing up his next two novels after the war with Heinemann, instead of his usual three: 'I feel that if I am in charge after the war at E. and S. it may very well be a good thing to change . . . After all a *salary* is something to cling to.' He then added, as if he felt the war had ended his career as a writer, 'I may not feel like writing any more books, except very occasionally.'[11]

It is extraordinary that Greene wrote this letter soon after he had completed one of his greatest entertainments, *The Ministry of Fear*, but one of his biggest fears was that the creative vein would run thin or run out entirely. The move to the commercial world of publishing was a means of protecting himself and his family. It made good business sense to Greene to change publishers after developing Eyre & Spottiswoode's fiction list, to move himself over in order to convince others to move also. Greene had a secret arrangement with Jerrold that Eyre & Spottiswoode would publish his future entertainments: 'say nothing to Charles [Evans, he wrote to his agent] about future entertainments being published by Eyre & Spottiswoode'.[12] But before that happened, he joined the firm, becoming a fully fledged publisher: 'I've been signing up my post-war future: 5 year contract with Eyre & Spottiswoode beginning at £1000 & going up by usual increments to £1500: in addition one's director's fee & entertainment allowance – of course the money from one's books. *In confidence*, Jerrold proposes to retire after giving me about 18 months training as a publisher & I shall then be in sole charge of the firm. This should be amusing.'[13] It wasn't entirely amusing. It was a desk job and Greene was busy. He was at his desk five days a week from ten o'clock till half-past five.

What was he like as a publisher? Anthony Powell, who had substantial private reasons for criticising Greene as a publisher, nevertheless praised him:

Greene . . . had spent the latter years of the war in the Secret Service. A man of very considerable practical ability (unlike many writers), his nervous energy, organising faculty, taste for conflict, sudden bursts of rage, would have made him successful in most professions . . . He soon set humming the veteran engine of Eyre & Spottiswoode . . . nevertheless, a chassis set rattling ominously under the force of the new dynamo.[14]

Some letters have survived which show Greene 'pushing' his authors. When sending out his autumn list, he approached leading reviewers such as J. C. Trewin of the *Observer*, mentioning first his 'best seller writers' – Mrs Parkinson Keyes, Major Yeats Brown, Algernon Cecil, David Masters and Arnold Lunn, who 'will obviously attract notice from their authors' reputations', but then singled out a number for special mention: Geoffrey Cotterell's *Then a Soldier*, 'one of the most amusing first novels which I personally have read in the last two years'; Colonel Wintle's *The Prisoner of Toulon*, 'the odd and extremely funny journal of a man who paints himself as something of a cross between a Blimp and a Card'; and Mervyn Peake's *Rhymes without Reason*, 'in the Carroll and Lear Tradition'.* 15

In February 1945 he sent Trewin his spring catalogue. He referred to other general books, but in speaking of novels selected only those which he felt he could genuinely recommend. Greene also began widening the scope of the Eyre & Spottiswoode list by bringing in foreign writers, specifically praising *Transit Visa* by the German communist Anna Seghers.16

In his final year as a publisher he selected Frank Tilsley's *Champion Road* for particular praise; again his judgment is succinct and accurate:

Tilsley . . . in spite of the praise he has received both from the intelligent and the popular critics, has always been hovering on the edge of writing his best book. *Champion Road* contains all that was to be found in his previous work – particularly that strain of almost obstinate honesty which has enabled him to dig out the truth from even an apparently banal situation – and in addition there is so much more. This is the book of Tilsley's which I have always wanted to publish and in it he reaches his maturity as a novelist.17

Greene started the Century Library, intending to bring back into print a series of forgotten classics. As he explained to Mrs Belloc Lowndes (the sister of Hilaire Belloc and author of the famous *Lodger*) the series would 'consist of a representative selection of the best fiction of this century'. Greene was not writing to Belloc Lowndes to suggest that he reprint one of *her* novels, but rather

---

* Peake, the author of the Gothic fantasy trilogy *Titus Groan* (1946), *Gormenghast* (1950), and *Titus Alone* (1959), was sick and in need. He was something of a genius and Greene's discovery.

approaching her because he thought she might know who the executors of Rhoda Broughton were, as he wanted to publish Broughton's *A Waif's Progress*. When he asked Evelyn Waugh to contribute an introduction to Saki's *The Unbearable Bassington*, Waugh replied that he would be delighted to do so, but refused payment by cheque ('because the state will snatch it') and suggested payment in kind:

> Money is not really much use these days . . . If you intend to publish a large number of novels in this series perhaps you might have the free intro. for a set; perhaps you could bind the *Unbearable Bassington* handsomely for me? Perhaps you would even give me some signed copies of your own work?[18]

Greene also approached George Orwell, whom he had met through a mutual friend, Michael Meyer, to write an introduction to any work by Merrick. Orwell jumped at the suggestion and offered to write one for *The Position of Peggy Harper*. Alas, when Greene left Eyre & Spottiswoode, Douglas Jerrold discontinued the Century Library and Orwell did not write his introduction.

*

On 1 August 1944 the Polish underground rose in Warsaw, but all were massacred. On 25 August the German commander in Paris surrendered to the Allies and Montgomery overran the V1 launching sites, but that only ended the first phase of the V1 bombing. The Germans then began releasing the V1s from planes and another 750 came over in the next few months. Then London had to face a greater and more sinister weapon of terror, the V2s.

The V2 rockets were 45 feet long and weighed 14 tons. They were silent, giving no warning, and were the most destructive weapons seen crossing London skies. It took only four V2s, falling on Croydon, to damage 2,000 homes. They travelled fast and the noise of the explosion, when it came, was very loud, like that of a gas explosion. Indeed, initially, the government put it about that they *were* gas explosions, but the great flashes of white light in the sky were enough for the general public to know that another secret weapon had arrived, one which gave no time for the anticipation of death.

During the period of the V1 and V2 bombing, Greene was on voluntary fire-watching duty, though not without causing trouble for staid, unimaginative authority, of the kind which always got up his sensitive nostrils.[19]

On one occasion Greene attacked Mr Webber because of his 'fantastically inefficient and childish ideas of organising a fire-guard':

Understanding that one had to report not later than half an hour before black-out, I arrived at 25 Gilbert Street last night about 10.15. I was told to go to 47 Mount Street and found the house locked. Half an hour later I tried again and found a guard there. He had an office chair to sit on – nothing else, not even a blanket.

With the help of a watchman, Greene eventually found his post, 'the absurd death-trap' at the head of a twisting iron emergency ladder, and set up his bed in room 2541 on the fourth floor below. There were no directions as to where a stirrup pump (to immobilise incendiary bombs) could be found or where water was available, and no issue of torches (in case of electricity failure). Greene ended his letter to Webber: 'If at any time you care to ring me . . . I will be delighted to tell you what you can do with your fire-guard duties.'[20]

Nine days later Webber replied to Greene in a detailed memo, which ended with a veiled threat: 'I am submitting a copy of this letter and the Fire Guard instructions together with a copy of your letter to the proper authorities in P.I.D. *for appropriate action.*'[21] Greene responded two days later denying most of Mr Webber's counter-charges and concluding: 'As I gather you wish to give a larger distribution to this personal memoranda, I enclose an extra copy for your convenience.'[22]

When Greene's quarrel with Webber was criticised, Greene gave a month's notice and tendered his resignation as a fire-guard.[*23]

*

But what was Greene, the publisher like at his office? We have his managing director's account, somewhat sardonic, certainly humorous, and often penetrating:

When he was a publisher he always came to our office very early in the morning, and always, from the first moment or so, in his favourite pose . . . of a man who had not been particularly early to bed and might leave again at any moment to get rid of his hangover at the Dog and Duck. He had usually announced his

---

* In fact, later letters to his mother show that he continued to fire-guard. Understandably so, since under the law men between the ages of sixteen and sixty could be compelled to fire-watch for at least forty-eight hours per month.

intention of going to be bored before leaving the previous evening, and when I asked him how the evening had passed off he always replied with a look of intense pleasure, 'It was perfectly ghastly' . . . His club must be what he calls 'the seedy club'; if he goes to a party it must be 'simply appalling' or 'perfectly ghastly'; even a quiet cocktail with two or three friends becomes, on leaving, 'a dreary little drink'.*[24]

Douglas Jerrold was excellent on how Greene spent the early part of his morning on arriving at his 'director's desk': 'He would settle down to the serious business of the day, telephoning with rapid succession to his bank, to his stockbroker, to his insurance agent, to his literary agent, to a film company or two, and, if it was really a busy morning, to two or three editors.' And Jerrold noted slyly: 'During these conversations the tortured conscience so frequently and so movingly on exhibition in his novels was notably absent.' Douglas Jerrold's distinction between the bright, capable publisher and Greene's wrestling with problems of good and evil is valuable: 'There was as much of the "Man Within" in the easy certainties implicit in the titles of the three novels of his maturity – *The Power and the Glory, The Heart of the Matter, The End of the Affair* – as in the un-ease with which the characters within the covers of these very fine books wrestle with the problem of good and evil, which is central to all Graham Greene's important writing.' And Jerrold went on to speak of the 'dangerous excited child': 'The child who, playing with the revolver, wanted sin without the guilt and now, in his maturity, wants the guilt without the sin'[25] which is too easy a judgement.

Part of this 'childishness' is reflected in Greene's pranks. Unlike the pranks of Victor Rhodes, the cuckolded husband in his 1959 play, *The Complaisant Lover*, Greene's pranks were on a more heroic scale. He would play a gigantic hoax on someone or some organisation, working the details out precisely. We can see this best in the case of Mrs Montgomery, a tale told by Jerrold but authenticated by Greene in interview:

Who is 'Mrs Montgomery'? The answer must be that there is no such person. She was invented to lighten his hours of work as a publisher . . . She began, with us, as the author of manuscript lost

---

* When Greene invited Kim Philby to become a member of the Authors' Club in Whitehall Court Greene gave as grounds, Philby later wrote: '(a) I was not an author and (b) it was the seediest club in London, so he said.'[26]

in the office and, not unnaturally, never found. In her righteous anger she summoned all and sundry by telephone to urgent meetings at impossible times in inconvenient places.[27]

Mrs Montgomery then took on a further reality. A notice from her biographer appeared in the *Spectator* asking to borrow any letters of Mrs Montgomery's which might be in the possession of others. This was followed by a letter from Mrs Montgomery protesting that the proposed biography 'was unauthorized and an impertinent intrusion on a life which she wished to remain private'.[28]

According to Jerrold, calls from Mrs Montgomery continued and when the manuscript could not be found, 'the spotlight fell on all Graham's colleagues, past and present, in turn'. Mrs Montgomery sent infuriated messages to all and sundry, for there can be no worse tragedy for a writer than the loss of a manuscript without a copy. Complaints came fast and furiously to colleagues at Eyre & Spottiswoode from many curious sources, even waiters, butlers, and bar owners. This is how Jerrold ended his story:

> I innocently asked the proprietor of our favourite bar if he had seen 'Mrs. Montgomery,' to be met with an enraged complaint that I was the sixth person who that morning had been badgering him about her. The next one who did so would be thrown out. He was!

Jerrold attributes the success of the prank to Greene's amazing attention to detail: 'It was [Greene's] care for detail, the meticulous attention to the psychology of the different recipients of messages and letters, the timing, the carefully concocted atmosphere of authenticity and urgency, which kept "Mrs Montgomery" alive among us for so long.'[29]

Greene once confided to me that he often acted like this during one phase of his depressive cycle:

> Mrs. Montgomery was a character I invented who sent a manuscript to Eyre & Spottiswoode which was unaccountably lost. Naturally they couldn't trace it. I had a woman [Dorothy Glover] phone up Jerrold as Mrs. Montgomery. Also I had 'Mrs. Montgomery' involved with a project for a magazine which would combine literature and psychoanalysis and I got a man (who was no friend of mine) involved in meeting Mrs. Montgomery to discuss the project. The rendezvous was made at El Vino's, whose manager I also didn't like. Thus I had it that

various other people converged on El Vino's asking for Mrs. Montgomery before the man was to arrive to discuss the project. By the time the man . . . arrived, the manager of El Vino's was half off his head and was very rough in turning him out of the bar.[30]

But eventually the hoax got curiously out of hand: 'And then a mysterious letter arrived from Edinburgh which wasn't part of the plot at all. I didn't know from whom it came. It referred to Mrs. Montgomery: it referred to the whole history and I thought that somebody else had interfered and taken a part in this, and it was time to finish the whole thing.'[31]

*

To improve the fiction list of Eyre & Spottiswoode, Greene decided he would try to enlist the French novelist François Mauriac. Knowing that Muggeridge was going to Paris, Greene asked him to seek out Mauriac and get him to agree to an English translation of his work. Promptly, in the early days of the Liberation, Muggeridge presented himself at the office of Mauriac's publisher, Grasset. Bernard Grasset had been a sympathiser if not a German collaborator and had, Muggeridge tells us, 'retired' to a psychiatric institution. His wife, a fierce red-haired woman, was left in charge, and when a uniformed Muggeridge appeared at their offices unannounced he caused some consternation. But Madame Grasset was greatly in favour of the translation and advised Mauriac to allow it. His acquiescence was by no means certain.

Muggeridge found Mauriac to be 'a frail, intense man of a kind often found among French writers and intellectuals, who seem to shake themselves to pieces with the vigour and urgency of their thoughts and words . . . . In his case, the impression was intensified by some impediment in his throat which caused him to speak always in a hoarse whisper.'[32]

Greene took up the story: 'Mauriac was very Anglophobic. I told Muggeridge to go to Mauriac and ask permission to bring out his books in a uniform edition. Mauriac, when he saw somebody in a British uniform come to his door, wondered what trouble he was in. When Muggeridge said, "I've come here on behalf of Eyre & Spottiswoode because they want to publish a collected edition of your books," why his whole attitude to England altered overnight. He became a great friend of mine.'[33]

The translation was brilliantly done by Gerard Hopkins and the first title, *La Pharisienne*, appeared as *A Woman of the Pharisees* in

1946. Greene brought Mauriac to England and with the help of the Oxford don, Enid Starkie (biographer of Baudelaire), 'wangled Mauriac an honorary degree at Oxford. I contacted Enid Starkie and got her in on it and we got it through. It was good for Eyre & Spottiswoode and of course it made Mauriac very pleased. The university bestowed on him an Honorary D.Lit. We had a party at a house I rented in Beaumont Street in Oxford.'[34] To his mother Greene wrote:

> I came back . . . in time for the party with eggs, ham and chocolates to help. The party was a huge success. Over 40 people and no one stirred till midnight. Mauriac stayed too to the bitter end. His address at the Taylorian (which I didn't go to) contained a great boost for me! We had a buffet in the dining room with some drinks, and more drinks in the drawing room and chairs and nightlights in the garden.[35]

To her son, as late as 1970, Vivien spoke about the party she prepared for Mauriac:

> Don't people remember, what the war, and YEARS following were like? The whole of the food was contrived by me and cooked by me, out of my own saved rations; (rations for one were 4 oz. butter weekly; eggs and tinned things like 'points' which meant you could have them if they were in stock and you happened to be lucky – say 1 or 2 eggs monthly) Well I fed 50 people, including Maurice Bowra, David Cecil, Rosamond Lehmann, etc.[36]

Mauriac and Greene, so different in character, shared a certain gloomy Catholicism in their creative artistry and admired each other. Mauriac wrote a preface to Greene's *The Power and the Glory*: 'There's really no news,' Greene wrote to his mother, 'except what is rather nice that François Mauriac has written a preface for the *Power and the Glory* in France – a very nice one which ends up with a personal apostrophe: "Dear Graham Greene, with whom I have so many ties . . . "' And then with his sense of personal world weariness, Greene added: 'This would have been beyond my dreams 20 years ago, at the time when one did dream.'[37]

'It is easy to understand the mutual admiration and affinity', the actor and writer Robert Speaight wrote, 'between Mauriac and Graham Greene. Each was a specialist in sin, and the possibility of salvation.'[38] Greene's loyalty to Mauriac had come at a time when he was in some despair. He had written his first three books – *The Man Within*, *The Name of Action* and *Rumour at Nightfall* – under the influence of his great predecessor Joseph Conrad. Unfortunately, it wasn't Conrad's great novels but his inferior melodrama *Arrow of Gold* that influenced him. In September 1932 Greene had been shown into his publisher's office, where Heinemann read him the riot act. They showed him evidence of the disastrous sales of his last two books and told him that there would be no further advances and no royalties on further books until all losses had been recovered. On the strength of his first novel's success, Greene had left the safety of *The Times*, even though they had tried strenuously to persuade him to stay. In the early 1930s he was desperately short of money and faced failure as a writer.

In 1932 one of Mauriac's best novels, *Le Nœud de Vipères*, appeared in English. Greene read it with an excitement which he remembered to the end of his life. For the first time, he saw the possibility of treating the contemporary world with the poetic realism he had admired in the Elizabethan and Jacobean dramatists. He turned his back on all he had written before. He had found a purpose to aid him in the 'long drudgery of authorship'.

At Eyre & Spottiswoode Greene intended to bring out not only the complete works of Mauriac, but those of Ford Madox Ford as well, whom he thought grossly underrated: 'No one in our century except James has been more attentive to the craft of letters,' he wrote. He took over all of Ford's best titles in order to produce a uniform edition. He was still very much the director and anticipated bringing them out within two years. However, before he could do so, he felt the need to offer his resignation.*

*

Greene was initially happy at Eyre & Spottiswoode and Muggeridge had a theory about this: 'One of the many funny things about Graham is that he likes routine work, likes going to an office. In fact, he so disliked not going to an office that he set up a kind of office for himself that he would go and work in. This is how he met Dorothy Glover. He hated working at home, he didn't like the life of an author, simply getting up in the morning and being all the time in the house.' Muggeridge saw quite a lot of Greene in his office at Ryder Street and in his office in Eyre & Spottiswoode, and was sure that Greene preferred to go to an office to having none.[39]

---

* The uniform edition of Ford Madox Ford had to wait until 1962–3, when he brought out Ford in three volumes while a director of Bodley Head.

Immediately after the war and while still in military uniform, Muggeridge visited the cramped quarters of Eyre & Spottiswoode in Bedford Street: 'If I had occasion to talk with one of them [Greene], I was keenly aware of the other's presence [Jerrold]; a telephone call by either produced a sort of anguished silence in which a third person found himself listening intently to every word spoken into the receiver, however softly.'[40] (No wonder Jerrold knew exactly whom Greene telephoned on his arrival at the office.) Writing to Vivien from his office, Greene hurriedly brings his letter to a close: 'I must stop now because Douglas is coming in and typing is rather noisy.'[41]

A publicity photograph has survived, taken in June 1947, in the offices of Eyre & Spottiswoode showing Jerrold sitting in publisher's pose behind his desk, Eyre & Spottiswoode books in row on row behind him, and Greene looking grim (as he often did). Greene had thought of a way of improving the fiction list as the caption below the photograph explains:

Graham Greene and Douglas Jerrold are two of the directors of Eyre & Spottiswoode. Graham Greene writes novels, short stories (two recently in the *Strand Magazine*) and films. Jerrold edits the right-wing *New English Review* and wrote the History of the Royal Naval Division in World War I. [How different they were in everything, but especially politics.] Eyre & Spottiswoode recently . . . offered for a first novel a prize worth 1,000 pounds – five hundred paid outright and five hundred in advance royalties. Their list includes Hugh Kingsmill, Neil Bell, D. B. Wyndham Lewis, Hesketh Pearson and R. K. Narayan.

Greene had been as good as his word and brought Narayan, Wyndham Lewis and Mervyn Peake over to Eyre & Spottiswoode.

According to Muggeridge, Jerrold 'gave an impression of being enormous. He dressed in an old-fashioned . . . way – black coat, striped trousers, stiff collar, foot-wear noticeably hand-made by Lobb. His head was tiny, thinly covered with sparse hair.' Hugh Kingsmill used to say that Jerrold looked like 'an inflated *hors d'œuvre*'.[42]

Muggeridge used to refer to Jerrold as 'Mr Forcible Feeble'. Not only did Jerrold dress sombrely, but he sounded immensely gloomy ('on the telephone as if already in Purgatory').[43] According to Anthony Powell, Jerrold could 'bring instantaneous and inextricable confusion to the simplest transaction'[44] and be verbose and pompous: ' "Douglas gets as much pleasure from writing me a pompous letter",

Hugh Kingsmill once exclaimed, "as other people do from having a good fuck." '[45]

Greene's desire to leave Eyre & Spottiswoode was due simply to the tedium of dealing with authors. Even when handling interesting problems, as evidenced by the following letter from Robert Kee, he paid the price of sacrificing his own writing. Greene had brought Kee's attention to certain rude words in *A Crowd Is Not Company* which demanded some compromises and Kee responded:

> As to alternative rude words for the book I'm not sure really that the best thing isn't to write 'B—s' for Balls (p. 44) – & this can't stand – and 'F—ing' for 'fucking' (p. 76); 'Put the shits up me' (p. 77) could become 'give me the shits' which is an equally favourite expression among such people. If you can't agree with blanks, 'Balls' could become 'Bull shit!' (or Bull?) and 'fucking' 'bloody'. The blank principle can be extended to cover phrases like 'well I'll be buggered' which I think comes in somewhere though I can't find it, and 'bugger off' (p. 139).[46]

But Greene truly admired Kee's novel, and set about 'pushing' it in a letter to Anthony Powell. 'I do pledge my shirt that Kee is a writer of extraordinary ability with a great future.'[47]

Now that he was a publisher, he had to lunch with writers: 'I went to a stiff lunch at the Ritz the other day given to a party of American authors who had been sent over here.' He'd only heard of two of them, Rex Stout, the detective writer, and Kay Boyle, 'as stiff and studied and silly as her books'.[48] Indeed, it was while he was a publisher that Greene developed the habit of having a dry Martini before meals: 'I had to have lunch with authors, and the idea of listening to these dreary people talking about their books right through a meal persuaded me that I had to give myself a boost to endure this drudgery.' Yet this 'drudgery' was endured for very good reasons: 'Are you by any chance a reader of the novels of Frances Parkinson Keyes?' he wrote to his mother. 'I'm not myself & don't know anyone who is, but they have enormous sales & pay for all our offices & staff & God knows what.'[49]

In spite of Jerrold's implied criticism that Greene in his first hour at work was doing everything but attend to publishing commitments, Greene was at times extremely busy trying to keep his writing alive while acting as publisher.

In an undated letter, but probably written early in 1947, Greene complains to his mother of not having written for a long time and of being very busy at Eyre & Spottiswoode: 'Douglas [Jerrold] has been in America, & I've been involved in the script [for the film] of *Brighton Rock* & altogether it's been a matter of all work & no play making me an extremely dull Jack . . . I feel very out of touch with my brothers & sisters, but lunch is my easiest meal so as not to break into my little time for work, & none of them are ever free for lunch.'[50] He then lists for his mother his many problems: 'First I had gastric flu . . . and now Douglas Jerrold is going to be away a month with flu,' and he contrasts Jerrold's behaviour with his own:

> I took 3 days holiday with my flu & went across to Paris where my film *Gun for Sale* was having a big success & where my [French] publisher wanted me to put in another appearance! I drank lots of wine & brandy & returned quite rested & cured . . . Next month I've let myself in for a talk at Downside. Film of *Brighton Rock* starts being made on 17th. Altogether there are not enough hours in the day. Sometimes wish I'd been a quiet stockbroker.[51]

In another letter, Greene reported that Jerrold was in America again: '& my chief editorial assistant is sick, & I find myself running the publishing with little more than a woman & a dog'. Moreover, these were difficult days as there were real shortages of paper, printers were closing down, and costs were up: 'On Sunday week, I'm off to Amsterdam & Brussels again over printing, to try & fight the crisis.'[52] Just before leaving he began a series of radio broadcasts, the first of which was about the crisis in printing and was transmitted on 9 March 1947.[53]

In October 1947 Greene spent a fortnight in New York City on business for Eyre & Spottiswoode. He arrived without the fanfare one might have expected for a famous British author, but that was the way he wanted it. While in New York, he was interviewed by a journalist who recorded: 'Mr Greene is tall and spare (a splendid example of English rationing, someone at a near table whispered), and looking a little bit like a young (40 year old) dispassionate Scotland Yard man.' In interview Greene played down his own entertainments: 'He doesn't see how people can care what happens to a Scotland Yard man . . . doesn't really like his psychological thriller books,' but played up his serious work: 'He's got a new, serious novel, *The Heart of the Matter*. It's a non-thriller, and he thinks it's good. Viking will publish it in the spring.'[54] Greene was probably also looking out for future excitement. From the Gotham hotel he wrote: 'I'm lunching on Wednesday and it's a lot of *Life* boys who are thinking of making me their special correspondent in India!'[55]

Such a contract with *Life* would have been impossible if he remained with Eyre & Spottiswoode. He was restless; he longed both to travel and write after three years as a publisher: 'I'm coming to a new arrangement with E. & S.,' he wrote to his mother, 'which after June 30 next year [1948] is going to give me much more time. I'm dallying with the idea of India at the end of next year, but that's between ourselves for the present. Just off to see the *New Statesman*. I'm thinking of becoming their dramatic critic!'[56]

*

Greene's departure from Eyre & Spottiswoode was more sudden than he had originally planned. Two possible explanations exist for it; Anthony Powell had one story and Greene the other.

Powell had written a small book about the seventeenth-century diarist John Aubrey entitled *John Aubrey and His Friends*. Finding that Oxford University Press's offer was 'unexciting', he offered it, on the advice of his friend Muggeridge, to Graham Greene. A contract was signed in May 1946, undertaking that the book would appear within nine months. Two and a half years went by and still *John Aubrey and His Friends* had not appeared. The delay was chiefly because of the shortage of paper, but also, as it transpired, because Greene felt that Powell's book was tedious and other books should take precedence. It was finally scheduled to come out in the late autumn of 1948.

In that autumn, Greene, Muggeridge and Powell met for lunch at the Authors' Club, 'an odd little backwater housed in Whitehall Court . . . dominated by Edwardian literary memories'.[57] Kingsmill, Muggeridge, Powell and Greene were all members – Kingsmill, according to Powell, 'virtually edited the book pages of the *New English Review* there' and 'was always to be found asleep every afternoon in one of the upright chairs; a coma from which he would emerge for tea at about four o'clock'. The club was closely linked with Douglas Jerrold, who was 'the most prominent member of its committee and in general guardian angel'.[58]

As Powell explained, it was during the course of the lunch that Greene revealed that *John Aubrey* would be delayed again, until the following year. Powell, in his modest way, recalled the events that followed: 'I made a fairly vigorous demur. There was a brisk exchange, in the course of which Greene said: "It's a bloody boring book anyway." '[59] Powell felt that such a comment from the managing director (Greene was in fact deputy managing director) of the firm responsible for marketing the book was discouraging, to say the least, and said he assumed Greene's words implied release from a contract that offered further books of his (of course these included his much more important novels) to Eyre & Spottiswoode. Greene agreed 'that consequence was implicit in the view he had expressed. The rest of the luncheon passed without incident.'[60]

This passage of arms found its way into Muggeridge's diary, an entry vaguely dated 15–17 September 1948:

> Curious lunch with Graham Greene and Tony. Started off with a stupid row about delay in Eyre and Spottiswoode's publishing Tony's book on John Aubrey. Hugh Kingsmill joined us and we laughed a great deal over a letter of protest which we drew up about the club silence room being abolished. Graham has a decided love of conflict. Very typical figure of this time – which is why his novels are so successful.[61]

And five weeks later, there is a further entry: 'Gathered from Douglas Jerrold that a row is brewing between him and Graham Greene, about Graham's agreement to release Tony Powell from his novel contract with Eyre and Spottiswoode.'[62]

At the time of the fracas Douglas Jerrold was in the United States. He came back to find a letter from the literary agent David Higham notifying Eyre & Spottiswoode that the contract Powell had signed for new novels was cancelled. The board of directors met, but was not prepared to withdraw from the contract. Indeed, in a letter to Powell dated 29 October, Jerrold stated firmly: 'Graham has no more power to release you from your contract with this firm than I have to sell the company's furniture and premises,' and he went on: 'Graham's commitments have since proved to be such that he has had to resign his executive position here and he is now only a valued member of our Board, with purely advisory functions, as he will tell you himself if you ask him.' From this it looks as if Greene's angry outburst at the Authors' Club led to his offering Eyre & Spottiswoode his resignation.

However, as late as 1981, Greene maintained that his resignation had nothing to do with Anthony Powell. 'That was a non-fiction book, and Jerrold had agreed to its publication, but because I had introduced it to Jerrold, to some extent I was keeping an eye on it, but I wasn't responsible for it. Tony Powell didn't realise about post-war paper rationing. Books couldn't be published as before the war.'[63] Nevertheless, Greene had not changed his mind about the book. He repeated to me what he had said more forcefully at the Authors' Club in 1948: 'It was a very dull book!'

The arrangement between Greene and Jerrold was that Greene should be responsible for the fiction list and Jerrold for non-fiction.

It was agreed also that while Greene was on holiday Jerrold would accept no fiction and while Jerrold was on holiday Greene would accept no non-fiction. Jerrold, according to Greene, broke this agreement.

When Greene returned from holiday he found that Jerrold had accepted 'a very bad imitation of *Brighton Rock*, full of soft porn'.[64] Also awaiting his return was a letter from Colonel Crosthwaite-Eyre, a former chairman of the board and a major shareholder in Eyre & Spottiswoode, who had retired to South Africa. In this letter (written to Greene because he was in charge of the fiction list) he told him that he had burned the book in his garden. Greene was indignant because he was blamed for a very bad novel which he had not accepted. At the next meeting of the directors, Greene circulated a little piece of paper on which he had written: ' "Agenda for next directors' meeting" – resignation of Director.' His resignation was accepted.

He left Eyre & Spottiswoode in 1948. He had had tremendous success with the publication of *The Heart of the Matter* and knew now that he could live on his writing and no longer needed to work for a publishing firm. To the Czech writer Egon Hostovsky whom he had taken on, Greene wrote in January 1949: 'I had meant to write to you some time ago and tell you that I have left Eyre & Spottiswoode. It became more and more impossible to carry on publishing and my own writing as well . . . I hope one day we may meet again, this time as fellow authors and not author and publisher!'[65]

He left the firm then over a disagreement with Douglas Jerrold, who was the chairman, but it was a friendly disagreement: 'Really I was fed up with being a publisher.' But Greene was not revealing the whole truth of the affair, as a letter to Powell reveals. It suggests that their argument did bring about Greene's resignation. *After* Jerrold had written to Powell saying that Greene had resigned and that Greene had no power to release Powell from his contract, Powell wrote to Greene in a cold professional manner: 'Your statement that Eyre & Spottiswoode released me from my contract with them seemed to me both authoritative and explicit when we discussed the matter in September. Can you confirm this?'[66]

Greene's response was close to an admission of error:

I expect you have heard by this time that I have resigned from the board of Eyre and Spottiswoode. Your case really brought matters to a head but the boil had been growing for many months. It is quite true that I offered to release you from your novel contract

. . . I did, however, very much hope after our meeting in the Authors' Club that the whole thing might blow over and I heard from David Higham that it was unlikely you would press the withdrawal of your novels.[67]

*

There was a sequel to Greene's resignation. Douglas Jerrold was always threatening to retire. Indeed, it was his half-promise that he would retire which persuaded Greene to go into the firm in the first place. Jerrold did do so, but not until ten years after Greene's resignation.

Sir Oliver Crosthwaite-Eyre, who had not forgotten Greene's genius as a publisher, offered him the opportunity to become chairman. By 1958, Eyre & Spottiswoode had joined with Methuen and Associated British Publishers and had increased enormously in significance. What Crosthwaite-Eyre offered Greene was the opportunity of a lifetime, a true family business which would have allowed his son Francis to enter a substantial publishing firm: 'What I would like to suggest to you is that we should make arrangements for Douglas to retire in the autumn, that you should join us as Managing and Editorial Director of the Publishers, that you would also join the board of Associated British Publishers and that of Eyre & Spottiswoode Limited.'[68] Crosthwaite-Eyre felt that Greene should have the three appointments, if he were to be kept properly in the picture as to the development the enlarged publishers would be undertaking. However, he tried to sweeten the offer by promising Greene that he would not have 'nearly so much "desk sitting" ' and, because he knew that Greene, then at the height of his fame, would need time off to write, suggested at least six weeks a year free to engage in his own work.

Greene liked and admired Oliver Crosthwaite-Eyre, and they had already discussed matters over lunch. At that time Greene had spoken rather cryptically: 'When you first spoke to me about it I turned the proposition down with little or no hesitation because at that moment I thought it possible that I should be living a great deal of my time abroad. That situation no longer exists and it is highly unlikely that the circumstances would recur.'

There is some evidence here of Greene negotiating terms but also deliberately talking himself out of a job:

I am first and last a writer . . . I cannot help fearing that without the necessity of writing I might abandon it altogether. This is a psychological problem for me alone and I think I would risk this particular danger. But if I am to continue writing and not to have an acute attack of claustrophobia I do think that the minimum time which I would have to spend out of the country for work would be two months in a year and I am not sure whether that would really meet the case. I think I would require a guaranteed two months and the possibility if the occasion arose of taking a further month. This from your point of view can hardly be very satisfactory. It is not a financial question as some of this period could always be regarded as unpaid holiday, but if I were you I should feel uncertain whether sufficient drive could be put into the strategy of the firm by a managing director who might be absent for such a period in any year.[69]

He asked to be allowed to brood on the matter until after Easter. He also encouraged his friend to 'feel at complete liberty to approach anybody else in the meantime'. But Oliver Crosthwaite-Eyre was interested only in Greene; he made a further offer: 'He offered me very good terms for those days,' Greene told me, 'of 5,000 pounds a year plus a car plus a chauffeur plus *three* months leave a year for my own private work and it was with some hesitation I turned it all down.'[70]

He was right to do so. On a postcard to Greene, John Betjeman put the situation in his own inimitable fashion: 'Old top . . . Dear old E&S publish better books than almost anyone. You are a great novelist. I hope you haven't stopped writing for publishing. Our brave new world will probably stop us all. I am as good as dead. John B.'

15

The Unquiet Peace

In this weak piping time of peace.
— SHAKESPEARE

O N 20 March 1945 Greene recorded what must have been the last V2 to hit London:

> On Sunday, I was lying late in bed and there was a huge crash, followed by a terrific rumble and the sound of glass going . . . I could see a pillar of smoke go up above the roofs . . . it was quite a long way away and a very lucky rocket. Just inside Hyde Park at Marble Arch where the tub thumpers would have been later in the day. I went and looked. The blast had missed the Arch and swept through the poor old Regal which was on the point of reopening after being flybombed and knocked out the windows in the Cumberland.[1]

It was a damp squib; the British Home Guard was standing down; the war was coming to a close: 'It really looks at last', Greene wrote to his mother, 'as though the war may be over soon.' But he concluded: 'One feels one won't have much energy for peace.'[2]

In the spring of 1945, the world mourned the death of President Roosevelt, but celebrated the violent demise of the dictators of the Axis forces. Italy's Benito Mussolini, captured by Italian partisans, had his body (and that of his mistress, Clara Petacci) strung upside down from meat hooks in a Milan petrol station on 28 April. On the eve of the Russian occupation of Berlin, with troops only several hundred yards away, Hitler went through a marriage ceremony with his mistress Eva Braun, before both committed suicide in the Chancellery bunker. William Joyce made his last broadcast on the day his hero Hitler poisoned himself. He roared drunkenly into the microphone a final '*Heil Hitler* and farewell.' Joyce, who at the height of his fame had sixteen million listeners tuned into the 31-metre band, was later convicted of treason and hanged.

The Third Reich, which was to have endured for a thousand years, had suddenly ended. Interviewed in later years, Greene, with Hitler in mind, said, 'Even if one persists in rejecting the idea of eternal damnation, how can one deny the existence of total evil?'[3]

On 7 May the news of the unconditional surrender of Germany was picked up from German radio. The next day, Winston Churchill broadcast to the nation at 3 p.m., formally announcing the end of the European War and pronouncing VE (Victory in Europe) Day. Churchill then went from 10 Downing Street to the House of Commons, the mass of people literally pushing his car up Whitehall.

The blackout was over; prominent buildings were illuminated: Big Ben, the Houses of Parliament, St Paul's Cathedral, Nelson's Column and Buckingham Palace. The exhilaration was immense. St Paul's was full of worshippers: 'We give thanks to God for all that this victory means for us and for the world,' said the Archbishop of Canterbury, advising the country not to 'forget the millions in Europe, dispossessed, scattered, hungry and homeless'.[4] High and low, rich and poor praised the day. The searchlights, which in wartime had sought enemy planes, now illuminated the night sky and helped bring pleasure to the massed crowds assembled below. King George let his young daughters, Princess Elizabeth and Princess Margaret, mingle with the excited Britishers, concerned, as he noted in his diary, that his 'poor darlings' had 'never had any fun yet'.[5]

Greene did not go to Oxford to celebrate VE Day with his wife. Vivien had moved from Trinity College, the home of her friends the Weavers, to 15 Beaumont Street. Greene sent his wife a curiously anaemic telegram on the day of victory: 'LOVE AND HAPPY PEACE TO YOU – GREEN', the final 'e' being missed off his name.

Vivien's reply gives no evidence of unhappiness: 'Your wire *quite* adorable and pie-worthy.' She and Francis, then aged nine, walked through Oxford from 10 p.m. to 1 a.m. to see the illuminations, floodlighting, rockets, and the fairy-lights on the private houses. A fire engine rushed up and down Beaumont Street pursued by a cheering crowd. But it was the enormous bonfires, 'huge leaping pyres', that drew 'the crowds of intent faces round them'.

The most beautiful one was just outside Queens, the firelight picking out the columns and cupola and statue, the steps crowd[ed] with young men and a mass of them in the street –

deep blue night sky above, and showers of gold sparks shooting up forty feet into the air. Magdalen floodlit looked as if it had been cut out of white paper, quite unreal – undergraduate piping the Road to the Isles and 'the tune of the 51st Highland Division played on entering Cambrai' . . . and a crowd clapping and cheering – a few doing a Highland fling . . . In Trinity Garden quad the men stood silently round a huge bonfire until again a Scottish undergraduate in a kilt played a rather sad air. The crowd very gentle, not very noisy – and having been told for six years not to be optimistic, naturally the habit clung.[6]

Although without her husband, she was determined to celebrate in a small way: 'Last night I had iced coffee and cake and 9 people came in. Drawing room looked lovely and I had one window quite up [open] and cushions on the balcony window sill . . . I didn't go out except just down St. Giles again and to the Memorial bonfire . . . '[7] There is a small reference to Graham in the last lines of her letter: 'I so missed you to go about with. Oxford is a good place for such things as the architecture looked so lovely: no street lights, just windows, and coloured lights and firelight.'

After the victory celebrations, Greene explained to his mother why he'd not gone home to Oxford to celebrate the peace with his wife and family: 'Having watched the blitz through I thought I'd see the peace in London but there was precious little to see but some floodlighting & still less to eat or drink. Everything very much more decorous than the Jubilee or Berkhamsted in 1918.'[8]

Greene took Dorothy down to St James's Park on the evening of VE Day to watch the celebrations. In *The End of the Affair* this experience is transferred to Sarah Miles and her husband Henry: 'It was very quiet beside the floodlit water between the Horse Guards and the palace. Nobody shouted or sang or got drunk. People sat on the grass in twos, holding hands. I suppose they were happy because this was peace and there were no more bombs.' Sarah's comments to Henry express Greene's own view: 'I don't like the peace.'[9]

The real reason for not visiting Vivien was not given to his mother. Dorothy would have been made very unhappy by his departure on VE Day. He was living with her, but no longer deeply in love, his loyalty increasing as love diminished, and Dorothy, that courageous comrade-in-arms, had seventy-six reasons to ensure Greene's presence in London – the seventy-six nights of the blitz endured together.

To repay Vivien for not having returned to her for VE Day,

Greene took her on holiday to the Osborne estate on the Isle of Wight:

> I had got leave to see O. which is closed to visitors & the old surgeon-admiral in charge just let us wander at our own sweet will by ourselves through the State Rooms. Wednesday we went over to Alwin Bay – Thursday we went to Godshill – a very bogus self-conscious village where however we had a strawberry tea & found an absurdly cheap olde antique shoppe where we got a pair of Regency candlesticks for 8/6d, a very nice 1850ish case of fruit & tea knives & forks – a dozen of each, very elegant in a very nice case for 3 guineas & a pair of Regency vases for a guinea.[10]

Such trips were to serve Vivien's passion for collecting, not Greene's, and his patience with such domestic holidays sometimes wore thin.

Vivien knew that she had to make a special effort before she moved into Beaumont Street in 1944, if she was to save her marriage: 'My aunt had left her flat in Warwick Square and I realised that it gave him the fright of his life when I wrote and said that she – this was just near the end of the war when the bombs had finished – offered it to me at the same rent because she was moving away and that I could have it. I thought it would be lovely to be in one's own home – there was a certain strain living with Stella Weaver. Graham provided a good many reasons why it would be a mistake and that it wouldn't do.'[11]

Before the end of the war, Greene suggested to Vivien that another child might be in order:

> I'd always talked about a third one to be called Mark, and here at the end of the war he [Graham] suddenly said, 'Have Mark,' and I felt a sort of outrage. In a physical sense the marriage ended just before the war. He said, 'We don't want any children in the war.' There was no pill then. I always think how different things would have been with the pill . . . When he suggested having Mark, I thought to myself, 'You've had all these women and you live with them and you say you love them and then come back after all these years to me, and expect to pick up everything just as it was,' and I said to him, 'No, no, nothing like that,' and he said, 'Oh very well,' quite cheerfully.[12]

The war meant a great deal to Greene: he'd believed for a long time it would solve his problems. When he was twenty-one, and before his marriage to Vivien, he wrote: 'I can't help wishing sometimes, darling, that something would happen to solve all problems once & for all. Something like war with Turkey & Russia & Germany, which would destroy all thought of the future, & leave only a certain present.'[13] He was not a pacifist: at the end of 1940 with the blitz raging in London, he wrote: 'If war were only as the pacifists describe it – violent, unjust, horrible, useless – it would have fallen out of favour long ago.'[14] When the war ended, its termination left a worm of depression: 'I have very little nerve for peace,' he wrote a few days before the Germans surrendered,[15] and after the VE Day celebrations, he added: 'I think everyone feels very flat with the peace.'[16]

There were other reasons to feel flat about postwar Britain. Returning soldiers were looking for a world fit for heroes. But conditions in England were not good. Shiploads of returning soldiers, sailors and airmen felt that they were arriving home to a defeated country: 'A grey limbo of ruins, rubble, exhausted faces.'[17] Demobilised servicemen wandered from one Government office to another getting ration cards and clothing coupons, dealing with temporary, often officious, seemingly always superior Civil Servants. There were long queues for everything, and in September 1945 it was reported, 'Many British parents, not in financial or local reach of hotels, restaurants, clubs and canteens have found it extremely hard to feed their children properly.'[18] People who could afford to eat out did well enough: those staying at home frequently had a meagre time of it.

The first few years of peace were dreary. After a diet of bombs and blackout the country now had to endure austerity, 'utility' goods, dried eggs and no lemons. Vivien recalled the twelve years of rationing: 'Twelve years you did without things, even queuing for toothbrushes for the children and shoes. You couldn't complain when the fighting was going on, but after the war it was worse, and bread rationing didn't happen till after the war.'[19] But it wasn't the discomforts of postwar Britain that troubled Greene; it was the immense boredom peace would bring.

*

In an attempt to keep boredom at bay, Greene sought to fill his time with work. In addition to his duties at Eyre & Spottiswoode, he began reviewing for the *Evening Standard* in 1945. But his great days as a reviewer, for the *Spectator* (1933–41), were virtually over. Reviewing for a popular newspaper like the *Evening Standard* was limiting (too few words, too popular a style) for Greene. The day before his first review appeared on 22 June 1945, he wrote to his mother that he was starting a weekly book article 'for three months in the *Evening Standard* on Fridays tomorrow! I asked for 35 gns. a week really hoping they'd say no – but alas they said yes!'[20]

GRAHAM GREENE ON BOOKS was the newspaper's leader. It described Greene as the author of a dozen books, 'every one of which has become famous', and nearly every one of which had been translated into every European language. He was also characterised as the adapter of films made from his novels and stories. The newspaper extolled the variety of his work – his range (from *Brighton Rock* to the brilliant *The Power and the Glory*), and spoke of his worldwide reputation for style and 'his knowledge of human values'.[21]

His reviews tended to denigrate various popular writers: Louis Bromfield is a producer of cellophane fiction: 'once a man with promise, but a lifetime of too easy success . . . [his books] guaranteed untouched by human hand and judging from the description on the cover the publisher has not found it necessary to open the book. Another well-wrapped Bromfield has simply shot down the conveyor belt to the distributing department.'[22] 'Mr. [Nevil] Shute is too confident that his gift of readability will allow him to get away with anything. There is a sense of laziness about his talent. Too often he chooses situations . . . that only a fool could muff.'[23]

Even admired writers and friends were reprimanded for failing to do their best: 'When we come down to Maugham, the case is different. There is such immense talent, couldn't he, we feel, have tried for something a little more difficult, couldn't he sometimes take a few risks . . . ?'[24] He felt impelled to refer to Dickens (an author he admired after all) as 'That gay Deceiver', and spoke of Dickens slandering his father in the character of Micawber, of doing very little for his own children (less than his own father had done for him), of making too much of his own experience of a blacking factory: 'How any Etonian of that period, embarked on a painful drudgery of eight years' schooling would have envied Charles Huffam his brief spell in commercial life.' Although Dickens was world famous by the age of twenty-three, he was, 'next to Gladstone, the most unlovable figure of his age'. 'The legend of the novelist who had learned in suffering was Dickens' most successful deception.'[25]

But Greene could take a courageous stand when a work of great distinction appeared, as in the case of George Orwell's *Animal Farm*: 'In wartime there has to be a measure of appeasement . . . [the writer] must not give way to despondency or dismay, he must not offend a valuable ally, he must not even make fun . . .'

Greene castigated his old employer, the Ministry of Information, 'that huge cenotaph of appeasement', because when Orwell first completed *Animal Farm*, a Ministry official to whom he sent the manuscript took a poor view of the satire: 'Couldn't you make them some other animal,' the official is reported as saying in reference to the dictator and his colleagues, 'and not pigs?'[26]

Orwell and Greene were not destined to be friends for long. Orwell could not really stand Greene's Catholicism and wrote a powerful condemnation of *The Heart of the Matter* in the *New Yorker* in 1948. Orwell suffered from fierce blind spots, yet he was remarkably honest. A year after his harsh review, he wrote to T. R. Fyvel: 'You refer to [Greene] as an extreme Conservative, the usual Catholic reactionary type. This isn't so at all . . . Of course he is a Catholic and in some issues has to side politically with the church, but in outlook he is just a mild Left with faint C[ommunist] P[arty] leanings. I have even thought that he might become our first Catholic fellow-traveller . . . '[27]

Greene's last review for the *Evening Standard* appeared on 4 October 1945. Speaking of Inez Holden, he stressed that her best stories 'leave in our minds the stirring and excitement that comes from the genuine creative act', which was what Greene longed for passionately. But after the war, work on *The Heart of the Matter* went slowly and he sought in the interim to bring out a collection of short stories.

Greene's earliest volume of stories was *The Basement Room* (1935), which included eight. Some of these were worthy of inclusion in the new collection – 'The Innocent', 'A Drive in the Country', 'When Greek Meets Greek', and 'A Little Place off the Edgware Road'; some were undistinguished and should not have been considered.

Greene was scraping the bottom of the barrel. To Nancy Pearn he wrote on 23 August 1946: 'I enclose a couple of short stories ["The Second Death" and "The Lottery Ticket"] which I dug out of a drawer. They have not yet been published and I propose to include them in my volume of short stories. I suspect you have already tried them out before, many years ago when my books had not started booming!' Originally he collected eighteen, intending to call them *Eighteen Stories*, but finding another ('The Innocent'), he changed the title to *Nineteen Stories*.

He wrote a modest foreword: 'I am only too conscious of the defects of these stories . . . The short story is an exacting form which I have never properly practised.' The best are still those which appeared in his first collection – 'The Basement Room' and 'The End of the Party', both written in the compulsive shorthand of a terrified child.

Early in 1946 Heinemann decided to bring out a number of Greene's books in a uniform edition. Frere wrote to the printer: 'Greene is now a Director of Eyre & Spottiswoode, and from that position of eminence he has some ideas about production himself.'[28] Nevertheless, the uniform edition was appallingly produced. The first two titles published were *A Gun for Sale* and *Brighton Rock*, then *Stamboul Train* and *England Made Me*. *Journey Without Maps* was published in 1949 and *The Lawless Roads* followed. By 1952, *It's a Battlefield*, *The Ministry of Fear*, *The Power and the Glory*, and *The Heart of the Matter* had also appeared.

Bringing Greene's non-fiction into the uniform edition was unexpected. It happened because Greene wanted Heinemann to surrender the rights to *Journey Without Maps*, which was out of print. Greene wrote to Louise Callender at Heinemann reminding her that *Journey Without Maps* was withdrawn soon after it was published in 1936 (because a libel case frightened Heinemann).[29] 'My own view is that it would be only equitable for you to surrender the rights back to me personally, in which case I should probably give a licence for three years to either Pan Books or Penguin [he gave the licence to Pan Books], and after that, if I was still a publisher myself, I would bring it out with *Lawless Roads* through my own firm.'[30]

With eight books brought into a uniform edition, Greene believed Heinemann wouldn't have the paper or the inclination to reprint the travel book. Heinemann knew Greene had them over a barrel. They renounced the rights to *Journey Without Maps*, but kept some hold over the book by publishing it in the uniform edition. It is unquestionably one of the best travel books of the period.

*

Greene was often edgy, especially if his personal or writing life was going wrong. Staying in an old hotel near St James's, his nerves exacerbated by the noise of workmen drilling in the middle of the night, he took an electric bulb out of the bedroom light and chucked it on to the street.[31]

Gillian Sutro recalled the time he promised to come to her husband's birthday party in Belgrave Square:

> He said he was absolutely going to come, and then he said he wasn't going to come, but he at least would come for dinner. I chided him, 'You said you were going to come to the party, and you have broken your word.' He replied, 'I'm feeling very taut tonight and if you go on like that I will walk straight out again.' So I shut up because I knew he'd walk straight out again – literally.[32]

Although outwardly calm, Greene was a man of deep passions. When he reviewed Madame Maritain's book, *The Golden Measure*, his anger rose at the publisher's smooth empty words: '[a book for] those who love truth and beauty . . . [for those] who are solicitous of what is bound up with the destiny of the human person', to which Greene responded: 'Instinctively at the vague complacent phrases, with which we have so often heard an advertising man express his stifling reverence for the spirit, the reviewer feels for the safety catch of his revolver.'[33]

Greene lived on his nerves, oscillating between periods of high excitement and moments of intense depression. Even Desmond Pakenham, a calm, cautious man who knew Greene in MI6, stressed Greene's 'inexpressible melancholia – it seemed as if all the sorrows of the world were known to him and he couldn't get the horror out of his eyes. This was not noticeable in company but when he was walking alone, particularly then, his face always looked worn and sad.'[34]

This duality is revealed in some of his publicity photographs at this time. His friend Mario Soldati, the Italian film director and novelist, recalled that in the late 1940s:

[Greene] had what I would call a hurt, offended face, metaphorically bruised by events, the expression, not continuously but every once in a while, of an angry and hurt face even when something small went wrong . . . there was something unearthly in those eyes. I have always felt this, since the first time I met him. Blue fire in his eyes, the eyes of a demon.[35]

As a way of reducing tension, which was often linked with his recurring excited phase, Greene would play compulsive pranks. We have seen the lengths to which he was willing to go to carry out a hoax – Mrs Montgomery is a monumental fictional figure, a true creation – but when Greene had a real hate on, as in the case of Wilson Harris, MP, the *Spectator*'s editor, he would be unrelenting in pursuit of his victim. Wilson Harris was an unpleasant, snobbish, pompous, superior man and Greene's hatred never waned. To celebrate Wilson Harris's birthday, Greene sent him a condom stuffed with sweets.

Greene celebrated another of his birthdays by writing a note to the *Evening Standard*'s Londoner's Diary to the effect that the late Frank Harris, author of the notoriously pornographic work *My Life and Loves*, was the cousin of Mr Wilson Harris, MP, respected editor of the *Spectator*.[36]

Immediately after the war the general election took place which resulted in a Labour Party victory and Winston Churchill's defeat. Greene and Walter Allen had arranged to have a meal together at Rules, by chance on the day the results of the election were announced:

> He arrived and joined me at our table and almost immediately, his eye catching the banner-headline of someone else's *Evening Standard*, said 'Damn!' I was amused by the tone of peevish irritation. 'What's the matter, Graham?' I asked. 'Don't you approve of the election results?' 'Oh, I don't care one way or the other.* It's just that I'd planned to make a telephone call at three o'clock and now I won't be able to.'

On this occasion, assuming that Churchill would win the election, Greene had intended to telephone the Reform Club, where Harris lunched every day 'with his cronies', to announce that he was speaking from the Cabinet Office and ask the telephone operator to be sure to tell Mr Harris that he was to call on the Prime Minister at 3.30.[37] Such an invitation would indicate that Churchill was going to offer Wilson Harris high office.

There were other episodes. Once when Greene knew that Cyril Connolly was having a party at home, he rang him up at ten o'clock at night pretending to be a sweep:

> He came on the phone and I said, 'Oh, Mr. Connolly?' and he said, 'Yes', and I said, 'Well I'll be around as arranged at seven o'clock in the morning. You'll be careful won't you and put dust sheets over all the furniture because it's a dirty affair.' He said, 'What is this, what is this?' 'Well I'm coming to sweep your chimney.' 'But I've never asked to have my chimney swept.' 'Oh yes, but this is the office. I've had these orders from the office and I'll be around promptly at seven o'clock, but I do want you to have everything covered with dust sheets.' 'But I haven't ordered it.' I said, 'Well I can't help that, I've got my orders from the office and the office is closed,' and I think it put a damper on the end of his party.[38]

---

* At this time Greene was almost apolitical. His attitude is expressed in an undated letter to his mother. Writing about the political battle going on in his area, he tells her that they have a straight fight in St Pancras between Conservative and Socialist: 'Reluctantly I shall vote Conservative. The Socialists are such bores! But if there were a Liberal I'd vote for him.'

Nor were the pranks limited to friends and enemies; complete strangers fell prey to Greene. Upon discovering another Graham Greene in the telephone directory, Greene rang the number: ' "Are you Graham Greene?" "My name is Graham Greene, but — ." "Are you the man who writes these filthy novels?" "No, I'm a retired solicitor." "I'm not surprised you're ashamed to confess you're the author of this muck." "No, really, I assure you — ." "If I'd written them at least I'd have the guts to admit it," ' concluded Greene.[39]

*

In October 1942 he had written to his sister explaining that his problem was that for the last four years he had been in love with 'two people as equally as makes no difference, the awful struggle to have your cake and eat it, the inability to throw over one for the sake of the other'. By 1946 in a Britain of shortages, rationing, and irritations, he knew that he now loved neither Vivien nor Dorothy. His personal life was arid and he was not writing anything of importance. He was ripe for an affair, but what followed refused to remain a modest adventure. It entirely changed his life. He would know his greatest love and greatest torment: the lightness of being and the dark night of the soul.

PART 4

Time of Catherine

The giant Ferris wheel in Vienna,
used in *The Third Man*

16

The Heart of the Matter

I can't get you out of my heart. You've splintered inside
it and surgeons are useless. They say one day I may die of
the splinter, but it can't be removed.
                                                    — GRAHAM GREENE

IN the postwar years Greene was to experience the most productive
and the most emotionally wrenching period of his life. This was
the time of Catherine. Catherine Walston dominated his thoughts
for over a decade and her influence was paramount during his great
creative period. She was the source of his creativity, for *The Heart of
the Matter* would not have been completed without her and *The End
of the Affair* would not have been started.

Catherine Walston was described kindly by Kitty Muggeridge as 'a
sort of belle dame', and acerbically by Malcolm Muggeridge as 'sans
merci but so belle'.[1] However, it was the description of the
Reverend Vincent Turner, SJ, the priest who received her into the
Catholic Church, which hit the target unerringly: 'She was
determined not to be chaste and yet she was deeply religious.'[2]

Catherine's Catholicism was a serious matter. Lady Melchett
remembers talking with her about religion: 'I said I believed in
Christ as a person and as someone incredibly good and a wonderful
prophet, but I couldn't even hope to believe in the whole package,
and Catherine turned on me: "Then you are saying Christ was a liar
and Jesus was a liar. You can't believe in a person if you think they
tell lies." She said, "Either you believe and if you believe you accept
it all. I believe." '[3] Greene was presenting the depth of Catherine's
convictions when Sarah in *The End of the Affair* says:

I believe the whole bag of tricks, there's nothing I don't believe,
they could subdivide the Trinity into a dozen parts and I'd believe.
They could dig up records that proved Christ had been invented by
Pilate to get himself promoted and I'd believe just the same.[4]

Catherine, an American, was married to Harry Walston of Thriplow Farm, later of Newton Hall. Walston was a rich landowner and, soon after the time of his wife's meeting with Greene, was agricultural adviser to Germany (1947 to 1948), attached to the Foreign Office. She was the daughter of David Henry Crompton and Lillian MacDonald Sheridan. Her father was English, though he lived in America. Essentially a gentle man, he was permanently saddened by the fact that his elder brother Paul, his wife and their six children were drowned when the liner *Lusitania* was sunk by a German submarine off the coast of Ireland on 7 May 1915.

A little stout as a child of six or seven, Catherine had blossomed into a great beauty by the age of thirteen. The children's nanny, Frances McFall,* knew that young 'Bobs', as Catherine was known to her family, was different. Catherine's youngest sister, Belinda Straight, recounts: 'On one occasion, Nanny took her from Rye (where we lived) into New York by train. She came back telling my parents: "I'm really worried about Bobs." "Well, why are you worried about Bobs?" asked my mother. "'Cause when she walked down the aisle of the train every eye – all the eyes of the men were upon her. Every head turned, and I'm afraid that there's going to be trouble ahead and she ought to be supervised very carefully." My mother thought that was greatly exaggerated.'[5] It wasn't. At fifteen Catherine had acute appendicitis and was operated on in Philadelphia. While still recovering, she climbed out of a hospital window to meet the intern who had been assisting in the operation. She was a law unto herself, yet her charm and attraction were extraordinary.

What was it that led people to look at her, since she often dressed simply?

It was true that when she went into a restaurant, people would look at her. She had a marvellous carriage, for one thing. She held her head high. She was dark-haired, sort of an auburn colour – and wonderful eyes and – short hair – and cheekbones that were fine cheekbones, rather widely spaced eyes, dark eyebrows, and she wore her clothes with great flair. She never showed that she was frightened of anything.[6]

---

* Frances McFall was the nanny for all the Crompton children. She stayed with the family all her life and is buried close to the Walston farm in Cambridgeshire: 'We all loved her and she brought us up. She was plain but incredibly wise. She understood a variety of peculiar people – including my family.'[7]

As a child Catherine couldn't be contained and was a bit of a daredevil. When her mathematics teacher told the class that it was dangerous to sit in the bathtub and pull a light chain because you could electrocute yourself, Catherine didn't believe him, made the experiment and survived. She learnt early in life that she could get away with things and handle people.

She did outrageous things, perhaps reacting against her sister Bonte (only one year older), who was favoured by her mother. Bonte, a serious child, was obedient to adults. When Bobs was eight and Bonte nine, they slept in the same room in twin beds. One night Bobs said to Bonte, 'Do you know what's very peculiar?' Bonte said she did not know and Bobs asked, 'Bonte, did you read in the paper the story about the little girl who died?' 'No, I didn't,' Bonte replied. 'Yes, there was a story about a little girl who was lying in her bed and it was dark and all of a sudden a light appeared under her bed, and that meant she was going to die. Bonte, I see a light under your bed.' At this point, Bonte ran screaming down the hall, rushed downstairs into the room where her parents were giving a dinner party and shouted, 'The light! The light!'[8]

According to Belinda Straight (Binny), Catherine showed no signs as a child of being interested in religion – although her sister Bonte went through a religious phase and painted pictures of Christ. The children's religious instruction was negligible; David Crompton was an agnostic (he disliked the idea of papal infallibility) and his wife only a mild believer who occasionally went to the Unitarian church. As Belinda Straight recalls: 'Our English nanny used to take us to Rye, New York, to the Episcopal church at Eastertime or Christmas where the Reverend Henshaw would intone, and we would sing the hymns. I don't remember anything about communion, whether Nanny went to communion.'[9] At fifteen Catherine visited a couple of churches with her friends. Once she showed both Bonte and Belinda some communion glasses. Nanny came into the room and seeing the glasses asked Catherine where she had got them. She had stolen them from a Catholic church – an interesting beginning for one who became deeply religious.

*

Unquestionably, Catherine was vivacious, outspoken and intelligent (though through her waywardness at school, not well educated).[10] She married Harry Walston when she was only eighteen. Her cousin John Sebastian Bach Booth had asked the Cromptons to arrange a skiing house party. Booth invited some student friends who had been at Cambridge University with him, among them Harry Walston.

Belinda Straight recalled tagging along as the younger sister of sixteen:

> All these people were very bright, they sang a lot of German Lieder songs, they had read the Communist Manifesto and various other volumes of interest including Proust and Lawrence, and we were all embarrassed because my mother talked about believing work should begin in the community rather than on a world scale. I thought she was very provincial then.

So they went skiing on Pack Monadack in the New Hampshire hills where the Cromptons had a farm; Harry, as Belinda remembers, hurt his back on the first day of skiing and had to stay at home. Catherine decided to stay behind with Harry and that was how they got to know each other and Harry to fall in love with her.[11]

Bonte's recollection differed only slightly: 'I only knew Harry one weekend. We went on a skiing weekend to New Hampshire and Bobs hurt her ankle and Harry stayed back with her and the rest of us went skiing. We came back at the end of the weekend and on Monday morning Harry Walston telephoned and proposed to Bobs over the phone. So it just took him three days.'[12]

Catherine announced her engagement shortly after the skiing trip. Her father interviewed Harry to find out whether he could support Bobs, and Harry (very wealthy even then) said he thought he could.[13] Harry was Jewish, but he had never attended Hebrew school or gone to synagogue. He was brought up as a Protestant at Eton. His father, who died when Harry was young, was a noted archaeologist, Sir Charles Walston (originally Walstein).

When Catherine and Harry arrived in England, Harry's mother, Florence, Lady Walston, decided to give a garden party to introduce her son's fiancée: 'The garden party was replete with women wearing flowered chiffon dresses and floppy hats and looking very staid, Bobs appeared in a bathing suit and did handstands and cartwheels on the lawn – this absolutely shocked Lady Walston and a number of other people and horrified my mother.'[14] Bonte Durán added: 'My sister didn't care a damn for Lords and Ladies and Earls . . . she simply turned cartwheels. She was a very daring young lady.'[15]

Perhaps Catherine was making a point to the formidable Lady Walston, who had been very upset by the engagement because she thought Catherine might be a fortune-hunter who had entrapped Harry. When she contacted a cousin of the Cromptons, Sir George Booth (head of the Cunard Line), his answer to her query 'Can you tell me something about the Crompton family?' was 'Can you tell me something about the Walston family?'[16]

The couple were married in Wilton, New Hampshire at the Unitarian church. The young men who had originally come to ski were the ushers and, the celebrations over, Catherine and Harry sailed for England.

Bonte realised that her sister was not in love with Harry Walston. On the day of her marriage, Catherine went for a walk with Bonte and said: ' "I am not in love with Harry." And I said, "But, Bobs, you cannot marry a man that you're not in love with." She said, "I like Harry; he's very nice, and I can't stand life here." '[17] Years later Catherine wrote to Belinda that she felt that her marriage with Harry was 'NEVER a marriage. At the time I married him I decided that I would give it a try, and if I found anyone I liked better, I would leave Harry and marry X.'[18]

Lady Melchett was puzzled by the couple: 'It was really weird because one never saw them intimate with each other. They sat next to each other and that was the only sort of outward sign that there was a deep bond between them. Certainly Harry must have felt that he did have this beautiful jewel of a wife. There was a sort of mystery about their relationship. I couldn't think of why this great beauty . . . could have married him. I mean, Harry was very nice, but he was a man's man . . . '[19]

Harry was long-suffering, almost masochistic, perhaps without realising it: 'I think being basically rather dull, she did bring a lot of excitement and drama into his life, and maybe he thought it was worth it . . . But there was a mystery about Harry. He was everyone's idea of an Englishman – you know, you can't show emotion, you hide all your feelings. Whether there was a lot of emotion underneath I don't know.'[20] Elizabeth Walston (Harry's second wife) described her husband as 'an enigma' and a 'most uncommon man' who had difficulty expressing his love.[21] His son William said, 'My father thought my mother was a wonderful person. Since that was the case, whatever she wanted, whatever she needed, he would support. Even in his happy second marriage he continued to think of the deceased Catherine and was waiting to be with her. Harry was agnostic (I don't know whether he thought there was an afterlife), but if there was the slightest chance of one he wanted to be united with her.'[22] Although Harry often gave no public display of his devotion to Catherine, he adored her and his will directed that his ashes be spread upon her grave.

When Catherine met Greene, she and Harry had been married for twelve years and he was not a man to censure his wife's love affairs.

He felt that Catherine was an individual and had every right to do what she wanted.[23] As Catherine wrote to Belinda: 'Our sex life broke down before it hardly got started. We have never decided whose fault it was, and of course, it doesn't matter . . . we have become very loving friends, almost twins – brother & sister . . . Certainly I could not live with him without his compassion, his fondness, justice, humour, willingness.'[24] Although she no longer had sex with her husband, there would be many times when Greene became angry and jealous over Walston, for it was Harry, not Greene, she went home to.

*

Vivien knew that her husband was living with Dorothy in London (though Greene tried to keep this from her), and that he had many other women: 'I knew there were many, very many. Once a woman called Annette [a prostitute] phoned him and I answered. It was just a voice, an anonymous message for Graham. I knew he went with that sort of woman. I knew about it before the war. I never said a word.'[25] She had her reasons for keeping silent: 'How would you approach somebody? I had two small children and a house and everything, and perhaps it would go away. Nor did he speak about it.'[26] However, the full extent of Greene's unfaithfulness was not known to Vivien for some years: 'After he left me, Graham told me he had had thirty-two women.* I don't know whether it was meant to be wounding or just unimaginative. I mean I knew that he was unfaithful, but I didn't really want to know. As long as one didn't *know*, the family was kept together – that was more important.'[27]

Vivien told me she felt a remarkable equanimity about Dorothy, but that Mrs Walston disturbed her deeply. Catherine was young, beautiful, slim, and had lovely clothes of the sort that Vivien could neither afford nor obtain. It was a painful embarrassment for Vivien to be in Catherine's company:

> I remember her coming to Beaumont Street in the most marvellous coat – apricot, Paris mohair. Very good looking, beautiful features and this marvellous coat – in those hard times,

---

* A list has survived of forty-seven women Greene slept with, mostly prostitutes and pre-war assignations. In *The Quiet American*, when Pyle asks Fowler (a surrogate for Greene) if he has had a lot of women, he admits that not more than four women have had any importance to him – or he to them: 'The other forty-odd – one wonders why one does it . . . I wish I could have those nights back . . . One starts promiscuous and ends like one's grandfather, faithful to one woman' (pp. 102–3). Three of the four women of importance to Greene must be Vivien, Dorothy and Catherine.

because she went back and forth to America and she was very rich, and of course when one was counting the coupons in ration books to get another pair of gloves, to see this staggering sight, and a huge topaz brooch on it – perfectly plain coat – gorgeously cut, gorgeous material, wonderful apricot colour.[28]

Vivien's first remembered humiliation occurred early in Greene's affair with Catherine or even before it started. The war had just ended, and the house in Beaumont Street was, Vivien told me, comparatively unfurnished. Catherine's visit to Greene must have been late in 1946, and its effect on Vivien was quite startling:

> She was with Barbara Rothschild, a great friend of hers. Graham and I were coming down Beaumont Street – I can almost remember the piece of paving stone – it was outside where the new extension of the Randolph Hotel is, and they came up and, quite ignoring me, said: 'Oh you'll be coming to the party' – Barbara speaking to Graham, and Mrs Walston with her. And Barbara said to Mrs. Walston 'Are you going to wear your rocks?' (This was a new expression to me.) And Mrs Walston said, 'Oh yes. I think it's that sort of occasion', and, 'What time will you be coming, Graham?' and so forth. They were simply talking about this with me standing there, not a word to me. I stood and I was looking at this paving stone where we were standing, and there was really nothing else for me to do, while they were talking about things they all shared.[29]

'Until he met Mrs Walston he was always very sweet,' Vivien recalled, 'but I consider that was a turning point. He turned into a different person. She was a very bad influence on him – he became indifferent to the children and had furious and terrible tempers.' Greene's brother, Hugh, agreed with Vivien. Accounting for the fact that he had few letters from Greene during the late 1940s and 1950s, he put the blame squarely on Catherine: 'She didn't take to me nor I to her,' and he added, 'Graham became harder then and less friendly. It was all Catherine Walston's fault.'[30] In another interview Vivien returned to the charge: 'I think the change was entirely and purely Mrs Walston. A very powerful woman, with very strong sexual drive, and I'm not deficient myself, but she had a great number of men and as I say with her money . . . '[31]

But what Vivien never forgot, and what truly vexed her, was that she had brought about their meeting:

Mrs Walston wrote to Graham to say that his books had so influenced her that she was going to become a Catholic and she rang me up because he hadn't met her and she hadn't met him. But this was a way of meeting him I think. And would he come to her reception – she was being received into the Church. When I reported to Graham that Mrs Walston had telephoned to me asking him to be her godfather because he had brought her into the Church, he said, quite laughingly, 'Oh yes, do go [and Vivien did] and say all the right things and could you send some flowers or something from me.'[32]

Father Vincent provided a group photograph, taken immediately after Catherine had been received into the Catholic Church. She is wearing a checked dress and looks serene. What is remarkable about this photograph is that whilst Catherine is sitting on a chair and looking carefree, behind her and standing to her left is Vivien. She is wearing a rather old-fashioned hat and is not looking directly into the camera. Her head is turned to one side as she gazes at Catherine; her expression is puzzled and not friendly. Could it be that she had a premonition of what was to happen or was she simply suspicious of the happy, unsuspecting girl in front of her?

Greene telegraphed Catherine on 25 September 1946 and it is clear he did not initially expect the correspondence to continue: 'Dear Mrs Walston. This is a shockingly belated wire of congratulations and best wishes. I gave my secretary a telegram to send but in the rush of work (I had been away on the continent for a fortnight) she never sent it. I feel I am a most neglectful godfather!' There was also some forced humour: 'I haven't even sent you a silver mug or a spoon to bite.' His wire made a casual reference to her reception into the Church, wishing he'd been there, and he ended, 'Again all my wishes for the future, Yours, Graham Greene.' It seems the telegram went astray because we know Catherine wrote to Greene and he quickly sent her an apology explaining his 'chilling silence' on her special day.

Little correspondence from Catherine to Greene has come to light, but in one letter Greene wrote of finding in a drawer an early letter from Catherine. It started, he tells her, ' "Dear Godfather" and ended, "Yours sincerely, Catherine Walston." Why did I keep it? These are mysteries.'[33]

Years later, Vivien bitterly recalled that it was 'so ironic that C.W. asked ME to ask Graham to be her godfather . . . so I was instrumental'.[34] She was very blunt about what Catherine was up to: 'I think she was out to get him and got him. I think it was a quite straightforward grab. I remember writing to Father Vincent Turner and saying that it was just as if you got into a railway carriage with somebody you knew very well and they got the tickets and sat down to read and presently they got up and simply opened the door of the carriage and heaved you out. It was as sudden as that in a way.'[35] In looking back to those tempestuous days, Vivien may have felt that the affair began suddenly. However, it did not.

Greene's brisk recounting of the start of their affair did not mention Vivien's role in bringing them together or his being Catherine's godfather. He recalled that Robert Speaight had arranged for them to meet:

I suspect it may have been through Bobby Speaight and she said to Bobby Speaight oh I'd like to meet him and so I went along and had a drink one evening. I described the Windmill Theatre to her [nudes were allowed to pose there but not move] and how I used to go and get free tickets when I was on *Night and Day*. We got on very well and then she invited me to see her place in the country and it was getting late after lunch and she said 'Oh I'll fly you back.' . . . And that was the beginning of the affair.[36]

In an undated letter to Catherine, Vivien, perhaps still unsuspecting (or at least not willing to countenance her fears), wrote: 'We were THRILLED by the flight – it was a marvellous "present". Graham arrived before 5!' Greene referred to the trip in a letter to his mother and spoke of Catherine (though he spelled her name Katherine, for he was not yet closely acquainted with her): 'I had lunch with her at the farm & the question of how to get to Oxford cropped up. It was five minutes to three & it would have taken by train till after 8. A bright idea struck her & she said "Why not fly? I'll come over with you & fly back." She rang up an aerodrome, we leapt into a car: out again into a little tiny plane, & I was at Kidlington outside Oxford in 45 minutes. Lovely flight over the snowy country.' Greene's frugality is apparent: 'The ride was simply put down to her account.'[37]

It was on the plane that they *knew* they would become close friends. Greene was impressed by her beauty, but also by the ease and freedom wealth gave her, a freedom he had never known. He was, as usual, preternaturally alert (the novelist never slept) and very curious about people he'd met for the first time: 'He listened with the intense interest one feels in a stranger's life.'[38] He always needed 'the green light' before responding even to friendship, and it was Catherine's simple 'I like you so much' to which he reacted. From her words he had an immediate sense of truth and their conversation gave them both a feeling of security.

We do not know whether Catherine was already thinking of an affair, but Greene felt they were safely divided: Catherine had a husband and five small children; Greene a wife and two children; she was his goddaughter and he her godfather. Yet in a letter to Catherine, one year after that plane ride to Oxford, he recalled how love came to him: 'The act of creation is awfully odd and inexplicable like falling in love. A lock of hair touches one's eyes in a plane with East Anglia under snow and one is in love.'[39] When the plane descended at Kidlington, he walked alone in the darkness and rain to where Vivien and his children waited. Thinking of Catherine, he felt 'an extraordinary happiness'.[40] 'The taste of the lipstick was like something he'd never tasted before and that he would always remember. It seemed to him that an act had been committed which altered the whole world.'[41]

On 20 December 1946 he sent Catherine a telegram: 'A MILLION THANKS FOR WONDERFUL PRESENT. ALL EXTREMELY GRATEFUL.' The following day, 21 December 1946, Vivien added her comments: 'We couldn't BEGIN to say thank you "properly" (as children say) for the utterly magnificent object [Vivien appended a sketch of a huge turkey] which at present swings despondently in our larder! Many many most grateful acknowledgements. It is so very good of you and my breath was simply taken away . . . with the good news.' Vivien then rambled, in a further expression of her nervousness and perhaps in an attempt to stress the importance of family life and Greene's essential role in it: 'The children broke up the next day & I have been as busy as you may imagine one to be who has a 5 storey house & no domestic! Our crib [of Jesus] was ready on Sunday and we decorate the tree this afternoon: I ice the cake tonight, for we have *The Tea* on the Eve & light the Tree then too . . .'[42] But whatever Vivien wrote to Catherine, her real feelings remained pent up. In 1977 she admitted to having been ashamed and angry that Mrs Walston was dispensing charity in the shape of a bird.

On Boxing Day Greene wrote: 'What a lovely turkey. We gorged on Christmas Day until the children were limp. You really are a perfect god-daughter!' But he seemed to have had an ulterior motive in writing, for he used the occasion to initiate a meeting between them: 'Are you going to be in town in the New Year – won't you ring me up and have lunch with me and tell me about Poland . . . I've always wanted to see the place where Conrad originated – Podolia wherever that is.'[43]

Catherine's involvement with the Greenes increased. Early in 1947 she found a house which she felt they would like, and invited Greene to visit her in Cambridgeshire to look it over. 'I've had an exciting weekend as I think I've found a house – or rather my beautiful goddaughter, Katherine Walston, found it for me,' Greene wrote to his mother. 'It's called The Queen's House & it's at Linton, a village about ten miles from Cambridge: a most beautiful little Queen Anne house with an Elizabethan brick back part. In perfect order . . . two bathrooms, 1/2 an acre of garden with a chance of later buying an orchard next door. Newly painted & decorated. Loveliest staircase I have seen.'[44]

Vivien also wrote warmly to Catherine: 'the Linton house sounds delicious', but then in her feline way went on to say: 'The only difficulty is [that] it sounds rather "fenced in" . . . I am not at all mobile, for I can't drive a car nor even ride a bicycle (through sheer incompetence, not because I don't love to go up to London or go about). Therefore, wherever I am, I have to really settle in, if it's in the country & that means room for rabbit hutches (for the children, of course) & somewhere to sit in a garden someone else works in.'[45] The phrase 'someone else works in' suggests that she was very conscious of Catherine's wealth and perhaps feared she might be taken for a poor church mouse. Subtly, she poured cold water on the advantage of moving to Linton. At the same time, she was defensive and protested too much: 'It's much, much nicer having a village of course – think of all the thrilling happenings that one wouldn't miss for anything! I'd love to be in a village or market town or such, or enough in it to be part of it & dive into the Teeming Group of village life! I have to realise that Graham will have to spend a lot of time in London for quite a bit, so no Lady of Shalott existence for me . . . It's extremely angelic of you to set things going.'[46]

Then on St Valentine's Day, Vivien wrote in the greatest haste telling Catherine (what Catherine must have already known) that Greene had bought The Queen's House and made it over to her: 'I'm longing to see it, but *please* don't decide to go away to California or Ireland before WE move in!'[47] There is a proprietary feeling to these letters – 'love from *both* of us', 'before WE move in' – which reads as an attempt on Vivien's part to cope with someone wealthier, prettier and younger.

Vivien recalled her true feelings about the Linton house episode:

They [Catherine and Graham] were going to live in Linton . . . Before, when I was looking for a house, Graham rang me up at Beaumont Street, and said, 'I've bought a house at Linton near Cambridge.' And I was very upset – I hadn't been asked –

nothing. And it was far away – I knew nobody there, and I had lived so much of my life in Oxford, and it was very important to know the grocer you were registered with. [This was at a time when there were serious food shortages.] And I was horrified. It was a rather pretty Queen Anne on the outside, but the back was awful. It was very medieval and had never been touched – great draughty doorways and up and down steps. I couldn't think how I was going to manage alone with the two children and I didn't know a soul. I said 'I don't see how I can manage it at all.' And quite suddenly he realised he was going to be deeply involved with Mrs Walston and having me at Linton near them was the last thing he wanted. So he immediately sold the house and we never went anywhere near it.[48]

Vivien was an intellectual and an omnivorous reader, but she could be nervous when she wasn't sure of herself. While sometimes condescending to those beneath her, she was rather uncertain of herself with those above her socially and Catherine Walston always set her teeth on edge. Her husband was well aware of her nature and how others reacted to her. In *The Heart of the Matter*, Scobie (modelled on Greene) is disturbed by young Fraser calling Scobie's wife Louise (partly modelled on Vivien) 'Literary Louise'. Aware of her 'kindly Lady Bountiful manner', Scobie goes on to speak compassionately about Louise in a way that Greene thought applied to Vivien: 'He knew every one of her faults. How often he had winced at her patronage of strangers. He knew each phrase, each intonation that alienated others. Sometimes he longed to warn her – don't wear that dress, don't say that again, as a mother might teach a daughter, but he had to remain silent . . . What right have you, he longed to exclaim, to criticize her? This is my doing. This is what I've made of her.'[49]

Yet the affair did not really become serious until Greene and Catherine went to Achill together in April 1947 to 'her' island (or rather the cottage on Achill which belonged to her and *not* to her husband). Achill was to be their escape from the world into their own particular Paradise.

In Greene's first novel, *The Man Within*, the hero's love for Elizabeth reflects uncannily young Greene's love for Vivien. The book is full of a youngster's devotion, even worship, and Elizabeth (Vivien in life) is seen as a saintly person. What Greene admired in Vivien *before* his marriage was her serenity, sanity and purity. She alone was able to give him a sense of peace. In *The Man Within*, the hero, Andrews, finds a private paradisal cottage, isolated on the

Sussex Downs where Elizabeth lives. But there is a serpent wriggling in the love nest.

Andrews loves his Elizabeth yet also finds it necessary to escape from her strong sense of sanctity. Referring to his own weakness of character, Andrews admits that he would be creeping out of the house to visit prostitutes before he'd been married a month. Here is Greene's nature.

Greene's love for Catherine was real, but it was also an escape from his manic London phase. In a sense it was a replica of the fictional love described in *The Man Within*, though Greene, no longer young and inexperienced, was now on the threshold of middle age. The originator of the seedy world called Greeneland had at times a desperate need to disappear from such a world, and what fitted his need psychologically was escape to a cottage like the one of *The Man Within*. The cottage at Achill had a corrugated roof, no running water and only a cold tap outside. It was not as Vivien imagined it to be (Catherine, with extraordinary chutzpah, wrote to Vivien about it): 'I can't quite visualise you on the earth floor in Ireland. It sounds as if it might be cold in February.' But then, responding to what would have pleased her (though *not* her husband), Vivien added: 'I think there must be the softest white lambskin rugs on it. With love from *both* of us.'[50]

*

'All arrangements made for April,' Greene wrote to Catherine. And love was to happen at Achill, an intense love described in his poem 'I Do Not Believe', which was written for Catherine but not published until 1983, five years after her death:

> I can believe only in love that strikes suddenly
> out of a clear sky;
> I do not believe in the slow germination of friendship
> or one that asks 'why?'
>
> Because our love came savagely, suddenly,
> like an act of war,
> I cannot conceive a love that rises gently
> and subsides without a scar.[51]

Greene's love would certainly not 'subside without a scar', for what was he to do with a wife whom he'd once described as 'the most important thing in life & the one thing it would be utter terror to lose' – and a mistress in Gordon Square who lived her life for him? Dorothy had shown herself, during the blitz, to be a heroine.

She had a more masculine courage than Vivien, and was the closest Greene ever came to having a lover, a drinking partner and a friend, in one person.

At first he carried on as if no problem existed. The idea of giving up either wife or mistress was unthinkable. He could not, to use Vivien's phrase, simply push them both out of the train. However, trouble was brewing, and he knew he'd have to lie.

Initially he involved himself in what he always knew was a vain struggle to maintain the lies. Of course, they were neither frequent nor necessary so far as Vivien was concerned. He visited his wife and children at Oxford only at weekends. His mistress was a different case, though he strenuously tried to avoid immediate discovery.

Dorothy (called 'my girl' or simply 'MG') was often the topic of Greene's correspondence with Catherine: 'She [Dorothy] is taking the line that this new Catholicism of mine won't last but that she'll play it [out] as long as I will.'[52] Soon Dorothy became suspicious: 'a bit of a row blew up before I left – she said I had changed so much in Ireland', but discovery of his new affair was, at first, containable: 'she still believes that it's simply that I've come under the influence of a pious convert!'[53] Catherine was pious and a convert, but Dorothy had underestimated her terribly.

Having slept with Catherine, Greene continued to desire her obsessively. Whatever he now did with Dorothy recalled Catherine: 'I missed you so much on Sunday. Mass wasn't the same at all. We went to 12 o'clock [Mass] at St. Patrick's Soho and had a drink afterwards at the *Salisbury* in St Martin's Lane.'[54] Greene felt restless. He tried to ring Catherine unsuccessfully from Charing Cross and went to bed depressed, but woke up 'blissfully' happy because he'd recalled their time on Achill and her saying to him, 'I like your sexy smell.' Then the next day Greene had a letter from her ('how beautiful your handwriting is') and got her on the phone: 'Result I feel cheerful and I've written 1,000 words!'[55]

Catherine's character and wealth did not make her an easy conquest for the famous novelist. He was never certain of her love – after all, she had had many lovers – and he often tried to persuade her that she did love him. 'And you love me – you do, you know, and I'll see you on Thursday.'[56]

Time after time Greene returned to those halcyon days on Achill: 'Oh how I want the peace of Achill and you, darling. I hate everything here.'[57] When at the cottage, the Atlantic would blow in through the top of the door, and there was a feeling of freshness and dampness on the skin when they went out in the night in their pyjamas. Perfectly ordinary things took on a symbolic importance when he described their days there – the list appears in numerous letters: 'I miss bread-making, candles, motor licence, graveyards more than I can say.'[58]

Later, when Catherine was returning to Achill alone, Greene wrote a note to remind her of three things – 'that I'm still terribly in love with you, that I miss you (your voice saying "Good morning, Graham" at tea time) and that I want you.' He remembered the sound of the rusty gate as it swung open; orange juice at three in the morning after sex; Catherine dressed in her pyjama top nursing the fire and filling the turf bucket; Catherine's whistling and the clink of washing up as he tried to work in the next room, and her bread-making.[59] It was the physical things and the memories of them that brought Greene a sense of peace, 'the most beautiful word in the language'.[60]

When Catherine suggested that they take John Hayward, their crippled friend, to Achill on their next visit, Greene worried: 'I felt your plan was doubtfully wise. I still think they won't understand the *three* of us, but I'm quite prepared to do what you want in this case. It seems a pity if one has to give up going to Achill together. It's got under our skin. Only yesterday I was longing to push the rusty gate and see it swing.' He went on to describe his depression:

> I feel very dry and dark nightish. I hope we get to Achill but it's as you wish . . . how I long for a spot of peace again, Cafryn [in letters Greene often shortened her name]. Sometimes I feel homesick for [Achill] . . . Don't let's give it up.[61]

*

If Greene sometimes felt 'dry and dark nightish' in the early days of his love for Catherine, and if she was an escape from intolerable conditions in his personal life – what were those conditions? There is a passage in *The Heart of the Matter* (there are many such passages) which reflects Greene's character:

> He laid his pen down again and loneliness sat across the table opposite him. No man surely was less alone with his wife upstairs and his mistress little more than five hundred yards away up the hill, and yet it was loneliness that seated itself like a companion who doesn't need to speak. It seemed to him that he had never been so alone before.[62]

Greene had his own wife and mistress in mind here (the last third of *The Heart of the Matter* was written *after* he'd met and fallen in love with Catherine): and was using his life as an intelligence officer in Freetown as the basis for Scobie's life. He transferred his problems with his wife and mistress to an African setting. In spite of the fact that Vivien led a solitary life in Oxford (with her two young children) while her husband was abroad, Louise, Scobie's wife, is based in part on Vivien's character as Greene saw it; Helen, Scobie's mistress in Africa, on his mistress Dorothy in London – the five hundred yards were three thousand miles and in another country.

The marital conditions described in *The Heart of the Matter* did not exist while Greene was in Africa, but developed after he returned to England. They represent the stage of his life just prior to the entrance of Catherine. The world war had ended: the private war between Vivien and Greene had begun. Moreover, there was growing unhappiness between Greene and Dorothy. His seven-year-old love affair was turning sour and causing both of them deep anxiety. The core of Greene's unhappiness was in his nature, that mixture of extreme sensitivity and sexual desire for females who came within his orbit. Guilt was the single most powerful emotion in Greene and he came to feel that he was bad for both his wife and his mistress. This guilt irrevocably bound him, through a sense of pity and responsibility, to both women when love died.

In discussing Greene's sense of guilt, Vivien commented: 'I've said to him often: "If only you'd forget your guilt you'd treat me more nicely." It's because of that that he's nastier to me. He's got no sense of guilt with [the] others. There's no vows. Guilt makes you hate yourself, and then that rebounds on the person.'[63]

A study of his autobiographies, *A Sort of Life* and *Ways of Escape*, and his unpublished letters to Catherine, reveals the state of his marriage and his relationship with his mistress Dorothy. But to begin to understand his personal experiences it is necessary to read his fiction, in particular *The Heart of the Matter*. Novels declare themselves as fictions not as personal histories, though they mine the personal terrain. Greene always felt that so long as he presented his intimate experiences as fiction his secrets would remain unrecognised, and this appealed to his guarded nature.

The first part of *The Heart of the Matter* bears witness to his marital troubles: the second to his disturbed relationship with his mistress. By the time Catherine came on the scene, Greene was as unhappy and as suicidal as Major Scobie.

Like Scobie, Greene realised that 'No man could guarantee love for ever.' Once love had fled, what remained was the responsibility to maintain happiness in those he once loved, but the burden became oppressive.[64] Scobie looks at his wife Louise, her 'eyes

bloodshot with tears' and sees the visible signs of his failure as a
husband. Greene was troubled by what Vivien had become because
of their marriage: 'Fifteen years form a face, gentleness ebbs with
experience . . . He had led the way: the experience that had come to
her was the experience selected by himself. He had formed her
face.'[65]

What disturbs Louise is that Scobie no longer loves her.
Recognising that Vivien knew that he no longer loved her, Greene,
like Scobie, determined not to admit this:

I shall try to talk about anything under the sun to postpone seeing
her misery (it would be waiting at the corners of her mouth to
take possession of her whole face) . . . People talk about the
courage of the condemned walking to the place of execution:
sometimes it needs as much courage to walk with any kind of
bearing towards another person's habitual misery ... . I'll talk and
talk, but all the time I shall know I'm coming nearer to the
moment when I shall say, 'What about [your day] darling?' and let
the misery in.[66]

Although the subject matter (Scobie's failure to obtain money for
his wife's holiday) was not drawn from Greene's life, *The Heart of the
Matter* may reveal the probable form of the arguments between
Greene and Vivien:

'Ticki, why are you such a coward? Why don't you tell me it's
all off?'
'All off?'
'You know what I mean . . . I'm not a child, Ticki. Why don't
you say straight out – "you can't go"?'
. . . Reluctantly he had recourse to the hated nickname. If that
failed, the misery would deepen . . . 'Trust Ticki,' he said. It was
as if a ligament tightened in his brain with the suspense. If only I
could postpone the misery, he thought, until daylight. Misery is
worse in the darkness.[67]

The misery grows; Louise cries dumbly before him. He tries to
console her, but then they have reached a new level: 'Louise said,
"I've known it for years. You don't love me." She spoke with calm.
He knew that calm – it meant they had reached the quiet centre of
the storm: always in this region at about this time they began to
speak the truth at each other.'[68]

The truth meant a great deal to Greene, for lies had the taint of mortality about them. There came a time, within two years of meeting Catherine, when he went to enormous trouble to rid himself (often causing chagrin and pain in others) of the white lies he felt he was forced to tell.

But at this stage lying was a necessity and seemed justified: 'The truth, he thought, has never been of any real value to any human being – it is a symbol for mathematicians and philosophers to pursue. In human relations kindness and lies are worth a thousand truths. He involved himself in what he always knew was a vain struggle to retain the lies. "Don't be absurd, darling. Who do you think I love if I don't love you?" '[69]

Louise's devastating answer has been expressed by Vivien in interviews: ' "You don't love anybody." "Is that why I treat you so badly?" He tried to hit a light note, and it sounded hollowly back at him. "That's your conscience," she said, "your sense of duty. You've never loved anyone . . . " "Except myself, of course. You always say I love myself." '[70]

With deadly accuracy Louise replies:

'No, I don't think you do.'
He defended himself by evasions. In this cyclonic centre he was powerless to give the comforting lie. 'I try all the time to keep you happy. I work hard for that.'
'Ticki, you won't even say you love me. Go on. Say it once.'
. . . 'And yet you want to go away from me,' he said.
'Yes,' she said, 'I know you aren't happy either. Without me you'll have peace.'

This was what he always left out of account – the accuracy of her observation. He had nearly everything, and all he needed was peace . . . If he had become young again this was the life he would have chosen to live; only this time he would not have expected any other person to share it with him . . .

'You are talking nonsense, dear,' he said, and went through the doomed motions of mixing another gin and bitters. Again the nerve in his head tightened; unhappiness had uncoiled with its inevitable routine – first her misery and his strained attempts to leave everything unsaid: then her own calm statement of truths much better lied about, and finally the snapping of his own control – truths flung back at her as though she were his enemy. As he embarked on this last stage, crying suddenly and truthfully out at her while the angostura trembled in his hand, 'You can't give me peace . . . You haven't any conception,' he accused her, 'of what peace means.' . . . For he dreamed of peace by day and night. Once in sleep it had appeared to him as the great glowing shoulder of the moon heaving across his window like an iceberg, Arctic and destructive in the moment before the world was struck . . . Peace seemed to him the most beautiful word in the language: My peace I give you, my peace I leave with you: O Lamb of God, who takest away the sins of the world, grant us thy peace. In the Mass he pressed his fingers against his eyes to keep the tears of longing in.

Louise said with the old tenderness, 'Poor dear, you wish I were dead . . . You want to be alone.'

He replied obstinately, 'I want you to be happy.'[71]

Louise makes a statement regarding Scobie's conversion which, in part, rings true of Greene: 'Ticki, I sometimes think you just became a Catholic to marry me. It doesn't mean a thing to you, does it?'[72] Although Greene's faith was very important to him, Louise's comments express Vivien's opinion: after Greene's death Vivien said that she did not believe her husband was a true Catholic. Like Louise, Vivien gave her husband the nickname of 'Ticki' – it was only one of the many nicknames Vivien used in verbal play with her husband[*] and gave me reasons why she used nicknames, acknowledging the effect it had on Greene – he disliked this habit of hers. What Vivien did not know was that Greene was also aware of why she used them: 'These things', says Louise, 'creep on you before you know where you are. Suddenly you are calling someone Bear [Vivien called her daughter Bear] or Ticki, and the real names seem bald and formal, and the next you know they hate you for it.'[73]

In letters to Catherine, Greene voiced a great longing to escape both from his wife and Dorothy – and for him, both Achill and Catherine symbolised *peace*. In one letter he tried to define this: 'The day was peaceful, but I don't use the word peaceful in the same way as peace. Peaceful is negative – means no scenes and no positive unhappiness. But peace is positive, and all sorts of unpeaceful things like being in love and making love can be part of it. I think even a sikh massacre could be part of it.'[74] Two days earlier he wrote: 'My dear, before you cropped up, I used to have odd dreams of peace – that dream of the moon I gave to Scobie for instance.'[75]

Louise recognises that if she leaves Scobie (in her case to go to South Africa), he will gain his peace, and she even says, as we've seen: 'Poor dear, you wish I were dead . . . You want to be alone.' This simple line comes from a terrible dream Greene had. In the

---

* See Vol. One, ch. 25, for others.

same letter to Catherine in which he wrote of the moon image and his need for peace, he writes: 'I also dreamed this last time that Vivien died. She was dying and I walking up and down trying to pray. I found I simply couldn't pray for her life, so I simply prayed that she wouldn't have any pain.'[76]

17

The Third Man and Other Friends

'It's just buggery, boys.'
— DAVID O. SELZNICK

WRITING to Catherine Walston in September 1947, Greene made a rare boast: 'O the Greene stock is booming. [The film] *This Gun for Hire* revived at the Plaza, reprint of *19 Stories* announced, two more of uniform edition and huge enthusiasm for script of "Basement Room".' Along the right-hand edge of the letter he wrote, 'After this burst of self-advertisement. Love Graham.'

Nothing in his letters to Catherine could have given any impression that the script he was writing in collaboration with the film director, Carol Reed, would lead to 'huge enthusiasm'. On the contrary, Greene's first reference to it suggests no excitement: 'They [Alexander Korda and Carol Reed] are buying a short story of mine called "The Basement Room" and want me to work on it. Once I suppose I'd have been excited and pleased . . . by all this (it means 3,000 pounds), but I feel dreary.'[1] And in successive letters, Greene expressed boredom, describing the work as 'a drudgery'.[2]

To some degree his comments masked his real feelings, for, in particular, Greene was beginning to feel a deep friendship for the film producer, Sir Alexander Korda. In his early days, Greene had vigorously attacked Korda, suggesting that he was great only as a publicist 'since he had put over so many undistinguished and positively bad films as if they were a succession of masterpieces'.[3] Yet here was Greene, with Carol Reed as director and Alexander Korda as banker, in the process of producing two of the greatest films of the immediate postwar era — *The Fallen Idol* (based on 'The Basement Room') and *The Third Man*.

Carol Reed recalled how their successful collaboration began. For some time he and Korda had been looking for a story to turn into a

239

film. In Korda's penthouse at Claridge's, Reed mentioned Greene's novel *England Made Me*. Korda countered with 'The Basement Room', and retired to bed to nurse a cold. When Reed finished reading the story, he went to Korda and found him 'lying with his head propped up against a lot of pillows. I said to him: "This is a wonderful story," and expressed the strong desire to persuade Greene to work with [me]. Alex stretched out an arm from under the blanket and caught the telephone. "Is 'The Basement Room' free?" "Yes." "Well, would you ask the author if he would lunch with Carol Reed and talk it over?"'[4] Ten minutes later the telephone rang. Greene would be at the restaurant of Arlington House (Korda's headquarters) the following day at one o'clock.[5]

As soon as Greene came into the restaurant, Reed saw what sort of man he was: 'frightfully to-the-point and practical. There was no wasting of time with him, even to asking "How are you?" and that sort of thing . . . I had put my question to him [and] he answered: "How do you see it?" Then we talked things over.'[6]

But Greene had reservations, believing that the subject matter of the story – 'a murder committed by the most sympathetic character and an unhappy ending' – was not filmable.[7] In the story the young boy Philip (the film version changed his name to Felipe and made him an ambassador's son) dies an embittered old man, his psychological character ruined by his premature initiation into an adult world he never quite understood. In the collaboration which followed, Reed and Greene changed the story 'so that the subject was no longer a small boy who unwittingly betrayed his best friend to the police, but dealt instead with a small boy who believed that his friend was a murderer and nearly procured his arrest by telling lies in his defence'. Greene thought this was a good subject, especially with Reed handling it.[8]

Greene found in Reed a 'fine film and literary intelligence'. In reviewing the film *The Stars Look Down* in 1940, he had praised his direction: 'He handles his players like a master, so one remembers them only as people.'[9] Reed had a strong desire to present in film terms the author's ideas: 'I think it is the director's job . . . to convey faithfully what the author had in mind.'[10] At last, Greene had met someone he could work with on an equal footing. Reed's principles would satisfy the most fastidious of authors: 'Unless you have worked with the author in the first place you cannot convey to the actors what he had in mind nor can you convey to the editor at the end the original idea. In making a picture you have got to go back to the first stage to see how important something may be in establishing this scene or that character.'[11]

During the collaboration Reed and Greene developed a strong professional and personal admiration for each other. They took a suite of rooms in a Brighton hotel with interconnecting doors, plus a room with a secretary between them. Greene started by making changes to his original, though he used the dialogue from his story whenever it seemed to fit, and in the first version of the script a great deal of the original dialogue was kept. Then, as the writer and director kept working, the words from the original story were 'slowly whittled down to reduce the dialogue as much as possible'. Greene knew what he was doing in turning his story first into a film treatment and then into a script, since the right rhythm in a book may seem unrealistic on the screen and need modification: 'Dialogue in fiction must have the flavour of realism, without having to be real, while on the screen the camera emphasizes the realism of the situation.' Curiously enough, you have to be closer in a film to real conversation 'in order that the dialogue will match the realistic furnishings of the setting'.

As Greene wrote the first draft, Reed suggested revisions which Greene either accepted or to which he offered alternatives. Once this draft was completed, Greene wrote ten more pages to fit the agreed new ending.[12] Reed remembered (wrongly) that the script took about ten days. In fact it was completed in four months, June to September 1947.[13]

The Fallen Idol was released in England in September 1948, and in America was entitled *The Lost Illusion*, the working title during the film's production. This was Greene's first *real* work for the cinema and his favourite among his film scripts. The film received substantial praise and deserved it. In New York it was spoken of as having subtlety, intelligence, unforced humour and tragedy, and most of all as being free from theatrical posturing.[14]

*

The Third Man is a classic film and is perhaps the story everyone identifies with Greene. It is a memorable and triumphant thriller, winning the Grand Prix for best feature film in the 1949 International Film Festival at Cannes. The fact that it is still being shown daily in Vienna is evidence of its continued popularity. As Greene told it, *The Third Man* had a casual birth: 'Sometimes one may turn them over [stories] after many years and think regretfully they would have been good once, in a time now dead. So it was that *long before* [emphasis added], on the flap of an envelope, I had written an opening paragraph: "I had paid my last farewell to Harry a week ago, when his coffin was lowered into the frozen February ground, so that it was with incredulity that I saw him pass by, without a sign of recognition, among the host of strangers in the Strand." '[15]

A year after *The Fallen Idol*, Greene was asked by Korda over dinner to write another film script for Carol Reed. Greene came up with the note he had written on the flap of an envelope about the last farewell to Harry – this paragraph only, because he had taken the story no further and had not an inkling of what would come next. This was an intriguing titbit to drop on the table beside Korda at dinner, but the story was in fact incorrect.[16]

As Greene told it, he took his 'note on an envelope' to Vienna because Alexander Korda wished to make a film about the city's four-power occupation. Vienna, in 1947, was divided into American, Russian, French and British zones, the inner city being administered by each power in turn. The battle-scarred, bombed-out ruins of the city fascinated Korda and he wanted to put them on film: 'He was prepared', Greene told me, 'to let me pursue the tracks of Harry.'[17]

On 28 September 1947 Greene wrote to Catherine of his feelings after completing a novel: 'I sent *The Heart of the Matter* to Heinemann yesterday, and I have no ideas for another book and feel I never shall . . . I feel very empty and played out . . . This is always the way when a book is finally cleared. It affects one badly, so that even one's religion doesn't mean a thing.'

But two days later the situation changed dramatically – the creative impulse for Greene was always somewhat miraculous. That night at 11 p.m. he wrote to Catherine, then in America:

I believe I've got a *book* coming. I feel so excited that I spell out your name in full carefully sticking my tongue between my teeth to pronounce it right. The act of creation is awfully odd and inexplicable like falling in love . . . Tonight I had a solitary good dinner where I usually go with My Girl and afterwards felt vaguely restless (not sexually, just restless) so I walked to the Café Royal and sat and read *The Aran Islands*, and drank beer till about 10 and then I still felt restless, so I walked all up Piccadilly and back and went into a Gent's in Brick Street, and suddenly in the Gent's, I saw the three chunks, the beginning, the middle and the end, and in some ways all the ideas I had – the first sentence of the thriller about the dead Harry who wasn't dead, the Risen-from-the-dead story, and then the other day in the train all seemed to come together. I hope to God it lasts – they don't always. I want to begin the next book with you in Ireland – if possible at Achill, but on Aran or Inishboffin or the Galway Hotel or anywhere.

Now I shall go to bed with lots of aspirin, but I shan't sleep.[18]

In a postscript he added: 'Today I read an article which said "Unlike such writers as James Joyce and Graham Greene . . ." – damn it. I'm not played out yet.'

Greene went to Korda's for dinner soon after he had had this extraordinary inspiration about a man risen from the dead. When he went to Vienna the following February, he had the beginning, middle and end of the story, not just the first sentence. The sentence scribbled on the back of an old envelope was not written *long before* he went to Korda's, and his knowledge of the development of the story was already substantial.

However, Greene had originally intended to set his story in London, not Vienna. To tie it into the complications of that occupied, ruined city clearly would cause difficulties – and it did.

Greene left for Vienna in February 1948 seeking first-hand impressions, but went reluctantly, for the tremendous desire to see more of Catherine grew upon him: 'I'm getting dissatisfied with small snippets of you.'[19] On the plane, he felt 'lonely, screw-eyed & miserable'.[20] He was looking forward to finishing his preliminary survey of Vienna so that he could rendezvous later with Catherine.

He was met at the airport by Elizabeth Montagu, daughter of Lord Montagu, who worked for Korda and had the job of looking after Greene, and making sure that he saw all he needed to. She introduced Greene to a friend of hers, the London *Times* correspondent, Peter Smollett (anglicised from H. P. Smolka), who was extremely knowledgeable about conditions and confusions involved in the four-power occupation. She took him to the opera (they were performing *Fidelio*); the theatre was one of the few not destroyed by bombing. There was rubble everywhere and Greene watched pedestrians picking their way through the mounds of it caused by the terrible Allied bombing. There was very little entertainment except clubs where nude dancing took place.

Elizabeth Montagu managed to get Greene a room in the famous Sacher hotel – difficult to do because it was the senior officers' transit club for British troops in Austria. When he arrived there was snow on the roofs and 'sleet driving along the tarmac'. At the terminal he had evidence of his increasing fame: 'a press photographer waiting to catch me unshaved, & the editor of the English paper'.[21] In that strange way which is typical of Greene he noted: 'How humiliating it is to be one of the victors because all the jokes are turned against the victors, never against the defeated!'[22]

In the script, Greene has a short, apt description of the city – it was the 'smashed dreary city of Vienna'.[23] That February Greene was struck by the dreadful circumstances of the Viennese, many of whom were collapsing in the streets from starvation. The narrator in the story, Colonel Calloway, in charge of the British Military Police in Vienna, echoes Greene's own experience: 'I never knew Vienna between the wars, and I am too young to remember the old Vienna with its Strauss music and its bogus easy charm; to me it is simply a city of undignified ruins which turned that February into great glaciers of snow and ice.'[24]

Elizabeth Montagu took Greene to the central cemetery, which he insisted they visit as a setting for Harry Lime's pretended burial: 'Vienna looks indescribably miserable. I spotted a good cemetery for my opening – with a tramline running beside it & opposite a half mile line of monumental stonemasons . . . Today it's been snowing for 24 hours & everything looks lovely under the snow . . . the main feature of my morning ride was the fantastic central cemetery with the monuments looking grotesque under snow – white moustaches when there shouldn't have been & white bonnets slipping over eyes of stone women who should have been stark naked.'[25] *The Third Man* closely follows his letter to Catherine:

The trams ran along the high wall of the Central Cemetery, and for a mile on the other side of the rails stretched the monumental masons and the market gardeners – an apparently endless chain of gravestones waiting for owners and wreaths waiting for mourners . . . the avenues of graves, each avenue numbered and lettered, stretched out like the spokes of an enormous wheel . . . The snow gave the great pompous family headstones an air of grotesque comedy: a toupée of snow slipped sideway over an angelic face, a saint wore a heavy white moustache, and a shako of snow tipped at a drunken angle over the bust of a superior civil servant . . . [26]

By 17 February 1948 he wrote: 'the story is crystallising & I'm longing to get away' – to Rome, where he had arranged to meet Catherine as soon as he felt the story was ready for writing. He missed Catherine dreadfully: 'One feels terribly lonely in a crowd of people being hospitable. I want to be on my own with you. This is the sort of life that stretches ahead:

Today: [Tuesday]
4.30 Austrian Catholic publisher.
6. American police chief.
7.15 – 1 or 2 [in the morning] *The Times* correspondent [Smollett].
Wed 12.30 A large jovial American Information Service woman.

4. A gigolo at the Casanova Bar.

7. British Council man.

Thursday. Lunch The 20-year-old actress [Alida Valli].

6. A hideous hawk-like American woman who won't take No for an answer.

Friday. Lunch. A playboy Austrian count.

Dinner. English couple.

Saturday. Elizabeth Bowen cocktail party.

Sunday. Lunching with an Austrian industrialist.

Monday. 6.30 a.m. off Thank God.'[27]

In *Ways of Escape*, Greene described dining with his friend Elizabeth Bowen, who had come to Vienna to lecture at the British Institute as a guest of the British Council. After dinner, Greene took her to the Oriental, a rather seedy night club:

'They will be raiding this place at midnight [Greene told Elizabeth].'

'How do you know?'

'I have my contacts.'

Exactly at the stroke of twelve, as I had asked my friend [Charles Beauclerk, chief information officer] to arrange, a British sergeant came clattering down the stairs, followed by a Russian, a French and an American military policeman. The place was in half-darkness, but without hesitation (I had described her with care) he strode across the cellar and demanded to see Elizabeth's passport. She looked at me with respect – the British Council had not given her so dramatic an evening.

*

On 12 February Greene wrote to Catherine: 'I have your photograph stuck up in a letter rack under the light, as though I was an undergraduate in love for the first time. Have I ever felt like this before?' As the time for their meeting in Rome drew nearer he longed for the isolation of lovers: 'Let's be really anti-social & lone wolves. I'm tired to death of company.'[28]

He thought of leaving Vienna by train because it would have been easier to reach Italy that way, but for the sake of adventure, he decided to fly: 'I suppose I could stop here & go down by train to Italy but that looks like missing an exciting story in Prague [it was thought that a revolution was breaking out there] & one's Catholic hosts then might think one was turning tail.'[29] Before leaving for Prague, Greene again expressed his longing: 'I . . . desire [you] very badly & I can't believe I saw you only a week ago today . . . If it wasn't for your photo I feel I should almost forget what you looked like – such aeons & centuries of days.'[30]

He arrived in Prague in the middle of a snow storm. There was no food on the plane, no food in the hotel, and no rooms to be had. He spent the night on a sofa. Eventually, scrambling for food, he found his way to the basement, where he discovered a ball for the staff in progress and suddenly there was food aplenty. He watched the Venezuelan ambassador dancing with the fat cook (wise man) and felt, if this was a revolution, it was a happy one. Early the next morning he was out in the streets seeking the blasts of riot and revolution to discover no more than a crackpot inventor who spoke of a parachute which could be guided for fifty kilometres after the drop, and, more extravagantly, a machine which could build a foot of wall every second.

Greene was in Prague for a week, still hoping to find himself in the middle of a revolution – but little was happening in the streets apart from marches and shouting crowds waving red flags. He remembered the novelist Egon Hostovsky sitting on his sofa bed, and telling him that Jan Masaryk, the Czech Foreign Minister (whose father, Thomas Masaryk, had earlier been president), had said goodbye to his staff and a few days later was dead, an apparent suicide which might well have been murder.

On 27 February 1948 a paragraph appeared in the *News Chronicle* about Greene the eternal traveller, under the heading of 'Czech-mate': 'A guest in Prague's most ambitious hotel, the Alcron, when it passed yesterday from private into public ownership, was novelist Graham Greene, who is in Prague at the moment to lecture for the British Council. He looked for his Communist waiter. He had been appointed national administrator.' To which Greene replied when the note came to his attention: 'the Alcron did not pass from private into public ownership, I am certainly unaware of ever having been served by a Communist waiter who had been appointed national administrator, and I was not lecturing for the British Council.'[31]

*

He met Catherine in Rome in late February and began writing the treatment for *The Third Man*. They visited Ravello together and, upon completing the story, he read it aloud to her in bed. Perhaps more important for Greene's future was finding a small villa in Anacapri, Rosaio, where most of his later books were to be written at least in part.[32] It was a magical place: 'There I can do more in three weeks than I could in three months at [home].'[33]

The villa had originally belonged to Count Cerio. It had been a refuge for Maxim Gorky, Norman Douglas and Jan Masaryk when they first arrived on the island. Immediately after the First World War Francis Brett Young lived there and then it was sold to Compton Mackenzie. According to John Cairncross, a friend from Greene's days with the SIS, Greene picked it up for a song 'because a South African, who had got it for his mistress, had to leave'.[34] Shirley Hazzard recalled that Greene bought the villa and its contents for only £3,000, a bargain he often referred to with satisfaction.

Visiting Rosaio one might expect to find photographs of wife or children or mistress, some pointers to Greene's private life. Not so. While the ground floor was not bare, it was not sumptuous either. His study upstairs was reached by a very short staircase to a door into the loft. The study was extremely small with only a skylight and contained a wooden trestle table of rough unplaned wood and a rough wooden bed at right angles to it. Nothing else. The walls were whitewashed and, apart from a small cross, without ornament – a monastic cell. This was his 'happy home' high in the mountains.[35]

He loved Capri. It was here that he made friends with the navigator Michael Richey (now over seventy and still sailing his boat *Jester* alone across the Atlantic); the brilliant writer Shirley Hazzard and her husband, the biographer Francis Steegmuller; and with Dottoressa Moor, of whom he wrote: 'in her moments of bawdry she resembled the Wife of Bath and in rambling sexual memories Mrs Bloom's monologue'. She had 'startling blue eyes, tough electric hair as alive as a bundle of fighting snakes, a small square body with big teeth' and she had a capacity for passionate living Greene had known in no other woman. She was the trusted doctor for the poor in Capri – she'd take the pulse of a peasant in the street, the blood pressure of a fisherman in her house – and she was paid in kind, a fish, a lettuce from a stall in Caprile, or fruit, sometimes a bottle of wine.[36] Greene was particularly friendly with the artist Countess Cerio (the leading Caprian on the island, whose grandfather was a friend of Joseph Conrad) and, unexpectedly, with Norman Douglas.

He met Douglas, hedonist and sybarite, in 1948 soon after he had bought Rosaio with the proceeds of *The Third Man*. Douglas was no longer writing; his masterpiece *South Wind* had appeared as early as 1917. His novels had never attained wide circulation and he was perennially short of funds. Greene was fascinated by him, especially by his philosophy, which he tried to adopt while on the island: 'find everything useful and nothing indispensable, and everything wonderful and nothing miraculous'.[37] Douglas was tolerant, pagan in outlook, and railed against hypocrisy, puritanism and smugness. All these qualities, but for Douglas's denial of the miraculous, suited Greene. Douglas had been a close friend of Joseph Conrad (whom Greene admired), had children, but was now living in Capri at the home of a friend. Greene's other friend Sir Harold Acton (himself a homosexual) was a little jealous of his friendship with Douglas: 'he did not think it right . . . Norman having this friendship and warmth for a heterosexual'.[38] There must have been something special about Douglas, for he was a strange man for Greene to like, because he was a homosexual.

Mario Soldati described Greene as 'a free man and without prejudice, but he had a kind of bitterness against homosexuals. He was full of contradictions . . . but at the same time he loved Norman Douglas immensely.'[39] Soldati recalled Greene's hostility to the playwright Terence Rattigan, who wrote the first treatment for the film *Brighton Rock*. Soldati pointed out that Greene's difference in attitude was not because he objected to Rattigan the homosexual but to Rattigan the hypocrite, the crypto-homosexual who retained the Victorian varnish of respectability.[40] If Greene had been a homosexual he would have been open about it like Douglas.

As soon as he arrived on Capri, Greene would write notes to his friends, especially those living on, not merely visiting, the island – to Dottoressa Moor, to Countess Cerio, even to Gracie Fields and Norman Douglas. A note to Norman Douglas has survived:

Albergo Terrazzo, Capri, 1 April 1948

Dear Norman Douglas,
    I'm back here again till Sunday. Would it be possible for you to have lunch with me tomorrow? I'd call for you any time you like, or meet you where you like. Would you ring up & leave a message?

Douglas returned Greene's letter writing the following note upon it: 'Dear Gr Gr, Come here at once, if you can, 9.10, to the Ristorante Savoia near the Piazza, where you will find friends galore. Else come to Caffè Vittorio on the terrace Tomonso at about 12.30 and then lunch with us. Norman.'
Douglas's response failed to reach Greene and found its way back to Douglas, so he wrote yet another note on the letter:

Dear Graham Greene,
    This [note] went all over town to try and find you but you still can make the Vittorio at 12.30.

During the years 1947–55 Greene often took Catherine with him to Capri. There he could be alone with her; they could be 'lone wolves' but not anti-social. A note to Catherine has survived: 'Seven o'clock on Friday night. Dear, I'm so happy to be loved by you. G.' At the bottom of the sheet he'd written at an angle: 'You are sitting on the roof . . . just over my head.' On another occasion, he left her a short note on Foreign Office notepaper: 'Strolling out towards the Church. Have done 600 [words] anyway, darling.' And thinking perhaps of a religious film he writes a tantalising short note: 'A camera shot of the Crucifixion: / From a new angle the strange tree. / The camera records without pity / The authentic Agony.'[41]

*

Greene returned to Vienna in June 1948, this time with Carol Reed and the film crew. Reed looked at Greene's treatment and compared it with the current reality: 'When Carol Reed returned with me to Vienna to see the scenes I had described I was embarrassed to find that between winter and spring Vienna had completely changed. The black-market restaurants, where in February one was lucky to find a few bones described as oxtail, were now serving legal if frugal meals. The ruins had been cleared away from in front of the Café Mozart [which Greene calls "Old Vienna" in the story]. Over and over again I found myself saying to Carol Reed, "But I assure you Vienna was really like that – three months ago." '[42]

What did Greene do in Vienna? His dedication in *The Third Man* suggests that he drank too much: 'TO CAROL REED in admiration and affection and in memory of so many early morning Vienna hours at Maxim's, the Casanova, the Oriental.' To Catherine he wrote: 'This trip has moments of fun, but I drink too much & work too much & miss you too much & think too much. I am getting terribly bored with the story & everybody except Carol who gets nicer & nicer on acquaintance . . . Vienna has begun to rot my guts already . . . Carol hates going to bed before 4.'[43]

But at whatever time he was drinking with Reed, or finishing up late at the Oriental, Maxim's and the Casanova, Greene continued to work: 'I have agreed to finish the first treatment before I leave Vienna and the story seems to get longer and longer. I do it straight on the typewriter, usually about two and half hours in the morning, then the first drink . . . then lunch: then a couple more hours and perhaps an hour on a bed with Hardy's poems: then the drinking starts again.'

On 23 June 1948 Reed and Greene went to the Russian zone. 'Feeling much more cheerful after a drunken evening with Carol annoying the Rs. [Russians],' he wrote to Catherine. His postcard shows the Prater prior to the Russian bombing, the funfair with its Arabesque steeples, and in the centre of the postcard the giant Ferris wheel. Although conditions had improved, the Russian sector was still terrible: 'the Prater lay smashed and desolate and full of weeds, only the Great Wheel revolving slowly over the foundations of merry-go-rounds like abandoned millstones, the rusting iron of smashed tanks which nobody had cleared away . . . '[44] The trees were splintered and there were shell holes everywhere. 'It looked like a sort of nightmare: something out of Hieronymus Bosch,' recalled Elizabeth Montagu. 'It was very dramatic. The wheel was still there, that was the amazing thing. It stood there. It was a very fragile thing but it hadn't got a direct hit.'[45]

Greene also spent time in the sewers of Vienna where Harry Lime, brilliantly played by Orson Welles, finally loses his life: 'We dressed in heavy boots and macintoshes and took a walk below the city. The main sewer was like a great tidal river, wide as the Thames, rushing by under a huge arch, fed by tributary streams.'[46] Greene mentioned in his story how these streams have fallen in waterfalls from higher levels and have been purified, so that only in the side channels is the air foul: 'The main stream smells sweet and fresh with a faint tang of ozone, and everywhere in the darkness is the sound of falling and rushing water.'[47] He described reaching the curving iron staircase, and the accumulation of debris in the shallows, a scum of orange peel, old cigarette cartons,[48] but he never spoke of the rats.

Elizabeth Montagu accompanied Greene into the sewers and mentioned to the sewer police who went with them that she had seen no rats. The sewer police* wore lint-white uniforms, like ski instructors, with trousers tucked into high boots to stop the rats taking a chunk out of a leg. They told Elizabeth to turn around slowly and not panic. As she turned, a policeman shone his huge torch behind towards the top of the sewer and there was a great army of rats, eyes glittering. The rats, which were very fierce and frightening, were the size of small dogs and had originally been raised on farms for their fur: 'They were a peculiar phenomenon because when the Russians came into Vienna they let all the rats out of their farms. They are the rats that make wonderful fur linings for winter coats.'[49]

---

* The sewer police worked the enormous system of sewers: there were no Allied zones in the sewers, and the Russians refused to allow the entrances, which were disguised as advertisement kiosks (and still are), to be locked. Thus agents could pass uncontrolled from one zone to another.[50]

Greene spent twenty days (10 to 30 June) in Vienna on this second visit – late nights, hard drinking, hard writing. In *Ways of Escape*, Greene described how, on his penultimate day, he met the future Duke of St Albans, Charles Beauclerk, then a young intelligence officer, who told him about the scandalous profiteering in watered-down penicillin which caused the deaths of children who in effect received little or no aid from the medication. '[The hospital] had bought some of this penicillin for use against meningitis. A number of children simply died, and a number went off their heads. You can see them now in a mental ward.'[51]

Beauclerk may well have provided Greene with information about the 'penicillin racket', but he may have already heard the story from another source. Five days before he left Vienna in February he spent a long evening with *The Times*'s correspondent, Peter Smollett. Smollett was better informed than the young intelligence officer about the dirty rackets then operating in Vienna. He and Greene spent several nights together and once visited the Russian sector so that Greene could call on an old, retired servant who had worked for his mother. The Russian guards were quite fierce and any informality out of place could lead to arrest. Having a British car with a uniformed driver and the Union Jack prominently displayed was a necessity.

The deliberate watering down of penicillin must have been part of the news of the day, but what makes it likely that Smollett was Greene's initial source is a statement by Elizabeth Montagu. She recalled that Smollett wanted Greene to look over some unpublished stories, one of which contained an account of the watered-down penicillin.

Although working on the film treatment, Greene continued to miss Catherine. He got rid of his depression with companionship and drink: 'A fit of the blues last night was dispelled by hard drinking and a night at Maxim's with an attractive half-Russian, half-German dancer who had yet read books. We talked about Spain and Venice and Lesbians and Oscar Wilde and Dr [Axel] Munthe and Capri . . . I didn't go to bed with her because she lived half an hour away and couldn't leave till 2 and I wanted an early night.'[52]

Greene's references to other women when writing to the woman he loved tormentedly seem to have been made to show her that he had the opportunity even if not the inclination for other affairs: 'Today at lunch a far prettier young actress of the Josephstadt than Greta – we go to her first night tomorrow, and tonight the beautiful Biddulph, and I feel abysmally uninterested. I think I have always been really, but now I feel more than ever out of the game and ready to pimp in an avuncular way for Carol . . . '[53]

Greene lunched with women who were looked upon as possible subjects for seduction: 'I am giving lunch to the beautiful wife of the unfaithful man on Wednesday (he's in England), but my heart is not in the game: so far avoided the twenty-year old actress [Alida Valli].'[54] Not only did Greene miss the opportunity of having an affair with her, but Orson Welles did also. Welles was deeply involved with an Italian actress at the time, and did not realise that Alida was 'the sexiest thing you ever saw in your life . . . I see her now and she excites me beyond words . . . *The Third Man* . . . [is] the only movie of mine I ever watch on television because I like it so much – and I look at Alida Valli, and I say, "What was in your mind when you were ten days in Vienna and you didn't make a move?" She drives me mad with lust when I see her in it!'[55]

Despite what he wrote to Catherine, Greene didn't stay away from all women. Elizabeth Montagu had the wearisome task of escorting him to midnight dives where the most haggard prostitutes would hang out. 'Hideous they were . . . where did such hags come from? . . . It was always late and I longed to prop my eyes open with a matchstick – such hags.' When she asked how Greene could go to such dives and remain a Catholic, he looked at her and said: 'I have my ways.'[56]

In a letter to Catherine written just before his departure from Vienna, he entertained her with a fictional sexual encounter in the style of Henry James rewriting *Fanny Hill*:

> Lying there his head cushioned, how cushioned only his great forebears, Tristram, Paolo, Anthony, Ronio & the incomparable Jules could have adequately conceived, cushioned against a softness, a furriness, an obscure yielding carpet of brown moss that the poets had sometimes compared to a forest, others to a lily pond, & the Eastern writer who had conceived the thousand and one nights to a rabbit, he felt an urgent wish to fasten his lips, nay to thrust his tongue between these outjutting coral cliffs, to speak in these hidden caverns – not the essential juices that now urgently, relentlessly demanded satisfaction in the same crevice, but the essential, the gourmet extracts edible also to the touch of crab & aguja, the feel of fungi and so raising his head he pushed, he propelled, he satisfied the first craving against her cunt, quickly, savagely, his tongue rasping like a cat, before he turned his attention to the imperative demands of his job.[57]

*

Once the script of *The Third Man* was completed, at the beginning of August, Greene and Carol Reed sailed to America on the *Queen Elizabeth*. Greene lamented having a huge twin-bed cabin all to himself. He observed that two passengers were reading *The Heart of the Matter* (which had recently appeared), and judged his fellow passengers as 'a dismal collection of drabs and drears, bloopers and hounds', with the exception of two: Kenneth McPherson, an intimate of Norman Douglas, and the actor Robert Morley.[58] On board ship, he and Carol Reed went to bed at the unprecedented time of 10.30 with hardly a drink: 'I suppose it's the sudden stopping of work & the temporary stopping of all problems – the stretched elastic sags.'[59] He knew only that he loved Catherine, that he hated the life he led, that he wanted quiet and peace 'with you & lie on a bed, reading St. John of the Cross'.[60]

He landed in New York and received an 'offer of a December [theatrical] production of *The Heart [of the Matter]* which I'm holding at arm's length. It's odd. Everybody seems to have read the bloody book.'[61] Finally, he and Reed flew out to California and met David Selznick at La Jolla. Selznick held the American rights in *The Third Man* and by the terms of the contract had to be consulted about the script.

On arrival Greene sent Harry Walston a picture postcard. On it is a drawing of a man like a Chinese mandarin, looking a little like Greene, sitting in a box and looking bleakly out. Beneath is the caption PEOPLE ARE NO DAMN GOOD. And his message to Walston was: 'All my prejudices are confirmed, except that I like Selznick enormously.'[62]

They moved on to Santa Monica to a luxurious suite, once the home of Marion Davies, the film-star mistress of the newspaper tycoon, William Randolph Hearst: 'For a while Carol and I could do nothing but laugh. It's very beautiful, about the size of the Palace of Luxembourg, & incredibly luxurious.' Everything was on a large scale – a bedroom as big as a huge living room, a bathroom the size of Greene's living room. Also there was plenty of liquor: 'On a table we found 2 bottles of Scotch, one bottle of gin, 1 Noilly Prat & a bottle of cognac from Cary Grant. The whole place needs to be seen to be believed . . . It's really balking not having a love affair in a place like this. A f—— wouldn't do! One wants to be sentimental too & not sleep till 5 in the morning.'[63]

But if Greene liked Selznick, he and Reed had much to put up with. Selznick went straight into the attack:

'It won't do, boys . . . It's sheer buggery.'

'Buggery?'

'It's what you learn in your English schools.'

'I don't understand.'

'This guy comes to Vienna looking for his friend. He finds his friend's dead. Right? Why doesn't he go home then? . . . It's just buggery, boys.'[64]

The conferences went on nightly never starting before 10.30 p.m. or finishing before 4 a.m. At their last meeting Selznick suddenly announced that he didn't understand something about the script: 'Why the hell does Harry Lime . . . ?' and he described some extraordinary action on Lime's part. 'But he doesn't,' Greene answered. Selznick looked nonplussed and then said, 'Christ, boys. I'm thinking of a different script.'[65]

The result of these conferences was forty pages of notes from Selznick that were, on the whole, ignored by Reed and Greene. Angry letters passed from Selznick to Korda, but when the film was a success all was forgiven and Selznick began to believe in it. He dropped his criticism of the title: 'Listen, boys, who the hell is going to a film called *The Third Man*?' He had suggested a title like *Night in Vienna*, 'a title which will bring them in'.[66]

When the film appeared in Britain in August 1949, Greene was indebted to Orson Welles for Harry Lime's famous parting speech to his friend, Holly. Holly meets his supposedly dead friend Harry on the mighty Ferris wheel:

When you make up your mind, send me a message – I'll meet you any place, any time, and when we do meet, old man, it's you I want to see, not the police . . . and don't be so gloomy . . . After all, it's not that awful – you know what the fellow said . . . In Italy for thirty years under the Borgias they had warfare, terror, murder, bloodshed – they produced Michelangelo, Leonardo da Vinci and the Renaissance. In Switzerland they had brotherly love, five hundred years of democracy and peace, and what did that produce . . . ? The cuckoo clock.[67]

*

After only six days in America, it was agreed that Greene would fly back to England and then on to Vienna. But it was not to be. 'I hate more & more theatrical & film people. Not Carol Reed who is sweet. Now I look like being imprisoned here another week. Last night I had to work from 10.30 in the evening til 5.15 this morning

& then the telephone woke me at 9.30.'[68] In the previous eighteen months Greene had written one-third of *The Heart of the Matter*, three complete film scripts, and a 30,000 word novelette [*The Third Man*] and he was exhausted.

The press briefly stated 'Graham Greene in New York Hospital'. The earliest reference was in the *Catholic Times* of 3 September 1948 – by which time Greene had returned to England. The headline was followed by a short note: 'famous writer, author of "The Heart of the Matter" and many other works, is at present recuperating from an operation in a New York hospital'. A letter to his mother gives more information: 'I should have written long before this to announce my safe return, but I was very tired & for a time not very well . . . I had to work like a galley slave roughing out a play [based on *The Heart of the Matter*] before I left again. When I got back I was wanted in Vienna but refused to go & have been resting quietly for ten days in the country.'[69] Malcolm Muggeridge recorded in his diary: 'Greene described having a haemorrhage in New York. He seemed to me in poorish shape.'[70] Even his letters to Catherine were circumspect: 'Cafryn darling, just as I'm catching the plane I've turned a bit sick. Nothing serious, but I have to stay over for a few days.'[71]

When asked about this mysterious illness Greene described what happened just as he and Reed were getting ready to leave for England:

I'd had rather a night on the tiles the night before with Jean Stafford, the American writer, and we'd drunk pretty well a bottle of whisky each, and Carol Reed was sitting on his bed telephoning his wife, saying that we were going to be back the next day, what time our plane was getting in. And I suddenly felt wet, and I looked down and saw . . . blood . . . soaking out from my trousers. It came from my penis. And the trouble was that I couldn't draw Carol Reed away from his conversation with his wife. I kept on saying, 'Carol, I'm bleeding!' 'Yes dear, we should be at Heathrow by such and such a time.' 'Carol, I'm bleeding!' I never got through for a long time, and then he summoned the house doctor, and I was pushed into a hospital nearby where they wanted to know how much money I'd got, and what kind of a room I wanted. I said, 'Well I haven't got any money so you'd better put me into your cheapest room, but I think Mr David Selznick will pay.' The doctor told me about three things which it could be, and two of them were very serious, and that he would have to examine me properly the next day under anaesthetic. When I came through the anaesthetic, he told me all was well, but I must be off the drink for a month.[72]

He was taken to the Medical Arts Center Hospital and Carol Reed flew back without him.

The following day Greene told Catherine how for twenty-four hours he had wondered whether all was up between them. On the plane back to Europe, he wrote her a cryptic note: 'Though I miss you, it will be *no* good seeing you.'[73]

18

Love as a Fever

My Love is as a fever, longing still
For that which longer nurseth the disease.
— SHAKESPEARE

No one touched Greene as deeply as Catherine Walston, even at a religious level. Although Greene became a convert to win Vivien, he felt a truer Catholic with Catherine: 'I nearly slept at Mass today. How dead it was – not dead in the amusing phosphorent way of last Sunday, aware of your shoulder half an inch from mine, but just limp and meaningless and boring. I'm not even a Catholic properly away from you.'[1] After going to Mass with Vivien, he wrote to Catherine: 'It's odd how little I get out of Mass except when you're around. I'm a much better Catholic in mortal sin! or at least I'm more aware of it.'[2] Yet Greene was troubled. Sometimes he wished that he and Catherine were pagans, 'anyway for ten years. I might relapse after that into Catholicism or after 17 years; when I am sixty and you are nearly 50.'[3]

Loving Catherine was a sin, and yet he felt keenly alive because of it. He took T. S. Eliot's phrase to heart: 'Most people are only a very little alive; it is only when they are so awakened that they are capable of real Good, but that at the same time they become first capable of Evil.'[4] Like Kurtz in *Heart of Darkness*, Greene took risks with his immortal soul. It was in his nature to go beyond permitted limits: he wanted to know, to experience, but most of all he wanted a great love. Both he and Catherine were religious and genuine Catholics, and yet they succumbed to sexual temptation. In later life, Greene scotched the notion of sexual sin altogether: 'I find the idea [of mortal sin] difficult to accept because it must by definition be committed in defiance of God. I doubt whether a man making love to a woman ever does so with the intention of defying God.'[5]

Greene was bewitched: 'I am in love with a Bacall profile, a wood in Cambridgeshire, Chesterfield cigarettes, bathrooms, and Rolls Royces, Austins and Fords, Irish Whisky.'[6] It was the attraction of opposites: Greene, in spite of his extraordinary fame, was still tremendously shy, while Catherine was an extrovert. She loved to say shocking things, 'not out of any sort of perverseness', but simply because it was her way.[7]

David Crompton described his sister as being attracted to famous people.[8] The guests at Thriplow Farm and Newton Hall were said to include George VI, Elizabeth II, Dwight D. Eisenhower, Bob Hope, Eddie Cantor and James Cagney. As Greene's lover, Catherine increased her friendships in literary and film circles. When she was curious to meet Evelyn Waugh, Greene arranged for him to come to London for lunch:

> Graham's flat is next to hers at 5 St. James's Street. The paralysed John Hayward [the writer and critic] was there, tenderly and candidly petted by Mrs W. Luncheon plainly had been brought from her flat for there was no salt. She sat on the floor and buttered my bread for me and made simple offers of friendship . . . Finally, I was asked to go with her to the country [Thriplow]. I couldn't that afternoon as I had to dine with the editor of the *Daily Express*. Very well they would pick me up after dinner. I couldn't do that as I was lunching with Father Caraman next day. Very well she would send a car for me at 2.30.[9]

At Thriplow Waugh met a side of life he had never seen before: 'very rich, Cambridge, Jewish, socialist, high brow, scientific, farming. There were Picassos on sliding panels & when you pushed them back plate glass & a stable with a stallion looking at one . . . The house a series of wood bungalows, more bathrooms than bedrooms. The hostess at six saying, "I say shall we have dinner tonight as Evelyn's here. Usually we only have Shredded Wheat. I'll see what there is." Goes to tiny kitchenette & comes back. "Well there's grouse, partridges, ham, a leg of mutton and half a cold goose" (literally). "What does anyone want?" There's a children's nannie dining with us called "Twinkle" . . . everyone talking to her about lesbianism & masturbation. House telephone so that generally people don't bother to meet but just telephone from room to room.'[10] One side of the dining room at Thriplow looked out on to the paddock and it was not unusual for Catherine to draw the attention of her dinner guests to the sight of the horses breeding. Whether this was done to amuse her guests or to shock them, it was an uncommon household.[11]

When Greene was staying at Thriplow, he would sometimes entertain the Walston children. Susan Walston recalls him reading Sir Arthur Conan Doyle's story 'The Speckled Band' to them, and Bill Walston that he read them G. K. Chesterton's Father Brown stories. The Walston children liked him because he was soft-spoken and gentle. They felt that their mother was very protective towards him, she would warn them not to disturb him in the mornings so that he could write.

Waugh noted that Catherine was 'barefooted and mostly squatting on the floor. Fine big eyes and mouth, unaffected to the verge of insanity, unvain, no ostentation – simple friendliness and generosity and childish curiosity.'[12]

She enjoyed being admired. Despite his overwhelming passion, Greene was very watchful of her character and he had her in mind in the following extract from Sarah's diary in *The End of the Affair*: 'I can't be alone for the rest of my life with Henry, nobody admiring me, nobody excited by me, listening to Henry talking to other people, fossilising under the drip of conversation like that bowler hat in the Cheddar Caves.'[13]

The Walston house was 'nearly always . . . full of men and all admirers of Catherine – whether they were priests or whether they were friends of Harry's they'd always gravitate around her and she liked that'. On the whole Catherine was not comfortable with other women, as Lady Melchett remembers: 'She didn't really like women . . . She knew I admired her so I was tolerated . . . '[14] But it was also true that her guests were drawn to her compulsively. Her daughter Susan recalls that when Catherine left a room it died and guests would soon leave for their own rooms.

It was a love affair of dangerous proportions. Despite Greene's doubts about whether Catherine reciprocated his overwhelming love, family and friends agree that Catherine did love Greene, that he was her greatest passion. Yet she was in control, if one can be in control of such turbulence: it was Catherine who would bring Greene to breaking point with Vivien and Dorothy, and Catherine who allotted the time they would spend together. In *The End of the Affair* Bendrix is desperate to see Sarah, who is taking care of a sick Henry, and Sarah coolly takes charge:

'Isn't there any way to see you?'
'But of course.'
There was silence for a moment on the phone and I thought we had been cut off. I said, 'Hullo. Hullo.'
But she had been thinking, that was all, carefully, collectedly, quickly, so that she could give me straightaway the correct answer.

'I'm giving Henry a tray in bed at one. We could have sandwiches ourselves in the living-room. I'll tell him you want to talk over the film – or that story of yours,' and immediately she rang off the sense of trust was disconnected and I thought, how many times before has she planned in just this way?[15]

Everyone was aware of their liaison. Even with Harry in the house, Catherine would say things like, 'You know, Graham and I were in bed all day and all night – that's why I'm feeling a bit jaded.'[16]

When Greene spent Christmas 1947 with the Walstons at Thriplow, he and Catherine managed to make love while her husband was in the house. The incident, in a different form, found its way into *The End of the Affair*.

There was never any question in those days of who wanted whom – we were together in desire. Henry had his tray, sitting up against two pillows . . . and in his room below, on the hard-wood floor, with a single cushion for support and the door ajar, we made love. When the moment came, I had to put my hand gently over her mouth to deaden that strange sad angry cry of abandonment, for fear Henry should hear it overhead.[17]

In the novel, Henry comes downstairs and greets Bendrix and goes back to his sick bed. Bendrix asks Sarah a curious question and the answer seems to fit Catherine:

'Do you mind?' I asked her, and she shook her head. I didn't really know what I meant – I think I had an idea that the sight of Henry might have roused remorse, but she had a wonderful way of eliminating remorse. Unlike the rest of us she was unhaunted by guilt. In her view when a thing was done, it was done: remorse died with the act. She would have thought it unreasonable for Henry, if he had caught us, to be angry for more than a moment. Catholics are always said to be freed in the confessional from the mortmain of the past – certainly in that respect you could have called her a born Catholic.[18]

Greene's obsession with Catherine gave her the power to change his moods, taking him from despair to euphoria. He felt as Bendrix did about Sarah: 'I have never known a woman before or since so able to alter a whole mood by simply speaking on the telephone, and when she came into a room or put her hand on my side she created at once the absolute trust I lost with every separation.'[19]

*

Greene's love for Catherine was complicated by his continued relationships with Dorothy and Vivien. Visiting Ireland with Dorothy in 1947, he wrote: 'I hate seeing Dublin with someone else, but when I promised that holiday I had no hope of you at all. And only three quarters of a thought.'[20] On this holiday Dorothy wanted to revitalise their love, but it was, unbeknown to her, a futile hope. In a postscript to a letter to Catherine, Greene wrote: 'My God, how bored I am.'[21] Dorothy could not duplicate the intense feelings experienced in Ireland with Catherine: 'A complete absence of onion sandwiches, turf fires, home made bread, candlelight.'[22]

Greene conveyed a hidden message in this letter. Like many lovers, he and Catherine shared a code. His letter from Ireland indicates an 'absence of onion sandwiches' and a postcard from Amsterdam bears the simple message: 'I love onion sandwiches.' 'There was one code word I did remember – "onions". That word had been allowed in our correspondence to represent discreetly our passion. Love became "onions", even the act itself "onions".'[23] While in Ireland with Dorothy, Greene intended to remain true to Catherine.

As a further twist to the story, it seems that onions were themselves a code, a joke between Greene and Catherine. Harry Walston hated the smell of garlic, so at Thriplow Greene and Catherine would eat it ostentatiously so Harry wouldn't break in suddenly in the middle of the night. Greene thought this so amusing that he used it in *The End of the Affair*, only changing garlic to onions so Harry Walston wouldn't realise what they had done.[24]

Greene had come down with a bad case of flu, felt miserable and was trying to remove himself from Dorothy's life: 'The long term prospects seem favourable. I think things are going to be arranged,' and knowing his own nature he added: 'though I shall probably need a shove or two later'.[25] The next day Greene reported: 'My companion's [Greene rarely used Dorothy's name in letters to Catherine] caught my cough and fever. Plans for the future are solidifying quite a bit. A lot of good sense has been talked between the coughs.'[26]

After Dorothy and Greene returned from Ireland, a sudden squall blew up between Greene and Catherine: 'I have been thinking hard about our telephone conversation and the odd series of events that have taken place since Achill . . . Isn't it rather odd that gossip should suddenly spring up within a few weeks of *your* knowing about the thing, when there was no gossip as far as one knows (it didn't even reach you for nine years). And the gossip is apparently spread by Speaight – whom you know? And the object? If the gossip drove me to break with my mistress and smooth Vivien down, it would obviously make our love affair more easily managed.'[27] It is difficult to tell from this single letter what the gossip might have been, but presumably it was peddled by Robert Speaight and given to him by Catherine (who loved gossip). It may have been gossip about Greene having a wife in Oxford, a mistress in London and now a second mistress, though it must have been much more serious than that, for Greene went on: 'if I'm right . . . the affair is not worth managing smoothly. Better walk out on each other now when it can be done without ill feeling because after all, you made no promise of secrecy when I so rashly told you that evening at Rules.' What could have been told to Catherine about his affair with Dorothy which, if it got about, would make Greene and Dorothy break up?

Greene had taken Dorothy at the start of their affair to one of those small hotels in Paddington where you can get a room any time of day for an hour or two. It had the look of a brothel and the landlady turned out to be someone linked with the film *Brighton Rock*. To have this story divulged as a joke at Dorothy's expense would have been highly distasteful to Greene. Though no longer in love with her, he was very close to her and admired her spirit.

Catherine's reply must have been unapologetic because Greene followed up with an accusation that her love for him was self-deception. Even if he told the truth about Dorothy to Vivien, it would still be a deception if he held back their love affair: 'What is the good of keeping *us* back? Within 12 months a new line of deception would have developed.' He also returned her letters: 'Well, my darling, you may as well have these letters. I think they are quite sensible. I expect this is the end. If it is, you've given me the best morphia I've ever had.'[28] He ended one of his letters to Catherine with the thought: 'Thank God, anyway that there's somebody I can't hurt.'[29]

They met again and the atmosphere cleared. Catherine flew out to Achill alone, and Greene was back in love, his letters pursuing her to Achill and reminding her of three things: that he was terribly in love with her, that he missed her voice, and that he wanted her. Still thinking that his love was unrequited, he admitted to great hopes that a trip to India (where *Life* considered sending him) would secure her love: 'It might be a way of being with you for 3 months and by God, I'd get into your *skin* before that time was over.'[30]

Catherine invaded his thoughts. When at work at Eyre & Spottiswoode, he stared at a present from her: 'Your briefcase looks lovely. It sits on a chair and looks at me and I miss you and wish it were you.' He felt the need to visit her in Ireland: 'The only way I get any happiness now is either with you or with work. And work is for the time being over.'[31] He'd just finished *The Heart of the Matter*.

The prospect of a holiday with Catherine had a magical effect on him and as the time of their meeting drew near he could barely contain himself, sending her three telegrams in three days:

Staying five nights would you like me to and would you meet me with sleeping bag.

Hurray arriving Shannon Airport at 5.30.

Longing for Thursday.

On 4 July 1947 Greene was light-hearted: 'I feel excited and cheerful and quite undespairing! I'm awfully nice to everybody. Will I really see you there? Where shall we spend the nights? In sleeping bags on a turf field – or in Galway City. I don't care a damn but *do* be there. Five nights anyway.' In a postscript the inevitable lie rears: 'Officially I'm in Holland on Guild Publishing.' Two days later he was in a fever of anticipation: 'Is it true that I'm going to see you in less than five days,' and then he burst out into verse: 'Long roads and stony ditches / And here's to nice girls / And to hell with riches.'[32]

The fear grew that something might prevent Greene from seeing Catherine: 'Don't let anything stop you. I can't settle to any book when I'm not going to see you. I can't read poetry. Now I'm to see you again, I take poetry down again, and it throws its stones at me to make me ache for you: "One careless look on me she flung / As bright as parting day, / And like a hawk from covert spring / It pounced my peace away."' And he answered the quote: 'Your looks weren't careless, and I had no peace but it makes me want you just the same.' And immediately he quoted another poem: 'You've stuffed my pillow, stretched the sheet / And filled the pan to wash your feet.' He ended his letter with the triumphant assertion, 'You are going to be so involved soon, you won't want another soul. You are in love and I'm in love and we are going to meet Thursday.'[33]

After five days with Catherine, he was able to face two weeks with Vivien and the children in Switzerland in August, but his thoughts strayed to Catherine and their sexual congress: 'Last Sunday, about an hour ago, we got out of the car and went to bush.'[34] This memory and its effect on Greene is more fully described in *The End of the Affair*: 'I lay there unable to sleep, one memory after another pricking me . . . a day in the country when we had lain down in a ditch out of view of the road and I could see the sparkle of frost between the fronds of hair on the hard ground and a tractor came pushing by at the moment of crisis and the man never turned his head.'35

Greene had no letters from Catherine while in Switzerland and he feared the silence: 'Catherine dear, I hope you meet me [at the airport] . . . I wish we could get away somewhere for two nights – I mean nights not afternoons . . . I long to hear something from you, but your handwriting would probably mean that you weren't meeting me. I'd hate that . . . I love you . . . I wonder whether you do.' To still his doubts, Greene answered his own question: 'Yes, I think you do.' He still felt cut off from her, and waking up with Vivien at his side he kept on having the curious notion that it was Catherine, but added: 'it was all wasted because we didn't like each other. Do you think we only like each other in Achill?'36

He couldn't stand Switzerland, though ironically he was to die there forty-five years later: 'This place is very pretty, very clean, very kind. I think it must be rather like Limbo. Music, fireworks, good plain food, contentment and good taste evenly spread. I prefer Achill and the choice of Heaven or Hell.' His confidence oozed away: 'Darling, let me know if you are *not* meeting me. I'd want to make other arrangements.' And he had written, then crossed out: 'I don't mean sexual.'37

But it was a working holiday for Greene; he was still correcting *The Heart of the Matter*. 'Nearly finished Karamazov but very disappointed on second reading. Maybe I can write as good as D. Cut larger chunks of the new novel and after all it may be good.'38 He had been reading André Gide's latest novel and felt encouraged: 'It makes me feel that perhaps after all my book [*The Heart of the Matter*] is not so bad. It's a damned sight better than his.'39

When he returned from Switzerland, Catherine met him at the airport but then went to the United States for three months until October. Back at work as a publisher in Bedford Street, he daydreamed between reading the scripts of 'two dull authors' and thought of his time with Catherine by Galway harbour: 'How one can go on *falling* in love with the same person . . . sometimes several times a day. My God how I miss you. It seems too good to be true that we'll be sleeping in that charming Galway hotel and driving up through Westport, picking up steaks on the way and with time, time to squander.' Still in the early exciting stage of love 'which just seems to go on and on'.40

There was another reason for his excitement. John Hayward, who

19 Catherine Walston

20 (*above left*) Catherine Walston, Greene's 'Bacall profile'

21 (*left*) Greene on Capri

22 (*above*) Greene and Catherine at Anacapri

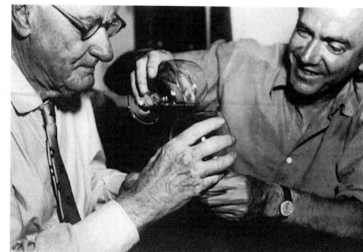

23 (above)
Greene with
John Hayward
at Thriplow

24 (right)
Norman Douglas
with Graham
Greene

25 Greene at
Achill, County
Mayo

26 Greene and Catherine on Capri

27 (*above left*) The *Elsewhere*, Alexander Korda's yacht

28 *(left)* Alexander Korda with Graham Greene on the *Elsewhere*

29 (*above*) With Catherine aboard the *Elsewhere* at Antibes

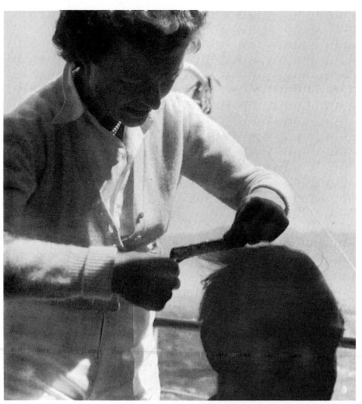

30 Catherine as barber

31 In Malaya with Major McGregor Cheers and two gurkhas

was sitting in judgment on *The Heart of the Matter*, had expressed his admiration and Greene admitted to being 'nearly cheered because John likes the book very much – I'm just off to see him now'. Expressing his desire to marry Catherine, he ran on excitedly, 'I've told the *New Statesman* that I'll do their dramatic criticism but now I'm begging to repent.'[41]

*

Greene's 'absurd grotesque [love] life' had its difficulties. Vivien always knew more than she admitted and kept quiet about it, but Dorothy was of cruder clay. From his Bedford Street office, Greene wrote:

> Feeling battered. Big scene which went on last night till about 2. One of the worst yet. I miss peace and you more than ever . . . We've been having rats lately and this morning [Dorothy] came face to face with it in the clothes cupboard and killed it with a shoe. This on top of last night's scene had left one a bit flat. The trouble is that with you away one will stay flat. It is like the court after Hannibal left for England . . . The scene last night did *not* end traditionally.[42]

Unable to break free, Greene placed Dorothy in the way of an affair and had high hopes of it: 'The girlfriend is really ripe for a love affair and I wish she'd take the plunge. Henri is in town and they are going to a party together tonight. I really pray for something to happen.'[43]

There is always the contrast between on the one hand, the loveless affair with Dorothy, the dead marriage to Vivien, and on the other the promise of periodic love from Catherine. From Vivien's house in Beaumont Street, Greene wrote: 'The dark night for me is *dryness* in extra boredom: with you I don't feel that – or despair either.'[44] That dryness of spirit, which afflicted Querry in *The Burnt Out Case*, the sense of total emptiness, is what Greene suffered after the completion of a novel. Having finished *The Heart of the Matter*, he experienced a withering of the creative spirit, and Catherine served as a narcotic, if not a cure.

Living in Beaumont Street for just a weekend was unbearable: 'O God, What a house. This is Sunday with both dullness and Vivien around. Nobody goes and tells somebody to do something. They shout from the basement.'[45] The house in Beaumont Street had a basement kitchen. Greene's nerves were on edge, but he denied this: 'Forgive this outburst, but at weekends I wonder which wears one down most: Oxford or London. I sometimes think that far from being nervy, I have the strongest nerves in Christendom. I want your peace and excitement again . . . I long to have you lazily stretched on an Achill sofa with a book and a pencil and interrupt you every ten minutes with something I want to talk about and every twelve minutes I'm in love.'[46] Greene, renowned for the prodigious sense of smell and decay reflected in his novels, then added: 'How it makes me hate the *smell* of other people.' His letter ends on a mysterious note: 'My dear, the important cigarette burn has completely gone. It must be renewed.'

It looks as if Greene enjoyed punishment. When interviewed, Vivien lamented the fact that Catherine changed Greene, but she felt 'After the war things would settle down and it would all be part of the past . . . But of course far from it – things just got worse.'[47]

But if Vivien practised a quiet forbearance, how did Dorothy react to Greene's infidelities? 'Dorothy was very jealous,' Vivien recalled, 'and when he had an affair with Catherine, she sent him postcards with grave stones on them. Metaphorically she simply threw plates at him and shouted and yelled and he did show great pride in the mark where she'd burned a cigarette on his hand, and I think that rough stuff rather appealed. He wasn't being bored and he could get bored to screaming point.'[48] Greene's secret malady was boredom unto madness. The despair he often felt when alone placed him in a region where 'laughter was like the unknown syllables of an enemy tongue'.[49]

Still he didn't know how to give up Dorothy. She wouldn't leave him and, after loving Catherine for a whole year, he was still living with Dorothy in Gordon Square. In order to be able to see Catherine more often, Greene persuaded Dorothy to travel to Africa: 'I am fixing up for my girl to go on a cargo ship toward Africa and back.'[50] Three days later, on 5 September 1947, he had completed the arrangements: 'Today I wangled her a passage on an Elder Dempster cargo ship down the West African coast and back, mid-September to mid-December – so she'll be happy.' He felt nostalgia for his past journeys: 'I must say when I saw the list of stops my heart missed a beat.' Las Palmas, Dakar, Bathurst – all places he had visited in 1934 during his travels, which appear in *Journey Without Maps* – Lagos, where he had been trained as a secret agent, and Freetown where he'd been stationed.

The projected journey softened Dorothy: 'I think this will be very good for her – getting away from me and new places and being made much more of – as any white woman is there. Elder Dempster too are treating her as a V.I.P.! She's been very sweet this last week and much more ready to accept the fact that one can love two people!'[51]

Greene hoped that during the two months she was away, Dorothy might fall out of love. 'As you once said,' he wrote to Catherine, 'absence doesn't make the heart grow fonder.' Given Catherine's partiality to others, he feared he might be left without anyone: 'All the same you mustn't walk out on me before she returns or I shall be left high & dry & desperately having to look for a love affair.'[52]

*

Greene was possessive of his love for Catherine. One night the Greenes were entertaining John Rothenstein, the director of the Tate Gallery, and his wife Elizabeth, both of whom knew of Catherine's affair with Greene. Later that evening Greene wrote to Catherine: 'Talking to John about God knows what. I hear the two women [Elizabeth and Vivien] slightly bitching you out of the corners of my ears and the blood all seemed to go to my head and I grinned and grinned at John and didn't hear a word of what he was saying.' The following day, he awakened with the firm knowledge: 'I don't like people who don't like you. If anybody is going to dislike you it's got to be me.'[53]

Though he longed to be Catherine's only love, Greene was not successful. Vivien once asked him: 'Don't you mind [Catherine's] other lovers, her being married and all that?' He responded rather primly, 'I wish you hadn't said that, it was very nasty' – and added defiantly, 'Why should I mind? I've had lots of other women.'[54]

But Greene did mind. His relationship with Catherine was strained by his jealousies, which compelled him to make the most terrible accusations against her. He portrayed this and her response to it in *The End of the Affair*:

'A frigid woman is never jealous, you simply haven't caught up yet on ordinary human emotions.'
It angered me that she didn't make any claim. 'You may be right. I'm only saying I want you to be happy. I hate your being unhappy. I don't mind anything you do that makes you happy.'
'You just want an excuse. If I sleep with somebody else, you feel you can do the same – any time.'
' . . . I want you to be happy, that's all.'
Insecurity is the worst sense that lovers feel . . . Insecurity twists meanings and poisons trust . . . . I would catch her out in small lies, evasions that meant nothing except her fear of me. For every lie I would magnify into a betrayal, and even in the most open

statement I would read hidden meanings . . . I saw intimacy in the most casual movement of the hand . . . 'I'd rather be dead or see you dead,' I said, 'than with another man. I'm not eccentric. That's ordinary human love. Ask anybody. They'd all say the same if they loved at all.' I jibed at her, 'Anyone who loves is jealous.'[55]

Greene refused to believe that love could take any form other than his own: 'I measured love by the extent of my jealousy, and by that standard of course she could not love me at all.'[56]

Greene did not trust Catherine to remain true to him, an aspect of their relationship mirrored in *The End of the Affair*. 'I went home that first evening with no exhilaration but only a sense of sadness and resignation, so again and again I returned home on other days with the certainty that I was only one of many men – the favourite lover for the moment.'[57]

What maddened Greene was his fear that he was merely 'a favourite', for Catherine was having other simultaneous affairs. Sarah, in *The End of the Affair*, clearly expresses Catherine's attitude to these liaisons: 'He thinks I still sleep with other men, and if I did, would it matter so much? If sometimes he has a woman, do I complain? I wouldn't rob him of some small companionship in the desert if we can't have each other there.'[58] And what Sarah says of Bendrix was also true of Greene: 'Sometimes I think that if the time came he would refuse me even a glass of water.'[59]

Catherine's letters from America seemed to indicate that she was having an affair with an old friend, Lowell Weicker, an American general who had been stationed in England during the war and had often visited Catherine at Thriplow. Greene was desperately unhappy and a great deal more jealous than Harry Walston: 'I didn't sleep on Sunday night. I suppose you were with Lowell. I feel the dreariness of my own character, Wilson [The MI5 spy in *The Heart of the Matter*], when he felt that embracing Louise was like writing on a damp pad. The letters blur too soon . . . I've a great deal of blurry myself.'*[60] Walston loved his wife without needing to possess her.

Greene prayed that Lowell didn't become too good a substitute for him, and added: 'I suppose you are out of the Church again. I wish I was the only one who put you out! And how I wish we could just have each other and no one else – anyway for a few years.'[62]

---

* The exact quotation is: 'For exactly an hour and a half the mark of his mouth had been the last on hers. He felt . . . dreariness of a man who tries to write an important letter on a damp sheet and finds the characters blur.'[61]

Catherine was away in America until 11 October 1947. Although they were to meet on her return, he was afraid she would fall out of love with him. When Greene felt he was only the favoured lover of the moment, his letters portrayed the worldly wise, experienced lover, an innocence lost. He put up a hard front, enticing her to stay with him, but also showing her that he could find others should she drop him.

There was, for instance, the 'Mystery Girl'. Peadar O'Donnell had arranged for Greene to have lunch with her and prior to their meeting, Greene imagined she had either 'a face like a horse or a body like a governess'. The 'Mystery Girl' proved to be a young widow with two children, a very luscious blonde, slightly wrong in teeth and accent. Greene shared with Catherine the kind of crude remark one man might make to another: 'she might fill up a gap . . . it would be fun to cuckold Bill!'[63]

Yet other affairs did not provide an answer: 'I would be just as angry because she refused to be jealous of my past or my possible future.'[64] It was only Catherine he worried about. Imagining that Catherine was having another affair in America, Greene had a bad night: 'What were you up to last night? Next month I shall see you. I hope. Feel very restless and disturbed today. I want badly to disappear from the bloody literary and sexual scene – like Bierce in Mexico, Rimbaud in Abyssinia or Gauguin in the South Seas. I wish I hadn't got a family and a sense of responsibility . . . I want you – badly and quite crudely. Substitutes don't work. Let's disappear together. I'm whistling hard. Won't you answer my whistle?' He ended the letter with the first profanity to appear in his letters to Catherine: 'What a bloody, not to say fucking fool I am, Cafryn. I can't stay out of love with you for more than 36 hours.' Nor was he able to do so even when his letters suggest she was writing to him about her escapades in Wilton, New Hampshire.

Greene was getting ready to take Vivien to America – her chance for a holiday – but he was dejected, partly because of the 'grim prospect of America without a dose of [Catherine] to help it down'. His emptiness was also due to the fact that he had sent Heinemann *The Heart of the Matter* on 27 September 1947, and had no ideas for another book: 'The only thing in the next month or two that could mean anything or that could bring one alive is loving someone. So I look to Ireland like an escape from Purgatory . . . Let's love more than a fortnight if it's humanly possible. Do you remember how cautious we were the first time against deciding on more than one week? I want to say to you, "Suppose we weren't pretending but were really in love." '[65]

Greene was certainly in love, but what made him doubt Catherine was her honesty:

> she was now five minutes late. It was my bad luck that she caught me looking at my watch. I heard her voice say, 'I'm sorry. I came by bus and the traffic was bad.'
>
> I said, 'The tube's quicker.'
>
> 'I know, but I didn't want to be quick.'
>
> She had often disconcerted me by the truth. In the days when we were in love, I would try to get her to say more than the truth – that our affair would never end, that one day we should marry. I wouldn't have believed her, but I would have liked to hear the words on her tongue . . . But she never played that game of make-believe, and then suddenly, unexpectedly, she would shatter my reserve with a statement of such sweetness and amplitude . . . I remember once when I was miserable at her calm assumption that one day our relations would be over, hearing with incredulous happiness, 'I have never, never loved a man as I love you, and I never shall again.'[66]

*

While in America with Vivien, Greene hoped that he would meet Catherine in New York on 11 October, but that became impossible as meetings and publisher's parties piled up: 'My engagements in New York so far on October 10 lunch with Frank Taylor. Cocktail party at the Cosmopolitan Club in our "honour." I wish you could be there, except that it wouldn't be fair to Vivien her first day. October 11, 12, and 13 my agent [Mary Pritchett] wants me and Vivien to go to a house she "got in Connecticut" but I have a date with you on 11th and dinner with John Carter on the 13th. I don't want to spoil Vivien's holiday. We've got October 31 and onwards. October 11 lunch with Carol Brandt and dinner with my publisher. 15th & 16th to Boston so it fills up.'[67]

Vivien well remembers that visit to Mary Pritchett's since it was where she spent her twentieth wedding anniversary: 'We were at Mary's and it was awful. I was snubbed and he was in a bad temper and somebody said: "Let's drink to that [the anniversary]." He was sort of wry. Not what you'd call wholehearted . . . He was aloof and irritable when we went to Massachusetts.'[68]

Since the war Greene's relationship with Vivien had remained strained and they had continued to move further and further apart. There is an account in the *Oxford Mail*, 26 April 1945, which illustrates how separate their lives were becoming: 'Mrs Graham

Greene's house is on the corner of Beaumont Street and Gloucester Street. I have been intrigued by this place ever since she first moved in and set up a notice: "This is *not* a Guest House or Hotel. It is not offices. It is *not* a Ministry!" ' The oddity of this notice attracted the journalist:

I don't know what it was but from the moment she [Vivien] arrived, the house had about it the stamp of a rare and distinctive personality. Perhaps it was the collection of coloured bottles she placed so gaily in her front window for all the world to see. And then at Christmas, there was a tree there and a wreath of holly on the door. In the end I could bear it no longer. 'I can't wait to be invited,' I told her one day (ignoring the instruction not to ring) – 'I want to come in – now!'

Inside I found a positive Hinterland of culture – gilded Récamier couches, early Victorian chairs of mother-of-pearl, dessert plates of cut mirror, the residue of a courageous as well as a cultivated mind. And then on Monday night, it spilled its treasures onto the street . . . The Regency striped curtains of candy pink and white were pulled right back, the candles flickered the chandeliers shone, and one remembered with gratitude that life may be short but art is long.[69]

Everything seemed to declare THIS IS VIVIEN GREENE'S HOUSE, not Greene's.

Vivien's passion for stately homes continued unabated, and while Greene did not publicly object to visits he made with his wife, privately his letters were critical: 'I *dragged* with her on Sunday to a meeting of the Georgian Group at Badminton, the Duke of Beaufort's house – four hours *hot* railway travel and a picnic lunch among flies – one needs to be in love to enjoy that kind of thing. I am beginning positively to hate beautiful houses and beautiful furniture and a private house open to public inspection seems more dead than a museum.'[70]

But it was an incident early in his affair with Catherine that forewarned Vivien of the altered nature of her relationship with Greene. Vivien and the children had gone to Bath for the day to visit cousins. When they returned to the house in Beaumont Street, they found Greene and Catherine together:

he had a very strange look on his face, and I realised that somehow he thought I'd gone for some other reason. Or maybe he even thought that I'd known he was coming. It was a very curious

271

look. She was very insouciant as usual. He said, 'We've come back from Achill Island.'

Vivien put the incident near the end of April 1947, the first magical visit for Greene to Achill with Catherine. 'I know that because I got the children's supper and the next day was the Feast of St Catherine of Siena, and I think that is the end of April.'[71]

Greene explained to Vivien that Catherine had a bad back and that given the long return journey to London, it would be best if they stayed the night.

> And I said, for something to say, 'I see it is your name day tomorrow. I am going to Mass anyway, it's only just round the corner.' She said, 'Oh, I'll come with you' and she came and she had Communion next to me. Some later time, I brought this up and I said 'How could you have brought her to the house?' and he said 'Oh there was nothing between us – we didn't even kiss each other when we were in the house.' I said, 'Going to Communion was very terrible,' [receiving Communion, the body and blood of Christ, in a state of mortal sin, is itself a mortal sin] and he said, 'Oh we both went to confession before we came here.' But they went straight on to London to live together and that was sort of sickening.[72]

What Vivien also objected to was that she had to have beds made up and the supper cooked: 'How could I say anything with two children there. It was impossible – it was a dreadful situation.' But it is not correct that Greene and Catherine 'lived together' in London: they never did. At this time he was still living with Dorothy during the week and Vivien and his family at weekends.

Although the children's presence made it impossible for Vivien to confront Greene, they later corresponded about the matter. In response to Vivien's complaint that the two were leagued against her in her own home, Greene wrote that he and Catherine had definitely given up their affair:

> We had already been to confession before that night . . . & had no intention of starting again. It was over & we didn't exchange a word of love or affection that night – she wouldn't have stayed over then if she had not been on the point of collapse.

From the moment it did start again, Catherine kept away from the house in Beaumont Street. 'I am not defending us in saying this,' Greene stated, 'only explaining something that may make the pain a little less. The affair to us seemed dead & buried in the Farm Street confessional.'[73] Because of the date of this letter (12 December 1947) it's probable that Greene took Catherine to his Oxford home *after*, not before he separated from Vivien.

But was it a true confession? Isn't this Scobie's dilemma in *The Heart of the Matter*: to love a mistress so much that a true confession cannot be made? Scobie enters the confessional box:

He could hear Father Rank close the door of his box and nausea twisted him again on his knees. 'O God,' he said, 'if instead I should abandon you, punish me but let the others get some happiness.' He went into the box. He thought, a miracle may still happen. Even Father Rank may for once find the word, the right word . . . Kneeling in the space of an upturned coffin he said, 'Since my last confession I have committed adultery.'
'How many times?'
'I don't know, Father, many times.'
'Are you married?'
'Yes.' . . .
'Is it one woman?'
'Yes.'
'You must avoid seeing her. Is that possible?'
He shook his head.
'If you must see her, you must never be alone with her. Do you promise to do that, promise God not me?' He thought: how foolish it was of me to expect the magic word. This is the formula used so many times on so many people. Presumably people promised and went away and came back and confessed again. Did they really believe they were going to try? . . . I am not going to try to cheat myself or God. He replied, 'It would be no good my promising that, Father.' . . .
Father Rank said, 'I don't need to tell you surely that there's nothing automatic in the confessional or in absolution. It depends on your state of mind whether you are forgiven. It's no good coming and kneeling here unprepared. Before you come here you must know the wrong you've done.'
'I do know that.'
'And you must have a real purpose of amendment. We are told to forgive our brother seventy times seven and we needn't fear God will be any less forgiving than we are, but nobody can begin

to forgive the uncontrite. It's better to sin seventy times and repent each time than sin once and never repent.' . . .

He's right, of course, he's right. I was a fool to imagine that somehow in this airless box I would find a conviction . . . He said, 'I think I was wrong to come, Father.'[74]

If Greene was not contrite, then Scobie represents his romantic courageous self. Did Greene lack the moral courage to promise to avoid Catherine in the Farm Street confessional?

It is difficult not to feel that Greene's defence of his actions to his wife was specious, but his sense of guilt after he had written the letter must have been intense. Greene was unable to mend his ways; it was his private hell and he shared his anguish with no one.

When in Italy in late 1949 Greene attended Mass with Padre Pio, the stigmatic. He recalled the occasion to me:

I can recall the stigmata, the dried blood sticking out. It would dry and then it would bleed again and then dry again. He also had to have his feet padded because they also bled . . . I was as near to him as I am now to you and those hands looked terrible, sort of circular pieces of dried blood.

Pio invited Greene to meet him privately, but although he longed to do so, he refused: 'I didn't want to change my life by meeting a saint. I felt that there was a good chance that he was one. He had a great peace about him.' Greene was afraid of losing his lover; the vow of chastity was one he could not keep. But there was also the difficulty of what would happen to faith if doubt were removed.

After Catherine's visit to Beaumont Street, Vivien was sure that the end of her marriage was near: 'I felt as if there was a thunderstorm coming up and you ask when is it coming, when is it going to come and I longed for something to happen, not for it just to go on and on. When he brought Catherine to my house to spend the night after they'd returned from Achill where she took her men, why, from that moment, I felt really there was no return.'[75]

19

Private Wars

A pity beyond all telling
Is hid in the heart of love.
— W. B. YEATS

THE death of her marriage is etched for ever in Vivien Greene's
memory: 'Graham left me on this Queen's wedding day – 20
November 1947.' What brought things to a crisis was a letter Greene
had written to Catherine from Beaumont Street. The letter was
addressed to her in New York, but by the time it arrived, she had
left and it was returned to the sender:

> We were having breakfast . . . it had been going on and on and I
> felt I must know one way or the other. In any case, I had an
> intuition and I took this letter and I thought, now I won't open
> this letter – it'll postpone whatever is going to happen. If I do
> open it something awful is going to happen. I had the letter and
> looked at it for a bit and I said to myself: 'I'll get it over – I know
> this is going to alter everything.' And when I read it, Francis had
> seen my face change . . . he got up and said, 'What's the matter?'

Vivien sent Francis off to school and continued to examine the letter.
Somebody had opened it and seeing 15 Beaumont Street, Oxford,
on the writing paper, had re-addressed it.*

> I opened it and of course it was a passionate love letter. I rang him
> up and said that we must talk, and I suppose I was shedding tears,
> and asked him to come down and he did. I said I've got a letter

---

* It is possible that Catherine was still in New York and had Greene's letter returned
to his wife or left instructions to return any mail to the sender. This certainly would have
brought matters to a head.

and I think you ought to know about it, or something like that. And he sounded as if he knew. I don't know how, but as if he knew that the thing had blown, as they say. He came down that afternoon from London. First of all he said, 'Oh that doesn't mean anything. You know how one writes.' And I said, 'No – I know what is real feeling and that is real.' And he said, 'Well, yes it is.' And he said, 'I am going to leave you. We'll be going away together – leaving here.'

Greene told Vivien that he would be sending someone to pack his books and clothes: 'It was very difficult with the children coming back soon from school. We went upstairs into the drawing room and then he left. And I thought, well, I'll probably never see him again and looked out of the window that was facing the street, and he looked back for a minute, didn't wave, but looked back.'[1]

This dramatic moment appeared eight years later in his novel *The Quiet American* as the hero Fowler, visiting the Caodaist festival in Tay Ninh, turns his memories over at random, memories which were Greene's – 'a fox . . . seen by the light of an enemy flare . . . the body of a bayoneted Malay . . . my wife's face at a window when I came home to say good-bye for the last time'.[2]

After he left, Vivien was stunned. She remembered the last Christmas and New Year in Beaumont Street – making up stockings for the children in front of the gas fire, listening to the trains at the station blowing their whistles at midnight to welcome in the New Year and sobbing. She found the whistles terribly melancholy and wondered what would become of her.

Upset by her husband's departure, Vivien wrote to Greene's mother, who replied in distress: 'I am ashamed of my son. It absolutely makes my heart bleed. I could never have believed it of Graham. What about his religion – surely one cannot get absolution if he confesses such sin. Like you, I am appalled at K. [Catherine] – too terrible. I could kill her, nasty minx. With everything in the world & 5 children . . . I hope he will keep away from K now. I think you are a saint. I feel like a murderer.'[3]

In another letter Marion Greene darted in anguish from one subject to another: 'Your letter distressed me beyond words – poor dear thing.' After speaking of 'that horrid woman', she stressed the parallels between Greene and his hero Scobie – the suicidal qualities of both: 'Of course Graham is too soft-hearted. I feel there is much of him in Scobie. I think the only way he can save himself is to cut clear of D[orothy] & the other woman & return to you & the children. Perhaps not in Oxford, quite a fresh start & let that woman commit suicide. I don't expect she would . . . Graham was a very sensitive child. You know the stories. He hated to be taken notice of or favoured in any way . . . Nobody could have been more in love than he was with you. I am sure his only salvation is to return. How does he go to confession – I cannot understand that part. As to K. she is his God-daughter. I thought you could not, in your church, marry God-children. You may commit adultery apparently. I don't know how that woman can – what does her husband know – all those little children too. It is just beastly.'⁴ Later Marion questioned whether Walston could divorce his wife if he condoned the adultery. She ended the last letter in deep sadness: 'I simply *cannot* understand such a tender-hearted person as he is being so cruel to you.' Vivien must earlier have given some explanation as to why he could be cruel, for Marion Greene's letter ends: 'I am sorry about drugs [benzedrine] & drinking. Oh dear, I am glad Da has not lived to know all this. I dread G. coming.'⁵

Greene did not remain unaffected. Early in the new year of 1948, Evelyn Waugh ran full tilt into his friend: 'Mass at 12 at Farm Street where I met the shambling, unshaven and as it happened quite penniless figure of Graham Greene. Took him to the Ritz for a cocktail and gave him 6d [to check] his hat. He had suddenly been moved by love of Africa and emptied his pockets into the box for African missions.'⁶

Later in the year, and soon after the publication of *The Heart of the Matter*, Greene was described by an unnamed interviewer in America in the *Saturday Review of Literature*: 'Tall, stooped, with bleak blue eyes, he is not incautiously called "complex". Admirers say he is shy, sardonic, sensitive, misanthropic, profoundly Christian.'⁷

Complex, certainly, and in despair over Vivien, Dorothy and Catherine. Vivien had not given up hope that she could bring Greene back to his family. Dorothy was still desperately and bitterly fighting to hold on, while Catherine remained an elusive yet obsessive dream.

A month after he had returned from Sierra Leone in 1943 and four years before his affair with Catherine, Vivien was still the 'best, the most dear person' he had ever known. After a visit to his family at Oxford, then living in the lodgings of the President of Trinity, Greene returned to the King's Arms, and spent the night drinking with friends of his brother Raymond. After the party, he wrote a letter to Vivien in the early hours affirming his love '*in vino veritas*' and adding: 'Life is sometimes so beastly that one wishes one was dead, and I go to places like Mexico and Freetown in a half hope that everything will be finished. Sometimes I wish I could twist a ring and skip twenty years and be old with you with this ragged business over. I've never wanted to be old but with you I could be old and happy' (something he was later to repeat to Catherine). After admitting he'd told a lot of lies in the last thirty-eight years ('or I suppose in 35 years, one couldn't lie from the cradle'), he admitted: 'but this is true. I hate life and I hate myself and I love you. Never forget . . . if I ever make you unhappy really badly and hopelessly or saw life make you that, I'd want to die quickly.'[8] How close these sentiments are to Scobie's, except that Scobie acts upon his desire 'to die quickly'.

Now all had changed; love did not reside in the Greene household: 'Have you ever seen a room from which faith has gone?' Greene wrote in his play *The Potting Shed*: 'You can fill it with Regency furniture . . . But a room from which faith has gone is quite different. Like a marriage from which love has gone, and all that's left are habits and pet names and sentimental objects, picked up on the beaches and in foreign towns that don't mean anything any more.'[9] The reference to 'Regency furniture' is to the furniture Vivien liked. Greene saw her house as a museum, not a home of love, and stressed this in interview. Their differences in taste and character are reflected in a letter he wrote just before the war ended, in which he refused Vivien's offer of a desk: 'About the Regency desk . . . If it was for you, I'd say go ahead. But if it's for me, I'd say no. The only kind of desk I can see myself writing my sort of books at is a flat one . . . not period or decorative . . . I couldn't write a word – except a delicate essay on Charles Lamb – at a Regency desk. Sorry.'[10]

Yet there was another reason for the break up of the marriage that one priest at least was unable to understand:

What a trying time to go to Confession. At Farm Street nobody, so I went unwillingly from previous experience to the Cathedral. After 3/4 hour I got a Fr. Pilkington & gave him the whole works to be on the safe side. You've never heard anything so fantastic. I had to start marital relations with my wife again & it was a sin to keep the separation going. Then about 'adultery' – I was agreeable to say I'll try, try, try, till the cows come home. But he wouldn't allow that. I must promise from this moment to give up seeing you etc. Finally I said, 'I'm sorry, Father, I'm afraid I must find another confessor' and walked out. I even had to teach him (perhaps that is why I was short) the elementary fact of life, that you couldn't have a woman without desire.[11]

The viewpoints of his wife and mother must be set beside a poem Greene wrote to Catherine in 1949, along with seven other poems dedicated to her and privately printed. The print run was only twenty-five, and the collection was entitled 'After Two Years'. It is not only an intense and genuine reflection of his feelings, but an accurate account of when his love for Catherine first dawned and a description of the magic of Achill:

> In a plane your hair was blown.
> And in an island the old car
> Lingered from inn to inn,
> Like a fly on a map.
> A mattress was spread on a cottage floor
> And a door closed on a world, but another door
> Opened, and I was far
> From the old world sadly known
> Where the fruitless seeds were sown,
> And they called *that* virtue and *this* sin.
> Did I ever love God before I knew the place
> I rest in now, with my hand
> Set in stone, never to move?
> For this is love, and this I love.
> And even my God is here.

The paradox of Greene's characters lies in the fact that out of the sinner comes the saint. In *The End of the Affair* hate is a source of love; in *The Heart of the Matter*, sin is a necessary concomitant of salvation. In this poem Greene celebrated the 'mattress . . . spread on a cottage floor', the old world gone with its easy distinctions of '*that* virtue and *this* sin', on the distinctive and contradictory grounds that he had never really loved God before he knew this place of adultery: 'For this is love, and this I love. / And even my God is here.'

In moments of deep depression, Greene felt abandoned by God: 'I've seen the mark of His footsteps going away,'[12] and experienced not only a sense of hopelessness, but what Coleridge called 'the dying away from him of all hope'. And in order to stand the strain he universalised his despair: 'nobody who lives escapes a private agony'. He also suffered from the sense of being locked into his own egotism, a place of captivity and misery, where the only means of escape were the palliatives of drugs, drinking, sexual adventures, and dingy night clubs (the seedier the better) or else the active sectors of the line: war, that 'ravaged and disputed territory between two eternities'.

*

Throughout these years Greene felt an angry longing for Catherine. Her familial and social responsibilities at Thriplow and Newton Hall forced her to ration her time with him. He was troubled by his sense that Catherine's feelings did not match his own. Again and again his obsessiveness and jealousy ruined his love.

There are references to his jealousy in his letters (or recalled in dreams) and diaries, but the point is put most succinctly in *The End of the Affair*:

[We] used to have long arguments on jealousy. I was jealous even of the past, of which she spoke to me frankly as it came up – the affairs that meant nothing at all . . . She was as loyal to her lovers as she was to [her husband], but what should have provided me with some comfort (for undoubtedly she would be loyal to me too) angered me. There was a time when she would laugh at my anger, simply refusing to believe that it was genuine, just as she refused to believe in her own beauty. . . .[13]

In the novel, Greene provides us with the heroine's private journal and this fiction reflects Catherine's true feelings. In one interview I had with him Greene hinted that Sarah's journal in *The End of the Affair* revealed either what Catherine had said to him in conversation or what she had written in her own diary. Their correspondence indicates that Catherine personally scrutinised and criticised *The End of the Affair*, not least because so much of it was culled from their life and love and turned into literature. Because Sarah's posthumous journal in the novel is based on Catherine's, Greene didn't wish to modify the order of events without her acceptance of the changes: 'Could you find time to look through [the revised typescript of the novel]? Nothing has been added, but . . . the order of the journal has been altered – one entry cut altogether.'[14]

Catherine's difficulty in dealing with this nervous, depressive genius is reflected in the passage in the novel dealing with the journal entry for 12 June 1944: 'Sometimes I get so tired of trying to convince him that I love him. He pounces on my words like a barrister and twists them . . . He is jealous of the past and the present and the future. His love is like a medieval chastity belt: only when he is there, with me, in me, does he feel safe.'[15]

But Greene was bound to feel vulnerable. He had left Vivien, and was in the process of leaving Dorothy, but they were rarely out of his mind. He could see with terrible clarity the conflict and suffering he had caused those he once loved. He felt that he had poisoned the lives of his wife and mistress just by withdrawing his love and therefore could never quite bring himself to depart altogether. He was aware of the pain he was causing Vivien, and wrote a year after he had left her: 'I never cease to be sorry about what I've done, & never cease to think of you with love.' Greene felt that he alone was guilty, and he felt deep remorse about Dorothy.

He could look coolly at Dorothy (with that splinter of ice in the heart) and knew her to be a little, dumpy woman whom he had befriended, loved and wished now to drop, but not unceremoniously. The exhausting battles of love and hate had to go on and they were persistent and noisy. Dorothy fought for Greene even after he'd left her. In any case his conscience dictated that it would be a gradual withdrawal. The knowledge that once love was over, he would replace it with a terribly engrossing pity made Greene's life painful: 'It was the face for which nobody would go out of his way, the face that would never catch the covert look, the face which would soon be used to rebuffs and indifference that demanded his allegiance.'[16] Greene knew how the shock would affect Dorothy when he told her he would be leaving to live elsewhere: 'her mouth a little open as though she were out of breath. He had the sense of an animal which had been chased to its hole.'[17] He could not easily be pitiless towards her and his escape from their home was relentlessly slow.

However much he was under Catherine's influence, however much he wanted to please her, he understood the feelings of his wife and mistress: 'Inexorably the other's point of view rose on the path like a murdered innocence.' He had sworn to Vivien that he would preserve her happiness: he had sworn similarly to Dorothy, but with Catherine he had accepted another and contradictory responsibility. He knew that the lies must end and that he would have to tell the truth without shading: he felt the wounds of the victims of his love and he raised a question: 'Was it the butterfly that died in the act of love?' But he knew the answer in the human world: 'Human beings were condemned to consequences. The responsibility as well as the guilt was his'.[18] 'I dread tonight,' Greene said to Catherine, eleven months after he had left Vivien 'but the choice of weapons is with [Dorothy], one has to be the servant of the one who suffers most or one injures.'

I remember Greene, his face absolutely wooden, an ingrained melancholy painfully apparent, speaking many years after the event: 'I've betrayed very many people in my life.' He selected only one for special mention: 'I betrayed Dorothy. Particularly Dorothy.' She had no marriage, no children (her companion, her widowed mother, in fact outlived her), and was resigned to her role in his life. What was there left for him to feel but an enormous pity? 'He knew from experience how passion died away and how love went, but pity always stayed. Nothing ever diminished pity. The condition of life nurtured it.'[19] And Greene, who was tied to a deep sense of guilt and pity, hated this aspect of himself, criticised it in his novels: 'Pity is cruel. Pity destroys. Love isn't safe when pity's prowling round.'[20] He desperately wanted to maintain happiness in those he had loved.

Of course, Greene really believed that it was absurd to expect happiness in a world so full of misery. Though he had moments of real joy, usually connected with the completion of a novel and the transitory sense that he had achieved something, or connected with the initial, wonderful euphoria of love, in his heart he felt that a happy man was either an extreme egotist or else living in absolute ignorance.

Greene suffered in slowly breaking off with Dorothy and even allowed himself to be humiliated by her – a most terrible thing for him to bear. As a child he had found humiliation more terrible than suicide. There was no question that Dorothy could be something or a termagant. The jealousy of the fat Portuguese captain's mistress in *The Heart of the Matter* is a modification of Dorothy's emotion, and Greene was writing there of his own condition and experience: 'she will take away my trousers so that I cannot go out alone; every day it will be drink and quarrels until we go to bed.'[21] On one occasion when she thought Catherine was in town and that Greene was going to visit her, she prevented him by hiding his trousers – Dorothy was a very spunky woman.

Arguments between Greene and Dorothy had gone on before he met Catherine, but then they argued about Vivien: ' "You are not protecting *me*. You are protecting your wife." "It comes to the same thing." "Oh," she said, "to couple me with – that woman." . . . "That woman," she repeated, watching his eyes. "You'd never leave her, would you?" "We are married," he said . . . "You'll never marry me." "I can't. You know that." "It's a wonderful excuse being a Catholic," she said. "It doesn't stop you sleeping with me – it only stops you marrying me." '[22] Greene knew that he was turning Dorothy into a Vivien in terms of parallel misery (though Vivien never fought vulgarly). It seemed to him that 'life always repeated, or perhaps his life repeated, the same pattern. There was always sooner or later, bad news that had to be broken, comforting lies to be uttered . . . to keep misery away.'[23]

Greene knew that he was among the legion of sinners and in *The*

Heart of the Matter and *The End of the Affair* he explored the depths of his own depressive character and the conflicts he, seemingly, engineered. They were conflicts which he knew he could not solve and he often came round to one solution, the solution that Scobie found – that of suicide. It appealed to him as the only way out of his absurd, grotesque and complicated love-life.

*

At the beginning of *The Heart of the Matter* Greene has a lead quotation from Charles Péguy: 'The sinner is at the very heart of Christianity.'[24] His activities give the sinner an intimate sense of the 'terror of life, of going on soiling himself and repenting and soiling himself again', a statement which appears in Greene's first novel, *The Man Within* (1929), and reappears in a letter to Vivien written nine months after he'd left her. She had written him a soft and mitigating letter, in answer to a stern letter which suggested she was out for revenge.

Throughout 1948 Vivien and Greene struggled over the form their separation should take: should they have a deed of separation or a judicial separation, the latter being a great deal more final than the former? Vivien had modified her stance out of dislike for vulgar argument, but also, I suspect, because she had received a letter from one friend who, although a friend of Catherine's, was trying earnestly to be an honest intermediary. She and certain Catholic priests tried hard to persuade Vivien not to go ahead with a judicial separation, but instead to sign a deed of separation. Greene's friends seem to have been disturbed about his suicidal tendencies.

It was this that made them write Vivien supportive letters, for as intelligent as she was, she could never have been a natural member of the Walstons' circle. She was neither worldly nor famous. She didn't fit into their circle just as Literary Louise didn't fit into the colonial society of *The Heart of the Matter*. The friend who knew both her and the Walstons assured Vivien that, if she behaved well, sooner or later Greene would return to her and Catherine's true position would be revealed as that of the woman standing between a wife and husband. The same friend wrote to Vivien to say that Catherine was able to justify herself as having nothing to do with the break up of Vivien's marriage. But, if Greene were to leave Dorothy, it would be clear that only Catherine stood between him and Vivien. Catherine had also insisted that Vivien must be told everything: 'It's only fair to the poor girl.'

Only later did it become clear that Catherine's insistence on Vivien being told as much as possible, that all Greene's weaknesses be laid bare, was an effort to turn Vivien against him; to make Vivien abandon any moral high ground and behave badly herself. The same friend warned Vivien about Catherine's experience in the arts of winning a man; and how, identifying Greene's suffering with Scobie's in *The Heart of the Matter*, many Roman Catholic priests were strongly supportive of him, despite his adultery.

The Reverend C. C. Martindale, a distinguished Catholic priest, wrote to Vivien, stressing that what he was about to say of Greene was gathered from his books ('which made me both esteem him and love him') and added: 'You are having to deal with a man to whom you have promised fidelity, and who has promised fidelity to you. Yet he is a tormented soul (as "Punch", I think, called him) and will often be defeated not only by personal weakness (as we all are) but by a kind of clashing of duties.' Having heard that Vivien was thinking of divorce, Martindale argued against it 'because it would give him the last push down into desperation, and also, create an awful scandal and give grounds to all such critics to say that he is not only a bad Catholic, but a bad *man*, which he isn't'.[25] It is likely that it was Martindale to whom Greene and Catherine went for confession.

In another letter, Martindale wrote: 'I imagine [Greene] has unconsciously put himself into the person of Scobie and expresses his own mind. If that is so, he must have suffered very deeply some time or other and have verified St Paul's words: "I see the better, yet follow the worse." ' Martindale went on to say of Greene, 'there is an enduring good kernel in a man who surrounds it with husk upon husk of wrong, and that it is this heart of good which survives when Purgatory (in this life or the next) has scorched off all the husks'.[26]

Taking notice of the advice, Vivien responded gently to Greene's letter, which suggested that *she* wanted a judicial separation in order to take revenge:

O what has happened to you, dear one? You have changed so dreadfully . . . Only think that you could write about 'having to PROTECT YOURSELF' from me and my 'revenge' . . . Those words seem to be from an hysterical malevolent woman not you, my friend for 20 years. You know absolutely and completely that I am your friend and you can TRUST me. You do know it in your heart, but you can't completely trust the people about you and you are psychically ill, or poisoned or afraid . . . You, rich, famous, free to wander and return when you like, without the anxieties of your family – to want protection from me (cooking in the basement or painting a dolls' house) – who has never in the whole of my life ever dreamed of hurting you or of doing you wrong or saying any word against you to friends or children.[27]

Vivien was fighting hard for his return: 'Long after I'd joyfully "forgiven" you about Dorothy I was loving and trusting you . . . and you can think of me in connexion with a wicked and vulgar notion of "revenge". Something fearful is happening in your mind and your heart about me – don't you realise what is being done to you . . . you are *being made to hate* someone who has only sadness and affection for you and you hit out to take away any last remaining feeling of security I have.'[28]

And she almost won, for he replied from California, from the Hotel Bel Air: 'I don't care a brass farthing about being famous. I'm very unhappy too & have been except for brief intervals for nine years. I don't believe this is the end of us . . . When I got your letter all my inclination was to throw everybody & everything up & return. Your pull was far greater than any other pull. But then I told myself hopelessly . . . what's the use? As soon as I give up C[atherine] I shall feel the pull back & within a few weeks I should begin to cheat.'[29]

On 3 June 1948 just before he went to Vienna with Carol Reed to start filming *The Third Man*, he sent Vivien an open and totally direct letter of the kind he felt a great need to write. He was at last writing as he'd always wished to; not tampering with a word, not altering a disagreeable fact: the lies in his life had to end. He discussed both his relationship with her and with Dorothy:

You know I am fond of you. Quite apart from that I am aware of the responsibilities I owe you & the children. But, mainly through my fault, we have lived for years too far from reality, & the fact that has to be faced dear is that by my nature, my selfishness, even in some degree by my profession, I shall always, & with anyone, have been a bad husband. I think, you see, my restlessness, moods, melancholia, even my outside relationships, are symptoms of a disease & not the disease itself, & the disease,* which had been going on ever since my childhood & was only temporarily alleviated by psycho-analysis, lies in a character profoundly antagonistic to ordinary domestic life. Unfortunately the disease is also one's material. Cure the disease & I doubt whether a writer would remain. I daresay that would be all to the good.[30]

---

* Greene is being unfair to himself here. His disease was genuine. He had been a depressive, with all that entailed, from the age of thirteen.

Greene then makes a full confession about Dorothy: 'For nearly nine years . . . I have had a second domestic life in London, but the fact that that has been without the ties & responsibilities of a husband, has not made it any more of a success. I have failed there just as completely as at Oxford, so that especially during the last four years [since 1944], though the strain began much earlier, I have caused her a great deal of misery. So you see I really feel the hopelessness of sharing a life with anyone without causing the unhappiness & disillusion − if they have any illusions.'[31] Greene then made Vivien an offer which was no offer, presumably leaving it to her to make the final break: 'If you feel that a life is possible for us in which, though Oxford is my headquarters, there are no conditions, no guarantees or time-table laid down for either of us . . . then let us try it. But, my dear, if as you reasonably may feel this arrangement (or lack of arrangement) would only make for more misery, then I think we had better have an open separation which will be less of a problem & nervous strain for both.'[32]

But this calm was only temporary and soon tempers were high once again. Some portion of the argument is revealed by Vivien to her Catholic lawyer in late September 1948, some three months after the publication of Greene's bestseller, *The Heart of the Matter*. Greene had invited himself down to Beaumont Street and she gladly agreed to his coming as a guest on a Saturday and staying till Sunday after tea. At first she found him truculent, saying she would find it very difficult to bring proofs of adultery and that if she insisted upon a judicial separation she would only get a minimal allowance. If there were a private separation then he would aim at the maximum possible. Later in the day 'he was entirely softened and wept very much and I felt very hopeful of the future, then'.

> The worst thing [was] still to come. Before he raised the question of the Personal notice in the papers he began to say 'why don't you divorce me; a judicial separation is the same as a divorce . . . You needn't think it will break up my relationship with C.W.; we could decide anyway to go away together permanently. Why don't you have a divorce and be done with it.' I said we had both and he in particular most violently, had been against it and I thought it disastrous for the children, both at Catholic schools. Then he became slightly hysterical and said, 'Well one good thing I have got out of Korda in America and that is five hundred Nembutal tablets and I can solve the whole business with that.' As you know, this is not the first time I have had threats of suicide and I said only 'whatever you have done to Francis, I can't believe

you would leave him a memory like that . . . ' He said 'They'd
never know and soon get over it anyway . . . '

When Vivien spoke of these suicide threats to the Reverend
Vincent Turner and the Weavers, their reaction was, 'People who
talk about it never do it.' But Vivien was concerned because, as she
told her lawyer, 'he had attempted it twice before I met him, and he
has this obsession that writers show in their writing the way they will
die, and this is a strong feeling with him. If he took an overdose, as
he has often threatened, it would be like Scobie in *The Heart of the
Matter* and – as in the book – I as his wife would be blamed by
everyone . . . Of course I realise that Mrs Walston and Graham can
set up house together and she can change her name by deed poll to
"Greene" and call herself Mrs Graham Greene. No one can stop that
and it is done every day . . . But even more suicide threats won't
bully me into a divorce.'[33]

*

Greene's continued passion for Catherine was having a serious,
physiological effect on Dorothy. 'I feel terribly sorry for her,' he
wrote to Catherine, 'physically the whole thing shows.'[34] Greene's
powerful sympathy for Dorothy came from knowing her condition:
'When you visualized a man or a woman carefully, you could always
begin to feel pity – that was a quality God's image carried with it.
When you saw the corners of the eyes, the shape of the mouth, how
the hair grew, it was impossible to hate. Hate was just a failure of
imagination.'[35] Greene was in pain, and whatever Dorothy's
retaliation it was his intense conviction that he deserved punishment.

To ease his conscience he took Dorothy to Paris. He and François
Mauriac had to go to Brussels to speak at Les Grandes Conférences
Catholiques at the Palais des Beaux Arts. Greene gave a brilliant
address on the threats to Christian civilisation to an audience of
3,000. The photograph of them which appeared in many newspapers
(though the *Catholic Times* missed the last 'e' in Greene) shows
Mauriac with his slightly twisted face, and Greene with his powerful
bulging eyes and pessimistic expression.

Afterwards, Greene and Dorothy went on to Paris, but the trip
was disastrous. He wrote to Catherine: 'as for love (in the f-sense) we
are two corpses'. In *The End of the Affair*, Greene applies a similar
image to Henry and Sarah, when Sarah writes in her journal: 'Henry
and I sleeping side by side night after night like figures on tombs.'[36]
He told Vivien that he hoped to take a flat by himself in London,
and that the present set up in Gordon Square would be materially

altered: '*though I am trying if it's humanly possible to save some relationship there*'.[37] Greene's method of saving part of the relationship, however, was unnecessarily complex.

He decided to take Dorothy on a long trip, first to Paris again, then to Marrakech and during that time, he planned to give her a letter explaining that they must part, that he was in love with another, and that he felt he'd have to leave their home in Gordon Square. When I asked him why he used such a roundabout method – after all he was living with Dorothy and could have approached her in London – he admitted he suffered from moral cowardice.

Although Greene's 'Dear Dorothy' letter has not survived, what has is Dorothy's letter to Greene (the only one) upon her discovery that he was having an affair. Dated 14 April 1948, the letter reflects Dorothy's direct, pungent style. It is sometimes indecipherable, sometimes ungrammatical, and reveals their disturbed relationship:

> I had lunch with Mr. Mellar today. Heard little except the story of you & Walston for an hour & a half. Everyone from Douglas [Jerrold] to the packers [at Eyre & Spottiswoode] it seems know you are behaving like a fool over an American blond [*sic*] as you have made no attempt to disguise it from anyone, everyone you know in London is talking about it too! Charles supplies the directors with information (he is in great demand as he has become part of the set up & drinks with you all) & your secretary deals with the lower orders & so on. They also know that you are prepared to break up Oxford for this woman.

That Dorothy was unaware that Greene had left his wife indicates something of Greene's secretiveness. She reported that although others had guessed about the Walston affair as far back as April 1947, their suspicions weren't confirmed until that autumn (while Dorothy was away) when the affair grew more intense and Greene completely 'lost his head'.

> They are of course 'very sorry for the other woman' [Dorothy] who they regard as a kind of Graham Greene specimen – something to be kept in private & never seen or mentioned . . . Mrs. Greene feels that you are going out of your mind as no man in his right senses would behave as you do over an American blond with a yearning for culture!

Upon hearing that Catherine had gone to Venice with Greene, Dorothy did a little sleuthing to check 'to see how far any of the story was true'. She saw little use in 'trying to build up any kind of life . . . you are not to be trusted to help make one in any way,' and then contemplated their future:

> I suppose we will go on living together for a while, checking our bags in & out & sleeping here between times. I feel I dont care either way; life has been so completely smashed for me during our time together & so much has had to be lost that nothing matters very much any longer. I'll go on with it all as long as the parent [Dorothy's mother] lives of course but I'll be glad when it's over.

Now that Dorothy was made aware of the affair, it explained Greene's thin excuses for many trips and his attitude towards her since her return from Africa, which she had found puzzling. She then questioned whether a promised holiday together would now be possible: 'a week or two with me will fall very flat after three months with a woman you are so madly in love with so cancel it if you like, it would be awful too to lie with one woman when all your thoughts are on another. I am glad I know all this as otherwise I would have tried to perk things up with us again in several ways, now I can simply live my life apart from you . . .'

Dorothy wrote the letter because she felt it was impossible to talk to Greene. Yet despite her bitterness and pain, she ended the letter by keeping the door of reconciliation open:

> I dont want a repetition of the last revolting afternoon with you, one only spits at someone you regard as a pretty low creature, not a woman who has lived so long with you & through so much . . .
>
> I will arrange as soon as possible for us to have separate rooms as I know you will prefer it, you couldn't of course suggest it as it would have meant telling the truth.
>
> If at any time you want to make a life we can share, or this thing with Walston breaks tell me, but any advance now I'm afraid must come from you.

D

*

On returning from Venice, Greene did not cancel his holiday with Dorothy, but set out for Marrakech. His letters to Catherine show how this baleful excursion developed. The first letter speaks of 'too long & dreary scenes . . . have started again. I'll take her to Africa, but the end is nearly on us.'[38] And the next is a postcard written five days later from Rabat: 'Everything fixed but life a bit grim – don't like Muslims much.' And then on 7 May he admitted: 'Letter has been delivered. Pretty ghastly results, but we go on to Hotel Jamais, Fez.'

The woman who stole Greene's trousers so he couldn't leave home to visit Catherine was not likely to accept the situation gracefully. On 11 May from Fez he described what happened: 'It's been a pretty grim holiday . . . I gave her the letter 24 hours before we left Paris. Ghastly, scenes, but we went on.' They arrived at Casablanca at four in the morning, to find the hotel closed. They then went to the railway station, where they had an accidental meeting with a French physicist called Boutry and waited together for the 7.50 train. It turned out to be a godsend since they were only able to get a room at Rabat through Boutry's influence. Now that the fatal letter had been delivered, half of each day would be pleasant and the other half 'an awful hell of tears, pain, melancholy . . . ' But Dorothy thought that perhaps the relationship could continue, at least on a trial basis:

Yesterday morning, after the worst scene yet when I was reduced to a nervous pulp, M.G. suddenly hit on a compromise that satisfied her . . . I can't see that it is much different from my letter . . . The idea is that I have the flat of my own, work there every day, spend the night there when I want to, go away when I want to, but still, except on these occasions, sleep at Gordon Square. The arrangement to be tried out for 3 months from when I come back from U.S.A. &/or Vienna, & if it fails – as of course it will – we split altogether. I shall test it out as soon as I return . . . by a weekend or midweek at Thriplow.[39]

Greene was hopeful that the arrangement would not last three months, that Dorothy would again go off to West Africa and perhaps marry the captain of the Elder Dempster ship, and that the holiday would go on quietly without fuss: 'Everything is quieter now, & last night we went & saw a couple of very bad naked dancers in a native brothel & smoked a pipe of hashish.'[40] But fighting threatened to break out at any time: 'Today I put on my corduroys & she spotted the guilt marks right away – in five seconds. She said she'd already found them on my grey flannels. However no scene – yet.'[41]

By 16 May, Greene and Dorothy were at Marrakech, and thinking of Catherine, Greene would strike off the days on his calendar waiting for the moment they'd be together again. Little wonder, for the holiday was even more ghastly than he anticipated: 'Yesterday we arrived here, hell opened again from 2 till 6 & I nearly got the plane back but the office was closed. There is no longer a chance, I think, of avoiding a complete split & this time has cleared my mind a lot about that & wiped out a good many memories.' He was quite frantic: 'No more lies or worries of that kind. No more telegrams . . . it will be a good time beginning & I'll write my best book yet.' What he wanted Catherine to do was to write, or wire, or telephone directly to him, whether Dorothy was there or not: 'All the deception is over for ever.'[42]

Greene and Dorothy moved on to Agadir, where there was a French Foreign Legion encampment, and life took on a certain pleasure: 'Got here yesterday by plane & the sweet one-armed Commandant of the Foreign Legion met us with his aide-de-camp & took us home to dinner. This a much nicer place than Fez or Marrakech: very like West Africa with a long, slow murmur of surf & one's clothes damp with humidity.' But to be with Dorothy was painful, for she had powers of persistence which recall Ida's in *Brighton Rock*. Although aspects of the film star Mae West were used by Greene in the development of Ida's character, Dorothy's beery behaviour in pubs also corresponds with Ida's. 'I feel terribly cut off. I think one is now going through the "worst" time you prophesied, but before the end of the summer one will be quite clear. You can't imagine the agonising boredom of these long strained days. I want to be with you & laugh & be silly & happy & write. Can't write today, but I'll have the story ready for when I get back. I think − so far − so good. Perhaps my last religious story before the great sex novel?'[43]

He was to return, certainly to Port Royal, at 6 a.m. on 28 May, but while travelling by plane he must have at least toasted his new novel which appeared on the bookstalls on the 27th. He sent a card to Catherine to 'drink to *The Heart of the Matter* on the 27th'.

Soon after returning to Gordon Square with Dorothy, Greene wrote urgently to Catherine because he was immediately leaving for Vienna with Carol Reed. He'd seen Catherine only once since his return: 'Cafryn dear, it seems about five years since Wednesday. Thursday proved an absolutely ghastly afternoon with the worst scene yet [with Dorothy].' Catherine had found him the flat next to hers at 6 St James's: 'I long for the 1st drink at No. 5 . . . It is an odd smorgasbord feeling of insecurity, knowing that Gordon Square is over. How I wish the sea captain would persuade m.g. to leave me . . .'[44] He also included a short note to Catherine's husband, Harry Walston: 'But I do want to tell you how I appreciated yesterday coming out of the storm to your welcome & your whisky. You were both so sweet to me.'

In Vienna, he wanted assurance that Catherine had got him a flat for he was determined not to return to Gordon Square: 'I hope all goes well about 5 St. James. It's like a promise of peace & life.'[45] In a letter written the next day, whilst describing in detail life in Vienna, he returned to the subject of the flat: 'I would love to walk bang into the flat on arrival and find you and a bottle . . . I long to be back, but now I wish that I had cleared the decks completely [with Dorothy] before I left, so that there would be nothing to dread.'[46]

Four days later he sent a telegram to Catherine: 'Arriving Northolt 8 pm Thursday will go straight St James's.' He had made his second escape – the first from Vivien and now from loyal Dorothy. Without a promise from Catherine to leave her husband, Greene had succeeded in removing two obstacles to their love and at just the right moment. With the publication of *The Heart of the Matter*, Greene was suddenly the most famous and most pursued writer in England.

20

A Vulgar Success

Do good by stealth, and blush to find it fame.
— ALEXANDER POPE

THE beginning of *The Heart of the Matter* contains the following disclaimer: 'No character in this book is based on that of a living person . . . I want to make it absolutely clear that no inhabitant, past or present, of that colony appears in my book.' However, as if to distance himself further from his characters, Greene also made an unusual statement (quoted by Waugh in his review): 'These characters are not my creation but God's. They have an eternal destiny. They are not merely playing a part for the reader's amusement. They are souls whom Christ died to save.'

This statement is not specious, yet it must be stated that Scobie is, to a great extent, Greene's emotional and psychological double. Scobie's problems – his love entanglements and serious religious commitment – reflect Greene's own, and by treating his life as fiction, Greene was able to disguise his torment.

Oddly enough, *The Heart of the Matter* may have had its origin in a dream Greene recalled twenty-two years prior to the publication of the novel. He was then in his twenty-first year and courting Vivien:

Oh my dear I had such bad dreams . . . We were on a platform and you were going away, and you laughed in the most heartless manner at my misery, and I grew furious and you got cold and taunting and the train came in, and an awful looking bounder 'considerably older than yourself,' came along to the carriage door and started talking to you, and you were fearfully affectionate, and gave him your photo. And then I began really to hate you, and I pushed the man away, and took hold of you, by the shoulders and forced you to look at me. And you twisted yourself away, very

293

white and contemptuous and said 'I won't have this. I'm sick of you.' So I got hold of you again and I wasn't furious, I simply hated you. And I said that I'd make you understand how miserable I'd been for 9 months because of you. And you struggled and I hit you . . . And then I thought of a revenge far better. And I said 'I suppose you are going to marry that man?' And you smiled and said 'Yes, I certainly am.' And I let go of you and said 'Then I'm done with you and everything' and rushed away to shoot myself. Not through love of you, but through hate. Because I felt you'd never get over the thought of having made a Catholic kill himself.[1]

There is something about Greene's mood: 'I'll undo / The world by dying,'[2] which indicates that suicide was never far from his mind. Whenever Greene felt cornered and deeply melancholic about his grotesquely complicated life, suicide seemed the only way out. Harried by his sense of responsibility to both Vivien and Dorothy, Greene's dilemma is faced by Scobie – how to fulfil his promise of love to both wife and mistress. After much personal conflict, Scobie accepts the possibility of his soul's eternal damnation and decides to commit suicide. This is the denouement of the novel.

Edward Sackville-West, a friend of Greene's, reviewed *The Heart of the Matter* in the *New Statesman*. The review explains for the non-Catholic reader the terrible implications of suicide for a Catholic: 'You may be maimed, bankrupt, deprived of friends, relations and all support, broken in health, persecuted, tortured, imprisoned, but there is one reprisal you must never take: suicide. To the non-Catholic it must seem that there are many worse – less pardonable – sins: relentless cruelty, for instance, and treachery, and meanness. To which the Church replies that whereas cruelty and treachery can be wiped out by repentance . . . the wretch who takes his own life has no time in which to repent of his sin. Suicide is unpardonable, quite as much because it is final, as because it is the goal of despair, than which no insult to God can be more profound.'[3]

Inevitably, the novel caused uproar among its readers and critics. However, Greene's letters reveal nothing of this or that he had an extraordinary bestseller on his hands: 'The Catholic Press are beginning to come out. A long article by Evelyn [Waugh] in the *Tablet* followed by silly little theological note by a complacent Canon. *Catholic Herald* [a] long, good but cautious review. A nice Elizabeth Bowen which I enclose. The non Catholics are going to like the book better.'[4] On the back of the envelope of a 21 June letter, Greene wrote: 'Nice long piece by Eddie Sackville-West in *New Statesman*.' Greene's references to the reviews are modest, but the reviews themselves show that a furore was rapidly developing.

It was the review by his friend Evelyn Waugh in the *Tablet* (5 June 1948) which initially helped the controversy along. Waugh began his review with a splendid accolade: 'Of Mr Graham Greene alone among contemporary writers one can say without affectation that his breaking silence with a new serious novel is a literary "event". It is eight years since the publication of *The Power and the Glory*. During that time he has remained inconspicuous and his reputation has grown huge.'

But Waugh was at pains to stress that 'thousands of heathens will read it with innocent excitement, quite unaware that they are intruding among the innermost mysteries of faith'. Waugh's review was full of praise, and he made two points which were taken up by others and became the basis for many letters to the press. First, 'the reader is haunted by the question: Is Scobie damned?' Second, he spoke of Scobie's 'sacrilegious communions' and of his suicide: 'He dies believing himself damned but also in an obscure way . . . believing that he is offering his damnation as a loving sacrifice for others.' Waugh felt it essential to state that 'the idea of willing my own damnation for the love of God is either a very loose poetical expression or a mad blasphemy'.

In the same issue a letter appeared from Canon Joseph Cartmell. Cartmell responded both to the novel and Waugh's review of it:

> Mr Evelyn Waugh's comments on the theology of this book are, in my view, unimpeachable. Father Rank, to console the widow, expressed his opinion that Scobie really loved God. He could hardly mean it in the literal sense, unless he was assuming that Scobie's sins were undeliberate, the involuntary acts of a warped mind – an assumption which is against the whole tenor of the book. Scobie is a deliberate sinner up to and including the taking of the poison. Whether he was damned is another question, to which we do not know the answer . . .
>
> Making his first bad communion, he prayed: 'O God, I offer up my damnation to you. Take it. Use it for them [Louise and Helen].'

With a fierce sense of his own theological superiority, Cartmell went on: 'I do not think that Mr Greene means to assign any real value to this offering. You cannot do evil that good may come of it. Such an offering could have no worth with God. It is, as Mr Waugh says, a mad blasphemy. Indeed, no positive good came of Scobie's death . . . The only good was a negative one, the removal of himself as a source of sin to them. Scobie was in fact a very bad moral coward. He could have escaped from his entanglement by a comparatively simple resolution. He would not take it. His attempt to give an air of moral respectability to his sins and his suicide, as though they were helping others, was, objectively, pure sham.'

Greene wrote privately to his friend Bishop Butler (who had written in support of Greene to the press): 'I find Canon Cartmell's rather textbook statement of when the love of God is possible and when it is not a little lacking in reality.' And he ended a letter to Evelyn Waugh: 'I thought the Canon rather complacent. Can't one write books about moral cowards?' The letter was undated, but must have been written about the middle of June 1948 as it is full of joy over Waugh's review: 'You've made me very conceited. Thank you very very much. There's no other living writer whom I would rather receive praise (& criticism) from.'

Waugh's thoughtful praise for his friend's book was tempered by the belief that:

> Many Catholics . . . will gravely misunderstand [the novel], particularly in the United States . . . where its selection as the Book of the Month will bring it to a much larger public than can profitably read it. There are loyal Catholics here and in America who think it the function of the Catholic writer to produce only advertising brochures setting out in attractive terms the advantages of Church membership. To them this profoundly reverent book will seem a scandal. For it not only portrays Catholics as unlikable human beings but shows them as tortured by their Faith. It will be the object of controversy and perhaps even of condemnation.[5]

*

Greene's 'profoundly reverent book' scandalised many Catholics. The controversy raged in the letter columns of leading Catholic newspapers. One Captain Stanley Norfolk thought it incredible that any Catholic could approve of the novel or that it could have been written by a Catholic: 'Faith, Hope and Charity – all are conspicuously absent, and the whole story is permeated with the stench of the latrine . . . no good whatever can result from publicising it, while the book's potentiality for harm is immense . . . If ever there was a book that should be banned surely this is it.'[6]

The editor of the *Catholic Herald*, whilst disagreeing with such a response, admitted that many of his readers supported Norfolk.

Subtler minds than Captain Norfolk, such as a certain Ronald Brownrigg, also argued for its suppression:

> Great minds think differently on the subject of Mr Greene's latest *opus*. This fact is, to my mind, a strong argument against its publication . . . I wonder if your correspondents can conceive, as I most certainly can, of mentalities that will be muddled by *The Heart of the Matter* into thinking that what Christ said was 'If you love me, break my commandments'?[7]

Bishop Brown, writing to the *Universe*, attacked *The Heart of the Matter*'s portrayal of adultery: 'Adultery is adultery whatever attempts may be made to disguise it by not using the hard word.' But his argument was similar to Brownrigg's. 'No doubt many could read it without it making much impression on them but there will be others on whom it will act as a bad book.' Brown's condemnation belongs to a world which died before the First World War: 'There is also a painful want of reticence about things which modesty teaches should not be mentioned.'[8]

Another writer, Denys Blakelock, suggested that he had taken to hiding from his Anglican friends books like Greene's which portray sinful Catholics while upholding the truth of God and of the Church he founded. A person who signed her letter 'Irishwoman' had the perfect answer: 'Mr Blakelock might as well hide the New Testament from his Anglican friends because it shows that the first Pope told three cowardly lies and disowned his Lord.'[9]

Evelyn Waugh, Edward Sackville-West and Raymond Mortimer had attached much importance to the probability of Scobie being a saint. This idea was intolerable to some readers as a letter from William Goodger shows: 'Scobie commits adultery, sacrilege, murder (indirectly), suicide in quick succession. In three of these cases he is well aware of what he is doing . . . he takes communion in mortal sin because he can't bear to hurt his wife's feelings. This isn't the way a saint behaves . . . According to all the rules (accepted without argument by all Catholics, including Greene and Scobie himself) Scobie is bound for Hell as he has deliberately denied God.'[10]

The Reverend John Murphy's unfavourable review is disturbing, for by reducing the novel to simple terms his argument strikes home:

> [The] vortex [of plotting] sucks poor Scobie down at last . . . Scobie is a Catholic with a conscience of the highest sensitivity and insight whose weak will ultimately leads him to adultery, sacrilegious Holy Communions, responsibility for a murder [in the

novel Scobie's faithful servant Ali is murdered because Scobie no longer trusts him] . . . and for full measure, to a suicide . . . To be precise, he fears woman more than he fears God — two women, his wife and his mistress, and what he really fears is hurting them. He is afraid to tell his wife that he has a mistress, not knowing that she knows it; and he is afraid to tell his mistress that he must give her up . . . How can you account for the fact that a man commits suicide in order, among other things, to avoid making any more bad Communion? But the answer is obvious: Because he despaired where he should have repented.[11]

The captivating simplicities expressed here were challenged by the brilliant Jesuit, C. C. Martindale. The question Martindale wished to raise was whether we could say that Scobie finally despaired: 'No one doubts that Major Scobie committed many sins, suicide included: but did he "finally despair"? . . . The poison took long to act: during that time what was truly in his "heart," the real man fought its way through the clouds of his tortured mind . . . and he avowed that he was sorry and that he loved.' And then Martindale made a sensitive distinction. In speaking of Scobie, he was also, though perhaps not deliberately, speaking about Greene's affair with Catherine Walston which he was privately aware of: 'Its essence is that an honest but rather superficial Catholic [Scobie] finds that in proportion as he sins, his faith in Him against Whom he sins is intensified.' This is the basic irony of Greene's affair with Catherine Walston.

In dealing with the question so many readers raised in their letters to the press — does Scobie go to Hell because of his suicide — Martindale wrote: 'Only when he reaches the peak of wrongdoing does the vision of God's holiness fully dawn.' And finally, though speaking of Scobie, Martindale came to a conclusion about Greene which he hinted at in his private letter to Vivien: 'Priests surely often meet the enigma of the co-existence of *seeming contradictories in one man* — of evident innermost righteousness with the apparent committing of mortal sins.'

Martindale's peroration is moving:

I am glad that prudent priests and experienced laymen think as I do — that this is a magnificent book, both theologically accurate and by a layman who 'knows as much as any man can know about human nature.'

I know one, a hard-headed man to whom this book has given the last necessary stimulus to becoming a Catholic, and many who, like me, will continue to draw from re-reading it a deeper love of suffering distraught humanity and of God.[12]

So Greene had the spirited support of various Jesuits and laymen, as a letter from M. M. Farr suggests: 'I should like to put on record the fact that one great sinner was so moved by Mr Greene's last book that he has completely changed his way of life and returned to the practice of the Faith.'[13]

But Murphy and other like-minded Catholics were not alone: there was at least one famous writer whose review reflected his nature; a clear, unambiguous mind fitted to a clear, unambiguous style. To George Orwell, Scobie was incredible because the two halves of him did not fit together:

> If [Scobie] were capable of getting into the kind of mess that is described, he would have got into it years earlier. If he really felt that adultery is mortal sin, he would stop committing it . . . If he believed in Hell, he would not risk going there merely to spare the feelings of a couple of neurotic women. And . . . if he were the kind of man we are told he is – he would not be an officer in a colonial police force.[14]

What a simple, straightforward, absolutist mental world George Orwell lived in. Our betrayers are often not outside ourselves, but within. It was not Stalinist dictatorships which troubled Greene, it was the hounds of Heaven. Like Scobie, Greene felt he was the source of suffering in those he loved most.

It was Canon Cartmell who responded, as we have seen, to Scobie's communion when he prays: 'O God, I offer up my damnation to you. Take it. Use it for them': by suggesting that Mr Greene did not mean to assign any real value to this offering. 'You cannot do evil that good may come of it.' Indeed, in his letter to Waugh, Greene denied this reading of Scobie's actions: 'I did not regard Scobie as a saint, & his offering his damnation up was intended to show how muddled a mind full of good will could become when once "off the rails".'[15]

But Greene may have had a curious notion about prayers, seeing them as a sort of brokering with God, and his answer to Evelyn Waugh smacks of special pleading. In *The Heart of the Matter*, Greene has Scobie, in a scene of great imaginative power (the first hundred pages of this novel are the most moving he ever wrote) visit a makeshift hospital that housed the survivors from a ship sunk by a German submarine, who had endured forty days in an open boat. At one point, Scobie is with a dying child, and again his prayers take the form of bargaining with God. Scobie's first prayer is that nothing should happen until Mrs Bowles, a missionary's wife acting as nurse, returns. He listens to the child's heavy uneven breathing, as 'if she were carrying a weight with great effort up a long hill'. He longed to be able to carry the weight for her:

> He thought: this is what parents feel year in and year out, and I am shrinking from a few minutes of it. They see their children dying slowly every hour they live. He prayed again, 'Father, look after her. Give her peace.' The breathing broke, choked, began again with terrible effort. Looking between his fingers he could see the six-year-old face convulsed like a navvy's with labour. 'Father,' he prayed, 'give her peace. Take away my peace for ever, but give her peace.'[16]

He hears her small scraping voice from the bed repeat 'Father'. He watches her blue and bloodshot eyes watching him. He can see her breast struggling for breath to repeat the word. He acts out the part of a father, telling her not to speak. He remembers how he used to make, with the help of a handkerchief, the shadow of a rabbit's head:

> 'There's your rabbit,' he said, 'to go to sleep with. It will stay until you sleep. Sleep.' This sweat poured down his face and tasted in his mouth as salt as tears. 'Sleep.' He moved the rabbit's ears up and down, up and down. Then he heard Mrs Bowles's voice, speaking low just behind him. 'Stop that,' she said harshly, 'the child's dead.'[17]

Later in the novel, he institutes another pact: 'O God . . . if instead I should abandon you, punish me but let the others get some happiness.'[18]

Vivien Greene said to me how absurd this business of bargaining with God was, that it was not the way of a real Catholic. But in a letter from Greene published in *Dieu Vivant*, 17 November 1950, Greene speaks openly about Scobie's prayer over the dying child:

> one did have in mind that when [Scobie] offered up his peace for the child it was genuine prayer and the results that followed. I always believe that such results, though obviously a God would not fulfil them to the limit of robbing him of a peace for ever, are answered up to a point as a kind of test of a man's sincerity and to see whether in fact the offer was one merely based on emotion.[19]

In an undated letter to his wife about *The Heart of the Matter*, Greene recorded that 'this book has been the devil to do, worse than the P and G and that was a brute'. But if it was 'the devil to do', it stands along with *The Power and the Glory* as one of his two pre-eminent works in the trinity completed with his next work, *The End of the Affair*. Daniel George writing in the *Daily Express* felt justified in regarding *The Heart of the Matter* as a masterpiece; for George Painter in the *Listener*, Greene was now 'a great Catholic writer (for such, in *The Power and the Glory* and his present novel, he has securely become)'; for George Malcolm Thomson in the *Evening Standard*, Greene had produced a novel 'of distinguished quality and power'. And finally Lionel Hale in the *Observer* conceded: 'What a writer this is! If he chose ever to rest on his laurels how safe he would be!' This was a possibility Greene never entertained.

*

Immediately after the war, and before he met Catherine, Greene felt he would probably never write anything of significance again. However, with the publication of *The Heart of the Matter* on 27 May 1948, and the appearance of two films, *The Fallen Idol* (September 1948) and *The Third Man* (August 1949), he had finally achieved great success and renown, but they brought him little happiness.

Greene, who hated fuss and always wanted to go unnoticed (in his early school photographs he always seemed to be hiding), was suddenly a media figure. His name appeared everywhere, he was a person to be seen, wondered at, and his autograph was avidly sought: 'At Heathrow the trouble began. Associated Press girl reporter, autograph album of buffet girl, photo on the steps of plane. I want to hide. I want to build a house of bricks with Harry [Walston] & disappear.'[20] He might have had the world at his feet, but he still saw life with fiercely jaundiced eyes.

He wrote to Catherine on 21 June 1948, a little under a month after *The Heart of the Matter* had appeared, 'Really apart from you & a few things connected with you, life doesn't offer much. Perhaps if one was a failure, instead of a vulgar success, one would have success to look forward to.'[21] In his melancholy, Greene never allowed himself to win. 'The hours run out: I count them and wonder how few are worth the bother of counting or living.'[22]

The pressure of fame genuinely troubled Greene: ' "Fame" is an unholy bore. It would have seemed exciting at 24 . . . but yesterday I wanted to finish *A Lear of the Steppes* . . . & the captain of the aircraft would sit & talk: at Amsterdam I was quietly reading when the manager of the hotel & staff appeared with autograph albums: at

Hamburg, getting into a car, a microphone was shoved under one's nose: at every nightclub *The Third Man* is played.'[23]

It wasn't only the newspapers that publicised Greene. In reviewing French and German notices, one critic described Greene as an extraordinary innovator:

> To England belongs the credit of producing an author who has done more than most to make European Catholics question their whole outlook on faith and holiness . . . Until recently it was scarcely possible to pick up at any rate a German Catholic review without an article devoted to Graham Greene; now he is generally accepted as having introduced a new type of sanctity to the world; his whiskey-priest is compared, not with characters of fiction, but with saints who actually lived in the past. The recognition of the unorthodox saint of fiction has also led to a new appreciation of holiness in paths hitherto unnoticed even by those who knew that the way to heaven was hard.[24]

However, Greene's deep-seated concern was not controversy or fame, but the possibility that he might lose Catherine: 'Will you still love me if I'm excommunicated? Because you do love me   What a lot you do for me – getting me a home, giving me hope . . . '[25] Whenever he had to be away from her, in the United States or Europe, he became terribly worried. When not in personal contact, he felt unable to fight for Catherine's continued love and thought that without his presence she would get too disturbed over their situation as godfather and goddaughter who were also lovers and that she would then leave him.[26]

As a devout Catholic, Catherine knew that she had sinned and felt that she could not just go to confession and soon afterwards repeat the sin. They both knew what to do, and although they made efforts to end the affair, they didn't succeed. With Greene at his most persistent and obsessive, she knew the solution was not easy to come by.

Knowing Catherine would be at a retreat when he ended his visit to America and fearing Catholic pressure, Greene used scabrous language: 'I hope the little shits won't gather around you too much in the next three weeks.'[27] In the same letter he repeated this slightly differently: 'I love you & trust you & hope the priests & the shits won't work on you when I'm away.'

All the time the novel was selling enormously. Greene received letters of support, such as one from Adele Rudd, an avid reader of Greene. Her letter quoted a letter from a Jesuit priest in America: 'I am thrilled by *The Heart of the Matter*. Greene is powerful and penetrating. The book is startling but certainly true to life. I have little patience with Catholic critics who refuse to admit Catholics commit such sins.' And the Jesuit added: 'It is selling by the thousands here.'

If it was selling well in America, it was shooting to the top of the bestseller lists in England. Greene's publisher Heinemann did an initial printing of 10,000 copies, which sold out in six days after George Malcolm Thomson chose it as the *Evening Standard* Book of the Month. A second edition of 10,000 was rushed out in *eight days*. By the middle of June (the book had only appeared in the bookshops at the end of May) the second edition was exhausted and a third edition, a further 10,000, was ready by the end of the month. Meanwhile orders were coming in from all over the country.

The book received a further fillip. In July the Government of Eire banned it on the grounds that it was 'indecent in tendency'. Whilst it was true that the Catholic clerics on the Irish Censorship Board had opposed the ban in the first place, the laity were in the majority and the ban stuck until the publishers appealed. Of course, the banning helped to sell copies. The ban was lifted early in October, though the controversy continued.

So Greene had his 'vulgar success'. When invited to Paris six months later in January 1949 by his publisher Robert Laffont, Greene was genuinely surprised at the response:

> You can't believe how famous I am here. Passed through customs and police in two minutes at Le Bourget . . . It's all too fantastic. My books in every shop – a whole display in the Rue de Rivoli. Three different people writing books on me for three different publishers. The Professor of English at the Sorbonne has asked me to lecture & says that he can fill the hall twice over.[28]

What pleased Greene was that he had vanquished his *bête noire*, the novelist and drama critic Charles Morgan. Like Greene, Morgan was a winner of the Hawthornden, but Greene thought so little of his work that the fact that Morgan was a prior winner of the Hawthornden prevented Greene from taking pleasure in the award: 'Three of [Morgan's] past graduate pupils writing theses on me, one on "L'Univers de G.G.," one on "Le Malheur dans Les Oeuvres de G.G." & one on "The Technique of the novels of G.G." Priests flock reverently around.' Greene adds: 'I'd really be rather enjoying it if I believed it, but I don't quite . . . common sense tells me it's all a joke that will soon pass.'[29]

21

Boston Tea Party

Although it swings from fun to gloom
It may evade its rightful doom.

— NOËL COWARD

HAVING achieved immense success as a script writer with *The Third Man*, Greene emerged as a playwright in the summer of 1949 with a dramatisation of *The Heart of the Matter*. Basil Dean was to direct the play in New York and Boston with the assistance of the producers Richard Rodgers and Oscar Hammerstein and it was scheduled to open on Broadway in the autumn. Although Greene had originally intended to write the script in collaboration with Dean in New York, circumstances forced them to work in England.

In an effort to keep a check on inflation, the Chancellor of the Exchequer, Sir Stafford Cripps, had instituted a programme of austerity with strict taxation and a voluntary wage freeze. The Bank of England turned down Greene's proposal for the financing of his stay in America, viewing it as a bad risk. On 21 June Greene wrote to *The Times:*

one department of the Bank of England still appears to regard [writers] as an inferior race, or at least as distinct outsiders . . . I asked the Bank of England for the usual business man's allowance of 10 pounds a day to keep me in New York during the period of writing. Royalties had already been advanced to me by Rodgers and Hammerstein to enable me to visit New York for the preliminary consultations last year, and it is unreasonable to expect further advances before the play is written.

Even if the play were unsuccessful, by the terms of the contract the dollars earned could not fail to equal the small amount the Bank of England was asked to sanction. If the play were a success, the dollars accruing to this country would be incalculable. The

Bank of England, however, tells me that it cannot gamble on an unknown quantity to the extent of 350 pounds, the amount asked for . . . The Bank of England has offered to sanction a daily allowance of 4 pounds, on which it is impossible to live and work in New York under present conditions. I have therefore had to cancel my contract. One wonders how many other authors have been prevented in the same way from earning dollars for this country.[1]

Greene's letter to *The Times* led to questions being asked in Parliament. In answer, Sir Stafford Cripps denied that Greene had stated in his application that he had a contract or that the dramatic version had to be written in New York under the terms of the contract or that royalties had been advanced to him already: 'or even if the play were unsuccessful the dollars earned would reimburse his expenditure'.[2]

Greene replied promptly (ever ready to do battle) though his manner was modest. He wanted to correct the impression conveyed by Cripps: 'In all but the omission of the word "contract", Sir Stafford Cripps has been misinformed. My application stated definitely that I wished to visit New York by arrangement with Messrs Rodgers and Hammerstein, the theatrical producers, in order to dramatize my book *The Heart of the Matter* for them. The Bank of England replied that they were only prepared to allow me a maximum amount of 4 pounds a day; when they were satisfied that the application was a genuine one. There was no question . . . of their allowing a larger amount.'[3]

Life expressed the opinion of many when it noted that it was extraordinary that the Bank of England thought Greene's venture too risky an enterprise to let such a small sum of money leave the country – '[it] strikes us almost speechless'.[4] Three months after the 'affaire Greene', in September 1949, Cripps devalued the pound.

Now that Greene and Dean had been forced to write the play in England, they put up in a hotel to hammer out the script. Greene pushed himself hard and by 7 September he looked forward to the appearance of a secretary – 'a change from Dean's face' – and hoped to have the first draft of the play completed by Thursday lunchtime.[5] Nineteen days later, apart from having taken Evelyn Keyes to see *The Third Man*, Greene 'worked, worked, worked with Dean'. Evelyn Keyes had fallen in love with Greene, but he felt nothing sexual towards her and avoided any relationship: 'One sticky evening, but last night was pleasant & friendly & unemotional.'[6]

On 26 September, feeling pressured to complete the play, Greene told Catherine that he was back on benzedrine 'to try to get this bloody thing finished this week. I'll stop it in good time so that you won't have to suffer from my nerves.' But during the whole time he was writing the play, he had his mind centred on writing *The End of the Affair*: 'I want more than anything to get on with the "I" book, but it's not a book I can write in driblets.' Still work on the play went on: 'I'm rather flat out . . . At work all day trying to flog a dead horse into life, & I'm feeling the effect of 3 days benzedrine running.'[7] Not only did Greene have to contend with the after effects of the benzedrine, but also with a nerve-racking drama played out in an adjoining room:

> tonight a woman was having a hysterical seizure next door while we were trying to work. I've never heard anything so ghastly. Poor devils. Dean after half an hour insisted on calling the manager. He was right because the manager packed the man, who had never spoken above a whisper while she shrieked the abuse at him, to a separate room. Awful how after twenty minutes she was cooing down a telephone to her girl friend as though nothing had happened. And the friend of course would never have believed in the shrieking maniac & imagined her husband exaggerated.[8]

Dean and he were hard at it: 'A lot [of] benzedrine, & only 2 hours sleep . . . No benzedrine yesterday, ten hours sleep last night with the help of a tablet.' On 30 September he reported to Catherine that he had 'a revolutionary idea for the play', but he did not give any details.

On his forty-fifth birthday, 2 October 1949, Greene wrote to Catherine that he was racing her to the end of life. Although still working doggedly to complete the play, Greene celebrated the day by going to early Mass at Farm Street. He received a book of poems from the poet Kathleen Raine: 'One was dedicated "For Graham". Not a love poem thank God, but quite a good one. It seemed . . . hermaphroditic having a poem dedicated to one.'*[9] Greene was also remembered by Vivien and Dorothy; Vivien sent him Burton's *Travels in West Africa*, and Dorothy Glover an anthology of John Clare's poems.

Greene had hoped that Ralph Richardson would take a part in his 'new' play, but after having lunch with Richardson, he discovered it

---

* The second stanza of the poem runs: 'I prayed for love that should be all in all, / But in a fancy less substantial than a dream / Thought that my hands were nailed together to the wall.'

was not to be: 'Lunch with Ralph Richardson was a disappointment
– he seemed rather lukewarm about the play. What he really wanted
was me to write a film for him & Myrna Loy. I said I could do
nothing before December. November is absolutely booked – you [a
holiday in Italy] & the novel [*The End of the Affair*]. I long for both,
the first always, the second sometimes. But I love the combination.'[10]
Later that day, he took Evelyn Keyes to see Richardson in *The
Heiress* and came to the conclusion that he didn't want him in his
play, which was 'nearly finished': 'A final grand reading by Dean on
Tuesday.'[11]

Greene finished the play on his birthday about 6.30, and had a
double gin with Basil Dean to celebrate; then suddenly he saw that
the first act was all wrong, and that it needed to be reshaped.[12] But
however tired of writing Greene might be, he was more troubled by
the depression he would experience on finishing the play (as he
inevitably did after any exhausting piece of writing) and the
approaching emptiness in his life after returning from his holiday
with Catherine: 'I think it would be more sensible to go [abroad]
after Italy in that dreary patch when one spell of happiness is over
and there's nothing to look forward to.' He then admitted: 'I'm
always a bit unbearable those days.'

Thinking of Paris, Greene realised 'with horror' that about three
out of the five times he had gone there alone since the war 'he had
picked somebody up'. But Catherine had changed all that: 'second
strings aren't any good and a monastery's the only possible substitute
for you! . . . I want you and nothing but you for the rest of my
life.'[13] Like Bendrix's love for Sarah in *The End of the Affair* Greene's
passion for Catherine 'had killed simple lust for ever. Never again
would I be able to enjoy a woman without love.'[14]

When he was in Italy with Catherine in November it appears that
events conspired to make the holiday less paradisal than anticipated,
as an undated letter to his mother suggests:

> The weather in Italy was rather awful & Rex & Barbara Warner*
> stayed with us nearly the whole time which we did not intend.
> Towards the end we went across to Naples for a day's house
> shopping – & were stuck for four days because the boats didn't
> sail.[15]

But he must have enjoyed Italy more this time than last, for he

---

* Rex Warner, a novelist, had a good reputation both just prior to and after the war.
Barbara Warner, née Rothschild, was a close personal friend of Catherine's.

had expressed reservations about their previous trip in March to his mother:

> I have been most of my time in Anacapri – which I don't like very much: I may sell the villa again – apart from a few days in Rome & in Florence (Florence bored me). Now I have been staying for a few days in Ravello near Amalfi with the Huntingdons (she is Margaret Lane who wrote the life of Beatrix Potter) & I've enjoyed that a lot.[16]

*

After completing the play in October, Greene decided that he and Dean would travel to West Africa in December. The trip was to be the antidote to the void he would feel when Catherine returned to her husband: '[Africa] will help one get over the post-Italy depression. Work is the only constant possible in life: if only one *could* work. Everything is like benzedrine, a postponement.'[17]

Greene tried to arrange his journey to Sierra Leone from Paris, but he had trouble getting a yellow fever certificate from French officials. He spent the night at his publisher's: 'Last night at Laffont's. I gloomily consented to return & in Paris, arriving here on the 18th – dinner with the Comtesse Beaumont; on the 19th book signing & press reception & lunch with the *Dieu Vivant* people on the 20th, returning to England the evening of the 21st.' One thing he refused to do again was to sign books in Paris: 'I simply cannot face another book signing . . . At the last one I was signing steadily for well over three hours and it is too exhausting.'[18]

Frustrated by the difficulties over his yellow fever certification and by being in Paris without Catherine, Greene writes drearily: 'O dear, this is the silliest of all impasses – I don't really want to hang around these empty streets for a week – they echo with you . . . I don't really care a damn where I am – the whole routine of existence seems awfully pointless when our only contacts are telephone calls, letters, etc., but I'd prefer to be somewhere without memories or else absorbed in something that scares or excites me . . . there's nothing to do now except look at the rain & wait for lunch.' Greene feared that the trouble over the certificate would force him to return to England: 'it looks as though the only news will be a return to No. 5 [St James's] & watch the rain from there.'[19] But suddenly and jubilantly at the end of the letter: 'Hell of a day with officials, all well (D.V.!) Off tomorrow & love you so dearly . . . More from Freetown.'

Two days later, Greene was stuck at Dakar. The officials were unhappy about his lack of a certificate as Dakar had a bad record of yellow fever: 'Hope to go on tomorrow where if the Freetown officials want to show their disapproval of me, they can slap me into quarantine.'[20]

Now that he was on a trek to unknown experiences, Greene's melancholia disappeared like snow on the desert. His desire for extinction also vanished as he moved among the eccentric characters of his beloved Africa. Greene had been warned by Air France that if there were a problem with his yellow fever certificate in Dakar, it would be useless to go to the consul-general for assistance as he was always drunk after 8 a.m.:

> We called at 4 & after ringing twice, the doorway opened, not by a servant but by a white man, who swayed slightly. 'Is the Consul-General in?' I said. 'It's him in person,' he said. We stayed about half an hour, unable to get any sense out of him, & he developed a strong dislike of Basil [Dean] & an embarrassing liking for me – perhaps he scented someone who liked a drink too. He insisted on Basil photographing him & me & a black servant ('good fellow – I knock him around a bit') on the steps under the Royal Arms & urged me to come and stay with him: 'Got two beautiful women to dinner tonight. Your friend – don't know his name – nor yours – looks short tempered. You stay with me any time. Always have a room for you.' I'd rather like to spend a night with him & see what happens. Another of his *bons mots* was after an embarrassing silence (he had been too drunk to get his telephone to work) he spread his arms wide and with a twinkle at me, 'Tell me the latest story from London.' Gin alas, not whisky is his drink.[21]

Finally, Dean and Greene were able to leave Dakar. Greene obtained a bogus medical certificate to say that he and Dean were unfit to be inoculated, which allowed Air France to put them on the plane, 'but we may be still questioned by the strict English when we get to Freetown'.[22] There were many comings and goings and wires to be pulled, but finally they arrived, after an awful journey, at the transit camp. Dean was depressed, not so Greene:

> but suddenly getting under a mosquito net in the damp stuffiness, I felt at home – a familiar austere narrow home of four muslin walls. And this morning the light was beautiful & the black women passed by the window in robes of the loveliest colours, slouching by, chewing their sticks. I can never get this part right out of my system.[23]

Re-experiencing his past in Freetown helped to chase Catherine away or rather attach Greene to her in a different way. There was an alternative world to his frustrating but all-encompassing passion for Catherine:

> I am too happy to be in West Africa . . . to mind what happens. (Dean is still asleep.) Next to you I love this hot wind and the black decorative women & the rather oafish friendly men in shorts & the mosquito net & the camp bed & the washed out madame behind the bar & this grey bright light. If I couldn't be with you, I'd like to be here.[24]

Greene looked forward to the sights and smells of Freetown and hoped that he'd reach it the following day. He planned to seek out Ali, his servant during the war, 'who is in the police band now'.

The acerbic Greene disappeared in Africa. He loved the French customs officials who were not troubled by his and Dean's failure to have proper documents, but jovially warned them of what might happen when they passed through British customs in Freetown:

> At the airport at 1 in the morning people were so charming – the Sante man who roared with laughter at our yellow fever letters but passed us through 'Tell me what happens,' he said, 'Eight days quarantine. My English colleague's very strict. You are the first British I have seen without proper certificates. O what fun you are going to have. 8 days quarantine. We French, we know how to dance,' & began to dance on the floor. 'We dance this way, that way, we dance . . . '
> ' . . . The polka,' I said.
> 'Yes, the polka, but my English colleague, he doesn't know how to dance.'[25]

In this same letter, one of Greene's longest to Catherine, he expressed his love of Africa and Catherine in the same breath: 'I have loved no part of the world like this & I have loved no woman as I love you. You're my human Africa. I love your smell as I love these smells. I love your dark bush as I love the bush here, you change with the light as this place does, so that one all the time is loving something different & yet the same. I want to spill myself out into you as I want to die here.'[26]

When Greene arrived in Freetown he visited his old haunts: 'I am sitting on the balcony where Wilson sat at the City Hotel & saw Scobie [in *The Heart of the Matter*]. It's very very hot & sticky & I love Freetown . . . It's too hot to write properly, & for the first time I don't miss you physically (it's too hot to make love) only mentally . . . Alas! There are no schoolgirls in the window opposite, but a horrible radio blares a woman resident's impressions of Trinidad.'[27] Wilson, who has only just come out from England, is sitting on the balcony of the hotel, when a man called Harris joins him:

> 'Look down there,' Harris said, 'look at Scobie.'
> A vulture flapped and shifted on the iron roof and Wilson looked at Scobie. He looked without interest in obedience to a stranger's direction, and it seemed to him that no particular interest attached to the squat grey-haired man walking alone up Bond Street. He couldn't tell that this was one of those occasions a man never forgets: a small cicatrice had been made on the memory, a wound that would ache whenever certain things combined – the taste of gin at mid-day, the smell of flowers under a balcony, the clang of corrugated iron, an ugly bird flopping from perch to perch.[28]

Greene met again the one-time Provincial Commissioner, 'old Sayers . . . with a black mistress & black children', now a public relations officer. And he wrote wistfully to Catherine: 'Sometimes I have a crazy desire to ask for a job as assistant P.R.O. or something & simply stay in this place. When one of our holidays is over & there's none on the horizon, life seems over too, & if one's going to walk about as a ghost, this would be an agreeable place to haunt. Whisky is only 1/6 a glass, & gin even cheaper.'[29]

By travelling to Africa Greene rescued himself from the dark side of his character, but the happiness of his two weeks there did not last. He had travelled up-country as he had done in the old days and suddenly he desired Catherine again. He tried hard to switch his thoughts away from her at night in order to get through it. He wrote to her as an adolescent in the throes of first love would write, the first sentence deliberately emphasised: '*Please make a plan for us to see each other soon*. Do you think sometime this Christmas you could meet *my Mum*? And can we go to Paris please in January for a week & either find a house or a dinette & have our old suite at the Ritz.'[30] Because his hand was 'pouring with sweat', Greene stopped writing, but not before expressing his jealousy of Harry Walston: 'I *hate* going to sleep without you & I can't help hating the thought of the other bed beside you. Every night I have to switch the thoughts. One isn't only jealous of sex – one is jealous of company & the first words on waking.' In a postscript he repeats his thoughts of love and suicide:

'O my dear, I miss you so much at night to lie down beside & sleep – how I sleep then. It's at these times one wishes one was dead. Let me see you soon. It's all I live for. God bless you & pray for me.'[31]

*

Soon after his return from Africa and Paris, Greene planned to travel to America on the *Queen Elizabeth* in early February 1950. He was desperately needed in Boston, for Basil Dean was running into serious difficulties in directing the play. If Greene had known the sad state of affairs he would have travelled by air.

Greene boarded the *Queen Elizabeth* and at 9.10 p.m. that night recalled his last sight of Catherine: 'Dear heart, I still see your hand against the window of the car. Never, never have I felt going away from you more.'[32]

On board ship, he was pleased that his name was not on the passenger list, and he felt at peace. He passed the time by reading George Orwell's *Nineteen Eighty-Four*, which he found 'very good except the sex part. That's ham.'

Greene met a man who was a hero of his, and he found it odd and rather sad that life should 'reduce' one's heroes:

> First Mauriac, whom one is used to now. This evening I was having drinks with a little man, a Spanish basque, who had read my books & who turned out to be one of my heroes of the 30's – the President of the Basque Republic [José Antonio Aguirre, 1904–60], the Catholic who fought Franco (I tried to fly to Bilbao during the siege & broadcast from there). Now the Hero had suddenly become just a man of my own age who liked *The Power and the Glory*. Thank God, Captain Scott & Captain Oates are safely dead & can't turn into retired naval officers who read novels.[33]

Throughout the voyage thoughts of Catherine were with him by day ('Like the Hail Marys that fit into the corpus of one's thoughts, so I say over & over again, I love you, Catherine') and night: 'I dreamed of you last night & as a result miss you more than ever: "When I waked / I cried to dream again." '[34] As usual, his letters soon returned to marriage: 'Do think hard of living with me & eventually (I'm sure) really marrying in the Catholic Church. In a few years your children will all be away from home, & there'll be just you & Harry. It won't be so very long before we are both old, but you are the only person (+ a few priests) that I want to be old with . . . I want to be with you when even desire is dead.'[35]

On arriving in New York Greene discovered that the bookings

for the play were not going well: 'Rodgers & Hammerstein have appealed to me to give interviews. They say I'm their only card, as the English cast is unknown.'[36] Greene was seen on to the train to Boston by a representative of David Selznick and arrived there at 9 p.m. only to find no one about. Hammerstein called the next morning and walked with him to the theatre through the snow. Greene had lunch with Basil Dean before the dress rehearsal. He found that the play was 'a terrible affair except for the last act'.[37] The next day his diary records exhausting activity: 'Typed out notes & went through them with Hammerstein at noon. They are having terrible trouble with Dean & are glad of my coming . . . Down to theatre where Dean hopelessly behind schedule . . . having light rehearsal (enormous trouble taken that resulted in fiasco at rehearsal). Dress rehearsal call postponed from 6.30 [p.m.] till 8.15. Actually started at 10.30. First act went smoothly in spite of its faults. Second act very poor. Finished about 3. Cast nervous, despairing, exhausted.'[38]

The rehearsals came as a bad shock to Greene. Although he did not care about the success of the play too much, he did care whether what he'd done was competent. Although Dean's direction was the cause of many of the production's problems, Greene thought the fault rested with the play itself:

Basil of course has slave driven the cast & reduced them to bad nerves. His production too is old-fashioned. The dresses are awful. But it's no use pretending that the main fault is that it's a bad play.

I had to have a press conference on Wednesday with the dramatic critics – about two dozen of them. We got on well, & the result is a kindly intelligent Press – they might have torn the whole thing in pieces especially with all the things that went wrong on the first night in the way of stage management. Poor Oscar Hammerstein was more fussed than me. I like him enormously. Rodgers less so. Dean has treated both very badly, so that they have welcomed me all the more.

I think I've spotted the main faults of the play. Today I've revised the last act & part of the second, cutting two scenes altogether. We should get that into rehearsal tomorrow. Next week I'm going to alter the whole character of Wilson & practically rewrite the first act. Maybe it won't be a bad play when it gets to New York.[39]

The *Boston Daily Globe*'s headline read: 'BRITISH NOVELIST GRAHAM GREENE TURNS PLAYWRIGHT – AND LIKES IT.' The journalist admitted that Greene didn't fit preconceived notions of the famous author of *Brighton Rock*, *The Power and the Glory* and *The Heart of the Matter*. 'Tall and a little stooped with a serious but friendly face, he did not look at you either austerely or analytically. Those eyes which had seemed so sharp in photographs were pale-blue, but neither penetrating nor cool. Obviously a shy man, he did not fit the conventional idea of a cosmopolitan world traveller, as he faced the circle of questioning Boston newspaper people. But his ease asserted itself – and drew a sympathetic laugh from the group – when asked if such collective interviews were done in England, he replied in his soft voice and with a laugh: "No, thank God." '[40]

Greene described to the press how he and Basil Dean worked on the dramatisation: 'Part of it they wrote together, part separately, and then compared their work. Greene now feels the theatre to be fascinating and wants to do a solo play . . . Mr. Greene has another book in mind [*The End of the Affair*] and also another film play for a director in Italy [*The Stranger's Hand*, directed by Mario Soldati]. But the idea of doing a solo stage play is actively in his mind.'[41]

Greene was trying hard to improve the play before it got to New York: 'Friday: Typed out 6 pages of notes suggesting changes. At the theatre all the afternoon, while Dean rehearsed some changes. Had dinner with Dean at hotel & then with Hammerstein to first night . . . Terribly embarrassing performance with everything going wrong. Post mortem till 2 a.m.'[42] The following day Greene worked all day to compress Act 3 into three scenes, which were ready in time for the Sunday afternoon rehearsal. On the Monday he rewrote the Bamba scene (in the novel, the occasion when the assistant District Commissioner commits suicide) and changed the end of the first love scene. On the Tuesday he wrote the epilogue, retouched the Bamba scene and then went to sleep, but in the afternoon when he was asked to dinner by Rodgers and Hammerstein he guessed the worst. In his diary he wrote: 'Play to be withdrawn. Face-saving announcement of production in Autumn. Sat up very late trying to comfort Dean.'[43] On 1 March the announcement appeared in *The Times*:

The producers of the play *The Heart of the Matter*, the dramatization by Mr. Graham Greene and Mr. Basil Dean of Mr. Greene's novel of the same name, have decided to end its run in Boston on Saturday night and to defer until next season any further performances. It was to have opened here on March 16. The reason given for the withdrawal was that too much rewriting was necessary in the short time given to the adapters.[44]

Greene had failed in his first attempt at writing a play and was more hurt and disappointed than he admitted. As a letter to Basil Dean in July shows, he was reluctant to revive any interest in the play, in himself or others:

I have read the new version of THE HEART OF THE MATTER and I am afraid that I cannot agree to its production in Liverpool or elsewhere. There is no use in pulling punches on this matter, and it seems to me to be a far worse version than the original. The original at least did contain a certain amount of good scenes and also the subject of the book. The good scenes in this case have got the guts removed from them and the new material has not to my view any value whether of dialogue or drama. The whole subject of the book has not only been lost but been sentimentally travestied. You will understand therefore my desire not to go on with the matter as I am not prepared to do any more work myself on the play. In fact the new version could not be made presentable from my point of view however much work I did on it.[45]

*

Most people would have been deeply unhappy about having so much work come to nothing, but the Boston disaster didn't trouble Greene as much as his inability to bring Catherine to his side. Even before Rodgers and Hammerstein closed down the play, he was on the verge of a breakdown:

I feel desperate, darling. If you walked in the door now I should break down & cry (like I've been crying in bed). I can't sleep more than three or four hours & that's with the help of pills. It's like after West Africa only worse. I've raised the price for anybody with a gun now to 5000 [pounds]. I look at the nembutal with such longing but people would say it [the suicide] was because I'd written a flop. But I don't care a damn about the flop – it's this working & working on something dead, & the tightness, & the hearing so little of where you are & what is happening to you . . . I can't get you out of my mind & I don't know how to keep going. This is all nerves & tiredness & the bloody American atmosphere . . . And for 1947 & 1948 [breaking up with Vivien and Dorothy] I'd exchange this for the break up time willingly. It was awful, but there was something to look forward to the other side, & this beastly loneliness wasn't then. I say Our Fathers & Hail Marys but it doesn't work, & I can't telephone to you or the Jesuits. I can't even see anybody.[46]

22

Wildly, Crazily, Hopelessly

Who invented the human heart . . . show me the place
where he was hanged.

— LAWRENCE DURRELL

G REENE loved Catherine 'wildly, crazily, hopelessly':[1]

And the sense of a world that grew more dear
Because of the feet that walked & the tongue that spoke
And the breath how quiet in sleep,
And my joy that woke
In Rome, Ravello & Capri
Siena, Venice every day
Touching you where you lay
And knowing you are here,
My dear.[2]

But by the summer of 1949 it appeared that some restriction had
been placed on his visits by Harry, and Catherine's letters became his
lifeline increasingly: 'I loved getting your letter. I still feel in a
curious way knocked out by Thursday & the awful Friday when I
believed an iron curtain had dropped & you had chosen the other
side of it.'[3] 'You don't know what letters do to me,' Greene wrote.
'From the depths of gin blues I was suddenly ready to kiss any
beggar's sores from sheer happiness when your letter arrived.'[4]
Melancholia often descended upon him: 'I'm nervy with wanting
you & feel scared at the time still ahead as I have no certainty of
when I shall see you. And the depression comes down when I think
of the years ahead, with scraps and bits of you, probably smaller
scraps & bits.'[5]

It was a particularly difficult time. In Catherine's company Greene exhibited quick mood changes: he was desperate one minute and happy the next, his anchor being Catherine. Productive, volatile, potent sexually – he was not bored. With Catherine by his side in Italy, especially in Anacapri, Greene was elevated and expansive, working with great concentration and fluency of thought.

Greene's moods could swing swiftly. His exaltation could descend to morosity and sudden bouts of irritability and accusation that seemed to bring an end to love: 'My dear, my dear, I'm so sorry. I failed you again. I always tell myself that it's the last time & then it happens . . . I love you, but what does that mean when one is of no use to you? It's the thing I want most & the sense of being useless of being able to do nothing for you grows & becomes an obsession . . . I know you'd be better off without me, but to be without you, would make all the years one had lived meaningless.'[6]

Greene had been a depressive since his school years at Berkhamsted. Many times he dealt with his depressions and deep sense of ennui by drinking heavily, and he was not the first writer to do so. He also used benzedrine, especially when he had a strict deadline, to complete work on time. He mentioned his use of it in *Ways of Escape*, when he was working on *The Confidential Agent* in the morning and *The Power and the Glory* in the afternoon, but he continued using it during his attempts to turn *The Heart of the Matter* into a play and later still when in Malaya and Vietnam. Earlier he had used morphia. He used alcohol constantly, which provided relief from restlessness, irritability and extreme agitation; however, alcohol is itself a depressant.

Greene realised his nature could be a trial for Catherine: 'I love you more than all the world and I wish it could make me into a perpetual sunny Jim, but it can't.'[7] Although his mood swings were difficult for Catherine, she understood that they were as painful for him: '[He] is very shy, and cannot conceive of anyone wanting him. He is a strange tormented person but intelligent, kind, and I think, tremendously good. I love him very much and wish so much that he did not suffer so much with a very real melancholia.'[8]
She could recognise when he was particularly disturbed:

one suffers with and because of someone that you love, and Graham's misery is as real as an illness . . . He has no work, no family, no friends whom he has any responsibility for, and every hour of every day he has nothing to plan for or no one to consider but himself, and for a melancholic by nature, this is a terrible breeding ground, and all I do, really, is to make things worse in the long run by my own fears of abandoning him.[9]

On occasion she would press him to see his psychiatrist, Dr Eric Strauss. She tried hard to be gentle with him. 'When I get irritable & crass,' Greene wrote, 'you are so sweet & patient & good to me. You never say the nasty things I say to you. That is not the difference between a man & a woman; it is the difference between you & me. You give me back all the peace that other people take away.'[10]

Often she felt she was the cause of these near breakdowns: 'I am a coward and cannot bear to watch him suffer because of things that I do . . . Were I really nice and good and brave, I would walk out, as I am convinced for HIM that's the best thing. But then, how seldom do I ever behave in the way that I know is best? He is very sweet to me and tries very hard, and occasionally when he fails he is overcome with remorse. But anyway, it's hard to know, and even when you know, it's hard to act.'[11]

*

Having separated from Vivien and moved out of Dorothy's flat, Greene, intermittently but with real determination, attempted to persuade Catherine to leave her husband and marry him. He was unremitting, always planning ahead, trying to see how he could find his way through the labyrinth to win her over.

Yet the responsibility and pity Greene still felt for Dorothy troubled Catherine and were difficult for her to understand, although he expressed his feelings precisely: 'When one says to someone, "I can't live without you," what we really mean is, "I can't live feeling you may be in pain, unhappy, in want." '[12] With respect to Dorothy, Greene felt an automatic pity that goes out to any human need; any victim demands allegiance, especially the victim you have created. It is also possible that Greene was unable to let go of any woman he had cared for.

A year after Marrakech, in the early summer of 1949, he offered Dorothy a new holiday. She chose Italy, which she knew to be Catherine and Greene's personal preserve. So, for once, it was Catherine's turn to be upset. 'My dear,' Greene wrote, 'I hated hearing your voice going dead & discouraged on the phone.'[13] He promised that though the trip might be Hell, it 'won't go wrong in the wrong way. If she has any hope in her mind of that (I don't think she has) this will dispel it for ever.' Once in Rome he felt 'very strained. I try to keep away from the places we went to, but your footsteps are everywhere & at every street corner.'[14]

Catherine's reaction was not to write to him while he was on holiday with Dorothy: 'Your silence weighs on one all the time &

makes me nervy . . . The trouble is you have such power to make one miserable as you have to make one happy. I miss you so much . . . I got very drunk last night to try to forget your silences & nearly got very stupidly involved. Every day the post comes there's nothing from you.'[15] That Catherine should punish Greene for taking his ex-girlfriend on holiday is unusual, for she was the least jealous of people.

Throughout 1949 and especially after July Greene pleaded with Catherine to marry him. On every possible occasion he returned to the Sisyphean task: 'If we were married we could have both the yacht & the house here [this was in Lymington where Greene anchored a small yacht, the *Nausikaa*, which he'd bought to avoid tax payment] & the cottage in Ireland & the flat in London & we could let Anacapri & take our holidays in Torcello.'[16] Telling her that his books would soon overrun his small flat in St James's, he wrote: 'I don't know what I shall do then . . . I think you'd better come and live with me and we'd take a bigger flat with room for all our books, and we'd send more to Capri . . . and more to Achill. I think two houses and a flat would be enough for us.'[17]

Given the matrimonial bent of his thoughts, Greene could not get too upset about the gossip their friend John Hayward was spreading: 'Well, as far as I'm concerned, I no longer care. I only wish I could shout you from the housetops. I like you, I admire you, I'm proud of you, and I love you. You are not only the best lover a man could have in his wildest dreams, but you've got the best brain of any woman I know . . . I wish I didn't have to do without the body and the brain for such a hell of a time.'[18]

How different Christmas 1949 was to be compared to the first Christmas Greene spent after his separation from Vivien. In 1947 Greene celebrated Christmas at Thriplow, and then Harry was 'one of the nicest people who ever lived'.[19] Greene was given the freedom of the house and on 29 December 1947, after a night of love, he wrote to Catherine: 'Darling, I have loved this Christmas. [Though not without having to apologise for being nervous and high-strung] . . . Don't think of my irritable outbursts – mere symptoms of night starvation . . . My dear, I love you & miss you so much before I leave even. It seems so natural to hear you around in the next room upstairs, talking in the kitchen. I am in love with you. I wish I could turn my ring & make time move.' But by 1949 everything was different. He could only see Catherine if her husband was engaged: 'I do hope Harry has a lot of work in town on his return & that I can keep you company . . . I'll be your saviour in all senses of the word. And sex-starved too.'[20]

As Christmas approached Greene was in Paris, extremely busy – dinner with the Comtesse Beaumont, book signing, press reception – and in despair:

> I found myself crying. I don't know what to do. It was all right yesterday when I spoke to you, but one can't telephone all the time. Then I hold you at bay till 3 in the morning drinking with Marie [Biche, his French literary agent] but one can't go on doing that . . . You captured Rome & Dublin, and now at the second assault you've captured Paris. I talked to Marie last night about the house and she's going to set about finding one, but what's the good? My dear, my dear. I used to like being alone, but now it's a horror. One thinks of times when we were happy & one tries to shut off thought. It's horrible that one can't be happy thinking of happy times like one can in an ordinary relationship. I don't know what to do about next year. One wishes over & over again that one of these planes will crash & they never do . . . I so long for your company – I don't at this moment, want to make love. I want to sit on the floor with my head resting between your legs like at the Ritz & be at peace . . . I never knew love was like this – a pain that only stops when I'm with people, drinking. Thank God, from tomorrow there are lots of engagements . . . You can always cure this pain by coming in at a door.[21]

*

What brought about this separation in 1949? If we were to rely solely on the surviving Walston–Greene correspondence – apart from a small number of undated letters, there is a gap from October 1948 until January 1949 and no letters for the month of June – we would be no closer to the truth. This was deliberate, as Greene wrote on 21 July 1949: 'if anybody ever tries to write a biography of me, how complicated they are going to find it and how misled they are going to be'.

Lady Selina Hastings, daughter of the Earl and Countess of Huntingdon, who were close friends of Greene and Catherine, told me that her father had heard a rumour that Catherine had had an illegitimate child by Greene. This story was repeated a number of times by different sources. Sylvia Luling (the pseudonym of Sylvia Thompson, the novelist) described seeing a child in the Walston nursery whom she spoke of as Greene's. Lady Melchett said casually: 'I think Catherine was very much in love with Graham. I was always led to believe that one of the Walston children was theirs.'[22]

Although a conspicuous number of letters have gone astray, there is no evidence in the remaining letters to suggest that Catherine had a child during this period, except perhaps the following: 'If when Twinkle [nanny to the Walston children and a friend of Catherine's] leaves you want a companion in your hotel to sally out after dark, telegraph me here or the Authors' Club.' In the same letter Greene added: 'I feel more than ever it was foolish not to tell her the truth – she must be extraordinarily dense not to guess it.'[23] These intriguing remarks were sent to 39 Percy Place in Dublin, the place of birth, as indicated in Dublin's Registry of Births and Deaths, of James Patrick Francis Walston, who was born on 18 July 1949. His mother is recorded as Catherine Macdonald Walston (formerly Crompton) and his father as Henry David Walston of Thriplow Farm. On 21 July 1949 Greene wrote to Catherine: 'Trouble may possibly start at Vivien's end with the news.'

But the child born in Dublin was not Catherine's, though he may have been Harry's. The weeding out of correspondence would still have been necessary since the circumstances surrounding the birth would have to be kept secret whether the child was Catherine's and Greene's or Harry's and an unknown woman's. The situation becomes more curious. Greene sent a telegram of congratulations to Harry at Thriplow and not to Catherine in Dublin, which surely was odd if the child was not Harry's or if Catherine had actually been pregnant. After the birth of the child, Greene mentioned in a letter that Ernie O'Malley had called: 'I suppose he'll be looking you up, though curiously he never said a word about you or the recent event.'[24]

The story from impeccable sources is that during this period Catherine wore pillows under her clothes and then larger pillows as the 'pregnancy' developed. A friend of Catherine's, who was sleeping with Harry, became pregnant and therefore he could well have been the father. However, she was also sleeping with another man at the same time.

There is no physical resemblance between James and Harry Walston: Harry and two of his sons, apart from James, are short, squat, broad shouldered – fleshy and with broad noses. James is tall, thin, willowy and with a fine bone structure and brown eyes. Catherine, Greene and Harry had blue eyes. Physical resemblance is not conclusive, but suggests that Harry might not have been the father either.

The solution to the difficult problem of what to do about her friend suddenly came to Catherine. She took matters into her own hands so her friend wouldn't have to contend with the shame of being a single mother, and persuaded Harry to agree to her extraordinary solution of faking pregnancy and taking on responsibility for the child. Presumably the biological mother was staying at 39 Percy Place and at birth the baby was moved secretly to Catherine's room and the pillows dispensed with. Catherine enjoyed the nine months of 'pregnancy' with the pillow game, which appealed to her sense of the extravagant. She was cocking a snook at the conventional world and in the process enjoying herself immensely.

The incident of a pregnant unmarried woman who was rescued by a friend found its way into Greene's 1969 novel, *Travels with My Aunt*:

> The girl . . . refused to marry your father, who was anxious . . . to do the right thing. So my sister covered up for her by marrying him . . . she padded herself for months with progressive cushions. No one ever suspected. She even wore the cushions in bed, and she was so deeply shocked when your father tried once to make love to her – after the marriage but before your birth – that, even when you had been safely delivered, she refused him what the Church calls his rights. He was never a man in any case to stand on them.[25]

In the last year of his life Greene and his niece, Louise Dennys, were discussing the difference in moral temper between the 1950s and the present day. Greene recalled how Catherine would visit him with pillows stuffed up her dress. She would fling herself down on the sofa and pull the pillows out with great relief and they would both be laughing.

*

The intensity of Catherine's passion for Greene must have disturbed Harry Walston. Although he was capable of 'profound forgiveness',[26] at one point he admonished Catherine for being too public about her affair with Greene and told her that she was causing her children embarrassment at school.[27] By the end of January 1950 the Walstons' marriage was strained. Harry and Catherine were seriously considering separation, for she was totally consumed by Greene.[28] Greene immediately took advantage of the difficulties and offered her marriage, arguing brilliantly for victory:

> I'm so sorry that all the trouble has started again. Please remember that I love you entirely, with my brain, my heart & my body, & that I'm always there when you want me. I don't like or approve

of Harry's judgements. When a man marries, he is like a Prime Minister — he has to accept responsibility for the acts of a colleague. My marriage failed (only God can sift all the causes), but the *responsibility* for the failure is mine. One can't lay the blame on one's wife. Your marriage, intrinsically, had failed before I knew you, & the man must accept responsibility — which doesn't mean guilt. It had failed because marriage isn't maintaining a friend, a housekeeper or even a mother. The Catholic service says 'with my body I thee worship' & if that fails the heart has gone out of it.[29]

Greene was certain that he could make Catherine happy and that any plan he would lay out for their living together would not exclude the Church. Although Catherine would be unhappy, it would only be for a short time. He reassured her that Harry could not deny her rights to her children: 'Harry could not divorce you without your consent, & *therefore* he could not shut down the doors between you & the children. You could insist on sharing them in any separation, just as if I chose I could insist on mine. He is not legally in a position to lay down terms or order a way of life for you.'[30]

In another letter he asked her forgiveness for presenting his case so persistently ('I wouldn't love you so much if I wouldn't fight to the last ditch'), but he must press it if 'the curtain is liable to fall'. He made ten points and entitled them '*Order of Battle in the unlikely event of your choosing me*':

1. During the 'unhappy period' we would consider losing ourselves on Achill and Anacapri, or we would take a long trip into strange territory . . . South Seas, India, Palestine, what you will.

2. We would immediately begin steps to see whether I could get my marriage annulled on two possible grounds.*

3. In the meanwhile proper arrangements would be made for you to have access to your children.

4. While the annulment proceedings went on, it might be

---

* It's difficult to say what grounds for annulment Greene had in mind here. Perhaps he thought to seek an annulment on the grounds that Vivien had no wish for further children and that they had not slept with each other for a number of years.

worthwhile considering changing your name by deed poll to mine, for two reasons

1)   I think it would make the whole business go down with your family
2)   It would enable us to economise when we travelled in only taking one room!

5. I would hand over to you half my controlling shares in the new company which would in effect give you 1/3 of all film & theatrical earnings in perpetuity.

6. Our finances – apart from my arrangement with Vivien & the children – would be in common & we would make a mess in common or a success in common.

7. Whenever we settled for any length of time, we would have two rooms *available*, so that at any time without ceasing to live together & love each other, you could go to Communion (we would break down again & again, but that's neither here nor there).

8. I love your children, & you would spend any time you wanted with them.

9. My love for you will go on till death, & I would guarantee never to break up our relationship except by your wish. No 'tipsy frolic' would make me walk out. It might make me sore as hell for 24 hours, but so far I don't think I've managed to be sore that time!

10. I would tell the truth to you always. Your part of our life should be yours. I trust you as I trust no other living person. I am yours entirely. I love you & will always love you. As I said in Paris you are the *saint of lovers to whom I pray*.[31]

We do not know the results of these bountiful offerings, but the correspondence which follows is very gentle and loving.

Greene then left for New York to work with Basil Dean on salvaging the production of *The Heart of the Matter*. Prior to his departure on the *Queen Elizabeth* he and Catherine managed to meet and he left her a simple love letter written on the reverse side of a letter from the bookseller David Low, which he had kept in his pocket during the journey to Calais:

> You are asleep & this is all I have to write on because you are holding my left hand . . . I love you more than I've ever loved you I believe. But that feeling happens again & again.
>
> Wouldn't it be odd if really I had never been married before & that's why the pseudo-marriage went wrong & one went in for tarts & love affairs. But I feel more married to you than I've ever felt. I want to be with you to have you to talk to & ask advice of about this and that. My dear, you are infinitely dear to me.
>
> . . . I believe in
>
> 1. God.
> 2. Christ.
> 3. All the rest.
> 4. In your goodness, honesty and love.
>
> I would live with you gladly & keep you *in* the church as much as I humanly could until the time when we could marry – as I believe we could. Perhaps I'm a swindler – I don't think so. I love you far more than life.[32]

When in New York, Greene visited Catherine's sister Bonte and her husband General Gustavo Durán (a famous Spanish Republican general, praised by Hemingway in *For Whom the Bell Tolls*) at their Long Island home, Apple Green, Old Westbury: 'Catherine was unhappy with Harry, felt warm towards him but it had nothing to do with physical love,' Bonte Durán said when I asked her to offer reasons for Greene's visit. 'I never knew why Catherine felt she needed my permission. Graham asked me to tell Catherine that it wouldn't be a terrible thing to leave Harry. He simply said to me: "I want to marry her." '[33]

Greene's work on the production of *The Heart of the Matter* was going badly, as we have seen: 'I'd pay back my expenses & slip away on a plane & thumb my nose at them, but there's Basil [Dean] & the cast & all the rest of them.'[34] The pressure of 'working & working on something dead' and the absence of any news from Catherine had brought Greene to the verge of a breakdown. By the time Rodgers and Hammerstein closed the play on 1 March 1950, Greene had reached crisis point.

He left New York on 8 March, delighted that Catherine had decided to meet him at the airport on Thursday. But then he was delayed and sent a succession of telegrams from Newfoundland:

THE USUAL BUGS NO HOPE ARRIVING BEFORE EARLY FRIDAY MORNING DEEPLY DISAPPOINTED.

AS USUAL HELD UP TWO HOURS GANDER DO WAIT.

EXPECT ARRIVE ABOUT I AM SO LEAVE MESSAGE WHERE YOU ARE.

Greene's plane was in fact seventeen hours late. He was stuck at Gander all night and did not reach London until 4 a.m. on Friday. Feeling 'wildly disappointed' that he had missed Catherine, he was delightfully surprised to find her in his flat at 5 St James's fast asleep on his sofa. They lit a fire and poured drinks, since for Greene it was midnight. It was, as Catherine described it, 'a superb piece of debauchery drinking whiskey at 6 am'.[35]

Catherine and Greene spent a wonderful day together and he spoke about his visit with the Duráns: 'I told her about our [his and Bonte's] conversation & she was very very moved, pleased, encouraged. It means more to her, you know, than even Binnie's [Belinda Straight's] sympathy. Anyway she needed it all that weekend.'[36]

And indeed Catherine did, for she and Greene had decided to confront Harry. Greene was to do what Bendrix in *The End of the Affair* longed to do:

'What's troubling you, Henry?' I asked . . .
'Sarah,' he said.
Would I have been frightened if he had said that, in just that way, two years ago? No. I think I should have been overjoyed – one gets so hopelessly tired of deception. I would have welcomed the open fight if only because there might have been a chance, however small, that through some error of tactics on his side I might have won. And there has never been a time in my life before or since when I have so much wanted to win. I have never had so strong a desire even to write a good book.[37]

They arrived at Thriplow in time for brunch on Saturday and it was Catherine who took the offensive:

The war guilt was Catherine's if you take the legal definition of who crosses whose frontier first – she flew out at Harry, & they both retired to the bedroom to have it out. Nothing of course came 'out'. Later that day I persuaded her we'd got to clear the air & have this thing in the open: she was being torn in pieces as things were. Things, things. I'm sorry, Bonte, don't look for style or even much clarity in this letter to you. Anyway, while the three of us were together, discussing endlessly C.'s nerves without even producing the real reason, she signalled to me that I could bring it out & so I told Harry what the reason was – that she couldn't make up her mind between non-marriage with him & marriage with me. We were all very quiet & civilised, but nobody slept more than an hour or two that night. Catherine had the worst time, with Harry lying awake crying. Next day, I would have left, but Harry obviously realised that I wouldn't in that case be able to return & the issue would then be clear . . . [38]

I was told that after their passionate reunion Greene had at last succeeded in persuading Catherine to leave her husband. Harry was in bed and she went up to tell him. He just looked at her and started crying, turned away and did not say a word. Harry's tears that night kept her at Thriplow.[39]

The next day Harry suggested that they take a walk together. Greene tried to make him talk about the situation but he wouldn't, though they chattered together amiably and cheerfully. Elizabeth Walston explained that this was Harry's way of dealing with relationships. He believed that if he did nothing about a problem it would go away or sort itself out.[40] He was, as the Reverend Thomas Gilby described him to Greene, 'a floater. Whatever happens . . . he'll float.'[41]

That evening it was arranged by all three that Catherine and Greene would have time together in Paris. They spent four peaceful days there, with Catherine relaxing and drinking less than Greene had known her to drink in the previous twelve months. After Paris, Catherine returned to Thriplow and Greene went to visit his mother. It was agreed that they would go to Italy together for five weeks in May. Greene wrote to Bonte that the confrontation with Harry was right and that it had cleared the air:

I think in a way [Catherine's] no longer 'scared' of Harry, now that the t's are crossed & the i's dotted. She was very brave & clear-headed when once the conversation opened up – the initial hurt has been taken out of her hands & I think that's what she feared more than anything.[42]

Greene had to wait for six weeks before he could meet Catherine again, for his confrontation with Harry had made him an unwelcome guest. Until then Greene could only wait for the future, living off the crumbs which from time to time Catherine offered – a day in a week, a night in London, a concocted visit to the home of mutual friends (the Huntingdons) – and always this passion to marry: 'Marry me, Catherine, in the church when we can, outside it any time. How many times one writes the same words till they must be stale as dry bread to you, that never has one conceived the possibility of loving so completely before. Lust has lost its meaning – it exists now only for you . . . "All longings, folly, grief, despair, / Day dreams & mysteries." The poems one liked in youth suddenly come alive in one's head.'43

Before their trip to Italy on 15 May, Greene had to travel to Germany. So close to winning Catherine, he feared that his 'stupid jealousies' might have ruined his chances: 'Why, O why was I beastly to you on the only two nights I had a chance of being peaceful & at home? I feel such fear of losing you through my own stupidity.'44

Greene realised that there would be times when they would be apart even if they were married: 'There would be trips you wouldn't want to come, but there'd always be the feeling "when I'm back we'll be together for days & days, or weeks & weeks." And always I'd want you to come.'45 Although he tried to distract himself with drink and danger, he could not ease his longing for Catherine:

> I've drunk a schnapps & eaten a Wiener Schnitzel & drunk two huge glasses of wine & it doesn't stop the longing. I stopped it for a while last night, standing on top of a wardrobe & taking a flying leap onto a bed, & agreeing to walk, over into the Russian zone with the Russian wife – but her husband wouldn't let her. Fear would be better than drink in driving you into the back part of my mind . . . I pray every night for you or death – I'd prefer the first, but the second would be a good second-best.46

He also travelled along the edge of the Russian zone until he was stopped by a tree trunk: '& the East German police invited one to step over, & one half longed to; one wants you or disappearance . . . I literally can't contemplate life without you.'47 This seems a dubious preparation for their Italian holiday in May, but it appears as if Catherine's latest letters tentatively suggested that she wasn't going to leave her husband: 'but I'll take any kind of life if sometimes for a period of weeks or days I can be with you'.48

When asked by a Russian girl, 'What do you want most?' Greene replied, 'To be married to someone.'49 In another letter comprised almost entirely of initials,50 he repeats his greatest hope:

D d d,

       I l y c,
       I w y t s i m b.
       I w t f y,
       I w t b y,
       I w t m l t y
       I w t k y

and above everything else in the world,

       I w y t m m.
       W a m l,
         G.

His letters are extreme: like a young lover he dreamed of serving with her in some medical mission, of finding a way to serve God with her, and of dying with her: 'All this means Catherine is that I love you more than my work, more than any person that's ever lived, & the only way I can learn to love God more than you is with you.'[51]

Catholic though he was, Greene no longer viewed their affair as adulterous:

St. Theresa stands by my bed & every time I turn to her . . . I pray for us. But I'm afraid my prayer is always that God's will shall be in favour of our love. Don't be too sure that it may not be & who knows whether the peace we have so often got together has not been *with* him, instead of against him? I feel no wrong in this love for you, I feel so often as though I'm married to you, only desperately sad sometimes at being separated from my wife (you, I mean).[52]

His petitions to St Theresa were always the same: 'Dear Saint, some of us have a vocation to love God. Some of us only have a vocation to love a human being. Please let my vocation not be wasted. I've proved it badly in the past, but *this* time I've entered my Order for life.'[53]

Greene threw everything into his battle for Catherine and explored the possibility that God was not against their love. He quoted a passage from Jean-Pierre de Caussade's *Self-abandonment to Divine Providence*, his reading matter when depressed: ' "Nothing happens in this world, in our souls or outside them, without the design or permission of God; now we ought to submit ourselves *no less to what God permits* [Greene's italics] than to what He directly wills." I just can't believe that the plane trip [from] Cambridge to

329

Oxford was not designed, any more than I believe that there's anything wrong in loving you with my body as well as my mind: "With my body I thee worship." '54

He turned to his older brother Raymond for help. Raymond Greene, who was still a doctor in Oxford but soon to move to Harley Street, arranged to meet Catherine and look, with an orderly, unromantic eye, at the nature of their love. Greene delivered Raymond's judgment:

I spent an evening with Raymond who has the hygienic strictly honest view of a doctor . . . I assume that apart from shades of misunderstanding he told the truth.

1) He said that you had quite decided in your mind *never* to leave Harry.

2) That on certain prompting from him you said you realized you would have a much more peaceful & happy life if you washed me out, but you didn't feel able to do that because you felt 'responsible' for me.

3) That though you loved having me at Thriplow my presence there always caused nerves & gloom.

4) That when I was not at Thriplow there was a perfectly peaceful atmosphere (this seems to conflict with the 'scenes with Harry').

5) That you were worried by my 'sexual energy.'55 Raymond said you gave the impression that this was 'rather a nuisance' to you.

I ought to add that he got the impression that probably unconsciously you were putting on an act & not telling the truth about a great many things.56

Greene wanted the facts at once and in detail: 'Now, my dear, for goodness sake tell me the truth. Then we can face anything. 3) is obviously true since Christmas. Were you telling the truth about 1) 2) 4) & 5)? You need not have responsibility for me, & my sexual energy can be put off altogether if it's a nuisance. If 4) is true, why invite me down & why prepare a room where *we* can work? . . . Anybody can stand & face facts, but what wears the nerves is half-truths, half lies, deceptions of any kind or another.'57

But none the less he admitted that even if all the points were true, he would still go to Italy. Moreover, if Catherine had decided *never* to leave Harry, Greene felt that it would be a relief in a way: 'One never wants to cherish a completely false hope.' Now that he had laid his cards on the table, Greene advised Catherine to 'play them straight & with courage. I love you, I want you, as a mistress, &

much more as a wife . . . I want to trust you to tell me the truth even when it's unpleasant. There's no future in half-truths.'[58]

Catherine's reply is missing, but clearly she raised a point that must have held some irony for the man who had left both wife and mistress for her: 'You wrote quite rightly about how does one found a life on complete abandonment of one's family etc. I tried it & failed.'[59] Although she was deeply in love with Greene, Catherine felt that there was no one as patient, loving and generous as Harry.[60] But she could not bring herself to be as completely honest with Greene as she was with others. In a letter written to Bonte three years later, she confessed that, 'Through cowardice, fear, love, stupidity and selfishness, I have allowed a situation and relationship to grow out of hand, and have never made my position clear enough . . . do I remain because I am selfish or unselfish, for good or bad motives? Maybe some of both . . . '[61] The future, which had looked so promising when Greene wrote to Bonte after confronting Harry, had suddenly become bleak.

*

Each day until their holiday in Italy was interminable and the strain was so great that Greene felt the need to see his psychiatrist: 'I'll see Strauss of course if I can get back from the second trip . . . '[62] The separation Greene had to endure bred the jealousy which often troubled their relationship. 'Now that you know that this L. affair isn't dead,' Greene wrote, 'would you *try* not to have times alone with him? [this is the same advice Greene received from his confessor] or have you found that after all he's very important, more than we are?' Greene pleaded with her not to let their affair 'crash': 'If we crash there's only tarting & self-disgust & three women a week'.[63]

Greene was told that Catherine was having an affair with a 'Swiss friend': 'I can't keep my imagination quiet yet. It's morbid & I hate it . . . There's so much to understand too: that story of *not* meeting your Swiss friend . . . Please *make* me understand. I feel hopeless. Suppose he [Harry] had become Ambassador, this would have happened all the time. Please try to make me see what happened, how. Would you ever have told me yourself? I'm lost. I don't know what to believe any more. Please pray for me as you've never done before.'[64]

The distance between them made Catherine's purported affair more difficult to bear:

Perhaps when we've got through this, we shall be closer than ever, but it's so difficult to get through separate. I long for night because then I can take pills & sleep. Then I wake & begin talking bitterly to myself, hurting myself, & poisoning the past. If I was with you, I might be beastly, but the boil would burst & the poison drain away, & we could be close again. There are so many weeks before I see you, & even then there'll be the strain of twenty-four hours & more – & one's bitterness comes back & one thinks, that's a strain he didn't have to put up with . . . How much better it is to be a labourer who beats his woman & forgets![65]

Though Italy was still ahead, Greene had almost given up hope: 'the Strauss business seems a little futile now & motiveless, as well as depressing. I am inclined to deep analysis or nothing.'

Catherine's reply is clear from the almost off-hand way he began a paragraph: 'O yes, of course we'll get things straight.' Then he quietly asked for answers which would help him reach a decision: 'It would help if you let me know by letter *before* Italy if there's been any more Lowell incidents since April 4 – or other incidents, including Harry.' Catherine and Harry were on holiday and Greene felt that with the help of French wine and his knowledge of the conflicts between Catherine and Greene, Harry would do his best to save his marriage.[66]

Greene promised he would still go to Italy, but he was already thinking how he could fill his time with adventure, trouble, and physical disaster to escape from his perpetual but futile passion: 'I think it would be best for all of us if I went off to Goa for six months – perhaps in the autumn . . . I feel very hopeless because now there's nothing whatever to hope for.'

He continued seeing Strauss until he left for Italy, and the sessions left him calmer and quieter:

One Strauss this week already, & another tomorrow. Three next week. He refuses to deep analyse me – has objections to it in all but profoundly maladjusted types, & agrees that it either leaves a person uncured but too conscious of his neuroses or produces a dull if happy simpleton; he says he notices the sense of humour is the first to go . . . I still find the seances depressing – the object is too patent, to shake you out of my mind. I'd rather have no mind.[67]

Strauss's treatments were beginning to have results. Greene had wanted electric shock treatment, but Strauss suggested instead that he write a long autobiographical piece: 'I like Strauss enormously . . . There's something of a saint in him . . . Another one this morning.'[68]

Without hope he went to Italy, but the very thought of seeing Catherine again affected him powerfully: 'I shall be seeing you in an hour & my hand trembles, & my heart beats like any adolescent in love. I went to bed this morning at 2 & woke at 5 & couldn't sleep again for thinking of you.'[69]

He was writing *The End of the Affair*, which he had begun in the Hotel Palma in Capri during an early visit just before he bought his 'happy' home in the mountains of Anacapri in 1948. He worked on the novel with tremendous vigour and happiness during May 1950 while with Catherine in Capri.

He called the novel his 'I' book – maybe because it is such a close transcript of his triangular relationship with Catherine and Harry, or simply because it is written in the first person. Inevitably after the euphoria of writing at such a great pace and with great power, he became melancholic:

Felt very depressed yesterday and pretty so-so today. There seems so little point in anything now that our holiday's over; back to snatched moments & restless hoping for telephones so little to come back to compared with what we've had & so little to live for . . . I hardly get any melancholia with you except for specific reasons & now without you it descends again. I've done 5000 words since our holiday [in Italy]. Yesterday I went to Mass at 6 and did 900 words by 8.30 before breakfast. But work's not enough . . . I feel very physically disturbed at you and not being available after the four weeks [the length of their holiday together] of being able to make love.[70]

Alexander Korda offered him a means of escape. He cabled Greene in June 1950, inviting him for a holiday on his yacht *Elsewhere*: 'I HOPE WILL BE ON ELSEWHERE FROM END OF THE MONTH WOULD YOU BOTH CARE TO JOIN ME.'

Greene was sorely tempted, but Catherine was unable to cruise on the *Elsewhere*. Korda loved Greene's company and sent another cable: 'LEAVING TOMORROW MORNING FOR ZURICH SATURDAY FOR ROME STOP HOPE BE MONDAY ON BOAT BUT ONLY FOR FEW DAYS STOP REAL HOLIDAY WILL START FOURTH JULY SOMEWHERE IN NORTH MEDITERRANEAN STOP TEMPTATIONS SHOULD ALWAYS BE YIELDED TO LOVE = ALEX.' Greene sent the cable to Catherine and added in his minute hand: 'How I wish you could come!'[71] But he could not persuade her and ended one letter: 'I could weep with longing to hear your voice.'[72]

By the first week of July, he was on the *Elsewhere* and asking

Catherine if she'd meet him at one of the yacht's many ports of call: 'we'd pledge each other for life . . . I'd fix everything, I'd see to everything. You'd never have too many things to think about only enough to keep you busy! Nicely busy. I'd write lots of books and see only the people we wanted to see for meals.'[73] The front of the postcard advertised a restaurant in Capri which they had both frequented, OSTERIA DEGLI AMICI – CAPRI. The card bore the motif of two hands clasped in love, and Greene repeated his heart's desire: 'They've left out the ring. Dear love, one word telephone wherever I am & I'd come to fetch you or to meet you', followed by the initials 'I W T M Y' [I want to marry you].[74]

And Catherine did join him on the yacht for a short period, for on 9 August he wrote of their visit to the Prince of Monaco's boat with Korda and their last kiss over the hedge at Nice airport. Greene also described life in the seaport in Antibes – he could not then have imagined that he'd spend the last thirty years of his life there – 'the scarlet woman with the thin legs . . . left her third husband last night . . . The Guinness yacht is back alongside with lots of children and wives . . . There are so many traces of you on board. Even the silences are full of you.'

By the middle of August, the yacht had reached San Remo and he told Catherine that his younger brother Hugh had gone off to Malaya: 'last night I dreamed he was dead and woke in tears!' Greene was still working hard on the first draft of *The End of the Affair*. 'I've written 61,000 words and should finish in 2 more days . . . I wish you were here to drink to the last word.'[75] He wrote his last thousand words, and the manuscript, then called *The Point of Departure*, ends:

> I found the only prayer that seemed to serve the winter mood: 'O God. You've done enough, my mind is broken like steps [?] I can't jump. I can't get beyond human love. O God I hate myself. Don't bother me any more. Leave me alone forever.
> [no. of words] 63,162
> Aug. 19 *N Y Elsewhere* 7.55 a.m.

This differs slightly from the final version found in the first edition:

> O God, You've done enough, You've robbed me of enough, I'm too tired and old to learn to love, leave me alone for ever.[76]

On finishing the novel, Greene left the yacht and flew back to London.

And so the troublesome relationship continued. He was obsessed but, unable to visit her at Thriplow, was seeing her for an evening only once a month. At times his frustration ran deep: 'Pray for me in the Achill church. My mind has been very twisted lately, but it will untwist when we are really together. You are absolutely necessary to me . . . there'll be no trouble this time in France. I am completely & solely in love with you.'[77]

In September, while visiting Vivien and the children, Greene realised that although he had considered returning to his wife should Catherine never marry him, there was no going back. While Vivien was 'perfectly nice', that door had been closed and even Greene's psychiatrist 'could never work that miracle'. Knowing he could not 'go home again', he wrote:

> Do you remember what David [Crompton] said about 'home' requiring an illusion of being indispensable to somebody. I feel particularly useless and so homeless. Paris, Goa, Malaya, London – there's no point beyond myself in being anywhere. I have ceased being of use to anybody.[78]

On reading about the Kon-Tiki expedition, Greene wished that he could write a cheerful travel book instead of his pessimistic kind: 'I wish I could write an optimistic one, but that, like verse, needs hope, & I haven't got hope. If I went to Malaya, after Hugh, or to Goa, I feel this monotonous rather stupid gloom would fall over the book. If only you could come with me – to Korea, or Goa, or Malaya. *Then* one might write a cheerful travel book.'[79]

Greene was preparing to leave for Malaya to observe the communist insurgency there. Because he was leaving, Catherine met him for a day: 'You've just gone, but I can smell the *Sous le Vent* all through the room, so that it's at least soaked with your scent, though you know the scent I prefer. You left that behind, dear heart. I loved you very very much today. Malaya is an unhappy excitement to work out. I wish, you were my wife, so that when one went away, one came home – to the place you shared and the bed you shared.'[80]

Greene asked for a last meeting before he left for Malaya, suggesting 21, 22 and 23 November, but then requested in his typical way that she add one more day: 'We shan't have any others to squeeze for a very long time.' He suggested that she ask the Duff Coopers (who were mutual friends) to invite them both to dinner, and thus gain an extra evening. He ended his letter: 'I kiss your mouth, your eyes, your "secret hair".'[81] In *The End of the Affair*, Bendrix, seeing a photograph of Henry in the *Tatler* with his wife on his arm feels the same desire for that secret place: 'She had lowered her head to escape the flash, but I would have recognised that close knotty hair which trapped or resisted the fingers. Suddenly I wanted to put out my hand and touch her, the hair of her head and her secret hair.'[82]

*

Again and again Greene fought with Catherine because she would not marry him, but afterwards he was always contrite and deeply troubled: 'I'm sorry that I've failed you again . . . I do such bad things to you. For God's sake – please ring me up & tell me how you are. You are all I have in the world & I make such a mess of things. Pray for me.'[83] But he never spoke better about his love affair with Catherine than in *The End of the Affair.*

When I began to realise how often we quarrelled, how often I picked on her with nervous irritation, I became aware that our love was doomed: love had turned into a love affair with a beginning and an end. I could name the very moment when it had begun, and one day I knew I should be able to name the final hour. When she left the house I couldn't settle to work: I would reconstruct what we had said to each other: I would fan myself into anger or remorse. And all the time I knew I was forcing the pace. I was pushing, pushing the only thing I loved out of my life. As long as I could make-believe that love lasted, I was happy – I think I was even good to live with, and so love did last. But if love had to die, I wanted it to die quickly. It was as though our love were a small creature caught in a trap and bleeding to death: I had to shut my eyes and wring its neck . . .

We remember the details of our story, we do not invent them. War didn't trouble those deep sea-caves, but now there was something of infinitely greater importance to me than war, than my novel – the end of love. That was being worked out now . . . the pointed word that set her crying, that seemed to have come so spontaneously to the lips . . . My novel lagged, but my love hurried like inspiration to the end.[84]

Yet the end of their love affair did not come so swiftly, though Catherine was often upset at the seemingly endless battles. Greene was going out to Malaya, and later Indo-China, and then Kenya, where the terrible revolt of the Mau Mau was taking place. He had nothing to live for he felt, and he was fearlessly waltzing forward into the active zone, in the direction of the battlefield.

PART 5

The Death Seeker

General de Lattre de Tassigny

23

War of the Running Dogs

The jungle is neutral.
— F. SPENCER CHAPMAN

IN the 1950s Greene wrote: 'I had travelled too much that year / and the roads were rough; / I came to this village as the dark dropped, / I had come far enough . . . ' In the years 1950 and 1951, he travelled far, though distance never allowed him to forget Catherine.

Apart from Greene's desire to escape Catherine's decision to remain with Harry Walston, a delicate situation involving his Danish publisher may have heightened his interest in a trip to Malaya. On 22 October 1950 Greene visited Copenhagen. After a few days there he travelled to Stockholm prior to the selection for the Nobel Prize for Literature. He thought he had a fair chance of being chosen and in a letter to Hugh Greene quoted a newspaper joke about his visit to Stockholm: 'two months too early is the newspaper crack'. Greene identified the three leaders for the Nobel: 'Pier Langerquist (the favourite), Faulkner & self. Odds on the Swede or Faulkner – but perhaps next year . . . ' He mentioned that a member of the Swedish Academy was coming to dinner: 'so I shall have to behave better than in Copenhagen, even though Westerman [Greene's Danish publisher] is putting in an appearance without his daughter or a shooting party'.[1] Greene had had a letter from Hugh inviting him to visit Malaya, where he was serving as the head of Emergency Information Services. In response to his brother's letter, Greene wrote that he was 'feeling exhausted as I had my Danish publisher on my back last night'.

It seems that Paul Westerman felt he was an aggrieved father, for his daughter Yvonne had broken off her engagement and given up her law studies as a result of a flirtation with Greene. 'One should

never flirt with 20 year olds, but she was very sweet & pretty.'*
Greene soothed Westerman by admitting that he wished his
publisher 'could be an injured father-in-law'; Westerman invited
Greene to go shooting with him in Africa and they 'drank & drank
& got friendlier & friendlier'.

Greene felt that his own retelling of the incident was in the worst
of taste: 'but I felt so relieved when the meeting went off so well, &
this is the steam from the relief. Alas, I wish I could marry & live
quiet with a pretty Dane. I pointed out the difference in age, but he
scouted that – said it was a minor matter. It *was* a curious evening.
The daughter had written to warn me that he was coming to see me
& I half expected him to have a big game gun or a sjambok.'[3]

Somehow the story got around. When I interviewed Vivien
Greene, she recalled her shock when the *Daily Express* telephoned
her with the news that her husband was to marry a Dane. It would
have been news to Greene if approached, but by this time he was in
Malaya.

Romantic entanglements aside, Greene's spur was the prospect of
adventure. To Hugh he wrote:

> I was fascinated by [your letter] & it sounds just my meat. Life on
> the frontier again – why, after all, should I try to write different
> books? Could you . . . let me have some facts for financial
> calculations? There'd be no point in coming for less than 6–8
> weeks. How much, do you calculate, life would cost me per
> week, or month, having as much drink & moving about as I
> wanted? Would it be hotel life or what? Add in a bit extra for my
> Chinese girl on occasion. Where would I fly to? Kuala Lumpur?
> . . . I suppose one would have to use a car a good deal. Could that
> be laid on officially on any excuse? The *Express* owes me rather
> more than a thousand, but a great deal of that would go on the
> return ticket – perhaps it's extravagant to take a return ticket.

Greene ended his letter suggesting that he'd not come out until
Christmas: 'All seasons are the same, aren't they?'[4]

Once he'd decided to go, Greene couldn't wait until Christmas
and on 31 October told Hugh he'd be leaving for Malaya on 25
November, arriving in Singapore on the 27th, and then on to Kuala
Lumpur. Although Greene knew West Africa, he was a very new
boy travelling in Malaya. He wrote to Hugh, concerned about the

---

* Yvonne Westerman was a quiet girl, well liked by men. She was pale with light
blonde hair, almost like an albino: 'There was something almost snobbish in her.'
Eventually she married twice, the second time to a baron.[2]

clothes he would need: 'What do you wear in the evening at parties, an ordinary dinner jacket or what? Do I need mosquito boots?' Telling Hugh that he'd already had his cholera injections and vaccination, he wanted to know whether he should bring quinine to deal with malaria.[5]

Hugh's letters have not survived, but it is clear he was doing his best for Greene: 'I would love to do the trip round Pahang in the armoured car with you, so I hope you won't do it before I come.' He also assured Hugh that when he was acclimatised he'd like to do a tough patrol: 'The trouble, I am warned, is that the Army is apt to put on show patrols for Generals and visiting politicians and I would like to avoid one of these.'[6]

Moreover, he wanted to avoid anyone who smacked of authority: 'I particularly don't want to stay with Sir Henry Gurney [the High Commissioner at the time of his visit] or Ross if it can be avoided without offence.'[7] Greene believed that 'it prevents one seeing life at anything other than an official level'.[8] Also, he felt he'd find 'the burden of hospitality appallingly tiring' – he had had more than he could take in Europe, he told his brother. He ended his letter: 'If you cannot meet me at the Airport will you send a message as to where I am to go.'[9]

On 13 November Hugh booked Greene into the Majestic hotel in Kuala Lumpur. Greene had worked out the general terms of what he was going to do in Malaya; he agreed that he needed to spend time 'with the planters who are in the danger area', and also 'a patrol with the Gurkhas would be a very good thing'. As always when preparing for a journey, he sought letters of introduction. His friend Bishop David Matthew wrote to the bishop of Malacca and also to the Superior of Catholic Missions in Malaya and the Far East. Greene told Hugh that *Life* magazine had offered him a minimum of $2,500 for anything he wrote about Malaya – 'This may help matters with the authorities,' he added.[10] Also he carried on his journey a letter from his friend Norman Douglas which contained a semi-humorous warning: 'Look out for syphilis – a friend of mine came back from Malaya in a deplorable condition – I am in a pretty groggy way myself.'[11]

*

What the British delicately referred to as the Malayan 'emergency' was called by the communist guerrillas the 'War of the Running Dogs', a contemptuous name for those in Malaya who remained loyal to the British. War had come to Malaya after the Japanese occupation and a State of Emergency was to last from 1948 until 1960.

The war took on a new urgency when three British planters were murdered. On 16 June 1948 Arthur Walker was at work on his estate in Perak. His wife was shopping in the town of Kuala Kangsar. At 8.30 in the morning three young Chinese rode up to the manager's office, leant their bicycles against the building, and walked into Walker's office. The Chinese followed their polite greeting, 'Tabek, Tuan', with shots to Walker's head and chest. They then calmly remounted their bicycles and rode away.

Half an hour later, only ten miles from Walker's estate, John Allison and his young assistant, Ian Christian, were at work on the Sungei Siput estate. Two Chinese walked into Christian's office, tied his hands behind his back, then went into the manager's room and tied his hands. They said to the clerks, 'These men will surely die today; we will shoot all Europeans,' and shot them. A fourth European manager escaped because his jeep had broken down while he was on his rounds of the rubber estate. Three Chinese had ridden up to his office also, but became worried by his delay and left without killing him.

The previous High Commissioner, Sir Edward Gent, had had no wish to declare a State of Emergency, but there was such an uproar (reflected by a newspaper editorial in the *Straits Times*, 'Govern or Get Out') that he yielded. Many, especially the planters and tin miners, felt that Sir Edward saw their problems as simply an increase in lawlessness instead of a highly developed attack by the communists aimed at bringing down the lawful Government and ending a hundred years of generally beneficent British rule. Malcolm MacDonald, then Commissioner-General for South-East Asia, was aware that Gent would not recognise a wart on his nose, never mind a war, and told him he was going to telegraph Whitehall to replace him. Whitehall recalled Gent to sack him, but when his plane reached London the York freighter aircraft he was travelling in collided with another and he was killed. The Malayan proverb would describe this as not only falling from the ladder, but having the ladder fall on you.

In the vast jungles, Chin Peng, Secretary-General of the Malayan Communist Party, felt sure he could replicate Mao Tse-tung's success in China. Chin Peng was setting out to run a nationwide guerrilla war, an insurrection on a massive scale similar to the one developing in Indo-China. His army was made up of 5,000 communists who faced 4,000 British and Malay soldiers without jungle experience. There were also 10,000 police officers, who were untrained for jungle guerrilla warfare.

By the time Hugh Greene had arrived in September 1950 the war did not seem to be going well for the British. During that year almost 650 civilians had been murdered and another 100 were missing. Hugh, who was with the BBC, was on loan for one year to General Sir Harold Briggs, the Director of Operations in the war. Hugh's task was to fight for the hearts and minds of the Malayan people: Chinese, Indian and Malay. His primary goal was to bring back to the fold those communists who had once fought alongside the British as guerrillas against the Japanese during the wartime occupation of Malaya.

He established a sound information service and conducted a highly successful campaign of psychological warfare against the communist terrorists. He knew he had to increase the belief of the public in the fairness of the British administration, undermine the morale of the communist underground (the Min Yuen) who were supporters of the communists in the jungle, and try to separate the rank and file from their leaders. He determined that there would be no exaggeration in the reports sent out from his office by radio, pamphlet or letter.

He understood the limits and the power of psychological warfare: 'The task of propaganda is to persuade a man that he can safely do what he already secretly wants to do because of disillusionment, grievances or hatred of life in the jungle and to play on those feelings.'[12] Various ingenious methods were used to get his message through, not only to the general public, but to the guerrillas. Captured documents were studied to give a guide to valuable intelligence. It was Hugh Greene who suggested printing surrender leaflets on waterproof paper (so that they could survive the incessant jungle downpour) which would show the dead faces of their comrades: 'Would you rather be dead like these? Or surrender and live like these?' He also contrasted scenes of the dead with photographs of local people living a civilised existence – visiting coffee shops, the cinema and the park – while the communists lived a hard life in the jungle without amenities.

Soon after he arrived in Malaya, Hugh Greene experienced two pieces of good fortune which were to assist him in developing his programme. The first was his appointment of C. C. Too, a brilliant Chinese who had had personal experience with the communist character, as his assistant. The second coup was the defection of Lam Swee, an important leader who had fallen out with Chin Peng and had surrendered rather than be executed.

His surrender meant that Hugh Greene could rely on his intimate knowledge of the killer squads lying deep in the jungle. It was Lam Swee who ghosted a letter, supposedly written by a communist called Chin Kuen, to persuade the rank and file to surrender. It was known that the ordinary communist in his jungle hideout missed female companionship and that sometimes the only man to have a woman would be the leader of the group. Half a million copies of this simple but effective letter were dropped by plane over the jungle: 'I surrendered after my commanding officer had stolen my girl-friend . . . Have you a girl-friend? The upper ranks can make love in their huts, but if you want to find a lady friend then you will have to wait until there is one left over from the upper ranks.'

Hugh Greene also approached the authorities about the need to increase the bounties for leading terrorists. When the Government substantially raised the reward for betrayal the *Straits Times* provided a full price list: '$60,000 on Head of No. 1 Bandit', $50,000 for members of the Malayan communist politburo; $40,000 for members of the central committee; $30,000 for State, town and regional committee secretaries; and $2,000 for information on, the capture of, or the killing of ordinary party members. If a communist brought in another communist he was offered only half the reward. Greed sometimes led to terrifying consequences, as when a communist brought in the severed head of his leader to collect the reward. Unquestionably, playing on man's cupidity was an important means of bringing about a steep decline in the morale of the communist terrorists.

*

On 27 November Greene wrote: 'Arrived 1/2 hr early at Singapore at 1.30. Overjoyed to see Hugh waiting.'[13] The next day he flew to Kuala Lumpur and had dinner with Noel Ross, adviser to the sultan. At once he was discussing his journeys and seeking information about the conditions of war: 'Discussed doing the danger area of Pahang with Gurkha adjutant . . . Young Chinese ex-member of Ferret Force who wants to return to jungle.' The aptly named Ferret Force was a group of mainly British soldiers who lived for weeks at a time in the jungle like the terrorists, trailing and attacking them wherever found. The British brought in Dayaks from Borneo, skilled trackers, to read the signs of the jungle and to help hunt down the ambushing terrorists. The terrorist stalker was himself being stalked.

It was very hot in Kuala Lumpur, the mosquitoes took their pint of blood and Greene slept in bed with what the locals called a Dutch wife: 'this is a bolster in my bed which I am supposed to sleep with like a woman and sweat into, but it doesn't feel a bit like you,' he wrote to Catherine.[14] When Greene stayed at the Majestic in 1950 there was no air conditioning, only an overhead fan, so a Dutch wife

32 The Continental Palace hotel in Saigon

33 In an opium fumerie

34–5 (*left and below*) On patrol with French troops at Phat Diem

36 (*right*) René Berval's apartment on rue Catinat, used by Greene for Fowler and Phuong in *The Quiet American*

37 (*far right*) Phuong and René Berval with their black dog

38 (*below right*) Larry Allen, the original for Granger in *The Quiet American*

39 (*below far right*) Greene with Colonel Leroy and Leo Hochstetter ('Q.A.') at Bentre

40 The bell tower at
Phat Diem

41 Phat Diem: 'The
canal was full of bodies'

42 A ceremony at the
Cao Dai temple

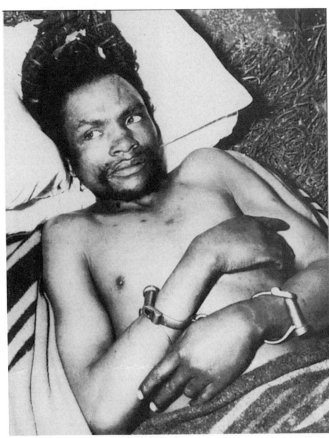

43 Dedan Kimathi, leader of the Mau Mau, after his arrest in 1956

44 Greene at a wild animal farm in Kenya

45–7 (*above*) Death in rue Catinat: the massive bomb explosion
outside the Continental Palace hotel in Saigon, 1952

48 Greene (*left*) with the elder Mathieu sister. Her younger sister, the
original for Phuong in *The Quiet American*, is seated extreme right

49–50 (*below left*) The bishop of Phat Diem with Trevor Wilson; (*below right*) Charlie Chaplin, Joan Reinhardt, Oona Chaplin and Graham Greene at Vevey

51 Our man in Havana

was a necessity. By wrapping both legs and arms around the bolster, sweating skin was separated from itself which prevented painful prickly heat.

Two days in Kuala Lumpur seemed enough for Greene: 'Last night's train to Singapore was dynamited so there aren't any trains today. I fly down tomorrow [to Singapore] and Father Frost is to meet me. K.L. bores me and I want to get away.'[15] But his journal shows that he was extremely active: 'Afternoon read secret document on Malay Communist organisation. Drinks with Ross & then very sticky formal black tie dinner with Commissioner of Police [Nicol Gray, an old Palestinian hand] & two of his officers. A terribly conceited &, outside his work, unintelligent man.'[16]

To avoid depression, Greene kept his days filled: 'On December 1–3 I'm in Singapore, then back to K.L., then December 9, 10 and 11 to Malacca with Ross the Adviser, then December 12 to 22 in Pahang [the terrorists were particularly active here] . . . People think I have rather perverted tastes in going to Pahang . . . The main dangers are staying with planters and patrolling with Gurkhas. Then with Hugh to Malacca for Christmas, 23–26 and quiet.'[17] Greene had brought the unrevised manuscript of *The End of the Affair* and by 1 December he started 're-revising the novel . . . I'm not nearly so gloomy about the book. I've reached p. 87 and taken out quite a bit – a few "narrow loin" cuts do make an enormous difference . . . The book is working out. I really think that with Eddie's [Edward Sackville-West's] help, I see what is wrong and I'm going to rearrange the journal – all chronological except the first entry which will be a different one. I believe the book won't be bad after this revision.'[18]

By now he could have had his Chinese girl, for his journal records that he visited Chinese and Malayan dance halls (where taxi girls dance with you for a small sum of money and you have the opportunity of taking them home or to a hotel – subject to paying the Mammasan) and took a trishaw to one called the Happy Land. However, he wrote to Catherine that he loved and missed her, '80% of my waking time. I carry you around like a sore.'[19] With a touching sense of how unimportant he might be to her, Greene asked: 'Dear heart, you will tell me, won't you, if this absence makes you want to be free of me?'

Greene soon grew tired of Kuala Lumpur and was restless for danger and anticipating death: 'everything is happening elsewhere – there are about half a dozen [terrorist] incidents every day in the country, but K.L. is completely peaceful'.[20] The city did not know what was going on in the countryside for the terrorists never attacked the capital. Thus the British Civil Servant and businessman of Kuala Lumpur could still drink in peace at the famous Spotted Dog (the Kelantan Club) facing the padang, where cricket was played in a calm, relaxed atmosphere. It was just the scene to make Greene shudder.

Among the rubber plantations and tin mines terror often reigned. Posters attached to trees demanded blood: 'Destroy the Running Dogs', or 'Death to the Running Dogs'. During the time Greene was in Malaya, and for the rest of 1950, war conditions were bleak. There were over 6,000 communist terrorist incidents, calculated to instil fear in Asians and Europeans alike. For example, in the isolated village of Jurantut in Pahang, the first villager found in the street was tied to a telegraph pole and formally executed; the police station was set on fire; the labourers' quarters of a near-by rubber estate were raided while the terrorists demanded food and subscriptions. When one of the labourers tried to fight the terrorists he was killed. The dead man's wife and child were tied up, placed in a bamboo hut, and the hut set on fire.[21] The labour force on the rubber plantations was always in danger because dispersing it was a means of disrupting the economy and destroying the profitability of the rubber industry.

The killing of children was another terror tactic used to get the Europeans to return home. Soon after Greene left, a two-year old, Susan Thomson, was murdered. The British instituted registration cards, which, of course, the communist terrorists did not possess. When particular groups accepted registration the terrorists would attack families. On an estate near Kota Tinggi four labourers' children and the planter were shot dead; only his fourteen-year-old child escaped, into the jungle. In Johore Bahru a six-year-old saw her father shot dead and an eight-year-old was burned to death with her family after her father had refused to surrender his registration card.[22]

In the midst of all this violence Greene kept his eyes open for copy: 'Strange little points emerge. The other day [in Singapore] a man who had escaped from the terrorists got into a crowded Singapore bus with bleeding hands tied together and nobody in the bus would even untie them. He went on with his hands tied until the bus reached the police station.'[23]

Yet war was not the only source of violence. Before Greene left for Pahang to visit a planter, serious riots took place in Singapore over a young girl named Maria Hertogh. Through no fault of her own she belonged to two separate, opposed communities and religious groups. Greene wrote to Catherine about meeting her:

I prayed this morning, not for you but for this little Dutch child. Yesterday I was driving round all day with . . . ex-Anglican-

Catholic priest and he asked me to have a cup of tea with the nuns
of the Good Shepherd. When we got to the Convent we found it
surrounded by armed police with Tommy guns. The Dutch child
Maria had been put into their care pending the foster-mother's
appearance and they were being guarded against a Malay attack.
The child had just arrived – a pathetic little creature who looked
younger than 12 [she was 13], in a Malay Sarong and little gold
earrings with a resentful dignity and a sense of great strain. The
nuns were innocently delighted and the Mother Superior managed
to make her smile once. They were quite unaware of the
ambiguity of the novel situation – the child had been baptised a
Catholic and she was being saved for the church. Maybe, but one
was reminded of a 'liberated' town. When she arrived at the
Convent she carefully and emphatically asked to be allowed to
wear her sarong and said firmly, 'You will not expect me to attend
your prayers, will you? I am a Moslem.' The nuns had already
abstracted a Koran from her suitcase. They were so kind and so
gentle and so sure that they were right.[24]

Maria's parents were Dutch Eurasians and when the Japanese overran
Indonesia where they once lived her father was made a prisoner of
war. Mrs Hertogh insisted that she had only let Maria stay with a
Malay woman, Che Aminah, for a few days. Che Aminah said that
she became the child's foster-mother.

After the war the Hertoghs were repatriated to Holland and tried
to get Maria back, but Che Aminah had disappeared. When she was
finally found in Singapore, Mrs Hertogh brought suit for the custody
of her thirteen-year-old daughter. The case was complicated by the
fact that Maria had been brought up as a Muslim and had married a
young Malay school teacher. The parents argued that she should be
returned to them because the marriage was null and void since Maria
was under age and they had not granted permission. But Maria did
not wish to return with her parents to Holland; she considered
herself a Muslim, knew her Koran, and spoke only Malay.

Greene arrived on the day that Maria was returned to her mother:
'[Maria] slept the last night in a room in the Girls' Home of the
Convent of the Good Shepherd, in Thomson Road, Singapore.' The
poor girl was not allowed to see her husband and Mr Justice Brown
declared that her marriage to Inche Mansoor Adabi was invalid and
indeed a 'discreditable manoeuvre designed to prejudice these
proceedings'. But the affair was not to end here. A Malay friend of
the foster family uttered prophetic words: 'We are very poor in
contrast to the Dutch, but we have thousands . . . of supporters.'

Eight days later in the *Straits Times*, 3 December 1950, the headlines read: 'FIVE DEAD, 100 HURT IN RIOTS: MOB RULE IN S'PORE STREETS: Cars, Buses Burned: Troops Called Out.' At the end of the rioting the death toll stood at eighteen, with over 180 injured. The rioters set up their own roadblocks and were armed with wooden sticks, iron rods, clubs, bottles, and bricks to use against Europeans and Eurasians travelling in cars or buses. Some drivers were knocked out cold or blinded by the objects thrown through their car windows. When the cars crashed or overturned, the occupants were hauled out and severely beaten or stabbed with broken beer bottles. These attacks took place in the Muslim sections of Singapore, and even though Muslim leaders appealed to the Malay crowds to disperse their microphoned voices were lost in the mad shouting of the mob.

Meanwhile, up-country nothing had changed and three other European planters were murdered by 'bandits'. On the train from Singapore to Kuala Lumpur Greene was made aware of war's reality: 'The train crammed with troops and police guards is just going to start . . . A notice in the carriages: "Terrorism: In the event of firing on the lineside passengers are advised to lie on the floor of the carriage and on no account to leave the train . . . " At the last stop – whole village load of Chinese were corralled by police beside the lines. They were being questioned over somebody's death in an ambush.'[25]

Returning to Kuala Lumpur, Greene found letters from all kinds of people offering him hospitality and especially one from a railwayman who had been in fourteen ambushes in twelve months: 'he wants to show me his side of things'.[26] The invitations held out the promise of adventure which Greene longed for as an antidote to depression. He wrote to Catherine from the Majestic hotel in Kuala Lumpur:

How often you've talked me out of melancholia in Thriplow, in Italy, in London, but you can't talk me out of it over 8,000 miles. Tonight it's very bad – the worst I've had since Germany. It seems so senseless to come all this way to be so bored and depressed. Perhaps next week when there'll be a tiny bit of danger things will look up . . . I'd like to take a big sleeping draught and wake up with another day gone . . . In this mood one can't work or even read properly . . . If only I could twist my ring and be in Anacapri with you . . . Tonight I feel like hell and long to pick up the telephone, but I don't even know your number. [The Walstons had moved from Thriplow Farm to Newton Hall during his absence.] I love you . . . more than God, more than all my family lumped together. I feel a wretched, useless failure when I'm away from you.[27]

Greene asked Catherine to pay no attention to his 'lonely wail' since by the time she got his letter he would be patrolling with the Gurkhas or drinking hard with his eccentric planter and would be feeling better. Three days later he put his need for her and his response to his nature succinctly: 'I love privacy when you are with me and hate my own company when you are not.'[28] And again he prayed: 'Dear God, give me Catherine or give me death.'

*

On 10 December Greene was driven by car to Malacca, a loaded revolver between the driver and him in case of sudden ambush. The next day he went to St John's fort: 'lovely view. Mount Ophir, the islands, the kampong among the coconut palms', and later visited a huge hillside Chinese burial ground: 'the semi-circular graves that from a long way off look like huge hoofmarks in the turf, the ruins of the old church in which St. Francis Xavier was buried is in the ground of the residency'. He entered the tomb and prayed to St Francis Xavier that it might be God's will that he marry Catherine.[29]

He went to a Chinese temple in Heeren Street and noticed how domestic the temples were: 'In one a bicycle and two girls and a man having his evening meal.' He compared one of the temples with a Catholic church: 'joss sticks instead of candles; shrines instead of saints – for any occasion. The shrines for particular purposes like our saints – for safety at sea, for students entering an exam, for children born ailing . . . The altars with inscribed tablets that take the place of our Masses for the dead.'[30] Greene was then driven to Port Dickson and had lunch at a Chinese hotel: 'The smarmy landlord: the terrible fat gold toothed waitress with her coyness & advances. Hotel rooms used as brothel at night, only separated from diners by curtains.'[31] They continued their journey and the evidence of war became more apparent: 'Drove via Seremban to Kajang. Lots of activity. Incident reported an hour before & an operation setting out.'

Greene liked Malacca; he found its people open and friendly. It was a wonderful change from Kuala Lumpur. But before he returned to spend Christmas there with Hugh, he came across his *bête noire* in Kuala Lumpur – A. H. Wheeler. As a boy Wheeler (called Watson in *A Sort of Life* because Wheeler was still alive) had befriended Greene in school, shared his secrets with him, but then betrayed him to Carter, the young boy who successfully brought Greene to breakdown and his first attempt at suicide. Wheeler, the source of the many Judas figures in Greene's novels, remained in his mind: 'I found the desire for revenge alive like a creature under a stone. The only change was that I looked under the stone less and less often . . . But still every few years a scent, a stretch of wall, a book on a shelf, a name in a newspaper, would remind me to lift the stone and watch the creature move its head towards the light.'[32]

When Greene accidentally met Wheeler in the cold storage shop, it was apparent that he was quite oblivious to Greene's hatred for him. Wheeler remembered that Greene used to help him with his Latin preparation, though Greene had forgotten this:

A man came up to me in the Cold Storage shop when I was buying drinks – a tall foxy faced rather heavy man who introduced himself as Wheeler. Wheeler was at school with me and belonged to the bad period. We were in the junior school together and then in the same house . . . . The real misery of that time began when he was suborned on to the side of my great enemy, Carter (who he told me the other day was dead) [Wheeler was misinformed; Carter did not die for another twenty-one years] I put Carter in *The Lawless Roads* – 'spreading terror from a distance'.[33]

Greene admitted that a 'lot began with Wheeler and Carter – suspicion, mental pain, loneliness, this damned desire to be successful that comes from a sense of inferiority'. And now after thirty-two years Wheeler was in a shop in Kuala Lumpur: 'rather flush, an ardent polo player and instead of saying what hell you made my life 30 years ago, one arranged to meet for drinks'.[34]

Greene drove back to Singapore with Noel Ross, missing bandits on the road by only an hour.[35] He spent a few days with Ross visiting the east coast on the China Sea: 'everything is much prettier from trees to women'. He stayed the night in a Malay-style house 'on a beach with the monsoon surf of the China Sea beating away and the trees like very delicate firs with silver drops of spray hanging from every twig'.[36] He found it peaceful but he hadn't come to Malaya for peace.

*

In his article on Malaya in *Life* (reprinted in *Ways of Escape*), Greene wrote first of the false view of planters pressed home by the popular press, a view which he held before visiting Malaya: 'a group of men, the harsh overseers of great capitalist enterprises, intransigent, unconstructive exploiters of native labour, drinking stengah after stengah in the local club . . . in the Somerset Maugham manner making love to each other's wives'.[37] But the planters were made of sterner stuff. In these violent times they ran a sweepstake on who would be killed next, where and when.

The reality of the planters' life came home to Greene when he stayed with Billy Litkie (in the article and in *Ways of Escape* he is called 'X') and his wife, Betty.

He lived with his wife in a small house of two floors surrounded by barbed wire, the ground lit at night by search-lights as far as the first trees. He was a man of late middle age, a former prisoner of the Japanese, who should have been looking forward to the final, easier, more prosperous years . . . But the life that remained for him was very different . . . this slow approach of inevitable violence.[38]

Earlier, on a day six people were killed, Litkie was ambushed a mile from his house, but shot his way out: 'Night and day the telephone rang at half-hour intervals from the nearest village to make sure the line had not been cut.'[39]

His assistant, Mansell, had been murdered on the estate a short while before Greene arrived and Litkie could not find a replacement. Communists had come on to the estate to question Litkie's tappers about his movements and his assistant had made the mistake of visiting the 'blocks of the estate in regular order at a regular time'. The communists so terrified the workers on the rubber plantations that no one was safe from betrayal. When Litkie moved outside the wire, even a hundred yards away:

he carried a Sten gun over his arm, an automatic pistol on his hip and two hand grenades at his belt . . . He would not contemplate retirement – he is in the front line for life and there was no expectation of peace but death.[40]

Litkie drank brandy and ginger ale with his breakfast instead of coffee: ' "Dutch courage," he said to me, pushing the starter of the little inadequately armoured car, setting off for a round of the estate or moving slowly out at the blind corner past which the road to the village ran and where one day, from the jungle opposite, a Sten gun would almost certainly open fire.'[41]

Litkie took Greene into the village, where they drank warm beer in the company of a Chinese shopkeeper who bought Litkie's cheap rubber, acted as his banker, and 'probably reported his movements to the guerrillas'. The planter would have a pink gin at the rest-house 'before he drove back along the lonely two-mile stretch, slowed down at the turn before that jungle wall, ten seconds of stretched nerves . . . One morning he and I were half an hour late in returning, and his wife waited with the anger of love for the sound of the engine, until he was safely back in the prison of wire. That night the radio announced the murder of three more planters.'[42]

Writing about the Litkies to his mother, Greene described how they 'fought each other from morning till night, but that, I suppose, was nerves'. He described the atmosphere at the estate as 'distinctly electric'.[43] In his journal Greene noted: 'Mrs. L's nerves very strained, but unlike most women here no physical signs of it. In the evening rather bitched L.: "You've never been in love . . . you've never been a husband." Secrets of married life . . . L. went to bed & Mrs. L & I continued with brandy till nearly 1. Discussion on boredom.'[44]

His last journal entry about Litkie records a final journey into Jerantut to get cheques, 'paid out 10,000 dollars just like that. Warm beer, Chinese candles. Sten gun & revolver laid on milk chests . . . [Story of] Disembowelling by bandits of trussed victims – in one case 3 children.'[45]

Terrorist squads did not limit their activity to rural villages and rubber estates. Trains and railway towns were attacked, railway and police stations burnt down. Always the killing was on a small scale: 300 terrorists burned down the station and the homes of the station master and inspector (two British railway engineers found asleep in a siding were killed). Trains were derailed, wrecked and set on fire. British troops moved by railway were often ambushed. On one occasion, the terrorist position, situated above the roof of the train, allowed the attackers to shoot through the roof with devastating results.

Greene also spent time at Gemas with a railway superintendent called Carrapiet. It was a stretch of line which had endured forty derailments in less than a year – on average about once a week. But Greene was unlucky; there were no derailments for him; instead the area had the worst rains in twenty-five years. He recalled the telephone ringing at intervals throughout the night, as at the Litkies; the activity was unceasing:

At 1 a.m. on Saturday the power plant was flooded and electricity failed. At 2.15 a.m. the Communists emerged from the jungle and derailed the breakdown train. At 4 a.m. the junction was completely cut off by road and the East Coast line was cut by floods. By breakfast time the water supply had failed – an odd added discomfort in the pouring rain. Even the station a quarter of a mile away must now be reached by wading. To the north a new landslide had taken place.[46]

In the evening Carrapiet and Greene waded through to the station and 'sat in the little refreshment room by the light of candles while the messages came in. Even the signal boxes were lit only dimly by oil lamps; figures disappeared in the dark of the long platform, and the whole obscure station and its wet acres had a strangely Victorian air as though electricity had not yet come into use. At 6 p.m. there was a washout to the south, and another landslide to the north. At 8.45 p.m. an East Coast train was derailed – by floods this time, not Communists. All the labour of the little town had to be called in to load freight cars with ballast by the light of lamps, but was there enough labour, enough ballast, enough freight cars?'[47]

Greene described Carrapiet without mentioning him by name: 'And at intervals the big patient man padded away and padded back to his glass, laughing at the wet, the cold, the enemy, waiting unruffled for the next telegram of disaster. One talks in terms of soldiers; and civilians, but there was never a better soldier than [he].'[48] Greene was sure of the courage of men like Carrapiet and Litkie and he made the point: 'perhaps you do not find courage where there is no danger [as in Kuala Lumpur], and love, too, may be a product of active war'.[49]

But Greene wasn't satisfied and couldn't leave Malaya until he had gone on a trek with the Gurkhas: 'Gurkhas gave their British officers absolute loyalty, and their officers returned them a quality of love you would not find in any other unit. Officers of the British Regiments complained that their colleagues in the Gurkhas never stopped talking about their men.'[50] Gurkhas are famed throughout Asia for their fighting qualities, they are mercenaries with a reputation sometimes sufficient to make the terrorist vacate his ambush in fear of their name.

On 12 December Greene was ready to make his journey with the Gurkhas. He noted in his diary that he visited a Police Operations Room and looked at the incidents' chart: 'Casualties of civilians heaviest, police next heaviest. Already well over 400 civilians . . .' His testing in the jungle was about to begin: 'Collected jungle kit from police stores.' The trip to the Gurkhas didn't get under way till 2.30 and then they stopped at 4 at the mess of the Scots Guards for tea and waited for a fresh convoy to take on the fourteen Gurkhas and one officer, Major McGregor Cheers, known as Hooray: 'Rode with Cheers in jeep with two Gurkha guards. Fresh convoy three lorries and scout car. Reach the Gap at twilight . . . into Pahang in darkness. Winding road . . . Shadows of lorry illuminated by scout car cast on forest wall.' That night he went to his tent at the army camp and slept well; it would be his last restful sleep for three days.

Before leaving Malaya Greene would know about the jungle: 'A far denser jungle than that of Burma, it restricts movement to less than a mile an hour. Visibility is sometimes 20 feet. Almost every day water pours down upon it, making the steep slippery slopes of the innumerable hills a cruel effort to climb. One is never dry and at night one is never in quiet – the ugly din of birds with their barnyard cries comes between the newcomer and sleep. When you pause for a halt on the march you see the leeches make for your boots – thin matchsticks looping with blind purpose across the wet leaves, later to swell into fat grey slugs if they find an opening in your clothing. And always there is the jungle stench – the heavy odor of decaying vegetation. It clings to your clothes. When you come out, your friends will avoid you if they can until you have bathed and changed.'[51]

The jungle nights were long: 'By six it is dark except for the shine of phosphorescent leaves: by midnight the rain will be falling down on yesterday's soaked leaves, and long after the storm is over the rain will continue to drip from the reservoirs of foliage. There will be nearly twelve hours of virtual darkness . . . '[52]

On 15 December Greene recorded: 'Left on patrol, pack & revolver. They struck out through the kitchen quarters, through the thin belt of rubber and into the jungle.' The next three days were to be the most arduous of his life:

> A Gurkha patrol worked by compass, and not by paths. It moved as the crow flies . . . but far less comfortably . . . only nine miles separated us from our objective, the main road on the other side of the block of jungle, but it took two and half days of walking and two nights to get there. We had started late and we began to camp after five hours' march. When our position was plotted we had penetrated rather more than three miles. There had been an interminable succession of 500-foot hills, the slippery laterite slopes set at an angle of almost 45°. Even the Gurkha sometimes slips and falls as he holds himself up by the branches of trees, the rubber soles of his jungle boots taking no grip in the mud and slime of leaves.[53]

And the reason for the Gurkha's method of patrol? 'If . . . you patrolled by paths you avoided the worst hills, which sometimes rose in this area to two thousand feet, and you never have to carve your way through the undergrowth, but you were staking all on finding tracks on the one path you followed. The Gurkha technique meant that in the course of a day you cut across many paths in your search for signs of the enemy; a newly broken bamboo with the juice still wet might be the only indication.'[54]

Greene's exclamation, 'even the Gurkha sometimes slips and falls', suggests that Greene did. In a letter to his mother written on 23 December from Kuala Lumpur, he spoke of his experience: 'I got back yesterday from a rather rough week in Pahang. I found a 3 day jungle patrol with the Gurkhas in full kit a bit of a strain! It was an interesting but at the time horrible experience. No bandits but complete exhaustion. They are quick movers . . . up & down 500 foot hills with slippery clay slopes at this angle \ hauling oneself up by trees.' In spite of its cryptic style Greene's journal gives an intimate taste of that gruelling journey:

Delicious taste of tea & rum at first halt. Before the end feeling completely whacked. Staggering in tracks. Terribly slippery – wet clay slopes \ with rubber soles. Scratched to pieces. Hill of over 500 feet at end. The camp. Double bed of logs & leaves for Cheers & self. V. depressed & worried in case I hold them up. Would welcome bandit bullet. Whole score 2 abandoned [terrorist] camps. Torrential rain at night & both rather sleepless with cramp.[55]

A halt had been made by 4.30 and the Gurkhas with their kukris cut down boughs to make 'shelters for men in pairs with one ground sheet stretched over-head to keep out night rains . . . Darkness has begun to fall when the kukri becomes a can-opener . . . Gurkha ration – rice, raisins, curry powder, tea, sugar and a little spirit lamp. The small flames glow like nursery night-lights in the dark.'[56]

On the second day an air drop was due at 10 a.m.:

Wireless not working. Clearing made with kukris. Great trees falling. Smoke bombs white & green colouring. Plane 30 mins late. Parachutes crashing down 20 feet outside area not larger than tennis court . . . Missing brandy. After lunch on. The area of the air strikes . . . Camp near stream & lovely baths, but afterwards feel sick. Leech has been at my right buttock. Bad night, too small log bed, rain getting in. Dreamed I was at Ritz with C[atherine] but the back against mine was only that of Major McGregor Cheers of the 2/7 Gurkha Rifles.[57]

In his *Life* article Greene recalled McGregor Cheers's concern with ornithology: 'My companion stands upright listening, but not for Communists. He whispers, "There is one bird I always listen for – at dark and at dawn. There it is. Like a bell. Do you hear it?" I could hear nothing but the clamour of the jungle barnyard. At 6 in the morning he is standing by our bed in the new mud of the night's downpour. "There. Do you hear it?" he whispers. "Like a bell." '58

Greene's thoughts about his experiences reflected public school standards:

> It was three days and two nights . . . in the jungle and it rained continually . . . The first night I was thoroughly tired and seriously contemplated putting a shot in my head because I thought if they had to send – there were only twelve of us – two men back with me, and they were hunting two hundred communists – I mean it was hardly a sporting effort and I'd be an awful nuisance to them.59

The following day, 17 December (a Sunday), he recorded again the strain and the struggle of the patrol: 'On again feeling sick. At first halt broke security silence with my retches [according to McGregor Cheers SILENCE had to be observed and conversation was reduced to a minimum (whisper) or by hand signal]. Another leech removed from my neck. Terribly steep hill finished me. Retching & retching. Have hardly eaten these three days.' Greene wrote in his journal, 'Relieved of pack & that way kept up in spite of 1500 ft. hill,' but then crossed this embarrassing acknowledgment of failure out of the text. The entry was followed by the glorious words: 'At last out of jungle.'

He should not have felt his conduct was an embarrassment. The operation was recorded as follows in the regimental history: 'During Operation "Stymie" we received a visit from Mr. Graham Greene. He was collecting material for . . . *Life* magazine . . . He insisted upon going on a patrol in spite of his lack of physical fitness. It was a short strenuous operation with every likelihood of meeting terrorists. On one occasion he passed out with exhaustion but carried on to the end regaled by an air-drop of brandy and ginger ale.'

McGregor Cheers told me that no special arrangements were made for Greene except that a Gurkha orderly had instructions to keep Greene in sight, not lose him in the jungle and, if necessary, to push him up the hillsides. Until the end, when he was quite sick, he carried a full kit and was fitted out like anyone else in the patrol. McGregor Cheers's last word on Greene was that he survived the 'ordeal' extremely well, but was astonished with the gruelling conditions the patrol worked under and the very strict discipline maintained.

One final word about Greene's experience of McGregor Cheers: 'On that first night's sleep – one was sleeping on the ground on a mackintosh, with a mackintosh tied on the trees above one's head to keep the rain off. In the middle of the night, McGregor Cheers rolled over on his side and put his hands around my throat and began to squeeze. I can only suppose he thought he had come on the communists.'

On 10 January 1951 Greene received a telegram in Kuala Lumpur from Catherine, saying she would meet him in Paris. It had the usual effect: 'Life seemed good again & as a consequence began to be nervous of bandits.'[60] But any optimism was shortlived, for, two days later, Greene awakened depressed: 'Worried by so few letters from C[atherine]. Despair of the future settling over me again.' He was still in search of trouble and by 15 January, whilst not involved in action, there seemed every possibility of it. There is a detailed entry in his journal for that day, cryptic though it is:

With Adler 1 1/2 hrs. by scout car to jungle camp. Damaged telegraph wires. More Communist posters. European officer was out on patrol. Reported bandit ambush of 200. Patrol had asked for transport. Went down & joined transport, then to tin mine. Arrival of patrol with naked body strung on pole. The bicycle. The identification at tin mine. The pillow. The old manager – 'My best boy: he was absolutely fearless.' The scowl & open mouth of death. Beaten about the mouth, stabbed through the heart. Like a new joint at the butcher's. Feeling off meals & off-colour afterwards . . . Restless night with bad dreams.[61]

He described these final experiences in Malaya to his mother: 'One day we found the murdered body of a young Malay constable – stripped naked & stabbed through the heart [with a bayonet]. He had only been dead a few hours – an ugly sight. I had to nerve myself to take a close-up photo of him.'[62]

Three years later he placed this event as an incidental memory of his hero Fowler in *The Quiet American*: 'I turned my memories over at random like pictures in an album . . . the body of a bayoneted Malay which a Gurkha patrol had brought at the back of a lorry into a mining camp in Pahang, and the Chinese coolies stood by and giggled with nerves, while a brother Malay put a cushion under the dead head.'[63]

Greene left Kuala Lumpur for Singapore on Wednesday, 24 January 1951, having spent almost two months seeking war and danger. By now his greatest desire was to leave Malaya; he had seen all he could see, and as he wrote his mother: 'I feel I've had enough of this place & I'll be glad to move on & gladder still to find myself in Europe. I don't find the East has any glamour.'[64] So he left Malaya, steaming 'away under the almost daily rainfall, sapping the energy of tired, overworked men'.[65]

Reaching Singapore, he records in his journal: 'Up at 4.30. Airport 5.15. Left 6. Arrived Saigon & met by Swan 10.'[66] Greene could not have known upon arrival that his experiences in Saigon and Hanoi would reveal to him that glamour which he had told his mother the East did not possess.

24

Bonjour Saigon

Some may, perchance, with strange surprise,
have blundered into paradise.
                              – FRANCIS THOMPSON

IN Vietnam Greene entered a world of civil war. The odds were
heavily stacked against the French; their opponent Ho Chi Minh
was both a communist and a nationalist. Although not in favour of
French colonialism, the Americans feared that the success of Ho Chi
Minh in Vietnam would have a domino effect. If Indo-China fell, so
would Indonesia, and in short order so would Malaya, Singapore,
Burma and Thailand. India would be extremely vulnerable and
Australia unenviably exposed.

In March 1946, five years before Greene arrived in Vietnam, Ho
had negotiated with the French, recognising that their departure
would leave a vacuum. France spoke of Vietnam becoming a free
state within the French Union, to which Ho seemed agreeable.
Indeed he attacked his pro-Chinese comrades:

> Don't you realize what it means if the Chinese stay? . . . The last
> time the Chinese came, they stayed one thousand years!
>   The French are foreigners . . . Colonialism is dying out.
> Nothing will be able to withstand world pressure for
> independence. They may stay for a while, but they will have to go
> because the white man is finished in Asia. But if the Chinese stay
> now, they will never leave.
>   As for me, I prefer to smell French shit for five years, rather
> than Chinese shit for the rest of my life.[1]

Ho may have been anti-Chinese, but he did not refuse the Chinese
troops and arms sent to aid him.

Ho was immensely popular and even General Eisenhower had to

admit that in democratic elections Ho would have won 80 per cent of the votes. But the French (and Americans) no longer trusted him. The French solution was to support the Emperor, Bao Dai. This failed chiefly because the Vietnamese public thought he was a French puppet. The 37-year-old Bao Dai was easy to criticise. He had a reputation as a playboy and debauchee, and he had, as a secret American legation telegram showed, corrupt financial dealings with the Binh Xuan: 'The Binh Xuan honorarium to Bao Dai from his gambling concession amounts to between twenty-four to thirty million piasters annually according to Nguyen Phan Long, former Prime Minister of Vietnam.'[2] Yet Greene, who interviewed him, found him to be 'an intelligent and subtle man, resolved not to compromise himself, and to survive'.[3]

It looked as if France's postwar rule in Vietnam was rapidly coming to an end. Its expeditionary force was being decimated, its troops on the verge of a rout. In a secret note Dean Acheson, then American Secretary of State, observed that the Asian communist principle in war was to use mass in terms of men, while the Western principle used mass in terms of firepower, and admitted that the Asian principle was more successful for 'they seem able [to] capture any French post at will and destroy [the] garrison'.[4]

The French losses overall were so great that they decided to evacuate the garrison at Lang Son when it was not even in difficulties. Adding to their fear was the decision to evacuate French women and children from the capital Hanoi. Confidence ebbed; no one, not even the French, believed the Vietminh could be defeated.

The French then recruited a secret weapon in the shape of a 61-year-old French hero, General de Lattre de Tassigny, and gave him the powers of a dictator. De Lattre's only son was at that time serving in Indo-China and it was rumoured that he had written to his father saying: 'What we need is a leader who leads, fresh blood and new machinery, and no more niggling, small-time warfare; and then, with the morale that we still have in spite of it all, we could save everything.'[5]

The position offered to de Lattre was not to be taken lightly: how could anyone win against the Vietminh, led by Ho, whom the peasants loved and followed, as opposed to Bao Dai, the emperor-puppet? It looked hopeless. But de Lattre had the reputation of being a brilliant, erratic, bad-tempered and heroic man. Seymour Topping (the Associated Press Correspondent), who, like Greene, had a number of furious passages of arms with him, nevertheless admitted that he was a magnificent soldier:

he was a terrific soldier . . . a great soldier. Later on when I came back to Vietnam with the Americans and saw all these American generals who were amateurs in comparison to de Lattre in terms of knowing the country and the tactics and the terrain and everything else, it was just incredible to me that they could carry on.[6]

De Lattre arrived in Saigon on 17 December 1950 (only five weeks before Greene), when the French army was still tasting defeat. Edmund Gullion, then second in command at the American legation, remembered that de Lattre impressed him even before he had set foot on Vietnamese soil:

French Vietnam was then a valley of discontent, of despair. Period. And [de Lattre] arrived and they had all turned out, everybody, to meet him, everybody: the army, the diplomatic corps, the Church, school teachers, all lined up there. And he arrived over the plain and he circled it several times so that he could touch down at exactly the same hour that the gun salute took place and he got the maximum salute, borrowing this from American and British military services (they don't do that particular thing in France normally when arriving) . . . His plane came in and de Lattre stood at the top of a flight of stairs, on the platform, the gangplank and he turned his profile this way. He had a magnificent profile (something like MacArthur), and watching him arrive, he seemed seven foot tall, stiff and straight and he took white gloves and pulled them carefully on his hands, like that – a very symbolic gesture, symbolising in the honour of the corps a gentleman aristocrat was in office. But the symbolism of pulling on the gloves was lost to no one . . . He was coming down to clean up this mess.[7]

As he descended from the plane the band began playing the 'Marseillaise'. When a wrong note was struck by one of the bandsmen, they all received a severe tongue lashing – everyone had to know that there was a new master controlling events. When he landed in Hanoi two days later he sacked the area commander within five minutes of his arrival because he considered the Guard of Honour sent to greet him was sloppily turned out. He then assembled all the officers, but particularly addressed himself to the junior officers (one of whom was his son Bernard): 'To you Captains and Lieutenants, it is because of you that I have agreed to take on this heavy task. I guarantee that from today you will be commanded.'[8]

On 1 January 1951 the American consul in Hanoi, Wendell Blancke, sent a secret telegram to the State Department about de Lattre: 'This New Year morning De Lattre received civil and military leaders, made a moving speech which had most eyes swimming, Vietnamese as well as French. Theme was, they shall not pass, plus slogan "confidence and resolution". Said Vietnamese independence and national army must soon become reality . . . added his wife now arriving Saigon, will leave her in Hanoi . . . as earnest of confidence and family feeling.' The evacuation of women and children from Hanoi was abandoned, as were plans to give up the Tonkin delta. He stated that the French army would fight and if it had to be, be destroyed, but it would *not* evacuate. Bringing his wife to live in Hanoi did much to restore the morale of military and civilian personnel: 'I shall often be among you. I shall come with my wife . . . ' This was an act of genius and won him complete confidence. Having lost entire companies and prepared for the worst by evacuating its civilians, the French High Command, in the person of de Lattre, now stood firm and assured.

With his Napoleonic jaw and Roman nose, he looked messianic. An electrifying speaker, he delivered his speeches in a husky voice ranging from a whisper to fortissimo.[9] When he addressed the down-hearted troops, he made them see their mission in a new light. He expressed his objective to an American journalist:

We have abandoned all our colonial positions completely. There is little rubber or coal or rice we can any longer obtain. And what does it amount to compared to the blood of our sons we are losing and the three hundred and fifty million francs we spend a day in Indochina? The work we are doing is for the salvation of the Vietnamese people. And the propaganda you Americans make that we are still colonialists is doing us tremendous harm, all of us – the Vietnamese, yourselves and us.[10]

This political philosophy was commendably on the side of the youth of Vietnam:

This war, whether you like it or not, is the war of Vietnam for Vietnam. And France will carry it on for you only if you carry it on with her . . . Certain people pretend that Vietnam cannot be independent because it is part of the French Union. Not true! In our universe, and especially in our world of today, there can be no nations absolutely independent. There are only fruitful interdependencies and harmful dependencies . . . Young men of

Vietnam, to whom I feel as close as I do to the youth of my native land, the moment has come for you to defend your country.[11]

Edmund Gullion recalled de Lattre inviting Vietnamese students to fight for Ho Chi Minh: 'If any of you young men want to fight for your country and don't think it's this country, then go, go and fight for Ho Chi Minh.'[12]

*

General Giap began the Vietminh offensive in the middle of January 1951. He was out to test de Lattre and decided to invest Vinh Yen, twenty-five miles north-west of Hanoi. He made an initial attack on the 13th and by nightfall the French were forced up against a marshy lake. It looked desperate for the French – 6,000 French troops faced 20,000 Vietminh. De Lattre flew into Vinh Yen in a light plane and took charge of the battle. He ordered major reinforcements from as far as South Vietnam. On the 17th he took a great risk and committed his reserve troops. Shortly after noon the Vietminh forces quit the field of battle, leaving behind them over 6,000 dead. It was a disaster for Giap.

On 23 January Wendell Blancke reported: 'DELATTRE left town yesterday rather like bull fighter turning his back on fixed bull. As trophies he bore congratulatory effusions from BAO DAI, HUU . . . which tickled him so he could not wait next days press splash and called in British Consul [Trevor Wilson] and me to crow over them.'[13]

Blancke's praise of de Lattre or as he called him in the telegrams CINC (commander-in-chief) was grudging: 'It is true CINC has restored confidence and his personality overshadows all at moment.' Blancke believed, as did many others, that if de Lattre had not come to Vietnam to replace General Carpentier, Hanoi would have fallen. Success also came because the French used close air support and dropped napalm for the first time. Under napalm there was panic among the Vietminh troops – who could blame them for running into the forest screaming?

The life of the military and political world in Indo-China seemed to be picking up because of the arrival of one man – de Lattre. It was even reported in a secret memorandum dated 21 September 1951 that the *Echo du Vietnam* noted that 'Vietnam will honor General de Lattre by building a temple to him as a "Tutelary Deity".' Edmund Gullion responded to the foolish article by adding tartly: 'The Legation by no means intends to detract from the honest praise of which the General is so genuinely deserving. It is perhaps a little too early, however, to place him among the immortals.'

*

Greene arrived in Saigon on 25 January 1951, after de Lattre's great success. He entered a world of nightly bombings, anonymous grenade throwing, and the frequent assassination of both communist terrorists and government officials. Greene came seeking refuge. His troubled spirit, so often darkened by melancholia, lifted while in Vietnam. The country was to get firmly under his skin: 'the spell was first cast . . . by the tall elegant girls in white silk trousers, by the pewter evening light on flat paddy fields, where the water-buffaloes trudged fetlock-deep with a slow primeval gait . . . the Chinese gambling houses in Cholon, above all by that feeling of exhilaration which a measure of danger brings'.[14] It was a love he shared with thousands of others, including many retired *colons* and officers of the Foreign Legion whose eyes would light up at the mere mention of Saigon and Hanoi.[15]

His initial enthusiasm is revealed in his journal:

What a difference between Saigon & K[uala] L[umpur]. Gaiety in spite of grenades. Lunched with J[enkins, of Reuters] who drove me around afterward . . . Begin to see my programme clear. So much happier here. Met Fr. journalist to hear about the *Cao Dai* at 7. 8 Swan fetched me to dinner. Vietnamese Minister of Information. French I[ntelligence] officer with pretty wife. Invitation from General de Lattre. All is set. To bed at 1.[16]

That first day he wrote to his brother Hugh: '*This* is the country, not Malaya. The women . . . really lovely & beautifully & sophisticatedly dressed. The situation is fantastic. One lunches and dines behind iron grilles or wire netting to keep out the grenades. Good food, good wine, & tremendous friendliness.'[17] He gave the impression that the French authorities were perhaps more accommodating than the British in Malaya; there was certainly a difference in style:

A car was put at my disposal at once: within a few hours of arriving I was asked to dine informally (no black ties) with General de Lattre who lives in a magnificent place, 200 men changing guard to music.[18]

The original meaning of the name Saigon was 'gift to the foreigner', and so it was to the French. Ninety years of French occupation had turned a simple village of palm trees and atap huts into something very French — wide, straight boulevards, gracious squares, solid main buildings, all speaking loudly of France even today, for there has been little rebuilding in the twenty years of communist rule. In the Majestic hotel the colonial trademark of the Lyons manufacturer is still in the lavatory bowl.

The Majestic stands on the banks of the Saigon river (the river smells when you get too close, and you get too close if you live there as Greene did). In Greene's day it had an enormous bar; it still had in 1993, but the jazz pianist, who used to play the latest Parisian hits, has gone. Now, as then, ships are at anchor in front of the hotel, though two of them are tourist attractions – the tourists being chiefly Australian, not American or French.

The once gracious rue Catinat, the street where Fowler and the beautiful Phuong lived and loved in *The Quiet American*, with its plane trees shading out the hot afternoon sun, is treeless now: the pavements cracked and heavily pock-marked. But Saigon in the 1950s was in the midst of war. In the downtown area civilians and military would congregate: the Majestic hotel was at one end of the rue Catinat, the Continental Palace hotel at the other, with no more than 300 yards between the two. The street was known as 'Radio Catinat' because war gossip flourished in the French cafés. There were chairs in the streets, civilians and soldiers relaxing over *café au lait* and croissants; minute bars where soldiers and sailors sat drinking cognac and Dubonnet. There was the aroma of French bread and the *maisons de coiffeur*, where the French women went to have their hair washed, combed and set – hopeless in a climate so humid. In the Place de Pagneau de Behaine by the great red-brick cathedral (which Greene found ugly), Vietnamese nuns, black robed, padded softly by. It seemed a peaceful world.

*

The Saigon river is only a few hundred yards wide and the countryside on the opposite shore was, in Greene's day, controlled by the Vietminh, enemy country. Looking from the Majestic balcony, you can see launches plying back and forth. From the roof, beyond the riding lights of the ships, in the early 1950s you might have seen tracer bullets shooting across the sky, or the bombing of a village and its fiery end. 'One trishaw driver pedalled slowly by towards the river-front and I could see lamps burning where they had disembarked the new American planes,' wrote Greene in the first paragraph of *The Quiet American*.[19] Unloading took place at night to disguise the fact that the military supplies were American – American insignia were quickly stripped from the planes and replaced with French.

Life in the streets of Saigon remains much the same: families work from their little shops from dawn to dusk; carpenters chip away at sailing junks; tailors turn out a made-to-measure suit in twenty-four hours; Saigon's beggars place their specially made crutches and their amputated arms or legs in your direct line of vision in the hope of money for another day's existence.

There was always fear of sudden attack by the Vietminh in the city. When Greene arrived it was thought that 15 per cent of the local Vietnamese were secret Vietminh supporters and activists – a ready-made fifth column (later the enemy within would increase three-fold). Saigon lived with the nightly terror of bomb explosions or grenade assaults – the assassin a mere boy on a bicycle cycling fast. One such killing took place at noon: there were two victims (one white, the other brown) and soon in the heat the flies began to circle the bodies. Seymour Topping, who knew Greene, recalled his first night in Saigon after booking into the Continental Palace hotel with his wife:

We'd checked into the hotel after a long flight and had just sat down on the huge bed under a ceiling fan barely stirring the air, when a shattering explosion ripped the square under our windows. We rushed to look . . . A score of cyclo drivers who pedalled the bicycles (pushing the rickshaws ahead of them) were streaking away from the café in all directions. One of the cyclo drivers had thrown the plastic bomb. The cyclo drivers took off in all directions to divert the police. Thus the one that had actually thrown the bomb wouldn't get caught. French soldiers and sailors, dead and wounded, lay amid overturned tables and shattered glass inside the café. Outside on the sidewalk terrace, where they'd been sitting sipping drinks, a badly wounded soldier gripping his groin stumbled into the street.[20]

In response to the French resurgence, the Vietminh were escalating their terrorist campaign. De Lattre realised this would increase civilian deaths, but he was determined to shake up the police and judiciary. He had ' "thrown out" the judge of the military tribunal who had been handing down acquittals for fear of Vietminh reprisals',[21] but the fear of the judges was entirely understandable. In response to the charge by Nguyen Van Tam, head of the Vietnamese Sûreté, that he gave easy acquittals, one judge said: 'I have nine children. Who will feed them if the Vietminh kill me because of my sentences?'[22]

Saigon was an informers' paradise. Tam, known as the Tiger of

Cailay, was as ruthless as the Vietminh in meting out justice. When he discovered that his trusted secretary belonged to the Vietminh, he acted with extreme dispatch, executing him that evening. Vietminh agents were often summarily executed, their dead bodies left with a notice which read, 'X is a communist murderer executed for his crimes.' Those agents Tam didn't have killed he passed over to the French military courts – he had no faith in the Vietnamese courts.[23]

C. L. Sulzberger reported in the *New York Times* that almost daily some individual on the 'death list' of the Vietminh was murdered 'by a chosen executioner who vanishes into a crowd past unarmed policemen. Hand grenades are rolled down movie aisles or pitched into unsuspecting groups of innocents.' And Sulzberger gave a comic example of how people were reacting under the strain: 'Early this month when retiring Premier Nguyen Phan Long and his successor Tran Van Huu were speaking at Saigon's Town Hall a champagne cork popped and everyone ducked instinctively.'[24]

Top military personnel were targeted for assassination. On 31 July 1951 General Chanson, a right-hand man of de Lattre's, was killed by a 25-year-old member of a suicide battalion who ran suddenly towards him and the local provincial governor. A grenade exploded, killing all three.

Abandoned corpses were often found and the killing never ceased. Greene himself recalled the case of a local girl who became a human bomb. She blew herself up, taking with her a party of sailors from a warship anchored in the Saigon river. Edmund Gullion recalled unexpectedly witnessing the assassination of the head of the French Sûreté on 28 April 1950:

It was in the morning but I hadn't come from my flat, and I walked by the square and I saw Bazin [the head of the Sûreté] just about to get into his car, and he was carrying this leather folder. And in front of him was another car parked with some Vietnamese in it. As he started to get into it, this other Vietnamese jumped out of the parked car right in front of him, holding an enormous revolver in two hands, the way they do in American movies now, two-handed, and pumped shots into his belly. I was right across the street from him, a narrow street, and I ducked behind a barber's chair [in the open]. Then the assassin got into the car and drove away. The irony of it was that they were expecting some kind of ceremony and there was a French squad rehearsing for it, and I remember seeing this fellow go right past them – and he was never found.[25]

Just before his death Bazin had told a French journalist: 'Every day the Vietminh radio says, "Bazin, you are going to die." ' He knew that his killers had already arrived in Saigon. He had hoped that he would get them before they got him.

*

Prostitutes still work the street near the cathedral and the Palace Norodom in Cholon, but in Greene's day the district was populated by little opium dens and brothels, often housed together so you could move from one to another. The life of Cholon goes on all night, a chaos of noise and light. There is a tremendous sense of life; numberless Chinese live cheek by jowl. Greene went there to the whorehouses and to the opium dens; to the Palais de Jade and the Arc-en-Ciel for Chinese food and taxi girls. Here any eroticism could be catered for, everything could be bought or sold.

An American friend, John Getz, who worked for the American legation and had been given the task of looking after Greene by Edmund Gullion took Greene to his first opium den (because Greene asked him to), although Seymour Topping also claimed that privilege.

Greene dated his first opium experience as 31 October 1951 in a letter to his mother: 'had my first opium soirée (I rather liked it) and so back here [Hanoi] feeling quite recovered. The trouble however at present is that everything is pretty quiet & the French take far too much trouble about one's personal security. Everybody is afraid of getting into a row if anything should happen – rather cramping.'[26] After taking opium he had a dream in which religion and sex were inextricably linked.

Going back in time to the year AD 1, Greene was living not far from Bethlehem and decided to walk to a small town to visit a brothel. He had with him a gold coin with which to pay the girl he chose. As he approached the town he saw a strange sight: a group of men in Eastern clothes bowing and offering gifts to a blank wall. Greene stood quite a while watching the strange scene and then something, he could not say what, impelled him to throw his coin at the wall and turn away. Time moved rapidly forward and he found himself lying on his bed reading in the New Testament about some Eastern kings coming to a stable in Bethlehem. He then realised that this was what he had seen. Greene's first thought was: 'Well, I went to Bethlehem to give that gold coin to a woman and it seems that I did in fact give it to a woman, even though all I saw was a blank wall.'[27]

This was the beginning of Greene's passion for opium. He never let it get out of hand, but as with alcohol he used opium to control his depression. In the detailed account in *Ways of Escape*, Greene indicated that his first experience occurred when he was taken to a small apartment in a back street by a French official: 'I could smell the opium as I came up the stairs. It was like the first sight of a beautiful woman with whom one realizes that a relationship is possible: somebody whose memory will not be dimmed by a night's sleep.'[28]

Realising that Greene was a *débutant*, the madame insisted that he have only four pipes. This ensured that his first experience would not be spoilt by nausea from over-smoking. The atmosphere appealed to him:

> The *ambiance* won my heart at once – the hard couch, the leather pillow like a brick – these stand for a certain austerity, the athleticism of pleasure, while the small lamp glowing on the face of the pipe-maker, as he kneads his little ball of brown gum over the flame until it bubbles and alters shape like a dream, the dimmed lights, the little chaste cups of unsweetened green tea, these stand for the *luxe et volupté*.[29]

Each pipe, from the moment the needle plunges the little ball home and the bowl is reversed over the flame, lasts no more than a quarter of a minute – the practised inhaler drawing a whole pipeful into the lungs in one inhalation. After two pipes Greene would feel drowsy, after four his mind would feel alert and calm – fear and unhappiness only dim memories.

The effect of the opium was curious. Greene would normally have been shy at exhibiting his inadequacy in speaking French. However, on this occasion, he found himself reciting to his companion Baudelaire's poem of escape, 'Invitation au Voyage'. When he got home he experienced for the first time the 'delightful "white night" of opium':

> One lies relaxed and wakeful, not wanting sleep. We dread wakefulness when our thoughts are disturbed, but in this state one is calm – it would be wrong even to say that one is happy – happiness disturbs the pulse. And then suddenly without warning one sleeps. Never has one slept so deeply a whole night-long sleep, and then waking and the luminous dial of the clock showing that twenty minutes of so-called real time have gone by. Again the calm lying awake, again the deep brief all-night sleep.[30]

Once after smoking Greene went to bed at 1.30 a.m. He rose at 4 to catch a bomber to Hanoi, but in those few hours had slept all tiredness away.[31] Opium became a 'wonderful substitute for the unimportant act of sex':

Working differently, as it does, on a man and a woman, it is not a substitute for love, and it has broken many marriages, but for the traveller who does not want the unimportant act (to give his gold piece in a brothel) it is a wonderful pacifier. I remember smoking once in a brothel in Saigon . . . I was restless with the long absence from someone I loved [Catherine], and when I came into the backroom and saw the sprawl of the lovely and graceful [girl] on the big couch I prepared to surrender to the unimportant . . . I asked my companion for two pipes. After that, I thought, I will go upstairs, and as she lay with her head in my lap I looked forward to the release in after two more pipes. But when I had smoked four, I no longer desired her, though she had lost no grace or beauty, I wanted only to smoke yet further pipes and then to lie down on my own bed alone and enjoy the white night.[32]

The preparation of the pipe, the way the lamp shines on the face of the pipemaker, Greene's desire to quote Baudelaire, the diminishing effect smoking had on his sex drive, are all reflected in the first few pages of *The Quiet American*:

Now she [Phuong] was kneading the little ball of hot paste on the convex margin of the bowl and I could smell the opium. There is no smell like it. Beside the bed my alarm-clock showed twelve-twenty, but already my tension was over. Pyle had diminished. The lamp lit her face as she tended the long pipe, bent over it with the serious attention she might have given to a child. I was fond of my pipe: more than two feet of straight bamboo, ivory at either end. Two-thirds of the way down was the bowl, like a convolvulus reversed, the convex margin polished and darkened by the frequent kneading of the opium. Now with a flick of the wrist she plunged the needle into the tiny cavity, released the opium and reversed the bowl over the flame, holding the pipe steady for me. The bead of opium bubbled gently and smoothly as I inhaled.[33]

Fowler takes a second pipe. They talk about Pyle, about his willingness to marry Phuong, which successfully takes Phuong from Fowler. She asks if he'll have a third pipe and he accepts:

I wondered whether she would consent to sleep with me that night if Pyle never came, but I knew that when I had smoked four pipes I would no longer want her . . . 'Pyle won't come now,' I said. 'Stay here, Phuong.' She held the pipe out to me and shook her head. By the time I had drawn the opium in, her presence or absence mattered very little . . .

'Don't worry. He'll come. Make me another pipe.' When she bent over the flame the poem of Baudelaire's came into my mind: '*Mon enfant, ma sœur . . .*'*[34]

Once in Hanoi and aware of the unfriendliness and sadness of that capital city (in contrast nothing quenches the spirit of Saigon) on the edge of battle, Greene and Trevor Wilson took a girl to the hotel from an opium house. Greene felt that Catherine had lost interest in him and their long affair was over: 'She would only undress in the dark, and in bed she twittered like a bird on the pillow.' Because of the opium, Greene had little desire. They had tossed up to see who should have the girl first, but Greene was unable to perform. At 2.30 in the morning he took her down to poor Wilson, still waiting, but the opium had affected him adversely too. Greene ended his journal entry: 'She was friendly, she was home, and I have lost here the sense of home.'[35]

When Seymour Topping, 'Top', mentioned that he and his wife Audrey had tried opium, '[Greene] was anxious to go and we couldn't resist his desire':

We found the best opium den in Hanoi. There was a man, a tall black man from US military, he knew about it. The four of us went and I think the black fellow was the one who knew where to go. Anyway, all I remember is going down alleys, in a maze of alleys and having secret raps at the door and everything's full of intrigue and adventure, and we go into this place and all the women are floating around in white gossamer gowns and there were like double decker bunks and everybody laid down and the women prepared the opium for us. We took our shoes off . . . like

---

* In Greene's undated 'Saigon journal', in thinking about his experience with women he becomes philosophically sexual:

> I woke in the plane from Saigon, and some sexual dream compelled by the beat of the plane engine made me wonder why the cry of a woman's orgasm is always sad: the sound that seems to be torn from her unwillingly, in pain, rather than pleasure? Do they know the sound they make and the words they use, with each woman so invariable?

the Japanese. There were French and Vietnamese there. We were the only foreigners but they welcomed us in. So we were the first people to 'corrupt' Greene [laughing]. We didn't mean to. We saw he wanted it for the adventure. He wanted to know what it's like to go to an opium den in Hanoi and we wanted to know too. So we went in and it was just, you know, the atmosphere was perfect, perfect atmosphere. And they lay down and they all rolled up in little black balls. We had long pipes. I was on the opposite bed to Graham Greene. He seemed to go right into it as if he'd been there all his life. And we had five pipes. We each had five pipes and by the end of three I was levitating. We were also flaking around and enjoying ourselves and Greene was not really asking any questions or anything. He was just there observing. His pale blue eyes lit up as he absorbed detail which later went into *The Quiet American*. So when it was over, we went back to the hotel where we were all staying and we sat up and talked all night. And Top was telling Graham how to write novels [laughter] and he was telling Top how to write newspapers [more laughter].[36]

If his journal mentions brothels and opium dens, his dreams at night were often about Catherine. He was desperate and angry, feeling that he had lost her:

November 2 [1951]: At night woke sadly quarreling with C. & carried on awake like early last year.

November 4: In how many odd churches in strange places has one prayed the same prayer [that Catherine would marry him]. The depression of having nothing to look forward to . . . I could be happy these weeks [in Vietnam] if there was a future like there always has been. Cafryn very bad.

November 5: Awful dream of C. & woke in the night angry & quarrelling. Oddly enough erotic dream of D[orothy Glover] but full of regret because her sex smell was not C's . . . Dreams of C. but not bad only sad dreams this time.

He was desperately unhappy about Catherine and trying to anaesthetise himself with drink and opium.

*

In many ways Greene's *The Quiet American* is based on his own personal observations and is, more than any other novel, direct *reportage*. Many of his experiences find their way directly into the novel and what can be discovered about the people he came to know illustrates his creative process.

During Greene's January 1951 visit to Vietnam he journeyed to the battleground in the Catholic enclave of Phat Diem, a coastal port near Hanoi on the fertile Red River delta, which is known as the rice bowl of Vietnam. He flew in a plane lent by General de Lattre with Trevor Wilson. His initial impressions of Phat Diem, of its prince bishop and a Belgian priest they met were not complimentary:

> the two of us went off in tiny morain plane to Phat Diem to spend night with the warrior bishop. Fantastic number of churches. Guard of honour. The sad sincere relentless face of the bishop. Strange Cathedral, ex. Buddhist temple. Visit top hospital with the unpleasant Belgian priest. The Viet-Minh prisoner gangrening. Broken limbs splinted with bamboo. No plaster . . . The Belgian priest's amateur surgery.[37]

This Belgian priest, Father Willich, who was the bishop's general factotum, appears in the novel in the extraordinary bell tower, from which you could see the mortar shells burst and watch the enemy and the French parachutists moving in single file along the canals and the great market burning fiercely: 'Even the priest who sat in a corner of the tower never changed his position as he read his breviary.'[38] Audrey Topping remembers him as ugly looking. 'He was bald headed and had a big nose and I remember that vividly – I mean, they all shaved their heads.'[39] Greene met the Belgian priest on his second visit to Phat Diem in December 1951, drank with him and found that he had a 'rough amusing Belgian cunning'. He also added that he 'smelt in his dirty black soutane'.

A confidential report to the State Department from the American legation concerning a visit from Father Willich (31 March 1951) confirms what Greene reported about the Belgian priest and his hospital: 'Phat Diem has received 150 cotton blankets of American aid, and *nothing else* . . . At present, in his 70-bed hospital, the Father, who is also chief (and sole) surgeon, in addition to his religious duties and functions as professor of mathematics and public works engineer, is obliged to perform intricate operations without proper sterilization of his instruments.'[40]

The priest in the novel, whom Fowler comes to know in the bell tower at Phat Diem, shares many of Willich's characteristics and experiences. Like Willich, the priest is European but not French – and the bishop, while hating the communist Vietminh, also hates the

French. The fictional priest and Father Willich both act as the sole surgeon for the hospital:

> 'We have the only hospital in Phat Diem [says the priest in *The Quiet American*], and our only nurses are these nuns.'
> 'And your surgeon?'
> 'I do what I can.' I saw then that his soutane was speckled with blood.[41]

The priest asks Fowler whether he came up the tower to find him. When Fowler responds that he was merely getting his bearings, the priest replies:

> I asked you because I had a man up here last night. He wanted to go to Confession. He had got a little frightened, you see, with what he had seen along the canal. One couldn't blame him.[42]

Whilst Fowler is certainly based on Greene's life and many of his characteristics are found in the character of Fowler, Fowler's atheism was not shared by Greene. Fowler feels, as a non-Catholic, that there is something unmanly about confession, 'kneeling in one of your boxes. Exposing myself to another man.' What is fascinating is that the unnamed character ('I had a man up here last night. He wanted to go to Confession') was Greene. Trevor Wilson told me that he and Greene met Father Willich twice: 'Graham always left me and made a confession to Willich.'[43] It is revealing of how Greene worked as a novelist – transferring his own personal experience to an unnamed character.

To Catherine, about his contact in Phat Diem with the death of civilians, he wrote: 'especially . . . a poor woman and her small boy who had got in the way of war, drove me to Confession'.[44]

Greene left Vietnam on this first visit believing that the Catholic area of Phat Diem could look after itself (this turned out to be monumentally incorrect). He felt that the Catholics were inspired by an idea equal in strength to the communist Vietminh, a view he put forward in *Life*:

> The other day at Phat Diem, in the north of Indo-China, I watched the Viet Namese Catholic bishop inspect his outposts, the unpaid militia who had helped clear the bishopric and who now held it free from the Communist enemy. I heard the young men sing their hymns; I watched the platoon leaders come up with their bouquets of flowers for their bishop. There were only 2,000

of these men here, and there were not enough uniforms yet to go round, but I would have felt more confidence fighting in their ranks than in the ranks of the 1,000,000 armed Malay police. They reminded me a little of the Home Guard in 1940. The Home Guard was never tested as these few men so often are when the guerrillas seep up across the wide flat paddies, but their strength was an idea, and that idea love of their country. Christianity too is a form of patriotism. These Vietnamese belonged to the City of God and were proud of their city that lay behind the no man's land of rice. 'You see,' I wanted to say to my friends in Malaya, 'it can be done.' An idea was fighting an idea.[45]

When Greene returned to Phat Diem eight months later in October 1951, he discovered that 'an idea fighting an idea' was not enough.

*

In spite of the excitement of Vietnam, Catherine Walston remained of profound concern to Greene. Before leaving Malaya for his visit to Indo-China, he admitted that he was 'getting tired of peaceful atmosphere with no hope of a bullet'. This was true especially when he felt that he had no hope of persuading Catherine to leave her husband and family. It was at this time that he had a depressing dream in which Catherine said to him: 'I've got something rather sad to break to you.' She told Greene that she was forbidden ever to come to Italy with him again.

However, six days later he received a telegram from Catherine announcing she'd meet him in Paris.[46] Just prior to catching a plane on the first leg of his journey, he noted: 'Depressed & worried. Will C. be tired of it all?' On the plane he wrote her some verses entitled 'After Four Years':

> I went as far as China to forget you,
> But in the razed village on the plain,
> In a footprint, on the laterite, I met you,
> So it's not worth going there again.

He could not lose Catherine in the marshes south of Saigon, there was no forgetting, she was everywhere.

When Greene's plane arrived in Paris at 10.35 p.m. it was over two hours late. Expressing his longing to wake up in the night and feel her against him, Greene had cabled Catherine to bring his briefcase, her red shoes and four shirts. She met him with warm clothing. They spent a week together at the Pont-Royal hotel in rue

Montalembert, before leaving for London. Afterwards he wrote: 'No one has ever been more loved than you except the saints. Remember you're the central object & purpose of a life.'[47]

He told his mother that he loved his first visit to Indo-China – 'a very strange medieval place'; that the High Commissioner General de Lattre was very kind to him, providing him with everything from cars to tiny aeroplanes for his journeys; that he was shot at once, but discovered it only afterwards – and that he wanted *to return* to Vietnam.[48] But first Korda's charm and blandishments (and a desire to escape his eternal boredom) found him again aboard the *Elsewhere*.

25

Interlude on *Elsewhere*

We've added about ten feet to give it a rounded stern so
it will be about one hundred feet long and we'll put
bulwarks up . . . so it will look more elegant.

        – ALEXANDER KORDA

IN June 1951 Greene was sailing in the Aegean on Korda's yacht,
the *Elsewhere*. He knew that he needed to go back to Indo-China;
the war was heating up in the Catholic Phat Diem area and *Paris
Match* wanted him to write on Indo-China as France's 'Crown of
Thorns'. Yet his thoughts always returned to Catherine. He could
not but be aware how rarely they now met:

> I live from holiday to holiday with you. Hope deferred is a strain
> . . . *Paris Match* is pressing for a date for Indo-China, & sometimes
> there seems so little left. Each year there's a downward graph – I
> wish I hadn't kept a diary: one might not notice how steeply it
> was . . . [1]

When the *Elsewhere* arrived at Hydra, the island was decked out
for a festival: bells clanged, fireworks were set off, a play was
performed in the street and, on the quayside, Greene saw a chauffeur
he and Catherine had used on their last visit. At Nauplia was yet
another chauffeur they always used, which brought memories
flooding back of inland trips he had made with Catherine. Greene
persuaded Korda to take them to Mycenae – 'wonderful heavy ruins
of the Homeric age which were legendary ruins already when the
Parthenon was building'. Another old chauffeur had candles in his
pouch to light up Agamemnon's extraordinary beehive tomb. Their
next stop was Epidaurus, where the Vienna Symphony Orchestra
was playing in the Greek amphitheatre:

> It was awful getting there, but once there it was very lovely – the

sun sinking, stars & moonlight & cigarettes going on & off like lighthouses: about 12,000 people & the King & Queen sitting on pillows. First Mozart's Jupiter Symphony (which I liked perhaps because a faint idea for an Indo-China novel stirred).

When it was quite dark the orchestra played Beethoven's Fifth Symphony – 'incredibly romantic'.[2] He looked forward to London because when he got home he could speak again to Catherine: 'but the agonising part of being in love starts again'.

By the middle of August, it seemed that Harry Walston was forbidding Catherine to see Greene. Greene suspected that the imminent publication of *The End of the Affair* was behind Walston's ultimatum – it was published in September, but he received copies in August, which he gave to special friends. On 15 August, after he had returned to London, he wrote to Catherine that her sister Belinda (Binnie) had given him strong advice:

> Binnie's just gone. She couldn't tell me much. I'm so sorry for all those miserable days for you. I gave her a copy of the book [*The End of the Affair*]. How sad & ominous the title now seems to be. Binnie obviously felt that I should take things into my own hands & clear out of the picture. *I would if you asked me to*, but it would be like death. I would like to hear from you calmly in writing . . . if you would like me to disappear. I'd sublet the flat & go abroad or something.

It seemed that Harry Walston was threatening divorce. Greene answered that four and a half years of condonation put the possibility out of the question: 'Harry *can't* threaten anything. Morally he had every right 4 1/2 years ago; now he hasn't even the legal right . . . For him to bring down a curtain *now*, after you've got used to me & our life together is cruel & unwarranted.'[3]

Harry Walston had forbidden his wife to see Greene, not only at Newton Hall, but elsewhere also: 'If for even a couple of weeks by doing nothing you accept Harry's right to forbid you to see me aren't you making it impossible *without a major trouble* ever to be with me again? Harry can dictate about Newton, not about your life outside.'[4]

Greene left it to Catherine: 'if you decide against me & the "affair" (if that's what one calls these four years between the first Achill & the last Italy) must be over, then I clear out without question', but he added a caveat: 'Sooner or later the old promiscuity for both of us probably. There's something terribly wrong in *that* alternative.'[5] Telling her he was grateful for the years she had given him, he added that he wanted to carry on with her until death.

In March 1950 Greene had sent the manuscript of *The End of the Affair* to Catherine because he wanted to give her a sentimental present. In the letter with the manuscript he wrote: 'Because I'm going to Germany tomorrow: because I hate myself today, because all the best part was written with you (I remember coming out of my workroom while you were washing up & reading one sentence & saying "isn't that good" – "virtue tempted him in the dark like a sin") and because I love you & bastard as I am, I'm married to you by this ms. Graham. Put up with me for another year or two.'[6] He gave her also a typescript of *The Heart of the Matter* and wrote on the flyleaf: 'For Catherine with love, a book which would never have been finished without "the graveyard, rock & sea".'*

The dedication in the English edition of *The End of the Affair* read: 'To C.' – few readers would know to whom this referred. But in the American edition, it was to read: 'To Catherine with love.' When Walston brought pressure to bear on Catherine to limit her visits to Greene, Greene wrote to her to ask: 'Would you like me to cable America to try to stop the dedication?' It was not changed, however.

With publication came Harry Walston's latest refusal to allow Catherine and Greene to meet. The whole of literary London would believe not only that Greene was Mrs Walston's lover – literary London knew that already – but that Greene had written a close account of their affair.

Catherine's sister, Belinda Straight, wrote a firm letter to Catherine objecting to the fact that the novel revealed the Walston family too easily and too obviously and was, in a sense, a betrayal of Harry Walston. However, when she complained, Catherine responded that it wouldn't be right to expect a creative writer to change his text. (Belinda had asked for the name of Crompton to be replaced – after all she was a Crompton herself. Greene had called one of his characters Father Crompton.) Belinda was astonished when Walston wrote to her to say that she had hurt her sister by her remarks – a remarkable man. Belinda then advised Harry Walston to sue Greene for the undeniable resemblance between himself and Henry Miles, the cuckolded husband. He never did, but his

---

* Greene also left her the typescript of *The Point of Departure*, the working title of *The End of the Affair*, with the words: 'for Catherine with my only love, the night we went to a medium & the day before we went back to Rome, Passetbois, Anacapri, Aniello, Norman [Douglas], everything. From Graham.' He also gave Catherine his fat black fountain-pen as a souvenir.

relationship with Greene was spoilt even further by the appearance of the novel.

To add more constraints to their love, it appears that Catherine had suggested that though they should continue to see each other, they should no longer have sex. She opted for 'intellectual companionship'. There is a strong possibility that the Dominican priest Thomas Gilby, a close friend of both Walstons and the author of *Morals and Marriage: The Catholic Background to Sex*, was behind Catherine's remarks:

> You say the last 4 1/2 years have been a fairy tale. Thomas has probably said that, but he hasn't lived them. It was at least a fairy tale which might have lasted another five before one side of the relation died slowly & naturally out. The fairy tale you are substituting is one in which one will be afraid to come into the same bedroom, afraid to kiss, afraid to touch you, when we shall be so self-conscious that the body will be always in one's mind because never at peace.[7]

Greene could not be persuaded that their sexual relationship was wrong, given the depth of their love. He quoted Browning. 'Better sin the whole sin sure that God observes.' Again and again he put forward the view that the only way they could continue to stay together for life '*is* to go back & back to Confession & Communion after every time or period, but I *don't* believe – even Thomas doesn't believe in the possibility . . . of suddenly switching a relation into the unphysical level.'[8] He then became sophistical, speaking of eventual and immediate intention. If Catherine's intentions were immediate then Greene thought it better to end their affair promptly. But he warned her and he warned himself what that would lead to: 'I hope & pray you don't [end it] because life would be a real desert without you, & God knows what shabby substitutes one would desperately try to find. But try & answer clearly.'[9]

Catherine continued to hold out some hope only to dash it later. Unable to stand the situation, Greene came out with his own ultimatum, a statement of three alternatives:

> I can't stand this situation – I simply haven't got the strength. There are only three things possible to choose.
>
> 1) I know you won't, but that's to come away with me to Italy, start annulments – you'd have your children half their holidays,

we'd marry as soon as we could, & if possible have one of our own . . .

2) Be as we were minus Newton [because he was no longer allowed by Walston to visit Newton Hall]. Sometimes going away for a little, getting back to confession or communion all the time. But in between be lovers.

3) I disappear completely as from tomorrow. My dear, last night shows that I *can't* be with you & not your lover. I'm too in love for that. I'd just ask one thing & that's for you to take my bureau key & take away your letters in the top right hand drawer. I tried the other day to destroy them, but it meant seeing them & I couldn't.* If it's 3 try not to be corrupted & lie around. I'll try not.

You said it was not the love relationship that Harry minded – it was that you 'worked to sew on fly buttons', but no one, not even the church, has a right to demand that you shan't love in that way. Our love's been a good love . . . I have been your husband . . .

Please put 1, 2, or 3 on a piece of paper. It won't be 1, but if it's 3 I think I must go away tomorrow . . . Your lover – probably for the last time of writing it.[10]

It seemed the end, but it was an end he sought to prolong.

Korda was pressing Greene to join him again on his yacht, *Elsewhere*. Flamboyant yet friendly, Korda had a great fondness for Greene. Greene wrote a sketch of the man under the name of Dreuther in his 1955 entertainment *Loser Takes All*:

He had just ordered himself a Pernod and he was talking with easy familiarity to the barman, speaking perfect French. Whatever the man's language he would have spoken it perfectly. Yet he wasn't the Dreuther of the eighth floor now – he had put an old yachting cap on the bar, he had several days' growth of white beard and he wore an old and baggy pair of blue trousers and a sweat shirt.[11]

The cruise on the *Elsewhere* was to begin on 27 September. Greene had promised Evelyn Waugh that he would spend ten days

---

* At his home in Antibes on 14 December 1983 Greene told me he had destroyed Catherine's letters.

with him beforehand. Waugh, unaware of the troubles between Catherine and Greene, had invited them both to stay. His wife had taken the children away for a month and he was on his own: 'Is there any hope of having you for a visit (if with Catherine, better still) to cheer me up . . . Do come if you can bear the thought.'[12] He warned Greene that his cook was also on holiday: that only a village woman would take her place so they might have to live on scrambled eggs; that his butler had gone sick and 'all my comforts & yours depend on him'. He went on to tell Greene, who hated any formality of dress, that he wore a dinner jacket in the evenings – 'but there's not the smallest reason why you should do so'. He couldn't even promise constant hot water as the boiler was one of the things his sick butler attended to: 'Plenty of coke if you know about fuelling. It will be Swiss Family Robinson Life.'[13]

These limitations on comfort did not deter Greene: 'I like boiled or scrambled eggs and can do without hot water indefinitely. I can't drive . . . but Catherine can . . . The Swiss Family Robinson life is exactly what Catherine and I used to live when the world allowed us to . . . I look forward so much to this visit. Perhaps I'll be able to work again.'[14] Greene's fear of losing Catherine had stopped him from producing his daily 500 words.

Greene wrote to Catherine on 3 September: 'what can one write about, when one can't write about one's longing? . . . please come to Evelyn's as planned for Sep. 11, 12 & 13. I shall probably be going away on Sept. 27. Korda has asked me to go on his boat & work on a film story I've suggested to him. Olivier & Vivien Leigh will be there too. From Athens to Istanbul.' And he added that he was frightened of the memories of previous occasions on Korda's yacht, this time without her, but that he was surrounded by memories in London too.

Catherine wrote to Waugh before their visit. He replied: 'Of course I won't tell Graham you wrote . . . I shall love you to come if you can bear the discomforts. It will not even be Swiss Family Robinson.' She was clearly worried about the visit: 'Please believe that I am far too depressed by my own odious, if unromantic, sins to have any concern for other people's.'[15] To Catherine's suggestion that Greene might be happier if she didn't come along, Waugh responded: 'But when you say Graham is sometimes happier without you, that is another matter. You know & I don't. I did detect in his letters a hint that he looked forward to a spell of solitude. Only you can decide whether that mood is likely to persist. If you think it a bad time, come later when Laura [Waugh's wife] is home.' Waugh then added a slyly comic postscript about the Walston wealth: 'the Donaldsons tell me you live in great magnificence with a domestic chaplain, butlers in black coats and groaning tables of delicatessen. My conservative newspaper tells me you have got away with wads of public money & are starting to grow ground nuts in Cambridge. But, dear Catherine, I don't listen to gossip about you.'[16] Waugh is probably making fun here of the abortive ground-nuts scheme in Tanganyika initiated by socialist Minister John Strachey – and Harry Walston was a very rich socialist.

Waugh wrote to Nancy Mitford about their visit (Catherine stayed only for three days and Greene a week): 'Greene behaved well & dressed for dinner every night. Mrs Walston had never seen him in a dinner jacket before and was enchanted and will make him wear one always.' And then added: 'G. Greene spent his days patrolling the built up area round Dursley noting the numbers of motor-cars. He takes omens from them.'[17]

Martin Stannard, quoting this in his biography of Waugh, comments 'the last two sentences were a humorous allusion to Bendrix's obsession rather than Greene's'. However, Greene confirmed that at this time he collected car numbers when bored. What was true of Bendrix in the novel was true of Greene: 'During the last year . . . I've been so bored I've even collected car numbers. That teaches you about coincidences. Ten thousand possible numbers and God knows how many combinations, and yet over and over again I've seen two cars with the same figures side by side in a traffic block.'[18] What Greene felt he had to do, and he couldn't cheat, was first to spot the number 1 by itself and then work numerically upwards. Greene never explained his hobby. When I asked him what he was atoning for, he answered casually – 'Oh, I was just bored.'[19] However, in a letter to Catherine he wrote jubilantly that he'd seen a car with the number 206.

Both Catherine and Greene enjoyed themselves at the Waughs'. In a letter to Greene, she admitted she liked being with Waugh, especially since he was able to cheer Greene up enormously. Greene made the same point to Waugh: 'I enjoyed myself with you so much & you eased what would have been a very bad period for me.'[20]

Immediately following his visit, Greene went on his voyage with Korda: 'I told Korda I'd go with him. We had dinner all by ourselves & he was very sweet. He's going to Rome on 27th with his party but I couldn't bear these nights at the Grand Hotel, so I shall fly out on the 29th & join him for one night. Then Athens. If the Hanoi business comes off, I shall go straight on, so I don't know when I'll be back in England.'[21]

Catherine had decided that they would be parted for seven months, so the future held some hope, but Greene seemed to despair even then: 'I can't believe that after seven months – even if some of them are dreary & sad – you'll want to start the wear & tear of me again. It'll be so much easier for you to stay put. But I . . . live only in hope of being with you again.' The date chosen for their reunion was the end of April: 'On April 30 the bells of Assisi will be clashing for the patron saint of husbands – & you are the only wife I've ever really had.'[22]

Greene's voyage on *Elsewhere* was scheduled to finish at Istanbul. His sister Elisabeth and her husband Rodney Dennys were at the British Embassy and Greene asked Catherine to write from 29 September until further notice c/o Rodney Dennys, British Embassy, Istanbul. Doubtful that they would ever get together again, he admitted he was working against his conscience: 'It says do the time. You are better with Catherine, it's right to be with her.'[23] As he prepared to leave on Korda's yacht, he had little doubt that it was over: 'The days are awful. I hate the telephone that will never ring & I have so little hope now.'[24]

Once on board he enjoyed the company of Laurence Olivier and Vivien Leigh ('I quite like the Oliviers – he is nicer, but she has more brains.')[25] and ballerina Margot Fonteyn. On 24 October 1951, his short respite over, he caught a plane from Orly airport at three in the morning. He lunched at Bahrein, spent the night in Karachi, and arrived in Calcutta on the following day. Brief entries in his journal record his thoughts as he flew across India: 'Over India – where are the swarming millions? The sense of empty wastes . . . The terrible squalor – this is all we [the British] had done in 110 years.'[26] He had wired family friends from Paris, who met him at the airport. They took him to tea and later to dinner. Greene liked them both, but thought their child 'hopelessly spoilt'. He described his visit in a letter to his mother:

It was a 'dry' day (every Thursday is) in Calcutta, so we had to do all our drinking at their home before dinner & then in my bedroom . . . Put up by the airline at the Grand Hotel – everybody but me had to share rooms, but luckily to the French a writer is much more important than a colonel. The night's stop was only till 1.30 in the morning, when we were given eggs & bacon & driven through streets with the pavements lined with sleeping figures & occasional sacred cow. The cows kept themselves to themselves & seldom shared a pavement with a human.[27]

It had been a very slow journey by a rather seedy service, but once Greene landed in Saigon he felt 'very happy & at home'.

26

A Crown of Thorns

In a narrow bed
drop down dead.
— S. W. BRUNT

THE Far East had an exciting yet disturbing effect on Greene. It gave rise to doubts as evidenced by an untitled (and unknown) manuscript begun on 30 December (probably 1953):

> nothing is more disquieting than the East. It calls into question all one's beliefs, religious or political. The awful poverty of Macau, the pullulation of Hong Kong. Does one believe in quite the same way in the East in personal survival . . . ? It's so easy in Europe to believe that everyone in the street, the café, the cinema will survive, separate and distinct — there are only a few million of them — does one really believe any more there is the separate survival of every spider one does not deliberately kill, every ant one avoids with the foot?[1]

While questioning his belief in survival after death, Greene retained his curious desire for death, becoming a death seeker.

Libby Getz said that Greene wanted 'to be crucified on an anthill in a third world country'.[2] He sometimes slipped in his death wish as an aside, as when, on returning to Malaya for a short visit after he'd failed to get killed in Vietnam, he wrote: 'Tomorrow I go by rail to K[uala] L[umpur] to give the Communists another chance.'[3]

On a later trip in January 1954 Greene travelled with a convoy to the fortified village of Thui-nai in Vietnam, which was approached by a narrow causeway between canals. Seconds before the convoy entered an unknown minefield, the commandant decided to send ahead a mine-detecting patrol. Greene's jeep was stopped just before it went over a mine enclosed in a wooden box, with a piece of wood over the detonator. He and his driver had narrowly escaped being blown sky-high. He received his reprieve grudgingly:

It was difficult to thank God with any sincerity for this gift of life. I have much to look forward to in another fortnight for a month [he was to be with Catherine] . . . but afterwards stretches the long period of indeterminate blight when one is depressed, bored, melancholic. The consciousness that in the long run there is nothing to live for and that the best bet is on the black.[4]

On occasion his longing for death came at moments of ecstasy: when deeply in love or when moved by beauty. Only death had the power to capture happiness eternally. When he was twenty-one Greene had written to Vivien: 'Loving you is like being drowned in a moment of ecstasy, during a clean, swift stroke, when the whole arc of blue is caught up by the eye, & death comes & leaves eternally pictured on the mind the clean blue sweep of the sky, & indelibly carved on thought, frozen in death, your head & eyes & hair . . . .'[5]

This is the extravagance of youth, but at forty-seven Greene felt the same desire. At Phat Diem, he was struck by the beauty of the area:

The path through the water covered paddy fields with churches the only visible buildings – half a dozen at a time: two facing each other fifty yards apart . . . Sunset over the strange mountains, gold in the water which slowly turns to blood orange & pewter. The fisherman. The strange cranes that left the nets like huge midges. The long field of ripe rice like corn. A Sunday of childhood. The blue flowering weed. Longed for death to come here with an ambush, on this coloured evening.[6]

Fowler, the cynical Englishman in The Quiet American, ('What a shit he is!' said Evelyn Waugh in a letter to Greene[7]) has, in spite of his nature, many of Greene's qualities. He raises questions (and provides answers) which reflect Greene's spiritual autobiography:

Why should I want to die when Phuong slept beside me every night? But I knew the answer to that question. From childhood I had never believed in permanence, and yet I had longed for it. Always I was afraid of losing happiness. This month, next year, Phuong would leave me. If not next year, in three years. Death was the only absolute value in my world. Lose life and one would lose nothing again for ever . . . Death was far more certain than

God, and with death there would be no longer the daily possibility of love dying. The nightmare of a future of boredom and indifference would lift.[8]

His problems with Catherine had left Greene with a strong sense that he had no future. On his return to Vietnam on 23 October 1951 he felt impelled to place himself in the midst of the conflict.

On 15 November Greene went on a bombing raid – perhaps death would come that way. He recorded the experience in his journal:

> Left for Haiphong. Arrived Cat-B: 10.30. Colonel said no chance of bombing mission that day . . . Drinking afterwards with Capt. Pinquet of Gascogne dive-bombing mission turned up. He had been told to send me only on horizontal bombing but under influence of drink all went well. Started at 3. Over target, Phong-To, a recently captured post & village [by the Vietminh] at 4.15. Spent 3/4 of an hour bombing & gunning. 14 dives – one from 9,000 to 3000 (highest range for Vietminh heavy m.g.s). On way home shot up sampan on the Red River from 200 feet. Shower of vertical sparks. Extraordinary rose light on mountains & gold on paddy. Dinner party at Jardines. Very tired and stoned & little overturned.[9]

He gave a radio talk about the raid on the BBC, the text of which was printed in the *Listener* on 15 September 1955, three months before *The Quiet American* was published. The changes in the two accounts are negligible.[10] Here is the passage in the novel built up from the notes in his journal:

> At Haiphong I had friends in the Squadron Gascogne, and I would spend hours in the bar up at the airport . . . orders had gone out from Hanoi that I was to be allowed only on horizontal raids – raids in this war as safe as a journey by bus, for we flew above the range of the heavy machine-gun; we were safe from anything but a pilot's error or a fault in the engine . . .
>
> One morning in the mess . . . as I drank brandies and sodas with a young officer . . . orders for a mission came in. 'Like to come?' I said yes . . . Driving out to the airport he remarked, 'This is a vertical raid.'
>
> 'I thought I was forbidden . . .'
>
> 'So long as you write nothing about it. It will show you a piece

of country up near the Chinese border you will not have seen before. Near Lai Chau.'

'I thought all was quiet there – and in French hands?'

'It was. They captured this place two days ago. Our parachutists are only a few hours away. We want to keep the Viets head down in their holes until we have recaptured the post. It means low diving and machine-gunning . . . Ever dive-bombed before?'

'No.'

'It is a little uncomfortable when you are not used to it.'

. . . I was crammed on to a little metal pad the size of a bicycle seat with my knees against the aviator's back.[11]

Captain Pinquet (called Trouin in the novel) took Greene over the Red River (and the Red River at this hour was really red). To Fowler it seemed that he had gone far back in time and was seeing it with the first geographer's eyes. They then turned away at 9,000 feet towards the Black River. Soon they were over the village to be attacked.

We circled twice above the tower and the green-encircled village, then corkscrewed up into the dazzling air. The pilot . . . turned to me and winked. On his wheel were the studs that controlled the gun and bomb-chamber. I had that loosening of the bowels, as we came into position for the dive, that accompanies any new experience – the first dance, the first dinner-party, the first love . . . On the dial I had just time to read 3,000 metres when we drove down. All was feeling now, nothing was sight. I was forced up against the navigator's back: it was as though something of enormous weight were pressing on my chest. I wasn't aware of the moment when the bombs were released; then the gun chattered and the cockpit was full of the smell of cordite, and the weight was off my chest as we rose, and it was the stomach that fell away, spiralling down like a suicide to the ground we had left . . . As we climbed in a great arc I could see the smoke through the side window pointing at me.[12]

Before the second dive Fowler felt fear, the fear that he would humiliate himself by vomiting over the navigator's back, or that his 'ageing lungs' would not be able to stand the pressure. After the tenth dive, he was aware only of irritation, the bombing run was going on too long.

And again we shot steeply up out of machine-gun range and

swerved away and the smoke pointed. The village was surrounded on all sides by mountains. Every time we had to make the same approach, through the same gap. There was no way to vary our attack. As we dived for the fourteenth time I thought, now that I was free from the fear of humiliation, 'They have only to fix one machine-gun into position.' We lifted our nose again into the safe air – perhaps they didn't even have a gun. The forty minutes of the patrol had seemed interminable, but it had been free from the discomfort of personal thought. The sun was sinking as we turned for home: the geographer's moment had passed: the Black River was no longer black, and the Red River was only gold.[13]

They turned homeward but as they came towards the river the plane aimed its cannon at a small sampan, shattering it in a shower of sparks. The bomber didn't wait to witness whether any victims survived, it just climbed and returned home. Fowler found it disturbing: 'There had been something so shocking in our sudden fortuitous choice of a prey – we had just happened to be passing, one burst only was required, there was no one to return our fire, we were gone again, adding our little quota to the world's dead.'[14]

*

During Greene's two-month stay, he again visited Phat Diem because fighting there had intensified. A *New York Times* article of 10 May 1951 reported: 'commercial traffic flourishes between Phat Diem and insurgent territory, most of it done by coastal junks'. The Vietminh's objective was often rice: a minimum of 90,000 tons per year was needed to feed 300,000 men (150,000 combatants and as many coolies).

The *New York Times* also spoke of the peculiar nature of the area and of bishops who had medieval powers of life and death. The headline read: 'TWO BISHOPS RULE AREA IN TONGKING: *Catholics Administer Districts Independently of the French, Bao Dai or [Communist] Insurgents*' and the article described the influence of the bishops who were leaders of the Church, the army and the state in the war against communism; they operated virtually as autonomous powers, each bishop with his own army. The area's Catholicism* had made people strongly anti-communist and for more than a year it had successfully

---

* Catholicism had come with the Portuguese in the sixteenth century. Phat Diem is still a land of churches, which loom out of the rice fields. Greene observed that in a land of pagodas, suddenly, upon reaching Phat Diem, you felt you were back in Europe, in the Netherlands – the straight canals running off to the sea and in every village a church as big as a cathedral.[15]

resisted communist penetration: 'and today . . . reputedly the most peaceful regions in all Vietnam'.

De Lattre was not as optimistic about the region remaining peaceful. Dean Acheson, the American Secretary of State, discovered that de Lattre was disillusioned with the Catholics in Phat Diem because he believed they had withheld information about the major Vietminh attack. If the French had received notice twenty-four hours earlier much bloodshed might have been saved. General Cogny said that while the French followed Vietminh troop movements and had expected an attack in the area, they had to depend largely on villagers for news of actual attack preparations. The Vietminh, on the other hand, seemed amply informed about French movements. The French were angry because French troops and French blood kept the Vietminh menace away from Phat Diem, yet the local people continued to be indifferent and sometimes hostile towards the French.

De Lattre's bitterness was due primarily to the loss of his only son, Bernard. Young Bernard de Lattre commanded a company which was sent to relieve a naval commando unit in the area. The French High Command (and de Lattre) were extremely irate because villagers had spotted the Vietminh assembling for attack, but had made no effort to warn the French garrison. There were a reported 10,000 Vietminh in the area. De Lattre suffered from the bitterness of a soldier accustomed to having people either for or against him – he couldn't stand deceit. He felt personally hurt by the ambivalence of Vietnamese and Catholics, whose champion he considered himself to be. He was suspicious of the Catholics in the area, particularly Bishop Le Huu Tu, who had made a vociferously anti-French speech. The British consul in Hanoi, Trevor Wilson, witnessed the speech and afterwards became implicated in it in de Lattre's mind.

Though Greene was not to arrive until four months after this particular attack on Phat Diem, nevertheless he was extremely well informed. He saw that Phat Diem illustrated the bizarre nature of the conflict: 'a medieval episcopal principality . . . [which] only . . . collapsed [after the 19 June attack and had to be] saved by French parachutists . . . The present Bishop is Monsignor Le Huu Tu, a former Trappist. He is an austere man with the face of a sad, meditative monkey . . . a dusty skull contemplates him from the other side of his desk.'[16]

Greene knew his bishop:

He is a nationalist and his number-one enemy is the French, after which come the Communists. Even with a foreigner, he makes no mystery of this order of preference. He knows the French (they took his army from him).[17]

By the time Greene returned to Phat Diem on 16 December, the war was intensifying. Just before dawn on 10 December Phat Diem came under attack from a large Vietminh force.

The French were secretive about the Vietminh attack on Phat Diem and two accounts (given to the US legation by spies in the field) were found to be incorrect. Not until 16 December could Wendell Blancke send a corrected account of the raid to Washington:

Sunday Dec 9. first day of two-day religious festival VM troops quietly entered town at midnight in considerable strength took up positions and systematically set up communications equipment. Many townsmen aware their presence *but none alerted military authorities* [emphasis added]. At 4.45 a.m. Dec 10 two big explosions gave signal and small arms fire broke out as all posts in town [eight posts comprising Vietnamese] were attacked simultaneously. Most of these fell in matter of minutes; only one resisted as long as quarter hour and was finished by VM bomb. [In *The Quiet American*, Greene is again spot-on as to the nature of communist infiltration: he speaks of the religious festivals, the long line of the religious procession and 'Nobody noticed the Vietminh agents who joined the procession too and that night . . . the advance agents struck.'[18]] Six Fr-controlled posts across river held out and were not taken. At dawn VM invited populace into streets to look VM troops over and witness they had harmed no (rep no) one nor pillaged civilian property.

VM did not immed retire as first reported but continued firing on Fr-held posts till paratroops arrived about 1500 hours Dec 10, source estimated a battalion of latter dropped nearby from 21 planes. VM then blew bridge on Vac-Gianj River, isolating Fr-held posts from town. At 2100 hours VM left Phat-Diem withdrew to positions unknown to townspeople but not far off. Fr laid down heavy artillery and other fire on Phat-Diem outskirts all night. Townspeople were terrified but next day saw no shelling damage . . . Only casualty was large central market of thatch which took fire. Next day Franco-Viet forces from posts across river moved into town without resistance and reinstalled Vietnamese troops in abandoned posts.

Source confirmed Vietnamese troops in captured posts were turned loose after arms taken . . . VM casualties unknown but one woman saw some 50 their corpses carted away near her river property.[19]

The townspeople were amazed that those officials who had not fled were not rounded up or interrogated. Even known grafters were left in peace; perhaps, some conjectured, because they were Vietminh agents 'who behaved badly in office to destroy confidence in governmental regime'.

Greene entered Phat Diem on 16 December, so we are able, as it were, to parachute ourselves into the area at the same time, since Blancke's account parallels in certain important respects Greene's journal and the account he wrote in *The Quiet American*.

Greene's journal starts cryptically:

Dec. 13. [1951] Thurs.
Woke refreshed by pipes [opium] at 5.30. Taxi 6. Plane 7. Met by Bonneville [Sûreté]. Lunch Ballion. Think Phat Diem was momentarily in Vietminh hands . . . Wrote to [General] Salan asking permission to go to Nam Dinh [this was the only way to approach the war area] & received reply within an hour . . . that lot of P.D. had been blown up & had been in V.M. hands for 2 days . . . Drink before that with Salan's a.d.c. who carefully separated from de Lattre's attitude [de Lattre's turning against Trevor Wilson and Greene].

On 15 December Greene caught a plane to Nam Dinh, where he met Captain Mathei, who invited him to accompany him to Phat Diem, which was then under attack.

December 16 Sunday.
Mathei had to go by plane. A day of waiting for a marine boat . . . Finally got on board at 1 a.m. rather the worst for wear. Boat started at 3 a.m. & arrived at Marine H.Q. about 8 a.m.
First sight of near Phat-Diem very shocking. One quarter opposite the officer's house like a street in London during the blitz. The same sense of desertion, charred beams & plaster. The empty desert of streets. Night of Dec. 9–10 advance agents probably entered at the tail of Fatima procession.

In *The Quiet American*, Greene wrote that the bishop had acquired a devotion to Our Lady of Fatima after a visit to Europe and celebrated her feast day each year with a procession. He also had a grotto built in her honour in the cathedral precincts.

Greene's journal went on to describe the attack on Phat Diem and its aftermath:

Surprise attack 4 a.m. on three sides officers' quarters etc. Radio wrecked & only communication by telephone to Marines. Col. woke by barking dogs. Captain Boissithis had his verandah collapse over his bed. His life saved by Vietnamese soldiers. The [French Foreign] Legion officers driven up to the top floor. Fight on staircase.

Went out and saw parachutists who were sweeping between the canals. The canal thick with bodies. The mother & child dead in a ditch. Afterwards to find [Father] Willich at the Cathedral. The whole of Phat-Diem crowded into & around Cathedral with their furniture, cooking pots. Like a huge market day where everyone was sad. Watched by unsmiling faces. At top of bell tower Willich reading his breviary. Watched planes bombing & bringing supplies. The constant explosion of mortars like bombs in the blitz. Flames burning in Phat-Diem. The burning market, the flames becoming more brilliant as dark fell. Extraordinary that there were only 20 deaths – no officers.

Woken from 2 onwards at intervals by mortar fire. (The silence of VM attack shoulder to shoulder, I'm told) The awful anonymity of the grey faces in the canal.

December 17th Monday.

A frustrating day . . . . The note wrote relieving anybody of responsibility. Arrival of [Colonel] Sizaire with a suggested 24 hours with the Navy & then Phuly to get me out of Phat-Diem. Accompanied by another Col to Marine . . . long wait for landing craft & found myself on way back to Nam Dinh . . . Slept at Sizaire's. This was a genuine mistake. His order to the Navy had been misunderstood.

The following day Greene waited all morning for Colonel Sizaire, only to find that the colonel had 'forgotten' him and gone back to Phat Diem alone. Later that day Greene left by plane for Hanoi. It is likely that the French feared their famous guest would be killed or, if not killed, would write an account unsympathetic to them – the Vietminh had after all won a victory in Phat Diem. That Greene was allowed into Phat Diem is itself surprising for a secret memorandum speaks of two newsmen trying to visit the town: 'They received a gruff answer that roads and transport facilities were so taxed by campaign that it made a trip [to war zone] impossible.'[20] Greene told me in interview he went where no newspaper man was allowed – rebels were all round within 600 yards, with flames, far too many corpses and constant mortar fire.

Comparison of Greene's journal accounts, the historical records and *The Quiet American* shows how much personal experience he used in the novel. Both Fowler and Greene arrived by landing craft, though Greene arrived at 8 a.m. and Fowler before dawn:

> I had come in before dawn in a landing-craft from Nam Dinh. We couldn't land at the naval station because it was cut off by the enemy who completely surrounded the town at a range of six hundred yards, so the boat ran in beside the flaming market. We were an easy target in the light of the flames, but for some reason no one fired. Everything was quiet, except for the flop and crackle of the burning stalls . . .
>
> I had known Phat-Diem well in the days before the attack – the one long narrow street of wooden stalls, cut up every hundred yards by a canal, a church and a bridge . . . In its strange medieval way, under the shadow and protection of the Prince Bishop, it had been the most living town in all the country, and now when I landed and walked up to the officers' quarters, it was the most dead. Rubble and broken glass and the smell of burnt paint and plaster, the long street empty as far as the sight could reach, it reminded me of a London thoroughfare in the early morning after an all-clear: one expected to see a placard, 'Unexploded Bomb'.
>
> The front wall of the officers' house had been blown out and the houses across the street were in ruins.
>
> Coming down the river from Nam Dinh I had learnt from Lieutenant Peraud [presumably Captain Mathei] what had happened . . . [21]

It took four days, with the help of parachutists, to push the enemy back half a mile around the town. The parachutists often failed to net the army, according to American secret reports, because the supposedly trapped Vietminh filtered through their military encirclements by swimming under water in the canals using reed pipes to breathe. 'This was a defeat: no journalists were allowed, no cables could be sent, for the papers must carry only victories.'

What follows in the novel is absolutely true. Greene had first asked General Salan (a personal friend of Trevor Wilson's) for permission to visit Nam Dinh, which was outside the war zone. Although he had encountered some resistance from Colonel Sizaire, this was a great deal less than if he had asked permission from Hanoi.

General Salan would most certainly not have given Greene permission to visit Phat Diem: 'The authorities would have stopped me in Hanoi if they had known of my purpose, but the further you get from headquarters, the looser becomes the control until, when you come within range of the enemy's fire, you are a welcome guest – what has been a menace for the *Etat Major* in Hanoi, a worry for the full colonel in Nam Dinh [Colonel Sizaire], to the lieutenant in the field is a joke, a distraction, a mark of interest from the outer world.'[22]

Having arrived at Phat Diem, Fowler, like Greene, accompanies a small group of legionnaires – Greene joined two actual sorties into one fictional account. Fowler crosses two canals and takes a turning which leads him to a church, where he finds a dozen men sitting on the ground in parachutists' camouflage. He asks to accompany them (in this war a European face proves itself a passport in the field) and gets permission to go with the combatants.

They go behind the church in single file and stop for a moment for the soldier with the walkie-talkie to contact the patrols on either flank. The patrol waits behind the church until it is thirty strong. The lieutenant explains to Fowler that they are headed for a village where 300 Vietminh have been reported, perhaps massing for an attack. They move on in silence:

'All clear,' the lieutenant whispered with a reassuring wave as we started. Forty yards on, another canal, with what was left of a bridge, a single plank without rails, ran across our front. The lieutenant motioned to us to deploy and we squatted down facing the unknown territory ahead, thirty feet off, across the plank. The men looked at the water and then, as though by a word of command, all together, they looked away. For a moment I didn't see what they had seen . . .

The canal was full of bodies: I am reminded now of an Irish stew containing too much meat. The bodies overlapped: one head, seal-grey, and anonymous as a convict with a shaven scalp, stuck up out of the water like a buoy. There was no blood: I suppose it had flowed away a long time ago. I have no idea how many there were: they must have been caught in a cross-fire, trying to get back.[23]

In an article in *Paris Match*, Greene put it differently, suggesting that the bodies were Vietminh, but he could not know for sure: 'It is hard to assess the losses of the Vietminh: here and there the canal was filled with a thick gruel, heads floating above the accumulation of bodies below.'[24]

The carnage is a reminder of the finality and anonymity of death:

I . . . didn't want to be reminded of how little we counted, how quickly, simply and anonymously death came. Even though my reason wanted the state of death, I was afraid like a virgin of the act. I would have liked death to come with due warning, so that I could prepare myself . . . [25]

Fowler is struck by the comradeliness of the patrol's movements, 'as though they were equals engaged on a task they had performed together times out of mind. Nobody waited to be told what to do.' The patrol tries to cross the plank but finds that the weight they are carrying makes it impossible except a few inches at a time. When another man finds a punt, Fowler and five others pile in:

Six of us got in and he began to pole towards the other bank, but we ran on a shoal of bodies and stuck. He pushed away with his pole, sinking it into this human clay, and one body was released and floated up all its length beside the boat like a bather lying in the sun. Then we were free again, and once on the other side we scrambled out, with no backward look . . . we were alive: death had withdrawn . . . *[26]

The group of parachutists are crossing a farmyard when they hear two shots fired to their front. Long minutes afterwards one of the sentries reports and Fowler catches the phrase, 'Deux civils'. They move on to find the two civilians: 'Twenty yards beyond the farm buildings, in a narrow ditch, we came on what we sought: a woman and a small boy. They were very clearly dead: a small neat clot of blood on the woman's forehead, and the child might have been sleeping. He was about six years old and he lay like an embryo in the womb with his little bony knees drawn up. "Mal chance," the lieutenant said. He bent down and turned the child over. He was wearing a holy medal round his neck . . . There was a gnawed piece of loaf under his body. I thought, "I hate war." '[27] In his *Paris Match* article Greene wrote about the same incident: 'the bodies of a woman and her small boy caught in a crossfire between the parachutists and the enemy. This mother and child suddenly lost their anonymity when I realized that

---

* At one point not mentioned in the novel, but in his journal, in the furore Greene accidentally lost contact with the French legionnaires and found himself stumbling between the parachutists and the Vietminh in some fear.

their faith and mine were the same.'[28]

Greene spent the night in the officers' mess, but it brought only cold comfort as he wrote in *Paris Match*: 'the Colonel was awakened at 4.30 in the morning by the explosion of a bazooka shell which blew out the façade of the house where the officers were billeted'.[29] In *The Quiet American* he dealt with the experience more fully: 'Dark had fallen by the time I reached the officers' quarters, where I was spending the night. The temperature was only a degree above zero, and the sole warmth anywhere was in the blazing market. With one wall destroyed by a bazooka and the doors buckled, canvas curtains couldn't shut out the draughts.'[30] 'One slept in one's clothes,' Greene told me, 'in a half-wrecked mess with a revolver on the pillow.' Afterwards he returned to Hanoi, as does Fowler, but not before graciously signing a note to exonerate the French of any responsibility for taking him on patrol.

*

The Vietminh had gained a great propaganda victory in Phat Diem. Reports came to the Americans that whilst the Vietminh were scrupulously 'correct' during their brief occupation of the town, the Franco-Victnamese forces, when they returned, burned, looted and generally made themselves intolerable.[31] So far as Phat Diem was concerned, the Vietminh had won their objective: the supply of arms. By their careful behaviour the Vietminh also did much to offset Catholic aversion to the communists. As for the bishop of Phat Diem, despite his recent assurances to de Lattre, he was soon fulminating against the French once more.[32]

By 4 July 1951 the French army had lost 35,000 soldiers, of whom 800 were St Cyr graduates, the *crème de la crème* of their professional troops. No wonder that leading American diplomat David Bruce felt de Lattre had bitten off more than he could chew. Even de Lattre recognised that had it not been for American military aid the French could not have contained some of the Vietminh attacks in 1951. Inevitably Bruce and the Americans had doubts about de Lattre's timetable. They felt that although de Lattre believed that he could clean the situation up in twelve to eighteen months if there was no invasion, by Chinese volunteers or regulars, this was whistling in the wind. Recruitment to the Vietminh had suffered because of the increase in French military activity, and the Vietminh knew themselves to be in a fierce firefight. However, an order of the day as found on a dead soldier was: 'Whatever may be our losses and however large they may be, we must exterminate the enemy.'[33]

27

A Quiet American

Over there, over there . . .
The Yanks are coming, the Yanks are coming,
The drums rum-tumming everywhere.
— GEORGE M. COHAN

IN *Ways of Escape* Greene stressed that his characters in *The Quiet American* came from his unconscious: 'The exception was Granger, the American newspaper correspondent. The press conference in Hanoi where he figures was recorded almost word for word in my journal at that time.'¹ Greene's journal entries are cryptic but provide him with the material to enlarge upon later: 'Dec. 14 [1951] Friday. Lunch with Kulti, Graham Jenkins & Allen of A.P. Drank all afternoon with W. & A. at Tavern Royale. Then to Press Conf. Goussot's evasive gestures, pretty boy approach. Allen's harsh rudeness. W. & A. complain that their messages are always held up by censor till the Fr. correspondents have put through theirs.' He developed this in *The Quiet American*:

> Granger . . . was there. A young and too beautiful French colonel presided. He spoke in French and a junior officer translated . . .
>
> The interpreter said, 'The colonel tells you that the enemy has suffered a sharp defeat and severe losses — the equivalent of one complete battalion. The last detachment are now making their way back across the Red River on improvised rafts. They are shelled all the time by the Air Force.' The colonel ran his hand through his elegant yellow hair and, flourishing his pointer, danced his way down the long maps on the wall. An American correspondent asked, 'What are the French losses?'

The colonel answers with patient ambiguity.

> 'The colonel says our losses have not been heavy. The exact number is not yet known . . .'

'Is the colonel seriously telling us,' Granger said, 'that he's had time to count the enemy dead and not his own?' . . .

'The colonel says the enemy forces are being overrun. It is possible to count the dead behind the firing-line, but while the battle is still in progress you cannot expect figures from the advancing French units.'

'It's not what *we* expect,' Granger said, 'it's what the *Etat Major* knows or not. Are you seriously telling us that platoons do not report their casualties as they happen by walkie-talkie?'

The colonel's temper was beginning to fray. If only . . . he had . . . told us firmly that he knew the figures but wouldn't say. After all it was their war, not ours. We had no God-given right to information. We didn't have to fight Left-Wing deputies in Paris as well as the troops of Ho Chi Minh between the Red and the Black Rivers. We were not dying.

The colonel suddenly snapped out the information that French casualties had been in a proportion of one to three, then turned his back on us, to stare furiously at his map. These were his men who were dead, his fellow officers, belonging to the same class at St Cyr – not numerals as they were to Granger. Granger said, 'Now we are getting somewhere,' and stared round with oafish triumph at his fellows . . . [2]

The bullying American correspondent existed and was well known in his own right. He was Larry Allen, once called 'the most shot-at United States foreign correspondent'. Like his fictional counterpart, Allen was delighted to touch the colonel (whose name was Gousset) on the raw.

When Greene met him in 1951, Allen was forty-three. He was a hard-drinking, hard-talking, hard-driving person who, in drink, could be outrageous. He had won the Pulitzer Prize for his reporting of the Second World War nine years earlier. He was honoured for his ability to be where the action was thickest (a characteristic he shared with Greene), and for the fullness of his written accounts. During the war in Europe he was often to be found at sea and was on the aircraft carrier *Illustrious* when it miraculously survived a seven-hour attack by fifty Stukas and torpedo planes. As a journalist he was a stormy petrel, always getting into trouble wherever he was. Or so it seemed; but by the time he reached Vietnam he had got through most of his career and was no longer seeking danger. The contrast between his reputation and his current activities was made clear by Greene. Granger himself described how he worked as a correspondent:

They give us a car to Press Camp. They lay on a flight over the two towns they've recaptured and show us the tricolour flying. It might be any darned flag at that height. Then they have a Press Conference and a colonel explains to us what we've been looking at. Then we file our cables with the censor. Then we have drinks . . . Then we catch the plane back.

The American attaché in the novel praises Granger and a famous article of his: 'What did you call it? Highway to Hell – that was worthy of the Pulitzer. You know the story I mean – the man with his head blown off kneeling in the ditch, and the other you saw walking in a dream . . . ' Granger answers:

'Do you think I'd really go near their stinking highway? Stephen Crane could describe a war without seeing one. Why shouldn't I? It's only a damned colonial war anyway. Get me another drink. And then let's go and find a girl. You've got a piece of tail. I want a piece of tail too.'[3]

'By the time he had reached Vietnam,' Seymour Topping sadly related, 'Allen had lost his heroic qualities, had been drinking too much and was rather obese and sloppy in manner, in his personal demeanour and in his work as well. He was not a reliable reporter of the Indo-China experience. He lacked integrity. He looked like a larger version of the film actor Peter Lorre. Big bags under his eyes.'[4]

Howard Simpson's description of Allen, in his account of his own time in Vietnam, coincides with Greene's fictional portrayal: 'While other journalists were rushing from province to province seeking action, Allen put his stories together with a few telephone calls and discreet inquiries over a few drinks at the Hotel Metropole [Hanoi] or the Café Normandie. When he did venture into the field, his sources had already assured him the displacement would be worthwhile.'[5]

We meet the journalist Granger when he arrives, drunkenly and unceremoniously, at the Continental. Fowler, Pyle, and the American economic adviser Joe are drinking on the terrace as two trishaw drivers come pedalling furiously down the rue Catinat and draw up in a photo-finish outside the hotel. In the first is Granger, who begins to argue with his driver about the fare. ' "Here," he said, "take it or leave it," and flung five times the correct amount into the street for the man to stoop for.'[6] Drunk as he is, Granger makes ugly passes at Fowler's girlfriend, the beautiful Phuong. When it becomes apparent that she is unobtainable, the journalist brings the conversation to an end: ' "Break it up," Granger was shouting. "Can't waste the whole night here. I'm off to the House of Five Hundred Girls." '7

It is possible that Allen, Granger's model, did go with Greene to the House of Five Hundred Girls (actually the House of Four Hundred Girls). Greene, writing of a corrupt Minister in the Vietnamese Government, mentioned how, having closed the Grand Monde, the gambling centre of Cholon, he sacrificed a great deal of his income: 'to recoup himself [he] opened a great new brothel like a shabby garden city, little houses set among shrubs and flower beds, neon lighted so that the faces of girls and flowers have the appearance of unhealthy sweets'.8 A number of commentators mention it: it was called Le Parc aux Buffles (pen for buffalo) and so known as the Bull Ring. A better-class brothel for officers was in the same complex.

Four days after his arrival, Greene described his visit in his journal:

Then to other ranks brothel. After hours. The huge courtyard with the girls sitting in groups. The little lighted rooms. Strolled around. Enormous bonhomie. The Fr. police post inside the brothel. The girl stretched across two pairs of knees. The white elegant crossed legs under the light. Price asked 30 pesetas – 8/6d. Then directed to officer's brothel. Much less attractive place, though better girls. To go inside would have made getting out difficult. Price 300 pesetas.9

It must have been one of the world's largest emporia for the sale of flesh – all those cubicles forming a square around the open courtyard. Greene visited it with two companions, one of whom described it later:

It was the soldiers' brothel. The soldiers who went there were like animals and the girls came for money and certainly had to earn it. Outside the iron gate stood a soldier with a sub-machine gun. We tried to persuade Graham not to go in. The guard warned him not to do so either. When Graham went in, the girls pounced on him and Graham came out with his shirt sleeve torn off and his arm bleeding.10

Greene transferred his unexpected manhandling to the loud-mouthed Granger:

When I reached the House of the Five Hundred Girls, Pyle and Granger had gone inside . . .

It was the hour of rest in the immense courtyard which lay open to the sky . . . The curtains were undrawn in the little cubicles around the square – one tired girl lay alone on a bed with her ankles crossed. There was trouble in Cholon and the troops were confined to quarters and there was no work to be done: the Sunday of the body. Only a knot of fighting, scrabbling, shouting girls showed me where custom was still alive . . . I caught sight of Granger flushed and triumphant; it was as though he took this demonstration as a tribute to his manhood. One girl had her arm through Pyle's and was trying to tug him gently out of the ring . . . I . . . called to him, 'Pyle, over here.'

He looked at me over their heads and said 'It's terrible. Terrible.' . . . It occurred to me that he was quite possibly a virgin.

'Come along, Pyle,' I said. 'Leave them to Granger . . .'

I got hold of Pyle's sleeve and dragged him out, with the girl hanging on to his arm like a hooked fish.[11]

What Greene didn't reflect was the sentimental side of Allen: 'I remember sitting in a night club one night and they played "Bewitched, Bothered, and Bewildered",' said Audrey Topping. 'I looked over at Larry and there were big tears rolling down his cheeks. He was rather fat and repulsive.'[12] But there is a scene late in the novel where Granger first criticises the Englishman Fowler: '[Granger] made a feeble attempt to mock my accent. "You all talk like poufs. You're so damned superior. You think you know everything."' This is followed by Granger unburdening himself; he'd had a cable from his wife that his eight-year-old son had polio.[13] Even though he doesn't believe in God, Granger tells Fowler that he'd prayed: 'I thought maybe if God wanted a life he could take mine.'[14]

*

Larry Allen was not the only historical person to find his way into *The Quiet American*. When the quiet American, Pyle, asks Fowler, an old hand in Indo-China, about conditions in Vietnam, Fowler talks about the Cao Dai: 'And . . . there's General Thé. He was Caodaist Chief of Staff, but he's taken to the hills to fight both sides, the French, the Communists',[15] the thought being that the true nationalist must fight both the French and the communists. Caodaist Chief of Staff Colonel Trinh Minh Thé is the bandit in *The Quiet American* with whom Pyle as a CIA agent has secret contacts.

In the cables sent from the American legation in Saigon to

Washington there are a number of references to the original Colonel
Thé (a self-styled general) – Greene seems to have used him in the
novel without adding or subtracting anything. Colonel Thé's mutiny
took place on 7 June 1951, though it wasn't reported in the *New
York Times* until 14 June. Donald Heath, the American ambassador,
reported it to the Secretary of State and mentioned that the
authorities (since there had been no leaks to the press) were keeping
it dark:

> Tran Van An reports that 2500 Caodaists, led by Chief of Staff
> Col. Trinh Minh Thé, left Tay Ninh on June 7 taking with them
> 300 rifles and 60 auto rifles, as protest against policy of Huu Govt.
> These troops, which include 'Best Caodaist cadres' are said to have
> crossed border into Cambodia and are awaiting developments . . .
> Pope Pham Cong Tac is alleged to have stated that, 'Thé shld
> have consulted me before his departure, but had I known why he
> was leaving, I wld not (rpt not) have stopped him.'
>
> If this development, which has not (rpt not) been mentioned in
> local press, is true, Leg[ation] considers it rather alarming. Thé has
> reputation of being real brains of Caodaist mil org and his
> defection, even had it not been accompanied by that org
> followers, wld have been itself an unfortunate incident.[16]

Thé acted swiftly to create uneasiness in the Vietnamese
Government and the French. He sent a letter to all chiefs of
diplomatic and consular missions explaining the reason for his action:
that the French, instead of co-operating with Vietnamese nationalists
to combat communism, were on the contrary trying to divide and
weaken nationalists with a view to returning a colonial regime to
power. The following extract gives some idea of Thé's style:

> We openly proclaim our non-cooperation with the French, who
> have evil intention of enslaving us, and appeal to all peoples of
> French Union who are fighting under the French flag to wake up
> and stop this wanton shedding of blood in our time. We appeal
> earnestly to democratic peoples throughout the world, who are
> fighting to overthrow communism and camouflaged colonialism,
> to help us in this struggle to re-establish peace and human
> justice.[17]

An account of the Cao Dai appears in a secret enclosure sent to
Washington from the legation in Saigon. It assured Washington that
although a number of dissident Caodaists were collaborating with the

insurgent Vietminh, the movement's spiritual leadership and its numerous communities supported the present political arrangement in the country:

> The Cao Dai Pope at Tay Ninh, known as the 'Radiant Sun of the South' is perhaps the most significant spiritual leader of the movement today . . . The Tay Ninh organization which has cooperated closely with the present Government maintains the most important Cao Dai armed forces, numbering about 15,000 troops in varying stages of training and equipment.[18]

The account goes on to say that the religious principle of Caodaism attempted to synthesise the world's great religions: its ethical principles were largely Confucian, its inspiration spiritualist, its ritual Buddhist, its hierarchic organisation Catholic. Greene made a number of visits to the Cao Dai and found them, of all of France's allies, the most amazing:

> At the entrance to the fantastic, technicolour cathedral are hung the portraits of three minor saints of the Caodaist religion: Dr Sun Yat Sen, Trang Trinh, a primitive Vietnamese poet, and Victor Hugo, attired in the uniform of a member of the Academie Française with a halo round his tricorn hat. In the nave of the cathedral, in the full Asiatic splendour of a Walt Disney fantasy, pastel dragons coil about the columns and pulpit; from every stained-glass window a great eye of God follows one, an enormous serpent forms the papal throne and high up under the arches are the effigies of three major saints: Buddha, Confucius, and Christ displaying his Sacred Heart.
>
> The saints, Victor Hugo in particular, still address the faithful through the medium of a pencil and a basket covered by a kind of movable ouija board . . . [19]

Greene came away convinced this 'world' religion was bogus (he puts this in *The Quiet American*), and with the image of a chain-smoking pope discoursing hour after hour on Atlantis and the common origin of all religions. Founded in 1926, the Cao Dai were pacifist, yet they supported an army of 20,000 men, using a primitive arsenal to guard against an eventual stoppage of French arms – mortars fabricated from old exhaust pipes.

The Caodaists made no attempt to recapture Colonel Thé, although according to *The Quiet American* he had kidnapped a cardinal. However, it was rumoured that he had done this with the pope's connivance. Greene was reflecting the rumours about Thé circulating during 1951. On Greene's last visit to Tay Ninh in 1954, he was told secretly that a meeting with Colonel Thé could be arranged in the Holy See itself. As Greene said, 'The eye of God watched the Caodaists from every window, but sharp human eyes were also very much required.'[20] He refused to meet Colonel Thé, although Thé was the master-mind behind ruthless and little justified events in Saigon, which were duplicated in the novel.

Thé had started life as a ferryman. He hated graft, but nevertheless had a capacity for ruthless action, coupled with an uncontrolled hysteria. Well organised, he set himself up as the leader of the self-styled National Resistance Front.[21] The Americans were in contact with him, which is the source for Greene's dislike of the Americans in Vietnam, symbolised by Pyle.

Through a nephew, the political delegate Le Van Hoach, Colonel Thé made a request for US aid for medicines under the economic aid programme.[22] But the US ambassador, Donald Heath, strongly pro-French, added to one telegram: 'Of course I do not (rpt not) believe we can or shld undertake any policy excursion of this sort apart from Vets. govt. and French command . . ,'

Thé was a difficult enemy to have and troubled even de Lattre. He interested Greene critically because his equal hatred of the French *and* the communists provided a catalysing agent, in *The Quiet American*. Without him there would be no tragedy.[23]

*

Where were the central figures in *The Quiet American* drawn from: Fowler, the cynical English newspaper reporter, Phuong, the Vietnamese girl, and Pyle, the quiet American (as opposed to Granger, the ugly American)? Greene was quite certain about their origin: 'So the subject of *The Quiet American* came to me, during that talk of a "third force" on the road through the delta and my characters quickly followed, all but one of them [Granger] from the unconscious.'[24]

While he was writing *The Quiet American*, Greene was still fighting for Catherine, and some of his problems between Vivien, Catherine and himself are reflected in the novel. While in Hong Kong, Greene received a letter from Vivien's friend Stella Weaver which deeply disturbed him. Stella was very concerned because on the night of Saturday, 22 December 1951 a man had broken into Vivien's house and attacked her in the bathroom.

He probably thought she was alone in the house as she very often is. But Lucy and Francis, having arrived the day before, were there. Lucy was in bed and asleep. Wakened by Vivien's screams, she rushed out of her room into the bathroom, seized hold of the man, and he fled.[25]

Vivien was unharmed except for a bruise and a cut on the lip. She was, however, 'terribly shaken and shocked and frightened', and still very upset. The Weavers had 'been anxious about her for some time. She is desperately unhappy and lonely.'[26]

On receipt of Stella's letter, Greene wrote at once to Catherine on 16 January 1952:

I've written and telegraphed to Vivien, but what can I do? I've told her that I'll sell their house and get her a larger flat wherever she likes, and I've told her frankly that it's no good my saying that I'll come back and stay with her, because I'm still in love with another woman and I could never stay the course. I feel desperate and hopeless, but not so depressed and hopeless as poor Vivien. I do seem to muck up everyone I love.

In a postscript comes a plaintive cry of his need for Catherine and for the wretched (but inevitable) way he had treated Vivien:

O, how I'm in need of your voice. I can't again go through another six months like this. And then, I think, poor Vivien has had four years. It's her *hope* that makes her miserable. If only we could have been like the other lovers who go away together and marry again, she would have been better off. Perhaps if I'd let her divorce me she'd been better off.

In *The Quiet American* Fowler is somewhat desperate because his girlfriend Phuong is being courted openly by the American Pyle. Fowler writes to his wife Helen in England asking for a divorce, and because he had always been truthful to her he does not try to put himself in the best light. This was extraordinarily true of Greene: it was the truth that mattered, not whether the events cast him in a good light – they often didn't.

The letter Greene wrote to Vivien has now disappeared, but it seems likely that Fowler's letter to Helen is based on it. As he indicated to Catherine, it was full of sympathy, but without any hope of a reconciliation. In order further to diminish that hope, he may have suggested they should at last divorce – certainly it was on his mind ('Perhaps if I'd let her divorce me . . . '). His thinking must have been that his long affair was at a dead end, and that these terrible six-month separations (initiated by Catherine) made any future life with her doubtful. Perhaps he now felt that a divorce would clear the air – at least he would not then be guilty of continuous adultery.

Fowler's letter to Helen in *The Quiet American* seems to invoke from her the decision he does not want – for Helen to say *no* to him in spite of the fact that he greatly fears the loss of Phuong. The letter is a revelation of Greene's character as well as Fowler's. How easily Greene could have had Fowler put the right gloss upon his activities in the Far East, but Fowler does not, as Greene also would not have done:

Dear Helen, I am coming back to England to take a job of foreign editor. You can imagine I am not very happy about it. England is to me the scene of my failure. I had intended our marriage to last . . . To this day I'm not certain what went wrong (I know we both tried), but I think it was my temper. I know how cruel and bad my temper can be . . . You have been very generous to me, and you have never reproached me once since our separation. Would you be even more generous? I know that before we married you warned me there could never be a divorce. I accepted the risk and I've nothing to complain of. At the same time I'm asking for one now.

. . . I could wrap this up and make it sound more honourable and more dignified by pretending it was for someone else's sake. But it isn't, and we always used to tell each other the truth. It's for my sake and only mine. I love someone very much . . . but I know I'm not essential to her [how true this seemed to be in Catherine's case] . . . It's stupid of me to tell you this. I'm putting a reply into your mouth. But because I've been truthful so far, perhaps you'll believe me when I tell you that to lose her will be, for me, the beginning of death.[27]

I asked Greene if he had asked his wife for a divorce some years after his separation. He told me that he had. When I asked Vivien, she admitted he had but thought it was no more than a telephone conversation. Greene had a passion for getting the details of any event correct, so it seems likely that he wrote to Vivien about it just as Fowler wrote to Helen. If Greene did write to Vivien she would have responded by letter, as is her practice. Helen's response to Fowler's letter seems to be the kind of letter Vivien could have written. Vivien was greatly hurt by losing her husband to another woman and her wound seems never to have healed entirely. Helen's letter is subtle yet pained:

> I am not surprised to get your letter and to know that you were not alone. You are not a man, are you? to remain alone for very long. You pick up women like your coat picks up dust. Perhaps I would feel more sympathy with your case if I didn't feel that you would find consolation very easily when you return to London. I don't suppose you'll believe me, but what gives me pause and prevents me cabling you a simple No is the thought of the poor girl. We are apt to be more involved than you are.[28]

In the novel, Greene writes of Helen's 'sexual wounds . . . remaining' over the years. Fowler, through not choosing his words with skill, has set them bleeding again and so does not blame her for seeking out his scars in return. The character of Anne referred to below parallels Catherine, and the enforced six-month separation from Catherine (assuming Vivien commented upon it) might have looked as if he had left her:

> I've always believed you loved Anne more than the rest of us until you packed up and went. Now you seem to be planning to leave another woman because I can tell from your letter that you don't really expect a 'favourable' reply . . . What would you do if I cabled 'Yes'? Would you actually marry her? (I have to write 'her' – you don't tell me her name.) Perhaps you would. I suppose like the rest of us you are getting old and don't like living alone. I feel very lonely myself sometimes. I gather Anne has found another companion . . . But you left her in time.[29]

Helen points out how difficult it would be for Phuong to live in London and then writes: 'Marriage doesn't prevent you leaving a woman . . . It only delays the process.' Greene comments through Fowler:

> Her pain struck at my pain: we were back at the old routine of hurting each other. If only it were possible to love without injury – fidelity isn't enough. I had been faithful to Anne and yet I had injured her. The hurt is in the act of possession: we are too small in mind and body to possess another person without pride or to be possessed without humiliation. In a way I was glad that my wife had struck out at me again – I had forgotten her pain for too long, and this was the only kind of recompense I could give her.

Unfortunately the innocent are always involved in any conflict. Always, everywhere, there is some voice crying from a tower.[30]

Helen questions whether going against her deepest convictions and saying yes would be good for Fowler and then sinks him with unanswerable logic: 'You say it will be the end of life to lose this girl. Once you used exactly that phrase to me – I could show you the letter, I have it still.'[31] Helen's final answer to Fowler's request is what Vivien's rebuttal might have been, and the passage echoes Vivien's faith as a Catholic:

You say that we've always tried to tell the truth to each other, but, Thomas, your truth is always so temporary. What's the good of arguing with you, or trying to make you see reason? It's easier to act as my faith tells me to act . . . and simply to write: I don't believe in divorce: my religion forbids it, and so the answer, Thomas, is no.

*

Was there a source for Phuong herself? Greene borrowed her house and name from the girlfriend of René Berval (editor of *France-Asie* in Saigon) and the flat they lived in (actually 104 rue Catinat). In his dedication to René and Phuong, Greene wrote: 'I have quite shamelessly borrowed the location of your flat to house one of my characters, and your name, Phuong, for the convenience of readers because it is simple, beautiful and easy to pronounce.' But Phuong, who is such a convincing presence in the novel, had a more real existence than the dedication implies.

When I asked Greene whether Phuong 'Berval' was the basis for the beautiful Phuong in the novel, he replied:

Phuong [Berval] was not really very attractive to my mind and the girl is meant to be attractive in the book. I mean René's girlfriend was much less attractive than most Vietnamese girls.

During a previous interview he had told me about two sisters who seemed reminiscent of the two sisters in the novel, one of whom is Phuong:

Oh, the mistress of the manager of the Majestic offering her younger sister. Yes. She was *very* attractive, the younger sister. I've got a photograph of her in the party I went to almost as soon as I arrived, the first in the Chinese quarter in 1951 . . . There's a bit of Chinese blood in her which goes quite nicely because the Chinese give a little bit of weight to the body as it were. On the other hand they don't like the Chinese suffer from duck's disease, you know, a bottom that falls down near the ground. And it's quite a good mixture. But her elder sister was becoming almost ugly . . . the younger one might have become so in time.[32]

The manager of the Majestic, who was also the owner, was a Corsican called Mathieu Franchini. He was very influential in Saigon, and had married into a Vietnamese family. Franchini was a 'fixer' and must have been a source of information for Greene. Greene's diaries prove that they often drank together at both the Continental Palace and the Majestic.

In a sense Greene had no luck with the original for 'Phuong'; for one thing he met her on the last full day of his first visit to Saigon. On Sunday, 4 February 1951 he was very tired and missed Mass. He had coffee with Elaine, 'wife of absent journalist' (who was to become Hugh Greene's wife), met the Toppings, had dry martinis with them and took them to lunch at the Vieux Moulin. After a siesta, he went to 'terrible reception by Alliance Française'. 'Anna, the ugly Chinese journalist', he writes in his journal, 'had brought her beautiful sister, but hemmed in with Lycée teachers.'[33] This sister became Phuong in *The Quiet American*.

He had seen her eight days earlier. He wrote in his journal: 'Intended to have early night but in Majestic bar picked up by manager to join his party – Chinese woman journalist, French doctor & pretty Ammanite wife. To Grand Monde. Journalist's two sisters – one with Thailand chargé d'affaires & one ravingly beautiful. V. disturbing.'[34]

René Berval, who knew the Mathieu sisters, helped Greene to meet them again. Back in Europe, Greene wrote to René on 4 May, wanting to know when the next main offensive by the Vietminh would take place so that his return could coincide with it. He ended his letter with a reference to the sisters: 'Do give my love to Anna and say that I am looking forward to seeing her and her sister again.'

Nothing happened during his second visit to Saigon, but on his third he commented in his journal:

Jan. 21. Monday. [1952]
Drink with René Berval. Lunch with Graham Jenkins . . . Saw Pierre & Moret [French Sûreté, the model for the Pascal-reading policeman Vigot in *The Quiet American*]. Dinner with Mathieus. Anna & the beautiful sister who turns out to be the air hostess.

Anna's vigilant eye on matrimony. 7 bicycle grenades today in the town.

In the novel Phuong's sister, Miss Hei, tries to ensnare Pyle into marriage with Phuong: 'I had seen her first, dancing past my table at the Grand Monde in a white ball-dress, eighteen years old, watched by an elder sister who had been determined on a good European marriage.' Meeting the sister for the first time, Pyle says of Phuong:

'She is very pretty sister . . . '
'She is the most beautiful girl in Saigon,' Miss Hei said, as though correcting him.[35]

Pyle answers that he can well believe it and Fowler says, 'It's time we ordered dinner. Even the most beautiful girl in Saigon must eat.'[36]
Greene left a record of meeting 'the most beautiful girl in Saigon'. In a letter dated 8 November to his mother, the year not mentioned, but most probably 1951, he wrote:

I spent three rather social but nice days [in Saigon] but then flew up here [Hanoi]. It's a very tiring flight of about four hours. I had to be at the airport at 5 a.m. very hot & pouring with sweat (which was sad because a very pretty little half caste Air France girl came & sat beside me at the bar).[37]

28

Innocence Abroad

To live in hearts we leave behind
is not to die.

— THOMAS CAMPBELL

'INNOCENCE', says Fowler, speaking of Pyle, 'is like a dumb leper who has lost his bell, wandering the world meaning no harm.' Alden Pyle, the very honest American, has fallen in love with Fowler's girl, but in his good-mannered way feels he must tell Fowler before approaching her. Pyle travels alone, taking the risk of being shot at by a naval patrol or a French plane or having his throat cut by the Vietminh — and all because honour compels him to tell Fowler that he's in love with his girlfriend. He finds Fowler in the middle of the war at Phat Diem, spending the night at the French officers' mess. Having told him, Pyle asks his advice about Phuong, but misunderstands Fowler's nature as he misunderstands Phuong's:

'I wouldn't trust my advice if I were you. I'm biased. I want to keep her.'

'Oh, but I know you're straight, absolutely straight, and we both have her interests at heart.'

Suddenly I couldn't bear his boyishness any more. I said, 'I don't care that for her interests. You can have her interest. I only want her body. I want her in bed with me. I'd rather ruin her and sleep with her than, than . . . look after her damned interests.'

He said, 'Oh,' in a weak voice, in the dark.

I went on, 'If it's only her interest you care about, for God's sake leave Phuong alone. Like any other woman she'd rather have a good . . . ' The crash of a mortar saved Boston ears from the Anglo-Saxon word.[1]

There is no evidence in his journals that during his numerous visits to Vietnam Greene met anyone remotely like Pyle, though he met most of the Americans in Saigon – in 1951 there were very few of them. He built Pyle's character up from a number of diverse elements.

When Greene first went to Saigon he heard of a British air attaché who was living with a Vietnamese girl in Saigon, made her pregnant and then was called back home. Hearsay has it that the attaché went home to his wife and children and paid his pregnant girlfriend 300 dollars before leaving. There is a passage in the novel where Pyle becomes angry over Fowler's 'dirty cracks' and asks: 'What can you offer her? . . . A couple of hundred dollars when you leave for England, or will you pass her on with the furniture?'[2] A young American then working in the American aid mission called Jim Flood decided (with a Pyle-like sense of injustice) that the air attaché's offer was not enough; the Vietnamese girl needed protection, so he married her in Saigon. Tom Peck, in the consular passport department, was Flood's best man at the wedding. Ambassador Donald Heath came to the reception for Flood (a junior member of his staff) and his bride. The story of Jim Flood's marriage was the gossip of the rue Catinat and Greene had heard it.

When *The Quiet American* was reviewed in the *New Yorker* on 7 April 1956 (the novel was published in December 1955 in England and March 1956 in America) the journalist A. J. Liebling masked his anger at Greene's portrayal of America under a contemptuous air. Liebling did however make an interesting point. Far from granting that Pyle was an American, his view was that Pyle was a perfect specimen of a Frenchman's idea of an Englishman – 'a naïve chap who speaks bad French, eats tasteless food and is only accidentally and episodically heterosexual', who is earnest in an obtuse way and physically brave through lack of imagination: 'Pyle's choice of idiom convinced me that he is a thinly disguised Englishman.'

This looks like clever bantering, but it may well be that Liebling had accidentally hit on some of the truth. To begin with Pyle is a little like Greene as a young boy, naïve, unmalicious, shy, a virgin. (He is also a caricature of Greene when he first fell in love.) Greene's earlier innocence is being criticised by the older, more experienced Greene, seeing himself as Pyle sees Fowler – 'a man of middle age with eyes a little bloodshot, beginning to put on weight . . . less noisy than Granger perhaps but more cynical, less innocent'. The notion of creating a character who was fundamentally naïve would also have appealed to Greene because he saw a way of symbolising a too-young nation, ignorant of colonial responsibility and hating colonies because, long ago, it had been one.

Pyle looks upon Phuong as a perfect lady, not as a taxi girl now living with an older Englishman with little chance of marriage. It is Pyle, watching a troupe of female impersonators perform ('in low-cut evening dresses, with false jewellery and false breasts and husky voices, they appeared at least as desirable as most of the European women in Saigon'), who is embarrassed: 'I was astonished by the sudden violence of Pyle's protest. "Fowler," he said, "Let's go. We've had enough, haven't we? This isn't a bit suitable for her." '[3]

Fowler asks Pyle when he fell in love with Phuong and he admits that it was while he was dancing with her at the Chalet, with Fowler watching: 'it was seeing all those girls in that house [of prostitution]. They were so pretty. Why, she might have been one of them. I wanted to protect her.'[4] When Fowler lies to Pyle, saying that rumours that he's being called back to London for a promotion are untrue, Pyle again speaks like an Englishman or rather like an English schoolboy: 'You'd play straight with me, Thomas, wouldn't you?' Fowler examines Pyle's question: 'Are you playing straight?' and says that it belongs to a psychological world of great simplicity, 'where you talked of Democracy and Honor without the u as it's spelt on old tombstones, and you meant what your father meant by the same words'.[5] Of course, and why not? Pyle is straight out of a good quality public school – in essence he *is* English.

It may well be that Greene had an actual Englishman in mind, at least in the initial stages of creating Pyle's character. He had met an Englishman in Malacca who was a good but naïve man, and who had, as Pyle has, an obsession with a taxi dancer. He died because he completely misjudged his girlfriend's character.

In Malacca, on 10 December 1950, a month before his first visit to Saigon, Greene went to the City Park Dance Hall where there were attractive Chinese taxi dancers. Here he met a young Englishman called Jollye (written in his journal as Jolly). Greene described Jollye as a young man 'who was crackers about Macao, dreamed of going back and living there (the earthly paradise), could talk of nothing else. We met in the City Park Dance place and he had a Chinese girl with him whom he fondly believed was a virgin, "see her home every night: can't touch her". He had extraordinary clear, wild blue eyes and loved the Chinese.'[6] When Greene returned to Malacca with his brother Hugh for Christmas, he went back to the same dance hall and saw Jollye's girl: 'she was taxiing [being hired out for dancing] and I was afraid of seeing him because I couldn't remember his name for introductions. I described him to our companion [Cunningham-Brown, who met Greene at the Residency in Malacca, and later told me that Greene 'was burnt up inside by Catholicism, fighting against his desires which he failed to

understand']. He said, "Oh, that was Jolly." Jolly I know as the name
of a young man who was shot a week ago. I had noticed his tiny
absurd car and had said to Noel Ross, "That would be good for an
ambush," but they put five bullets in him very accurately in spite of
the tiny car. It was oddly sad being afraid to meet him and seeing his
"virginal" Chinese girl taxiing and then finding he wasn't here or
back in Macao or anywhere at all. He was a young Resettlement
Officer. He had told his Chinese taxi girl where he was going next
day and the information was passed down the line to the terrorists.'
So Jollye died and Pyle died, each killed by a communist assassin:
Jollye was reported by his girlfriend to the communists; Pyle by his
friend Fowler.

Jollye's British public school character remains in Pyle – when did
an American, even from Boston, speak the following lines? Fowler
and Pyle are in the officers' quarters at Phat Diem and Pyle has just
declared to Fowler that he's fallen in love with Phuong:

> He looked up from his bootlaces in an agony of embarrassment. 'I
> had to tell you – I've fallen in love with Phuong.'
> I laughed. I couldn't help it. He was so unexpected and serious.
> I said, 'Couldn't you have waited till I go back? I shall be in
> Saigon next week.'
> 'You might have been killed,' he said. 'It wouldn't have been
> honourable. And then I don't know if I could have stayed away
> from Phuong all that time.'
> 'You mean you *have* stayed away?'
> 'Of course. You don't think I'll *tell* her without you knowing?'[7]

Pyle is abiding by a well-established British code: you have to be fair;
you cannot in love or war take unfair advantage of your opponent.
Not until Fowler breaks the recognised code between them by lying
to Pyle – saying his English wife will divorce him, thus allowing him
to marry Phuong – does Pyle fight aggressively for Phuong's hand in
marriage.

Everything about Pyle suggests the product of a good English
background – good family, good training, the true type of English
gentleman. He is complicated by his sense of fair play, by his
sensitivity and the idealism of extreme youth; he is really an
imperishable British product. He tries on the personal plane to act
honourably, to treat friendship as important and to save a friend's life
when the occasion demands. How far Fowler has fallen from these
standards of gentlemanly behaviour becomes clear when, after Pyle
has saved his life, he responds: 'If it had been you, I'd have left you.'[8]

Another candidate as source for Pyle is an American, Colonel Edward Lansdale, who had at that time a tremendous reputation for his work in Intelligence. Moreover, he himself thought that Greene had used his background to create Pyle. It's rare to find a book on Vietnam which doesn't automatically accept that Greene used Lansdale as his source, the latest to do so being Howard Simpson's *Tiger in the Barbed Wire*: 'Lansdale, who became the model for the lead character in Graham Greene's *The Quiet American*'.[9] Lansdale's biographer, Cecil Currey, had no doubts that Lansdale was Greene's source:

One of [*The Quiet American*'s] two focal characters was Alden Pyle, patterned after Lansdale and other Americans Greene observed in Vietnam, and thus Greene became the first author to caricature Lansdale's real-life exploits. Greene did not like what he knew of them and he made this fact very clear in this text. He described Pyle as a young man with . . . a crewcut, and an earnest, 'unused' face. Pyle had been sent to Vietnam by his government, ostensibly as a member of the 'American Economic Mission,' but that assignment was only a cover for his real role as a CIA agent. His orders called for him to create a political force in Vietnam that could resist a communist takeover after the French departed. His duties included funneling money and explosives to a warlord general.[10]

Currey then quotes Lansdale's recollection of the one occasion he and Greene crossed paths. It was 1954 and Lansdale had been invited to dine at the Continental Palace hotel with Peg and Tillman Durdin, a husband-and-wife team of American correspondents who had just returned from an interview with Ho Chi Minh (which Lansdale had helped to prepare them for).

When Lansdale arrived, he saw a large group of French officers at the sidewalk terrace and Greene sitting with them. Later, as he and the Durdins were leaving, Greene said something in French to his companions and the men began booing Lansdale. The Durdins knew Greene, and Peg stuck out her tongue at him, turned and gave Lansdale a hug and a kiss, and said, 'But we love him!' For some reason Greene banged the table at which he sat. Lansdale smirked and thought, 'I'm going to get written up some place as a dirty dog.' He later commented, 'I had the feeling that Greene was anti-American.' The rancorous feeling between the two men was mutual. Greene called the widespread notion that Lansdale provided the basic model for Pyle a 'myth' and observed that he 'never had the misfortune to meet' Lansdale, whom he 'would never have chosen . . . to represent the danger of innocence'.[11]

'Graham Greene once told someone', Lansdale commented, 'that he definitely did not have me in mind when he created the character Alden Pyle. I sure hope not . . . On the other hand, Pyle was close to Trinh Minh Thé, the guerrilla leader, and also had a dog who went with him everywhere – and I was the only American close to Trinh Minh Thé and my poodle Pierre went everywhere with me.'[12]

Lansdale was certainly one of America's best-known CIA operatives, not in itself a quality to be praised in a spy, but by the time Greene and he encountered one another, Greene had almost completed *The Quiet American*. Lansdale went to Vietnam after the fall of Dien Bien Phu in May 1954 and Greene began writing *The Quiet American* as early as March 1952, completing it in June 1955. The first draft was completed earlier however, which precludes the possibility of Lansdale influencing the novel. As for Lansdale's dog, which he thought Greene had used, the one Greene had in mind was René Berval's big black dog.

The idea for *The Quiet American* came to Greene when driving back to Saigon after spending the night with Colonel Leroy, who was in charge of Bentre province:

Less than a year ago [Greene wrote in 1952] when we had toured together [Leroy's] watery kingdom, it was in an armoured boat with guns trained on the bank, but now as night fell we moved gently along the rivers in an unarmed barge furnished, not with guns, but with gramophones and dancing girls. [Leroy] had built at Bentre a lake with a pagoda in imitation of one at Hanoi, the night was full of strange cries from the zoo he had started for his people, and we dined on the island in the lake and the colonel poured brandy down the throats of the girls to make the party go and played the Harry Lime theme of *The Third Man* on a gramophone in my honour.

I shared a room that night with an American attached to an economic aid mission – the members were assumed by the French, probably correctly, to belong to the CIA. My companion bore no resemblance at all to Pyle, the quiet American of my story – he was a man of greater intelligence and of less innocence, but he lectured me all the long drive back to Saigon on the necessity of finding a 'third force in Vietnam'. I had never before come so close to *the great American dream* which was to bedevil affairs in the East as it was to do in Algeria.[13]

When Pyle quotes a journalist called York Harding – 'York wrote that what the East needed was a Third Force' – he seems naïve but in fact was voicing an underlying facet of American policy. The Americans were looking for an incorruptible, purely nationalist Vietnamese leader who could unite the Vietnamese people and provide an alternative to the communist Vietminh:

'I heard [Pyle] talking the other day at a party the Legation was giving to visiting Congressmen . . .

'He was talking about the old colonial powers – England and France, and how you two couldn't expect to win the confidence of the Asiatics. That was where America came in now with clean hands . . .

'Then someone asked him some stock question about the chances of the Government here ever beating the Vietminh and he said a Third Force could do it. There was always a Third Force to be found free from Communism and the taint of colonialism – national democracy he called it; you only had to find a leader and keep him safe from the old colonial powers.'[14]

There is a real possibility that what the unnamed American said on the long drive back to Saigon is reflected in this paragraph, but Greene must have heard the argument from a number of sources. The date of this visit to Bentre excludes the possibility that the source was Colonel Lansdale.

In interviewing various consular officials and CIA agents in Washington and elsewhere who operated in Vietnam during Greene's years there, I asked if they had visited Colonel Leroy in Bentre. Those who had were possible candidates for the original of Pyle, or at least for his views. Some half a dozen had visited Bentre, some as Colonel Leroy's guests – but they had not been there with Greene and had not given him a taste on the way back to Saigon of the 'American Dream'.

Greene had a small snapshot in his possession and on the reverse he had identified the people in it. Leroy was in the middle, and on his left was someone Greene identified as Q.A. In interview Greene could remember no more about him than he'd written in *Ways of Escape* – even his name escaped him but he thought it was Teutonic.

Various US legation people looked at the photograph and finally Paul Springer recognised Q.A. as Leo Hochstetter. Hochstetter had died, but his wife was alive; a letter also exists which Greene wrote to Hochstetter at the American legation in Saigon, dated 17 April 1952:

My dear Leo, It may amuse you to have this souvenir of our day and night with Colonel LeRoy and perhaps you would pass on one of the two copies to him. I certainly look as if I am going through a melancholy mood. I often look back with nostalgia to Saigon and wish an opportunity would arise of revisiting the place.

Hochstetter worked under Robert Blum, head of an economic aid mission and a friend of Edmund Gullion. They both had strong views on the need for a third force, views which Hochstetter supported. 'Leo was colourful, loquacious,' said Tom Peck, 'with opinions on everything that came along . . . Everyone else in ECA [the mission] in Vietnam seemed to have a specialty that bore directly on Vietnam's economic needs that the US might be able to help with. But Leo had no such qualifications that I can recall. My guess is that he wanted to do something to help his country and got the job through political pull of some kind.'[15] Paul Springer recalled that Hochstetter was number two in the economic aid mission. He was short and pudgy and of dissolute appearance: 'street smart' defined him best. He was loquacious and irreverent.[16] John Getz agreed that Hochstetter 'talked constantly, and loved to play the clown at a party, singing comic songs and delivering witty lines that *he* appreciated more than anyone else. He was public affairs director for the economic aid mission.'[17]

Mrs Hochstetter said that her husband liked Greene:

coming home from seeing Colonel Leroy apparently they'd been insulting each other all the way back in the car. They were both suffering from horrible hangovers and he called Leo 'Cock' and Leo described him as half-cocked and full of unanswered questions. That Greene was doing great harm by being a communist fellow-traveller. But they ended up a mutual admiration society, more or less.[18]

There were fundamental differences between Pyle and Leo Hochstetter. Pyle was gentle, modest and quiet, Hochstetter was powerfully gregarious; by using the talkative, versatile Leo Hochstetter as one source for Pyle, with his simplistic moral standards, Greene was probably playing a private practical joke. However, only he knew who his source was and only he could appreciate the joke, but that would be enough for him.

Pyle often speaks with a naïveté which is not justified, but Greene is stressing not only Pyle's inexperience in Indo-China but the dangers of innocence in a complex and difficult society like Vietnam.

In 1951 there were no more than thirty-eight Americans in the ECA and in the MAAG (the military aid organisation), but over the years the numbers increased greatly. And though there were intelligent operatives, they were young and without question profoundly exhilarated by the fact that they were in Indo-China and standing up to communism. It was a heady time for them all.

Nancy Baker, the young wife of Charles Baker, who was among other things consular security officer at the legation in Saigon, gives an authentic description of how it was for those American consular and aid officers arriving in Saigon for the first time – for what Pyle would have felt:

> The town is gradually being taken over by the Americans, what with visiting military missions, medical missions, etc. There is absolutely no more room at the [Continental Palace] hotel to take care of a stray pigeon. And mostly before lunch or before dinner, you'll find a good percentage interspersed in the crowd at the hotel's café and sidewalk café.[19]

> Saigon never ceases to amaze us with its paved streets lined with trees, its water system, its substantial-looking buildings and villas, its monstrous cathedral, its parks . . . That they have not yet disintegrated into dust when each step in the process of doing anything around here is done so slipshod, so carelessly, is a monument to the French and their blood, sweat, tears, and lost tempers. But they have to leave and in the meantime they hate us as economic imperialists who are going to stab them in the back by feathering our nests when they get out. While, surprisingly, the Vietnamese have received us most cordially but with restraint and wonder. They respect power and money, and the US has both, and they are willing to believe in the good will of the US, but not quite.[20]

By linking the young naïve Pyle to the murderous activities of Colonel Thé, Greene could attack American naïveté in dealing with a bandit whom they saw as a third force leader. In his *New Yorker* review of *The Quiet American*, A. J. Liebling charged that Greene 'apparently resented passing on world leadership to the Americans'. The ill will was understandable. It was 'part of the ritual of handing over', but there was a difference 'between calling your over-successful offshoot a silly ass and accusing him of murder'. Is it Liebling who is being naïve here?

29

Death in rue Catinat

Go and try to disprove death,
death will disprove you.
— TURGENEV

ON 5 January 1952 the *New York Times* reported that General de
Lattre had been operated on in Paris: 'Neither the nature of his
illness nor of the operation has been disclosed.' By 11 January the
heroic soldier was dead; it was a time of mourning in Vietnam, as a
letter sent home by Nancy Baker shows:

> For about 4 weeks the latter part of January and the first of
> February, the local French and Vietnamese officials and the
> Diplomatic Corps were in mourning for the death of de Lattre.
> Not that I was in agreement for that long length of time of
> mourning, we still had a very enjoyable time staying home in the
> evenings, reading, or have small dinners.[1]

With de Lattre gone, hope died that the French could win the war
in Vietnam. The United States and France held opposed views on
the country's future, and if the US State Department did not press
France hard this was only because it felt that France might throw in
the towel, to stem the loss of its best sons. There were real divisions
in the American legation in Saigon also. On the one hand
Ambassador Heath was a genuine supporter of the French leadership
symbolised by de Lattre. Edmund Gullion thought the French were
wrong and that they were not serious about independence. He and
Robert Blum were strongly against the survival of colonialism and in
favour of building up a nationalist army. They both advocated ways
of winning the war which the French authorities found
unacceptable.
Blum, like Pyle in *The Quiet American*, was looking for a third

force to capture the nationalist interest of the Vietnamese people. He felt that only if the Vietnamese were fighting for democracy and independence would they begin to take a powerful personal interest in defeating the communist Vietminh. Without a third force, he and Gullion both believed the French could not succeed. As Blum said:

> We wanted to strengthen the ability of the French to protect the area against Communist infiltration and invasion, and we wanted to capture the nationalist movement from the Communists by encouraging the national aspirations of the local populations and increasing popular support of their governments. We knew that the French were unpopular, that the war that had been going on since 1946 was not only a nationalist revolt against them but was an example of the awakening self-consciousness of the peoples of Asia who were trying to break loose from domination by the Western world.[2]

Blum wanted the United States to be looked upon as a friend to a new nation, not as a supporter of colonialism (that was an anathema to the Americans).

After visiting Vietnam in 1951, Congressman John F. Kennedy went home to preach the gospel of those forward-looking Americans in the legation. Speaking of how America had allied itself to the desperate effort of the French regime to hang on to the remnants of an empire, Kennedy concluded: 'the French cannot succeed in Indochina without giving concessions necessary to make the native army a reliable and crusading force.'[3] Emperor Bao Dai feared that if the Vietnamese army were expanded into a nationalist army, it might defect *en masse* to the Vietminh. His tragedy was that he was expressing a truth that initially looked like cynicism.

Because Bao Dai proved so disappointing the Americans felt they had to find someone who represented the new nationalism, someone who opposed the French, someone without the taint of colonialist power, who was also strongly opposed to the communist Vietminh. Thus Colonel Thé became significant.

At the time that Greene was visiting Vietnam and beginning to write *The Quiet American*, Colonel Thé had not yet become important to the Americans. They knew he was small beer, but in the early days of his revolt from the Cao Dai his statements expressed his opposition to both the French and the communists. It was only later, after Dien Bien Phu in 1954 when the French were in the process of leaving Vietnam, that the Americans decided on their third force figure – the Catholic strong man Ngo Dinh Diem, who had spent much of the war in a monastery in New Jersey. Thé then came into his own by joining forces with Diem. He was brought back out of the jungle to support Diem by Colonel Lansdale with the help of CIA money. To the French Thé was a murderous reptile: to the ordinary Vietnamese a romantic hero. Howard Simpson, an American writer in Saigon, described overhearing an 'incongruous melodrama' (his words) involving General Nguyen Van Vy, a pro-French Bao Dai loyalist and chief of staff of the Vietnamese army, and Colonel Thé:

> Cao Dai general Trinh Minh Thé, in civilian clothes, is lecturing Vy while armed members of Thé's newly formed pro-Diem 'Revolutionary Committee' have taken up positions by the doors and windows . . .
>
> General Vy is being asked to read a prepared statement calling for an end to French interference in Vietnamese affairs, repudiating Bao Dai, and pledging his loyalty to Ngo Dinh Diem. Vy is responding to Thé's harangue in a low voice, trying to argue his case. The veins on Thé's forehead are standing out . . . Suddenly Thé pulls a Colt .45 from his belt, strides forward, and puts its muzzle to Vy's temple. Thé pushes Vy to the microphone, the heavy automatic pressed tight against the general's short-cropped gray hair. I wince, waiting for the Colt's hammer to fall. The repetitive clicking of a camera is the only sound in the tense silence . . . Vy begins to read the text into the mike, the paper shaking in his hands. His face is ashen, and perspiration stains his collar. Thé complains he can't hear and demands that Vy speak louder. When Vy finishes, Thé puts his automatic away. General relief sweeps the room.[4]

*

Thé's influence is central to the plot of *The Quiet American*. He is the catalyst who reveals Pyle's 'special duties'. Thé's desperate actions in the novel are based on historical fact. Greene also asserts, both in the novel and in his non-fictional writing, that the CIA was involved with Thé, providing him with the material to carry out nefarious actions. This is what so scandalised Liebling in the *New Yorker*: 'There is a difference . . . between calling your over-successful offshoot a silly ass and accusing him of murder.'[5]

In his dedication to René Berval and Phuong, Greene mentioned that he had rearranged historical events: 'the big bomb near the Continental preceded and did not follow the bicycle bombs. I have no scruples about such small changes.'

On 25 January 1952 the *New York Times* reported:

> Saigon, Indo-China, Jan. 21. Seven plastic time bombs, all of them attached to bicycles by *Communist terrorists* [emphasis added], exploded in the crowded streets here today, injuring twenty-four persons, eight of them seriously.[6]

Greene made the incident into a mystery and greatly increased the number of plastic time-bombs. He was in Saigon at the time and his diary entry shows he knew exactly how many time-bombs were planted: he was deliberately making this a humorous episode in the novel:

> Just at that time that the incident occurred of the bicycle bombs . . . The whole affair . . . was not worth more than a paragraph, and a humorous paragraph at that. It bore no relation to the sad and heavy war in the north, those canals in Phat Diem choked with the grey days-old bodies, the pounding of the mortars, the white glare of napalm.[7]

Fowler's Indian assistant, who seems to have some contact with the Vietminh, arranges a meeting for him with Mr Heng (clearly a Vietminh agent). Fowler meets Mr Heng after waiting fifteen minutes beside a stall of flowers in the boulevard Charner. A truckload of police drive up with a grinding of brakes and the squeal of rubber from the direction of the Sûreté Headquarters in the rue Catinat:

> the men disembarked and ran for the store, as though they were charging a mob, but there was no mob – only a zareba of bicycles . . . Before I had time to adjust my camera the comic and inexplicable action had been accomplished. The police had forced their way among the bicycles and emerged with three which they carried over their heads into the boulevard and dropped into the decorative fountain . . .
> 'Opération Bicyclette,' a voice said. It was Mr Heng.
> 'What is it?' I asked. 'A practice? For what?'
> 'Wait a while longer,' Mr Heng said.[8]

Idlers start approaching the fountain where 'one wheel stuck up like a buoy' and are stopped by a policeman. Heng examines his watch, the hands standing at four minutes past eleven. Fowler has just time to say that his watch is fast, and for Heng to admit that it always gains:

And at that moment the fountain exploded over the pavement. A bit of decorative coping struck a window and the glass fell like the water in a bright shower . . . A bicycle wheel hummed like a top in the road, staggered and collapsed. 'It must be just eleven,' Mr Heng said . . . That day all over Saigon innocent bicycle pumps had proved to contain bombs which had gone off at the stroke of eleven . . . It was all quite trivial – ten explosions, six people slightly injured and God knows how many bicycles. My colleagues . . . called it an 'outrage' – knew they could only get space by making fun of the affair. 'Bicycle Bombs' made a good headline. All of them blamed the Communists. I was the only one to write that the bombs were a demonstration on the part of General Thé . . . [9]

On 25 January 1952, four days after the event, Tillman Durdin of the *New York Times* came out with the news that it was the dissident Caodaist Colonel Thé who was responsible for planning the incident, and not the communists. A secret memo from Donald Heath to the State Department reads: 'He [Tran Van Tuyen, secretary of the Phuoc Quoc Hoi nationalist group] told Durdin . . . "Third Force" had set off second set "exploding bicycles".'[10] A secret agent of the American legation (cover name Pierre) gave further information:

Pierre states that the bicycle explosions Jan 21 have been definitely traced to Colonel Thé, many of whose men hold regular Cao Daist passes and can enter and leave city without hindrance from security organizations. Source adds that one of Colonel Thé's majors has been arrested, and revealed everything, including name of Colonel Thé's pyrotechnical expert. There was the added suspicion that a French colonel who had been a former liaison officer with the Cao Daists had also been arrested under suspicion of complicity in the explosions.[11]

A much more serious bomb explosion took place in Saigon on 9 January, two days before de Lattre's death. The *New York Times* headline read: 'RED'S TIME-BOMBS RIP SAIGON CENTER: Missiles Kill 2 and Injure 30 in Spectacular Vietminh Strike in Indo-China.' Later newspaper issues raised the dead to 8 Vietnamese, 2 Frenchmen, and thirty-two injured. Again Tillman Durdin had the story:

Agents here of the Vietminh forces this forenoon staged one of the most spectacular and destructive single incidents in the long history of revolutionary terrorism in Saigon.

Two time bombs were exploded at 11 o'clock in the crowded center of two main downtown squares, killing two persons and injuring thirty. Thirteen automobiles were blasted and burned, walls were pitted, windows knocked out and plaster jarred loose in buildings all around the scene of the explosions.

The bombs had been left in two parked automobiles. One blast went off in the Place de Théâtre, which is overlooked by the Opera House, the Hotel Continental and a complex of stores and office buildings. The other blast occurred in the square in front of the City Hall, a block away. The two explosions occurred within two minutes of each other. The police believe that the two cars, which had false license plates, had been driven up and parked only a short time before the bombs went off. The perpetrators of the crime had time to leave the cars and get away safely before the explosions occurred . . . several arrests were made but the actual carriers of the bombs are believed still at large and the city is being combed for suspects.[12]

The French soon relinquished the idea that the bombing was the work of the Vietminh for, as the *New York Times* reported on 26 January 1952, 'radio broadcasts from the headquarters of the opposition Caodaists had virtually taken credit for the terrorism'. The French were profoundly angry over Thé's killing of innocent civilians in the square. General Salan, de Lattre's successor, asserted that he reserved the execution stake for such as Thé.

*

Greene used the bombing near the Continental Palace in *The Quiet American* (though he made no reference to the second bomb going off simultaneously as it would have complicated his story unnecessarily) and linked Pyle, the CIA undercover man, with Colonel Thé and the bombing. Pyle is providing Thé with plastic explosive for the bombs and, the suggestion is, the know-how for producing a time-bomb – a method not previously used in terrorist attacks. By suggesting that the American legation knew about Pyle's connection with and involvement in terrorist activities, Greene turned the incident into an unsavoury episode. Fowler suspects that Pyle is more deeply involved with Thé and his activities than he should be and advises him not to rely on the Colonel:

Perhaps there is a prophet as well as a judge in those interior courts where our true decisions are made [says Fowler to himself].

'We are the old colonial peoples, Pyle, but we've learnt a bit of reality, we've learned not to play with matches. This Third Force – it comes out of a book, that's all. General Thé's only a bandit with a few thousand men: he's not a national democracy' . . .

'I don't know what you mean, Thomas.'

'Those bicycle bombs. They were a good joke, even though one man did lose a foot. But, Pyle, you can't trust men like Thé. They aren't going to save the East from Communism. We know their kind.'

'We?'

'The old colonialists.'

'I thought you took no sides.'

'I don't Pyle, but if someone has got to make a mess of things in your outfit, leave it to Joe. Go home with Phuong. Forget the Third Force.'[13]

But Pyle doesn't forget the third force, as Fowler discovers.

It is half-past eleven in the morning and Fowler is visiting the Pavilion (in reality La Pagode), the coffee centre for European and American women in rue Catinat. He sees two young, tidy, identically dressed American girls ('it was impossible to conceive either of them a prey to untidy passion') sitting at the next table scooping up ice-cream. They finish their ices and one of the young ladies looks at her watch. 'We'd better be going,' she says, 'to be on the safe side.' The young American girls leave the café, where there is only an old French woman carefully and uselessly making up her face. Suddenly the two mirrors on the wall fly at Fowler and collapse half-way. The dowdy French woman is on her knees in a wreckage of chairs and tables; her compact lies open and unhurt in her lap. The explosion has been so close that Fowler's eardrums have still to recover from the pressure. He thinks it is another joke bomb like the bicycle bombs, but when he gets into the Place Garnier, he realises by the heavy clouds of smoke that this is no laughing matter:

> The smoke came from the cars burning in the car-park in front of the national theatre, bits of cars were scattered over the square, and a man without his legs lay twitching at the edge of the ornamental gardens. People were crowding in from the rue Catinat, from the Boulevard Bonnard. The sirens of police-cars, the bells of the ambulances and fire-engines came at one remove to my shocked ear-drums.[14]

Suddenly Fowler remembers that his ex-girlfriend, Phuong, now living with Pyle, must be in the milk bar across the square, since she always goes there at eleven. He tries to get across, but is stopped by the police. He looks up and sees Pyle and urges him to use his legation pass to cross the square to find her. Pyle insists that she isn't there, that she isn't there because he specifically warned her not to be. Fowler remembers the two American girls leaving the coffee shop to be on the safe side and suddenly the pieces fall into place. He realises that the Americans were aware that there was going to be a bomb explosion and Pyle had warned Phuong for the same reason: Pyle was involved in it. Finally they both cross the square to the scene of carnage:

A woman sat on the ground with what was left of her baby in her lap; with a kind of modesty she had covered it with her straw peasant hat. She was still and silent, and what struck me most in the square was the silence . . . the only sounds came from those who served, except where here and there the Europeans wept and implored and fell silent again as though shamed by the modesty, patience and propriety of the East. The legless torso at the edge of the garden still twitched, like a chicken which has lost its head. From the man's shirt, he had probably been a trishaw driver.

Pyle said, 'It's awful.' He looked at the wet on his shoes and said in a sick voice, 'What's that?'

'Blood,' I said. 'Haven't you ever seen it before?'

He said, 'I must get them cleaned before I see the Minister.' I don't think he knew what he was saying. He was seeing a real war for the first time . . . I forced him, with my hand on his shoulder, to look around. I said, 'This is the hour when the place is always full of women and children – it's the shopping hour. Why choose that of all hours?'

He said weakly, 'There was to have been a parade.'

'And you hoped to catch a few colonels. But the parade was cancelled yesterday, Pyle.'

'I didn't know.'

'Didn't know!' I pushed him into a patch of blood . . . 'You ought to be better informed.' . . .

'They should have called it off.'

'And missed the fun?' I asked him. 'Do you expect General Thé to lose his demonstration? This is better than a parade. Women and children are news, and soldiers aren't, in a war. This will hit the world's Press. You've put General Thé on the map all right, Pyle. You've got the Third Force and National Democracy all over your right shoe. Go home to Phuong and tell her about your heroic dead — there are a few dozen less of her people to worry about.'[15]

Fowler leaves Pyle standing in the square and goes in the direction of the cathedral. He considers that he had reason to be thankful:

wasn't Phuong alive? Hadn't Phuong been 'warned'? But what I remembered was the torso in the square, the baby on its mother's lap. They had not been warned: they had not been sufficiently important. And if the parade had taken place would they not have been there just the same, out of curiosity, to see the soldiers, and hear the speakers, and throw the flowers? A two-hundred pound bomb does not discriminate. How many dead colonels justify a child's or a trishaw driver's death when you are building a national democratic front?[16]

Unquestionably Greene was condemning the CIA for involving itself with a killer and providing that killer with weapons. Worse, he charged them with knowledge of what Thé was doing, and with conniving with him. 'There mustn't be any American casualties, must there?'[17]

Greene never moved an inch from his conviction that the CIA were involved, though he took a different tack when he answered Liebling's condemnation and argued in *Ways of Escape* in favour of American involvement:

When my novel was eventually noticed in the *New Yorker* the reviewer condemned me for accusing my 'best friends' (the Americans) of murder since I had attributed to them the responsibility for the great explosion — far worse than the trivial bicycle bombs — in the main square of Saigon when many people lost their lives. But what are the facts, of which the reviewer needless to say was ignorant? The *Life* photographer at the moment of the explosion was so well placed that he was able to take an astonishing and horrifying photograph which showed the body of a trishaw driver still upright after his legs had been blown off. The photograph was reproduced in an American propaganda magazine published in Manila over the title 'The work of Ho Chi Minh', although General Thé had promptly and proudly claimed the bomb as his own. Who had supplied the material to a bandit who was fighting French, Caodaists and Communists?[18]

This is a weak argument. This was the day of home-made bombs and it was as true for the Americans as it was to anyone living in Saigon at the time, 'to be wary; to be always afraid; to be alert'.[19] Photographers, obsessed with getting a scoop, might well have been in the square – do newspaper photographers ever relinquish the camera except in sleep? Grenade attacks and assassinations took place in that area, often in broad daylight, and *Life* was renowned for scooping the opposition and taking photographs that other magazines were unable to. As Tom Peck said, 'but *Life* had a reputation for being "Johnny on the spot" when a newsworthy event occurred'.

In fact, the photograph of the trishaw driver was not originally a *Life* photograph, though it appeared there. The photographs were taken by a Vietnamese photographer. He always carried his camera and when the bomb exploded in front of his eyes he took the photographs, for obvious commercial reasons. Both Charles Baker and Tom Peck were able to buy their own copies the next day: they were on sale. *Life* described the scene more fully than Greene did:

> This devastation-filled street scene is the usually placid Place du Théâtre in Saigon. At 11 o'clock [Greene in his novel puts the explosion ahead by one hour] . . . a powerful bomb planted by Vietminh Communists, exploded in the trunk of an auto parked in the crowded, busy square. The bomb blew the legs from under the man in the foreground and left him bloody and dazed, propped up on the tile sidewalk with his broken left ankle twisted beneath him. It killed the driver of the . . . delivery truck as he sat at the wheel. It riddled and set fire to the truck, made a torch of a cloth-topped jeep, smashed and burned more autos and raked the square with fragments and flame.[20]

Initially the authorities thought that the bomb was the work of the Vietminh. For days the Vietminh had been broadcasting that that day was the first anniversary of the death of On, a student who had been killed in a demonstration in Saigon. Calling Saigon an 'occupied zone', they asked supporters to make it a 'day of hatred'. Ambassador Heath was troubled by the explosion because the Vietminh had not used these tactics before. He wrote to the American Secretary of State: 'While feat selected is less exhibition strength than of VM willingness indulge in cowardly and brutal acts of terrorism, exploit was carried out with grim efficiency and will undoubtedly be heralded as Commie triumph.'[21] Colonel Thé's claim that it was his handiwork was therefore first thought to be an idle boast.

Greene, in *Ways of Escape*, offered proof – to the extent that proof can ever be offered when secret organisations are involved. It is clear that Greene thought the CIA were involved in this particular explosion:

> There was certainly evidence of contacts between the American services and General Thé. A jeep with the bodies of two American women was found by a French rubber planter on the route to the sacred mountain [where General Thé had his hideout] – presumably they had been killed by the Vietminh, but what were they doing on the plantation? The bodies were promptly collected by the American Embassy, and nothing more was heard of the incident. Not a word appeared in the Press.[22]

This seems an odd story, but when I checked it out with American Intelligence, they confirmed that Greene's comments were accurate – two American women were murdered, though why remains a mystery.

The next incident Greene uses to indicate that the CIA were up to 'dirty tricks' is more intriguing and no one in Washington would recently admit to this strange tale: 'An American consul was arrested late at night on the bridge to Dakow (where Pyle in my novel lost his life) carrying plastic bombs in his car. Again the incident was hushed up for diplomatic reasons.'[23]

CIA contacts cast serious doubts on the authenticity of this story. This supposed incident of Greene's allowed him to enlarge upon an American consul being arrested, presumably by the French authorities, for carrying plastic bombs (it is Pyle who provides the plastic explosive that leads to the devastation in the square). But Greene himself doubted the information the first time he was told. It came from his friend Trevor Wilson, who told Greene his source was impeccable – the French commander-in-chief, General Salan. Greene followed it up after Salan had left Hanoi and he and Wilson flew out to Paris. Salan was adamant. His information was genuine. Greene never stated his source publicly, but he referred to it in a letter to Catherine Walston, written on his fifty-second birthday, 2 October 1956:

> I had an interesting visit to General Salan, the ex-c. in c. Indo-China. He once arrested a U.S. Vice-Consul in the act of carrying plastic – an answer to one's questions. He said from personal experience I had got the native girl's character [Phuong] absolutely right.[24]

But could there be any truth in the allegations: was American Intelligence in contact with Thé before 1954 when Colonel Lansdale befriended him? Did the French get it right this time or was their source suspect (secret informers sometimes are)? The only information comes from a telegram Donald Heath sent to the State Department describing some documents obtained from a Cao Dai sympathiser, a French official in the commissariat who for money handed over French secrets to the Cao Dai: 'Some of the documents', wrote Ambassador Heath, 'seem suspect.' Some Heath suspected were true: 'we have to judge ourselves which we can believe in'. The French of course were afraid of the Americans and believed that they had their own scenario for the future. Certainly from documents which came into the American legation's hands, the French believed the Americans were in touch with Thé and that legation officers had certain leading Vietnamese in their pay:

> It suggests Fr Mil operations against Thé, but warns of danger because Thé real natlist. It expresses fear that reaction wld provide US with opportunity strengthen hold on country and states that Tran Van Tuyen, Tran Van An and Nguyen Huu Tri are Amer agents. Finally, it accuses Thé of responsibility for Ja 9 explosions and claims explosive devices were provided by US.[25]

Leaving aside the truth of these remarks, and Heath does not comment on the truth or falsity of them in his report, we must assume that these comments are indirectly taken from the French Sûreté. If the Sûreté's judgment was accepted by French officials (with whom Greene had good relations), and perhaps by General Salan himself, then Greene would feel that he could use such remarks as truth in his novel. Assuming that contact between Thé and the CIA took place, that the CIA provided the explosive devices, and that Greene had been told of these facts by the French, but was asked not to divulge this information in any public way, then surely Greene would speak as here – as if he knew more than he was able to say: simply telling the unrelated story of some consul picked up with plastic bombs in his car and omitting private statements made to him by the Sûreté and Salan.

Still assuming for the moment that the CIA did provide Thé with explosives and did co-manage the terrorist activity (as in the novel), then Greene's reasoning is strange for it begs the question of who else could have helped Thé but the CIA. However, there is another possibility. Thé was an inventive man who hated the French, who from a certain perspective had heroic qualities. He could well have acted on his own initiative. He had a strong desire to be original, and in the bomb explosions he was, for usual terrorist activity by the Vietminh in Saigon amounted to grenades thrown from a bicycle or the periodic assassination of those working for the French. There was no need for Greene to opt for a conspiratorial view of the world, though as a one-time intelligence officer, it is perhaps understandable that he might do so.

Pyle's warning to Phuong not to be in the milk bar in the square* and that Americans were to be away from the area no later than eleven twenty-five is shocking, but if one part of the scheme is true (that it was the Americans who gave the explosives to the terrorist Thé) then it is probable that the other part is also. Yet as someone who knew Greene and also lived in Saigon at this time said, 'This was a war zone and there were explosives all over the place. Thé could have gotten them almost anywhere.'[26] Thé could have scavenged for the bomb parts and, as Greene reported about the Cao Dai, made his own weapons. '[The Cao Dai had] its own primitive arsenal . . . mortars are fabricated from old exhaust pipes,' he wrote in *Paris Match*, and in the novel he came back to this point when Fowler tells Pyle: 'They know enough to turn your exhaust pipe into a mortar. I believe Buicks make the best mortars.'[27]

I checked security legation correspondence from Saigon to Washington to see if any Americans were in the vicinity of the bomb explosion in order to test Greene's statement in *The Quiet American* that 'there mustn't be any American casualties'.[28] The following security telegram from the legation was written the day after the explosion (10 January 1952):

No US citizens or employees injured in yesterday's explosions downtown Saigon tho several escapes seem providential. Wife and infant son of NA Killen were in part across from Catinat blast site only few minutes earlier; wife of FSO Leonhart drove from parking area where charge was placed within five minutes of explosion; wife of V.C. Baker was in Indian shop across street at time of blast, had presence mind to fall to floor behind counter (shop was damaged).

Nancy Baker, who seemed to be the nearest to danger and therefore most knowledgeable about the event, said:

---

* The milk bar was in fact in the rue Catinat half a block away from the square. Phuong would have heard the report of the explosion: she would not have been in any personal danger.

I had missed being in the square by a minute, leaving it and going into the rue Catinat. Just as you entered rue Catinat, some thirty yards away from the square where the massive explosion took place I looked into a fabric store window, went in. An Indian clerk came up to me to speak and the bomb went off. We leaped under a wooden table. I thought at first it was an aerial attack. I was in shock and rather frightened. It went off exactly at 11 o'clock. I had a six month old baby, my first. I was afraid.[29]

Some years later, when in Bangkok, Nancy sat next to Tran Van Dinh, a Vietnamese public relations officer, at a dinner. Tran Van Dinh, having read *The Quiet American*, said that the Americans had alerted the clerks and secretaries to leave the area before the explosion. 'I got quite agitated. I said that this was a most inaccurate account. I said it could not be true else I wouldn't have been in the area.' Charles Baker then spoke up: 'I was post security officer in Saigon and my job would have been to alert people of the danger. I was only married a year and I had this young baby. If I had heard I would have most certainly warned my wife to stay indoors that day.'[30] And Americans and French needed to be vigilant, as a note in the *New York Times* in February 1952 shows:

The United States Legation here today warned all the city's American residents that the Vietminh Communist rebels were planning demonstrations here tomorrow against the French and Americans. The legation advised them to be on the look-out for bomb throwers. There are 300 Americans in Saigon.[31]

Edmund Gullion was adamant that neither the legation nor the CIA had any dealings with Thé at this time: 'The idea of an independent force springing out of the rice paddies was not something that we were really concerned with. There were disaffected people, and people like Diem who held themselves aloof from the French for a long time and we thought they were a more likely independent force.'[32] A CIA agent told me, quite categorically, 'To my knowledge no single agency official was – *at that time* [emphasis added] – in contact with Colonel Thé,' and he added: 'And I would know.'

PART 6

To America with Love

Greene on stage with Eric Portman
and Dorothy Tutin during rehearsals
for *The Living Room*

30

Visa Not for Sale

All claim to special righteousness awakens in me that scorn and anger from which a philosophical mind should be free.

— JOSEPH CONRAD

CHRISTOPHER SYKES, Evelyn Waugh's biographer, recorded a meeting in the autumn of 1953 in White's club between Waugh and a number of friends, one of whom was Greene. It was at the time of Senator Joe McCarthy's anti-communist campaign. Greene was planning to go to the United States and was 'in a state of indignation'. McCarthy's informers had found out that Greene had been a member of the communist party and as a result he had been denied a visa:

> Graham fulminated against this injustice . . . ending up by saying, 'Anyway it's given me an idea for a political novel. It will be fun to write about politics for a change, and not always about God.' . . . 'Oh' [Waugh] responded on his high note, 'I wouldn't give up writing about God at this stage if I was you. It would be like P.G. Wodehouse dropping Jeeves half-way through the Wooster series.'[1]

McCarthy's informers (it was the US Customs and Excise which formally denied Greene his visa) discovered that he had been a member of a proscribed organisation because Greene deliberately gave out the information to test the McCarran Act.[2] He first let it be known that he had been a member of a proscribed organisation when a nineteen-year-old student at Oxford. His picture was on the front cover of *Time* for the issue of 29 October 1951. Greene is looking pensive. Above his head and in the left-hand corner is a Catholic cross (very small); beneath his picture is the legend: 'NOVELIST GRAHAM GREENE: Adultery can lead to sainthood.' In the article (*The End of the Affair* was being reviewed) Greene released the information that as a prank at Oxford he had been a dues-paying member of the communist party for six weeks. 'When he found that party membership would not get him a free trip to Moscow, he dropped out.'[3]

Greene explained that these facts had not been 'cleverly unearthed' by the CIA but had been disclosed 'rather naïvely' by himself: 'the First Secretary of the American Embassy in Brussels, where I happened to be for a debate with François Mauriac . . . told me that the State Department were anxious for cases which expose the absurdity of the Act. So I mentioned my past to a *Time* correspondent. The plastic curtain fell immediately and was not lifted again until John Kennedy was President.'[4]

A confidential letter dealing with the question of Greene's communist membership was sent by air pouch by Robert McClintock, Chargé d'Affaires in Brussels. It said that Greene had 'lectured last night [30 October 1950] in Brussels on the subject of the "Paradoxes of Christianity". He is a zealous convert to Catholicism and could not very well today be regarded as a Communist or a totalitarian.' However, he had proffered the information that he had been a probationary member of the communist party for three months (actually no more than six weeks). Robert McClintock told Greene that the Department of State was applying the Internal Security Act of 1950 as it was written: 'However, I suggested that, if Mr. Greene should wish to become a *cause célèbre*, I should be glad to take his application for a visa.' He added: 'This invitation will probably not be accepted since Mr. Greene is leaving the end of this month for Kuala Lumpur where his young brother, whom he termed as a "stripling of about 40", is head of the Political Warfare Section of the British Forces fighting Communists in Malaya.'[5] Greene, as we know, went on to Malaya and then to Vietnam and was unable to visit America until 1952 during Joe McCarthy's rise to prominence. Testing the waters in 1948 would not have appealed to Greene, it would have been too safe; but by 1952 it had become a battle worth fighting, a move from the quiet to the active sector of the line.

In his view the McCarran Act's blanket exclusion of all alien communists from the United States was fatuous. Philosophers like Michael Polyanin, novelists like Alberto Moravia and the anti-communist Arthur Koestler (whose masterpiece *Darkness at Noon* surely has us all in his debt), were all at different times excluded.

Greene wished to place himself under the ban imposed by the McCarran Act because many 'were excluded by this Act and were unable in their anonymity and poverty to bring their case before the Attorney-General . . . I applied for a visa because I was in a position to secure a measure of publicity against McCarthy and McCarran.'[6]

Greene's visa problems began while in Singapore. He wrote in his journal: 'January 14, 1952: French Consulate for transit visa & Am. Consulate. Great difficulty about Am. visa.' The difficulties persisted:

Saigon: Jan. 22. Tuesday: Long morning at American Legation with Getz & the Minister Heath, who are trying to deal with my visa problem.

Saigon: Jan. 25. Friday: No Visa news.

Saigon: Jan 27. Cable from *Life* that makes one decide to wait on a little for American visa.

Saigon: Jan 29 Tuesday. Tea with Bervals. Feeling pretty low. No sign of Am. visa.

On 1 February Greene lunched with Graham Jenkins of Reuters and had drinks with 'noisy Am correspondents & concocted news story on unobtainable visa'. Two days later, a short piece appeared in the *New York Times* and from there spread across the world. The *New York Times*'s article was headlined: 'Graham Greene Visa Held Up for Inquiry', and went on to say that Greene's entry visa into the United States was under investigation by the State and Justice Departments 'in conformity with the requirements of the Internal Security (McCarran) Act; that the 47-year-old author had applied for a visa in Saigon; and that the authorities in Washington thought the case merited further attention'. The McCarran Act automatically barred visas to anyone who had been a member of any subversive group, such as the communist or Nazi parties.

Greene's American publisher, Harold Guinzburg, was concerned about his not being able to visit the United States, and sent a telegram to the Majestic hotel, Saigon: 'HOPE YOU WONT ALLOW TECHNICALITY OF A STUPID LAW KEEP YOU FROM AMERICAN VISIT. WOULD LOVE SEE YOU HERE GREETINGS.'[7] But it was too early to expect a relaxation of the McCarran Act while McCarthy flourished; officials were afraid of being labelled 'sympathisers'.

While still in Saigon Greene received a normal visa (usually a visa is operative for a year), but it was then changed. Tom Peck, the US consular official in Saigon, said in interview:

The visa took a long time, two months, as I remember it, but then when permission finally came, I stamped it for one year (which is the normal amount of time given to applicants). But then in rereading the Attorney-General's note, I realised that Greene had only been given a period of three months to visit the U.S. I was frightened that if I didn't get to Greene soon, he would be off with a year's visa which I was instructed this could not be. So I telephoned the Continental hotel and asked if I could come and see him. I took the elevator but don't remember the number, knocked at the door. I remember thinking how tall he was (for I'm six foot and he stood above me). The ceilings were very high and ceiling fans spinning around – no air conditioning. For some reason I recall that the windows either small or the room heavily curtained but I remember there was very little light in the room. I asked to see his passport and looked at it and then pulled out my cancellation stamp, and quickly stamped it CANCELLED and dated it across his visa. When he saw me doing this he shouted, rising from his chair, 'What are you doing!' I told him, that I'd made a mistake in giving him a visa for a year when the Attorney-General had given him only a three months' visa. I immediately issued a new one there and then for three months. He was hopping mad I never saw him again.[8]

Greene was a fighter when roused and the bureaucratic rigmarole would cost the United States dear in terms of reputation. Charles Stuart Kennedy, a retired consul-general, recalled that when he entered the United States Foreign Service in July 1955, he endured a basic officer's course which concentrated heavily on visa matters. Among other things they were told to use some common sense in applying the strict visa law and the case of Greene was used as a horrible example of what not to do:

As we were told it, a vice consul refused Greene a visa for having been a member of the Communist Party at Oxford for a few weeks. As a prominent Catholic writer who obviously was not a mouthpiece for Moscow the vice consul should have sent a telegram to Washington explaining the matter. This would undoubtedly have resulted in his being granted a waiver of the prohibition against communists or former communists getting visas. By the bureaucratic insensitivity on the part of the vice consul Greene was ticked off and wrote *The Quiet American*.

Kennedy went on to use this case for thirty years in training new vice consuls, telling them that they had to use some discretion in administering the immigration law: 'If in doubt, or if the matter might create a public relations problem, for heaven's sake let me know about it or refer the damned thing to the Department of State for its opinion.'[9]

Greene's visa problems would continue for many years, but at least now he could go to Hollywood, where he was to advise on the film *The End of the Affair*. Mrs Young, his secretary, sent a postcard to Greene's publisher A. S. Frere at Heinemann: 'Graham's story to the Press has done the trick and the U.S. visa has been produced! I had a cable this morning saying he'd not now be back [in England] until about Feb. 20th and that letters should be sent to him c/o Mrs Pritchett marked "Please Forward".'[10] A letter written to his mother just prior to getting his visa reveals his ambivalence: 'I think if I do get over there, I shall be turned out of the country after a couple of interviews.'

Greene left Saigon rather sadly on 9 February 1952 for Hong Kong: 'I left Saigon early yesterday – with certain regrets. I had one or two good friends there. Especially during this last stay. Perhaps I'll write the "entertainment" I thought of and go back and film it one day. People have been nice to me.'[11]

René Berval and Trevor Wilson had been good friends, but Greene had in mind the kindness shown by the Americans – the Toppings, the Getzs. There is no feeling here that he had been badly done to by the Americans in Saigon: no ugly Americans, and no anti-Americanism from Greene. In his journal he wrote of John Getz and his beautiful wife Libby. Just before his departure from Saigon, he took the Getzs out for dinner to the Jade Pavilion and to gamble at the casino. The day before he left for Hong Kong he 'phoned Libby who insists on seeing me off'. The next day, Libby and John Getz called for him at 6.45 in the morning. 'Kissed Phuong farewell through the grill. Libby [Getz] v. sweet & rather disturbing.'[12]

He left for Hong Kong at 8 a.m. and, writing to Catherine Walston, he stressed it was 'odd to have hot water again, to be wearing my tweed suit and one of your Dublin ties'.[13] On the 11th he arrived in Tokyo at 5 a.m., was given an early morning drive round selected temples, viewed the garden of the concubines, and visited but did not stay in the 'incredibly ugly Imperial Hotel like an air-raid shelter . . . The Press everywhere after that.' He went to the zoo (sited on the top of a department store), to a Japanese theatre, and after a lunch which was too rich for him he went to the airport 'rather knocked out'.

*

On his arrival in the United States Harold Guinzburg sent Greene a cable: 'RELIEVED THAT YOU'RE IN AND THE NATION STILL STANDS.'[14] Greene went to Hollywood to see about the filming of *The End of the Affair* and, as he put it to Catherine: 'I had a quiet time here fixing up the files of *your* novel – except for Mass with Claire Booth Luce in a church so clean and so rich that I longed to be with you in the little grubby Anacapri church where nobody's rich.'[15] He also mentioned that he went for a drink with Charlie Chaplin.

In Hollywood he learnt how seriously McCarthyism was entering its soul. When he arrived in Los Angeles he felt he had entered a city under 'a reign of terror'. He found that Hollywood's film studios 'took extra measures toward anyone under the threat of McCarthyism' and against anyone of 'liberal tendencies' or who was linked with a left-wing movement. 'People seem to be completely at the mercy of the man [Senator Joseph McCarthy],' he remarked, 'and if a man answers yes, he had been a member of the Communist party, he is expected to give the names of friends in the party.'[16]

Greene returned to New York to consult with the editors of *Life*, and to receive the 1952 Award for Fiction from the Gallery of Living Catholic Authors for *The End of the Affair*. He was interviewed, among other newspapers, by the *New York Herald Tribune*. The headline was strong: 'Graham Greene Says U.S. Lives in Red-Obsessed "State of Fear"'.

Mr. Greene arrived in New York about 2 p.m. yesterday and a few hours later when he granted an interview in his room at the Hotel Algonquin, immediately expressed concern over what he said is happening to American freedom because of the country's growing fear of Communism.

He considered his own case rather comical, he remarked, because he had been a Roman Catholic since 1926, and is certainly no friend of the Communists. But he doesn't consider the anti-Communists' policy in America with its pattern of 'smearing and besmirching' very funny.

'I'm speaking this way because I like America and Americans . . . This land of freedom. People came here not to win television sets or refrigerators but to gain freedom from the house spies, the informers, the military regimes.' He added sadly, 'But there are a lot of informers going around here now.'[17]

Greene was at pains to stress not his own case but what Senator McCarthy of Wisconsin was doing, and he spoke out directly, as a Catholic, to Catholics: 'As part of their religious beliefs all Catholics should be opposed to this.' It was almost the duty of Catholics to oppose such laws as the McCarran police-state law and the general nature of McCarthyism. He quoted President Roosevelt's statement in his first inaugural: 'The only thing to fear is fear itself,' and then Thomas Paine, who had done so much for the American revolution: 'We should guard even our enemies against injustice.' He felt bewildered by the nature of America's fear complex and felt that this obsession was being noticed in other parts of the world: 'America's allies are beginning to wonder if their concept of democracy is the same as yours. The fear of one man – Stalin – is not found in England or Europe.'

An editorial in the *New York Times* agreed with Greene and spoke of the puerility to which 'our immigration laws have been allowed to sink'. 'We never were really worried about Mr. Greene, whose transgression apparently was that he belonged to the Communist party for about a month some twenty years ago, prior to his conversion to the Catholic faith.' People like Senator McCarran attempted to create a 'kind of intellectual *cordon sanitaire* about the United States – an attempt which has seriously damaged our reputation as a liberal democracy abroad and has encouraged the forces of reaction, parochialism and xenophobia at home'. It pointed out that rigid barriers set up by its immigration laws played into the hands of its enemies: 'What hope have we . . . to hold out to defectors from the Communist regimes, what inducement are we able to offer the former Communists who are among the most effective enemies of communism, when we automatically slam our doors in their very faces?'[18]

*

According to his biographer, David Robinson, Charlie Chaplin embarked for England on the *Queen Elizabeth* on 17 September 1952. He had been at sea for two days when the radio announced that the US Attorney-General (who had only recently and reluctantly granted Greene a limited visa) had ordered that Chaplin be detained by the Immigration and Naturalisation Service upon his return to the United States. Chaplin had lived in America for forty years but had kept his British passport. It would now have to be decided whether he could re-enter the country under US laws. It was a deliberate insult to America's most famous living comic. Immediately, in a great rage, Greene wrote an open letter to Charlie Chaplin, which appeared in the *New Statesman* on 27 September 1952. The letter first spoke of 'the great pyramid of friendly letters that must be awaiting' Chaplin in London, for of course he was the world's but certainly England's favourite son:

> Your films have always been compassionate towards the weak and the underprivileged; they have always punctured the bully. To our pain and astonishment you paid the United States the highest compliment in your power by settling within her borders, and now we feel pain . . . at the response . . . from those authorities who seem to take their orders from such men as McCarthy.

The main accusation against Chaplin seemed to be that he had spoken when Russia was invaded by Hitler's troops in her defence at a public meeting in San Francisco. His speech had been made at the request of President Roosevelt, but, as Greene recorded, the authorities' accusation was based mainly on the fact that Chaplin had addressed his audience as 'comrades' – a dangerous term signifying communist sympathies. Greene referred to conditions in England when Catholics were persecuted. He compared McCarthy and the Un-American Committee with Titus Oates, who in 1678 fabricated evidence to prove a popish plot to assassinate Charles II, which resulted in the frenzied persecution of Catholics throughout the land and in the hanging of three innocent people.

He ended his open letter to Chaplin:

> They will say it is no business of ours. But the disgrace of an ally is our disgrace, and in attacking you the witch-hunters have emphasized that this is no national matter. Intolerance in any country wounds freedom throughout the world.

His letter was reprinted in America by *New Republic* on 13 October 1952 with an excellent introduction, presumably by the editor:

> At 63, THE MAN who made buffoons of dictators is threatened with the dictatorial McCarran Act. When Charlie Chaplin tries to pass the Statue of Liberty, he will be held at Ellis Island until he convinces the Attorney-General that he is pure. His is the burden of proof. Accused of non-conformism and contempt 'for the high state of womanhood', Chaplin is lumped with Costello as an 'unsavory character' . . . Chaplin's re-entry permit implies absence of cause to deport him. Threatening him once he has left is dishonorable and the world knows it.

Greene received a tremendous response to his letter, much of which supported him, though Evelyn Waugh wrote to him rather defensively: 'It is no good pretending I wasn't shown your letter about Chaplin in the *New Statesman*.'[19]

Not everyone responded favourably. One letter in particular Greene saved in his archives and also sent to the *New Statesman*. It is a letter which conveys 'more vividly than press reports the atmosphere of smear, suspicion and unreason that McCarthy, like Titus Oates before him, has managed to impose on a section of his countrymen' Greene wrote in his cover note. The letter came to Greene because, in applying for a second visa to return to America churlishly he was offered one for only eight weeks. That did not allow him to work on his play *The Living Room*, then being produced on Broadway, and he refused it. Greene thought the letter was a bizarre and macabre joke:

Dear Mr Greene,

You have earned the gratitude of the American people by refusing a visa to the United States. You will please us still further in the future by not even applying for one. There are enough of the home grown variety of ex-Communists and fellow travellers here already. No need for any 'furriners'. May I suggest instead that you turn your talents to securing a visa to Russia where you will be welcomed with open arms. I anticipate much less trouble for you there. We beseech you please do not on any account honor us with your presence in this country. It is enough to have to live in the same world with you.

Unfortunately, my womanly intuition tells me that if you have not already landed here you will all too soon come to these shores – your half-baked statements to the contrary. No truer words were ever writ than 'A man is known by the company he keeps' to which may be added also by the periodicals he contributes to.

Sincerely L. Ettinger.

P.S. If this is a publicity gag then I feel sorry for you to have to sink so low. Won't you make 150,000,000 Americans happy and stay on your side of the ocean?

Public figures receive hostile letters, but Greene's public statements aroused vindictive responses:

In our sympathy for the underdog it's easy to forget he sometimes is indeed a dog. A mad dog who calculatingly clothes his treachery

445

with the loose fitting robe of liberalism . . . forfeits the respect due an honest straightforward enemy . . .

Despite his conviction on the charge of fathering the child of a young actress never included among his numerous wives, Chaplin's present troubles are political . . . the moral reptile of today is free to slink about pretty much as he pleases, to chain-marry wives . . . to write, direct and act in his own movies and even compose his own music . . . The American is proud of his citizenship . . . He . . . holds . . . the right of a nation to deny its hospitality to the criminal, the diseased, the anarchist, the world revolutionist . . .

Nothing but the certainty of a refusal has prevented his applying long ago for American citizenship: the threat of deportation has been like a vulture, patient but always alert, at his shoulder for many years . . . I'll agree Charlie Chaplin is an artist of great merit . . . I do not concede to a man possessing his Marxist-Leninist-Stalinist theories the right to remain out of prison or to stay alive; my love for the music of Prokofieff and Khachaturian will not unsteady these hands on the bombsight when the time comes.[20]

Victor Lasky, who had looked on Greene as a favourite author, wrote to him saying he was totally bewildered by the fact that Greene was now so anti-American.[21] Greene thought that Lasky confused his criticism of certain American personalities and certain American acts with being anti-American and concluded that he did not consider himself 'anti-American any more than I consider myself anti-Romanian or anti-Italian, but I do think we are at liberty to criticise what we consider injustices or dangerous tendencies in other countries, especially when those countries are tied as closely to us as America . . . In England we have not noticed any particular slowness on the part of America to criticise our policies in, say, India or Palestine, but it would be absurd necessarily to label such critics as anti-British.'[22]

*

Greene's visa troubles continued throughout the 1950s, but he remained as determined as ever to attack the McCarran Act. In September 1954 it seemed that he was in further trouble with the US Customs and Immigration Service, for an FBI radiogram carried the following information to the Director of the FBI in Washington:

GRAHAM GREENE, SMC. INS ADVISED GREENE ARRIVED SAN JUAN, PR LAST NIGHT AT 8.55 PM VIA DELTA . . . AIRLINES FROM

HAITI. INS ADVISED SUBJ INADMISSIBLE TO U.S. BECAUSE OF MEMBERSHIP IN COMMUNIST PARTY OF ENGLAND. WAS PLACED UNDER GUARD BY INS AND RETURNED TO HAITI ON DELTA . . . AIRLINES DEPARTING SAN JUAN 7.30 AM AT THIS DATE SUBJ ADVISED INS THAT HE WAS A NOVELIST AND WAS GOING TO NYC TO CONTACT AN AGENT FOR HIS BOOKS. HE SENT TWO CABLEGRAMS WHILE IN SAN JUAN, ONE TO QUOTE . . . MARY [PRITCHETT] UNQUOTE IN NEW YORK STATING QUOTE TURNED BACK. CAN'T LUNCH. LOVE GRAHAM UNQUOTE AND THE OTHER TO QUOTE [PETER] BROOKS MYRTLE BANK HOTEL, KINGSTON, JAMAICA. CAN'T LUNCH WITH L. PHOEDE TURNED BACK. GRAHAM. UNQUOTE SUBJ STATED WHILE IN CUSTODY OF INS THAT HE HAD BEEN A MEMBER OF THE CP. OF ENGLAND YEARS AGO WHEN HE WAS 19 YEARS OLD; THAT HE WAS GOING TO WRITE A BOOK ABOUT HIS EXPERIENCE IN SAN JUAN AND THAT HE WOULD MAKE A LOT OF PUBLICITY OVER HIS BEING DETAINED. SUBJ DESCRIBED AS FOLLOWS: BORN FEBRUARY 10, 1904 [*sic*], ENGLAND; HEIGHT 6 FEET [*sic*]; WEIGHT 180 POUNDS; SANDY, THIN HAIR; OCCUPATION, BRITISH NOVELIST; NO ADDRESS AVAILABLE. SUBJECT INDICATED HE WOULD RETURN TO ENGLAND FROM HAITI VIA DUTCH AIRLINES.

Time picked up the story: 'British Novelist Graham (*The Third Man*) Greene, who is something of an internationalist . . . out to smash the . . . McCarran Act, stepped off a plane at San Juan airport, Puerto Rico and snapped a sharp yes when immigration officials asked the routine: "Have-you-ever-been-a-Communist?" question. Greene, who was *en route* to London from a vacation in Haiti, was politely detained overnight, next morning took off for Havana for a few days' nightclubbing and the chance to bemuse reporters with his story.' Greene told the now old story of how he became a communist for a joke, and added of the Immigration Service: ' "They couldn't have picked on a person who is less a Communist," he said of his Puerto Rico detention. "It's all very silly." '[23]

If he was planning to confront the Customs and Immigration Service, his letter to Catherine just before his departure from Haiti, where he had been on holiday, doesn't reveal it:

I'm coming back by Puerto Rico and New York . . . I have 8 hours at the airport, but Mary Pritchett is going to come out to lunch and the strange Truman [Capote] has written to some American girl whom he swears is 'a mutual fate' – 'no doubt of it: you'll only take one look at each other. I can even tell what dishes she'll choose from a strange menu.' I don't believe in this, but she will be a very odd girl if she does present herself at the airport for lunch.[24]

But it was a 'mutual fate' that they should *not* meet, for Greene was not allowed to go beyond Puerto Rico and was deported the next day.

Greene described in detail what happened, giving the impression that he was not testing the McCarran Act but merely saw his return to England by the quickest route as being first to San Juan, then New York and then to London. It seems that when in Port-au-Prince he asked the American ambassador if he could grant him a transit visa without application to the Attorney-General. The answer was no. The ambassador told him it was legal to be in transit without a visa if he had no objection to being locked in a room at the airports in San Juan and New York. Greene had no objections, but had a strong instinct that the ambassador's plan wouldn't work, which it didn't. However, he was not locked in a room at the airport at San Juan but was treated by the authorities with commendable respect and kindness: 'If you give us your word of honour not to escape you can spend the night at a hotel in San Juan.'[25] Greene was to be put on a plane back to Haiti the next morning. Two plainclothes detectives were to be in the room next to his and would wake him up at 6.30 in the morning to take him to the airport.

Greene invited the officers to drink with him in the bar of the hotel. They had whiskies and more whiskies, and then one of the plainclothes officers felt it would be a shame if Greene didn't see something of San Juan. They didn't see much – save for a lot of bars. The next morning one of the officers was suffering from a bad hangover and Greene was *not* on his way back to Haiti. The captain of the plane took pity on him and took him on to Havana instead.

Was it deliberate? Was Greene having another go at the American leviathan? It had become a game or rather that is how Greene treated it in his own account: 'It was, I think, in 1954 that I was deported from Puerto Rico, an occasion I shall always remember with pleasure.' It was certainly news that flashed round the world and no doubt embarrassed various officials: 'I expect you've heard how I hit the front page in the war against U.S.', he wrote.[26]

Part of Greene's attitude towards the United States was that of having fun baiting the authorities. But it wasn't all fun, for when he arrived at customs invariably he was made to wait long periods at the port of entry and that can seem more painful than any punishment.

If I wished to visit the United States I had to get special permission from the Attorney-General in Washington – this took as a rule about three weeks and my stay was limited to four. I had to inform the authorities on which planes I would arrive and leave, and mysterious letters and numbers were inscribed on my temporary visa which always ensured a long delay at Immigration. I rather enjoyed the game.

He did not always enjoy the game, however, for if you play with authorities sometimes you get burnt. Jacques Barzun, the writer and scholar, recalled meeting Greene in the early 1950s at a small cocktail party given by Viking Press:

I was present and curious to meet the author of what he called 'entertainments' and what I thought of as a hybrid genre of crime fiction.

After standing about for some time, chatting with literary friends and the Viking people – Marshall Best, Pat Covici, and Harold Guinzburg – we were told that Mr. Greene had been delayed by Immigration officials and would be a little late. He finally arrived, looking grim and not at all appreciative of the proffered hospitality. After possessing himself of a tall glass he made the rounds of the small groups, piloted by Marshall Best, who was trying hard to impart some sociable ease to the occasion.

In vain: Mr Greene could speak only of the indignity he had suffered on entering this country. He was under suspicion of being a Communist, his name apparently on a list. He was questioned hard and long about his connections, his writings, his purpose in coming, his sponsors and publishers. He made a point of saying that the Viking Press had not been known to his examiners, who looked as if they thought it an underground and subversive printing press . . .

There was very little the guests could say except to express their commiseration and regret, and assure Greene that the rest of his visit would be 'one continuous welcome': 'These promises fell on deaf ears. Mr. Greene did not smile and manifestly did not believe: he had come to an unfriendly and bigoted philistine country.'[27]

31

Drama and the Man

Close the drama with the day.
— BISHOP BERKELEY

DESPITE the disaster of the production of *The Heart of the Matter* in 1950, Greene told journalists in Boston that 'the idea of doing a solo stage play was actively in his mind'.[1] He began writing what was to be his first play, *The Living Room*, in Vietnam: '21 Nov. [1951] Worked on play . . . after dinner. 6 pipes. Sat up to 3 talking.' On 28 December: 'Did a little work on play. Less depressed.' And by 8 January 1952, when he was in Kuala Lumpur, he recorded in his journal, 'Finished play.' As was usual with Greene when he had nothing further to write, he became depressed: 'v. depressed with nothing to do'.

There are no further references to the play until Greene sent a telegram to Catherine dated 3 April 1952: 'LIVING ROOM TAKEN FOR IMMEDIATE PRODUCTION AM I CLEVER'. The following day he sent her a letter: 'Isn't it exciting about the play. I wonder if you got my wire. Peter Glenville is going to produce [he directed the play as well]. The book must be dedicated "To Catherine with love." May it be?' And that is the dedication in both the British and the American editions of the play. Greene then added, 'And you've got to hold my hand brazenly on the first night.'

Greene had had the play in mind years before he began writing it. In Peter Glenville's personal copy Greene wrote: 'For Peter with great gratitude & affection, from Graham, June 1, 1955. Begun in Achill, continued in Anacapri & finished in Kuala Lumpur.' The first sketch of the play was written on the back end-papers of Greene's copy of the *Devotional Poets of the XVII Century* (one of the Nelson Classics). The sketch was the briefest of notes in pencil:

The Living Room
Act 1. Sc. 1.

Arrived. Living Room. 1 hr. ·
Then keeping things dark. Curtain.
'Oh yes, I said his wife'

Scene 2. The family conference. Curtain – 'But this was not a confession'

Scene 3. The willing of communications. The brown party. Lover old now, priest no guts. Giving the religion?

Act 2. Scene 1. The appeal to the priest. The wrong word.

Scene 2. The shifting of the furniture.

On the other back end-paper he wrote the cast. Apart from calling the psychologist Henry Dale instead of Michael Dennis, and not giving the daily woman a name, the cast of characters had already been worked out. Part of the play is based on the untitled (and unpublished) typescript of a novel now housed in the Humanities Research Center in Austin, Texas, which contains two chapters: 'The Funeral of a Father' (in the play the funeral is changed to the funeral of the young heroine's mother) and 'The Oldest Friend'. In the play Rose, the young, pretty, sensitive girl gives herself adulterously to Michael, her mother's executor, and the oldest friend of the family. Rose is an innocent, ardent for life. She cannot bear the pain of leaving Michael, who is married to a Catholic woman who refuses divorce.

Rose knows about the marriage, but has never met Michael Dennis's wife. When she does she is profoundly disturbed by the meeting. When she asks her uncle (in a wheelchair – the symbol of paralysed goodness) to advise her, he replies: 'And if I say, "Leave him"?' She answers that she could not bear the pain, and he says, 'Then you'd better go with him, if you're as weak as that.' Her dilemma is that she cannot bear the wife's pain either. Not until Michael's wife arrives unexpectedly to persuade Rose to give him up does she become real: 'She was just a name, that's all. And then she comes here and beats her fists on the table and cries in the chair. I saw them together. I've seen him touch her arm.'[2]

Greene's play had its première in Stockholm in October 1952 when his personal fame was at its height. He wrote to his Swedish friend and publisher Ragnar Svanstrom that 'it might be rather fun to come over for the first night', especially since the play had been postponed until the spring of 1953 in England. Critical response was mixed – from the sublime to the remorseless.

'The public who went to the play included the *whole* of literary Stockholm,' said one critic, '[and they] appreciated to the full incomparably the most fascinating production of the autumn season.' The critic went on: 'when Graham Greene himself stepped on to the stage, I thought the applause would never stop. It was, perhaps, rather for one of the greatest novelists of our time, than for the dramatist, but either way, it was well-meant.'[3] Greene was described as the 'new world-dramatist'. Another reviewer called the play 'positively agonizing':

How far can one go with scenes of sheer torture on the stage before the audience can endure it no longer? At the Little Dramatic Theatre last night there were, in fact, people who found it difficult to remain in their seats during the big scene in the second act of Greene's drama of passions, *The Living Room* where a young girl is literally harassed to death. Olof Molander had so horribly readily lent the emphasized reality and hard discipline of his production to Greene's sadism – an emotional state which seems essential to this author to awaken his creative genius . . . His play has been the incentive for a production of such power, magnitude and brilliant lucidity that at times it is positively agonizing . . . The world première gave the impression of a gala performance with the whole of Stockholm crowded about the object of gala – the author. But the predominant feeling of the audience at this most remarkable Dramatic Theatre first night was one of uneasiness, deep emotion and – as I said – sometimes agony.[4]

There was one powerful and angry voice, full of deep hatred for Greene and an equal hatred of Catholicism – the voice of Artur Lundkvist. Lundkvist would pay Greene back for being Greene: such appalling fame, such success, such backwardness as expressed by his Catholicism, and such hatred, the critic felt, for modern psychology. Unfortunately Lundkvist, who had great power in the literary world of Stockholm, was chairman of the committee which decided future Nobel Prizes. He was on record as saying that Greene would only receive the Nobel Prize for Literature over his dead body. His hatred carried on for most of his life and his death in the same year as Greene's barred for ever the possibility of a Nobel Prize.

Admitting that the theatre public 'appeared at times to be deeply moved', he was troubled by an audience who 'tittered delightfully every time the priest on the stage spat out the word psychology or the name Freud'. According to Lundkvist: 'the play consists of Catholic propaganda of the most vulgar type, to which is added artistic and intellectual cheating'.

He went on: 'The most dangerous and unpleasant thing about Greene's play is the way in which it attacks modern psychology. The means are clearly dishonourable – a number of foul blows below the belt.' He felt that Greene's dislike of psychology – which was not for a moment true – was shared by many in the audience, those who kept 'guard over their tangled complexes, dread elucidation and analysis . . . And yet . . . it is psychology that we have to thank for the progress that has been made during the latter generations as regards candour, naturalness, inner freedom and increased consciousness.'

He also thought that the priest often had the best lines. Whilst the priest rejected all claims to logic and psychological knowledge in the interests of paradoxical faith, yet it was he, not the psychologist, who was allowed to carry off the victories in this field also. The doctor of psychology in Lundkvist's view didn't command even the rudiments of psychological general knowledge and clear reasoning which should counteract the priest's misleading mystifications. Not only was the play 'a monstrosity of anti-psychology', it was from start to finish 'sadistic in the name of human sympathy'! Sympathy becomes terrorism, it falsifies its claims 'so that only self-sacrifice is possible': 'This Jesuitically exploited sympathy coerces, oppresses, lies and is used as rank blackmail. The result is the girl's suicide.'

'The one person in the company who is most able to cope with life [Rose] must be sacrificed in order that obsolete dogma and morbid hysteria shall triumph . . . What sort of victory has been won? Catholicism's claims to oppression have triumphed, the Church has been avenged against one who has dared to escape her, reason and human feelings have been trampled underfoot. Mr. Greene and his sympathizers should feel satisfied.' Lundkvist averred that there must be few who refused to agree with 'this cynicism or perverse charlatanism'. Yet he felt that the play unmasked itself as 'a warning against Catholic distortion, its inhuman demand for sacrifice, its abuse of power behind its so-called solicitude for the soul'.

Lundkvist's last blows show a profoundly prejudiced man: 'Graham Greene's development (degeneration) has long been suspect. In this play he reveals himself as a morally dangerous writer in league with the darkest powers of present-day western reactionism. The plague flag should be raised over the Dramatic Theatre Studio.'[5]

Greene himself was commendably modest in speaking to the audience: 'I allow my characters to live their own lives once I have created them. They are, as a rule, full of contradictions and can be interpreted in many different ways. I myself, perhaps, had imagined some of them in another way than they appeared tonight, but I don't know that my way of seeing them was the right one.'[6]

On the first night, the audience was kept waiting for Greene – 'It seemed as though the Almighty had borrowed one of Greene's own dramatic tricks when He locked the author in Dr Gierow's lift while the audience sat waiting in the theatre . . . The Almighty [also] allowed some imp of mischief to spatter candle grease over the famous author's dinner jacket in order that he should not take his first night too grandly. Nor did he . . .'[7]

Back in England, the play went on tour in the provinces before it faced a London audience. It went first to Edinburgh, then Glasgow and finally Brighton. To his brother Herbert Greene wrote: 'I shan't go to Brighton to see the play as I shall already have had to follow it around in Edinburgh and Glasgow for the purposes of making any changes that are necessary & I shall want to have a rest from it before the London first night.'[8]

Greene learned that unlike a film script, where the writer is excluded from the act of creation once the script has been completed, the playwright doesn't become a forgotten man. He thought he would be 'an unwelcome stranger lurking ashamed in the stalls', but it was not so. He discovered that with a play the writing continues after the play goes into production: 'It would extend through rehearsals and through the opening weeks of tour.' He thoroughly enjoyed rehearsals and was struck by the fact that the actors all played a part in suggesting improvements: 'in the play as a whole . . . nearly a dozen lively informed intelligences criticising and suggesting'.[9] He enjoyed the process more than dramatising his novels: 'One newcomer has been very happy in the theatre, in the deserted stalls at rehearsals, at the note-takings on the stage after performance, in the corridors and the bars and dressing-rooms.'[10]

He went to the first performance in Edinburgh. The play was a success and Evelyn Waugh wrote to him about hearing of one man's response: 'I was delighted to hear from an American, who journeyed to Edinburgh on your account, that your play is brilliantly successful.'[11] Greene went to Edinburgh with his friend Mario Soldati, the Italian film director. He liked Soldati because he was unconventional, not stiff or formal. In a letter to his mother, he described him as 'that nice but hysterical Italian film director'. While they were there, Greene, Soldati, and Greene's friend John Sutro had an encounter Greene described as 'bizarre' in a *Picture Post* article:

> The theatre has brought even certain bizarre experiences the cinema never offered: a struggle on a hotel floor at two in the morning with a breeder of prize bulls.[12]

After the performance on the first night, Greene, Sutro and Soldati returned to the hotel for a drink. Greene recalled that he was reading *A Life of Chekhov* which he had under his arm and that he was wearing a red tie (as he always did with a dark suit):

> a mysterious Scotsman began to glare at me and finally said: 'Have you contributed to the flood relief fund?' because there had been big floods in Edinburgh. I was taken aback and I said 'no' because, thank God, I'm only a quarter Scotch. He then came around behind me and seized my tie and pulled it down and so then we all went into a scrabble. And he was much heavier than I was and I thought I was winning but it was because Mario Soldati was pulling him from behind. But then Mario got a crick in his back and subsided on a chair, so that I was really the beaten one. But then there was a great scene of shaking hands.[13]

Mario Soldati remembered the story differently:

> It was below freezing point and we were drinking black velvet which Graham had introduced me to − a mixture of Guinness and champagne and we were drunk and talking about fucking and cunt and a man on the other side of the room − we were talking loudly − was even more drunk than we were. After a while he came across to us and said: 'You two must be communist buggers' and Graham said 'Why not communist fuckers' and the man tried to hit Graham and they wrestled and I tried to separate them.[14]

In a copy of *The Living Room* which he gave to Mario Soldati, Greene wrote, 'For helping me in the battle of the Edinburgh hotel'.

When the play went on to Brighton it had a tremendous reception. The lure of Greene's name, the fact that this was his first play, coupled with the name of film star Eric Portman in the cast and a new star, Dorothy Tutin, made it an irresistible draw.

Although local people still regarded Greene as having stabbed

Brighton in the back in *Brighton Rock*, there was almost universal agreement that this was a remarkable play. The *Brighton and Hove Herald*'s drama critic said that Greene needed a stage to torture himself and that the real protagonist was the 'conscience of Mr Greene tying itself in knots and taking heavy punishment in the process'.[15] The critic spoke of 'the icy uncompromising wastes of Graham Greeneland', describing the main tenet of the play as a choice between 'suffering our own pain or suffering the pain of others'. Another critic spoke of people being 'hypnotised by the name of Graham Greene'. And the result? 'An orgy of sin, suffering and tragedy in the true Graham Greene manner. It is of course, executed with considerable artistic skill and Mr Greene displays an unerring sense of theatre.'[16]

After touring the provinces, *The Living Room* opened in London on Thursday, 16 April 1953, at the Wyndham's Theatre. The ballerina Margot Fonteyn wrote soon after it was afloat: 'I hear that you were a tremendous success here . . . All I know is that 2 people did something 27 times in 3 weeks.'[17] And it was a truly tremendous success, chiefly because the character of Rose, who commits suicide, was played by the young, still untried actress Dorothy Tutin. Greene in some correspondence called his play the Tutin play, a pointer to her achievement.

It made the front cover of the *Picture Post* with a superb photograph of her. Inside there was a photograph with Greene in the background, just behind Eric Portman and Dorothy Tutin. The play was a triumph: the *Daily Express* reported that Greene 'writes about chill misery', but 'sells like hot cakes'. The journalist John Barber described Greene, 'tall, gaunt, haggard-eyed', and recalled how, after the first night, Greene heard cheers for Dorothy Tutin ('a newcomer of 22 with the frailty of a lapwing in a storm'); cheers for Eric Portman and loud cries for 'Author', 'Author', and when he came up on to the stage he refused his accolades:

Do not call me a success. I have never known a successful man. Have you? A man who was a success to himself? [Barber thought his 'china-blue eyes were bloodshot' as Greene went on] Success is the point of self-deception. Failure is the point of self-knowledge.[18]

On Tuesday 14 April there were eight curtain calls at the end of the play. Margot Fonteyn led the crush of people to congratulate Dorothy Tutin. Greene came in and hugged her. Two nights later the play and the acting brought forth an astonishing fourteen curtain calls.

Evelyn Waugh promised to 'clap hands and call "Author" ',[19] but his response to the play was not entirely happy. Waugh wrote to Greene that the play had held him breathless, but that Greene's 'hospitality before & during the performance dulled my old nut a bit and I must return in very cold blood to enjoy much that I missed. All I was able to realize was that you had written a first class play . . . Messrs [Raymond] Mortimer & [Edward] Sackville-West after the show were most enthusiastic. We vied in your praises.'[20] His diary entry was less sanguine:

> To London with Laura for the first night of Graham's play . . . Champagne first at Claridge's. Odd party – Korda, Eddie Sackville-West . . . Barbara Rothschild. Went to play in high spirits which the performance failed to dispel. More champagne between acts. With result that I was rather inattentive to the final scene which presumably contained the point of the whole sad story. On reflection I felt the tone was false. The piety of the old Catholic ladies wasn't piety. The tragic love of the heroine wasn't tragic; her suicide clumsy.[21]

On the whole Catholics did not like the play, and for obvious reasons. Vincent Cronin writing in the *Catholic World* criticised the young heroine Rose from the point of view of a Catholic: 'She has, after all, given herself adulterously on the very night of her mother's funeral, and she takes her own life (in full knowledge of what that entails) because she cannot get her own way without hurting others . . . Yet because she dies reciting the Our Father, her suicide is clearly meant to arouse our sympathy, when surely on all rational grounds it should arouse our shame.'[22]

*

On 22 August 1953 a totally unexpected letter appeared in *The Times*, which led to the birth of a society. Given Greene's lack of partiality for clubs and societies, the letter was extraordinary:

> Sir, – May we beg the courtesy of your columns to announce the formation of the Anglo-Texan Society? The society has the general object of establishing cultural and social links between this country and the state of Texas which occupies a special historical position not only in relation to the United States but also in relation to Great Britain. It is hoped, when funds permit, to establish special premises in London for welcoming visitors from Texas and – if our ambitions are realized – of providing them with

a hospitality equal to that which Texas has traditionally given to English visitors. Those interested are asked to communicate with the undersigned at 1, Montague Square, London, W1.

> We are, Sir, yours, &c.,
> GRAHAM GREENE, President
> JOHN SUTRO, Vice President

The letter troubled Alan Pryce-Jones, who was attached to the *Times Literary Supplement*, and he asked Sir William Haley, editor of *The Times*, why he had published it. Did he think the Anglo-Texan Society was serious? Sir William replied: 'Mr. Pryce-Jones – the names themselves were a guarantee of the seriousness of the letter.' But if Haley had known anything about John Sutro he would have realised that he was a court jester – a wonderful man given to practical jokes, as of course was Greene.

Greene and John Sutro had gone up to Edinburgh to see a play in which their friend Trevor Howard was acting. They were having drinks beforehand when a party of Texans arrived. The Texans had been on a conducted tour of Norway and were passing through Edinburgh:

> There were two very attractive looking girls in the party, and so I sent a note by the waiter to them asking if they would like to share our box at the theatre. And the waiter returned – a typical dour Scotch Puritan – slammed my note back on the table and said: 'they said it's not for them' or words to that effect.[23]

John Sutro added a further comic note to the scene. The waiter, he said, took the note originally to an old lady, who was outraged to receive it.[24] Greene then arranged that he and Sutro should leave the bar at the same time as the girls, and went up to them and said: ' "I'm sorry if you were offended but I thought perhaps you'd like to come for the play." And they said, "Oh but we didn't think it was true. We thought it was a joke. We'd love to come." ' And so, accordingly, they all went to the play together: 'We had a nice time, a perfectly innocent evening, and afterwards drove them around Edinburgh.' Neither Greene nor Sutro could remember their names, but they were a Miss Crosby and a Miss Alexander: 'Coming back in the train the next day we thought in memory of these sweet people we would found an Anglo-Texan Society.'[25] According to Sutro, 'We sat in the restaurant car drinking black velvets all the way. And by the end of it we said how awful it was that Texans in England had got such a bad deal and we concocted a letter to *The Times*, which I posted off. Graham went off to Kenya the next day and I went off to Paris. The letter went off and we thought, "Oh they will never publish it, will they." And then two days later in Paris . . . the telephone rang in our flat – it was the Associated Press: "What is this about the Texans and an Anglo-Texan Society – you and Graham Greene?" And I said, "Well there it is – the bonds between Great Britain and Texas are great and it's so sad that nothing is done." They said, "Thank you." And then I went back ten days later and found over ninety letters, including one from Sir Hartley Shawcross and Samuel Guinness the banker.' Sutro couldn't resist responding to this extraordinary hoax: 'So I had a huge cocktail party at the Garrick and it was formed, notepaper was printed and we've never been able to stop it.'[26]

Only one newspaper scented a hoax and incidentally revealed what the intelligent man in the street felt about Greene, though the passage in the *New York Times* (11 October 1953) had also its own tongue in cheek:

We could not believe our eyes. We remembered only too vividly Mr Greene's controlled but consuming anger towards us because of what he considered was a reactionary reign of terror over here . . . We can feel scepticism, like a calcium deposit, residing right in our bones. Mr Greene may be on the side of God, but he has created some fascinating diabolisms and plenty of hells in his time, and we wonder whether Mr Greene doesn't have some insidious plot underfoot. Maybe like getting Texas, our richest, vastest, proudest state to secede from the union.[27]

The interest was astonishing – accidentally Greene and Sutro had tapped a deeply felt need. On one occasion, 'aided in its flight', as Greene put it, 'by the irresponsible genius of Sutro', Sutro organised a vast party at the Denham studios. He was helped by the American air force and the Houston Fat Stock Show, which dispatched three steers – three 'bawling doggies' was the comment in the American air force's newspaper – 2,500 pounds of prize Texan beef. Around 1,500 Texans and Anglo-Texan Society members turned up for the greatest event in Anglo-Texan relations or in Texanian terms: 'Just about the biggest Texas blowout in the history of Great Britain.' The United States ambassador, Winthrop Aldrich, was there and was redesignated by the governor of Texas, Allan Shivers, Texan ambassador to Great Britain. So for one day Texas was *truly* the Lone Star state: the 'richest, vastest, proudest state' had seceded from the

Union, and the flag of Texas was handed over by '*Texas* ambassador to Great Britain' to a jubilant John Sutro. What started this great event (Greene's description) was 'the ignoble hilarity of two tipsy travellers when they plotted their little joke'.[28]

The society was also serious and did some good. A letter from the British consul-general in Houston made an offer to the President, Graham Greene, which he could not refuse:

> As you are President of the Anglo-Texan Society I feel that I should endow the society with a contribution, and have pleasure in enclosing the bill for one million dollars! If you should wish any more money, please let me know and I shall be delighted to make up any further differences between the red side of your bank account and the black side that you may require.[29]

Greene was so astonished that in reply he fell back on cliché: 'No word of mine can adequately express our appreciation of your kindness in assuming all responsibility for our debit balances.'[30]

The society was still active in 1976, though sadly it no longer exists today. The flavour of old Texas is in numerous letters sent to Greene:

> As my Grandfather Carl Dyer fitted out the Schooner 'Sarah Lee', filled it with 200 cut-throats at his expense and went to fight in Mexico, ending up by being in charge of Santa Anna* after the battle of San Jacinto . . . I, as the last serving descendant, am naturally interested in your proposal to form the Society. From my point of view it might help me to locate the Bible Santa Anna gave to my Grandfather and also the latter's sword.[31]

Such are the vagaries of fame. When John Sutro died his obituaries made special reference to the fact that, with Greene, he had formed the Anglo-Texan Society in the 1950s to promote friendship between Britain and Texas.

---

* General Santa Anna was captured by the most famous of all Texans, Samuel Houston. Santa Anna later became President of Mexico.

32

Among the Mau Mau

And under the totem poles –
the ancient terror.
— LOUIS MACNEICE

GREENE left John Sutro to 'start' the Anglo-Texan Society because he was flying to Kenya the next day to report on the Mau Mau rebellion for the *Sunday Times*. To Catherine he wrote: 'My plane leaves at 3.50 and I get to Nairobi at 2.30 p.m. tomorrow . . . Did you see my Texas letter in the *Times*? I never thought I'd catch them.'[1]

Nairobi did not appeal to Greene – like Kuala Lumpur. It was the seat of government and he hated it: 'This is the dreariest of dreary holes and I long to get out of it.'[2] He wanted desperately to get into the field where settlers were fighting Mau Mau, but for the first week of his month-long stay he was tied up seeing British officials. He needed their help if he was to arrange his trip up-country, but he was bored: 'Lunch with Brigadier Gibson; Dinner with Father Tasell who talked & talked for an hour. Very tired.'[3] As always he was picking up information, using his powers of observation and attention to detail (he never seemed to take notes) to present a faithful record of the facts of the case. He was so famous that everyone wanted to discuss the conditions up-country and the Mau Mau with him: the editor of the local African weekly; Anderson, owner of the daily newspaper the *Standard*; Michael Blundell, political leader of the settlers; the Commissioner of Police O'Borke ('very friendly & helpful'). Among others Greene saw his old college friend Sir Robert Scott, then High Commissioner for East Africa (whom he spoke well about in *Ways of Escape*). He was invited to call on Scott, though they had lost touch for thirty years:

It was indeed Robert. He sat in the enormous gleaming room

461

completely unchanged, Gaelic, dark, brooding, somehow nervous, behind his great bare desk, fingering a pipe. At Oxford he had always fingered a pipe as though it kept him by a finger's breadth in touch with reality, because the odd thing about this heavy blunt figure, who always seemed to speak with some reluctance, after a long pondering, with a gruff Scottish accent, was that at any moment he was liable to take flight into the irrelevant, irrational world of fantasy . . . For instance there had been the affair of the young barmaid of the Lamb and Flag in St Giles's whom we all agreed resembled in her strange beauty the Egyptian Queen Nefertiti.[4]

He wrote in his diary: '26 August 1953. Robert Scott – unchanged – the bore he always was. Bare office. Adoring elderly secretary. A long way from the Lamb and Flag barmaid.'

And so it went on: 'To Gov. House for dinner with another Balliol man, Sir Frederick Crawford . . . Botched lunch with Michael Blundell. Vasey Member for Finance. Metheson to dinner at his home with Campbell of Time Life. Grim wife like a gypsy & grimmer mother who was either drunk or mad.'[5] The next day, Friday, he met General Sir George Erskine, in charge of the army ('commander-in-chief nice and cooperative') at eleven and that evening he met Group-Captain Ayers: 'to fix air stuff'.[6] A letter to Catherine enlarged on what Greene wanted: 'I've hired a car and a driver so as to be reasonably independent and the two points of real interest during that time seem to be a stay in a mission near Fort Hall in the Kikuyu Reserve, and doing night flying near Nyeri over the Aberdare mountains, spotting gang fires. I hope this comes off.'[7] There were Mau Mau gangs in the Aberdares and Nyeri was one of the areas where they were most active. Sighting gang fires would indicate a Mau Mau hideout, which would be radioed to the British troops operating in the bush below.

Just before he left to go up-country, Greene wrote a very direct letter about Kenya:

This is a dreary & dull spot & my time is taken up by listening to people talk to me from the C. in C. (a very nice man) down. Every day I feel more pro-Kikuyu & more anti-settlers who many of them are a kind of white Mau Mau. On Monday I'm moving off into the Kikuyu reserve with a car . . . Kitui – Fort Hall – Nyeri – the names won't convey much . . . Now I've got to go off to discuss my programme with the man in charge of the R.A.F. here – over whiskies. Priests, soldiers, policemen, government officials, settlers (all but the last quite sympathetic characters) leave one little time but the total effect so boring. The settlers make such a howl & yet only about 20 have been murdered: they ought to try Malaya for a change – or Indo-China. A tremendous show of revolvers which they continually mislay to the benefit of the Mau Mau.[8]

Greene's sympathies were always on the side of the persecuted, the underdog, but sometimes victims changed.

*

The Mau Mau was a secret insurgent organisation formed from the Kikuyu, the largest tribal group in Kenya, and bound by oath to expel white settlers by force. In 1952 the Mau Mau began to take reprisals against the Europeans, especially in the 'White Highlands', and a time of terror began for visitors and settlers alike. The Mau Mau killed not only white settlers but hundreds of loyal Kikuyu, although it was from the ranks of the poorest Kikuyu that they drew their support. As the leader of the Mau Mau, the self-styled Field-Marshal Sir Dedan Kimathi, said in a letter quoted by Greene in his article: 'I am explaining clearly that there is no Mau Mau but the poor man is the Mau Mau and if so, it is only Mau Mau which can finishing Mau Mau, and not bombs and other weapons.'[9]

'General' Kimathi was a simple, vain and cruel man and, as Greene described:

He was fond of writing letters, to the police officers, district officers, even to the Press (signed sometimes 'Askari of the Liberation'). They varied from absurd claims to be head of a Defence Council covering the whole of Africa, from touches of pathetic vanity when he refers to his tours of Africa and Palestine (who knows the satisfaction he may get from such dreams cooped up with his followers in the caves and hideouts of the Aberdare mountains?) to moments of moving simplicity that recall the last letters of Sacco and Vanzetti.[10]

For his followers, Kimathi was charismatic and a remarkable orator, who inspired tremendous personal loyalty and maintained discipline among his troops by the gun or by garrotting them. When 'General' Kago disagreed with Kimathi's proposal that women coming to the camp as food carriers should stay and become sexual partners, Kimathi had him arrested, tried and sentenced to death for questioning his will. Kago would have died on the spot but for the fact that men loyal to him slashed the rope and killed the two hangmen.

Converts to the Mau Mau cause were forced to take an oath whose intention, however bestial, was to prevent betrayal and ensure the loyalty of those forced to join. The Kenyan Government discovered that 90 per cent of the Kikuyu had taken the oath, at least up to the third grade; higher grades of the oath moved into bestiality. The Government wrote a press release quoting the oathing ceremony: 'place a piece of meat in the anus of an old woman, prick human eyes with a thorn, bite a human brain, drink menstrual blood, eat the brain of a dead European, drink the urine of a menstruating woman'. It went on: 'place an erect penis into a living sheep's vagina seven times (without ejaculating); take a dead goat's penis and insert into a prostitute's vagina (the prostitute will be lying down for the purpose) seven times; force a dog to insert its penis into a prostitute seven times after which the initiate licks the dog's penis also.' If a traitor was killed, his blood, liver and heart would be used in a future oathing ceremony. Not all ceremonies used ritual cannibalism, but it was known that some did.

The brutality made Greene sympathetic to the European settlers, although sometimes their treatment of black Kenyans was singularly crude. In his first *Sunday Times* article he quoted a view held in London that political leaders like Kenyatta or Kimathi should not be excluded from political power. But he recognised that from London 'you could not see the group of burnt huts, the charred corpse of a woman, the body robbed of its entrails, the child cut in two halves across the waist, the officer found still living by the roadside with his lower jaw sliced off . . . a hand and foot severed . . . For here was the political power of Kimathi, the power of the panga [razor-edged choppers – something like a billhook].'[11]

Greene wrote the first *Sunday Times* article while staying at the 'Mau-Mau-ridden Fort Hall Reserve'. He was fifteen miles from the scene of the Lari massacre, 'where 150 wives and children of the Kikuyu Home Guard were hacked to death'. These were not whites but blacks employed by the Kenyan Government. *The Times* headline ran: 'MAU MAU MASSACRE OF LOYAL KIKUYU 150 men, women and children dead.'

The Mau Mau waited until most of the men had left on duty as Home Guard and then at 9.30 in bright moonlight they made their attack: 'One group fastened the doors of huts . . . another group, carrying torches, set fire to the grass roofs, and a third armed with pangas, swords, and hatchets, struck down men, women and children as they made desperate attempts to escape from the burning huts. All were terribly mutilated, and some . . . died in the flames . . . Vultures and storks wheeled all day over the scene of the massacre.'[12]

Greene went to the trial of those accused of the massacre. 'Some argued', he wrote, 'that as the Mau Mau had declared war on their own tribesmen, their own tribesmen might be allowed to try them, and certainly it could be argued that it would be better for a wild African justice to prevail than for British justice to alter the strict requirements of evidence. There are occasions when Pilate's gesture might well be imitated.'[13]

He also wrote: 'It would be easier to draw Kimathi as a heroic figure if we could put out of our minds those bestial ceremonies with the living sheep and the dead goat and the naked woman, or the pictures of mutilated bodies, the white farmer lying hacked wide open in his bath, and the little Ruck boy cut to pieces on his bed beside the toy railway track. Heroes should behave like heroes.'[14]

The Ruck massacre had taken place six months previously: a father, mother and young boy had been quickly wiped out, betrayed to the Mau Mau by a trusted servant who only a few days earlier had carried the child tenderly back to his mother after he had fallen from his pony. It was this aspect that plagued the white settlers. Prior to the Mau Mau they had trusted their servants. Greene summed up their feelings:

When the revolt came, it was to the English colonist like a revolt of the domestic staff. The Kikuyu were not savage, they made good clerks and stewards. It was as though Jeeves had taken to the jungle. Even worse, Jeeves had been seen crawling through an arch to drink on his knees from a banana-trough of blood; Jeeves had transfixed a sheep's eye with seven kie-apple thorns; Jeeves had had sexual connection with a goat: Jeeves had sworn, however unwillingly, to kill Bertie Wooster 'or this oath will kill me and all my seed will die'.[15]

'It was unreasonable to expect people to talk reasonably,' because, said Greene, 'there was too much bewilderment and too much fear.'

In part he was sympathetic to the settlers because he was sympathetic to one woman in particular whom he had met and liked immediately – Maria Newall. He had heard of her long before he met her. A courageous woman, she lived alone running a farm without European assistance on the edge of the Mau-Mau-ridden forest. Greene spent a few nights with her and, as his diary entries show, he was disturbed:

12 September 1953: Drove to Nakuru. Herd of about 60 giraffe. Met Maria Newall at club. Had lunch there & then drove to her house via that of a woman whose husband had committed suicide. Liked M.N. immediately. A civilised human being of great courage living alone on the edge of forest, running 500 acre farm without another European & without a guard . . . Slept badly, conscious that if attacked could do little to [save her] . . . M[aria] trousers & scarf looked very lovely. Must have been v. beautiful 15 years ago. During war ran her own ambulance unit. Torpedoed on way to Middle East.

Sunday 13 September 1953: Drove up to farm to inspect new Kikuyu labour. Didn't like look of one old man & one young one who had slipped into party without knowledge of head man. Paper showed he had been bound over for membership of a proscribed society. Decided to take him over to police station where he could be taken . . . to collect his papers & be looked over . . . In the evening police reported they had let youth go. M[aria] rather upset. Told me story of her life over dreary supper. Divorce [Maria Newall was a strong Catholic]. Remarriage outside church. Husband swindled by Lord Carlyle. Suicide. Her love affair with Walter Monckton with whom after 12 years still in love. His semi-impotence. Pathological jealousy . . . Suddenly without warning departure with Biddy[?] Carlyle whom he married . . .

Greene spoke with deep regard of Mrs Newall, who he said was a legend in Kenya: 'She was a standing reproach to frightened settlers dreaming of a safe retreat to England.'[16] Greene learned to judge acquaintances he made in the Kikuyu area by their attitude towards her:

She offended the frightened, she offended also the hysterical (who clamoured for the internment of the whole Kikuyu tribe), and she offended the inefficient . . . Not only has Mrs Newall designed and built her own house with native labour – civilised house in a land where such houses are few . . . not only with the dreaded Kikuyu labour was she running alone her 2000 head of cattle and her pyrethrum, she was capable of arresting an oath-taker singlehanded and driving him at midnight to the nearest police post twenty miles away . . . Her life can be more easily imagined by an American with his historic memory of the early settlers than it can be by the average Englishman at home. Substitute for the

Mau Mau the Red Indian, for the panga the tomahawk and the situation is not very different: sleep behind locked windows with a shotgun beside the bed . . . [17]

Greene remembered her sitting in the evening by her fire, among the books and pictures, in a room from which you could swear you heard the drone of London traffic, but outside only the forest and the mountains, a dog on the watch and the servants locked out, and in her lap a loaded revolver because *this* night may be *the* night.[18] A letter she wrote to Greene gives some idea of her character and her spunky response to danger. The youth who was released by the police had taken on the task for the Mau Mau of killing Maria Newall: 'That boy has been arrested again for not paying Tax. The oath administered [and his] task was to GET me & Edwin my head man.' He then escaped and one of her Kikuyu came up to her and said: 'He didn't get you yet.' She lost her headman and had to take on another, whom she felt afraid of. She related her conversation with him to Greene:

I have a kikuyu who rejoices in the name of Stephen – a christian of the . . . type 3 wives & 11 children, a bible under his arm over his treacherous heart for I have just been told he is mau mau – as well as being a police informer – he was indeed rewarded with a shop site in Elburgar for his help & 'loyalty'. I have however decided to keep him as it is far better than someone I *think* I can trust. I had to call him up & tell him if he put a foot wrong he was for 10 years H[ard] Labour. It was terrifying to see any human quail before an old woman – I added that if I found him breaking the curfew I should have no hesitation in shooting him – the interview then over I wouldn't like to say who was the more shaken!!![19]

*

Greene did not travel in a hired car as he had hoped, instead he was taken up-country by young officers. He was seeking trouble as always: going to the Fort Hall area; to Kapenguria where the mass trial over the Lari massacre was taking place; to Father McGill, whose mission had been attacked, and on into Mau Mau country – 'Up to H[ome] G[uard] camp. Terrible road. Rain. Cold. Back to Kojima. Nearly plunged over ravine.'[20] This brief entry was more of an *aide-mémoire* for the writer. Greene later expanded on the whole episode:

This young officer with whom I was travelling was in a landrover or jeep in the Aberdares, the mountains in Kenya. We turned corners very narrow, more paths than roads and just ahead of us with its back turned a rhinoceros. They go for a jeep like a ton of butter. He stopped quickly and whispered to me can you get up that bank and there was a bank about as high as this room, and I said no. And on the other side was a steep drop of a few hundred feet. So he said keep quiet and we waited. And the rhinoceros moved its head sideways a bit and then ambled on. And we gave it a good twenty minutes start before we went on again.[21]

In his diary he notes: 'Tense moment when we came on rhino. Watching it move its head uneasily. Nervy drive back. More fear of Rhinos than Mau Mau.'[22]

Another who drove him into the Mau Mau area in Fort Hall was a young officer named Candler whom Greene liked very much: 'Drank in police post. Eventually C[andler] turned up. Nervy night in his unprotected house with two former prisoners & two ex-Mau Mau bodyguards . . . Lunch with Candler. Attractive young wife.'[23] On 24 March 1954 he wrote: 'Poor Candler's been killed by the Mau Mau . . . in a typically horrid way. He had a very sweet wife.'[24]

In interview Greene described his expedition with Candler in his hushed voice: he would bite off the ends of his sentences when disturbed. Candler had a bodyguard of ex-Mau Mau men and was going to disarm a Home Guard up at the top of a mountain. Why they should assist the Mau Mau was unclear, but perhaps they meant to flush the Mau Mau from their hideout, providing them with a clear way down the mountain to steal and thereby open them up to attacks by British soldiers. The young officer refused ever to sleep inside a police station so they spent the night in an empty house outside town:

the Mau-Mau (ex-Mau-Mau) kept guard all night and we talked. We'd had quite a lot to drink. He'd got a gun: I hadn't. But I had no belief in his guard and I thought this time they'll come in and get the opportunity to cut our throats. They didn't. We went up and made a speech to the Homeguard and took away all their guns. And coming back it was very steep, wet road of clay and the car skidded and the front wheels began to go over, and there was about a thousand foot drop below. And it stopped. I didn't say anything – he just had time to say, 'We've had it.'[25]

Greene wrote about this incident to Catherine: 'The D.O. said quite calmly, "Now we've had it", and we mounted the bank and the front wheels went over a ravine.' And as when Greene had recorded an earlier narrow escape in Vietnam (when his jeep was stopped before it went over a mine), so now he experienced a similar feeling: 'It was the nearest I've ever come to my desire.'[26]

Candler was killed about six months later. Greene mentioned that Candler had been ambushed by the Mau Mau: 'His bodyguard stood by him. One went off to get help and when help came his guards were dead and his head had been cut off.' The pressure and anguish which Greene experienced are clear in his first article about Kenya, 'Photo of trunk from which the head has been severed remains long in the memory'.[27]

The battle of the Mau Mau was not concluded when Greene left Kenya. His final remarks about the outcome were still relevant:

> For good or ill the future of the Kikuyu seems to depend on Christianity − either they will be won by the Christianity of the priest in the execution pit or by the strange religion . . . where they are taught that there was a white God and a white Bible and every text had a secret meaning which the African was not expected to notice: 'Eyes have you and see not' − this meant, the teachers said, that you did not see what these white people and their white God intended for you and your children, and the black God lay in hiding like Mau Mau in the bamboo forest.[28]

Despite everything, Greene liked the Kikuyu: 'A young Kikuyu guide yesterday asked me if I had a gun. I said no. He said, "You trust in the goodness of God." ' And it was Father McGill at the Mission of the Annunciation whose mission had been burnt down (ten schools had been destroyed by the time Greene arrived in Kenya) who told him that the Mau Mau 'die like angels':

> When so many hundred times you have had to descend into the pit below the gallows to give the last rites to the broken-necked carrion lying there, each body becomes the body of an individual. You are in a different world from the courtroom at Githenguri . . . [29]

It was the same priest who would spend the last night with condemned prisoners: 'They ask unanswerable questions. They say to me: "Didn't God make a land for each people to live in, black and white, and didn't he put the sea between so that we shouldn't interfere with each other?" '[30]

33

No Man Is Neutral

He who does not bellow the truth when he knows the
truth makes himself the accomplice of liars and forgers.
— CHARLES PÉGUY

IN the 1950s Greene seemed to have taken on the role of unofficial
ombudsman — investigating complaints about what he saw as
unjust official acts. He used his fame to protect the vulnerable and
fight for the underdog. He had an incorrigible sympathy for the
outcast.

But if you seek the role of a David, Goliaths will appear. Not only
did Greene attack America, he attacked other countries and
individuals as well. In France he attacked his own church and the
highest prelate of the land. On 3 August 1954 the French novelist
Colette died. The first French woman to be honoured with a state
funeral, she was denied a religious funeral at the Eglise Saint-Roch.
Cardinal Feltin, Archbishop of Paris, refused on the grounds that
Colette had been twice divorced. Greene was among the mourners
who came to pay their last respects: 'On Saturday I had a seat in the
Goncourt Tribune for the funeral of Colette: a big cenotaph covered
with flags in the middle of the Palais Royale, a platoon and a band
of the Garde Républicaine, ovations and outside in the streets masses
of people and police.' He was moved to write an open letter to the
archbishop. Old poor women came up to him and complained 'of
the archbishop of Paris and his interdict'.[1] His letter appeared on the
front page of *Le Figaro littéraire* on 7 August 1954:

Those of us who loved Colette and her books gathered today to
honour her in a ceremony that must have seemed strangely
curtailed to Catholics present. We are used to pray for our dead.
In our faith the dead are never abandoned. It is the right of every
person baptised a Catholic to be accompanied to the tomb by a

priest. This right cannot be lost . . . due to some crime or misdemeanour, because no human being is capable of judging another or of deciding where his faults begin or his merits end.[2]

Admitting that everyone knew the reason why the archbishop had refused Colette the presence of a priest, Greene asked why two civil marriages were so unforgivable, for as he pointed out 'some of our saints provide worse examples'. Of course the difference was that the future saints repented, Colette had not: 'But to repent means to rethink one's life, and no one can say what passes through a mind trained in habits of lucidity when it is confronted with the imminent fact of death.' Greene accused the archbishop of making his condemnation on insufficient evidence: 'for you were not with her then, nor were any of your ministers'. He charged that the impression had been given that the 'Church pursues the fault beyond the grave'. Finally, Greene rounded on the archbishop: 'Your Eminence, through such a strict interpretation of the rule, seems to deny the hope of that final intervention of grace upon which surely Your Eminence and each one of us will depend at the last hour.'

Many Catholics wrote to Greene objecting to his stance, though many did not. His friend Evelyn Waugh, so much more conservative in his approach to the Church, strenuously objected to it in a letter to Nancy Mitford: 'Graham Greene's letter was fatuous and impertinent. He was tipsy when he wrote it at luncheon with some frogs & left it to them to translate & despatch. He is dead to shame in these matters.'[3] When Mark Amory, the editor of Waugh's letters, approached Greene about this letter, Greene answered: 'I was not tipsy with alcohol when I wrote the letter but tipsy with rage.'[4]

*

On 9 October 1954 French Foreign Legion buglers in Hanoi blew a sad refrain as the tricolour was lowered, and the defeated French slipped away. The French had lost Vietnam on the battlefield at Dien Bien Phu and they were given eighty days to pack up and leave. The following day 30,000 Vietminh soldiers came marching into the city to celebrate and 80,000 Vietnamese, mostly Catholics frightened by the godless communists, fled south. Buildings were suddenly covered with slogans to celebrate the arrival of the Vietminh. One popular slogan expressed the somewhat idle hope: 'May President Ho Chi Minh Live a Thousand Years.' He lived seventy-seven years and lies in a mausoleum in Hanoi – badly embalmed so that he looks more dead than the dead.

After the French defeat the country was divided into two at the seventeenth parallel. The north was given to the communists, and in the south the Americans discovered their third-force leader in the Catholic Ngo Dinh Diem, who was made president of the republic.

Norodom palace in Saigon, once overflowing with French advisers, military and civilian, was now overflowing with American advisers. American newspapers, the American legation, and the many young Americans in Saigon genuinely believed they could do better than the French. They were ready to take over to defeat the communists – and colonialism too: 'Little by little, the folks back on the farm will realize that the world is theirs, whether they want it or not, for good or evil.'[5]

At this time *The Quiet American* was published. Greene had finished it in late June 1955 and it was brought out in England, in less than six months, by 5 December. It received powerful supportive reviews: Christopher Sykes in the *Tablet* thought it Greene's best book; Donat O'Donnell, the pen name of Conor Cruise O'Brien (*New Statesman*) called it 'The best novel for many years, certainly since *The Power and the Glory*'; Nancy Spain (*Daily Express*) thought it 'as near a masterpiece as anything else I have ever read in the last twenty years'; whilst Evelyn Waugh (*Sunday Times*) found the work 'Masterly, original, and vigorous'.

Greene touched a raw nerve among certain American reviewers, touchy about his portrayal of their national character as reflected by Pyle – so young, so naïve, so democratic in the face of the complex oriental mind. To some extent Greene had prepared the way for the novel's hostile reception with his much-publicised anti-McCarthy, anti-McCarran stand, especially his remark that Americans lived in a 'red-obsessed "state of fear"'. But Greene's particular enemy was *Newsweek*. Its headline was 'This Man's Caricature of the American Abroad' and the article which followed questioned Greene's purpose in inventing such a shallow figure, a cardboard lampoon, as Pyle. *Newsweek* answered its own question by suggesting that Greene had become overtly anti-American because in 1952 he had been 'temporarily denied a visa to the United States' by the consul in Saigon on the grounds of his membership of the communist party as a youthful prank for a few weeks in 1922. Greene's anti-Americanism was seen as arising out of personal pique.

The oddity about the review was that the novel was not published in America until March 1956, yet the review appeared on 2 January. One can only guess why the magazine decided it should attack a book so much in advance of publication. Presumably *Newsweek* was determined to put an end to the popularity of this British gadfly, this provoker and irritator; perhaps the magazine's sympathies were with Senator McCarthy.

Later that year *Newsweek* returned to the attack under the headline 'When Greene is Red' because it had discovered that Greene's novel was popular in Moscow:

> Wonder of wonders, the Kremlin has discovered Graham Greene. Not the Greene of the breath-taking 'entertainments', like 'Orient Express', 'This Gun for Hire', not the Greene of 'The Heart of the Matter' and 'The End of the Affair' whose characters wander through a haze of tortured religiosity. But the political Greene of 'The Quiet American', the controversial novel about Indo-China which has aroused many American tempers.
>
> Joining a chorus of acclaim from Soviet journals and newspapers, Pravda itself called the novel 'the most remarkable event' of recent British literary history and gave it five precious columns of comment . . . why [are] the Reds shouting over the work of a Roman Catholic novelist? It seems that the Soviet critics found a key to the secrets of the novel. All the leading characters turn out to be cut-and-dried political symbols, rather than the complete fragments of humanity which Greene intended (but hardly achieved).[6]

Thus Fowler, the 'cynical, world-weary, opium-smoking British newspaper correspondent, stands in *Pravda*'s view for humanitarianism triumphant: Alden Pyle, for anti-humanitarianism repulsed . . . "Pyle", *Pravda* now says, "is a symbol of the antihuman forces with which Fowler no longer wants to associate himself." When he decides to "become a human being" Fowler "commits an act of great courage" by entering into a conspiracy to murder Pyle.' Here was proof, thought *Newsweek*, of Greene's 'dreary stereotyping of his American characters'; 'Greene may take American criticism of *The Quiet American* somewhat more seriously, now that the communists have proved the woodenness of characters by making them over so effortlessly into Marxist stereotypes.'[7] *Newsweek* did much to establish in the minds of Americans that Greene hated America.

Greene often said that he was *not* anti-American but 'anti American foreign policy'. What he disliked was the vast influence of America spreading inexorably around the world. He wrote in his Congo journal in 1959 when rebellion had broken out in the Belgian colony: '[the bishop] feels – as I cannot – that the tribal framework must be broken and material incentives be given for that purpose.

Doesn't this lead straight to the gadget world of the States? He spoke of the necessity for a mystique, but is there any mystique in America today, even inside the Catholic church?'[8]

Yet were Americans not right to be disturbed at Greene's more provocative statements, for example when he said that he would prefer to end his days in the USSR rather than the United States? Greene later said that he meant the comment to be ironic:

> I think that the writer is taken more seriously in Russia than he is in the United States. In the US I could attack anything until the cows come home, as long as my books sold, they wouldn't object. But if in the USSR I wrote as I felt, I would soon find myself in a labour camp or some prison. I would end my days fairly soon but at least I'd have the compliment of being taken seriously.[9]

The explanation is still anti-American, though a variant of it found in Malcolm Muggeridge's diary makes more sense:

> I ran into Graham Greene, whom I hadn't seen for a long time. We were affectionate with an undercurrent of hostility. Greene described having a haemorrhage in New York. He seemed to me in poorish shape on the whole, talked a lot about how Russian domination would be less terrible than American, etc. I mentioned the Church and he said Russians only destroy its body, whereas the Americans destroy its soul. Altogether, he's as difficult as anyone I know, but I still like him.[10]

Not every American reviewer thought *The Quiet American* deserved the attacks it received. Robert Clurman in the *New York Times Book Review* felt it was high time that Greene ('a most quiet Englishman while Americans were frothing at the mouth over his book') said a word or two. The question which needed answering was how literally was one to take the Englishman Fowler, whom many readers interpreted as a spokesman for the author. In a letter to a friend, quoted by Clurman, Greene replied:

> If one uses the first person the point of view has obviously got to be I, and one must put one's self in I's skin as intensely as possible. It would be absurd, however, to imagine that the author is Fowler any more than he is the boy gangster in *Brighton Rock* . . . As Pyle stood for complete engagement, Fowler obviously had to stand for an equally exaggerated viewpoint on the other side. Those who have read my war articles on Indochina will know that I am *myself*

by no means a neutralist. I share certain of Fowler's views, but obviously not all of them – for instance, I don't happen to be an atheist. But even those views I share with Fowler I don't hold with Fowler's passion because I don't happen to have lost a girl to an American.[11]

While the novel *is* anti-American, it is also anti-British in the sense that Fowler, the tired cynic, commits the greatest sin in Greene's catechism – the fatal betrayal of a friend. In life Greene's loyalty to friends knew no limits. Fowler involves himself with the Vietminh because he discovers that Pyle's naïve dealings with the rebel Colonel Thé have led to the deaths of innocent civilians.* Pyle is involved in political intrigue beyond his capacity to manage.

The Quiet American is based on Greene's experiences, but it is based on other people's as well. Pyle, as we have seen, has no single source. The young unfortunate Jollye, whom Greene met in Malaya, alone made an important contribution to the creation of Pyle in the sense that Jollye's naïveté and lack of cunning gave Greene his notion of how to develop his fictional character. That an Englishman was one source for the American is ironic. *Newsweek*'s title for its review. 'This Man's Caricature of the American Abroad' need not have burst any American blood vessels for Pyle was also 'This Man's Caricature of an Englishman Abroad'.

*

Absorption of a place and its atmosphere was a necessity for Greene. He searched for exactitude in order that his characters could come alive in their setting. He felt, as did Conrad, the necessity of doing 'justice to the visible universe'.

American journalists on their way to Vietnam, after the French had withdrawn, took in their backpacks a copy of *The Quiet American*. It was the most reliable account of what it was like in Vietnam: it was also prophetic. Americans writing later about the Vietnamese debacle, when they in turn lost to the Viet Cong, felt that American policy-makers should have listened to Greene. It was the truth of the situation he found in Vietnam that was important, so since he was such an accurate chronicler of the period, anti-Americanism in some form had to appear in the novel because strong anti-Americanism was historically present, most of it emanating from

---

* When Greene interviewed President Diem, he asked him why he had allowed Thé to return when he was responsible for killing so many of his own people. Greene recalled that Diem burst into peals of laughter and said: 'Peut-être, peut-être.'[12]

the French. The Americans were pouring in arms and economic aid of all kinds, but it did not make them loved by the French – generosity often provokes envy. France had entered its colonial twilight. The French rulers knew in sober moments that the tale of their day was told and that their Far Eastern possessions would be lost. American prodigality often aroused in the French an impotent malice. The Americans were the new Romans, the new super power, and this political phenomenon was difficult for the French in particular and the West in general to face, and harder still to swallow. The journalist Howard Simpson recalled running into a group of French legionnaires in the company of a famous colonel who had lived in Vietnam since 1940. They were drunk and out of their mouths came the questions which many Frenchmen were asking the new *peaceful* invaders:

> The colonel loosed a barrage of barbed questions that raised my boiling point. Why were the Americans in Indochina? What did we think we'd accomplish? How much time had I spent in Vietnam? Did I know anything about the country?[13]

Lucien Bodard, the French foreign correspondent, described America's secret policy: 'They were only waiting for the chance to back nationalism once more – since Ho Chi Minh was a Communist, the right patriotic nationalist had to be found, the one who would beat Ho Chi Minh and his Communism far better than the repressive French.' Bodard's anti-Americanism leaps out from the page:

> All the Americans in Saigon, those in the embassy, those in the military mission and the special services and the USIS, to say nothing of the American journalists, were ill with Francophobia, virtuously ill at the spectacle of the French setting up 'colonialism' once more. They had such a wonderfully deep and sincere belief in the essential evil of it all. And they were so sure that America would do so much better than France . . . How passionately they all longed for a real Vietnam, a friend of America, instead of this Vietnam given over as a prey to the French.[14]

It was Bodard's view that the Americans were secretly working against the French in their zeal to stamp out colonialism. Moreover they gave arms to such bandits as Colonel Thé:

> Americans of every kind whispered to Vietnamese of every kind,

'Ask for more. Don't give in. Don't let yourselves be swayed by the French . . . they are trying to get out of their difficulties by disguising their colonial problem as anti-Communism.' It worked one hundred per cent against the French. By every means, and above all by the use of dollars, the Americans built themselves up a following. The secret services for their part went further: they gave arms to Bacut [leader of the Hoahao], to Thrinh Minh Thé, the Caodaist, and to all the leaders within the sects who went on hating the French and killing them in the name of nationalism . . . [15]

Despite official pronouncements promoting Franco-American friendship, the French only saw that their influence was being undermined by a 'flood of goods "made in USA" ':

it was the whole gamut of Yankee civilization, from DDT to canned cheese. And each parcel was sewn a huge label with the crossed flags of Vietnam and the United States and the words 'A gift from the people of America to the people of Vietnam'.[16]

The economic aid mission (to which Pyle belongs) was most dangerous to French interests:

It was the experts of the Economic Aid Mission who carried out the free distributions. They travelled all through Indochina telling the crowds, 'The French are your exploiters, but the Americans are your friends.' Nothing diminished their zeal . . . How ardently, in spite of their racial prejudices, they tried to love the Vietnamese.
. . . what fury, what bitterness, what cries of impotence against the high-ups who understood nothing, and against the French, who went on being kings of the castle! Naturally all these little Americans, eaten up by their consciences and carried away by zeal, went beyond their orders and joyfully did everything they could think of against the French . . . [17]

Bodard also stressed the Americans' lack of sensitivity to the Vietnamese culture. When two US officers were taken to visit a purely Asian unit they were honoured with a banquet of Vietnamese delicacies – a lacquered piglet, quantities of shrimps and *nem* (rice-flour fritters):

At the sight of the feast the Americans shuddered: then, apologizing, they took sealed packets out of their briefcases, cellophane-wrapped germ-free food. The Annamese NCO went pale as they started to eat their hygienic sandwiches without so much as touching the dishes he offered them: he was mortally offended.[18]

The Americans' preference for the cellophane-wrapped germ-free food seems likely to be an anecdote. Greene described Pyle's eating habits:

'Like a sandwich? They're really awfully good. A new sandwich-spread called Vit-Health. My mother sent it from the States.'
'No, thanks, I'm not hungry.'
'It tastes rather like Russian salad – only sort of drier.'
'I don't think I will.'
'You don't mind if I do?'
'No, no of course not.'
He took a large mouthful and it crunched and crackled.
In the distance Buddha in white and pink stone rode away from his ancestral home, and his valet – another statue – pursued him running. The female cardinals were drifting back to their house and the Eye of God watched us from above the Cathedral door.
'You know they are serving lunch here?' I said.
'I thought I wouldn't risk it. The meat – you have to be careful in this heat.'
'You are quite safe. They are vegetarian.'
'I suppose it's all right – but I like to know what I'm eating.'
He took another munch at his Vit-Health.[19]

In contrast to the French anti-Americanism, Greene's 'anti-Americanism' is tame.

When Fowler and Pyle are holed up for the night in the watch-tower in Phat Diem they argue about the war and its meaning: Pyle speaks of political ideas, Fowler of war's personal impact:

'You and your like are trying to make a war with the help of people who just aren't interested.'
'They don't want Communism.'
'They want enough rice,' I said. 'They don't want to be shot at. They want one day to be much the same as another. They don't want our white skins around telling them what they want.'
'If Indo-China goes . . . '
'I know the record. Siam goes. Malaya goes. Indonesia goes. What does "go" mean? . . . I'd bet my future harp against your

golden crown that in five hundred years there may be no New York or London, but they'll be growing paddy in these fields, they'll be carrying their produce to markets on long poles wearing their pointed hats. The small boys will be sitting on the buffaloes . . .'

'They'll be forced to believe what they are told, they won't be allowed to think for themselves.'

'Thought's a luxury. Do you think the peasant sits and thinks of God and Democracy when he gets inside his mud hut at night?'[20]

When Pyle cries out, 'You should be against the French. Their colonialism,' he is reflecting the arguments that went on in bars and restaurants of Saigon in the 1950s. Fowler's point of view is not sound, but perhaps it is an argument which was heard then:

'Isms and ocracies. Give me facts. A rubber planter beats his labourer – all right, I'm against him. He hasn't been instructed to do it by the Minister of the Colonies. In France I expect he'd beat his wife. I've seen a priest, so poor he hasn't a change of trousers, working fifteen hours a day from hut to hut in a cholera epidemic, eating nothing but rice and salt fish, saying his Mass with an old cup – a wooden platter . . . Why don't you call that colonialism?'

'It *is* colonialism . . . it's often the good administrators who make it hard to change a bad system . . . So you think we've lost?'

'That's not the point,' I said. 'I've no particular desire to see you win. I'd like those two poor buggers there to be happy – that's all. I wish they didn't have to sit in the dark at night scared.'[21]

Greene provided surprising support for colonialism, suggesting the relativity of his political beliefs. Elsewhere he wrote: 'the writer should always be ready to change sides at the drop of a hat. He stands for the victims, and the victims change'.[22] In an article for *Paris Match* he took a more Olympian view:

It is a stern and sad outlook and, when everything is considered, it represents for France the end of an empire. The United States is exaggeratedly distrustful of empires, but we Europeans retain the memory of what we owe to Rome, just as Latin America knows what it owes to Spain. When the hour of evacuation sounds there will be many Vietnamese who will regret the loss of the language which put them in contact with the art and faith of the West. The injustices committed by men who were harassed, exhausted and ignorant will be forgotten and the names of a good number of Frenchmen, priests, soldiers and administrators, will remain engraved in the memory of the Vietnamese: a fort, a road intersection, a dilapidated church. 'Do you remember,' someone will say, 'the days before the Legions left?'[23]

Speaking of Pyle, Fowler says: 'What's the good? he'll always be innocent, you can't blame the innocent, they are always guiltless. All you can do is control them or eliminate them. Innocence is a kind of insanity.'[24] There is a fearful price to pay for Pyle's righteous innocence, an innocence linked with power, the power of America. In Greene's view, the innocent do harm to the innocent: 'Is there any solution here the West can offer?' he wrote in his Indo-China diary, and added, 'the bar tonight was loud with innocent American voices, and that was the worst disquiet'.

34

The Honourable Correspondent and the Dishonourable Friend

Trust not him with your secrets, who when left alone in
your room, turns over your papers.
                    — JOHANN KASPER LAVATER

SHORTLY after Greene's arrival in Vietnam, the chief of the Sûreté
in Vietnam brought de Lattre a secret report on Greene. The
report indicated that Greene's brother Hugh was the 'patron' of the
Secret Services in Malaya and that Greene was an 'honourable
correspondent': in the vocabulary of espionage, a spy with a cover.[1]
De Lattre's suspicions were confirmed.

Greene first became aware of a certain coolness in de Lattre's
attitude upon his return to Vietnam in October 1951. Before, de
Lattre had treated Greene as an honoured guest, presenting him with
a shoulder-flash of the First French Army (which de Lattre had
commanded) and inviting him to a reunion of his old comrades. But
now Greene's friend Trevor Wilson had been ordered out of the
country and Greene's relationship with de Lattre had deteriorated.
By this time de Lattre had lost his only son and 'his rhetoric of hope',
as Greene put it, was wearing thin:

Now in a strange sick manner he linked the death of his son with
my visit to Phat Diem and the fact that both Trevor Wilson and I
were Catholics. He had shifted on to us, in his poor guilt-ridden
mind, the responsibility for his son's death (he had sent his son to
join a Vietnamese battalion to break up his relationship with a
Vietnamese girl who was a former mistress of the Emperor). He
reported to the Foreign Office that Trevor Wilson, who had been
decorated for his services to France during the war, was no longer
persona grata. Trevor was thrown out of Indo-China, and the
Foreign Office lost a remarkable Consul and the French a great
friend of their country. He had already gone when I returned to

Hanoi, but he was allowed to come back for two weeks to pack up his effects.[2]

The head of the Sûreté went even further and told de Lattre that 'Graham Greene has come here with precise instructions.' To which de Lattre responded: 'All these English, they're too much! It isn't sufficient to have a consul who's in the Secret Service, they even send me their novelists as agents and Catholic novelists into the bargain.'[3]

De Lattre was convinced that Trevor Wilson had dual roles, one as British consul in Hanoi and the other as a 'spy' for the British Government. Wilson's opposite number in the CIA in Hanoi told me there was no doubt about this:

Trevor Wilson was very shrewd – always on the look out for information and he hired a British girl in Hanoi married to a French foreign legion officer to be his office manager and this was another source of information for Trevor. There is no question that Trevor was doing two jobs. On the one hand he had his Consular diplomatic job. On the other he was SIS, visiting Maurice Oldfield his chief in Singapore. Oldfield was in charge of Trevor because he was the operational head [controller of MI6 then located in Singapore] who later became head of SIS in London – C himself.[4]

According to Greene, suspicion peaked when he received a telegram from Wilson announcing his imminent arrival from Paris: 'It was', said Greene, 'his eccentric economy never unnecessarily to sign a telegram, but obviously to the censorship this was a deliberate attempt to deceive.'[5] (It is probable that Wilson *was* trying to avoid recognition by not signing his telegram, for I have viewed copies of other telegrams Wilson sent to Greene and in every case they are signed: Greene was protecting his friend here.)

Greene guessed matters were coming to a head when, through the head of the Sûreté, he was commanded to have lunch with de Lattre. During the meal nothing was said, but the general came over to him afterwards saying, 'Le pauvre Graham Greene', and because de Lattre had not found time to speak to Greene he invited him back to a cocktail party and dinner the same evening. Greene, with commendable restraint, went back a second time to a party that went on and on, with musical entertainment by a soldiers' choir. He had heard the rumours that de Lattre would be leaving Hanoi, and, more ominously for France's future in Vietnam, would not return.

If I had known he was a dying man perhaps I would have perceived in him again the hero I had met a year before. Now he seemed only the general whose speeches were too long, whose magic had faded . . . a dying flame looks as if it had never been anything but smoke.

At ten o'clock the singing stopped and the general turned to me. 'And now, Graham Greene, why are you here?' His broken English had an abrupt boastful quality he did not intend. I said, 'I have told you already. I am writing an article for *Life*.'

'I understand you were in the Intelligence Service in the war. For three years.'

I explained to the general that under National Service we did not pick our job − nor continue it when the war was over.

'I understand that no one ever leaves the British Secret Service.'

'That may be true of the Deuxième Bureau,' I said, 'it is not true with us.' A servant announced dinner.

I sat next to the general and we talked polite small talk. Madame de Lattre eyed me sternly − I had disturbed the peace of a sick man whom she loved, on his last night in Hanoi, the scene of his triumph and his failure. Even though I was unaware how sick he was, I felt a meanness in myself. He deserved better company.[6]

When they rose from the table Greene asked de Lattre if he might see him alone. When the other guests left, which was not until one in the morning, the general sent for Greene to come to his study:

I had prepared in my mind what I thought was a clear narration, which included even the amount I was being paid by *Life* for my article. He heard me out and then expressed his satisfaction with some grandiloquence (but that was his way). 'I have told the Sûreté, Graham Greene is my friend. I do not believe what you say about him. Then they come again and tell me you have been here or there and I say, I do not believe, Graham Greene is my friend. And then again they come . . . ' He shook hands warmly, saying how glad he was to know that all was a mistake, but next day, before he left for Paris, his misgivings returned. I had received yet another dubious telegram, again unsigned − this time from my literary agent in Paris, 'Your friend will arrive on Thursday. Dorothy under instruction from Philip.'

The last sentence referred to my friend, Dorothy Glover . . .

who had decided to become a Catholic, and Philip was Father Philip Caraman, the well-known London Jesuit, but it was obvious what the Sûreté made of it. 'I knew he was a spy,' de Lattre told one of his staff, before boarding his plane. 'Why should anyone come to this war for four hundred dollars?' I had forgotten how uncertain his English was – he had mislaid a zero.[7]

In his journal, Greene recorded his feelings about his final interview with de Lattre: 'Said he had taken my part against the police but was worried by reports they brought in. Accepted my word. But does he? Felt I had not defended T[revor] enough, but the prejudices there are too great.'[8]

Wilson lost favour with de Lattre as a result of his contact with the bishop of Phat Diem, Monsignor Le Huu-Tu, who was outspokenly no friend of the French. Because Phat Diem was vulnerable to attacks by the Vietminh he had approached the French for weapons, but once they were in his hands he spoke from the safety of his cathedral against the French colonists: 'I have what I need for dealing with the French.' He had also had considerable contact with the Vietminh and at one time (in 1946) had agreed to be Ho Chi Minh's 'Supreme' adviser.

De Lattre was anglophobic and was profoundly upset by the fact that Bishop Le Huu-Tu had singled out Wilson before an applauding crowd by saying 'Long live the King of England': it was the sons of France (including de Lattre's own son) who were losing their lives in Vietnam, not the British. Indeed the French believed, according to my CIA sources, that Wilson encouraged the bishop's antagonism towards the French: 'Trevor was a very, very smart intelligence officer, as well as an important consul. He knew what was going on. He pushed too many buttons and he got into a jam with the French . . . He was out every night, to the bars, whatever was going on, parties, everywhere. That was his job if he was going to do it well and he did it well.'[9]

The fact that Wilson was an ardent Catholic and knew the Catholic hierarchies at Phat Diem and Bui Chu was a matter of some political significance, for they were a law unto themselves and felt themselves to be separate from the French administration. Greene, through Wilson, also had close contact with Bishop Le Huu-Tu and interviewed him for *Paris Match*. The article brilliantly, and unexpectedly, described him as 'an austere man with the face of a sad, meditative monkey'. This description at least should have pleased de Lattre, but it did not:

De Lattre rages when he learns about all the ceremonies organized for that [secret] agent. He foams at the mouth when he is told about the length of the interviews between the bishop and the novelist: The Englishman had devoutly kissed his ring, the Englishman had taken communion, the Englishman had displayed his most emotional smile. It is finally that same Englishman who found the best noun, the unique, the true, the necessary noun, 'monkey' which had escaped Dannaud, [General] Cogny, and Goussault. That's what it means to be a properly famous novelist.[10]

Greene's relationship with Wilson and consequently with the bishop of Phat Diem made him, in de Lattre's eyes, guilty by association.

There was much Intelligence interest in Phat Diem. The Catholics, an important political group in North Vietnam, were well organised: 'They have the infrastructure: the churches are full of meeting places where you can meet clandestinely: they know how to operate: they know how to send messages securely: they *are* good spy potential . . . And the Catholics were the true Third Force in Vietnam.'[11]

Both the CIA and the SIS were on a similar mission of assessment. Both wanted to know whether the French were trying to retain a colonial regime under a new form of colonialism – which the Belgians also tried later in the Congo. The Government would be local as would be the titular minister, but the *Number One* adviser would be French. 'The British were very interested in this and needed information as to how it was going.'[12] The Labour Government wanted to abdicate its colonial responsibilities, yet some of the trading companies had a strong desire to see the re-establishment of a colonial or pseudo-colonial regime.

Wilson's mission was not to try to influence de Lattre, but to inform the British Government what was happening. De Lattre in turn would have wished Wilson to be sympathetic to the French point of view and to influence American participation. However, Wilson was not sympathetic towards an excessive anti-colonialism, though neither did he hold the American belief that the communists were a monolithic block stretching through Indo-China ready to join forces with the Chinese.

Indeed, the following anecdote about Greene and Wilson at one of de Lattre's famous dinner parties reveals Wilson's rather 'undiplomatic' summary of the political situation:

The two men Greene and Wilson boozing together, would talk whole nights until dawn. One evening when they were supposed to dine, both of them, at de Lattre's, the consul had already drunk one glass too many. When he was half drunk, which was a semi-permanent state, he expressed what he was thinking and nothing could make him shut up, not even the furious face of the General. Wilson began telling him abominably scandalous things: 'You are going to lose the war. The whole people is Vietminh. You are fighting against the entire people! With your mercenaries you are already condemned, you're going to be defeated!'

De Lattre knows very well that the job isn't easy, but if it was child's play, why did France call him? He was there to conquer and he believes that he WILL win. He has, at this point, no doubt at all. In any case, it will be the 'Great Game'. It's HE who will save Asia . . . not this ridiculous boozer, a John Bull boozer – a living wine skin pierced with eyes at the same time too lively and too bloodshot – treats him as if he belongs to the ridiculous lineage of all incapable, incompetent French generals . . . He says such things in front of his companion, this so called writer, of whom he is the mentor. He says such things before the whole entourage and even before Madame de Lattre. It's intolerable![13]

It is probable that this drunken outburst by Wilson was the final straw for de Lattre and the cause of Wilson's expulsion from the country.

Once Wilson was ejected did Greene work for the SIS, even if on an informal basis, when he was in Vietnam? Was he, as the French reported, 'a spy with a cover' – an 'honourable correspondent'? Evidence that Greene helped out the 'old firm' comes from the Sûreté in Vietnam and CIA agents who knew him there. My CIA source had no doubt that the file the Sûreté kept on Greene was accurate (he had been astonished by the depth and accuracy of the file amassed on his own activities): 'And Trevor got kicked out, so that from then onwards Greene, who had been introduced to the political bishops by Trevor, *took on part of that job* [emphasis added].'[14]

Wilson's exile was not permanent. After de Lattre's death, Wilson was allowed back into Vietnam, only this time under the cover of a leather goods distributor:

Greene brought Trevor back in almost as his assistant. The French would all chuckle because they knew him thoroughly. They put a tail on them both and they watched them. But Graham was in effect giving a reverse cover to Trevor. The French wanted it to look right even though they knew it wasn't right. When Graham went back, he was doing *a short-term operational assignment* because Trevor was gone.[15]

So Greene was seeking information about the war, about political attitudes, and possible military and political outcomes as any good spy would do, but with the added oddity that His Majesty's former consul was now Greene's assistant.

Greene was approached by the SIS prior to his second trip to Vietnam in October 1951.* The initial contact was made through his friend Alexander Korda. Korda was no stranger to intrigue, having received a knighthood for Intelligence work done during the war. At the height of the blitz, when many of those who could afford to escape from London were doing so, Korda left London for America. From the perspective of the British people, the famous film mogul had ratted, gone to America – out of the war, out of the blitz, out of danger:

> [Churchill] instructed Alex to set up offices in New York and Los Angeles, and to link them to a worldwide motion picture corporation. These offices would exist for their own sake as a moneymaking enterprise of Alex Korda's, but they would also serve as 'cover' for British agents working in what was then neutral America. American isolationists had made it difficult for British intelligence operatives to work freely in the United States, but a movie company offered unparalleled opportunities for concealing intelligence work, and Alex could even himself act as courier . . . It was made clear to him that certain risks were involved. The least of these was public criticism of his departure.[16]

Korda continued to assist the SIS when he could and in the 1950s he was surveying Yugoslavian waters for the SIS while Greene was on *Elsewhere*. In Greene's journal there is a direct reference to the SIS which is enlarged upon in an undated letter written to Catherine (autumn 1951). Greene told her that Korda had again asked him to join him on his yacht *Elsewhere* and added, ' "The old firm" has asked Korda if I'd do a job for them. I don't know what. K's arranging a meeting when I get back from Evelyn [Waugh's].'

On his second visit to Vietnam, from 23 October to 22 December

---

* This is not to say that the SIS did not keep in touch with Greene. During his first visit to Saigon, Greene mentioned in his journal that he was met by Donald Lancaster and John Taylor – both men, I've been told, were SIS officers. The next day, 28 January 1951, he made another entry in his journal about yet another SIS man: 'Beazley from Jakarta – obvious member of the "old firm".'

1951, (after having learnt from the 'old firm' through Korda what was expected of him) he mentioned in his journal one Doug Bollen. On Sunday 11 November he went on a picnic with Bollen and the Toppings to a grotto. In an undated letter to his mother, he wrote: 'Yesterday I had a nice picnic in the country by a little pagoda among tombs with two old friends from the "old firm" [Donald Lancaster and John Taylor].' He heard the news of the final bust up between Trevor and de Lattre from Doug Bollen:

> Later while changing Bollen turned up & told me about General & T[revor]. General wants to see me tomorrow. Under circs. B. thought it best not to be seen there with me so whole thing called off. Dinner alone with B . . . Very disturbed.[17]

After his final meeting with General de Lattre, he wrote to Catherine: 'depressed by the whole T. business. Wish I was back on Korda's boat. Foolish to have left it when I did. Foolish to have come here.'[18] However, the next day Wilson returned, having been allowed two weeks to pack. The Sûreté had both of them watched.

If Greene was a 'casual' spy, then he was a man of many faces and he revealed other secret personalities beneath the personalities already revealed. Knowing of his continued relationship with the SIS, Greene's overt anti-Americanism may be viewed from a different perspective and his curious friendship with the greatest double agent England produced, Kim Philby, may have served a special purpose.

*

However extreme the circumstances, Greene could not be persuaded to abandon a friend (the opposite was also true – he never relented in his instantaneous dislikes). One night, at his home in Antibes, I quoted to Greene his own words about his childhood betrayer, Wheeler, whom he never forgave: 'I found the desire for revenge alive like a creature under a stone.' I asked him whether he still agreed with his description of what constituted a nightmare: 'What would be the point in preparing to prevent an attack when your best friend might suddenly, without any reason, turn into your worst enemy?'

Once he agreed, I suggested that Philby had acted like Wheeler, only Philby's betrayal, as in the case of the infiltration of Albanian revolutionaries into Albania, had had fatal consequences. Philby sent his *own* agents into Albania and then betrayed them to the Russians. They were caught on landing and shot. Greene's answer sounded as if he'd been briefed by Philby: 'They were going into their country armed to do damage to that country. They were killed instead of killing.'[19]

In giving this answer, Greene became highly flushed – the only occasion I remember the edge of his wrath. He thought that I had tricked him into agreeing with his earlier definition of what constitutes a nightmare before discussing Philby. 'In Philby's case it wasn't for personal gain,' he kept insisting. That his friend had acted out of a belief in communism, acted idealistically, was enough for Greene to forgive Philby – or so it would seem.

Greene's passionate belief in friendship carried conviction and is best described by E. M. Forster's famous but somewhat asinine phrase: 'If I had to choose between betraying my country and betraying my friend, I hope I should have the guts to betray my country.' Greene made this point in reverse in his introduction to Philby's memoirs *My Silent War*: '[Philby] betrayed his country, yes, perhaps he did, but who among us has not committed treason to something or someone more important than a country?' Now Greene was fascinated by persons on the verge of losing their faith, persons with divided loyalties, but Philby, as he himself tells us, never lost his faith in communism.

Nicholas Elliott, who knew Philby better than anyone, admitted that though outwardly a kindly man: 'Inwardly he must have been cold, calculating and cruel – traits which he cleverly concealed from his friends and colleagues.'[20] Possibly Philby wasn't a communist: he was a nihilist. Only nihilism truly embraced gives the strength for continuous, conscientious betrayal. It was the author John Le Carré's view that Philby never altogether left the world he forswore: that he enjoyed the Establishment, its camaraderie and institutional warmth, and remained to the end dependent on the people he deceived because he belonged – the right school, the right accent.[21]

Certainly to the end Philby 'expected and received the indulgence owing to his moderation, good breeding and boyish, flirtatious charm'.[22] Philby's view of himself comes out with remarkable clarity in one of his love letters to his third wife, Eleanor Brewer: 'I am full of faults and weaknesses, of course, but nevertheless in some odd way lovable.'[23] In some odd way lovable – that's what Philby thought would bring him through and save him from the punishment he warranted and from which he escaped when he defected to Russia on 23 January 1963.

Greene came to Philby's rescue on 14 July 1963, when an article appeared in the *Sunday Times* entitled 'Security in Room 51'. He wrote the humorous piece with the intention of reducing the hysteria surrounding Kim Philby's defection and flight to Moscow.

He recalled the war years when he and Philby were intelligence officers together in Ryder Street: 'Often during these last weeks, as the word "security" becomes more and more an ugly one, I look back with nostalgia to the happy carefree months I spent in 1943 and 1944 working in a large Edwardian house off St. James's Street.'

'Security in those days', he wrote, 'was quite a flippant word; we were not concerned with the fate of Governments, we were free from Press and Parliament, we were able to enjoy our small secrets. Even MI5 was only a voice down the telephone.' The United States and Britain had their separate agencies in the same house, but on different floors: 'The house was divided between two organizations. On the upper floor lived a group – rather suspect to us – belonging to the O.S.S., the predecessors of the C.I.A.'

To reduce the significance of 'betrayals' by double agents Burgess, Maclean and Philby, and to turn the tables, Greene speculated: 'what treacheries may yet be disclosed under a different regime? Which of us in the far past at Oxford and Cambridge had become corrupted by the capitalist way of life?'

Indeed, Greene made fun of the whole question of security: 'Security was a game we played less against the enemy than against the allies on the upper floor', and 'secrets' because of a danger from bombs 'might be blasted one night over the whole of St. James's, with all kinds of documents drifting into Boodles and White's'. Describing a rule that all secret documents be locked in a safe before the owner left the building, Greene recalled another mischievous prank carried out by him in his war with officialdom. Those on fire-guard duty had to search the building and deposit any documents left exposed on the night duty-officer's desk. The culprit next day would be reprimanded and fined.

> My own turn of duty as fire-guard came round once a week. I looked forward to that night with pleasure, because I had discovered a steel cupboard in one of the O.S.S. offices which was buckled. With a little effort I could insert my fingers and pull out sheaves of paper marked Top Secret.

He stacked the OSS documents on the duty-officer's desk, choosing a moment when he was not in the room. The next morning a fine was exacted 'from our puzzled and harassed allies'. The game went on for some weeks before the source of the documents was discovered. He thought it possible that he gave himself away to his boss Kim Philby 'over drinks in the King's Arms behind St. James's Street, where we would meet between sirens'.

One day he found an office order on his desk: '*For Fire-Guard Officers. In future the steel cupboard in room 51 is to be regarded as a safe and documents locked in the cupboard are to be regarded as secure.*' 'Gently, tactfully, without publicity,' Greene noted, 'the rules of security had been altered to contain rather than to close the leak.'[24]

It was the amusing side of their work that both Greene and Philby described when speaking of Ryder Street. Philby gave the impression in his letters to me that counter-espionage was a schoolboy's game, not a life dealing with betrayal and death: 'Much of our work had to be taken as a lark if one wanted to stay compos mentis.'[25]

In the penultimate decade of his life, Greene spoke more soberly about the dangers of being an agent:

> The 'turning' of a KGB man, for instance, would never surprise me, because the profession can become a sort of game as abstract as chess: the spy takes more interest in the mechanics of his calling than in its ultimate goal – the defence of his country. The 'game' (a serious game) achieves such a degree of sophistication that the player loses sight of his moral values.

But he still sought to praise Philby: 'I can understand a man's temptation to turn double agent, for the game becomes more interesting. Perhaps my childhood experience of divided loyalties has helped me to sympathize with people like Kim Philby, who have gone to the limit with their divided loyalties. I myself would not be capable of such courage, of such a force of conviction.'[26]

No doubt Greene liked and admired Philby – many did. Here was a man raised in the traditions of integrity and public service, ostensibly the best kind of Briton, a brilliant intelligence officer, suddenly revealed as a traitor to his country. His friends must have felt deeply his duplicity and betrayal. Only Greene remained a staunch supporter, becoming Philby's leading, and sole, apologist: this support earned him the opprobrium of the nation's journalists.

In his introduction to Philby's autobiography, *My Silent War*, Greene suggested that Philby's betrayal was prompted by his idealistic concern with the future of his country: 'In Philby's own eyes he was working for a shape of things to come from which his country would benefit.' And Greene placed Philby's betrayal in an historical perspective by comparing his betrayal with that of the English Catholic conspirators who worked for a Spanish conquest of their own country during the reign of Queen Elizabeth; and argued that a kindly Catholic 'must have endured the long bad days of the Inquisition with this hope of the future as a riding anchor. Mistakes of policy would have had no effect on his faith, nor the evil done by some of his leaders.'

What follows is a statement to be marvelled at as Greene defended his friend: 'If there was a Torquemada now, he would have known in his heart that one day there would be a John XXIII.' Surely an immediate evil is not mitigated by a future good four hundred years hence. Greene must have known that the future is made up of any number of possibilities none of which we can foresee. How could his subtle mind indulge in such intellectual folly? Such an argument allowed Philby to ignore the personal burden of responsibility, which we all share. When Philby sent his own agents to Albania and certain death, he made himself a privileged executioner of unsuspecting victims.

Philby was captivated by his old friend's willingness to write an introduction to his autobiography. It was a daring thing to do, for it brought them permanently together in a mutual challenge to non-communist authority. In the mind of the general public, such continued friendship was disturbing, but it seemed Greene was untroubled by his public reputation. In many commentators' eyes, so popular was his work, so welcome was the clarity of his letters to the press, so engaging the outspokenness of his views – he was for the victim and aren't we all victims? – that he was looked upon as the joker in the pack and allowed any freedom.

Greene's consistent support touched Philby and when asked in 1975 what he would like if he had a magic wand, he replied: 'Graham Greene on the other side of the table, and a bottle of wine between us.' Philby got his wish. In 1987 alone Greene visited the Soviet Union three times and met Philby on four separate occasions.

In the last year of Philby's life, Greene showed himself to be a genuine friend by urging the authorities to relent and let Philby visit England with impunity and again spoke of the purity of Philby's motives. Did Philby ever secretly visit England? Probably only in a dream of Greene's:

In January 1980 Kim Philby came to see me secretly in London. He was not as I remembered him – he was furtive and sharp-featured, and I was disappointed . . . He had come from Havana by an English boat and I asked him whether he wasn't afraid of being arrested . . . but he gave me vaguely to understand that he was safe now. All the same, when he came to leave he readily accepted my offer to walk in front of him. There was one man in particular he had seen come out of a room into the corridor who was dangerous.[27]

We can only speculate whether Philby visited England, but he did visit Havana (I have a copy of a postcard and follow-up letter he sent to Greene from Cuba) and for security reasons was only allowed to travel by boat.

Greene never commented about his attitude towards those who attacked him, but he had to endure virulent criticism from journalists and scholars alike over the years. A. N. Wilson's article, 'GRAHAM GREENE AND A COMPANION OF DISHONOUR', whilst a little more vituperative than most, sums up the opinion of many. The article speaks of how Greene's actions may be seen as praiseworthy from a certain perspective:

> By certain codes of conduct there could even be said to be something noble in Mr Greene's refusal to drop an old friend just because he happens to be a traitor who betrayed agents to their death . . . There are two answers to that. One is a general answer. The other relates specifically to Mr Greene. First the general answer. In the world of public school from which Mr Greene has never really escaped there is or used to be a code of heroic friendship. If you were friends with a chap you went on being friends even when all the other chaps said he was a rotter . . . even if he . . . was actually expelled from school for misconduct. This code to a large degree continues into grown-up life for a high proportion of middle class Englishmen. A friend goes on being a friend however badly he has behaved.

But Wilson asserts, 'Moscow isn't the parish of St. James. And Philby is not just a naughty boy who was thrown out of school for smoking behind the gym. He is a dangerous traitor.' Since Greene had had a holiday with Philby, Wilson excoriated Greene: 'To have a holiday with Philby, is morally on a par with having a holiday with Dr Goebbels while this country was at war with Nazi Germany.' This last was a piece of extravagance, but the article saw Greene as mischief-maker and the wayward darling of the Establishment: Philby as a 'pathetic drink-sozzled bore'.[28]

The editorial that appeared in the *Daily Telegraph* when Philby died examined the view of Greene and other left-wing sympathisers: 'More than a few journalists and Left-wing sympathizers have chosen to find [Philby] an amusing rogue, who merely chose the other side in The Great Game, in much the same spirit that a Zimbabwean cricketer might decide to build a Test career playing for England. Mr Graham Greene appeared to find Philby veritably companionable.' The editorial added, 'This faction regards the intelligence services with derision, and official secrets as a source of mirth.'[29]

Was Greene's attitude chiefly based on his expressed desire to support those 'who lie outside the boundaries of state approval', or could the off-the-cuff remarks of Evelyn Waugh unexpectedly carry genuine weight? 'I think Greene's a secret agent on our side and all his buttering up of the Russians is a cover up.'[30]

I am certain that Greene saw himself as a genuine friend of Philby's, but as extraordinary as it may sound, I believe he was serving a larger purpose in remaining a close friend of Philby's: he bore deliberately the burden of scandalised criticism from his literary, political and religious enemies in order to sustain a special loyalty to his own country.

Interviewed by Anne-Elizabeth Moutet in 1987, Greene gave the game away slightly when speaking of his personal correspondence with Philby: ' "Well, if there was anything political in it, I knew that Kim would know that I would pass it on to Maurice Oldfield [then head of SIS], so it was either information or disinformation . . . " he says, letting his voice trail off.'[31] What is important here is his admission that Philby's letters, if 'political', would be handed over to the SIS.

The correspondence was of greater significance than simply letting Greene know where Philby was at any given time. I suspect that SIS Philby-watchers never gave up the hope that he might contact someone in the West clandestinely; there was only one friend Philby could have used – Greene. Indeed Philby had tried earlier on, unsuccessfully, to lure his old friend Nicholas Elliott to a meeting in Helsinki. Later, when 'the formidable' Maurice Oldfield became 'C', the head of the SIS, he, I believe, hit on the idea of using Greene for this task.

One reason Philby might have needed such a contact was to enable him to carry on the 'game' of espionage, perhaps as an antidote to *taedium vitae*. He would wish to continue his double life, if this were possible, in any country and on any side – a double agent on the lookout to become a triple agent. It would not have been beyond his conceit. In spite of public honours he received in Russia, his Order of the Red Banner, his Order of Friendship of Peoples, his Order of Lenin (plaintively Philby said to Philip Knightley: 'It's equivalent to a K. you know'), he might have wished to contact the West precisely because he was *not* trusted by the KGB.

There is evidence for this in an anecdote related by Greene. When the Russian poet Yevgeni Yevtushenko came to visit Greene, Yevtushenko became critical of the KGB. Jokingly, Greene warned him to be careful for he had a friend who was a general in the KGB, which momentarily disturbed Yevtushenko. Yevtushenko guessed that Greene had Philby in mind:

> 'What, that traitor?' 'Yes, but he's not a traitor. He's a communist.' Yevtushenko replied, 'Do you *believe* that?'[32]

Although Philby may have had the privileges of a general in the KGB, and though he himself spoke of holding the rank of a general in the KGB, in fact he was never a general or even an officer in the KGB. Throughout his life in Russia he remained an agent known by the simple codename of 'Tom'.[33]

During his early years as a defector, Philby came to realise that the KGB had no intention of using him to his full potential. At least two successive heads of the KGB, Shelepin (1958–61) and his protégé, Semichastni (1961–7), distrusted Philby. Even those Russians who liked and admired him, especially Generals Kalugin and Lyubimov, never fully trusted him. His one time handler, Yuri Modin, said as recently as 1992: 'I wonder whether Kim cheated us like he cheated everyone else?'[34]

Certainly the authorities placed Philby under certain restrictions. When he first defected, he was denied an opportunity to visit his friend Guy Burgess, who was dying of alcoholism, and when visiting Cuba he was permitted to go only by ship, to forestall any attempt he might make to leave Russia. He was not even allowed to visit KGB headquarters until fifteen years after his defection – so much for his boast that he had the implied rank of a KGB general.

The second reason Philby might have for getting in touch with Greene was that over a long period Greene had been angling for him to do so. He was the big fish in the Russian sea and only Greene could hook him. To contact Philby might well have been important even in the higher reaches of office since it provided a private contact between the British and the Soviet Governments by way of the KGB. I have an extraordinary letter dated 22 January 1980 and addressed to the head of the SIS, which is tantalising in the speculation it engenders:

> I enclose herewith a xerox-copy of the postcard which Kim sent to Graham in January last year from Cuba. I also enclose a copy of a letter from Kim to Graham dated 2nd January this year, together with a xerox-copy of the envelope. Graham has the originals. The postcard came out of the blue, and Graham replied to it. Kim refers to this reply. The next communication was a letter Graham wrote to him on the subject of Iran, suggesting that there could be mutual action between the two great powers which could vastly

aid Salt II and that to establish a common frontier, with a face to face position, was less dangerous perhaps than playing games against each other in neutral territory. Kim is referring to this Iran letter from Graham, which Graham had written before Afghanistan, and therefore Afghanistan is Kim's own addition to the correspondence.

One has always assumed that everything Kim wrote was vetted by the K.G.B. Kim's latest letter is therefore of great significance as he mentions, for the first time, that he is in close touch with 'the competent authorities'.

In view of this, the fourth paragraph of his letter is uncommonly important, particularly the last sentence at the bottom of the first page and the rest of the paragraph at the top of the second page. The following paragraph is also interesting.

I have felt, for some time, that the KGB were probably doves rather than hawks and this seems to bear it out. Is it, do you think, a tentative feeler for the initiation of a dialogue between the KGB and SIS? No doubt you possess a canteen of long spoons. The fact that Kim, in one of his recent letters, asked Graham to send his regards to me may be more significant than I thought at the time. Old spies never die, and Kim must assume that I see old friends from time to time, and he probably also assumes that his letters to Graham are passed on. After all, no-one in his senses would maintain a correspondence with such a hot potato as Kim without letting it be known.

As you know, during the War I worked pretty closely with him from time to time, and got to know him about as well as most people. He had a remarkable flair for strategic deception, combining imagination with audacity. Is his latest letter a gambit in that game?[35]

To the extent that he established contact with Philby after his defection, Greene was helping his country's intelligence services, and, in a larger sense, was patriotically defending its security.

If Greene was approached by the 'old firm' to remain 'publicly' a friend of Philby's for the purpose of setting up a very English spider's web, then the SIS made an excellent choice. Greene, of all Philby's friends who were once close to him, was the only man Philby could trust in the West. If Philby did cheat Moscow, it must have been with Greene's help.

Greene gained the friendship of many left-wing leaders like Fidel Castro, General Omar Torrijas, Salvador Allende and Daniel Ortega; each held a significance for the 'old firm'. Perhaps to the end Greene played the Scarlet Pimpernel.

35
White Night in Albany

The unbearable lightness of being.
— MILAN KUNDERA

JOHN CAIRNCROSS, a friend from Greene's Intelligence days, recalled that when Greene and Catherine Walston started their affair they believed it would not last, they would grow tired of each other, but then it became 'something much more firm and binding'. When Cairncross suggested that they make things more permanent, Greene responded: 'We don't want to upset things – the children are growing up as good Catholics, and she doesn't in any case regard her existing marriage as valid because it was not a Catholic marriage.'[1] The suggestion here was that everything in the relationship was fine and under control.

However, everything was not fine nor under Greene's control. His relations with Catherine were becoming strained, the periods of separation imposed by her brought need for distraction – his work, his travels, his death wish, opium dens and brothels, and his 'substitutes' for her. His greatest desire still was to make her his wife, but more and more it seemed only a dream, a dream she did not share.

On occasions when the 'embargo' was lifted, Greene was like a nervous bridegroom. He went to the United States to see about filming *The End of the Affair* in February 1952 and the possibility arose that they might meet in New York since Catherine would be in Long Island visiting her sister. Greene booked into the Algonquin hotel and wrote urgently to Catherine, afraid that she might bring her sister too. They hadn't seen each other for six months:

Please, please be alone. Come up to my sitting room at the Algonquin . . . First let's look at each other like that time in Paris

497

. . . In case it's possible for you to spend the Wednesday night in New York I've got tickets for the new Rodgers-Hammerstein show, but I know it's probably impossible. If only you could, I'd get another room for you [an attempt to be discreet as Greene was so much in the news because of his visa problems]. Dear dear dear I can hardly believe I'm going to see you . . . I'm so in love with you.[2]

After Catherine left he wrote of being anaesthetised 'by life starting all over again and being with you after the beastly months. You are so dear . . . to me in New York and now another of the world's capitals has become simply you', and thanking her because she existed, he suddenly ended his letter humorously: 'Somebody has doodled the word FUN FUN FUN all over this blotting pad in different frames. The bastard must have been out with you.'[3]

Whenever Greene returned to London he was profoundly aware that the embargo on his seeing Catherine, except irregularly, was back in place:

Last night, I had dinner with Ingrid Bergman and Rossellini . . . I start to be sorry to be home. I drink far more away from you than with you, especially where your ghost haunts . . . Elisabeth [Greene's sister] and I got through 4 cocktails and 3 bottles of wine or 4 – one night. I found myself getting odd blackouts of memory . . . I love you and miss you and *hate* our new life of bits and pieces.[4]

It seems as if they could only see each other secretly and he was therefore always trying to persuade her to go for quick (and short) trips abroad: 'But let's go soon to Paris and do a dress show and a dinner at Vifors and a lunch in the Ritz grill.'[5]

There were times when Catherine disappointed Greene (the reference may be to *The Living Room*): 'It's all wrong that you are not at the play tonight.' Yet in spite of the difficulties Greene was *still* tremendously in love with Catherine in 1953.

She was the least jealous of people and if Greene were to be denied her, he would create some temporary happiness with others. Trevor Wilson (so often with Greene during his visits to Vietnam) said:

He likes women. They have to be attractive to him, and he would immediately go after the lady. In Bangkok, we were at the airfield, and he suddenly saw a lovely lady – a beautiful person and he said

'I must go and look at her'. He went over to see her and he made a date in Singapore. She was the wife of a hunter and he'd go off, and she'd say come down to Singapore and we'll have a nice time there – that's where she lived you see – so he booked a plane the next day and went off to Singapore. The beautiful woman stood up and he went after her. He appears to be shy to talk but somehow or other he manages it very well. But with men it's quite different. He only met people that I knew for certain reasons. There are two things that he'd go to the ends of the earth for: to get information: to know, and to contact a beautiful woman.[6]

There were some very depressing nights in November 1951 in Hanoi, as his diary testifies. He lacked hope for any future with Catherine and felt a wistful sadness over a lost opportunity with Margot Fonteyn:

November 4 Sunday [1951]
Woke feeling a bit ill. Pouring with rain. Felt a bit dismal & lonely at Mass which always makes me miss C. In how many odd churches in strange places has one prayed the same prayer. ['Dear God, let Catherine and I stay together always and one day let us be married.'] The depression of having nothing to look forward to. Only distraction from C to think of Margot. If I had stayed on the boat that might have developed enough . . . I could be happy these weeks if there was a future like there always has been . . . Cafryn very bad.

He had met Margot Fonteyn on Alexander Korda's yacht. They had been on the verge of an affair, but he left the yacht too soon to return to Vietnam. In interview Greene commented:

we became close and the last night I had to leave . . . [the *Elsewhere*] to go off to Vietnam. And the last night we went out together and Vivien Leigh insisted on pushing herself in but then got hopelessly drunk and then we'd been drinking heavily and nothing happened, but we agreed to meet when I came back from Vietnam, which we did. We used to go to greyhound racing together but by that time somebody had intervened. This was before her marriage, to a man I knew called Peter Moore whom I didn't like – he was one of Korda's people. She was a very nice person and we had every intention – she wrote to me in Vietnam, but Peter Moore slipped in between us.[7]

Margot Fonteyn's letters to Greene have a wonderfully open style, but only one of them mentions the affair that did not come off:

> Now that you seem to be living in space it is very difficult to contact you by phone . . .
> Our season finishes in two weeks on 27th of this month [June] and I fly off to Spain early the next morning . . . I'm not really sure of my holiday plans but if I don't see you before I leave I will ring as soon as I am back – by which time you will probably have gone to Indo China! When I think of it, it is just as well that we never started that affair as we would have had very little chance to continue it.[8]

If there could be nothing but friendship between Margot Fonteyn and Greene, the same could not be said for others. John Cairncross recalled visiting Greene in his flat at the bottom of St James's Street and finding Greene with 'an extremely attractive Australian girl' – Jocelyn Rickards: 'This was a girl', said Cairncross, 'who had been brought to a party of mine by Freddie Ayer [A. J. Ayer, the philosopher] . . . and later there she was, obviously very much launched with Graham.'[9]

I asked Greene about Jocelyn Rickards:

> I did meet her at a cocktail party, and I'd got to give dinner to a man, a German, a Catholic who wanted to write a novel, a Prince or a Count. And I'd got Rose Macaulay coming and I felt I did need somebody else and this girl had been very sweet at the cocktail party and had fought her way to the bar and got me a dry martini, and I said will you have dinner with me at a little party . . . So that was the beginning at a cocktail party. And we had an affair which lasted over a few weeks, you know. And we remained friends ever after.[10]

Greene spoke of Jocelyn as 'an old friend of mine – we'd had a bit of an affair'.

Such affairs were inevitable since he was only allowed to see Catherine rarely. But Catherine, after almost eight years, was still his first love: 'I don't even want a substitute for you – anyone would be such a dreary second best.'[11]

In August 1954 Greene went on holiday to Haiti. While there he stayed with Peter Brook (the theatre and film director) and Truman Capote. Greene found Capote 'rather endearing and very funny'.[12] He had an 'odd psychic quality about him':

I like Truman Capote very much . . . He is telling my fortune, and it gives one the creeps because one half believes . . . Between September 1956 and February 1957 I marry a girl 20 years younger who is either Canadian, American, New Zealand or Australian. I am very much in love and she is 5 months gone with a daughter who proves herself a genius by the time she is 18 . . . My whole life changes. We have a house abroad by the sea where we are very happy and about the same time I finish (or start) my best book. When I am in the seventies (I remain sexually active till the end!) we spend the summer in the mountains and the winters in the desert. We are very happy, but before we marry I go (in about 2 years' time) through a great crisis with myself. There it is — watch out. I'm oddly depressed by it. I want to be with you till death.[13]

*

In the past Greene's happiest times had been with Catherine in Rome and Capri, but in the mid 1950s he often went there alone, so that there were others to talk about in his letters to Catherine:

Rome: 19 March [1954]
Did I tell you I'm lunching with the nice Robert Graves' daughter and Diana today?

Grand Hotel, Roma
I've grown to like Claudia — spent yesterday at sea with her and the children. Tonight I dine with Barbara [Rothschild] and a couple of German Monsignori. If I hadn't this story to finish I'd take a plane to Guatemala. I wish you'd write and invite me to Paris or Brighton or a movie or to C.6 [Albany] so that I had some motive to return. I can't go to Capri now as I've lent the villa to a rather wet pretty South African with a small girl who has run away from her rich lover. The stupid things one does when in drink.[14]

The nightmare worsened when he had nothing at the moment to write about, leaving him open to depression and boredom: 'Nothing to distract me in Rome. Everybody's away. I've finished all my books and even the paper stalls are shut.' He spoke of taking a car the next day and scrambling down paths but that there'd be no fun in that:

I long for the 19th [when he and Catherine were to meet] — I'm heavy with longing for it, but it will be over so quickly. How I hope we can have a few weeks to live for. I dread long periods without you – everything, even the things one enjoys, is flat without you . . . one longs for you like a medicine that takes away the pain.[15]

Greene continued working in 1954 on *The Quiet American*, but Catherine was rarely with him. On 27 June he wrote: 'sickness, two elections and Binnie. We've seen less of each other this year than any other year.' Harry Walston had had nothing but bad luck in trying to become a Labour member of parliament. He had contested the 1945 election as a Liberal candidate and failed; he stood again as a Labour candidate for Cambridge in 1951 and 1955, then in 1957 and 1959 and failed again.

Catherine, who helped Harry during elections, had to keep scandal to a minimum, which was probably a further reason why she and Greene met more and more abroad and not in the vicinity of the Walstons' home. 'I'll be seeing Harry this evening,' Greene wrote, 'and I'll see if he's really concerned, or just thinks it would be a little nicer.'[16] Although it appears that Harry allowed Catherine to go off on these jaunts with Greene, they had to be spaced out and not disrupt family matters.

During the period 1954 to 1956 Greene's love for Catherine was undiminished, but she was making it increasingly difficult for it to flourish. Catherine often suffered a deep religious guilt:

I know that you are worried [Greene wrote] and unhappy at the conflict which you feel between your relation with me and Catholicism. That means that I *know* – and it's always a grim thought – that *in that way* you'd be happier if I left you. And that for a lover is a horrid thought. One wants to give happiness to somebody one loves . . . and not take it away.

My case, you see, is different. I would still stay in the fringes of the church if you left me – perhaps not even in the fringes, for almost all my *Catholic* writing has been done since I knew you and I have certainly been to the sacraments far more often in our five years than in the previous eight. So with me – as far as you are concerned – there's no real conflict, and sometimes I hate the conflict I cause in you.[17]

In June 1955 Greene was still working on *The Quiet American* at Anacapri. He loved to have Catherine by his side when working on a novel. In a letter to her he had quoted William Faulkner's praise of

The End of the Affair, then added: 'So don't let Philip [Caraman] or anyone make you think you are *bad* for my writing. You've produced perhaps the best book.'[18] This time it was possible for Catherine to join him in Anacapri for a short visit. By 24 June she had returned to Newton Hall and he was missing her: 'Work goes on, but without much fun as you and Scrabble [then a new and popular game] aren't waiting.'

By Monday, his last promised week to finish *The Quiet American*, he admitted he'd reached 60,000 words, but what was troubling him was their failure to see each other often enough. If she had been there he would have finished his book earlier: 'much easier with you around . . . So much of the trouble between us and the lack of contact has been a) physical with mental effects – lives like the irascible old colonels from India have b) absences – we've seen less of each other this year.'[19]

Greene was becoming very uneasy about any possible future with Catherine. He had been happy with her at Anacapri, but the holiday was marred by the memory of a crisis: 'It was a lovely working holiday but I wish "Rome" hadn't happened. It made me feel I live on a precipice.'[20]

He returned to England and went down to Sussex to see his mother and sister Elisabeth and her husband Rodney, but he was melancholy: 'It's a beastly day . . . the rain pressing on the window, and there isn't a film to be seen, and no one to talk to . . . I think sometimes I ought to get out of England and stay away. [He moved to France in 1966.]' His love for Vivien now seemed 'very tiny and far distant, more distant than childhood. One looks back across a huge chasm . . . I wish you weren't this side of the chasm and everything else so separated.'[21] On 7 July 1955, he wrote: 'Just [received] a parcel of the uniform edition of *The End of the Affair* . . . that book of ill omen.'[22]

Greene's anxiety that the great love of his life was slipping away is obvious. As always, periods of silence on Catherine's part worried him:

Catherine, Catherine, I wish you had the imagination to know what mental torture you can cause . . . I am sending this into the blue and telegrams because nobody knows where you are or when you are returning. It's a pain speaking and there are other things we have to talk to you about . . . This is the worst period and the worst strain since April 1950 – or was it 49. I don't know whether it's not the end. My dear, my dear. I wish you knew what you do to people. And I thought it was only my craziness.[23]

It appears from the correspondence that Catherine was becoming increasingly close to Thomas Gilby, the Dominican priest who often stayed with the Walstons. Harry Walston, who knew of her relationship with Gilby, had a genuine fondness for him. A letter from Newton Hall from a member of the family suggests that Catherine was besotted with Gilby and Greene was losing her.

The strain of the previous few years began to tell on Greene's health. In July 1955 he suspected that he had harmed his liver: 'If there was anything wrong with my liver it's cured . . . I had hoped for some physical explanation of my melancholia . . . '24 In August of the same year he spent time with his daughter at Green Park Ranch in Calgary in Canada, which he had generously bought her. His liver was on the mend: 'my liver is becoming like a baby's because of the absurd liquor laws. I never have a drink till evening, and then never more than two whiskies before dinner . . . By 9.15 one is in bed.'

In 1956 Greene had numerous X-rays. He was ill and his doctors were seeking to find out if he had cancer of the colon. In February he had barium X-rays: 'Just been for my fourth X-ray. My fifth tomorrow.'25 A few days later his gall bladder was examined. In March, and in bed sick, he wrote to Catherine that he believed they were at a critical stage:

> I feel guilty because at least twice I've prevented & fought against the idea of finishing, even though that may be better for you. The trouble seems to me is that we both want to simplify our lives . . . & yet if you simplify you can only do it by excluding me (after all I'm a kind of barnacle on your boat) & if I should simplify it would be by . . . living abroad . . . We have to think a) whether we want to simplify enough to separate – except as friends who meet occasionally and b) whether it's possible to simplify & not lose each other . . . Call it a neurosis if you like, but I have the desire to be of use to someone, & in the last nine months particularly I have felt of little use & possibly of real harm to you . . . The simple thing that we probably both desire is to need & to be needed. I've fought too hard to make you stay . . . 26

When he was staying at the Royal Albion hotel in Brighton at the end of August, Greene came back to the same point:

> Of course, I want October/November but your last letter hinted that Harry might not agree, & sooner or later I have to decide whether I can go to rehearsals of *Potting Shed* [Greene's latest play to be produced and have its première in New York] in USA . . .

What worried him more than not seeing enough of Catherine was that he detected certain contradictions and ambiguities 'between the lines':

> For instance you were not to be allowed to go to Paris for the very sensible reason that with your diet etc. you should stay put, but apparently an island off Wales is less strenuous than lying in bed most of the day at the Ritz, & from your account of life at Newton it seems unlikely that our 'wild' Parisian life would be more tiring. But let's leave that. You said on the telephone that if something important were happening, of course you would come. But to me still the important thing is being with you – not a film or a first night as one of the bogus 'important' things which in the last year I've found myself inventing to bring you to town.

Perhaps the most serious were two statements Catherine had made in the middle of their lovemaking:

> One was that 'in a way' you would like our affair to come to an end – & that puts a certain responsibility on me; the other was that in the wildly unlikely hypothetical case that our respective partners died, you would not marry me. Now I've always felt that from the Catholic point of view there was an excuse for us in that we would marry if we could. But if that's not the case, what is our affair – except nights on the tiles, and that's awfully unimportant to [set] against breaking the rules. Personally I want to marry you & would marry you tomorrow if I had the chance, but an affair can't be important on one side only.
>
> Dearest Catherine, ever since I persuaded you over a long night & a long morning not to leave me (June last year) [the 'Rome' incident], I have at intervals felt guilt & uncertainty – guilt to you & uncertainty of the future.
>
> I used to go off & give you a breathing spell – Malaya, Indo-China & what not. This time I'm only giving you a three week one, but do think a bit & tell me how you really feel. I want to have this spell myself – a partial holiday in case we don't have our usual one & some hard thinking.
>
> . . . I love you & want to be with you & there's nothing I want more than our holiday. If the Far East is too strenuous, then I'd suggest the Canary Islands or the West Indies, but I'd be equally content with Bognor Regis if you were with me. That to me is the only 'important' point.[27]

On their last holiday together in Rome, Catherine had insisted on twin beds: 'it seems to make a gap before one sleeps & when one wakes,'[28] 'ever since Rome & that awful long night I've been afraid of pressing you.'[29] Greene felt that Catherine was slipping away from him, and she was. Eight years of turmoil and torment had taken their toll.

*

Back in England Greene was nostalgic for Vietnam and had brought back with him a sentimental souvenir: the last opium pipe he had smoked in a fumerie off the rue Catinat. He had got on well with the Chinese proprietor and had given him lessons in English. When the time came for him finally to leave Vietnam, the proprietor let him take the pipe with him. It lay in a dish in Greene's flat in Albany, slightly damaged in transit, a relic of happier days.

Greene had moved from St James's Street to Albany near Piccadilly Circus, close to the Ritz hotel (where he often stayed in later years after he had left England to live in France). His flat, number C6, was on the second floor and reached by a simple uncarpeted staircase like one you would expect in an Oxbridge college. The area was black with taxis, but the sound of London's traffic didn't penetrate the flat.

In Vietnam without the French there was no control of the roads, the watch-towers were left to crumble and anarchy was returning. Greene felt he would never again see the 'strange sunsets falling on the Baie d'Along or the lamp glowing on the cook's face as he prepared an opium pipe'.[30] The country was about to retire behind the plastic curtain, the last performance begun. The days of the rue Catinat were over, he would miss the pavement cafés, the good restaurants, the elegant women in the *ao dai*, their beautiful national dress.

On his last visit to Vietnam, Greene had smoked more than usual: normally he smoked no more than three perhaps four pipes, but on this occasion alone in Saigon and waiting for another visa, ironically a communist visa, he smoked himself inert. In his previous sessions, often with French officials, he had smoked no more than twice a week; now on three occasions he smoked ten pipes a night. Even then this amount was not enough to make him an addict. An addict, whittled down to extreme emaciation, cheeks sunken like twin wells, would need to smoke over a hundred pipes a day.

Greene hoped to recapture happier times and smoke his pipe once more. He recalled in an unpublished manuscript entitled 'Opium in Albany' what Sir Tan Cheng Lock had once said: 'I cannot see how anyone after the age of fifty can carry on his work properly without the aid of opium.' A friend had brought Greene back from Persia a slab of opium looking like a bar of chocolate and the possibility of smoking in the quiet of Albany became a reality.

He invited Catherine to share a last pipe with him. They had no lamp, so they tried a candle. First they tied up the loose parts of the pipe with scotch tape. It was an almost impossible task and they had only one pipe of scorched opium apiece out of the whole bar. Greene then remembered that Dottoressa Moor of Capri had given him a tin of opium already twenty years old. Greene found the tin, opened it and was astonished to find the opium in perfect condition: 'Like a great wine opium guards its quality over the decades.' It was a tremendous struggle because the candle flame turned and twisted, but they attained three pipes each: 'but what pleasure it was to recapture the smell and the quiet and the serenity, however crudely, just off Piccadilly. The quiet of Albany was very similar to the quiet of a fumerie where no one interrupts the repose of another.'[31]

*

Greene's escape into the 'white night of opium' was only a palliative, lessening the pain of his melancholia. There never seemed to be peace in his life, and sometimes when it came he turned away from it. Since his house at 14 North Side had been destroyed in the blitz, he had not had a permanent home. In the years of travel (and no man travelled more, as his diaries show) in the Far East, Greene had lost his sense of home.[32]

Reflecting on the 1950s, Greene said: 'It was a period of great happiness and great torment. Manic depression reached its height in that decade.'[33] He needed friends he could trust, like his sister Elisabeth and his brother Hugh. But others he had come to rely on would soon leave him.

His friend Alexander Korda once saved him from suicide by taking him out of himself: 'My dear boy, this is so foolish what you plan. Come with me to Antibes. You are bored. All right. We will go on the *Elsewhere*.'[34] Korda, whom Laurence Olivier had praised for his 'Godlike yet unobtrusive generosity',[35] died suddenly from a massive heart attack in 1956. In early 1961 Eric Strauss (head of the psychiatric department of St Bartholomew's hospital) died. Evelyn Waugh, writing to Lady Diana Cooper, said: '[Greene's] alienist Dr Strauss kicked the bucket last week. No one to keep an eye on him now.'[36]

Catherine had been central to his existence since the first days in Achill in 1947 and had helped to bring into being some of his greatest novels – *The Heart of the Matter* and *The End of the Affair*. Now she was gradually detaching herself and their relationship was fading. Ahead were Anita Bjork, the Swedish classical actress, and Yvonne Cloetta, who saw Greene into a distinguished old age.

But at C6 in Albany he was now with Catherine. Under the influence of opium they lay back with shoes off in spartan simplicity. The smell of the opium cleared the nostrils, the mind was racing, the body numb. They were soon to sleep the 'white night of opium'. In the future Greene would go to Haiti, the nightmare republic where the dictator 'Papa Doc' Duvalier flourished, destroying enemies and friends, using for the purpose the hated Tontons Macoutes (bogeymen in Haitian patois); he would go to Cuba, where Batista was taking too little notice of the young communist leader, Fidel Castro, fighting in the hills; he would go to the leper colony in the Congo, fulfilling his desire to be among lepers like Father Damien, whose life he had once hoped to write. He would continue to seek out the dangerous or the lost and forgotten places of the world. He was to have thirty-six more years wheeling obsessively round the world, compelled it would seem to wander the earth until death. Unending traveller, unending writer, he laboured like Sisyphus.

Even walking the streets he seemed homeless. Once in Antibes I became aware of his acute solitariness. Turgenev said that the heart of another is a dark forest, and as the twilight ebbed fast I watched him silently walk away, becoming a dark speck, until finally I lost him.

Notes

Wherever possible in the following notes I have referred to the Penguin editions of the works of Graham Greene because these are the most accessible and widely distributed. Although the pagination of some Penguin editions has remained unchanged for decades, others have been reset in recent years. Neither of these, however, contain the introductions in the Heinemann and Bodley Head uniform and collected editions. A full Bibliography of Greene's works and the sources used in this book will appear in Volume Three.

1   Rumours at Nightfall

1   Letter to Ben Huebsch, 25 April 1938.
2   *The Lawless Roads*, Heinemann uniform edition, 1955, p. 289.
3   *Ibid.*, pp. 287–8.
4   Letter to Ben Huebsch, 10 June 1930.
5   Diary, 14 September 1938.
6   *Ibid.*, 24 September 1938.
7   *Ibid.*, 25 September 1938.
8   *Ibid.*, 26 September 1938.
9   Letter to his mother, 23 September 1938.
10   *Ibid.*, 4 October 1938.
11   *Ibid.*, 26 December 1938.
12   Unpublished notebook.
13   Undated letter to Ben Huebsch.
14   Letter to Ben Huebsch, 9 April 1938.
15   *Ibid.*, 29 April 1939.
16   *Ibid.*
17   Letter from Ben Huebsch, 10 May 1939.
18   Letter from Vivien Greene, 23 November 1939.
19   *The End of the Affair*, Penguin edition, 1975, pp. 25–6.
20   Letter to Ben Huebsch, 12 June 1939.
21   Letter from Hugh Greene to his mother, December 1933 or January 1934.
22   Letter to Ben Huebsch, 13 July 1939.
23   In-house memo, 25 September 1939.
24   *Spectator*, 18 August 1939.
25   Undated letter to his mother.
26   Telephone conversation with Vivien Greene, 23 August 1990.
27   *Ways of Escape*, Penguin edition, 1987, p. 68.
28   Interview with Walter Allen, August 1976.
29   Interview with Vivien Greene, 23 June 1977.
30   *Ways of Escape*, pp. 68–9.
31   Letter to Ben Huebsch, 31 May 1939.
32   Letter from David Higham, 22 May 1939.

33 *Spectator*, 22 September 1939.
34 *Ways of Escape*, p. 69.
35 *Ibid.*
36 *Spectator*, 22 September 1939.
37 Letter to John Hayward, 20 October 1950.
38 *Ways of Escape*, p. 69.
39 *Ibid.*
40 Interview with Vivien Greene, 26 July 1979.
41 Undated letter to Vivien Greene, but written late August 1939.
42 Letter to Vivien Greene, 30 August 1939.
43 *Ibid.*, 4 September 1939.

2   Enter Dorothy

1   Interview with Graham Greene, 25 April 1981.
2   Interview with Malcolm Muggeridge, June 1977.
3   Letter to Hugh Greene, 7 April 1939.
4   Undated letter to Vivien Greene, probably written in September 1939.
5   Angus Calder, *The People's War: Britain 1939–45*, Panther edition, 1971, p. 41.
6   Letter from a friend to Vivien Greene, 5 July 1939.
7   Interview with Vivien Greene, 23 July 1977.
8   Undated letter to Vivien Greene, probably written in September 1939.
9   *The End of the Affair*, Heinemann edition, 1951, p. 48.
10 *Ibid.*, p. 49.
11 Interview with Vivien Greene, 23 June 1977.
12 Interview with David Higham, August 1977.
13 Interview with Sir Hugh Greene, 19 May 1981.
14 Interview with Malcolm Muggeridge, June 1977.
15 *Ibid.*
16 Interview with Vivien Greene, 23 June 1977.
17 *Ibid.*
18 *Ibid.*, 26 July 1979.
19 Letter to Vivien Greene, 26 October 1939.
20 *Ibid.*, 6 November 1939.
21 *Ibid.*, 4 January 1940.
22 Letter from Vivien Greene, 5 January 1940.
23 *Ibid.*
24 *Ibid.*
25 *Ibid.*, 24 January 1940.
26 Letter to Vivien Greene, 15 October 1939.
27 Letter from Vivien Greene, 7 December 1939.
28 *Ibid.*
29 *Ibid.*, 1 January 1940.
30 Letter to Vivien Greene, 14 October 1939.
31 Letter from Vivien Greene, 28 November 1940.
32 Undated letter to Vivien Greene.
33 Letter from editor of the *Strand* to Nancy Pearn, Greene's agent, 4 August 1939.
34 *Ways of Escape*, Penguin edition, 1987, p. 69.
35 *Ibid.*, p. 70.
36 Letter to Laurence Pollinger, September 1939.
37 Letter to Vivien Greene, 21 September 1939.

3   The Ministry and the Glory

1   F. H. Hinsley and C. A. G. Sinkins, *British Intelligence in the Second World War*, vol. 4, HMSO, 1990, p. 17.
2   Walter Allen, *As I Walked Down New Grub Street: Memories of a Writing Life*, typescript.
3   *Ibid.*
4   Letter from Barbara Wall, 14 March 1981. She recalled her last meeting with Greene in 1948 at Rules, Covent Garden: 'I longed to write another novel but was in despair as to a plot . . . He was his usual enchanting and unpresuming self (though by now the author of *The Heart of the Matter*) and suggested to me that I should look at the small news items in the evening papers, of the "body found in the river" type, and build a plot around that.'
5   Letter to Vivien Greene, August 1939.
6   Malcolm Muggeridge, *The Infernal Grove: Chronicles of Wasted Time*, vol. 2, Fontana/Collins, 1975, pp. 81–2.
7   *Ibid.*, p. 88.
8   'Men at Work', *The Penguin New Writing*, 1942, p. 18.
9   *Ibid.*, p. 19.
10   *Spectator*, 8 November 1940.
11   Interview with Malcolm Muggeridge, June 1977.
12   Letter to Laurence Pollinger, 17 May 1940.
13   Letter to Howard Spring, 23 May 1940.
14   Letter to Nancy Pearn about Storm Jameson, 22 July 1940, and also about Dorothy Sayers, 24 July 1940.
15   *A Sort of Life*, Penguin edition, 1974, p. 150.
16   *The Diaries of Evelyn Waugh*, ed. Michael Davie, Penguin edition, 1979, p. 470.
17   Unpublished diary provided by Barbara Wall.
18   Letter to Vivien Greene, 4 January 1940.
19   'That is to say that this book is addressed providentially to a generation that the absurdity of a crazy world is clutching by the throat. To the young contemporaries of Camus and Sartre, desperately prey to an absurd liberty, Graham Greene will reveal, perhaps, that this absurdity is in truth only that of boundless love.'
20   Letter to Vivien Greene, 24 November 1939.
21   *Ways of Escape*, Penguin edition, 1987, pp. 66–7.
22   *Spectator*, 8 March 1940.
23   Letter to Laurence Pollinger, March 1940.
24   Letter from Laurence Pollinger, April 1940.
25   *Ways of Escape*, p. 67.
26   *A Sort of Life*, p. 58.
27   Pastoral letter from Cardinal Griffin for Advent 1953. For a fuller quotation of the pastoral letter, see David Leon Higdon's article, 'A Textual History of Graham Greene's *The Power and the Glory*', *Studies in Bibliography*, 33 (1980), 234.
28   *A Sort of Life*, p. 58.
29   Letter to Vivien Greene from Marion Greene, 3 July 1940.
30   Interview with Vivien Greene, 26 July 1979.
31   *Ibid.*
32   Letter from Vivien Greene, February 1940.
33   Letter from Francis Greene to author, 18 March 1994.
34   *Ibid.*
35   *Ibid.*

4 The Blitz

1 Barbara Nixon, *Raiders Overhead*, Lindsay Drummond, 1943, p. 13.
2 A. P. Herbert, *The Thames*, Weidenfeld & Nicolson, 1966, p. 165.
3 W. R. Matthews, *St. Paul's Cathedral in Wartime*, Hutchinson, 1946, p. 35.
4 *Observer*, 8 September 1940.
5 Quoted by Norman Longmate, 'London's Burning', *Daily Telegraph*, 18 June 1990.
6 *Picture Post*, 28 September 1940.
7 *Observer*, September 1940.
8 The film was ready by 20 October 1940.
9 'At Home', *Collected Essays*, Penguin, 1981, p. 333.
10 *The Ministry of Fear*, Penguin edition, 1978, p. 28.
11 *Ibid.*, pp. 28–9.
12 *Ibid.*, p. 64.
13 Undated letter to his mother.
14 *Spectator*, 25 October 1940.
15 'The Strays', *ibid.*, 1 November 1940.
16 Interview with David Low, 24 August 1984.
17 Interview with Graham Greene, 25 April 1981.
18 *The Ministry of Fear*, p. 188.
19 *Ibid.*, p. 40.
20 *Ibid.*, p. 188.
21 'Lightning Tour', *Spectator*, 13 June 1941.
22 Paul Fussell, *Wartime*, Oxford University Press, 1989, p. 213.
23 'Domestic War', *Spectator*, 28 March 1941.
24 'A Pride of Bombs', *ibid.*, 14 February 1941.
25 Malcolm Muggeridge, *The Infernal Grove: Chronicles of Wasted Time*, vol. 2, Fontana/Collins, 1975, p. 111.
26 'At Home', p. 334.
27 *Ibid.*, p. 336.
28 *Ibid.*
29 Malcolm Muggeridge, *Like It Was: A Selection from the Diaries of Malcolm Muggeridge*, ed. John Bright-Holmes, Collins, 1981, p. 249.
30 Letter to Anthony Powell, December 1940.
31 *The Ministry of Fear*, p. 65.

5 The Destructors

1 *Ways of Escape*, Penguin edition, 1987, p. 84.
2 Interview with Graham Greene, 25 April 1981.
3 Hector Bolitho, *War in the Strand*, Eyre & Spottiswoode, 1942, pp. 77–81.
4 Letter to his mother, 18 April 1941.
5 Letter from his mother, 20 April 1941.
6 *Ibid.*
7 *The Confidential Agent*, Penguin edition, 1981, p. 115.
8 Interview with David Low, 24 August 1984.
9 Letter from Vivien Greene, headed 'For March 15, 1941'.
10 *Ibid.*, 12 March 1941.
11 Interview with Graham Greene, 14 December 1983.
12 Letter from Vivien Greene, 12 March 1941.
13 *Ibid.*, 4 April 1941.
14 Interview with Vivien Greene, 10 August 1983.

15 Letter from Francis Greene to author, 18 March 1994.
16 Interview with Vivien Greene, 15 August 1977.
17 Letter from Vivien Greene, 1941.
18 *Ibid.*, 1941.
19 Interview with Vivien Greene, 15 August 1977.
20 *Ibid.*
21 Letter to his mother, October 1940.
22 Malcolm Muggeridge, *Like It Was: A Selection from the Diaries of Malcolm Muggeridge*, ed. John Bright-Holmes, Collins, 1981, p. 317. Entry for 13 January 1949.
23 Interview with Vivien Greene, 23 June 1977.
24 Interview with Graham Greene, 25 April 1981.
25 *Ibid.*
26 Letter from Vivien Greene, 28 October 1986.
27 Muggeridge, *Like It Was*, p. 317.
28 Interview with Graham Greene, 25 April 1981.
29 Letter to Mrs Compton Mackenzie, 30 October 1940.
30 Letter to Anthony Powell, 16 December 1940.
31 Letter to Mary Pritchett, March 1941.
32 Muggeridge, *Like It Was*, p. 317.
33 Interview with Vivien Greene, 23 June 1977.
34 Vivien Greene's journal for 1978.
35 'The Destructors', *Twenty-One Stories*, Penguin edition, 1981, p. 11.
36 *Ibid.*, p. 16.
37 Letter to Vivien Dayrell-Browning, 21 August 1925.
38 Muggeridge, *Like It Was*, p. 249.
39 Letter to Vivien Dayrell-Browning, 1926, quoted in *The Life of Graham Greene*, Vol. One, 1989, p. 276.

6   Trivial Comedies, Shallow Tragedies

1 'The New Ambassadors Revue', *Spectator*, 25 July 1941.
2 'Time for Comedy', *ibid.*, 11 April 1941.
3 'Wednesday After the War', *ibid.*, 18 April 1941.
4 'Up and Doing', *ibid.*, 30 May 1941.
5 'Under One Roof', *ibid.*, 27 June 1941.
6 'Black Vanities', *ibid.*, 2 May 1941.
7 Malcolm Muggeridge, *The Infernal Grove: Chronicles of Wasted Time*, vol. 2, Fontana/Collins, 1975, p. 113.
8 'Revudeville', *Spectator*, 6 June 1941.
9 *Ibid.*
10 'Non-stop Vanities', *ibid.*, 27 June 1941.
11 Muggeridge, *The Infernal Grove*, p. 113.
12 'Dear Brutus', *Spectator*, 24 January 1941.
13 'Women Aren't Angels', *ibid.*, 25 April 1941.
14 ' "Bed-Exhausted" ', *ibid.*, 23 May 1941. Review of 'Australia Visited 1940' by Noël Coward.
15 'Blithe Spirit', *ibid.*, 11 July 1941, p. 34.
16 *Ibid.*
17 *Ibid.*
18 Letter from Rosamond Lehmann to the *Spectator*, 18 July 1941.
19 *Ibid.*
20 *British Dramatists*, Collins, 1942, p. 46.

21 *The Noël Coward Diaries*, ed. Graham Payer and Sheridan Morley, Little Brown, 1982, entry for 9 March 1953, p. 208.
22 Letter from BBC to Miss Cooper of Pearn, Pollinger and Higham, 25 June 1941.
23 Letter to Miss Cooper from Graham Greene, 26 June 1941.
24 *The End of the Affair*, Heinemann, 1976, pp. 65–6.

7   School for Spies

1   Letter to his mother, 7 April 1941.
2   Malcolm Muggeridge, *The Infernal Grove: Chronicles of Wasted Time*, vol. 2, Fontana/Collins, 1975, p. 127.
3   Herbert Greene, 'I Was a Secret Agent of Japan', *Daily Worker*, 22 December 1937.
4   *Ways of Escape*, Penguin edition, 1987, p. 73.
5   Interview with Rodney Dennys, 22 January 1992.
6   Letter to his mother, 2 September 1941.
7   *Ibid.*
8   Letter from Vivien Greene, 26 November 1941.
9   Letter to his parents, 3 October 1941.
10 *Ways of Escape*, p. 70.
11 'Memorandum on the Work of the Section of Civil Affairs & Security', British Intelligence Corps Library, Ashford, Kent. Quoted in Anthony Cave Brown, *'C': The Secret Life of Sir Stewart Graham Menzies*, Macmillan, 1987, pp. 761–3.
12 Undated letter to his mother, October 1941.
13 Letter to Laurence Pollinger, 8 October 1941.
14 Letter to Miss Pearn, October 1941.
15 Letter from Miss Cooper, 22 October 1941.
16 Letter to Miss Cooper, 23 October 1941.
17 Letter to Laurence Pollinger, 14 November 1941.
18 Interview with Graham Greene, 25 April 1981.
19 Undated journal entry.

8   Return to Africa

1   Journal, 9 December 1941.
2   *Ibid.*
3   *Ibid.*
4   *Ibid.*
5   Letter to his mother, 7 March 1942.
6   Journal, 9 December 1941.
7   'Convoy to West Africa', 9 December 1941, *In Search of a Character*, 1980, p. 84.
8   *Ibid.*, 10 December 1941, pp. 85–6.
9   Journal, 11 December 1941.
10 'Convoy to West Africa', 12 December 1941, *In Search of a Character*, p. 89.
11 *Ibid.*
12 *Ibid.*, 13 December 1941, p. 93.
13 Journal, 14 December 1941.
14 Journal, 15 and 16 December 1941.
15 *British Dramatists*, Collins, 1942, p. 32.
16 Letter to his mother, 14 February 1942.
17 Journal, 19 December 1941.
18 'Convoy to West Africa', 12 December 1941, *In Search of a Character*, p. 90.

19   *Ibid.*, 19 December 1941, p. 96.
20   F. H. Hinsley with E. E. Thomas, C. F. S. Ransom, and R. C. Knight, *British Intelligence in the Second World War*, vol. 1, HMSO, 1979, p. 334.
21   Journal, 18 December 1941.
22   *Ibid.*, 23 December 1941.
23   *Ibid.*, 1 January 1942.
24   *Ibid.*, 24 December, 1941.
25   *Ibid.*, 1 January, 1942.
26   Letter from Vivien Greene, 30 January 1942.
27   Journal, 30 December 1941.
28   *The Heart of the Matter*, Penguin edition, 1983, p. 101.
29   Journal, 3 January 1942.
30   'Convoy to West Africa', 3 January 1942, *In Search of a Character*, p. 106.
31   'The Soupsweet Land', *Collected Essays*, Penguin edition, 1983, p. 339.

9   The Soupsweet Land

1   Journal, 4 January 1942.
2   *Ibid.*
3   *Ibid.*
4   *Ibid.*
5   *Ibid.*, 5 January 1942.
6   *Ibid.*
7   *Ibid.*
8   Journal, 7 January 1942.
9   *Ibid.*, 6 January 1942.
10   *Ibid.*
11   'The Soupsweet Land', *Collected Essays*, Penguin edition, 1983, p. 455.
12   Journal, 9 January 1942.
13   *Ibid.*
14   Letter to Anthony Powell, December 1940.
15   'The Soupsweet Land', *Collected Essays*, pp. 455–6.
16   *Ibid.*, p. 456.
17   *Ibid.*
18   Letter from Kim Philby to author, 18 April 1978.
19   Journal, 10 January 1942.
20   *The Heart of the Matter*, Penguin edition, 1983, p. 31.
21   Greene was always alert to stories of sorcery, of the Big Bush Devil, and of evil and magic, which flourished in Freetown. He committed to his journal a story told by Mackenzie: 'a D[istrict] O[fficer] he knew who against all warnings went into the Porro bush: "If you go there, you get very ill." He went & pissed on the Porro stone. Down with bad malaria 3 days later, & on twice returning to the station immediately got malaria worse & worse."' Perhaps it was this entry that led him to commit to his journal the following idea for a story never written: 'Idea for a story: the agent who tries to invent a big bush devil for purposes of propaganda & finds himself involved in more & more murders.'
22   Journal, 11 January 1942.
23   *The Heart of the Matter*, p. 18.
24   Journal, 7 March 1942.
25   *Ibid.*, 14 January 1942.
26   *Ways of Escape*, Penguin edition, 1987, p. 74.
27   Journal, 19 January 1942.

28 Letter to his mother, 5 February 1942.
29 *Ibid.*
30 Journal, 18 January 1942.
31 Letter to Laurence Pollinger from Vivien Greene, January 1942.
32 *Ibid.*, 27 March 1942.
33 Journal, 24 January 1942.
34 *Ibid.*, 13 February 1942.
35 Letter to his mother, 14 February 1942.
36 Letter from Vivien Greene, March 1942. Vivien didn't receive Greene's letter until five weeks later.
37 Journal, 1 February 1942.
38 *Ibid.*
39 *Ibid.*, 26 January 1942.
40 *Ibid.*, 11 February 1942.
41 *Ibid.*
42 *Ibid.*, 29 January 1942.
43 *Ibid.*, 26 January 1942.
44 *Ways of Escape*, p. 74.
45 Journal, 12 February 1942.
46 *The Heart of the Matter*, p. 14.
47 H. E. Bates, *The Blossoming World*, Michael Joseph, 1971, pp. 174–5.
48 *The Heart of the Matter*, p. 65.
49 *Ibid.*, pp. 70–1.
50 *Ibid.*, pp. 71–2.
51 *Ibid.*, p. 147.
52 *Ibid.*, p. 166.
53 Letter to his mother, 14 October 1942.
54 'The Soupsweet Land', *Collected Essays*, p. 458.
55 Journal, 8 March 1942.

10 Our Man in Freetown

1 Undated letter to his mother.
2 *Ibid.*
3 *Ibid.*
4 *Ibid.*
5 Interview with Graham Greene, 25 April 1981.
6 Letter to his mother, 2 April 1942.
7 Letter to Elisabeth Greene, 2 June 1942.
8 Letter to his mother, 2 April 1942.
9 'The Soupsweet Land', *Collected Essays*, Penguin edition, 1981, p. 341.
10 Letter to Elisabeth Greene, 2 June 1942.
11 *Ibid.*, 30 July 1942.
12 *Ways of Escape*, Penguin edition, 1987, p. 75.
13 Letter to his mother, 4 May 1942.
14 *Ibid.*
15 *The Heart of the Matter*, Penguin edition, 1983, p. 115.
16 *Ibid.*, p. 21.
17 'The Soupsweet Land', *Collected Essays*, pp. 342–3.
18 *Ibid.*, p. 341–2.
19 *Ibid.*, p. 341.
20 Letter to his mother, 19 April 1942.

21 *Ibid.*, 11 June 1942.
22 Letter to Elisabeth Greene, 2 June 1942.
23 *Ibid.*
24 *Ibid.*
25 *Ways of Escape*, p. 75.
26 Letter to Elisabeth Greene, 20 April 1942.
27 *Ways of Escape*, p. 94.
28 'The Soupsweet Land', *Collected Essays*, p. 341.
29 *The Human Factor*, Penguin edition, 1978, pp. 46–7.
30 *Ibid.*, p. 47.
31 Interview with Graham Greene, 11 August 1977.
32 Letter from Kim Philby to author, June 1978.
33 'The Soupsweet Land', *Collected Essays*, p. 343.
34 *Ways of Escape*, p. 91.
35 Letter from Graham Greene to author, 27 February 1991.
36 *Ibid.*
37 OSS Files, National Archives, Washington, DC.
38 'Indo-China: Internal Affairs: 1950–4: Confidential US State Dept', Central Files, National Archives, Washington, DC.
39 Interview with Graham Greene, 25 April 1981. Richard Cox was at Balliol the same years as Greene, (1922–5), served in the Colonial Service, Sierra Leone from 1928 onwards and was still there during Greene's service with the SIS.
40 *Ways of Escape*, p. 183.
41 *The Heart of the Matter*, pp. 171–2.
42 Letter from Graham Greene to author, 20 March 1991.
43 *Ways of Escape*, p. 92.
44 *Ibid.*, p. 90.
45 *The Heart of the Matter*, p. 48.
46 *Ibid.*, pp. 49–50.
47 *Ibid.*, p. 50.
48 *Ibid.*, p. 51.
49 *Ibid.*, p. 52.
50 *Ibid.*
51 *Ibid.*, p. 55.
52 *Ibid.*, pp. 54–5.
53 *Ibid.*, p. 51.
54 *Ways of Escape*, p. 90.
55 Undated journal entry, 1942.
56 Letter to his mother, 22 July 1942.
57 Letter to Hugh Greene, 1 August 1942.
58 Letter from Peter Turnbull to author, 30 October 1981.
59 Letter from Graham Greene to author, 27 February 1991.
60 Interview with Rodney Dennys, 23 January 1992.
61 Letter from Kim Philby to author, 9 April 1974.
62 *Ibid.*
63 Letter from Graham Greene to author, 20 March 1991.
64 Letter to Elisabeth Greene, 2 June 1942.
65 *Ways of Escape*, p. 77.
66 *The Heart of the Matter*, p. 79.
67 *Ibid.*, p. 83.
68 *Ibid.*, pp. 83–4.
69 *Ibid.*, pp. 84–5.
70 *Ibid.*, p. 94.

11 A Mad Cook, a Suicide and a Nest of Toads

1   *Ways of Escape*, Penguin edition, 1987, p. 91.
2   Letter to his mother, 22 July 1942.
3   *Ways of Escape*, p. 91.
4   Letter to his mother, 12 August 1942.
5   *The Human Factor*, Penguin edition, 1978, p. 195.
6   Letter to his mother, 12 August 1942.
7   *Ibid.*, 22 June 1942.
8   *The Human Factor*, pp. 189–90.
9   *Ways of Escape*, p. 91.
10 *Ibid.*, p. 75.
11 *The Heart of the Matter*, Penguin edition, 1983, p. 26.
12 *Ibid.*, p. 77.
13 *Ibid.*, p. 69.
14 Interview with Graham Greene, 25 April 1981.
15 'The Soupsweet Land', *Collected Essays*, Penguin edition, 1970, p. 344.
16 *The Heart of the Matter*, p. 172.
17 *Ibid.*, p. 173.
18 Letter from George Neal to author, 27 January 1993.
19 Journal, 10 January 1942.
20 *The Heart of the Matter*, p. 173.
21 *Ibid.*, p. 174.
22 *Ibid.*
23 *Ibid.*, p. 175.
24 *Ibid.*, p. 86.
25 *Ibid.*, p. 85.
26 *Ibid.*, p. 194.
27 *Ibid.*, p. 88.
28 Letter from C. J. Mabey to author, 6 November 1975.
29 *The Heart of the Matter*, p. 88.
30 Letter from Vivien Greene to Laurence Pollinger, June 1942.
31 Letter to Laurence Pollinger, 19 June 1942.
32 Letter to his mother, 11 June 1942.
33 *Ibid.*
34 Letter from Vivien Greene addressed to Freetown, 28 February 1942.
35 Vivien Greene's journal, 7 April 1942.
36 Letter from Vivien Greene, 9 March 1942.
37 *Ibid.*, 6 April 1942.
38 *Ibid.*, 28 April 1942.
39 *Ibid.*, 25 May 1942.
40 *Ibid.*, 7 July 1942.
41 *Ibid.*, 12 July 1942.
42 *Ibid.*, 14 July 1942.
43 *Ibid.*, 1 August 1942.
44 *Ibid.*, 14 April 1942.
45 *Ibid.*, 26 August 1942.
46 Letter from Hugh Greene, 28 June 1942.
47 Letter to Elisabeth Greene, 15 October 1942.
48 *Ways of Escape*, pp. 92–3.
49 Letter to his mother, 19 April 1942.
50 Letter to Laurence Pollinger, 9 March 1942.
51 *Ibid.*, 22 May 1942.

52 Letter to his mother, 22 June 1942.
53 Letter to Laurence Pollinger, 22 May 1942.
54 Letter from Laurence Pollinger, 15 June 1942.
55 Letter to Laurence Pollinger, 17 July 1942.
56 *Ibid.*, 22 July 1942.
57 *Ibid.*, 4 August 1942.
58 *Ibid.*, 29 September 1942.
59 Cable from Laurence Pollinger, 25 September 1942.
60 Letter to Laurence Pollinger, 4 November 1942.
61 Letter from Laurence Pollinger, 17 December 1942.
62 Cable from Mary Pritchett, December 1942.
63 Letter from Laurence Pollinger, December 1942.
64 *Ibid.*
65 Letter to Vivien Greene, 24 December 1942.
66 Undated letter to Elisabeth Greene from an unidentified schoolgirl friend.
67 'Across the Border (An Unfinished Novel)', *Penguin New Writing*, Penguin, 1947, p. 70.
68 Interview with Vivien Greene, 23 June 1977.
69 *A Sort of Life*, Penguin edition, 1986, p. 21.
70 Interview with Vivien Greene, 23 June 1977.
71 *The Human Factor*, p. 169.
72 Letter from Vivien Greene, 23 March 1942.
73 *A Sort of Life*, p. 20.
74 *Ibid.*
75 Letter to his mother, 30 November 1932.
76 *The Heart of the Matter*, p. 155.
77 Letter from Marion Greene to Elisabeth Greene, 9 November 1942.
78 *Ibid.*
79 *The Potting Shed*, Penguin edition, 1971, p. 35.
80 *Ways of Escape*, p. 76.
81 *The Human Factor*, p. 55.
82 Graham Greene, *Irish Times*, 17 April 1978.
83 'The Soupsweet Land', *Collected Essays*, p. 345.
84 Letter to his mother, Good Friday, 1942.
85 *Ibid.*, 19 January 1943.
86 Letter to Elisabeth Greene, 15 October 1942.
87 Letter from Kim Philby to author, June 1978.
88 Interview with Graham Greene, 25 April 1981.
89 Letter from Laurence Pollinger to Vivien Greene, 29 January 1943.
90 Letter from Vivien Greene to Laurence Pollinger, February 1943.
91 *Ways of Escape*, p. 89.
92 Mario Soldati, *Fuori*, trans. Mario Curreli, Mondadori, 1968, pp. 419–21.
93 *Ibid.*, p. 421.

12 Carving *Brighton Rock*

1 Letter to Laurence Pollinger, 1 July 1942.
2 Letter from Margery Vosper, 10 July 1942.
3 *Ibid.*
4 Letter to Margery Vosper, 12 August 1942.
5 *Ibid.*
6 *Ibid.*
7 Letter from Laurence Pollinger, December 1942.

8   Letter from Vivien Greene to Laurence Pollinger, 15 December 1942.
9   Letter from Laurence Pollinger, 21 December 1942.
10 Letter to Laurence Pollinger, 1 January 1943.
11 Letter from Vivien Greene to Laurence Pollinger, February 1943.
12 Letter from Laurence Pollinger to Vivien Greene, 25 February 1943.
13 Letter to Laurence Pollinger, 4 March 1943.
14 *Ibid.*
15 *Ibid.*
16 *Ibid.*
17 Cable from Laurence Pollinger, 11 March 1943.
18 Letter to Laurence Pollinger, 13 March 1943.
19 Letter from Vivien Greene to Laurence Pollinger, March 1943.
20 Letter from Laurence Pollinger, 18 March 1943.
21 *Ibid.*, 29 March 1943.

13   Agents Three: Greene, Muggeridge and Philby

1   Anthony Cave Brown, '*C*': *The Secret Life of Sir Stewart Graham Menzies*, Macmillan, 1987, p. 250.
2   Undated letter, probably written in April 1943.
3   Malcolm Muggeridge, *The Infernal Grove: Chronicles of Wasted Time*, vol. 2, Fontana/Collins, 1975, p. 138.
4   Undated letter to David Low.
5   Letter from Kim Philby to author, 8 April 1978.
6   Milne was a particularly close friend of Philby's, having been at Westminster school with him. Sometimes they holidayed together in central Europe. They remained close friends until Philby left hurriedly for Moscow in 1963, an escapee from British Intelligence and the police.
7   Muggeridge, *The Infernal Grove*, p. 149.
8   Graham Greene, Introduction to Kim Philby, *My Silent War*, Panther Books, 1969, p. 9.
9   Letter from an unattributable source to author, 17 June 1977.
10 Letter from Kim Philby to author, 9 April 1974.
11 The following secret document written by Herbert L. Will from the headquarters of X2 in Ryder Street, typifies the type of information sought. X2, or double cross, was the American equivalent to SIS:

> Subject: Disseminate of Counter-espionage information to the X2 Branch, London.
> A good example of the type of information that X2 is interested in but which came first into the hands of SOE/SO is, as you will recall, the killing of a prominent member of one of the leading German intelligence services in Denmark. I refer to this example merely because it is fairly typical and, being a concrete case, may be helpful in indicating one type of information desired.
> cc: each SCI unit (Destroy).

12 Muggeridge, *The Infernal Grove*, pp. 164–5.
13 Interview with Malcolm Muggeridge, June 1977.
14 *Ibid.*
15 Information from an unattributable source.
16 Bruce Page, David Leitch and Phillip Knightley, *The Philby Conspiracy*, Doubleday, 1968, p. 111.
17 Muggeridge did well in some instances, for example kidnapping enemy agents and having

them taken across the border into British territory. In May 1943 Muggeridge kidnapped Alfredo Manna, the head of the shipping intelligence network operated by the Italian consul, Campini, who worked in close collaboration with Wertz. Muggeridge had Manna kidnapped, put across the Swaziland border (then British territory) and sent to Camp 020. After interrogation, Manna supplied a great deal of information about the Axis activities. Muggeridge also received a congratulatory telegram from 'C' for providing the precise bearings of a projected rendezvous with a German U-boat which led to its apprehension. *The Infernal Grove*, p. 166.

18 Interview with Graham Greene, 13 December 1983.
19 Information from an unattributable source.
20 Cave Brown, 'C', pp. 224–5.
21 Muggeridge, *The Infernal Grove*, p. 144.
22 Cave Brown, 'C', p. 227.
23 Muggeridge, *The Infernal Grove*, p. 144.
24 Hugh Trevor-Roper, *The Philby Affair*, William Kimber, 1968, pp. 37–8.
25 *Our Man in Havana*, Penguin edition, 1962, p. 215.
26 Cave Brown, 'C', p. 227.
27 Interview with Graham Greene, 25 April 1981.
28 *Ways of Escape*, Penguin edition, 1987, p. 183.
29 Information from an unattributable source.
30 *Ibid.*
31 Michael Howard, *British Intelligence in the Second World War*, vol. 5, HMSO, 1990, p. 63.
32 Information from an unattributable source.
33 OSS files, National Archives, Washington, DC.
34 *Ibid.*
35 *Ibid.*
36 Information from an unattributable source.
37 *Ibid.*
38 *Ibid.*
39 Interview with Graham Greene, 13 December 1983.
40 Kim Philby, *My Silent War*, Panther, 1973, p. 41.
41 Otto John, *Twice through the Lines*, Macmillan, 1972, p. 98.
42 *Ibid.*, p. 99.
43 Phillip Knightley, *The Master Spy: The Story of Kim Philby*, Knopf, 1988, p. 109.
44 Page, Leitch and Knightley, *The Philby Conspiracy*, p. 167.
45 Christopher Andrew and Oleg Gordievsky, *KGB: The Inside Story*, HarperCollins, 1990, p. 293.
46 Letter from Kim Philby to author, 8 April 1978.
47 *Ibid.*
48 *Ibid.*
49 *Ibid.*
50 Knightley, *The Master Spy*, p. 119.
51 Philby, *My Silent War*, Pan Books, 1989, p. 99.
52 Robert Cecil, 'Cambridge Comintern', *The Missing Dimension*, ed. Christopher Andrew and David N. Dilks, Macmillan, 1984, p. 179.
53 Interview with Graham Greene, 25 April 1981.
54 *Ibid.*
55 *Ibid.*, 15 December 1983.
56 Interview with Tim Milne, 1992.
57 Letter from Kim Philby to author, 8 April 1978.
58 *Ibid.*
59 However, Louise Dennys, Greene's niece, told me that Greene did not suspect Philby was a spy.

14   From Spy to Publisher

1   Interview with Graham Greene, 25 April 1981.
2   Evelyn Waugh, *Unconditional Surrender*, Butler & Tanner, 1961, p. 245.
3   Letter from his mother, 23 June 1944.
4   Interview with Graham Greene, 25 April 1981.
5   *The End of the Affair*, Heinemann, 1951, p. 80.
6   *Ibid.*, p. 81.
7   Letter to Laurence Pollinger, 1 July 1944.
8   Interview with Graham Greene, 25 April 1981.
9   Letter to his mother, 2 July 1940.
10 *The Comedians*, Penguin edition, 1981, p. 63.
11 Letter to Laurence Pollinger, 29 September 1942.
12 *Ibid.*, 4 August 1943.
13 Undated letter to his mother.
14 Anthony Powell, *Faces in My Time: To Keep the Ball Rolling*, vol. 3, Heinemann, 1980, p. 199.
15 Letter to J. C. Trewin, 18 September 1944.
16 *Ibid.*, 9 February 1945.
17 *Ibid.*, 12 July 1948.
18 Letter from Evelyn Waugh, Ash Wednesday, 1946.
19 During the time Greene was working with Kim Philby in Ryder Street, he was a member of the Reform Club. On fire-duty nights ('One had one's fire duty nights because the fire bombing was still going on,') he and Philby would go and have breakfast there ('a real good breakfast: eggs and bacon'). They took turns staying awake all night on duty: 'Then one day the head waiter changed and the new beastly head waiter refused to take my order for breakfast the next day when I was going to be on fire duty. So I resigned on the grounds that I could no longer subscribe to the Reform format.' Interview with Graham Greene, 25 April 1981.
20 Letter to William H. Webber, 22 January 1944.
21 Memo from William H. Webber, 31 January 1944.
22 Letter to William H. Webber, 2 February 1944.
23 Letter to Mr Kirkpatrick, 4 August 1944.
24 Douglas Jerrold, 'Graham Greene, Pleasure-Hater', *Harper's*, August 1952, p. 51.
25 *Ibid.*, p. 52.
26 Letter from Kim Philby, 8 April 1978.
27 *Ibid.*
28 *Ibid.*
29 *Ibid.*
30 Interview with Graham Greene, 25 April 1981.
31 *Ibid.*
32 Malcolm Muggeridge, *The Infernal Grove: Chronicles of Wasted Time*, vol. 2, Fontana/Collins, 1975, p. 263.
33 Interview with Graham Greene, 25 April 1981.
34 *Ibid.*
35 Undated letter to his mother, June 1947.
36 Letter from Vivien Greene to Francis Greene, 12 October 1970.
37 Letter to his mother, 1 November 1948.
38 Robert Speaight, *François Mauriac: A Study of the Writer and the Man*, Chatto & Windus, 1976, p. 177.
39 Interview with Malcolm Muggeridge, May 1977.
40 Muggeridge, *The Infernal Grove*, p. 216.
41 Undated letter to Vivien Greene.

42 Muggeridge, *The Infernal Grove*, p. 262.
43 Powell, *Faces in My Time*, p. 199.
44 *Ibid.*
45 *Ibid.*
46 Letter from Robert Kee, 29 October 1946.
47 Undated letter to Anthony Powell, 1948.
48 Letter to his mother, 20 October 1944.
49 *Ibid.*
50 *Ibid.*, undated, but probably early March 1947.
51 *Ibid.*
52 *Ibid.*
53 Both Vivien and ten-year-old Francis listened to the broadcast. Vivien felt her husband sounded 'very sad'; their son thought his father's words 'were very well chosen!' *Ibid.*
54 *New York Times* book review, 16 November 1947, p. 10, provided for author by Neil Brennan, Greene's bibliographer.
55 Letter to Catherine Walston, 18 October 1947.
56 Letter to his mother, 20 August (year undated, but probably 1947).
57 Powell, *Faces in My Time*, pp. 198–9.
58 *Ibid.*, p. 199.
59 *Ibid.*, p. 201.
60 *Ibid.*
61 Malcolm Muggeridge, *Like It Was: A Selection from the Diaries of Malcolm Muggeridge*, ed. John Bright-Holmes, Collins, 1981, p. 298.
62 *Ibid.*, p. 304. Entry for 25 October 1948.
63 Interview with Graham Greene, 25 April 1981.
64 *Ibid.*
65 Letter to Egon Hostovsky, 11 January 1949.
66 Letter from Anthony Powell, 12 November 1948.
67 Letter to Anthony Powell, 14 December 1948.
68 Letter from Sir Oliver Crosthwaite-Eyre, 4 March 1958.
69 Letter to Sir Oliver Crosthwaite-Eyre, March 1958.
70 Interview with Graham Greene, 21 April 1981.

15 The Unquiet Peace

1   Journal, 20 March 1945.
2   Undated letter to his mother.
3   Marie-Françoise Allain, *The Other Man: Conversations with Graham Greene*, Bodley Head, 1983, p. 157.
4   Archbishop of Canterbury's address, 8 May 1945.
5   Angus Calder, *The People's War: Britain 1939–45*, Pantheon, 1969, pp. 567–8.
6   Letter from Vivien Greene, May 1945.
7   *Ibid.*, 10 May 1945.
8   Undated letter to his mother, May 1945.
9   *The End of the Affair*, Heinemann, 1951, p. 124.
10 Letter to his mother, 21 June 1945.
11 Interview with Vivien Greene, 26 July 1979.
12 *Ibid.*
13 Undated letter to Vivien Greene.
14 *Spectator*, 6 December 1940.
15 Letter to his mother, May 1945.
16 *Ibid.*

17 Alan Jenkins, *The Forties*, Heinemann, London, 1977, p. 60.
18 *Sunday Times*, September 1945.
19 Interview with Vivien Greene, 26 July 1979.
20 Undated letter to his mother.
21 *Evening Standard*, 22 June 1945.
22 *Ibid.*, 13 July 1945.
23 *Ibid.*, 17 August 1945.
24 *Ibid.*
25 *Ibid.*, 31 August 1945.
26 *Ibid.*, 10 August 1945.
27 Quoted in Michael Meyer, 'Memories of George Orwell', *The World of George Orwell*, ed. Miriam Gross, Weidenfeld & Nicolson, 1971, pp. 131–2.
28 Frere asked the printer to set up specimen pages which he then sent to Greene. Greene was not easily satisfied, and Frere had to write to reassure him that his wishes would be carried out: 'Here are some more specimen pages, one of them set in Mon 45–11 point solid, as you requested.'
29 Letter to Louise Callender, October 1946.
30 Letter to Heinemann, 11 October 1946.
31 Interview with John and Gillian Sutro, 1976.
32 *Ibid.*
33 *New Statesman*, 9 September 1944.
34 Interview with Desmond Pakenham, 11 June 1977.
35 Interview with Mario Soldati, 18 May 1977.
36 Interview with Walter Allen, 1977.
37 *Ibid.*
38 Interview with Graham Greene, 25 April 1981.
39 Michael Meyer, *Not Prince Hamlet: Literary and Theatrical Memoirs*, Secker & Warburg, 1989, p. 124.

16 The Heart of the Matter

1 Interview with Malcolm and Kitty Muggeridge, June 1977.
2 Interview with the Reverend Vincent Turner, July 1991.
3 Interview with Lady Melchett, 15 August 1991.
4 *The End of the Affair*, Heinemann, 1951, p. 178.
5 Interview with Belinda Straight, 26 July 1992.
6 *Ibid.*
7 *Ibid.*
8 *Ibid.* On another occasion, Bonte was sitting in the bath and reciting poetry when a black hand emerged through the open window. Bonte screamed and ran downstairs without any clothes on to where her parents were having a dinner party. Bonte cried out about the black hand and everybody rushed upstairs. Bobs, who had climbed up on the roof and stuck her blackened hand in the window, was caught out as she was trying to get the black off her hand.
9 *Ibid.*
10 Catherine did not believe in her own intelligence, and in part needed mentors to educate her. She learned a great deal about paintings from Sir John Rothenstein, then director of the Tate Gallery. Her brother, David Crompton, said that she had to be told what was good art before she could appreciate it and that it was Henry Moore, the sculptor, who taught Catherine how to see through her own eyes.

When she met Greene, she embarked on a course of reading which he encouraged. He recommended *Deaths and Departures* by Dylan Thomas, and novels by

E. M. Forster, Henry James, Trollope, Mauriac, and Scott Fitzgerald. Greene's reading list in non-fiction included *The Journal of Alice James*, *The Craft of Fiction* by Percy Lubbock and the biography of Wordsworth by Herbert Read.

11 Interview with Belinda Straight, 26 July 1992.
12 Interview with Bonte Durán, 25 May 1992.
13 Interview with Belinda Straight, 26 July 1992.
14 *Ibid.*
15 Interview with Bonte Durán, 25 May 1992.
16 *Ibid.*
17 *Ibid.*
18 Letter from Catherine Walston to Belinda Straight, 31 January 1969.
19 Interview with Lady Melchett, 15 August 1991.
20 *Ibid.*
21 Interview with Lady Walston, 13 June 1992.
22 Telephone interview with William Walston, 14 June 1994.
23 Interview with Lady Walston, 13 June 1992.
24 Letter from Catherine Walston to Belinda Straight, 31 January 1969.
25 Interview with Vivien Greene, 26 July 1979.
26 *Ibid.*
27 *Ibid.*, 23 June 1977.
28 *Ibid.*
29 *Ibid.*
30 Interview with Sir Hugh Greene, 19 May 1981.
31 Interview with Vivien Greene, 26 July 1979.
32 *Ibid.*, 15 August 1977.
33 Letter to Catherine Walston, probably June 1947.
34 Letter from Vivien Greene to author, 15 January 1982.
35 Interview with Vivien Greene, 26 July 1979.
36 Interview with Graham Greene, 25 April 1981.
37 Undated letter to his mother.
38 *The Heart of the Matter*, Penguin edition, 1983, p. 138.
39 Letter to Catherine Walston, 30 September 1947.
40 *Ibid.*
41 *The Heart of the Matter*, p. 76.
42 Letter from Vivien Greene to Catherine Walston, 21 December 1946.
43 Letter to Catherine Walston, 26 December 1946.
44 Undated letter to his mother.
45 Undated letter from Vivien Greene to Catherine Walston.
46 *Ibid.*
47 Letter from Vivien Greene to Catherine Walston, 14 February 1947.
48 Interview with Vivien Greene, 23 June 1977.
49 *The Heart of the Matter*, p. 32.
50 Undated letter from Vivien Greene to Catherine Walston.
51 *A Quick Look Behind*, Sylvester & Orphanos, 1983, p. 23.
52 Letter to Catherine Walston, 6 May 1947.
53 *Ibid.*
54 *Ibid.*
55 *Ibid.*
56 *Ibid.*
57 An undated note on blue paper written in pencil.
58 Letter to Catherine Walston, 17 May 1947.
59 *Ibid.*, 27 June 1947.
60 *Ibid.*
61 Undated letter to Catherine Walston, probably October 1947.

62 *The Heart of the Matter*, p. 235.
63 Interview with Vivien Greene, 26 July 1979.
64 *The Heart of the Matter*, pp. 25–6.
65 *Ibid.*, p. 16.
66 *Ibid.*, p. 56.
67 *Ibid.*, p. 57.
68 *Ibid.*, p. 58.
69 *Ibid.*
70 *Ibid.*
71 *Ibid.*, pp. 58–60.
72 *Ibid.*, p. 25.
73 *Ibid.*, p. 77.
74 Letter to Catherine Walston, 27 August 1947.
75 *Ibid.*, 25 August 1947.
76 *Ibid.*, undated, probably 2 September 1947.

17   *The Third Man* and Other Friends

1   Letter to Catherine Walston, 11 June 1947.
2   *Ibid.*, 2 August 1947.
3   See *The Life of Graham Greene*, Vol. One, p. 590.
4   Nicholas Wapshott, *The Man Between*, Chatto & Windus, 1990, p. 195.
5   *Ibid.*
6   *Ibid.*
7   *Ibid.*, pp. 195–6.
8   *Ibid.*, p. 196.
9   *The Pleasure Dome: The Collected Film Criticism, 1935–40*, ed. John Russell Taylor, Oxford University Press, 1980, p. 265.
10 Wapshott, *The Man Between*, p. 196.
11 *Ibid.*
12 *Ibid.*
13 On 2 August 1947 Greene notes 'I am working and working at *The Basement Room* . . .' and only on 2 September could he announce: 'I've nearly finished the first work with Carol Reed (they begin shooting on September 13).' Letters to Catherine Walston, 2 August 1947 and 2 September 1947.
14 *New York Post*, quoted in Wapshott, *The Man Between*, p. 204.
15 *Ways of Escape*, Penguin edition, 1987, p. 96.
16 *Ibid.*
17 Interview with Graham Greene, 11 August 1977.
18 Letter to Catherine Walston, 30 September 1947.
19 *Ibid.*, 12 February 1948.
20 *Ibid.*
21 *Ibid.*
22 *Ibid.*
23 *The Third Man*, Penguin edition, 1971, p. 13.
24 *Ibid.*, p. 14.
25 Letter to Catherine Walston, 12 February 1948.
26 *The Third Man*, p. 20.
27 Letter to Catherine Walston, 17 February 1948.
28 *Ibid.*
29 *Ibid.*, 18 February 1948.
30 *Ibid.*

31 Letter to the *News Chronicle*, 27 February 1948.
32 *Ways of Escape*, p. 105.
33 Marie-Françoise Allain, *The Other Man: Conversations with Graham Greene*, Bodley Head, 1983, p. 150.
34 Interview with John Cairncross, 14 May 1977.
35 He also used as his work table a better-made desk of solid chestnut under a window on the ground floor.
36 *An Impossible Woman: The Memories of Dottoressa Moor of Capri*, ed. and with epilogue by Graham Greene, Viking, 1976, pp. 193–4.
37 Ian Greenlees, *Norman Douglas*, British Council, 1957, p. 28.
38 Interview with Graham Greene, 25 April 1981.
39 Interview with Mario Soldati, 18 May 1977.
40 *Ibid.*
41 Letter to Catherine Walston, 1 April 1948.
42 *Ways of Escape*, p. 98.
43 Letter to Catherine Walston from Hotel Astoria, 21 June 1948.
44 *The Third Man*, p. 14.
45 Interview with Elizabeth Montagu, 10 April 1991.
46 *The Third Man*, p. 113.
47 *Ibid.*, pp. 113–14.
48 *Ibid.*
49 *Ways of Escape*, p. 99.
50 Interview with Elizabeth Montagu, 10 April 1991.
51 *The Third Man*, Penguin edition, 1971, pp. 80–1.
52 Letter to Catherine Walston, 26 June 1948.
53 *Ibid.*
54 *Ibid.*, 21 June 1948.
55 Barbara Leaming, *Orson Welles, A Biography*, Penguin, 1986, p. 444.
56 Interview with Elizabeth Montagu, 10 April 1991.
57 Undated letter to Catherine Walston.
58 *Ibid.*, 4 August 1948.
59 Letter to Catherine Walston, 4 August 1948.
60 *Ibid.*
61 *Ibid.*, 5 August 1948.
62 Postcard to Harry Walston, 9 August 1948.
63 Letter to Catherine Walston, 14 August 1948.
64 *Ways of Escape*, p. 52.
65 *Ibid.*, pp. 52–3.
66 *Ibid.*, p. 51.
67 *The Third Man*, Lorrimer, 1968, p. 114, n. 78. Script from the 1949 film by Graham Greene and Carol Reed.
68 Letter to Catherine Walston, August 1948.
69 Letter to his mother, 1 November 1948.
70 Malcolm Muggeridge, *Like It Was: A Selection from the Diaries of Malcolm Muggeridge*, ed. John Bright-Holmes, Collins, 1981, p. 297. Entry for 13 September 1948.
71 Letter to Catherine Walston, 22 August 1948.
72 Interview with Graham Greene, 25 April 1981.
73 Letter to Catherine Walston, 23 August 1948.

18   Love as a Fever

1 Letter to Catherine Walston, 29 June 1947.

2   *Ibid.*

3   *Ibid.*, 18 August 1947.

4   T. S. Eliot, *Selected Essays*, Harcourt Brace, 1950, p. 380.

5   Marie-Françoise Allain, *The Other Man: Conversations with Graham Greene*, Bodley Head, 1983, p. 158.

6   Letter to Catherine Walston, 22 August 1947.

7   Interview with Lady Melchett, 15 August 1991.

8   Interview with David Crompton, 26 May 1992.

9   *The Diaries of Evelyn Waugh*, ed. Michael Davie, Penguin, 1979, p. 701.

10   Letter to Nancy Mitford, 4 October 1948, *The Letters of Evelyn Waugh*, ed. Mark Amory, Weidenfeld & Nicolson, 1980, pp. 283–4.

11   Interview with Lady Melchett, 15 August 1991.

12   Waugh, *Diaries*, p. 707.

13   *The End of the Affair*, Heinemann, 1951, p. 116.

14   Interview with Lady Melchett, 15 August 1991.

15   *The End of the Affair*, p. 54.

16   Interview with Lady Melchett, 15 August 1991.

17   *The End of the Affair*, p. 55.

18   *Ibid.*, p. 56.

19   *Ibid.*, p. 54.

20   Letter to Catherine Walston, 6 May 1947.

21   Letter to Catherine Walston, 16 May 1947.

22   Postcard to Catherine Walston, 18 May 1947.

23   *The End of the Affair*, pp. 31–2.

24   Letter from Yvonne Cloetta to author, 23 May 1994.

25   Letter to Catherine Walston, 16 May 1947.

26   *Ibid.*, 17 May 1947.

27   *Ibid.*, 4 June 1947.

28   *Ibid.*, 11 June 1947. An unusual ending to his letter but for the fact that his previous letter to Catherine spoke of her being right when she had warned him against taking morphia: 'It's going to be bloody curing myself – I hope I can do it in a week like you can.' (Undated letter, probably 4 June 1947.)

29   *Ibid.*

30   *Ibid.*, 27 June 1947.

31   Letter to Catherine Walston, 29 June 1947.

32   *Ibid.*, 6 July 1947.

33   *Ibid.*

34   *Ibid.*, 2 August 1947.

35   *The End of the Affair*, p. 60

36   Letter to Catherine Walston, 2 August 1947.

37   *Ibid.*

38   *Ibid.*, undated but written close to 5 August 1947.

39   Postcard to Catherine Walston, 4 August 1947.

40   Letter to Catherine Walston, 21 August 1947.

41   *Ibid.* Greene did one theatre review of Noël Coward's 'Point Verlaine', on 13 September, and a book review on Robert Liddell's *Treatise on the Novel* before the year ended.

42   *Ibid.*, 22 August 1947.

43   *Ibid.*

44   *Ibid.*, 24 August 1947.

45   *Ibid.*

46   *Ibid.*

47   Interview with Vivien Greene, 23 June 1977.

48   *Ibid.*, 15 August 1977.

49   *A Burnt-Out Case*, Penguin edition, 1977, p. 15.

50 Letter to Catherine Walston, 2 September 1947.
51 *Ibid.*, 5 September 1947.
52 *Ibid.*
53 *Ibid.*, 15 September 1947.
54 Interview with Vivien Greene, 10 August 1983.
55 *The End of the Affair*, pp. 62–3.
56 *Ibid.*, p. 61.
57 *Ibid.*, p. 53.
58 *Ibid.*, p. 108.
59 *Ibid.*
60 Letter to Catherine Walston, 2 September 1947.
61 *The Heart of the Matter*, Penguin edition, 1983, p. 81.
62 Letter to Catherine Walston, 2 September 1947.
63 *Ibid.*, 5 September 1947.
64 *The End of the Affair*, p. 61.
65 Letter to Catherine Walston, 28 September 1947.
66 *The End of the Affair*, pp. 31–2.
67 Letter to Catherine Walston, 12 September 1947.
68 Interview with Vivien Greene, 26 July 1977.
69 *Oxford Mail*, 28 April 1945.
70 Letter to Catherine Walston, 29 June 1947.
71 Interview with Vivien Greene, 15 August 1977.
72 *Ibid.*
73 Letter to Vivien Greene, 12 December 1947.
74 *The Heart of the Matter*, pp. 220–1.
75 Interview with Vivien Greene, 26 July 1977.

19   Private Wars

1   Interview with Vivien Greene, 26 July 1977.
2   *The Quiet American*, Penguin edition, 1974, p. 88.
3   Letter from Marion Greene to Vivien Greene, 7 January 1948.
4   *Ibid.*, 29 June 1948.
5   Letter from Marion Greene to Vivien Greene, 7 January 1948.
6   *The Diaries of Evelyn Waugh*, ed. Michael Davie, Penguin, 1979, p. 694.
7   *Saturday Review of Literature*, 10 July 1948.
8   Letter to Vivien Greene, 9 April 1943.
9   *The Potting Shed*, Penguin edition, 1971, p. 84.
10 Letter to Vivien Greene, 24 April 1945.
11 Letter to Catherine Walston, 13 April 1950.
12 *The Potting Shed*, p. 88.
13 *The End of the Affair*, Heinemann, 1951, p. 61.
14 Letter to Catherine Walston, 6 January 1951.
15 *The End of the Affair*, p. 107.
16 *The Heart of the Matter*, Penguin edition, 1983, p. 159.
17 *Ibid.*, p. 160.
18 *Ibid.*, p. 161.
19 *Ibid.*, p. 178.
20 *The Ministry of Fear*, Penguin edition, 1978, p. 218.
21 *The Heart of the Matter*, p. 51.
22 *Ibid.*, p. 179.
23 *Ibid.*, p. 191.

24 Charles Pierre Péguy (1873–1914), French publisher, poet and Catholic.
25 Undated letter from Father Martindale to Vivien Greene, 1948.
26 Undated letter from Father Martindale to Vivien Greene.
27 Letter from Vivien Greene, 31 July 1948.
28 *Ibid.*
29 Letter to Vivien Greene, 12 August 1948.
30 *Ibid.*, 3 June 1948.
31 *Ibid.*
32 *Ibid.*
33 Letter from Vivien Greene to Mr Bishchoff, 27 September 1948.
34 Letter to Catherine Walston, 27 January 1948.
35 *The Power and the Glory*, Penguin edition, 1983, p. 131.
36 *The End of the Affair*, p. 117.
37 Letter to Vivien Greene, 1948.
38 Letter to Catherine Walston, 29 April 1948.
39 *Ibid.*, 11 May 1948.
40 *Ihid.*
41 *Ibid.*
42 *Ibid.*, 19 May 1948.
43 *Ibid.*
44 *Ibid.*, 7 June 1948.
45 *Ibid.*, 26 June 1948.
46 *Ibid.*

20 A Vulgar Success

1 Letter to Vivien Dayrell-Browning, 18 January 1926.
2 John Donne, 'The Will'.
3 Edward Sackville-West, 'The Problem of Despair', *New Statesman and Nation*, 19 June 1948, p. 108.
4 Letter to Catherine Walston, 7 June 1948.
5 *Tablet*, 5 June 1948.
6 *Catholic Herald*, 6 August 1948.
7 *Tablet*, 10 July 1948.
8 *Universe*, 3 September 1948.
9 *Ibid.*, 16 July 1948.
10 Letter to *New Statesman and Nation*, 26 June 1948.
11 *Universe*, 18 June 1948.
12 *Ibid.*, 25 June 1948.
13 *Ibid.*, 16 July 1948.
14 *New Yorker*, 17 July 1948.
15 Undated letter to Evelyn Waugh, probably June 1948.
16 *The Heart of the Matter*, Penguin edition, 1983, p. 125.
17 *Ibid.*, p. 125.
18 *Ibid.*, p. 220. Greene uses the same bargaining prayer again and again in his work. In *The Potting Shed* (1957), Father Callifer recalls the loss of his faith despite the miraculous recovery of his nephew James (who in childhood tried to hang himself).

Father Callifer recalls holding James on his knees, praying, and experiencing a terrible pain as if he were the one being strangled: 'I couldn't breathe, I couldn't speak . . . then your breath came back and it was just as though I had died instead.' (*The Potting Shed*, Penguin edition, 1971, pp. 73–4)

Finally James persuades his uncle to recall exactly his prayer: 'I suppose I offered something in return. Something I valued . . . I said, "Let him live, God. I love him. Let him live. I will give you anything if you will let him live." But what had I got to give him? I was a poor man. I said, "Take away what I love most. Take . . . take . . . " ' (p. 75)

Callifer cannot remember his exact words and it is James, hearing the words upon coming back to life after attempting suicide who remembers for him: 'Take away my faith, but let him live?' (p. 75)

However, perhaps it is most crucial in *The End of the Affair*. Sarah recounts in her diary discovering her lover, Bendrix, in the ruins of a bombed house: 'I didn't see Maurice at first, and then I saw his arm coming out from under the door. I touched his hand: I could have sworn it was a dead hand . . . wouldn't I have recognised life if there was any of it left in touching his hand?' So Sarah prays: 'I'm a bitch and a fake and I hate myself . . . *Make* me believe. I shut my eyes tight, and I pressed my nails into the palms of my hands until I could feel nothing but the pain, and I said, I will believe. Let him be alive, and I *will* believe . . . Let him have his happiness . . . But that wasn't enough. It doesn't hurt to believe. So I said, I love him and I'll do anything if you'll make him alive. I said very slowly, I'll give him up for ever, only let him be alive with a chance, and . . . I said, People can love without seeing each other, can't they, they love You all their lives without seeing You, and then he came in at the door, and he was alive, and I thought now the agony of being without him starts, and I wish he was safely back dead again under the door.' (Heinemann edition, 1951, pp. 112–13.)

19 *Dieu Vivant*, 17 November 1950, pp. 151–2.
20 Letter to Catherine Walston, 7 June 1948.
21 *Ibid.*, 21 June 1948.
22 Undated letter to Catherine Walston, 1949.
23 Letter to Catherine Walston, 24 March 1950.
24 E. Equinn, *Dublin Quarterly*, 1950, p. 137.
25 Letter to Catherine Walston, 7 June 1948.
26 *Ibid.*, 26 June 1948.
27 *Ibid.*, 4 August 1948.
28 Undated letter to Catherine Walston, probably August 1949.
29 Letter to Catherine Walston, 19 January 1949.

21 Boston Tea Party

1 *The Times*, 21 June 1949.
2 *Ibid.*, 23 June 1949.
3 *Ibid.*, 24 June 1949.
4 'The Un-Midas Touch', *Life*, 4 July 1949, p. 18.
5 Letter to Catherine Walston, 7 September 1949.
6 *Ibid.*, 26 September 1949.
7 *Ibid.*, 7 September 1949.
8 *Ibid.*, 11 September 1949.
9 *Ibid.*, 2 October 1949.
10 *Ibid.*, 26 September 1949.
11 *Ibid.*, 2 October 1949.
12 *Ibid.*, 3 October 1949.
13 *Ibid.*, 2 October 1949.
14 *The End of the Affair*, Heinemann, 1951, p. 66.
15 Undated letter to his mother.
16 Letter to his mother, 1 March 1949.
17 Letter to Catherine Walston, 7 October 1949.

18 Letter to Heinemann, 10 March 1950.
19 Letter to Catherine Walston, 7 December 1949.
20 *Ibid.*
21 *Ibid.*, 9 December 1949.
22 *Ibid.*, 13 December 1949.
23 *Ibid.*
24 *Ibid.*
25 *Ibid.*
26 *Ibid.*
27 *Ibid.*, 9–12 December 1949.
28 *The Heart of the Matter*, Penguin edition, 1983, p. 13.
29 Letter to Catherine Walston, 9–12 December 1949.
30 *Ibid.*, 14 December 1949.
31 *Ibid.*
32 *Ibid.*, undated letter written on board the *Queen Elizabeth en route* for America, February 1950.
33 *Ibid.*
34 *Ibid.*
35 *Ibid.*
36 *Ibid.*, 21 February 1950.
37 Diary entry for 22 February 1950.
38 *Ibid.*, 23 February 1950.
39 *Ibid.*, 25 February 1950.
40 Cyrus Durgin, 'British Novelist Graham Greene Turns Playwright and Likes It', *Boston Daily Globe*, 24 February 1950.
41 *Ibid.*
42 Diary entry for 24 February 1950.
43 *Ibid.*, 25 February 1950.
44 *The Times*, 1 March 1950.
45 Letter to Basil Dean, 27 July 1950.
46 Letter to Catherine Walston, 28 February 1950.

22 Wildly, Crazily, Hopelessly

1 Letter to Catherine Walston, 5 August 1948.
2 'After Two Years', written in December 1949.
3 Letter to Catherine Walston, 10 July 1949.
4 *Ibid.*, 5 August 1948.
5 *Ibid.*, 6 August 1949.
6 *Ibid.*, 8 July 1949.
7 *Ibid.*, 26 August 1950.
8 Letter from Catherine Walston to Bonte Durán, 13 March 1950.
9 *Ibid.*, 16 June 1950.
10 Letter to Catherine Walston, 26 November 1949.
11 Letter from Catherine Walston to Bonte Durán, 16 June 1950.
12 *The Heart of the Matter*, Penguin edition, 1983, p. 155.
13 Letter to Catherine Walston, 9 May 1949.
14 *Ibid.*, 21 May 1949.
15 *Ibid.*, 25 May 1949.
16 *Ibid.*, 11 April 1949.
17 *Ibid.*, 25 July 1949.
18 *Ibid.*, probably August 1949.

19 *Ibid.*, 16 December 1947.
20 *Ibid.*, 26 September 1949.
21 *Ibid.*, 19 December 1949.
22 Interview with Lady Melchett, 15 August 1991.
23 Undated letter to Catherine Walston.
24 Letter to Catherine Walston, probably July 1949.
25 *Travels with My Aunt*, Penguin edition, 1972, p. 15.
26 Undated letter from Catherine Walston to Bonte Durán.
27 Interview with Lady Walston, 1 June 1992.
28 *Ibid.*
29 Letter to Catherine Walston, 30 January 1950.
30 *Ibid.*
31 *Ibid.*, probably January 1950.
32 *Ibid.*
33 Interview with Bonte Durán, 26 May 1992.
34 Letter to Catherine Walston, 28 February 1950.
35 Letter from Catherine Walston to Bonte Durán, 13 March 1950.
36 Letter to Bonte Durán, 19 March 1950.
37 *The End of the Affair*, Heinemann, 1951, p. 10.
38 Letter to Bonte Durán, 19 March 1950.
39 Interview with Lady Walston, 1 June 1992.
40 *Ibid.*
41 Letter to Catherine Walston, 19 July 1949.
42 Letter to Bonte Durán, 19 March 1950.
43 Letter to Catherine Walston, probably 28 March 1950.
44 *Ibid.*, March 1950
45 *Ibid.*
46 *Ibid.*
47 *Ibid.*, 30 March 1950.
48 *Ibid.*
49 *Ibid.*, 28 March 1950.
50 Much of the correspondence contains cryptic codes that cannot be interpreted now that the participants are dead. Greene ended one of his postcards to Catherine with the statement: 'Longing for my flat' and two lines in code which are repeated in numerous letters: 'T.M.C.' and 'YLMB.'
    When courting Vivien, Greene often used the code 143, sometimes covering the whole end of an envelope. The code was quite simple (the numbers representing the number of letters in the word): 1=I: 4=love: 3=you. If the code is equally simple, perhaps T.M.C. means 'To my Catherine' and 'YLMB' an assertion he wishes were true, 'You Love Me Bobs.' Or the first case could signify 'Touch me Catherine' or a statement of intent – 'To marry Catherine'.
    The last lines of one of Greene's letters to Catherine read: 'ROF ROF TMC TMC TMC ROF.' I am unable to decipher the meaning of ROF, but presumably it is something so intimate that the code must remain a secret shared only by the lovers.
51 Letter to Catherine Walston, 30 March 1950.
52 *Ibid.*, 1 April 1950.
53 *Ibid.*, 3 April 1950 (Palm Sunday).
54 *Ibid.*
55 There is little doubt about Greene's 'sexual energy'. In 1933, when he had been married six years, Vivien received a phone call for Greene from Anita (Annette), and she *knew* for the first time that he was involved with prostitutes. Vivien never told Greene of the incident. In interview, Greene told me a little about his relationship with Annette:
    NS: Was the prostitute related to the prostitute in *Stamboul Train*?
    GG: Oh, yes. I mean she was the prostitute I was a little bit in love with. She

suggested once that it was an absurd waste of my money to pay, but we could do a film together and both make money. But I said that I would be incapable of doing it – I mean it wouldn't work. This was early right back in the 1930s when I was a young man. Interview with Graham Greene, 25 April 1981.

56 Letter to Catherine Walston, 13 April 1950.
57 *Ibid.*
58 *Ibid.*
59 *Ibid.*, 24 April 1950.
60 Letter from Catherine Walston to Belinda Straight, 31 January 1969.
61 Letter from Catherine Walston to Bonte Durán, 22 May 1953.
62 Letter to Catherine Walston, 6 April 1950.
63 *Ibid.*, 26 April 1950.
64 *Ibid.*, 25 April 1950.
65 *Ibid.*, 26 April 1950.
66 *Ibid.*, 30 April 1950.
67 *Ibid.*, 3 May 1950.
68 *Ibid.*, 4 May 1950.
69 *Ibid.*, 13 May 1950.
70 *Ibid.*, 24 June 1950.
71 Cable to Catherine Walston via Radio France, June 1950.
72 Letter to Catherine Walston, 17 June 1950.
73 *Ibid.*, 7 July 1950.
74 *Ibid.*
75 *Ibid.*, 16 August 1950.
76 *The End of the Affair*, p. 237.
77 Letter to Catherine Walston, 31 August 1950.
78 *Ibid.*, 6 September 1950.
79 *Ibid.*
80 *Ibid.*, 26 October 1950.
81 *Ibid.*
82 *The End of the Affair*, p. 70.
83 Undated letter to Catherine Walston, probably September 1950.
84 *The End of the Affair*, pp. 37–8.

23 War of the Running Dogs

1 Undated letter to Hugh Greene, but probably 24 October 1950.
2 Interview with Peter Levring, 6 April 1993. Interviewed on my behalf by Carole Foote, research associate.
3 Letter to Hugh Greene, 24 October 1950.
4 *Ibid.*, 26 October 1950.
5 *Ibid.*, 31 October 1950.
6 *Ibid.*, 3 November 1950.
7 *Ibid.*
8 *Ibid.*
9 *Ibid.*
10 *Ibid.*, 13 November 1950.
11 Letter from Norman Douglas, November 1950.
12 Michael Tracey, *A Variety of Lives: The Biography of Sir Hugh Greene*, Bodley Head, 1983, p. 130.
13 Journal entry, 27 November 1950.
14 Letter to Catherine Walston, 30 November 1950.

15 *Ibid.*
16 Journal, 30 November 1950.
17 Letter to Catherine Walston, 30 November 1950.
18 *Ibid.*, 2 December 1950.
19 *Ibid.*, 30 November 1950.
20 *Ibid.*, 1 December 1950.
21 Noel Barber, *The War of the Running Dogs: The Malayan Emergency, 1948–1960*, Weybright & Talley, 1971, pp. 434–44.
22 *Ibid.*, p. 76.
23 Letter to Catherine Walston, 1 December 1950.
24 *Ibid.*, 2 December 1950.
25 *Ibid.*, 5 December 1950.
26 *Ibid.*, 6 December 1950.
27 *Ibid.*, 7 December 1950.
28 *Ibid.*, 11 December 1950.
29 *Ibid.*
30 *Ibid.*
31 Journal, 11 December 1950.
32 *A Sort of Life*, Penguin edition, 1971, p. 60.
33 Letter to Catherine Walston, 25 December 1950.
34 *Ibid.*
35 'Malaya, the Forgotten War', *Life*, 30 July 1951, pp. 51–65.
36 Letter to Catherine Walston, 31 December 1950.
37 *Ways of Escape*, Penguin edition, 1987, p. 111.
38 *Ibid.*, pp. 111–12.
39 *Ibid.*
40 *Ibid.*
41 *Ibid.*, p. 112.
42 *Ibid.*
43 Letter to his mother, probably 19 January 1951.
44 Journal, 18 December 1950.
45 *Ibid.*, probably 20 December 1950.
46 *Ways of Escape*, pp. 113–14.
47 *Ibid.*, p. 114.
48 *Ibid.*, p. 116.
49 'Malaya, the Forgotten War'.
50 *Ibid.*
51 *Ibid.*
52 *Ways of Escape*, p. 120.
53 'Malaya, the Forgotten War'.
54 *Ways of Escape*, p. 116.
55 Journal, 15 December 1950.
56 *Ways of Escape*, p. 117.
57 Journal, 16 December 1950.
58 'Malaya, the Forgotten War'.
59 Interview with Graham Greene, 28 April 1981.
60 Journal, 10 January 1951.
61 *Ibid.*, 15 January 1951.
62 Letter to his mother, probably 19 January 1951.
63 *The Quiet American*, Penguin edition, 1977, p. 88.
64 Letter to his mother, 19 January 1951.
65 'Malaya, the Forgotten War'.
66 Journal, 25 January 1951.

24   Bonjour Saigon

1   *The Pentagon Papers*, Senator Gravel Edition, vol. I, Beacon Press, 1979, pp. 49–50.
2   Telegram, 20 August 1952, 'Indo-China: Internal Affairs: 1950–4: Confidential US State Dept', Central Files, National Archives, Washington, DC.
3   'Indo-China: France's Crown of Thorns', *Paris Match*, 12 July 1952, reprinted in *Reflections*, trans. Alan Adamson, Reinhardt Books, 1990, p. 131.
4   Undated note from Dean Acheson, National Archives, Washington, DC.
5   Lucien Bodard, *The Quicksand War: Prelude to Vietnam*, trans. Patrick O'Brian, Little, Brown, 1967, p. 351.
6   Interview with Seymour Topping, 13 July 1992.
7   *Ibid.*
8   From a restricted telegram to Washington from Saigon, 21 September 1951, 'Indo-China: Internal Affairs: 1950–4: Confidential US State Dept', Central Files, National Archives, Washington, DC.
9   *New York Times*, 11 January 1951.
10   *The Pentagon Papers*, p. 67.
11   *Ibid.*, pp. 67–8.
12   Interview with Ambassador Edmund Gullion, 1 November 1992.
13   Secret report to Washington by Wendell Blancke, US consul to Hanoi, 23 January 1951, 'Indo-China: Internal Affairs: 1950–4: Confidential US State Dept', Central Files, National Archives, Washington, DC.
14   *Ways of Escape*, Penguin edition, 1987, p. 121.
15   *Ibid.*
16   Journal, 25 January 1951.
17   Letter to Hugh Greene, 26 January 1951.
18   *Ibid.*
19   *The Quiet American*, Penguin edition, 1977, p. 11.
20   Interview with Seymour Topping, 13 July 1992.
21   US Consul Hanoi, Wendell Blancke, to State Department, 2 June 1951, 'Indo-China: Internal Affairs: 1950–4: Confidential US State Dept', Central Files, National Archives, Washington, DC.
22   Bodard, *The Quicksand War*, p. 186.
23   *Ibid.*, pp. 179–82.
24   C. L. Sulzberger, *New York Times*, 10 May 1950.
25   Interview with Ambassador Edmund Gullion, 1 November 1992.
26   Letter to his mother, 31 October 1951.
27   *A World of My Own*, Reinhardt Books, 1992, pp. xviii–xix.
28   *Ways of Escape*, pp. 130–1.
29   *Ibid.*, p. 131.
30   *Ibid.*
31   *Ibid.*, p. 132.
32   Undated journal entry.
33   *The Quiet American*, p. 13.
34   *Ibid.*, p. 14.
35   Journal, 5 January 1951.
36   Interview with Seymour and Audrey Topping, 13 July 1992.
37   Journal, 31 January 1951.
38   *The Quiet American*, p. 46.
39   Interview with Seymour and Audrey Topping, 13 July 1992.
40   American legation report to US State Department, 31 March 1951, 'Indo-China: Internal Affairs: 1950–4: Confidential US State Dept', Central Files, National Archives, Washington, DC.

41 *The Quiet American*, p. 49.
42 *Ibid.*
43 Letter from Trevor Wilson to the author, 21 July 1977.
44 Letter to Catherine Walston, 25 December 1951.
45 'Malaya, the Forgotten War', *Life*, 30 July 1951.
46 Telegram from Catherine Walston, 10 January 1951.
47 Letter to Catherine Walston, 28 February 1951.
48 Undated letter to his mother, probably written 12 February 1951.

25   Interlude on *Elsewhere*

1   Letter to Catherine Walston, 5 May 1951.
2   *Ibid.*, 19 June 1951.
3   *Ibid.*, 15 August 1951.
4   *Ibid.*
5   *Ibid.*
6   *Ibid.*, 22 March 1950.
7   Undated letter to Catherine Walston, August 1951.
8   *Ibid.*
9   *Ibid.*
10 Letter to Catherine Walston, 15 September 1951.
11 *Loser Takes All*, Penguin, 1955, pp. 103–4.
12 Letter from Evelyn Waugh, 18 August 1951.
13 *Ibid.*, 21 August 1951.
14 Letter to Evelyn Waugh, 22 August 1951.
15 Letter from Evelyn Waugh to Catherine Walston, 25 August 1951.
16 *Ibid.*
17 Letter from Evelyn Waugh to Nancy Mitford, September 1951.
18 *The End of the Affair*, Heinemann, 1951, pp. 231–2.
19 Interview with Graham Greene, 26 July 1981.
20 Undated letter to Evelyn Waugh, September 1951.
21 Letter to Catherine Walston, 23 September 1951.
22 *Ibid.*
23 *Ibid.*
24 *Ibid.*, 25 September 1951.
25 *Ibid.*, 29 September 1951.
26 Journal, 25 October 1951.
27 Letter to his mother, 29 October 1951.

26   A Crown of Thorns

1   Untitled manuscript, 30 December 1953.
2   Interview with Libby Getz, 11 December 1992.
3   Letter to Catherine Walston, 1 January 1952.
4   Journal, 9 January 1954.
5   Letter to Vivien Dayrell-Browning, August 1925.
6   Journal, 25 November 1951.
7   Letter from Evelyn Waugh, 5 December 1955.
8   *The Quiet American*, Penguin edition, 1974, p. 44.
9   Journal, 15 September 1955.
10 In the *Listener*, Wembley Exhibition is changed to Festival Gardens; 'For forty seconds

Pyle had not existed: even loneliness hadn't existed' is shortened in the BBC piece to exclude Pyle; 'middle-aged lungs' (Greene was forty-seven) is changed in the novel to 'ageing lungs' since Fowler is an older man.

11 *The Quiet American*, pp. 147–8.
12 *Ibid.*, p. 149.
13 *Ibid.*, pp. 149–50.
14 *Ibid.*, p. 150.
15 *Reflections*, Reinhardt Books, 1990. p. 142.
16 'Indo-China: France's Crown of Thorns', *Paris Match*, 12 July 1952, reprinted in *Reflections*, trans. Alan Adamson, p. 131.
17 *Ibid.*
18 *The Quiet American*, p. 48.
19 Telegram from Wendell Blancke to Washington, 19 December 1951, 'Indo-China: Internal Affairs: 1950–4: Confidential US State Dept', Central Files, National Archives, Washington, DC.
20 Secret memorandum, 'Indo-China: Internal Affairs: 1950–4: Confidential US State Dept', Central Files, National Archives, Washington, DC.
21 *The Quiet American*, pp. 46–7.
22 *Ibid.*, p. 48.
23 *Ibid.*, pp. 51–2.
24 *Reflections*, p. 144.
25 *The Quiet American*, p. 52.
26 *Ibid.*, pp. 51–2.
27 *Ibid.*, p. 53.
28 *Reflections*, p. 144.
29 *Ibid.*, pp. 143–4.
30 *The Quiet American*, p. 54.
31 Security report, 22 January 1952, 'Indo-China: Internal Affairs: 1950–4: Confidential US State Dept', Central Files, National Archives, Washington, DC.
32 Wendell Blancke report to State Department, 17 December 1951, *ibid.*
33 Quoted in secret telegram from Wendell Blancke to US Secretary of State, 26 June 1951, *ibid.*

27 A Quiet American

1   *Ways of Escape*, Penguin edition, 1987, p. 129.
2   *The Quiet American*, Penguin edition, 1974, pp. 63–6.
3   *Ibid.*, p. 35–6.
4   Interview with Seymour and Audrey Topping, 13 July 1992.
5   Howard R. Simpson, *Tiger in the Barbed Wire*, Brassey's (US), Inc., 1992, p. 43.
6   *The Quiet American*, p. 34.
7   *Ibid.*, p. 36.
8   *New Republic*, 9 May 1955.
9   Journal, 29 January 1951.
10 Interview at the School of African and Oriental Studies, 7 July 1974.
11 *The Quiet American*, pp. 37–8.
12 Interview with Seymour and Audrey Topping, 13 July 1992.
13 *The Quiet American*, p. 184.
14 *Ibid.*, p. 185.
15 *Ibid.*, p. 25.
16 Secret report from Donald Heath to US Secretary of State, 14 June 1951, 'Indo-China: Internal Affairs: 1950–4: Confidential US State Dept', Central Files, National Archives,

Washington, DC.

17 Extract sent to State Department, 19 June 1951, *ibid.*

18 Undated secret enclosure to Washington from American legation in Saigon, *ibid.*

19 'Indo-China: France's Crown of Thorns', *Paris Match*, 12 July 1952, reprinted in *Reflections*, trans. Alan Adamson, Reinhardt Books, 1990, pp. 135—6.

20 *Sunday Times*, 21 March 1954, reprinted in *Reflections*, p. 163.

21 Confidential Security Information sent to Washington from Saigon legation, 19 November 1951, 'Indo-China: Internal Affairs: 1950—4: Confidential US State Dept', Central Files, National Archives, Washington, DC.

22 Telegram to Secretary of State, Washington, 22 June 1951, *ibid.*

23 See Donald Lancaster, *The Emancipation of French Indo-China*, Oxford University Press, 1961, pp. 233—4.

24 *Ways of Escape*, p. 129.

25 Undated letter from Stella Weaver.

26 Letter from Stella Weaver, copy sent to Catherine Walston, 16 January 1952.

27 *The Quiet American*, pp. 80—1.

28 *Ibid.*, pp. 117—18.

29 *Ibid.*, p. 118.

30 *Ibid.*, p. 119.

31 *Ibid.*

32 Interview with Graham Greene, 25 April 1981.

33 Journal, 4 February 1951.

34 *Ibid.*, 27 January 1951.

35 *The Quiet American*, p. 42.

36 *Ibid.*

37 Letter to his mother, 8 November (?1951),

28 Innocence Abroad

1 *The Quiet American*, Penguin edition, 1974, p. 59.

2 *Ibid.*, p. 78.

3 *Ibid.*, p. 45.

4 *Ibid.*, p. 58.

5 *Ibid.*, p. 90.

6 Letter to Catherine Walston, 25 December 1950.

7 *The Quiet American*, p. 57.

8 *Ibid.*, p. 112.

9 Howard R. Simpson, *Tiger in the Barbed Wire*, Brassey's (US), Inc., 1992, p. 61.

10 Cecil Currey, *Edward Lansdale*, Houghton Mifflin, 1988, pp. 196—7.

11 *Ibid.*, pp. 97—8.

12 *Ibid.*, p. 198.

13 *Ways of Escape*, Penguin edition, 1987, p. 127.

14 *The Quiet American*, p. 124.

15 Letter from Tom Peck to author, 21 January 1993.

16 Letter from Paul Springer to author, 28 December 1992.

17 Letter from John Getz to author, 23 December 1992.

18 Interview with Mrs Hochstetter, 4 October 1993.

19 Letter home to the USA from Nancy Baker in Saigon, 3 August 1950.

20 *Ibid.*, 17 November 1950.

29 Death in rue Catinat

1   Letter from Nancy Baker to home in USA, 26 February 1952.
2   *The Pentagon Papers*, vol. 1, Beacon Press, 1971, pp. 73–4.
3   *Ibid.*
4   Howard R. Simpson, *Tiger in the Barbed Wire*, Brassey's (US), Inc., 1992, p. 148.
5   *New Yorker*, 7 April 1956.
6   *New York Times*, 25 January 1952.
7   *The Quiet American*, Penguin edition, 1974, pp. 140–1.
8   *Ibid.*, p. 141.
9   *Ibid.*, pp. 140–2.
10 Secret memo from Donald Heath to State Department, 14 February 1952, 'Indo-China: Internal Affairs: 1950–4: Confidential US State Dept', Central Files, National Archives, Washington, DC.
11 Secret memo from Donald Heath to Secretary of State, 4 February 1952, *ibid.*
12 *New York Times*, 10 January 1952.
13 *The Quiet American*, p. 157.
14 *Ibid.*, p. 160.
15 *Ibid.*, pp. 162–3.
16 *Ibid.*, p. 163.
17 *Ibid.*, p. 161.
18 *Ways of Escape*, Penguin edition, 1987, p. 128.
19 Interview with Nancy and Charles Baker, 31 January 1994.
20 *Life*, 28 January 1952.
21 Secret telegram, 10 January 1952, 'Indo-China: Internal Affairs: 1950–4: Confidential US State Dept', Central Files, National Archives, Washington, DC.
22 *Ways of Escape*, p. 128.
23 *Ibid.*
24 Letter to Catherine Walston, 2 October 1956.
25 Security Information, Ambassador Heath, 14 February 1952, 'Indo-China: Internal Affairs: 1950–4: Confidential US State Dept', Central Files, National Archives, Washington, DC.
26 Interview with ex-consular official who served in Saigon during Greene's visit to Saigon.
27 *The Quiet American*, p. 87.
28 *Ibid.*, p. 161.
29 Interview with Nancy Baker, 1 February 1994.
30 Interview with Nancy and Charles Baker, 1 February 1994.
31 *New York Times*, 21 February 1952.
32 Interview with Ambassador Edmund Gullion, 1 November 1992.

30 Visa Not for Sale

1   Christopher Sykes, *Evelyn Waugh*, Little, Brown, 1975, pp. 357–8.
2   Called after Senator Patrick McCarran, who sponsored the McCarran–Walter Immigration and Nationality Act of 1952, which severely restricted entry and immigration to the United States.
3   *Time*, 29 October 1951.
4   *Ways of Escape*, Penguin edition, 1987, p. 162.
5   Robert McClintock, letter to State Department, 31 October 1950.
6   London Diary, *New Statesman and Nation*, 22 November 1952.
7   Telegram from Harold Guinzburg, 4 February 1952.
8   Interview with Tom Peck, 1 February 1994.
9   Interview with Charles Stuart Kennedy, December 1992.

10 Postcard from Mrs Young to A. S. Frere, 6 February 1952.
11 Letter to Catherine Walston, 10 February 1952.
12 Journal, 9 February 1952.
13 Letter to Catherine Walston, 10 February 1952.
14 Cable from Harold Guinzburg, 13 February 1952.
15 Letter to Catherine Walston, 18 February 1952.
16 *New York Times*, 20 February 1952.
17 *New York Herald Tribune*, 15 February 1952.
18 *New York Times*, 6 February 1952.
19 Letter from Evelyn Waugh, 7 October 1952.
20 Letter from Captain Ginn, 29 September 1952.
21 Letter from Victor Lasky, 11 December 1952.
22 Letter to Victor Lasky, 17 December 1952.
23 *Time*, 13 September 1954.
24 Letter to Catherine Walston, 30 August 1954.
25 *Ways of Escape*, p. 163.
26 Letter to Catherine Walston, 11 October 1954.
27 Letter from Jacques Barzun to author, 5 May 1984.

31 Drama and the Man

1 *Boston Daily Globe*, 24 February 1950.
2 *The Living Room*, Penguin edition, 1970, p. 73.
3 *Svenska Dagbladet*, 1 November 1952.
4 Ivar Havic, *Expressen*, 1 November 1952.
5 Artur Lundkvist, *Morgon-Tidningen*, 4 November 1952.
6 'My Characters Live Themselves: Greene's Words on the First Night', *Stockholms-Tidningen*, 1 November 1952.
7 *Ibid.*
8 Letter to Herbert Greene, 17 December 1952.
9 'A Stranger in the Theatre', *Picture Post*, 18 April 1953.
10 *Ibid.*
11 Letter from Evelyn Waugh, 27 February 1953.
12 'A Stranger in the Theatre'.
13 Interview with Graham Greene, 25 April 1981.
14 Interview with Mario Soldati, 18 May 1977.
15 *Brighton and Hove Herald*, 3 March 1953.
16 *Ibid.*
17 Letter from Margot Fonteyn, 15 April 1953.
18 *Daily Express*, 17 April 1953.
19 Letter from Evelyn Waugh, 7 October 1952.
20 *Ibid.*, 21 April 1953.
21 *The Diaries of Evelyn Waugh*, ed. Michael Davie, Penguin edition, 1979, p. 718. Entry for 16 April 1953.
22 *Catholic World*, September 1953.
23 Interview with Graham Greene, 11 August 1977.
24 Interview with John Sutro, 10 May 1977.
25 Interview with Graham Greene, 11 August 1977.
26 Interview with John Sutro, 10 May 1977.
27 *New York Times*, 11 October 1953.
28 *Daily Telegraph*, 22 November 1974.
29 Letter from British consul-general in Houston, 24 June 1954.

30   Letter to British consul-general in Houston, 16 July 1954.
31   Letter from A. O. Dyer, 23 August 1953.

32   Among the Mau Mau

1   Undated letter to Catherine Walston.
2   Letter to Catherine Walston, 28 August 1953.
3   *Ibid.*, 24 August 1953.
4   *Ways of Escape*, Penguin edition, 1987, p. 158.
5   Diary, 26 and 27 August 1953.
6   *Ibid.*, 28 August 1953.
7   Letter to Catherine Walston, 28 August 1953.
8   Undated letter to Catherine Walston.
9   *Sunday Times*, 27 September and 4 October 1953.
10   *Ibid.*, 4 October 1953.
11   *Ibid.*, 27 September 1953.
12   *The Times*, 28 March 1953.
13   *Sunday Times*, 27 September 1953.
14   *Ibid.*, 4 October 1953.
15   *Ibid.*, 27 September 1953.
16   Interview with Graham Greene, 25 April 1981.
17   *Sunday Times*, 4 October 1953.
18   Interview with Graham Greene, 25 April 1981.
19   Letter to Graham Greene, 23 January 1955.
20   Diary, 2 September 1953.
21   Interview with Graham Greene, 26 April 1981.
22   Diary, 7 September 1953.
23   *Ibid.*, 1 and 2 September 1953.
24   Undated letter to Catherine Walston.
25   Interview with Graham Greene, 26 April 1953.
26   Letter to Catherine Walston, 2 September 1953.
27   *Sunday Times*, 27 September 1953.
28   *Ibid.*, 4 October 1953.
29   *Ibid.*
30   *Ibid.*

33   No Man Is Neutral

1   Letter to Catherine Walston, 9 August 1954.
2   *Le Figaro littéraire*, 7 August 1954; reprinted in *The Portable Graham Greene*, trans. and ed. Philip Stratford, Penguin, 1984, pp. 595–6.
3   Letter from Evelyn Waugh to Nancy Mitford, 15 September 1954, *The Letters of Evelyn Waugh*, ed. Mark Amory, Weidenfeld & Nicolson, 1980, p. 429.
4   *Ibid.*
5   Letter from Nancy Baker to her family in the United States, 17 November 1950.
6   *Newsweek*, 1 October 1956.
7   *Ibid.*
8   'Congo Journal', *In Search of a Character: Two African Journals*, Penguin, 1971, p. 27.
9   Interview with Graham Greene, 16 August 1982.
10   Malcolm Muggeridge, *Like It Was: A Selection from the Diaries of Malcolm Muggeridge*, ed. John Bright-Holmes, Collins, 1981, p. 297. Entry for 13 September 1948.

11 Quoted by Robert Clurman, *New York Times* book review, August 1956.
12 Interview with Graham Greene, 16 August 1982.
13 Howard R. Simpson, *Tiger in the Barbed Wire*, Brassey's (US), Inc., 1992, p. 32.
14 Lucien Bodard, *The Quicksand War: Prelude to Vietnam*, trans. Patrick O'Brian, Little, Brown, 1967, p. 222.
15 *Ibid.*, p. 223.
16 *Ibid.*, p. 226.
17 *Ibid.*, pp. 226–7.
18 *Ibid.*, pp. 227–8.
19 *The Quiet American*, pp. 86–7.
20 *Ibid.*, pp. 94–5.
21 *Ibid.*, pp. 95–7.
22 *The Portable Graham Greene*, ed. Stratford, p. 609.
23 *Reflections*, trans. Alan Adamson, Reinhardt Books, 1990, p. 146.
24 *The Quiet American*, p. 163.

34 The Honourable Correspondent and the Dishonourable Friend

1   Lucien Bodard, 'L'Appel aux Américains', *L'Express*, 1967.
2   *Ways of Escape*, Penguin edition, 1987, p. 123.
3   Bodard, 'L'Appel aux Américains'.
4   Interview with former CIA senior officer.
5   *Ways of Escape*, p. 125.
6   *Ibid.*, p. 126.
7   *Ibid.*, pp. 126–7.
8   Journal, 18 November 1951.
9   Interview with former CIA senior officer.
10 Bodard, 'L'Appel aux Américains'.
11 *Ibid.*
12 *Ibid.*
13 *Ibid.*
14 Interview with former CIA senior officer.
15 *Ibid.*
16 Michael Korda, *Charmed Lives*, Avon, 1981, p. 147.
17 Journal, 17 November 1951.
18 Letter to Catherine Walston, 18 November 1951.
19 Interview with Graham Greene, 16 August 1982.
20 Nicholas Elliott, *Never Judge a Man By His Umbrella*, Michael Russell, 1991, p. 183.
21 John Le Carré, introduction to Bruce Page, David Leitch and Phillip Knightley, *The Philby Conspiracy*, Doubleday, 1968, p. 31.
22 *Ibid.*, p. 28.
23 Eleanor Philby, *The Spy I Loved*, Pan, 1968, p. 33.
24 'Security in Room 51', *Sunday Times*, 14 July 1963.
25 Letter from Kim Philby to author, 8 April 1987.
26 Marie-Françoise Allain, *The Other Man: Conversations with Graham Greene*, Bodley Head, 1983, pp. 183–4.
27 *A World of My Own: A Dream Diary*, Reinhardt Books, 1992, p. 23.
28 A. N. Wilson, 'Companion of Dishonour', *Daily Mail*, 1987.
29 *Daily Telegraph*, 12 May 1988.
30 Letter to Ann Fleming, 5 September 1960, *The Letters of Evelyn Waugh*, ed. Mark Amory, Weidenfeld & Nicolson, 1980, p. 548.

31 Anne-Elizabeth Moutet, quoted in Anthony Cave Brown, *'C': The Secret Life of Sir Stewart Graham Menzies*, Macmillan, 1987, p. 747.
32 Interview with Graham Greene, 16 August 1982.
33 Christopher Andrew and Oleg Gordievsky, *KGB: The Inside Story*, HarperCollins, 1990, p. 5.
34 Interview of Yuri Modin by Anthony Cave Brown, 1992. Philby only knew his controller by his cover name, 'Peter'.
35 I have since learnt that the letter was sent to the head of the SIS by Rodney Dennys, Greene's brother-in-law.

35 White Night in Albany

1   Interview with John Cairncross, 14 May 1977.
2   Letter to Catherine Walston, 18 February 1952.
3   Undated letter of February 1952. Greene was on his way to Boston by plane.
4   Undated letter to Catherine Walston.
5   Letter to Catherine Walston, February 1952.
6   Interview with Trevor Wilson, 11 March 1977.
7   Interview with Graham Greene, 27 April 1981.
8   Letter from Margot Fonteyn, undated, Sunday.
9   Interview with John Cairncross, 14 May 1977.
10 Interview with Graham Greene, 25 April 1981.
11 Letter to Catherine Walston, 30 January 1953.
12 Undated letter to Catherine Walston, probably August 1954.
13 Letter to Catherine Walston, 30 August 1954.
14 Undated letter to Catherine Walston, probably July 1954.
15 Letter to Catherine Walston, 15 August 1952.
16 Undated letter to Catherine Walston.
17 *Ibid.*, probably July 1952.
18 Letter to Catherine Walston, 29 February 1952.
19 *Ibid.*, 27 June 1955.
20 *Ibid.*, 24 June 1955.
21 Undated letter to Catherine Walston.
22 Letter to Catherine Walston, 7 July 1955.
23 Undated letter to Catherine Walston, 1952.
24 Letter to Catherine Walston, 7 July 1955.
25 *Ibid.*, 9 February 1956.
26 *Ibid.*, 7 March 1956.
27 *Ibid.*, 31 August 1956.
28 *Ibid.*, 12 December 1956.
29 Undated letter to Catherine Walston.
30 'Last Cards in Indo-China', *Sunday Times*, 28 March 1955.
31 Graham Greene, 'Opium in Albany', unpublished manuscript.
32 Journal, 4 January 1953.
33 Interview with Graham Greene, 25 April 1981.
34 *Ibid.*, 13 December 1983.
35 Michael Korda, *Charmed Lives*, Avon, 1981, p. 464.
36 *The Diaries of Evelyn Waugh*, ed. Michael Davie, Penguin, p. 721. Entry for 5 June 1953.

Acknowledgments

I must thank Graham Greene (who helped me right up to the day before he died) and his family: his wife Vivien, who in these trying days when she is almost blind made strong efforts to be helpful; likewise his daughter Caroline, who was always friendly and helpful, and his son Francis, now his father's literary executor, whose comments on my text revealed that Greene's penetrating mind had been passed on to his son. Greene's sister Elisabeth Dennys, to whom I dedicated Volume One, assisted me (as did her husband Rodney Dennys) with the many difficult problems which are inevitable in so complicated a life lived by so subtle a mind as her brother's. Her children, Amanda, Louise and Nicholas, have all been helpful, in particular Amanda, who took on the complications of looking after her uncle's correspondence and literary affairs when Greene was alive and still continues with that task. I must also thank Yvonne Cloetta, who lovingly lived with Greene during his last thirty years. Other friends of Greene's from his Capri days, Countess Cerio, Shirley Hazzard and Francis Steegmuller, also assisted me.

I am blessed by the friendship of Graham Carleton Greene, who is now my literary agent; and am grateful to Dan Franklin, dedicated, sharp and intelligent publishing director at Jonathan Cape, Tony Colwell, a genius where photographs are concerned and indeed in all matters of publishing, and Liz Cowen, my editor, who made splendid and necessary changes to the final text and showed an uncanny ability to know what I intended to say even before I wrote it. My thanks to Leigh Priest, the admirable indexer, and to Joanne Hill, most competent of proof-readers; both of whom worked on Volume One. I would also like to thank Jenny Cottom, managing editorial director at Jonathan Cape, who again held the many strings together and saw the book through its final stages.

Catherine Walston's family have been helpful without exception: first among them her younger sister Dr Belinda Straight, whose razor-sharp mind she sometimes disguises so as not to make man afraid; also her older sister Bonte Durán, an outspoken intelligence; their brother David Crompton, soft-spoken but, like all the family, aware of the world; and Catherine Walston herself, whom I was only able to interview once in 1976, then crippled but with warm, understanding eyes. The Walstons' children – Susan, now in Australia, and Bill in Cambridge (twins who both spoke with a refreshing directness and honesty), Oliver, the eldest, farmer, traveller and successful radio broadcaster, and James – all have that directness of spirit which characterised Catherine Walston.

Dr Ronald Calgaard, president of Trinity University, San Antonio, Texas, continued to be a strong supporter and in strenuous months during the last year of writing enabled me to hire a much-needed researcher. The dean, William Walker, and Vice-President Ed Roy have shown a strong interest in the biography, and Harold Herndon, senior trustee of the university has always been a good friend to the book. Nor can I leave unrecorded the friendship of Bernard Lifshutz to the book and the author. Auberon Waugh kindly allowed me to quote from his father's letters.

I must thank Georgetown University and the many senior personnel there who assisted me: the Reverend Royden B. Davis, S.J., the past dean of Georgetown College and the Reverend Robert B. Lawton, S.J., the present dean (men of sterling character); Dr Claire Z. Carey (no dean in this sublunary world ever had a worthier assistant dean); and in the Department of English the friendly John Hirsh suggested people I should meet to prosecute my research. At the Georgetown University Library I must also thank Dr Susan K. Martin, the thoughtful, intelligent librarian; George M. Barringer, the only man who could decipher on the run Greene's sometimes impossible script; Nicholas B. Scheetz, whose off-the-cuff remarks on Greene are worthy of publication in themselves and who is always ready to assist visitors in 'his' Special Collections; and Lisette C. Matano, Michael J. North and Jon K. Reynolds. We all owe Joseph E. Jeffs thanks – his friendship with Greene enabled Georgetown to develop its unrivalled collection of Greene's material. My thanks also to Charles Stuart Kennedy; the knowledgeable one-time Consul-General Dr Cleveland C. Cram, to whom I owe more than I can ever express; also his friend E. J. Applewhite, a thinker walking his own road; and John Cairncross, Greene's friend of many years' standing. Those who were in Vietnam when Greene made his yearly visits gave me valuable background information for the period 1951–5 when very few Americans were there. In particular I want to thank William Colby, Tom Peck, David Whipple, John Caswell, Charles and Nancy Baker, Paul and Jean Springer, Ambassador John Getz and his wife Libby, Ambassador Edmund Gullion, Seymour and Audrey Topping, and Bill Igoe – a friend of Greene's, and of mine from when we first met in 1974, whose exciting comments will appear in the final volume. Gracious thanks also to Lucien Bodard for his distinguished account of Vietnam, and in particular his account of de Lattre in *L'Express*.

I offer my gratitude to the following: Dr Paul F. Betz; Mr and Mrs Eugene Quinn III; George and Nannette Herrick (who both read the typescript, Nannette waiting impatiently for her husband to pass her the next chapter); Charles de Salis; and Jacques Barzun, who recalled with his natural clarity Greene's visit to his American publishers in the 1950s. Anthony Cave Brown, Phillip Knightley and Stanley S. Bedington all educated me in the ways of espionage. I am enormously indebted to the late Kim Philby, who wrote to me from Moscow about his friend Graham Greene. John E. Taylor assisted me at the National Archives in Washington, DC. I was fortunate that my research led me to secret American legation documents sent from Saigon to the State Department. Numerous people were generous during my stay in Washington: Jackie Quillen, who offered accommodation whenever needed; John S. Monagan and his wife Rosemary, who both epitomised kindness in their actions; Robert and Brenda Hopkins; the Reverend J. Thomas Dugan, an eternal friend; Simon and Nicole Pinniger; Norma Smith, wife of Harry J. Smith, one of three friends to whom this book is dedicated; and Anthony V. Dresden, who introduced me to Mrs Hochstetter, wife of Leo Hochstetter the original Quiet American. I must thank too Katherine Henderson, who assisted me while studying the Greene archives at the Harry Ransom Humanities Research Center at the University of Texas, Austin.

I would like to thank Methuen London and Routledge in New York for permission to reprint 'The Ballad of Graham Greene' from *Noël Coward – Collected Verse,* Methuen, 1984; the unpublished poem on pp. 74–6 (copyright © 1994 the Estate of Noël Coward) is published by arrangement with the Estate of Noël Coward and Michael Imison Playwrights Ltd. The letter on pages 495 and 496 is reprinted by kind permission of the Estate of Rodney Dennys (copyright © 1994 the Estate of Rodney Dennys). Every effort has been made to trace relevant copyright holders and the publishers express their apologies if inadvertently any have been omitted.

As with the first book, I owe a great deal to Russ Newell's continued friendship, and of course the book will always owe much to Sylvia Sherry's good sense and intelligence. Once again I need to thank Neil Brennan, Greene's long-standing and outstanding bibliographer, who began working with the late Alan Redway (himself a distinguished bibliographer of Greene), and also Helen Redway, Alan's wife. Ronnie Challoner, honorary consul at Nice, has always offered assistance promptly and treated me with great kindness. My thanks also to Selina Hastings, future biographer of Evelyn Waugh and distinguished journalist.

After working all day on Greene, I used to retire to Martin's Tavern in Georgetown and so would like to pay due respect to the philosophers there: Herbie Angel, Ron Gittings, Nasirul Islam, Billie Martin, Jr, Bruce Sullivan, Keith Koffler, and especially the Socrates among them, Jay Flenner. Back in San Antonio I spent much time at the Seashore Restaurant. Thanks to the owners Majid Hashemi and Feridoon Amini, I was allowed to drink free coffee late in the afternoon as I corrected endless chapters. Thanks also to Ted C. Cooper, Jim Fogarty and Rey Leal, who entertained me with his scissor wit.

Throughout the last five years, while completing Volume Two, I have had a number of dedicated secretaries, students and a research assistant. Lucy Kilmer saw the beginning of the book, followed by Eleanor Kamataris, who always put in extra hours without pay. Edward Chism stayed over a year after graduating and committed himself strenuously to the book. Matt Hofer checked the proofs. Carol Wright Smith, my research assistant who collaborated with Tom Greene in drafting 'Before the War', taking over from Mr Chism, set a new standard in what dedication means.

A number of distinguished scholars and others helped to read the manuscript, in particular Peter Balbert, sterling supporter of the biography with his sharp, scintillating and unrivalled judgment; Robert ter Horst, whose eagle eye can spot an error in flight; Frank Kersnowski, who spent long hours reading the typescript, as did Cedric Watts, the leading Conrad scholar, who also read the proofs; Edwin Thumboo; the late John Kwan-Terry; the Distinguished Professor John Stoessinger, a friend to the book and the biographer; Professor George Leith, who dipped into selected chapters; Dr Bates Hoffer, whose passion for Greene has never wavered and who helped to bring me to Trinity University in the first instance; Professor John Carey, who was always willing to assist when needed; and Dr Ram Singh, a friend when I began writing this biography in 1976 and still a friend in 1994. My dear brother Alan Sherry patiently read my work with a willingness based on the fact that we are identical twins and continued to meet me at seaports and airports when I returned home. My thanks to Ian Carr, a man of great verbal fluency. Professor William Samuelson read the typescript and gave selflessly his support and encouragement. Carmen Flores worked incessantly on the book, checking the typescript from the first sentence to the last. I am ever in her debt. Dr Robert Still continued to look lovingly after my health. H. R. Gaines – better known as Illgotten, the northern recluse whose friendship with me has lasted many years (he speaks to no other apart from Ian Carr) – made interesting suggestions about the nature of non-possessive love as this is revealed in the biography. My thanks also to my friend Vinod Kumar.

I am conscious that I may have failed to recall all those who, in the long years of research, have assisted me. I ask their forgiveness. However, I can record my indebtedness to the following: Walter Allen, Dr William Breit, George Bull, Carmen Capalbo, the Reverend Philip Caraman, Ambassador Henry Catto, Bryan Cox, M.D., Mario Currelli, Nicholas Elliott, Philip French, Peter Glenville, Professor Samuel Hynes, Margarete Kleiber, Peter Levring, Nigel Lloyd, C. J. Mabey, Major J. McGregor Cheers, William David McInnis, M.D., Lady Melchett, Michael Meyer, Tim Milne, George Neal, Richard Gordan Newhauser, Rigel and Edwin Newman, Hoang Ngoc, my guide and translator in Vietnam, Erik Nielsen, Ian Ogilvie, Charles Orsinger, Jeffrey Richards, William Scanlan, Robert Shivers, Fay, William and Richard Sinkin, Banks Smith, Mario Soldati, John and Gillian Sutro, Peter Turnbull, the Reverend Vincent Turner, Hoang Tuy, distinguished scholar and researcher, the Honourable Mrs Elizabeth Varley, Florence M. Weinberg; also the Reverend Leopoldo Duran, Trevor Wilson and Michael Richey – friends of Graham Greene and believers in this biographer, and Barbara Wall, a lady of fine intelligence, who met Greene during the early part of the Second World War and always made my visits to her home an uplifting experience.

Norman Sherry

Trinity University
San Antonio, Texas
1994

Index

FOR THE BEST IN PAPERBACKS, LOOK FOR THE

In every corner of the world, on every subject under the sun, Penguin represents quality and variety—the very best in publishing today.

For complete information about books available from Penguin—including Penguin Classics, Penguin Compass, and Puffins—and how to order them, write to us at the appropriate address below. Please note that for copyright reasons the selection of books varies from country to country.

In the United States: Please write to *Penguin Group (USA), P.O. Box 12289 Dept. B, Newark, New Jersey 07101-5289* or call 1-800-788-6262.

In the United Kingdom: Please write to *Dept. EP, Penguin Books Ltd, Bath Road, Harmondsworth, West Drayton, Middlesex UB7 0DA.*

In Canada: Please write to *Penguin Books Canada Ltd, 10 Alcorn Avenue, Suite 300, Toronto, Ontario M4V 3B2.*

In Australia: Please write to *Penguin Books Australia Ltd, P.O. Box 257, Ringwood, Victoria 3134.*

In New Zealand: Please write to *Penguin Books (NZ) Ltd, Private Bag 102902, North Shore Mail Centre, Auckland 10.*

In India: Please write to *Penguin Books India Pvt Ltd, 11 Panchsheel Shopping Centre, Panchsheel Park, New Delhi 110 017.*

In the Netherlands: Please write to *Penguin Books Netherlands bv, Postbus 3507, NL-1001 AH Amsterdam.*

In Germany: Please write to *Penguin Books Deutschland GmbH, Metzlerstrasse 26, 60594 Frankfurt am Main.*

In Spain: Please write to *Penguin Books S. A., Bravo Murillo 19, 1° B, 28015 Madrid.*

In Italy: Please write to *Penguin Italia s.r.l., Via Benedetto Croce 2, 20094 Corsico, Milano.*

In France: Please write to *Penguin France, Le Carré Wilson, 62 rue Benjamin Baillaud, 31500 Toulouse.*

In Japan: Please write to *Penguin Books Japan Ltd, Kaneko Building, 2-3-25 Koraku, Bunkyo-Ku, Tokyo 112.*

In South Africa: Please write to *Penguin Books South Africa (Pty) Ltd, Private Bag X14, Parkview, 2122 Johannesburg.*

READ MORE GRAHAM GREENE IN PENGUIN TWENTIETH-CENTURY CLASSICS

> "Graham Greene was in a class by himself. . . .
> He will be read and remembered as the ultimate chronicler
> of twentieth-century man's consciousness and anxiety."
> —William Golding

Brighton Rock
Greene's chilling exposé of violence and gang warfare in the prewar British underworld features Pinkie, a protagonist who is the embodiment of evil. ISBN 0-14-018492-9

A Burnt-Out Case
A world famous architect anonymously begins working at a leper colony in order to cure his "disease of the mind." ISBN 0-14-018539-9

The Captain and the Enemy
Greene's final novel is a fascinating tale of adventure and intrigue that follows an Englishman from his childhood to gun-smuggling in Panama. ISBN 0-14-018855-X

Collected Short Stories
These thirty-seven stories reveal Greene in a range of contrasting moods, sometimes cynical and witty, sometimes searching and philosophical. ISBN 0-14-018612-3

The Comedians
Three men meet on a ship bound for Haiti, a world in the grip of the corrupt "Papa Doc" and his sinister secret police. ISBN 0-14-018494-5

The End of the Affair
A love affair, abruptly and inexplicably broken off, prompts the distraught Maurice Bendrix to hire a private detective to discover the cause. ISBN 0-14-018495-3

England Made Me
A tour de force of moral suspense, this is the story of a confirmed liar and cheat whose ultimate discovery of decency may cost him his job—and his life. ISBN 0-14-018551-8

A Gun for Sale
Raven's cold-blooded killing of the Minister of War is an act of violence with chilling repercussions, not just for Raven himself but for England as a whole. ISBN 0-14-018540-2

The Heart of the Matter
The terrifying depiction of a man's awe of the Church and Greene's ability to portray human motive and to convey such a depth of suffering make this one of his most enduring and tragic novels.

ISBN 0-14-018496-1

Loser Takes All
Greene offers up a tale of an unsuccessful accountant's second try at luck and love. ISBN 0-14-018542-9

The Man Within
Themes of betrayal, pursuit, and the search for peace run through Greene's first published novel about a smuggler who takes refuge from his avengers. ISBN 0-14-018530-5

The Ministry of Fear
This is a complex portrait of the shadowy inner landscape of Arthur Rowe, a man torn apart with guilt over mercifully murdering his sick wife. ISBN 0-14-018536-4

Our Man in Havana
In this comic novel, Wormwold tries to keep his job as a secret agent in Havana by filing bogus reports and dreaming up military installations from vacuum-cleaner designs. ISBN 0-14-018493-7

The Power and the Glory
Greene's masterpiece is a compelling depiction of a "whiskey priest" struggling to overcome physical and mortal cowardice and find redemption.

ISBN 0-14-018499-6

Stamboul Train
Set on the Orient Express, this suspense thriller involves the desperate affair between a pragmatic Jew and a naïve chorus girl.

ISBN 0-14-018532-1

The Third Man and The Fallen Idol
This edition pairs Greene's legendary thriller The Third Man with The Fallen Idol, in which a small boy discovers the deadly truths of the adult world. ISBN 0-14-018533-X

Travels with My Aunt
Henry Pulling's dull suburban life is interrupted when his septuagenarian Aunt Augusta persuades him to travel the world with her in her own inimitable style. ISBN 0-14-018501-1